Enforced performance of commercial sales contracts in the Netherlands, Singapore and China

Enforced performance of commercial sales contracts in the Netherlands, Singapore and China

Paula Kemp

eleven international publishing

Published, sold and distributed by Eleven International Publishing
P.O. Box 85576
2508 CG The Hague
The Netherlands
Tel.: +31 70 33 070 33
Fax: +31 70 33 070 30
email: sales@elevenpub.nl
www.elevenpub.com

Sold and distributed in USA and Canada
Independent Publishers Group
814 N. Franklin Street
Chicago, IL 60610, USA
Order Placement: +1 800 888 4741
Fax: +1 312 337 5985
orders@ipgbook.com
www.ipgbook.com

Eleven International Publishing is an imprint of Boom uitgevers Den Haag.

ISBN 978-94-6236-987-0
ISBN 978-94-6094-444-4 (e-book)

Table of Contents

Acknowledgements

This dissertation is the result of four years of research into the question of whether parties to a commercial sales contract are entitled to obtain the very thing they bargained for under the law of the Netherlands, Singapore and China and how the national solutions relate to the approaches taken by international contract and sales law instruments. This research has been a daunting but an extremely rewarding challenge, and it would not have been possible without the valuable and constant support received from my supervisors Professor Bart Krans and Professor Mark Wissink, who were always full of excitement and encouragement for my work. I am greatly indebted to them and would like to extend a heartfelt thanks for their valuable suggestions, unrelenting patience, profound belief in my work, and their guidance every step of the way. I have truly enjoyed each discussion.

For the first three years of my research, I lived and worked in Singapore. This would not have been possible without the support of Professor YEO Tiong Min. I would like to thank him for my appointment as Visiting Scholar at the Singapore Management University School of Law. This position allowed me to deepen my knowledge of Singapore law, to attend interesting discussions, and to visit seminars abroad on various contract law topics. I would also like to thank Dr. Garry Low for advice and invaluable comments on my work. During my stay in Singapore, I was also fortunate and honoured to meet Professor GOH Yihan, Professor THANG Hang Wu, Professor Locknie HSU, Associated Professor YIP Man, and many others. I am grateful for the new and indispensable insights they have provided me with. I would also like to give special thanks to Professor Maartje Visser for her kindness and incredibly warm reception.

As for my work on the contract law of China, I was fortunate to receive invaluable comments from Dr. XIONG Hao and Dr. JIANG Hao. I would like to thank them for reading my work, providing me with useful research advice and raising interesting points of discussion. I would also like to thank Dr. Michael Ng for giving me the opportunity to present my research at the Centre For Chinese Law, University of Hong Kong.

My deepest appreciation and gratitude are for the members of the Doctorate Committee, Professor A.G. Castermans, Professor J. Hijma, Professor Y. Li and Professor A.F.H. Loke. I truly appreciate their time and efforts in reviewing my dissertation and providing me with detailed insightful comments.

A very special massive thanks is due to Danny McGraddy for his invaluable advice, painstaking work in checking my drafts and always being so supportive. I would also like to express my gratitude to Jolien Spoelstra, Floor van Beek, Martina Mettberg-Lemière, Suzan Winkels-Koerselman, Joke Driessen and Minos van Joolingen for helping in whatever way they could during this challenging period. Finally to Rogier, who has been by my side throughout this PhD, living every single minute of it, and without whom, I would not have the courage to embark on this journey. And to darling Zoë Lynn. The only thing that made me forget the tiredness was seeing her unbridled appetite; that feeling of being swept away by a desire for life.

The research was concluded on 1 July 2019.

Abbreviations

AC	Law Reports, Appeal Cases (Third Series) (1891)-(England & Wales)
AELA	Application of English Law Act (Cap 7A, 1994 Rev Ed) (Singapore)
ALL ER	All England Law Reports (England & Wales)
art/arts	article/articles
BCLC	Butterworths Company Laws Cases (United Kingdom)
BW	Burgerlijk Wetboek of 1992 (Dutch Civil Code)
CCL	Contract Law of the People's Republic of China (1999)
CH	High Court (Chancery Division) (England & Wales); or Law Reports, Chancery Division (England & Wales)
Ch.D.	Law Reports, Chancery Division (1875-1890) (England & Wales)
ch/chs	chapter/chapters
CHN	China
CIETAC	China International Economic and Trade Arbitration Commission
CISG	UN Convention on the International Sale of Goods
Co	Cooperation
CPFTA	Consumer Protection (Fair Trading) Act (Cap 52A, 2004 Rev Ed) (Singapore)
CPL	Civil Procedure Law of the People's Republic of China (2017)
DCC	Dutch Civil Code
DCFR	Draft Common Frame of Reference prepared by the Study Group on a European Civil Code (2008)
e.g.	*exempli grati* (for example)
E.R.	English Reports (England & Wales)
ECL	Economic Contract Law of the People's Republic of China (1981, as amended in 1983)
ECLI	European Case Law Identifier
ed/eds	editor/editors
edn	edition
et al	and others
EWHC	High Court of Justice in England, together with the Court of Appeal and the Crown Court (England & Wales)
FCA	Federal Court of Australia
FEC	Foreign Economic Contract Law of the People's Republic of China (1985)
ff	and following

GCPL	General Principles of Civil Law of the People's Republic of China (1986)
HL	House of Lords
i.a.	*inter altri* (among others)
i.e.	*id est* (that is)
ibid	the same place
ICC	International Court of Arbitration
INCOTERMS®	International Commercial Terms of the ICC revised in 2019
KG	Kort geding (interim relief proceedings in the Netherlands)
Ltd	Limited
MJL	Malayan Law Journal
NJ	Nederlandse Jurisprudentie (Dutch case law)
NL	Netherlands
PACL	Principles of Asian Contract Law (draft articles 2016)
para/paras	paragraph/paragraphs
PECL	Principles of European Contract Law (1999)
PICC	UNIDROIT Principles of International Commercial Contracts (2004)
Pte Ltd	Private Limited
QB	Law Reports, Queen's Bench (England & Wales)
RJDC	Reports of Judicial Decisions China People's Courts
S&S	Schip & Schade (Ship & Damages) (Dutch law journal)
s/ss	section/sections
SCC	Supreme Court of Canada
SCPC	Renmin Fayuan nlixuan (selected cases of the People's Courts (China))
SGA	Sale of Goods Act (Cap 393, 1999 Rev Ed) (Singapore)
SGCA	Singapore Court of Appeal
SGHC	Singapore High Court
SGP	Singapore
SLR	Singapore Law Review
SLR(R)	Singapore Law Reports (Reissue)
SPC	Supreme People's Court (China)
UKSC	United Kingdom Supreme Court
UNIDROIT	Institute International pour l'Unification du Droit Privé/International Institute for the Unification of Private Law
v	versus; or volume
W	Weekblad van het recht (Dutch law journal)
WLR	Weekly Law Reports (England); or Weekly Law Reports (Singapore)
WPNR	Weekblad voor Privaatrecht, Notariaat en Registratie (Dutch law journal)

Table of cases

China

Binhai Entertainment Co Ltd of Haikou City, Hainan Province v Hainan Huaxin Realty Management Co Ltd [2001] SPC 16 May 2001

Changchun Foreign Economic and Trade Co v Changchun Chaouang Real Estate Development Co [1993] Changchun Intermediate People's Court and Jilin High People's Court (1993) SCPC (1992–1996 Collection) 202

Daqing Kaiming Wind Power Tower Manufacturing Co Ltd v Huarui Wind Power Technology (Group) Co Ltd [2015] SPC Gazette 2015, issue 11

Fuping Steel Rolling Co of Shaanxi Longmen Iron & Steel Co Ltd v Shaanxi Coke Chemical Co Ltd [2012] Shaanxi Higher People's Court 27 November 2012

Jiangsu Nanjing Xinyu House Property Development Limited Company v Feng Yumei [2004] Nanjing Intermediate Court 6 September (2004) SPC Gazette 2006, issue 6

Latex Gloves [1999] China International Economic and Trade Arbitration Commission [CIETAC] 13 January 1999 <http://cisgw3.law.pace.edu/cases/990113c1.html>

Wen Wufa v Guilin [1992] Commerce Bureau Guangxi Guilin Xiufeng District People's Court and Guilin Intermediate People's Court (1991) RJDC 1992, 1027

The Netherlands

ABB v Staat Dutch Supreme Court 4 October 1996, ECLI:NL:HR:1996:ZC2158, NJ 1997, 65

ABN AMRO v Malhi Dutch Supreme Court 5 April 2002, ECLI:NL:PHR:2002:AD8186, NJ 2003, 124

Artist de Laboureur Dutch Supreme Court 9 February 1923, ECLI:NL:HR:1923:175, NJ 1923, 676

Baris v Riezenkamp Dutch Supreme Court 15 November 1957, ECLI:NL:PHR:1957:AG2023, NJ 1958, 67

Batavus v Vriend's Tweewielercentrum Dutch Supreme Court 16 September 2011, ECLI:NL:HR:2011:BQ2213, NJ 2011, 572

Beliën v provincie Noord-Brabant Dutch Supreme Court 24 March 1995, ECLI:NL:HR:1995:ZC1674, NJ 1995, 569

Briljant Schreuders v ABP Dutch Supreme Court 20 February 1998, ECLI:NL:HR:1998:ZC2587, NJ 1998, 493

Brocacef v Simons Dutch Supreme Court 23 March 2007, ECLI:NL:HR:2007:AZ3531, NJ 2007, 176

Bunde v Erckens Dutch Supreme Court 17 December 1976, ECLI:NL:PHR:1976:AC5835, NJ 1977, 241

CBB v JPO Projecten Dutch Supreme Court 12 August 2005, ECLI:NL:HR:2005:AT7337, NJ 2005, 467
Claas v Van Tongeren Dutch Supreme Court 28 June 1985, ECLI:NL:PHR:1985:AC8976, NJ 1986, 356
Coolwijk v Kroes Dutch Supreme Court 28 May 1982, ECLI:NL:PHR:1982:AG4391, NJ 1983, 2
Corporate Web Solutions v Dutch company and Vendorlink BV Court of first instance Midden-Nederland 25 March 2015, ECLI:NL:RBMNE:2015:1096
De Beeldbrigade v Hulskamp Dutch Supreme Court 27 April 2012, ECLI:NL:HR:2012:BV1301, NJ 2012, 293
De Ruijterij v MBO Ruiters Dutch Supreme Court 14 June 1996, ECLI:NL:HR:1996:ZC2105, NJ 1997, 481
District Court Amsterdam 20 June 1876, W. 4212
District Court Arnhem 4 March 1999, ECLI:NL:RBARN:1999:BP4960
District Court Breda 16 August 2006, ECLI:NL:RBBRE:2006:AY6407, NJF 2006, 444
District Court Gelderland 18 December 2015, ECLI:NL:RBGEL:2015:8280
District Court Noord Holland 6 March 2013, ECLI:NL:RBNHO:2013:BZ5985
District Court Rotterdam 10 January 1921, ECLI:NL:RBROT:1921:46, NJ 1921, 384
District Court Rotterdam 24 June 2015, ECLI:NL:RBROT:2015:4417
District Court Utrecht 23 September 2009, ECLI:NL:RBUTR:2009:BJ8421, NJF 2010, 44
Dutch Court of Appeal Amsterdam 19 October 1877, W. 4200
Dutch Court of Appeal Amsterdam 14 April 1919, NJ 1919, 1101
Dutch Court of Appeal Arnhem 4 January 1972, ECLI:NL:GHARN:1972:AB6792, NJ 1973, 207
Dutch Court of Appeal 's-Gravenhage 8 April 1921, NJ 1921, 1151
Dutch Court of Appeal 's-Gravenhage 30 May 2000, ECLI:NL:GHSGR:2000:AK4304, S&S 2001/54
Dutch Supreme Court 21 June 1957, NJ 1959, 91
Dutch Supreme Court 19 December 1958, NJ 1959, 129
Dutch Supreme Court 27 February 1980, ECLI:NL:HR:1980:AC6832, NJ 1980, 352
Dutch Supreme Court 21 October 1983, NJ 1984, 804
Dutch Supreme Court 29 June 1990, ECLI:NL:PHR:1990:AD1189, NJ 1991, 337
Dutch Supreme Court 31 October 2003, ECLI:NL:HR:2003:AL8168, NJ 2006, 112
Dutch Supreme Court 7 December 2018, ECLI:NL:PHR:2018:692, NJB 2018, 2302
Endlich v Construction machinery Dutch Supreme Court 22 October 2004, ECLI:NL:PHR:2004:AO9494, NJ 2006, 597
Equinix v Rooq et al District Court Overijssel 7 January 2015, ECLI:NL:RBOVE:2015:363, JOR 2015, 96

Gerritse v Ontvanger Dutch Supreme Court 12 May 1989, ECLI:NL:HR:2000:AA5863, NJ 1990, 130
Hajzian Dutch Supreme Court 14 January 1983, ECLI:NL:HR:1983:AG4523, NJ 1983, 457
Haviltex Dutch Supreme Court 13 March 1981, ECLI:NL:HR:1981:AG4158, NJ 1981, 635
Intres v Walt Disney Company Dutch Supreme Court 1 December 1995, ECLI:NL:HR:1995:ZC1899, NJ 1996, 510
Kriek v Smit Dutch Supreme Court 12 June 1987, ECLI:NL:HR:1987:AC2558, NJ 1988, 150
Lauppe v Lelystad District Court Zwolle 27 March 1985, KG 1985, 124
Lundiform v Mexx Europe BV Dutch Supreme Court 5 April 2013, ECLI:NL:HR:2013:BY8101, NJ 2013, 214
Meegdes v Meegdes Dutch Supreme Court 21 December 1956, NJ 1957, 126
Meyer Europe v Pont Meyer Dutch Supreme Court 19 January 2007, ECLI:NL:HR:2007:AZ3178, NJ 2007, 575
Mol v Meijer Dutch Supreme Court 4 February 2000, ECLI:NL:PHR:2000:AA4728, NJ 2000, 562
Multi Vastgoed v Nethou Dutch Supreme Court 5 January 2001, ECLI:NL:PHR:2001:AA9311, NJ 2001, 79
Nieuwe Dam and Pereboomsloot v VVE et al Dutch Supreme Court 19 November 2010, ECLI:NL:HR:2010:BN7084, NJB 2010, 2202
NVB v Helder Dutch Supreme Court 27 April 1984, ECLI:NL:PHR:1984:AG4797, NJ 1984, 679
Oostenbroek v Nekami Dutch Supreme Court 8 December 1989, ECLI:NL:HR:1989:AG6222, NJ 1990, 474
Oosterhuis v Unigro Dutch Supreme Court 21 May 1976, ECLI:NL:PHR:1976:AC5738, NJ 1977, 73
Petermann v Frans Maas Dutch Supreme Court 2 February 2001, ECLI:NL:PHR:2001:AA9767, NJ 2001, 200
Plas v Valburg Dutch Supreme Court 18 June 1982, ECLI:NL:PHR:1982:AG4405, NJ 1983, 723
Ploum v Smeets II Dutch Supreme Court 25 March 2011, ECLI:NL:HR:2011:BP8991, NJ 2013, 5
Pluto Sport v VOF Marber et al District Court 's-Gravenhage 22 November 2011, ECLI:NL:RBSGR:2010:BO4625
Polak v Zwolsman Dutch Supreme Court 14 June 1968, ECLI:NL:PHR:1968:AC3608, NJ 1968, 331
Poot v ABP Dutch Supreme Court 2 December 1994, ECLI:NL:HR:1994:ZC1564, NJ 1995, 288
Pouw v Visser Dutch Supreme Court 29 June 2007, ECLI:NL:HR:2007:AZ7617, NJ 2008, 606

Ritzen v Hoekstra Dutch Supreme Court 22 April 1983, ECLI:NL:PHR:1983:AG4575, NJ 1984, 145

Staat v Shell Dutch Supreme Court 30 September 1994, ECLI:NL:HR:1994:ZC1460, NJ 1996, 196

Stichting Waterpakt v Staat Dutch Supreme Court 21 March 2003, ECLI:NL:PHR:2003:AE8462, NJ 2003, 691

Stierkalf arrest Dutch Supreme Court 7 March 1980, ECLI:NL:PHR:1980:AB7443, NJ 1980, 353

Stuyvers' Beheer v Eugster Dutch Supreme Court 15 May 1981, ECLI:NL:HR:1981:AG4190, NJ 1982, 85

Vaderschapsactie Dutch Supreme Court 22 September 2000, ECLI:NL:HR:2000:AA7204, NJ 2001, 647

Van Beers v Van Daalen Dutch Supreme Court 21 December 2001, ECLI:NL:HR:2001:AD5352, NJ 2002, 60

Van Dalfsen v Kampen Dutch Supreme Court 14 November 2007, ECLI:NL:HR:2008:BF0407, NJ 2008, 588

Van de Steeg v Rabobank Dutch Supreme Court 8 Februari 2013, ECLI:NL:HR:2013:BY4600, NJ 2014, 497

Van den Bos v Provincial Insurance Company Limited Dutch Supreme Court 29 September 1995, ECLI:NL:HR:1995:ZC1827, NJ 1996, 89

Van der Gun v Farmex Dutch Supreme Court 22 May 1981, ECLI:NL:PHR:1981:AG4192, NJ 1982, 59

Van der Leest v Gemeente Veghel Dutch Supreme Court 4 September 2008, ECLI:NL:HR:2008:BD3127, NJ 2010, 272

Van Genk v De Wild Dutch Supreme Court 21 June 1996, ECLI:NL:HR:1996:ZC2107, NJ 1997, 327

Van Oosterom v Majoor Dutch Supreme Court 16 January 1981, ECLI:NL:PHR:1981:AG4132, NJ 1981, 426

Verheijen Seed v Rijk Zwaan Dutch Supreme Court 23 Februari 1990, ECLI:NL:PHR:1990:AD104, NJ 1990, 663

Visser v Erven Kroon Dutch Supreme Court 12 November 1999, ECLI:NL:PHR:1999:AA3369, NJ 2000, 67

Vodafone v ETC Dutch Supreme Court 19 October 2007, ECLI:NL:HR:2007:BA7024, NJ 2007, 565

Vogelaar v Skil Dutch Supreme Court 31 May 1991, ECLI:NL:HR:1991:ZC0255, NJ 1991, 647

VSH v Shell Dutch Supreme Court 23 October 1987, ECLI:NL:PHR:1987:AD0018, NJ 1988, 1017

X v Bell Microproducts Dutch Supreme Court 27 April 2012, ECLI:NL:HR:2012:BV1299, NJ 2012, 294

Singapore

Abdul Jalil bin Ahmad bin Talib and others v A Formation Construction Pte Ltd [2006] 4 SLR(R) 778 (SGHC)
Adani Wilmar Ltd v Cooperative Centrale Raiffeisen-Boerenleenbank BA ("Rabobank Nederland") [2002] 2 SLR (R) 216
Alliance Concrete Singapore Pte Ltd v Sato Kogyo (S) Pte Ltd [2014] SGCA 35
Allplus Holdings Pte Ltd and others v Phoon Wui Nyen (Pan Weiyuan) [2016] SGHC 144
Bakery Mart Pte Ltd (in receivership) v Sincere Watch Ltd [2003] 3 SLR(R) 462 (SGCA)
Bankers & Traders Insurance Co Ltd v Insurance Services [1968–1970] SLR (R) 360
Bocotra Construction Pte Ltd and others v Attorney-General [1995] SGCA 51, (1995) 2 SLR(R) 282
British and Malayan Trustees Ltd v Sindo Realty Pte Ltd (in liquidation) and other actions [1998] SGHC 92, (1998) 1 SLR(R) 903
Chew Ai Hua Sandra v Woo Kah Wai and another (Chesney Real Estate Pte Ltd, third party) [2013] SGHC 120, (2013) 3 SLR 1088
Chia Ee Lin Evelyn v Teh Guek Ngor Engelin née Tan [2004] 4 SLR (R) 330 (SGHC)
Chiang Hong (Pte) Ltd v Ong Boon Pok Realty (Pte) Ltd [1983–1984] SLR (R) 481 (SGCA)
China resources (S) Pte Ltd v Magenta Resources (S) Pte Ltd [1997] (1997) 1 SLR (R) 103 (SGCA)
Chng Weng Wah v Goh Bak Heng [2016] SGCA 9, (2016) 2 SLR 464
Chua Chay Lee v Premier Properties Pte Ltd [2002] 2 SLR(R) 464 (SGCA)
Chua Kim Leng (Cai Jinling) v Philip Securities Pte Ltd [2006] SGHC 221
Chua Kwok Fun Kevin and another v Etons Management Consultants Pte Ltd and others [1999] SGHC 84, (1999) 1 SLR(R) 1088
Chuan Hiap Seng (1979) Pte Ltd v Progress Manufacturing Pte Ltd [1995] SGHC 17, (2015) 1 SLR(R) 122
Chuan Hong Petrol Station Pte Ltd v Shell Singapore (Pte) Ltd [1992] SGCA 35, (1992) 2 SLR(R) 1
Chung Khiaw Bank Ltd v Bajaj Textiles Ltd [1968–1970] SLR(R) 78 (SGGC)
Chwee Kin Keong v Digilandmall.com Pte Ltd [2004] SGHC 71, (2004) 2 SLR(R) 594
Chwee Kin Keong v Digilandmall.com Pte Ltd [2005] SGCA 2, (2005) 1 SLR(R) 502
CIFG Special Assets Capital I Ltd v Polimet Pte Ltd [2017] SGHC 22
CLAAS Medical Centre Pte Ltd v Ng Boon Ching [2010] SGCA 3, (2010) 2 SLR 386
Coastland Properties Pte Ltd v Lin Geok Choo [1999] SGHC 293
Computer-Aided Design (Asia) Pte Ltd v Sime Darby Singapore Ltd t/a Sime Darby Systems [1993] SGHC 195

Cooperative Centrale Raiffeisen-Boerenleenbank BA (Trading as Rabobank International), Singapore Branch v Motorola Electronics Pte Ltd [2011] 2 SLR 63 (SGCA)
Cytec Industries Pte Ltd v APP Chemicals International (Mau) Ltd [2009] 4 SLR(R) 769
De Beers Jewellery Pte Ltd [2002] 1 SLR (R) 418
Dynasty Line Ltd (in liquidation) v Sukamto Sia and another and another appeal [2014] 3 SLR 277
EC Investment Holding Pte Ltd v Ridout Residence Pte Ltd & Anor (Orion Oil Limited & Anor, Interveners) [2010] SGHC 270
EC Investment Holding Pte Ltd v Ridout Residence Pte Ltd and others and another appeal [2012] SGCA 50, (2012) 1 SLR 32
eSys Technologies Pte Ltd v nTan Corporate Advisory Pte Ltd [2013] 2 SLR 1200
Excelsior Hotel Pte Ltd v Hiap Bee (Singapore) Pte Ltd (OCBC Finance (Singapore) Ltd, intervener) [1989] SGHC 84, (1989) 2 SLR(R) 322
Export Services Singapore Pte Ltd v Idemitsu Chemicals Southeast Asia Pte Ltd [1998] 1 SLR 93
Federal Computer Services Sdn Bhd v Ang Jee Hai Eric [1991] 2 SLR(R) 427
Foo Jong Peng and others v Phua Kiah Mai and another [2012] SGCA 55
Foo Song Mee v Ho Kiau Seng [2011] SGCA 45
Forefront Medical Technology (Pte) Ltd v Modern-Pak Pte Ltd [2006] 1 SLR(R) 927
Fujifilm (Singapore) Pte Ltd (Formerly Known As Fuji Photo Film (Singapore) Pte Ltd) v Ultimate Packaging Pte Ltd [2012] SGDC 468
Gay Choon Ing v Loh Sze Ti Terence Peter [2009] 2 SLR(R) 332
Glahe International Expo AG v ACS Computer Pte Ltd [1998] 2 SLR(R) 764 (SGHC)
Glahe International Expo AG v ACS Computer Pte Ltd [1999] 1 SLR (R) 945 (SGCA)
Goh Guan v AspenTech, Inc [2009] 3 SLR(R) 590
Gold Coin Ltd v Tay Kim Wee [1985–1986] SLR(R) 575
Govindaraju and another v Ganasen and another [1994] SGCA 125, (1994) 3 SLR(R) 815
Grossner Jens v Raffles Holdings Ltd [2004] 1 SLR (R) 202
Guan Chong Cocoa Manufacturer Sdn Bhd v Pratiwi Shipping SA [2003] 1 SLR(R) 157
Hewlett-Packard Singapore (Sales) Pte Ltd v Chin Shu Hwa Corinna [2016] SGCA 19, (2016) 2 SLR 1083
Ho Seng Lee Construction Pte Ltd v Nian Chuan Construction Pte Ltd [2001] 2 SLR(R) 184
Holcim (Singapore) Pte Ltd v Precise Development Pte Ltd [2011] SGCA 1 (2011) 2 SLR 106
Holiday Inns Inc v Hotel Enterprises Ltd [1975–1977] SLR 336 (SGHC)
Hon Chin Kong v Yip Fook Mun [2017] SGHC 286
Hong Leong Finance Ltd v Tan Gin Huay, [1999] SGCA 1, (1999) SLR(R) 755
HSBC Institutional Trust Services Ltd v Toshin Development Singapore Pte Ltd [2012] SGCA 48, (2012) 4 SLR 738
Indian Overseas Bank v Cheng Lai Geok [1991] 2 SLR (R) 574 (SGHC)

Indian Overseas Bank v Cheng Lai Geok [1993] 1 SLR (R) 32 (SGCA)
Indulge Food Pte Ltd v Torabi Marashi Bahram [2010] 2 SLR 540 (SGHC)
iTronic Holdings Pte Ltd v Tan Swee Leon [2016] SGHC 77
Kajima Overseas Asia Pte Ltd v Glenn Industries Pty Ltd [1997] SGHC 11
Koh Lin Yee v Terrestrial Pte Ltd [2015] SGCA 6
Kong Swee Eng v Rolles Rudolf Jurgen August [2011] SGHC 300, (2010) 1 SLR 873
Lee Chee Wei v Tan Hor Peow Victor [2006] SGHC 116
Lee Chee Wei v Tan Hor Peow Victor and others and another appeal [2007] SGCA 22, (2007) 3 SLR(R) 537
Lee Cheng Kang and another v Lee Tian Kai [1996] SGCA 4, (1996) 1 SLR(R) 87
Lee Christina v Lee Eunice and another (executors of the estate of Lee Teck Soon, deceased) [1993] SGCA 56, (1993) 2 SLR(R) 644
Lee Seng Heng and others v Guardian Assurance Co Ltd [1932] SLR 110
Lim Beng Cheng v Lim Ngee Sing [2016] SGHC 282, (2015) SLR 524
Lim Check Meng v Orchard Credit Pte Ltd [1997] 3 SLR 795
Lim Kim Som v Sherriffa Taibah [1994] 1 SLR(R) 233 (SGCH)
Lim Xue Shan v Ong Kim Cheong [1990] 2 SLR(R) 102
Loh Wee Tin v Transvic Investment Pte Ltd [1995] 2 SLR (R) 251
Magenta Resources (S) Pte Ltd v China Resources (S) Pte Ltd [1996] 2 SLR (R) 316 (SGHC)
Management Corporation Strata Title Plan No 1166 v Chubb Singapore Pte Ltd [1999] SGHC 192, (1999) 2 SLR(R) 1035
Management Corporation Strata Title Plan No 473 v De Beers Jewellery Pte Ltd [2002] 1 SLR (R) 418
Meng Leong Development Pte Ltd v Jip Hong Trading Co Pte Ltd [1983-1984] SGCA 24, (1984) 6 SLR (R) 668
Metropolitan Electric Supply Co Ltd v Ginder [1901] 2 Ch 799
MP Bilt Pte Ltd v Edy Yumianto [1999] 2 SLR(R) 655
MP Bilt Pte Ltd v Oey Widarto [1999] 1 SLR (R) 908 (SGHC)
New Dennis Arthur & Anor v Greesh Ghai Monty & Anor [2012] SGHC 122
Ng Giap Hon v Westcomb Securities Pte Ltd [2009] 3 SLR (R) 518
Ng Lay Choo Marion v Lok Lai Oi [1995] SGCA 67, (1995) 3 SLR(R) 77
Norwest Holdings Pte Ltd (in liquidation) v Newport Mining Ltd [2010] 3 SLR 956 (SGHC)
Ong Chay Tong & Sons (Pte) Ltd v Ong Hoo Eng [2009] 1 SLR(R) 305 SGCA
Orchard Twelve Investments Pte Ltd v Golden Bay Realty Pte Ltd [1985–1986] SLR(R) 723
Oversea-Chinese Banking Corp Ltd v Daewoo Singapore Pte Ltd and another [2000] SGHC 104
Overseas Union Insurance Ltd v Turegum Insurance Co [2001] 3 SLR 330 SGHC
Philips Hong Kong Limited v The Attorney General of Hong Kong [1993] 1 HKLR 296
Phoenix Heights Estate (Pte) Ltd v Lee Kay Guan [1981–1982] SLR(R) 484

Premier Properties Pte Ltd v Tan Soo Tiong & ors [2000] SGHC 12
Pub 1997 Pte Ltd v Scorpion [1994] 1 SLR(R) 437
R1 International Pte Ltd v Lonstroff AG [2014] SGCA 56, (2015) 1 SLR 521
Rabiah Bee bte Mohamed Ibrahim v Salem Ibrahim [2007] 2 SLR(R) 655
Rainforest Trading Ltd v State Bank of India Singapore [2012] 2 SLR 713
RDC Concrete Pte Ltd v Sato Kogyo (S) Pte Ltd [2007] 4 SLR (R) 413 (SGCA)
Re Estate of Tan Kow Quee [2007] 2 SLR(R) 417
Regina v Willans [1858] 3 Ky 16
Robert Chua Teck Chew v Goh Eng Wah [2009] SGCA 40
SAL Industrial Leasing Ltd v Teck Koon (Motor) Trading [1998] 1 SLR(R) 501 (SGCA)
Seraya Energy Pte Ltd v Denka Advantech Pte Ltd and another suit (YTL PowerSeraya Pte Ltd, third party) [2019] SGHC 2
Simgood v MLC Shipbuilding [2015] SGHC 303
Straits Advisors Pte Ltd v Behringer Holdings (Pte) Ltd [2010] 1 SLR 760
Sun Qi v Syscon Pte Ltd [2013] SGHC 38
Sunny Daisy Ltd WBG Network (Singapore) Pte Ltd [2006] SGHC 130
T2 Networks Pte Ltd v Nasioncom v Nasioncom Sdn Bhd [2008] 2 SLR (R) 1
Tay Ah Poon and another v Chionh Hai Guan and another [1997] 1 SLR (R) 596 (SGCA)
Tay Joo Sing v Ku Yu Sang [1994] SGCA 45, (1994) 1 SLR(R) 765
TeH Guek Ngor Engelin née Tan v Chia Ee Lin Evelyn [2005] 3 SLR (R) 22 (SGCA)
The One Suites Pte Ltd v Pacific Motor Credit (Pte) Ltd [2015] SGCA 21, (2015) 3 SLR 695
The Vishva Apurva [1992] 1 SLR(R) 912
Toh Tiong Huat v PM Gunasaykaran [1995] 3 SLR(R) 627
Tomongo Shipping Co Ltd v Heng Holdings SEA (Pte) Ltd [1997] 1 SLR(R) 263 (SGHC)
WBG Network (S) Pte Ltd v Sunny Daisy Ltd [2007] SGCA 1, (2007) 1 SLR(R) 1133
Win Supreme Investment (S) Pte Ltd Joharah bte Abdul Wahab [1996] 3 SLR (R) 583
Wong Lai Keen v Allgreen Properties Ltd [2009] 1 SLR (R) 148
Xia Zhengyan v Geng Changqing [2015] 3 SLR 732
Yeo Long Seng v Lucky Park (Pte) Ltd [1968–1970] SGHC 20, (1970) SLR(R) 859
Yeoh Wee Liat v Wong Lock Chee and another suit [2013] SGHC 153, (2013) 4 SLR 508
Zurich Insurance (Singapore) Pte Ltd v B-Gold Interior Design & Construction Pte Ltd [2008] SGCA 27, (2008) 3 SLR(R) 1029

Other jurisdictions and arbitration
Austria: Oberster Gerichtshof nr 5, 21 June 2005 Ob 45/05m
Australia: Castel Electronics Pty v Toshiba Singapore Pte Ltd (2010) FCA 1028
Canada: Bhasin v Hrynew [2014] SCC 71
England and Wales: Abbot v Blair [1860] 8 WR 672
AG of Bengal v Ranee Surnomoye Dossee [1863] 15 E.R. 811

Associated Japanese Bank (International) Ltd v Crédit du Nord SA [1989] 1 WLR 255
Bankers Trust Co v PT Jakarta International Hotels & Development [1999] 1 Lloyds's Rep 910
Bell v Lever Brothers Ltd [1932] AC 161
Beswick v Beswick [1968] AC 58, (1967) 2 All ER 1197 (HL)
British Westinghouse Electric and Manufacturing Co Ltd v Underground Electric Rlys Co of London Ltd [1912] AC 673
Cassell & Co Ltd v Broome [1972] AC 1027
Cavendish Square Holding BV v Makdessi [2016] AC 1172
Chartbook Ltd v Persimmon Homes Ltd [2009] 1 AC 1101
Co-operative Insurance Society Ltd v Argyll Stores (Holdings) Ltd [1997] 2 WLR 898
Co-operative Insurance Society Ltd v Argyll Stores (Holdings) Ltd [1998] AC 1, (1997) 3 All ER 297
Couturier v Hastie [1856] 5 HL Cas 673, 10 E.R. 1065
Cud v Rutter [1720] 1 P Wms 570, 24 E.R. 521
Dent v Bennett [1839] 41 E.R. 105
Dickson v Dodds [1876] 2 Ch D 463
Douglas v Sidmouth Rly & Harbour Co [1866] 14 WR 361
Dunlop Pneumatic Tyre Co Ltd v New Garage and Motor Co Ltd [1915] AC 79
Eastwood v Kenyon [1840] 113 E.R. 482
Foley v Classique Coaches Ltd [1934] 2 KB 1
GPP Big Field LLP v Solar EPC Solutions SL [2018] EWHC 2866
Great Peace Shipping Ltd v Tsavliris Salvage (International) Ltd [2003] QB 679
Hill v CA Parsons Ltd [1971] 3 All ER 1345
Hilton v Tucker (1888) 39 Ch.D. 669
Howard E Perry v British Rly Board [1980] 1 WLR 1375
Johnson v Agnew [1980] AC 367
London Borough of Southwark v IBM UK Ltd [2011] EWHC 549
Marks & Spencer plc BNP Paribas [2015] UKSC 72
Mountford v Scott [1975] 1 All ER 198
Photo Production Ltd v Securicor Transport Ltd [1980] AC 848 (HL)
Quadrant Visual Communications Ltd v Hutchison Telephone (UK) Ltd [1993] BCLC 422
Rainbow Estates Ltd v Tokenhold Ltd [1999] Ch 64, (1998) 2 All ER 860
Routledge v Grant [1828] 4 Bing 653
Ryan v Mutual Tontine Westminster Chambers Association [1893] 1 Ch 116
Scott v Corp of Liverpool [1885] 1 Giff 216, 65 E.R. 851
Scott v Corp of Liverpool [1885] 3 De G & J 334, 44 E.R. 1297
Sky Petroleum Ltd v V.I.P. Petroleum Ltd [1974] 1 WLR 576
Smiths v Hughes [1871] LR 6 QB 597

St Albans City and District Council v International Computers Ltd [1996] 4 All ER 481
Strangborough and Warner's Case [1589] 4 Leo. 3; 74 E.R. 686
Taylor v Caldwell [1863] 3 B & S 826
Tito v Waddell (No 2) [1977] Ch 106 [1977] 3 All ER 129
Tsakiroglou & Co Ltd v Noblee Thorl Gmbh (1960) 2 QB 318
Wellmix Organics (International) Pte Ltd v Lau Yu Man, [2006] 2 SLR(R) 117
White and Carter (Councils) Ltd v McGregor [1962] AC 413 (HL)
Wilson v Northampton and Banbury Junction Rly Co [1874] 9 Ch App 279

Germany: Landgericht München nr 8, 8 February 1995 HKO 24667/93
Oberlandesgericht Koblenz nr 2 ,17 September 1993 U 1230/91
Oberlandesgericht München nr 23, 22 September 1995 U 3750
Schiedsgericht der Handelskammer, Hamburg, 21 March 1996, <http://www.unilex.info/case.cfm?id=195>

Malaysia: Chop Ngoh Seng v Esmail And Ahmad Bros [1948] 2 MLJ 93
Hock Hin & Co v Allwie & Co Ltd [1961] MLJ 232
Koek Tiang Kung v Antara Bumi Sdn Bhd [2005] 4 MLJ 525
MN Guha Majumder v RE Donoughare [1974] 2 MLJ 114

Spain: Tribunal Supremo 1 Juli 2013 <http://www.unilex.info/case.cfm?id=1823>

United States: Stephan's Machine & Tool Inc v D&H Machinery Consultants Inc [1979] Ohio Ct App 417 NE2d 579

Switzerland: Handelsgericht St. Gallen 5 December 1995, HG 45/1994 <www.unilex.info/case.cfm?id=190>

Arbitration: ICC Arbitration Case n 8128 (1995) <http://www.unilex.info/case.cfm?id=207>
ICC Arbitration Case n 8611 (1997) (Industrial equipment case) <http://cisgw3.law.pace.edu/cases/978611i1.html>

Table of figures

1 Introduction

[P]eople can understand each other even if their legal-cultural backgrounds are quite different. Understanding has to do with knowledge, and here it does not mean the same as acceptance, which is an attitude. We can understand without accepting and accept without understanding – such is the epistemic constitution of homo sapiens.[1]

1.1 Introduction

1. This research is dedicated to determine the availability of enforced performance of commercial sales contracts in the Netherlands, Singapore and China. More specifically, the focus is on the differences in the enforceability of positive non-monetary obligations in a commercial sales context and what this divergence means for the protection of the parties' performance interests. To rephrase this in more practical terms: this research deals with the ability of the courts to provide the parties to a commercial sales contract with the very thing they bargained for by ordering the promisor to specifically perform its obligations. In this regard, a multitude of non-monetary obligations (*e.g.* the seller's obligation to deliver certain documents) and potential non-actionable duties (*e.g.* the buyer's duty to take delivery) are discussed in order to reveal the dogmatic underpinnings of the key differences, particular points of concern for legal practice, and to what extent solutions can be found in international sales and contract law principles.

The main focus of this comparative research is on the enforceability of the seller's delivery obligation, because it is the most clear and common positive non-monetary obligation in a commercial sales context. Moreover, it is a useful tool to place the (diametrically opposed) civil and common law academic concepts for enforced performance of non-monetary obligations in the real world of commercial sales contracts. For example, an international retailer (buyer), located in a civil law jurisdiction, enters into a commercial sales contract with a wholesaler (seller), located in a common law jurisdiction, for the delivery of 100,000 custom-produced goods. The wholesaler refuses to deliver the goods and offers monetary compensation. The aggrieved buyer declines the offer and claims for enforced performance because it has a special interest in delivery of the goods. While civil law provides the buyer with a right to enforced performance in this situation, the common law tradition only allows for enforced performance of the seller's delivery obligation in specific circumstances and in the absence of counter-exceptions.

1 Jaako Husa, *A New Introduction to Comparative Law* (Hart Publishing 2015) 36.

Disagreement between the two legal traditions generally causes issues where a commercial sales contract is governed by civil law but the nature of the contract clauses is predominantly common law, or vice versa.[2] This may occur where parties use a standardised international commercial contract and where the strongest party, located in a common or civil law jurisdiction, 'forces' the other party to use a contract model that is not based on principles of the same nature as the law governing the contract.[3] For the purpose of bringing about new insights to bridge the gap between the two major legal traditions in this regard, the present study focuses exclusively on commercial sales contracts to reveal the main challenges in the realm of enforceability of non-monetary obligations to bring about a certain state of affairs.[4] The reason for the exclusive focus on one particular contract type is that it provides a better tool for analysing the multiplicity of interests in upholding the sanctity of a commercial contract, a reasoned examination of the applicable rules, and the varying results of the legal limitations to enforced performance.

2. Within the legal system of the Netherlands, Singapore and China, the current status of availability of enforced performance is influenced by statutes, court rulings, authoritative opinions and respective histories. These legal sources have been taken into account in ascertaining whether the available performance remedies have common features and also if there are variations requiring special awareness when dealing with international sales transactions governed by national sales and contract law or (domesticated or by choice of applicable law) international sales and contract law, such as the United Nations Convention on Contracts for the International Sale of Goods (CISG).[5] Consideration must thereby be given to the non-exclusive character of the CISG, which provides an opening for domestic courts dealing with international sales transactions to apply their own domestic contract and sales law principles,[6] although it instructs the courts to look beyond their national borders and apply principles from other jurisdictions if this serves a common interpretation

---

2 Rieme-Jan Tjittes, *Commercieel Contractenrecht: Deel I: Totstandkoming en inhoud* (Boom juridisch 2018) 32–33, 378–384.

3 Tjittes 2018 (n 2) 32, 33.

4 Nili Cohen and Ewan McKendrick (eds), *Comparative Remedies for Breach of Contract: International Studies in the Theory of Private Law* (Hart Publishing 2005) 50, 49.

5 The CISG came into effect on 1 January 1988. As of 15 February 2017, 85 States have adopted the CISG. Singapore and China (and the US) have made the so-called 'both parties' reservation, which means that a contract is only covered by the CISG if both parties are from a member state unless parties have agreed to 'opt-out' the Convention (the Netherlands does not have such a reservation). Thus, a sale between a Singaporean company and a Chinese or Dutch company is covered by the CISG. However, a sale between a Singaporean or Chinese company and a UK company is not covered by the CISG because the UK is not a member state. In case a Dutch company concludes a contract with a company from a non-member state, the CISG applies if the law of the Netherlands is appointed or the rules of international private law result in the application of Dutch law.

6 Art 7(1)(2), 28 CISG.

of the CISG. As a consequence, application of the CISG may result in unexpected decisions of courts who are not inclined to award a performance remedy if this is not in accordance with their own domestic sales law.[7] A key factor in this regard is that an international commercial sales contract falls under the sphere of the CISG if both parties have a place of business in a member state,[8] such as the Netherlands, Singapore or China.[9] It must, however, be noted that the contract law of Singapore is historically founded on the English common law model and England is not a member state.[10] Nonetheless, English common law principles and English case law may come into play when enforced performance of a non-monetary obligation arising from a CISG-contract (initially governed by Singapore law) is demanded.[11]

The CISG could also apply if only one of the parties to a commercial sales contract is from a member state.[12] Note, however, that Singapore and China have rejected the application of the CISG in cases where one of the parties does not have its place of business in a member state.[13] In this situation, the CISG does not apply if the parties designate the law of Singapore or China as governing the contract. That said, Singapore is currently considering withdrawing the reservation of applicability of the CISG, which would bring Singapore into line with the Netherlands, which has adopted the CISG without any declarations or reservations.[14]

7 See for a diametrically opposed viewpoint: E Allan Farnsworth, 'A Common Lawyer's View of His Civilian Colleagues' (1996) 57 Louisiana Law Review 227, 231. Professor Farnsworth holds the view that art 7(2) CISG provides the court with the option to apply the law that would govern the contract under the choice of law; Howard Hunter, *Law of Sales in Singapore* (Singapore Academy of Law, Academy Publishing 2017) para 10.16.

8 Art 1(1)(b) CISG.

9 The Netherlands has been a participating country since 1 January 1992 and has made no declarations or reservations. In 1996, Singapore adopted the CISG by enacting the Sale of Goods (United Nations Convention) Act (Cap 283A, 1996 Rev Ed) with the reservation that the Government of the Republic of Singapore will not be bound by sub-paragraph (1) (b) of article 1 of the Convention and will apply the Convention to the Contracts of Sale of Goods only between those parties whose places of business are in different member states. The CISG entered into force in PRC China on 1 January 1988 with a similar reservation.

10 In other areas, Singapore has also adopted principles which do not derive from the English common law system, such as the Consumer Protection (Fair Trading) Act (Cap 52A, 2004 Rev Ed).

11 Arts 28, 30, 46(1) and 62 CISG.

12 Art (1)(1)(b) CISG.

13 In accordance with art 95 CISG, Singapore and China have declared that they will not be bound by sub-paragraph (1) (b) of art 1 CISG; Ingeborg Schwenzer, Pascal Hachem and Christopher Kee, *Global Sales and Contract Law* (Oxford University Press 2012) 18; George T L Shenoy and Loo Wee Ling (eds), *Principles of Singapore Business Law* (2nd edn, Cengage Learning 2013) para 22.4.

14 Gary F Bell, 'Why Should Singapore Withdraw Its Reservation to the United Nations Convention on Contracts for the International Sale of Goods (CISG)' (2005) 9 Singapore Year Book of International Law 55–73; Shenoy and Loo 2013 (n 13) para 22.4.

3. It may be said that difficulties arising from the disagreement between the subject legal systems can be circumvented if the parties opt for a uniform principle that harmonises the approaches taken by the civil and common law traditions. This argument, however, fails to acknowledge that the main principles for determining the enforceability of non-monetary obligations under a commercial sales contract are integral to balancing the interest of the parties in actual performance and protecting the interest of the parties against abuse, from the moment the parties enter into the contract (and even before) until a judgement for enforced performance and judicial back-up measures are put in place. In other words, the mere implementation of a harmonised principle shall have a detrimental effect on the way a legal system balances the interests of contracting parties within its system.

Another point to consider when determining the effectiveness of a uniform principle is that cultural notions and legal traditions are (unconsciously) embedded in the understanding of academics and legal practitioners evaluating the best legal solution to overcome the disagreement between both major legal families to protect the parties' performance interest, and their view on the contract law regime that brings about the best legal practice. Nonetheless, a unification instrument which takes these points into consideration and does not encompass an escape route for interpretation or application of domestic contract law principles may provide the required relief on the matter for those involved in international commercial sales contracts. From a practical perspective, this solution would most likely only work if a supranational (*i.e.* not merely European) commercial court for global sales disputes is established. This seems inconceivable, as the commercial courts in the Netherlands, Singapore and China are feeding on their evolving positions as regional and international trading hubs. It also appears that the reluctance to accept an opt-out unification instrument as described above is also motivated by economic reasons, because favouring one system over another might affect the demand for domestic legal services. In other words, economic competition between the jurisdictions could play a role in the fact that the most important unification instrument for commercial sales contracts allows the domestic courts to seek recourse to their own national principles when confronted with a claim for enforced performance of a non-monetary obligation. The intricacies of this issue will be discussed later.

4. The distinct national perspectives on the question of whether enforced performance should be available makes it interesting to assess the three contract law regimes in view of the approaches taken by the CISG and the UNIDROIT Principles of International Commercial Contracts (PICC), which qualify as opt-out and opt-in codes respectively.[15]

15 The fact that the PICC is subject to mandatory domestic sales law indicates that relying solely on the operation of the CISG or the inclusion of the PICC into the choice of law is not sufficient to prevent the

In view of the goal of bringing about new insight to narrow the gap between traditional civil and common law views on enforced performance by ordering the promisor to do what it had promised to do, this research also takes into consideration the approaches taken by the Principles of European Contract Law (PECL), the Draft Common Frame of Reference (DCFR) and the draft of the Principles of Asian Contract Law (draft PACL).[16] For the sake of comprehensiveness, the legal instruments and model rules mentioned above are hereinafter addressed as unification instruments, unless otherwise specified.

To provide a complete picture, the mirroring function of the unification instruments is supported by a sprinkling of various legal case studies throughout this work. The examples used derive mostly from the database of international case law on the CISG and PICC,[17] but have been modified and adjusted to highlight specific problems that are worth thinking about when confronted with questions related to the availability of enforcing performance of a commercial sales contract across civil and common law borders. Notwithstanding these general considerations, the main reason for including the unification instruments as a mirror for the approaches taken by the three investigated jurisdictions follows from their transnational character, which (at various levels) reflect civil and common law values, their potential usage as a neutral legal regime and their incidence in national sales and contract law principles. The latter applies in particular to Dutch and Chinese contract law, which are both (indirectly) influenced by the CISG.[18] The relationship between the unification instruments, their fundamental traits and the incidence of the unification instruments in national contract law are illustrated below.[19] Interestingly, elements of the

application of purely domestic legal principles for commercial parties engaged in cross-border trade transactions.

16 The PACL is a private academic initiative by scholars from South-Eastern and Eastern Asian jurisdictions to harmonise contract law in Asia, and aims, *i.a.*, to serve – in the future – as a soft law instrument for cross-border transactions. The draft articles on performance and non-performance are inspired by CISG, PICC and PECL; Schwenzer, Hachem and Kee 2012 (n 13) para 2.135; Young June LEE (ed), *A Study on Draft Articles Principles of Asian Contract Law: Performance & Non-Performance II* (Asia Private Law Review No. 7 special 2016) 5; Francisco de Elizalde (ed), *Uniform Rules for European Contract Law?: A Critical Assessment* (Hart Publishing 2018), 192 *ff.*

17 www.unilex.info.

18 Although the incidence of the CISG in the contract law of the Netherlands and China is extensive, there are material differences. *E.g.*, the CISG adopted the requirement of a fundamental failure in performance for avoidance of the contract (arts 25 and 49 CISG). This requirement has not been adopted in the Netherlands and China. In contrast, Dutch contract law has adopted the principle that every failure in performance of one of its obligations gives the other party the right to set aside the contract in whole or in part, unless the failure, given its special nature or minor significance, does not justify the setting aside of the contract and the consequences flowing therefrom. As for China, art 94(4) CCL stipulates that parties to a contract may terminate the contract if the other party delays performance of its obligations, or breaches the contract in some other manner, rendering it impossible to achieve the purpose of the contract.

19 Sonja A Kruisinga, 'The Impact of Uniform Law on National Law: Limits and Possibilities – CISG and Its Incidence in Dutch Law'(2009) 13(2) Electronic Journal of Comparative Law <https://www.ejcl.org/132/art132-2.pdf> accessed on 2 January 2019; Stefan Vogenauer (ed) *Commentary on the UNIDROIT Principles of International Commercial Contracts (PICC)* (2nd edn, Oxford University Press 2015) 11 paras

sales law provisions under Dutch and Singapore contract law also share a common source, to wit, the 1999 EC Directive on the Sale of Consumer Goods and Associated Guarantees.[20] This shared foundation is restricted to consumer sales (which is not governed by the present research), but it would be interesting to monitor how these European principles develop in Singapore in view of the fact that a business purchasing an item incidental to its business may be regarded as a consumer [14], and the discretionary power of the courts to take into account local circumstances.[21]

23, 24; André Janssen and Samuel CK Chau, 'CCL and Unidroit Principles' in Larry A DiMatteo and Lei Chen (eds), *Chinese Contract Law, Civil and Common Law Perspectives* (Cambridge University Press, 2017) 447, 466; Lee 2016 (n 16) 1–6; Hunter 2017 (n 7) 11; Harriët Schelhaas (general ed), Danny Busch, Ewoud Hondius, Hugo van Kooten and Wendy Schrama (eds), *The Principles of European Contract Law and Dutch Law: A Commentary* (Kluwer Law International 2002) 13–19.

20 Commission Directive 1999/44/EC of the European Parliament and of the Council of 25 May 1999 on certain aspects of the sale of consumer goods and associated guarantees (1999) OJ, L171/12; Alexander F H Loke, 'The Lemon Law and the Integrated Enhancement of Consumer Rights in Singapore' (2014) Singapore Journal of Legal Studies 285–306.

21 <https://www.singaporelawwatch.sg/About-Singapore-Law/Overview> accessed on 14 March 2019.

Figure 1 Relationship between the unification instruments and the three subject legal systems

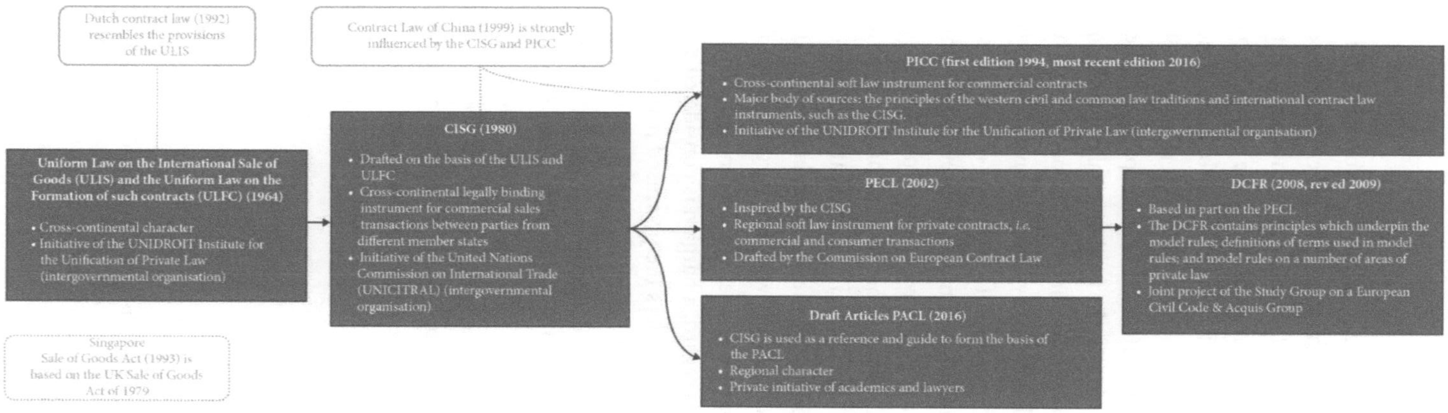

1.2 Research questions

5. Much has been written about the dogmatic qualification of enforced performance of non-monetary obligations (*i.e.* right *vs* remedy), the scope and potential forms of a claim for enforced performance, and the 'better law' in this regard.[22] However, to date there is no comparative work analysing the actual implementation of the universal *pacta sunt servanda* principle in relation to the operation of the common law bargain principle, and how both archaic principles influence the thresholds for establishing enforceable obligations under a commercial sales contract and the protection of each party's expectation of performance. The *pacta sunt servanda* rule embodies the fundamental principle, underlying most legal systems, that agreements that are legally binding must be performed.[23] Generally speaking, it is on the basis of this notion that most civil and common law jurisdictions have adopted the principle that enforced performance of a monetary obligation is generally available, provided that all other requirements are met.[24] However, in common law jurisdictions, this approach is typically not adopted for an action enforcing the promisor to do exactly what it has promised to do. This is because enforced performance of non-monetary obligations is considered an exceptional remedy that lies at the discretion of the court. The legal dogmatic justification is that the common law acts on the notion that the universal *pacta sunt servanda* rule interacts with the bargain principle, which encompasses the notion that an aggrieved party must be placed in an 'as good as position', as if the bargain had been performed. In this regard, a bargain is considered a reciprocal transaction in which each contracting party considers the promised performance as the price of the performance undertaken by the other.[25] Seen from this perspective, it is said that commercial parties to a sales contract primarily bargain for the monetary outcome of the transaction and not for obtaining the actual goods, which means in effect that an aggrieved party should be placed in the position as if the contract had been properly performed (*i.e.* the expectation measure). This proposition, however, is not as straightforward as it seems.[26] From a common law perspective, it is taken as axiomatic that a non-excused failure in performance should be remedied by monetary damages on the basis of the expectation measure. Only when damages are not adequate might an aggrieved

22 Cohen and McKendrick (n 4) 51, 222, 225.
23 Schwenzer, Hachem and Kee 2012 (n 13) para 45.87.
24 Schelhaas in Vogenauer 2015 (n 19) art 7.2.1 paras 1–3.
25 Melvin Aron Eisenberg, 'The Bargain Principle and Its Limits' (1982) 95 Harvard Law Review 741, 742.
26 Eisenberg 1982 (n 25) 798; J Dennis Hynes, 'Freedom of Contract, Fiduciary Duties, and Partnerships: The Bargain Principle and the Law of Agency.' (1997) 54(2) Wash & Lee L Rev 439, 444; Mindy Chen-Wishart, 'Contractual Remedies: Beyond Enforcing Contractual Duties' (2017) 85(6) George Washington Law Review 1617–1624.

party be entitled to claim for actual performance.[27] An analysis of the bargain principle from this viewpoint in the light of the *pacta sunt servanda* principle has already resulted in extensive discussions about the justifications for imposing limits on the application of the expectation measure.[28] In view of the proposition that the objective of a commercial contract is to bring about its monetary value, the primary status of damages is further substantiated with the argument that contracting parties are entitled to change their minds.[29] This is the same freedom underlying the ability to enter a contract and is also intricately interwoven with the doctrine of efficient breach. The bargain principle can also be addressed from a civil law angle.[30] That is to say, the idea that the bargain principle implements the internationally recognised legal concept of *pacta sunt servanda*. This approach seems logical because an order for enforced performance is more likely to provide the exact thing parties have bargained for, in contrast to damages, which are merely a legal relief measure.[31] Accordingly, the central premise of the present research is that a sales contract is the outcome of the effort the parties undertake to lay down certain rules for maintaining a good relationship rather than an instrument for obtaining a monetary benefit.

6. In view of the above, the main research questions are: to what extent does Dutch, Singapore and Chinese contract law balance out the interests of parties to a commercial sales contract in the principles surrounding the enforceability of performance obligations, and how do the domestic solutions relate to the approaches taken by the unification instruments? In order to answer these questions, attention is paid to the availability of enforced performance of non-monetary obligations available under the default contract law regime and to what (if any) extent enforced performance is limited.[32] Where the contract law system allows only for enforced performance in specific situations, it is considered to what extent enforced performance is affected by counter-exceptions.[33] The assessment of limitations and counter-exceptions is particularly helpful for determining the degree of flexibility by which a claim for enforced performance of non-monetary obligations of parties to a commercial sales contract, can be granted and given effect in the subject legal systems. This comparative inquiry goes beyond the primary understanding of the disagreement between civil and common law traditions because it adopts a holistic

27 Eisenberg 1982 (n 25) 799; Subha Narasimhan, 'Of Expectations, Incomplete Contracting, and the Bargain Principle' (1986) 74(4) California Law Review 1123.

28 Eisenberg 1982 (n 25) 799; Narasimhan 1986 (n 27); Chen-Wishart 2017 (n 26).

29 Chen-Wishart 2017 (n 26); Graham Virgo and Sarah Worthington (eds), *Commercial Remedies: Resolving Controversies* (Cambridge University Press 2018) 98–126.

30 Eisenberg 1982 (n 25) 741.

31 Melvin Aron Eisenberg, 'Actual and Virtual Specific Performance, the Theory of Efficient Breach, and the Indifference Principle in Contract Law' (2005) 93 California Law Review 975, 977.

32 Chs 2–4.

33 Chs 5–7.

approach by looking at the larger framework of principles related to performance obligations arising from a commercial sales contract. This is necessary in order to determine the degree to which the investigated legal systems are able to safeguard the performance interest of the aggrieved party and to protect the non-performing party against unjustifiable consequences of an order for enforced performance. The interests of these parties are balanced against the understanding of party autonomy and protection of public interest in the subject legal systems. The principle of party autonomy also brings about the question as to whether the parties may protect their performance interest by including a clause providing for an explicit right to enforced performance of the agreed obligations. This work examines the extent to which such clauses will be upheld and enforced by the courts. Another important feature of party autonomy that requires attention is the validity of provisions that encourages the promisor to do exactly what it has promised to do under the contract. This work only discusses the direct method of agreed sums payable upon a failure in performance, but indirect ways to encourage the seller to deliver the goods in accordance with the agreed terms should not be overlooked by contracting parties. For example, the contractual stipulation that the delivery of non-conforming goods entitles the buyer to terminate the contract without notice. This provision (if allowed) may give sellers an incentive to do what is agreed, because termination of the contract could diminish the seller's monetary benefits following from the bargain struck between the parties. A termination clause can, therefore, be considered as an indirect way of enabling the buyer to protect its performance interest.[34]

1.3 Relevance

7. This comparative work may be considered relevant for several reasons. The first reason is that the present comparative research provides an evaluation as to whether the investigated national sales and contract law principles are able to accommodate commercial parties engaged in cross-border contracting by providing a framework of legal enforcement rules that is sufficiently flexible for the limitless types of international sales transactions. Secondly, this research could potentially support the courts in the investigated jurisdictions when they are confronted with an enforcement claim concerning a commercial sales transaction across civil and common law borders. The final reason concerns the fact that, when adjudicating a commercial sales dispute, the CISG provides domestic courts with the right to limit the operation of a claim for enforced performance of a non-monetary

34 An analysis of the permissability of termination clauses goed beyond the scope of this work, which is focussed on direct ways to protect one's party's performance interest in performance of a commercial sales contract by ordering the other party to do what it has promised to do under the contract.

obligation if such court would not be bound to allow the claim under its own law. This effectively means that the CISG does not provide a solution for the intractable legal issue the different perspectives of the civil and common law traditions have on the availability of enforced performance of non-monetary obligations arising from a commercial sales contract. Hence, the danger exists that commercial parties to a CISG-contract are confronted with purely national contract and sales law principles. This work, therefore, could provide insights for determining the bindingness of non-monetary obligations under a commercial sales contract and to what extent the availability of enforced performance is best protected.

The findings provided in this study could be helpful for legal professionals, academics and national legislators who are seeking a new approach (at national and international levels) to overcome differences in the availability of enforced performance of non-monetary obligations under a commercial sales contract. The results are particularly relevant for commercial parties located in the three investigated jurisdictions, and more generally, for those involved in commercial sales contracts across civil and common law borders. This is because a close examination of the numerous international non-binding codes and model rules reveal that the drafters of these unification instruments have not managed to bring about consistent and universally recognised principles. This is especially true when taking into account the seemingly insurmountable divergence between the traditional civil and common law views on the thresholds for establishing an enforceable commercial sales contract, the dominant understanding of the availability of enforcing the obligations arising therefrom and the rules for giving effect to enforced performance.

1.4 APPROACH

8. This comparative research is built on the belief that a mere functional approach to contract law does not account sufficiently for the doctrinal differences between the concepts and terminology utilised in the three investigated jurisdictions and the unification instruments identified. This proposition follows from the focus of a functional approach on the effects of a rule and is not necessarily concerned with the underlying principles.[35] It is therefore submitted here that a functional method does not suffice to fully comprehend the approach taken by the various legal systems, how they operate and how their viewpoints relate to the development of international contract law. The reason for this is that concepts that might seem similar could actually operate quite differently due to their origin and domestic understanding. This premise applies in particular when comparing jurisdictions from the same legal tradition, when civil law is compared to common law and when the

35 Ralf Michaels, 'The Functional Method of Comparative Law' in Mathias Reimann and Reinhard Zimmerman (eds), *The Oxford Handbook of Comparative Law* (Oxford University Press 2006) 3.

approaches taken by systems that are on qualitatively different levels are taken into account. The present study, therefore, employs a horizontal and vertical analysis of the subject legal systems.[36] The horizontal dimension of this research is concerned with a comparison of Dutch, Singapore and Chinese contract law. The vertical dimension analyses the similarities and differences at the national level by looking at the approaches taken by the unification instruments identified. In view of these considerations, chapter 2 starts with an analysis of the historical and contemporary fundamentals of the contract and sales law of the Netherlands, Singapore and China. The key focus of this chapter concerns the degree to which the contract and sales law of the three investigated jurisdictions are rooted in legal and cultural traditions. The second step regards the ambit of a commercial sales contract in the investigated three jurisdictions and, where appropriate, to what extent they each restate the principles laid down in the unification instruments identified (chapter 3). The following topics are given special attention: the concept of sale, goods subject to sales law and the requirements for establishing an enforceable sales contract. The latter aims to reveal the overarching influence of the traditional civil and common law doctrinal principles, and to identify some of the theoretical and historical justifications for the existence and non-existence of judicial means to enforced performance in the national systems. The third step aims to identify the available judicial instruments to order the promisor to do exactly what it has promised to do, and to what extent the law relating to these actions has been influenced by their history (chapter 4). The fourth step encompasses an examination of three non-performance situations which are very common in commercial sales transactions (chapter 5). This concerns non-delivery, failure in taking delivery and discrepancies in quantity and quality of the delivered goods. The findings are used to determine the differences and commonalities, and to what extent the performance remedial regimes of the three investigated legal systems are in line with the approaches taken by the unification instruments.

9. A complete answer to the question as to when enforced performance of non-monetary obligations arising from a commercial sales contract is available also requires an examination of the legal principles and doctrines militating against enforced performance. Therefore, the influences of the traditional bars to obtain a court order for enforced performance are assessed in chapter 6. To determine the true value of a court order for enforced performance, it is also of paramount importance to examine the available enforcement measures to protect the parties' performance interest. In this context, chapter

36 Maurice Adams and Dirk Heirbaut (eds), *The Method and Culture of Comparative Law: Essays in Honour of Mark Van Hoecke* (Hart Publishing 2014) 59; Ugo Mattei, 'Comparative Law and Critical Legal Studies' in Mathias Reimann and Reinhard Zimmerman (eds), *The Oxford Handbook of Comparative Law* (Oxford University Press 2006) 12.

7 examines two specific issues: first, the way in which the investigated legal systems provide the aggrieved party with measures to execute a judgement for enforced performance other than straightforward enforcement proceedings; secondly, the admissibility of agreed sums to compel the promisor to perform as required by the law and the contract. Lastly, it is important to investigate the extent to which commercial parties are able to influence the availability of enforced performance by derogatory agreements, which (explicitly) allow or prohibit the aggrieved party to obtain a court order for enforced performance by way of ordering the promisor to do exactly what it has agreed to do. The possibility that such a contractual provision will be upheld and enforced under the law of the three investigated jurisdiction is discussed in chapter 8.

10. The selection of Dutch, Singapore and Chinese contract law, for this comparative study, is motivated by three considerations. Firstly, the three investigated jurisdictions represent an interesting foundation for exploring differences between a jurisdiction with strong roots in the French civil law tradition (*i.e.* the Netherlands), an English common law-based jurisdiction which is moving towards a more autonomous legal system (*i.e.* Singapore), and a jurisdiction which has combined socialist principles with German civil law, common law elements, and international sales and contract law principles (*i.e.* China).[37] Consequently, contract law in the Netherlands, Singapore and China differs fundamentally when considering the allocation of responsibility for safeguarding the actual execution of a commercial sales contract between the state and the contracting parties, and the protection offered by law against abuse. In this comparative study, the phrase 'contract law' is used to address the statutory principles and doctrines in the law of the Netherlands, Singapore and China, which form the legal framework for commercial sales contracts. This means in effect that the present work takes into consideration the Dutch Civil Code, the Singapore Sale of Goods Act, the Contract Law of the People's Republic of China as well as overarching legal doctrines and (uncodified) principles deriving from national case law. The second argument for comparing Dutch, Singapore and Chinese contract law follows from the fact that these jurisdictions all qualify as regional and international trading hubs, and each have ambitions to expand through building positions as regional and international legal hubs. The third motivating factor is closely related to this as it concerns the jointly shared ambitions of the three investigated jurisdictions to (i) develop trade-friendly domestic contract law systems, which stimulate economic growth by accommodating business-friendly contract law mechanisms;[38] (ii) by supporting the development of

37 See for the characterisation of Chinese contract law, Lutz-Christian Wolff, 'Impossibility of Performance and Contract Validity' in DiMatteo and Chen 2017 (n 19) 280.

38 NLD: *De toekomst van de nationale rechtsstaat* [The future of the national rule of law], Scientific Council for Government Policy Rapport nr. 270, 2002b and *Nederland Handelsland: het perspectief van de transactiekosten* [The Netherlands a trading country: the perspective of transaction costs], Scientific Council

overarching regional contract law;[39] and (iii) by adopting a court and arbitration system specialised in dealing with international trade disputes.[40]

11. Analysis and discussion of each topic are organised in the following manner. First, in the context of the civil law system of the Netherlands and the Singapore common law system, which are both based on Western notions of a sales contract, and then in the context of the Chinese contract law principles, which are influenced by various national and international legal traditions. The findings are contrasted against the relevant principles adopted by the unification instruments identified. This sequence is based on the premise that the civil law framework of the Netherlands and the common law regime of Singapore arise from opposing Western legal principles, whereas the contract law of China operates between cultural and social values, politics and (more recently) a mixture of civil and common law principles. One of the most striking features of Chinese contract law is the distinction between the elements of establishing a sales contract and the requirements for obtaining effectiveness. This means in effect that it first needs to be determined whether a legally enforceable contract is concluded by the parties by means of an assessment of the constitutional elements of the formation of a contract (offer and acceptance). Next, it needs to be ascertained whether the contract has gained effectiveness.[41]

In anticipation of a discussion of the formation of a contract and its effectiveness, it may be noted that in ancient China, a contract *(He Tong)* was only seen as evidence of an agreement *(Qi Yue)* between parties and, consequently, a written contract *(Qi Ju)* was

for Government Policy Rapport 2003 nr 66, 103, 194, 216; Kamerstukken II 2015–2016, nr. 1553; SGP: <http://www.singaporelaw.sg/sglaw/laws-of-singapore/overview/chapter-1> accessed on 21 October 2015; On 25 March 2015, Singapore signed the Hague convention of 30 June 2005 on Choice of Court Agreements, and the parliament has subsequently approved the Choice of Court Agreements Act to ratify the international pact. Briefly, if under the convention an exclusive choice is made for the Singapore court, the hearing has to be held in Singapore; CHN: In 1981, the Chinese government passed the Economic Contract Law (n 159 below) to regulate contracts between wholly foreign-owned enterprises and Chinese business entities, In 1985, the Foreign Economic Contract Law was promulgated to govern joint ventures between non-Chinese and Chinese parties; Chuan Feng, Leyton P. Nelson and Thomas W Simon, *China's Changing Legal System, Lawyers & Judges on Civil & Criminal Law* (Palgrave Macmillan 2016) 129, 135; Zhong Jianhua and Yu Guanghua, 'China's Uniform Contract Law: Progress and Problems' (1999) 17(1) Pacific Basin Law Journal <http://escholarship.org/uc/item/97t9s6th> accessed on 9 May 2016.

39 *E.g.*, the DCFR and the draft PACL as an answer to the efforts to establish one European contract law and the establishment of the ASEAN Economic Community (ASEC) respectively.

40 *E.g.*, the Singapore International Arbitration Centre (SIAC), the Singapore International Commercial Court (SICC), the Netherlands Arbitration Institute (NAI), the International Chamber of Commerce (ICC) for commercial disputes, the Permanent Court of Arbitration for investment disputes, the Netherlands Commercial Court (NCC) and the China International Economic and Trade Arbitration Commission (CIETAC).

41 Mo Zhang, *Chinese Contract Law: Theory and Practice* (Martinus Nijhoff Publishers 2006) 111.

regarded as the formal record of this agreement.[42] The Western definition of a contract – an agreement is, in essence, a contract – was only introduced in China in the 1970s and is reflected in article 2 of the Contract Law of China.[43] It should be further noted that in the legal system of China, the notion of embodiment of a combination of civil and common law principles is more accessible if the underpinnings of the civil and common law approaches are first discussed.

12. This work is based on an understanding of comparative research as a means of enhancing the understanding of domestic and international sales law principles, and not to determine the 'better law'.[44] The premises underlying this viewpoint are that diametrically opposed doctrinal perspectives may provide similar results, that identical legal principles may lead to diverging solutions, and that their appropriateness depends on the situation. The comparative approach adopted in this work also encompasses the idea that legal concepts can have different functions in different legal systems.[45] In other words, a certain legal phrase, term and label is not necessarily sufficient to determine the actual legal response. Therefore, the structure of the present research is based on practical situations that are not driven by specific civil or common law concepts. These situations are compared in the light of domestic and international contract and sales law principles, doctrines, literature, case law and discussions with academic researchers and legal practitioners. The inclusion of historical context is founded on the view that a legal system derives from experience, and on the reasoning that knowledge of the development of a legal system is essential to understanding the content of rules, principles, and doctrines in that legal system.[46] To clarify the operation of the findings, and because a mere theoretical undertaking is hardly sufficient to fully grasp the complexities of enforcement issues, the domestic legal responses are mapped out against specific cases.

1.5 TERMINOLOGY

13. *Preliminary* – This study aims to use neutral terms that are descriptive in nature, without, in any way, prejudicing the various terminologies used in the three investigated

42 This could also explain why contract law in China adheres to the evidentiary theory, which means that violation of a mandatory requirement that a certain contract must be made in writing, does not lead to a void, voidable or undeterminable contract; Zhang 2006 (n 41) 113.

43 Zhang 2006 (n 41) 25, 34.

44 Mark Van Hoecke, 'Methodology of Comparative Legal Research' (2017) 1 Comparative Law Methodology 127.

45 Husa 2015 (n 1) 137.

46 Pierre Legrand, 'Comparative legal Studies and Commitment to Theory' (1995) 58, 2 Modern Law Review 262, 265; Husa 2015 (n 1) 123, 155.

jurisdictions and unification instruments identified (*i.e.* CISG, PICC, PECL, DCFR and the draft PACL). In view of this, it is important to bear in mind that the terms used in the following chapters should not be axiomatically interpreted based on their traditional meanings (*e.g.* the common law term 'specific performance'). Furthermore, the choice of certain terms in this work does not indicate that the civil law interpretation of a legal concept is prioritised over the common law notion and vice versa.

14. *Commercial sales* – The enforceability of a sales contract is inextricably linked to the need to protect the divergent interests of the different parties involved in the transaction. Generally, this assessment depends on the type of transaction. That is to say, 'business to business transactions', 'business to consumer transactions' and sales between private individuals. However, the way the investigated jurisdictions make a distinction between commercial sales and consumer sales differ significantly. Moreover, as shown below, a transaction between two commercial parties is not always qualified as a non-consumer sales. Determining the boundaries put in place by the respective jurisdictions requires some attention due to the impact of the differing viewpoints on, for example, determining the availability of enforced performance to put a defect right (section 5.4).

Dutch contract law entails the principle that a consumer sale means the sale of a movable thing, entered into by a seller acting in the conduct of a profession or business with a buyer who is a natural person not acting in the conduct of a professional business.[47] The standard of interpretation for determining the nature of the transaction is subjective. It is said that this approach may significantly curtail the seller's interest where the latter, in light of the given circumstances, could reasonably have assumed that the buyer acted in the conduct of a profession or business.[48] A similar reasoning may apply when considering a commercial sales transaction between a self-employed buyer and a large international company and the former is the weaker party due to a significant imbalance in power. Only in exceptional circumstances, this may give cause to judicial protection of the self-employed professional buyer. Singapore courts also focus on the way parties have acted, but they deploy a different assessment for determining as to whether a transaction qualifies as a commercial or consumer sale. The starting point is the Singapore Unfair Contract Terms Act: a party deals as a consumer in relation to another party if 'he neither makes the contract in the course of a business nor holds himself out as doing so and 'the other party does make the contract in the course of a business'. This definition allows for a broad interpretation of a consumer sale when considering the Singapore Court of Appeal case *Koh Lin Yee v Terrestrial Pte Ltd* [2015] SGCA 6. The Court of Appeal decided that the phrase 'in the

47 Art 7:5(1) DCC.

48 J Hijma, *Mr. C. Assers Handleiding tot de beoefening van het Nederlands Burgerlijk Recht 7-I* Bijzondere overeenkomsten: Koop en ruil* 8th edn (2013) 77.

course of business' brings about the principle that a transaction qualifies as a commercial sale when it is clearly an integral part of the company's business, as opposed to being merely incidental to such business. In addition, a 'degree of regularity' is needed before a particular transaction could be considered a 'clearly integral' part of the business. This, in effect, means that a business may claim for enforced performance to put a defect right under the Singapore Consumer Protection (Fair Trading) Act when the purchase of certain goods is merely incidental and there is no evidence pointing to the regularity required to constitute a course of business (section 5.4). In China, the distinction between 'business' and 'consumer' transactions follows a different path due to a positive notion of a consumer (it does not mention the intention to use the goods for business or trade purposes) and limiting the coverage to daily consumption needs.[49] This premise follows from article 2 of the Consumer Protection Law which stipulates that 'when a consumer purchases or uses goods or receives services for the needs of daily consumption, their rights and interests are protected by this Law'. Although this definition offers the courts a high degree of flexibility to deal with the specific contemporary context of China, it is also said to introduce an increased level of uncertainty for small businesses.[50]

15. *Sales contracts and the concept of goods* – The present study discusses the legal framework of commercial sales contracts (excluding consumer transactions); however, it is difficult to provide an accurate definition of this undertaking, taking into consideration the common law distinction between an agreement to sell and the conclusion of a valid sale (section 3.2). Nonetheless, in this research, a sales contract is perceived as 'a reciprocal exchange of goods against an agreed purchase price'. Although this concept is adopted by the investigated legal systems,[51] the variegated definitions of goods that are found at the national and international levels require a case-by-case assessment of whether a commercial contract is governed by sales law legislation (section 3.3). At this point, it must be mentioned that most civil law jurisdictions adopt a broad notion of the concept of goods (section 3.3), whereas most common law jurisdictions restrict the definition to tangible goods.[52] Furthermore, various legal systems (civil and common law) make a distinction between movable and immovable goods.[53] In this research, goods are perceived as movable at the moment of delivery and include those that are either not attached to or detached from an

49 Art 2 Law of the People's Republic of China on the Protection of Consumer Rights and Interests, promulgated on 31 October 1993, amended on 27 August 2009 and on 25 October 2013, effective as of 15 March 2014.

50 Kristie Thomas, 'Analysing the Notion of 'Consumer' in China's Consumer Protection Law' (2018) Vol 6 n 2 The Chinese Journal of Comparative Law 294, 318.

51 NLD: art 7(1) DCC; SGP: SGP: SGA, s 2(1); CHN; Art 130 CCL; Schwenzer, Hachem and Kee 2012 (n 13) para 7.01.

52 Schwenzer, Hachem and Kee 2012 (n 13) paras 7.03, 7.04.

53 Schwenzer, Hachem and Kee 2012 (n 13) para 7.06.

immovable object. While it is not possible to provide an exhaustive list of items that are considered movable goods, money as a payment method is explicitly excluded. This approach is in line with the viewpoint adopted by the CISG.[54]

16. *Non-monetary obligations and payment of the purchase price* – The investigated (supra)national legal systems are all familiar with a judicial action to facilitate the enforced performance of non-monetary obligations under a commercial sales contract (*e.g.* the seller's obligation to deliver the goods in conformity with the contract, the handing over of ownership documents or safety certificates, and the delivery of spare parts). The process of enforced performance of such actionable non-monetary obligations should be distinguished from a monetary compensation for failure in performance, as this instrument does not provide the aggrieved parties with the very thing for which they bargained.[55] Similar reasoning applies for the remedies of the refusal of an aggrieved party to hold up its end of the contract (in civil law terms: *exceptio non adimpleti contractus*) and to put an end to the contract through the termination of the contract. The process of obtaining enforced performance of non-monetary obligations is also distinct from a claim for an agreed sum. The reason behind this is that actions for an agreed sum are normally not subject to the limitations that most legal systems place on the availability of enforced performance.[56]

17. *Actionable contractual rights and obliegenheiten* – Despite the broad scope of the concept of non-monetary obligations mentioned above, it does not relate to obliegenheiten, which are characterised by their non-actionability.[57] The term 'obliegenheit' originates in German and Swiss law and, in contrast to actionable contractual rights to performance, cannot be subject to a judicial order for enforced performance. Nonetheless, non-performance of a non-actionable duty is not without its consequences, because the non-performing party may lose its right to claim for enforced performance or damages. For example, a timber company located in country X and an importer of goods for barbeque events located in country Y conclude a contract for the sale of birch and juniper chips to be delivered at the premises of the buyer. The question arises whether the buyer is subject to an enforceable obligation to take delivery, and if not, if the buyer can be required to cooperate in order to enable the seller to make delivery, by providing information about the exact location of the premises and the times at which the seller can make the delivery.

---

54 Art 2(d) CISG.

55 GH Treitel, *Remedies for Breach of Contract: A Comparative Account* (Oxford University Press 1998) 43; Cohen and McKendrick (n 4) 227.

56 Treitel 1998 (n 55) 45.

57 See section 5.3 for a more detailed discussion.

18. *Enforced performance* – For the process of enforced performance of a positive obligation to do or convey something,[58] different terminology is used under the investigated (supra)national legal systems, which may cause confusion. The terms referring to a claim for enforced performance of non-monetary obligations are 'right of action' (the Netherlands), 'specific performance' (Singapore, PECL, DCFR),[59] 'continuance of performance' (China) and 'right to require performance' (CISG, PICC and the draft PACL).[60] In the present comparative study, the neutral terminology 'enforced performance' is used to address a claim for enforced performance of positive non-monetary obligations arising under a commercial sales contract, in order to avoid unnecessary confusion. In this regard, two issues are of specific interest: first, the common law remedy of (interim) mandatory injunctions is sometimes issued to enforce positive obligations [147-149]; secondly, the term 'enforced performance' is not used to lump together all substantive legal measures to bring about a performance remedy in the form of repair and replacement (section 5.4). This is because the availability of a claim for enforced performance does not necessarily require a failure in performance.[61] By contrast, it is axiomatic that a claim for repair and replacement is a response to a non-performance of the seller's obligation to deliver the goods in accordance with the terms of the contract. It is, therefore, separately discussed to what extent the investigated legal systems envisage the availability of enforced performance of a claim for repair and replacement in order to remedy a non-conforming delivery.

19. *Non-performance* – In addition to the differences in terminology to address an action carried out to obtain enforced performance, there is also a significant variance in the terms used for an infringement of a contractual obligation, in translations of domestic contract law as well as in the unification instruments. For example, 'non-performance' is used in the PICL, PECL, DCFR, the draft PACL,[62] and in the translation of the Dutch Civil Code.[63] The CISG is less consistent by using the phrase 'failure to perform' (this phrase is also used in the translation of the Contract Law of the People's Republic of China),[64] and 'breach of contract' for all situations where a contract is not properly performed.[65] The usage of the

58 *E.g.*, delivery of the goods, payment of the price and ancillary duties which enable the parties to fulfill their obligations.

59 SGA, s 52; Art 9:102 PECL; Art III–3:302 DCFR.

60 Art 6(1) CISG; Art 7.2.2(1) PICC; Art 7 Amendment Draft on Non-Performance PACL, see Lee 2016 (n 16) 198.

61 S 4.3.

62 Art 7.1.1 PICC; Art 8:101 PECL; Art III.-3:101 DCFR; Art 1 Draft on Non-Performance PACL.

63 *E.g.*, Section 3 Special Consequences of Non-Performance of the Obligations of the Seller in Warendorf Dutch Civil and Commercial Law Legislation.

64 *E.g.*, art 107 CCL for the right to enforced performance.

65 See for a failure in performance: arts 45 *ff*, 61 *ff*, 79 and 80 CISG; See for breach of contract: arts 25, 74, 77 CISG.

term 'breach' in the CISG may cause confusion because in common law jurisdictions, such as Singapore,[66] it is used to address a situation where the non-performing party is liable for damages due to a disturbance of a contract. To eliminate any uncertainty about what is intended in the present research, the neutral phrase 'non-performance' is used (in line with the PICC) in its most expansive form, without implying anything about the fault, attributability of the cause or liability for the failure in performance. Thus, the term 'non-performance' is also used for situations where a failure in performance is excused for damages under the law of the three investigated jurisdictions and the unification instruments.

20. *Parties to a commercial sales contract* – A variety of terminology and definitions is used in (supra)national contract law and literature to describe parties to a commercial (sales) contract, including 'promisor', 'promisee', 'obligator', 'obligee', 'debtor', 'creditor', 'non-performing party', 'aggrieved party' etc. In order to avoid ambiguity, the expressions 'promisor' and 'non-performing party' are used throughout this text to identify a party to a commercial sales contract who promised (and failed) to do or convey something. For example, the seller who promises to deliver certain goods and the buyer who promises to take delivery of the goods. The term 'promisee' is used to address the beneficiary of the obligations and duties arising from the contract. The above may cause confusion, as the promisee under a commercial sales contract is also the promisor of its own obligations. For example, the buyer is the promisee of the seller's delivery obligation and the promisor of its obligation to pay the purchase price. To provide the necessary clarity in this regard, the expressions 'seller' and 'buyer' are used in cases in which the type of obligation or duty is central to the discussion.

21. *Standard of reasonableness, fairness, good faith, fair dealing and honesty* – At the national and international level, different terms are used to address the standards regulating the legal duties owed by the parties to a commercial contract. The importance of providing clarity on the matter follows from the fundamental differences at a dogmatic and structural level between the views adopted by the subject legal systems. That said, the purpose of this paragraph is restricted solely to clarification of the main implications of the division. The starting point is that Dutch and Chinese contract law are familiar with a broad general principle in the form of the 'standard of reasonableness and fairness' and the 'principle of honesty and good faith' respectively (subjective and objective standard in both jurisdictions). There are, however, marked differences between the terms. Dutch contract law distinguishes between the 'principle of good faith' (which may apply, for example, to the seller of a

66 *E.g.*, SGA, s 52(1) for the availability of obtaining an order for enforced performance.

property containing asbestos), and the 'standard of reasonableness and fairness'.[67] The latter entails the notion that contracting parties are obliged to observe reasonable commercial standards of fair dealing.[68] The contract law of China takes a different approach by first stipulating that parties are obliged to adhere to the 'principle of fairness' when determining their rights and obligations.[69] This statutory standard is followed by the principle that parties are obliged to observe the principle of 'honesty and good faith' in exercising their rights and performing their obligations.[70]

In contrast to the approach adopted by Dutch and Chinese contract law, Singapore contract law follows the English law position, in the sense that it only recognises the principle of reasonableness for specific duties,[71] such as a reasonable price where a commercial sales contract is silent on the matter.[72] In other words, Singapore as a common law jurisdiction is not familiar with a formal and abstract duty of contracting parties to act in good faith. In view of the preceding considerations, it must be noted that the contract law of the Netherlands and China also encompasses a specific standard of reasonableness for the instance where there is no agreement on the price or the price is unclear.[73] This special principle, however, does not detract in any way from the fact that the agreement and conduct of contracting parties are also subject to the previously mentioned overarching expectation of general reasonableness and fairness, and the good faith standard. At the international level, the PICC, PECL, DCFR and the draft PACL have taken the same approach by adopting a broad general principle to act in accordance with good faith and fair dealing.[74] There are, however, differences in the scope of the obligation to act in accordance with good faith and fair dealing. The most pronounced example is that the PICC solely employs (1) autonomous, (2) international, (3) commercial, and (4) objective standards of good faith and fair dealing.[75] Under the PECL, 'good faith' is considered a subjective standard (*i.e.* good faith in mind), with 'fair dealing' (*i.e.* fairness in fact) being an objective standard.[76] The drafters of the DCFR have defined 'good faith' and 'fair dealing' as an objective standard of conduct.[77] Nonetheless, 'good faith' on its own may refer to a subjective mental attitude, often characterized by an absence of the knowledge of something that, if known, would adversely affect the morality of what is done. The draft PACL suggests

67 Arts 3:11, 3:12, 6:2, 6:248 DCC.
68 Para 53.
69 Art 5 CCL.
70 Art 6 CCL.
71 Para 54.
72 SGA, s 8(2)(3); What is a reasonable price is a question of fact dependent on the circumstances of each particular case.
73 Art 7:4 DCC; Art 6(2) CCL.
74 Art 1.7(1) PICC; Art 1:201 PECL; Art III.-1:103 DCFR; Art 1(2) Amendment Draft on Performance PACL.
75 Vogenauer 2015 (n 19) art 1.7 paras 14–16.
76 Arts 1:201 Comment E, 5:102, 5:101(1)(3) PECL; C Mak in Schelhaas 2002 (n 19) 47.
77 Art I.-1:103 and Annex 1 to the DCFR; Arts II.-8:101(1)(3)(a), II.-8:102 DCFR.

that the drafters envisage a subjective-objective standard.[78] That having been said, the imposition of a broad general duty to act in good faith by the unification instruments mentioned above, stands in stark contrast to the approach taken by the CISG, which only refers to the standard of good faith for the interpretation of the Convention and the (subjective) standard of reasonableness for the interpretation of the statements of contracting parties.[79]

78 Lee 2016 (n 16) 99–101.

79 Arts 7(1), 8(2) CISG; Tjittes 2018 (n 2) 377.

2 Historical and contemporary fundaments of sales law

2.1 Introduction

22. Parties to a commercial sales contract are subject to various obligations, which may follow from contractual stipulations and the law governing the contract. An assessment of these legal sources is, however, not a straightforward undertaking when comparing legal systems rooted in the civil and common law traditions. This is because these major legal systems are structured in a completely different way. When determining the obligations of the parties to a commercial sales contract governed by a contract law based on the civil law tradition, such as the Dutch or Chinese contract law, it is necessary to assess the general contract law principles and the law on sales contracts in a comprehensive way. This is because the obligations of the parties and the consequences of a failure in performance can found in the sales law provisions, but also in the general contract law. The contract law of Singapore is based on the common law tradition and, therefore, is structured in a different way in the sense that the obligations of the parties to a commercial sales contract are fitted in the Sale of Goods Act. Nonetheless, as Singapore is a common law jurisdiction, it is also necessary to take into account the general contract law principles in order to understand the precise nature and availability of the obligations laid down in the Sale of Goods Act. In view of the above, the present section delves into the historical development of the general contract law principles and sales law provisions adopted by the three subject jurisdictions. The central focal point is to provide a discussion of the development of the historical legal infrastructure on which the current principles underlying the availability of enforced performance are built. The 'high-level' aim of this brief undertaking is to enhance the understanding of the theories and the different legal approaches analysed in the following chapters.

2.2 Civil Code in the Netherlands

23. In the area of commercial sales law, there are in the statutory legal history of the Netherlands a number of important milestones. Three of them are discussed in the section below. These milestones concern the introduction of the Dutch Civil Code in 1838, the enactment of the recodified Dutch Civil Code in 1992 and, in the same year, the adoption of the CISG. To begin with the first milestone, at the end of the 18th century, the preparation

of the first centralised Dutch legal code aimed to replace the then existing variety of local laws, which had been based on Roman law and indigenous law.[80] A few years later, the efforts to codify and centralise regional law resulted in the promulgation of the Legal Code Napoleon (1809).[81] Somewhat later, the Kingdom of the Netherlands became part of the French empire and, as a result, the Legal Code Napoleon was replaced by the French Code Civil Napoleon and the French Code de Commerce.[82] In 1813, sovereignty was restored in the Netherlands and efforts were made to bring about a codification of Dutch law. Consequently, the French Code Civil Napoleon and the French Code de Commerce were both succeeded by the Dutch Civil Code and the Dutch Commercial Code (at least for the greater part of the Kingdom of the Netherlands) in 1838.[83] Although the names of these legal codes might suggest otherwise, the French Code Civil Napoleon was a major source of inspiration for the drafters of both legal codes.[84] Aside from some modifications due to changing social relations,[85] the Dutch Civil Code 1838 remained in force until, in 1992, recodified statutes were enacted.[86] This turning point can be traced back to a programme of revision that had begun as early as 1947.[87] The Dutch Civil Code of 1992 (hereinafter the Dutch Civil Code) shows many similarities with the forerunners of the CISG (*i.e.* the

80 The year 1798; Janwillem Oosterhuis, *Specific Performance in German, French and Dutch Law in the Nineteenth Century: remedies in an age of fundamental rights and industrialisation* (Brill Academic Publishers 2011) 198; YMI Greuter-Vreeburg and MJEG van Gessel-de Roo (eds), *Verbintenissenrecht, 1798–1814* (Werken der Stichting tot uitgaaf der bronnen van het oud-vaderlandse recht no 2002) pp XI–XIII; TJH Veen, *En voor berisping is hier ruime stof: over codificatie van het burgerlijk recht, legistische rechtsbeschouwing en herziening van het Nederlandse privaatrecht in de 19de en de 20ste eeuw* (Cabeljauwpers 2001) 7, 9; EOHP Florijn, 'Ontstaan en ontwikkeling van het nieuwe Burgerlijk Wetboek' (Dphil thesis, Universitaire Pers Maastricht 1994) 9; Arthur S Hartkamp, Marianne MM Tillema and Annemarie EB ter Heide, 'Contract Law in the Netherlands' (Kluwer Law International 2011) para 21; P Scholten, *Mr. C. Assers Handleiding tot de beoefening van het Nederlands Burgerlijk Recht. Algemeen Deel* (W.E.J. Tjeenk Willink 1974) Ch III, para 2.

81 The year 1809; Oosterhuis 2011 (n 80) 204; 15 februari 1808 in Greuter-Vreeburg 2002 (n 80) 162–163; 30 mei 1808 in Greuter-Vreeburg 2002 (n 80) 165–166.

82 The year 1811; Scholten, *Asser Algemeen deel* 1974* (n 80) Ch III, para 3; Oosterhuis 2011 (n 80) 208; E Holthöfer, 'Niederlande' in H Coing, *Handbuch der Quellen und Literatur der neueren europäischen Privatrechtsgeschichte* 3: Das 19 Jahrhundert 1: Gesetzgebung zum allgemeinen Privatrecht (C.H. Beck Verlag 1982) 1200–1202; Veen 2001 (n 80) 12.

83 Also called Burgerlijk Wetboek and Wetboek van Koophandel respectively; The Dutch Civil Code 1938 was promulgated in 1842 in the province of Limburg. See Oosterhuis 2011 (n 80) 216; Holthöfer 1982 (n 82) 12–13; Scholten, *Asser Algemeen deel* 1974* (n 80) Ch III, para 4.

84 Scholten, *Asser Algemeen deel* 1974* (n 80) Ch III, para 4; LC Hofmann and SN van Opstall, *Het Nederlands verbintenissenrecht: De algemene leer van de verbintenissen: Eerste gedeelte* (9th edn, Tjeenk Willink 1976) 1, 3.

85 Scholten, *Asser Algemeen deel* 1974* (n 80) Ch III.

86 Hartkamp 2011 (n 80) para 20.

87 Hartkamp 2011 (n 80) para 22.

ULFC and ULIS),[88] and enhances a layered structure of statutes. Consequently, the general overarching principles are first set out in the Dutch Civil Code and more specific principles follow in the subsequent parts. The present research is focussed on statutory provisions as laid down in Book 3 (Patrimonial Law in General), Book 6 (Law of Obligations) and Book 7 (Specific Contracts) of the Dutch Civil Code.

The principles mentioned above apply to contracts between Dutch parties, if the parties to a contract have explicitly chosen Dutch law (on the condition that the subject matter allows a choice of law) and if the principles of domestic private international law appoint Dutch law as the legal principles governing the contract. However, a sale of goods between a Dutch company and a party whose place of business is not in the Netherlands is governed by the principles of the CISG if the latter has its place of business in a member state or when the rules of private international law lead to the application of the law of a member state.[89] These principles are to be disregarded if the contracting parties have opted-out of the CISG by contract. In contrast to Singapore and China, the Netherlands has made no exception for the application of the CISG if one of the parties to the agreement is from a non-member state.[90] This means that the CISG also applies if only one of the contracting parties has its place of business in a member state and the private international law of the court adjudicating the dispute (the forum) calls for the application of the Convention.[91]

24. The Dutch Civil Code stipulates that obligations can only arise on the basis of the law.[92] This does not mean that every obligation has to be based on a statutory provision; it merely requires that an obligation must fit within the framework of the law.[93] Although this statutory framework is the starting point, judge-made law (*i.e.* legal precedents), viewpoints of scholars, considerations of relevant trade treaties) also play an important role in interpretation of contested and unclear statute(s) and filling any gaps through, for example, the doctrine of reasonableness and fairness.[94] In this respect, it may be noted that in the

88 Kruisinga 2009 (n 19); Convention relating to a Uniform Law on the Formation of Contracts for the International Sale of Goods (The Hague, 1964); Convention relating to a Uniform Law on the International Sale of Goods (The Hague, July 1, 1964).

89 Art 1(1)(a)(b) CISG.

90 Art 1(1)(b) CISG.

91 Ingeborg H Schwenzer (ed), *Commentary on the UN Convention on the International Sale of Goods (CISG)* (4th edn, Oxford University Press 2016) 39.

92 Art 6:1 DCC.

93 Dutch Parliamentary History Book 6 (Kluwer 1981) 42.

94 Hartkamp 2011 (n 80) paras 4, 5; C *Asser* and JBM Vranken, *Mr. C. Assers handleiding tot de beoefening van het Nederlands burgerlijk recht: Algemeen deel 2.* (W.E.J. Tjeenk Willink 1995) paras 83, 106, 116; 169 *ff*; Scholten, *Asser Algemeen deel* 1974* (n 80) Ch I para 1, and Ch III paras 19–28; The doctrine of reasonableness and fairness entails the requirement to act in accordance with reasonable standards of fair dealing, *i.e.*, to act in good faith and fair dealing. It must be noted that the concept of reasonableness and fairness marks a fundamental difference between the civil and common law tradition. Whereas the Dutch contract law employs a broad general standard of reasonableness and fairness, the English common law

past, the hierarchical status and usage of these instruments by the courts could not be determined by empirical research because legal precedents and academic works, which were taken into consideration by the court during deliberation, were generally not cited in the written ruling.[95] However, in recent decades, the Dutch Supreme Court began citing principles from earlier case law in its judgements.[96] A court can even provide a comprehensive overview of applicable judicial precedents in its ruling in order to prevent any misunderstanding of its decision.[97] There is, however, no formal rule of precedent under Dutch law. Nonetheless, it appears that the courts are bound by an informal restricted *stare decisis* principle in the vertical and horizontal sense when this is required in view of legal equality and legal certainty.[98] This means in effect that a court is bound by previous decisions, unless developments in society, the specific circumstances of the given case or unexpected consequences justify a deviation from decided cases.[99] Aside from the concordance of jurisprudence, vague principles such as the standards of reasonableness and fairness[100] may compel a court to take the applicable parliamentary history and the opinion of academic scholars into consideration if the rules laid down in the Dutch Civil Code do not provide adequate guidance for the specific circumstance of the case presented to the court.[101] See in this regard Figure 1 for an illustration of the influence of international and European contract law principles on Dutch contract law.

2.3 English common law roots in Singapore

25. In the statutory legal history of Singapore, there are also three major milestones for determining the basic framework of the written laws governing commercial sales contracts, namely the promulgation of the Second Charter of Justice in 1826, the passing of the

has taken the approach that the standard of reasonableness and fairness plays a role in identifying specific duties on a case-by-case basis. See for a detailed discussions John Cartwright, 'Redelijkheid en billijkheid: a view from English law', <https://openaccess.leidenuniv.nl/bitstream/handle/1887/42938/02-Cartwright_bwkj_30.pdf?sequence=1> accessed on 19 February 2019.

95 Vranken, *Asser Algemeen deel*** 1995* (n 94) 169.

96 *Stierkalf arrest* Dutch Supreme Court 7 March 1980, ECLI:NL:PHR:1980:AB7443, NJ 1980, 353.

97 *Gerritse v Ontvanger* Dutch Supreme Court 12 May 1989 para 3.1, ECLI:NL:HR:2000:AA5863, NJ 1990, 130; *Staat v Shell* Dutch Supreme Court 30 September 1994, ECLI:NL:HR:1994:ZC1460, RvdW 1994, 18; Vranken, *Asser Algemeen deel*** 1995* (n 94) 170.

98 This approach stands in stark constract with the English common law system, because the latter entails the rule that lower courts are obliged to follow the decisions of superior courts; See for the principle of *stare decisis* in a horizontal sense, OA Haazen, 'Precedent in the Netherlands' (2019) 11(1) Electronic Journal Of Comparative Law <http://www.ejcl.org/111/article111-12.pdf> accessed on 2 March 2019.

99 Vranken, *Asser Algemeen deel*** 1995* (n 94) 189; Hartkamp 2011 (n 80) para 4; Haazen 2019 (n 98).

100 Art 6:162(2) DCC.

101 Vranken, *Asser Algemeen deel*** 1995* (n 94) 172.

Application of the English Law in 1993,[102] and the adoption of the CISG by Singapore in 1996. The present section starts with the reasons behind the application of Western legal principles in Singapore and the role of England and the Netherlands in this regard. The political history of Singapore goes back to 1795 and is inseparably linked with the so-called Malay Peninsula.[103] Between 1795 and 1818, England and the Netherlands competed aggressively in this part of the world since the region was of great commercial interest to both countries.[104] In 1818, the British lost Malacca (a trading post in Malay) to the Netherlands, making England realise that it needed an alternative in the region to secure its trading interests.[105] On 28 January 1819, the Englishman Stamford Raffles arrived in Singapore to establish a trading post by concluding a treaty with the Sultan of Johore.[106] The Netherlands regarded this action as an infringement of their own alleged treaty with the representative of the Sultan of Johore in Singapore and negotiations over several years were, therefore, necessary before the Netherlands formally recognised England as the 'established power' in Singapore.[107] In return, England recognised the rights of the Netherlands in the rest of southeast Asia.[108] These acknowledgements on both sides were laid down in the Anglo-Dutch Treaty of London of 1824.[109]

Reverting to the 1819 arrival of Stamford Raffles in Singapore, an old English common law rule prescribed that if an uninhabited country is discovered by an Englishman, the English common law in being at that time is immediately there in force.[110] The English Second Charter of Justice of 1826 embodied this principle by formally introducing English common law in Singapore.[111] This was also the starting point for many difficulties in the

102 Statutes of the Republic of Singapore, Application of English Law Act (Cap 7A Rev Ed 1994).

103 The Malay Peninsula lies between the Andaman Sea of the Indian Ocean and the Strait of Malacca on the west and the Gulf of Thailand and the South China Sea on the east. It stretches south for c.700 mi (1,100 km) from the Isthmus of Kra, where it is narrowest, to Singapore. The northern part of the peninsula forms a part of Thailand; the southern part constitutes West Malaysia, the Malayan part of Malaysia. The peninsula forms a physical and cultural link between the mainland of Asia and the islands of Indonesia. Malay Peninsula; *The Columbia Encyclopedia* (Columbia University Press, 2015).

104 Anthony Webster, *The Richest East India Merchant: The life and business of John Palmer of Calcutta 1767-1836* (The Boydell Press 2007) 97.

105 Webster 2007 (n 104) 97.

106 Webster 2007 (n 104) 102; Shenoy and Loo 2013 (n 13) para 2.6.

107 Webster 2007 (n 104) 102; Shenoy and Loo 2013 (n 13) para 2.7.

108 Webster 2007 (n 104) 103.

109 Webster 2007 (n 104) 102, 103.

110 *AG of Bengal v Ranee Surnomoye Dossee* [1863] 15 E.R. 811 at 824.

111 Statutes of the Republic of Singapore, Application of English Law Act (Cap 7A Rev Ed 1994); In *Regina v Willans* [1858] 3 Ky 16 at 37 it was held that 'a direction in an English Charter to decide according to justice and right, without expressly stating by what known body of law they shall be dispensed and so to decide in a country which has not already an established body of law, is plainly a direction to decide according to the law of England'. Therefore, as a result of the Second Charter of Justice, Singapore received a court system on the prevailing English model; Helena HM Chan, *The Legal System of Singapore* (Butterworths Asia 1995) 4.

area of contract law. For example, it was not clear to what extent English commercial law was adopted in Singapore and whether the concepts of severability and suitability applied.[112]

In 1942, the development of a Singapore law system was put on hold by the Japanese occupation of Singapore, which lasted until the end of the Second World War.[113] After 1945, Singapore became a British Crown Colony. Nonetheless, the end of the war was also the beginning of the quest of Singapore for self-government, which in 1959 eventually led to a fully elected legislative assembly and a new state constitution.[114] However, this step did not result in an independent domestic administration. In order to achieve independence from England and for economic reasons, Singapore and Malaysia merged in 1963.[115] For various reasons, this merger only lasted until 1965,[116] when the current Republic of Singapore was established, and the development of an autochthonous legal system started.[117] An important aspect in this regard is the introduction of the so-called 'cut-off date', which means that from 1993 onwards the common law of England (including principles and rules of equity) remain a part of the law of Singapore, and shall continue to be in force, so far as they are applicable to the circumstances of Singapore and its inhabitants and subject to such modifications as those circumstances may require.[118] The introduction of the 'cut-off date' is the starting point of the development of an autochthonous Singapore legal system which is said to have resulted in an independent legal framework appropriate to

112 This uncertainty derives from the unclear wording of s 5 of the Civil Law Act (Cap 43, 1988 Rev Ed) which is believed to be the foundation of Singaporean commercial law. See for a detailed discussion of this topic Goh Yihan and Tan Paul, 'An Empirical study on the development of Singapore Law' (2011) 28 Singapore Academy of Law Journal 176, 184; Goh Yihan, Pearlie Koh, Lee Pey Woan, Andrew Phang Boon Leong and Tham Chee Ho, *The Law of Contract in Singapore* (Andrew Phang Boon Leong (ed) Academy Publishing 2012) paras 02.022–02.040; Andrew Phang Boon Leong, *From Foundation to Legacy: The Second Charter of Justice* (Singapore Academy of Law 2006) 27–35.

113 Shenoy and Loo 2013 (n 13) para 2.15.

114 Shenoy and Loo 2013 (n 13) para 2.20.

115 Shenoy and Loo 2013 (n 13) paras 2.22–2.25.

116 See for a detailed discussion Andrew Phang Boon Leong, *The Development of Singapore Law Historical and Socio-Legal Perspectives* (Butterworths 1990).

117 Shenoy and Loo 2013 (n 13) paras 2.26–2.35.

118 Statutes of the Republic of Singapore, Application of English Law Act (Cap 7A Rev Ed 1994), s 3 (1) (2) (hereinafter AELA 1993). The AELA 1993 clarified the application of English law in Singapore. For sales contracts this meant that the UK Sale of Goods Act (which was first adopted in 1993 and modified in 1979) continued to be a part of the law of Singapore in the form of the Sale of Goods Act (Cap 393, 1994 Rev Ed). Before the AELA 1993, the reception of English commercial law appears to derive from section 5, Civil Law Act (Cap 43, 1988 Rev Ed). Section 5 is repealed, but it should be noted that it was not clear as to whether the provision entailed the reception of the common law as well. See: Phang et al 2012 (n 112) Chapter 2; Phang 2006 (n 112) 27-35; Geoffrey Chevalier Cheshire, Micheal Philip Furmston, Cecil Herbert Stuart Fifoot, Andrew Phang Boon Leong, *Cheshire, Fifoot and Furmston's Law of Contract: Singapore and Malaysian Ed.* (Buttersworths Asia 1994) 6-16; Chan Sek Keong, 'A New Charter of Justice' in Goh Yihan, Paul Tan (eds), *Singapore Law, 50 Years in the Making*, Part A, Chapter 2.

Singapore's emphasis on international trade.[119] This proposition is reflected in the following viewpoint.[120]

> *The development of a uniquely Singaporean corpus of contract law continues apace. In addition, however, (...) broader factors and considerations are also important and it is very encouraging to note that the Singapore courts themselves are actively canvassing such issues which underscore, in turn, the integrated and holistic relationship between the universal and the particular, between theory and practice.*

26. Domestic sales transactions in Singapore are governed by the Sale of Goods Act and the principles of common law.[121] The Sale of Goods Act was amended in 1996 and 2014, which led to the adoption of the requirement (implied at law) that goods supplied under a sales contract be of satisfactory quality.[122] Further, a buyer of unascertained bulk goods (*i.e.* not properly defined goods), who has paid the purchase price, became at law entitled to acquire an undivided share in the bulk.[123] Lastly, a distinction was made between the right of a consumer buyer and a non-consumer buyer to reject goods which are delivered by the seller.[124] Aside from the Sale of Goods Act, the Singapore common law of contracts is of paramount importance for the present research because it provides insights into the essential fundaments of enforceable (sale) contracts, such as the interpretation of contractual terms and the default remedial scheme for contracts.[125]

27. Turning to international sales, in contrast to the UK, Singapore has adopted the CISG for non-domestic sale of goods.[126] The general rule is that the CISG applies to agreements between parties whose places of business are in the territory of states which are a member of the CISG, or when the rules of private international law lead to the application of the law of a member state.[127] In the view of Singapore scholars, this could result in the unintended application of the CISG between a party from Singapore and a party from a

---

119 Phang et al 2012 (n 112) paras 02.075–02.079.

120 Andrew Phang Boon Leong, Contract Law (2003) *Singapore Academy of Law Annual Review of Singapore Cases* 4, 127.

121 SGA, s 62(2).

122 SGA, ss 14(2), (6); Sale of Goods (Amendment) Act 1996, s 3, 4.

123 SGA, s 20A; Sale of Goods (Amendment) Act 1996, 6–8.

124 SGA, s 30.

125 Steven Chong, Cavinder Bull SC (eds) and a team of expert contributors, *Law Relating to Specific Contracts in Singapore* (2nd edn, Sweet & Maxwell 2016) 1043.

126 Effective date: 1 March 1996; the CISG was implemented by the Sale of Goods (United Nations Convention) Act (Cap 283A, 2013 ED).

127 Art 1 (a)(b) CISG.

non-member state.[128] Therefore, Singapore declared that the CISG only applies between parties whose places of business are in member states.[129] It is further noted that (in contrast to Dutch and Chinese contract and sales law) the influence of international contract and sales law does not extend to national legal provisions for commercial sales contracts.

28. In addition, sources of legal principles mentioned above, case law and academic legal works, such as textbooks and academic journal articles, should also be considered when discussing the intricacies of the performance remedial scheme of Singapore.[130] With respect to case law, Singapore courts adhere to the common law tradition that legal precedents must be taken into account by the court when adjudicating a legal dispute.[131] In this respect, a Singapore court is bound by the *ratio decidendi* of a superior court if the facts of the case do not materially differ and it does not concern an *obiter dictum* of the court (a statement of the court which does not affect the final ruling).[132] In contrast to *obiter dicta*, the operative reason of decisions of the Singapore Court of Appeal (*ratio decidendi*) are binding on the Singapore High Court, the District Court and the Magistrate's Courts, unless the court can distinguish the material facts of the case from those in the prior case.[133] The Court of Appeal does not have to follow its own previous decisions because its task is to develop the law.[134] The operative reasons of judicial decisions from other common law jurisdictions are not binding on Singapore courts.[135]

2.4 A MIXTURE OF LEGAL AND CULTURAL TRADITIONS IN CHINA

29. In the development of contract law principles of the People's Republic of China for commercial business transactions there are also three important milestones: the introduction

128 Chong et al 2016 (n 125) 1042.

129 Read art 95 CISG in conjunction with Sale of Goods (United Nations Convention) Act (Cap 283A, 2013 ED), s 3(2).

130 Wui Ling Cheah and Goh Yihan, 'An Empirical Study on the Singapore Courts of Appeal's Citation of Academic Works: Reflections on the Relationship between Singapore's Judiciary and Academia' (2017) 3 Singapore Academy of Law Journal <http://academypublishing.org.sg/Journals/Singapore-Academy-of-Law-Journal/e-First/ctl/eFirstPDFPage/mid/519/ArticleId/1090/Citation/eFirstPDF> accessed on 21 June 2017.

131 Shenoy and Loo 2013 (n 13) para 3.20.

132 Shenoy and Loo 2013 (n 13) paras 3.24, 3.42.

133 Cheah and Goh 2017 (n 130); <http://www.singaporelaw.sg/sglaw/laws-of-singapore/overview/chapter-1> accessed 14 June 2017.

134 *Ibid.*

135 *Ibid.*

of a set of special regulations for economic contracts in the 1980s,[136] the enactment of the PRC Contract Law principles, in 1999 and the accession of China to the CISG in 1986 (effective from 1 January 1988). The first steps towards a civil code for China were taken by the Qing Dynasty,[137] which aimed to introduce a civil code of China based on the German Civil Code (*Bürgerliches Gesetzbuch*).[138] It is argued that the proposed civil law structure was readily accepted because the ancient law of China already entailed a strong structured written code and moreover, the traditional Chinese mindset shared comparable principles with civil law traditions.[139] Nonetheless, it is held that the two prime reasons for the adoption of a German civil law framework in China, instead of the French Civil Code for example, is that young Chinese scholars conducted extensive research in Japan, which had already incorporated the German civil law structure into its existing law, and second, that Japanese legal experts supported the Qing legal reformers.[140] However, this civil code, the *Da Qing Min Lü Cao'an*, or Draft Civil Code of the Great Qing,[141] never came into force due to the fall of the Qing Dynasty in 1911.[142] The Chinese Republic assumed power and started in the same year with the second draft of the Civil Code of China, which was based on the framework of the first Japanese and German civil law inspired draft and introduced elements of the civil code of France, Italy and Switzerland.[143] Regarding western influences, the Civil Code of China did not deny the important role of

136 More particularly the later discussed General Principles of Civil Law of the People's Republic of China (1986); Lei Chen and Larry A DiMatteo, 'History of Chinese Contract Law' in DiMatteo and Chen 2017 (n 19) 5.

137 Lei Chen, 'The Historical Development of the Civil Law Tradition in China: A Private Law Perspective' (2010) 78 Tijdschrift voor Rechtsgeschiedenis, 159, 160–162; Lei Chen and Larry A DiMatteo, 'History of Chinese Contract Law' in DiMatteo and Chen 2017 (n 19) 4.

138 Chang Hanchu, *The Legal History of Contemporary China* (*Zhongguo Jindai Fazhishi*) (The Commercial Press 1973), 283; Yao Hui, 'The Modernization of Chinese Civil Law and the Contemporary Tasks', 3 Gansu Social Science (Gansu shehui kexue) (2008) 127; Zhang 2006 (n 41) 28, 29.

139 Chen 2010 (n 137) 475.

140 Consult He Qinhua, *Chinese Legal History* (3rd edn, Legal Press China 2002); W Jones, 'Some Questions Regarding the Significance of the General Provisions of Civil Law of the People's Republic of China' (1987) 28 Harvard International Law Journal 313; Wang Limin, 'The Reception of German Civil Law via Japan in Late Qing Period' (1997) 1 Law Science (faxue); Jianming Shen, 'The Remedy of Requiring Performance under the CISG and the Relevance of Domestic Rules [particulary in the context of China-related sales transactions]' (1996) *Arizona Journal of International & Comparative Law* 253–306 <https://www.cisg.law.pace.edu/cisg/biblio/shen1.html> accessed on 4 August 2017.

141 Zhang Jinfan, *On the Qing Civil Law* (Qingdai minfa zonglun) (Chinese University of Political Science and Law Press 1998) 249; D Reynolds, *China, 1898–1912: the Xinzheng Revolution and Japan* (Harvard University Press for the Council on East Asia Studies 1993).

142 M Schmiegelow and H Schmiegelow (eds), *Institutional Competition between Common Law and Civil Law, Theory and Policy* (Springer 2014) 58, 332; Guodong Xu, 'An Introduction to the Structures of Three Major Civil Code Projects in Nowadays China' (2004) 19 Tulane European and Civil Law Forum 37, 54 <http://biblio.juridicas.unam.mx/libros/4/1943/33.pdf> accessed 9 May 2017; Chen 2010 (n 137) 162; Shen 1996 (n 140).

143 Schmiegelow 2014 (n 142) 332; Chen 2010 (n 137) 169; Zhang 2006 (n 41) 29.

ancient Chinese civil law customs by starting from the premises that *'if there is no provision of law applicable to a civil case, the case shall be decided according to custom. If there is no such custom, the case shall be decided in accordance with the general principles of law'*.[144] Before the Civil Code of China was promulgated, some civil law principles, which later formed the general law of China,[145] had already been adopted by the Supreme Court.[146] The Civil Code of China eventually became a binding law in 1930, but it still used the ancient term of *Qi Yue* (agreement) instead of contract (*He Tong*).[147] An agreement was (and is) seen as an act of promise making (meeting of minds), and only the *Qi Yue* is subject to performance remedies.[148]

30. In 1949, the People's Republic of China (hereinafter China) was established by the new communist government.[149] This government replaced the civil code with a socialist system based on the Soviet model,[150] which was historically influenced by the French civil law tradition.[151] This indirect French influence also explains that, although the system of the new communist government was characterised by legal nihilism (a negative attitude toward law),[152] a form of codification of contract law could be found in the Provisions and Rules Regarding Contracts among Government Organisations, State-Owned Enterprises, and Collective Units.[153] However, contractual promises in the area of consumer transactions lacked any formal legal context and were subject to principles deriving from established customs.[154] In the following years, a number of contract law instruments were adopted to serve the planned economy, yet they were all discarded during the Cultural Revolution of the period 1966–1976.[155] From 1976 onwards, after the death of Mao Zedong, China's economic policy started to shift from a centrally planned economy towards a market economy.[156] In the 1980s, this development resulted in the introduction of the General Principles of Civil Law for non-economic contracts and a number of special regulations

---

144 Art 1 CCL.
145 Chen 2010 (n 137) 169.
146 Chen 2010 (n 137) 169.
147 Zhang 2006 (n 41) 30.
148 Zhang 2006 (n 41) 30.
149 Schmiegelow 2014 (n 142) 332; Chen 2010 (n 137) 173; Zhang 2006 (n 41) 30.
150 Schmiegelow 2014 (n 142) 58; Xu 2004 (n 142).
151 Zhang 2006 (n 41) 30.
152 Schmiegelow 2014 (n 142) 58.
153 Jianhua Zhong and Guanghua Yu, 'China's Uniform Contract Law: Progress and Problems' (1999) 17(1) UCLA Pacific Basin Law Journal 3 <http://escholarship.org/uc/item/97t9s6th> accessed on 9 May 2016.
154 Zhong and Yu 1999 (n 153).
155 Zhong and Yu 1999 (n 153).
156 Schmiegelow 2014 (n 142) 58; Chen 2010 (n 137) 175; Zhang 2006 (n 41) 36; Han Shiyuan, 'The Performance Interest in Chinese Contract Law' in Mindy Chen-Wishart, Alexander Loke and Burtong Ong (eds), *Remedies for Breach of Contract: Studies in the Contract Law of China* (Oxford University Press 2016) 41.

for economic contracts,[157] which eventually formed the basis of the complete Chinese Civil Code.[158] The special regulations for economic contracts were the Economic Contract Law of China (ECL),[159] the Foreign Economic Contract Law of China (hereinafter the FECL),[160] which excluded transport contracts,[161] Patent Law, Trademark Law and Succession Law, and the Law on Technology Contracts (LTC).[162] These three pillars were governed by the General Principles of Civil Law (GPCL).[163] However, contracts based on these particular regulations remained subject to intense state intervention because of their economic characteristics, which were inextricably linked with the state plan of China.[164] In this period, the status of the three laws also deteriorated due to overlapping and conflicting principles.[165] For example, the statutory right to terminate a contract only if the performance of the contract was rendered unnecessary by the other's party breach was removed from the ECL, but never from the LTC, which resulted in conflicting provisions for (domestic) economic contracts.[166]

31. In 1999, the aforementioned special regulations for contracts (ECL, FECL and the TCL) were combined into the Contract Law of the People's Republic of China (hereinafter the CCL).[167] The drafters of the CCL drew inspiration from international treaties and other legal systems, such as the German Civil Code. The adoption of the CCL abolished the distinction between civil contracts, economic contracts, domestic contracts and foreign contracts. Furthermore, the contractual capacity of individuals was accepted. This has strengthened the principle of freedom of contracting, which is reflected in the concept of

157 General Principles of Civil Law of the People's Republic of China (1986).

158 Xu 2004 (n 142).

159 Adopted at the Fourth Session of the Fifth National People's Congress and promulgated by Order No. 12 of the Chairman of the Standing Committee of the National People's Congress on December 13, 1981, and effective as of 1 July 1982 [expired].

160 Adopted at the Tenth Session of the Standing Committee of the Sixth National People's Congress and promulgated by Order No. 22 of the President of the People's Republic of China on 21 March 1985, and effective as of 1 July 1985 [expired].

161 Art 2 FECL.

162 Chen 2010 (n 137) 176; Chuan Feng 2016 (n 38) 129.

163 Adopted at the Fourth Session of the Sixth National People's Congress, and promulgated by Order No. 37 of the president of the People's Republic of China on 12 April 1986, and effective as of 1 January 1987. The current version was adopted at the Fifth Session of the Twelfth National People's Congress of the People's Republic of China on 15 March 2017, and come into force on 1 October 2017; Chuan Feng 2016 (n 38) 129.

164 Zhong and Yu 1999 (n 153).

165 Chuan Feng 2016 (n 38) 129.

166 Chuan Feng 2016 (n 38) 130; Lei Chen and Larry A DiMatteo, 'History of Chinese Contract Law' in DiMatteo and Chen 2017 (n 19) 6.

167 Contract Law of the People's Republic of China Order [1999] No.15 of the President of the People's Republic of China Contract Law of the People's Republic of China has been adopted at the Second Session of the Ninth National People's Congress on 15 March 1999, effective of 1 October 1999; Xu 2004 (n 142); Zhong and Yu 1999 (n 153) 130.

party autonomy.[168] The notion of freedom of contracting should, however, not be interpreted from a Western (European) perspective. Under the latter, the principle of freedom of contracting is paramount, although its impact may be affected where the contract is substantively unfair to one of the parties.[169] By contrast, under Chinese contract law, the principle of freedom of contracting is limited where the interests of the state are affected. It is held that this restriction entails a broad scope of concepts, such as public interest, market order, collective interests and interest of the Communist Party.[170] It is also said that the principle of freedom of contracting can be misused to justify unfair contract terms in commercial contracts between the state or a state owned enterprise and private (foreign) party, where a bad bargain affects the state's financial interest.[171] It is furthermore noted that contracts remain subject to the successor of the GPCL (the new General Provisions of the Civil Law of the People's Republic of China),[172] and specific pieces of separate legislation where appropriate. Furthermore, the CCL should be interpreted in view of the judicial interpretations of the Supreme People's Court concerning the application of the contract law of China.[173] These interpretations include opinions and answers on questions concerning the specific application of contract law principles and serve as a source of law for contractual issues (also called quasi-legislation).[174] The judicial interpretations clarify how the law should be applied in case of a failure in performance of the contract. Authoritative commentary and the judicial decisions published in the

168 Art 4 CCL stipulates that that the parties to a contract shall comply with the principles of voluntary participation; no party shall compel others to accept its will and no individuals or organisations shall unlawfully intervene; Zhong and Yu 1999 (n 153) 2, 9, 10; See for the proposition that party autonomy includes freedom of contract: Meng Zhaohua, 'Party Autonomy, Private Autonomy, and Freedom of Contract' (2014) 10(6) Canadian Social Science 212–216 <http://www.cscanada.net/index.php/css/article/view/5155 DOI: http://dx.doi.org/10.3968/5155> accessed on 22 February 2019.

169 Junwei Fu, *Modern European and Chinese Contract Law, A Comparative Study of Party Autonomy* (Wolters Kluwer Law & Business 2011) 170.

170 Fu 2011 (n 169) 171.

171 Hao Jiang, 'Freedom of Contract under State Supervision' (2015) SSRN Electronic Journal 253; Hao Jiang, 'Enlarged State Power to Declare Nullity, The Hidden State Interest in the Chinese Contract Law' (2014) 7(1) Journal of Civil Law Studies.

172 The General Provisions of the Civil Law of the People's Republic of China, as adopted at the Fifth Session of the Twelfth National People's Congress of the People's Republic of China on 15 March 2017, has come into force on 1 October 2017 (General Provisions 2017).

173 Interpretation I of the Supreme People's Court of Several Issues concerning the Application of the Contract Law of the People's Republic of China (Judicial Interpretation, 1 December 1999 (Judicial Interpretation (I) Contact Law); Interpretation II of the Supreme People's Court of Several Issues concerning the Application of the Contract Law of the People's Republic of China (Judicial Interpretation, 9 February 2009 (Judicial Interpretation (II) Contract Law); The English translation of both interpretations are published on http://en.pkulaw.cn/ (http://en.pkulaw.cn/).

174 Schmiegelow 2014 (n 142) 331; Judicial Interpretation I and II Contract Law (n 173); Interpretation on Issues Concerning the Application of Law for the Trial of Cases of Disputes over Sales Contracts, 31 March 2012 (Judicial Interpretation of Sales Contracts); Zhang 2006 (n 41) 31; Chuan Feng 2016 (n 38) 131.

Gazette of China also play an important role.[175] However, there is currently no central system which includes all relevant case law of China. Only a selection of important cases is published in the Gazette of the Supreme People's Court of China.[176] To solve this issue, the Supreme People's Court is working on a common law inspired guiding-case system, which in the future is intended to serve as a source of law.[177] That being said, decisions of the Supreme People's Court are currently not cited by lower courts unless the merits of the proceeding concerns a procedural matter,[178] which makes it difficult to ascertain the actual grounds of a ruling. Furthermore, it is worth noting that the words of the English translation of Chinese laws and case law are subsidiary to the original Chinese text. Regarding the sale of goods between a party from China and a foreign party, the CISG applies if both contracting parties have their relevant places of business in member states.[179] However, China (similar to Singapore) excluded the principle that the CISG also applies when the rules of private international law lead to the application of the law of a member state.[180] All told, the fact that China is a signatory country to the CISG limits the applicability of the contract law of China to domestic sale agreements and to international sale agreements between parties from China and non-member states. See in this regard Figure 1 for an illustration of the influence of international and European contract law principles on Chinese contract law.

2.5 CONCLUSIONS

32. This chapter has sought to lay out some of the historical and contemporary fundaments of the Dutch, Singapore and Chinese sales law principles. The starting point is that the respective contract law systems in the investigated jurisdictions were all extensively reformed between 1990 and 1999.[181] The contract law system of the Netherlands underwent a complete recodification in 1992, in order to keep pace with developments in society.[182] This means that, from a historical perspective, the examined statutory principles are new,

175 The Supreme's People's Court of the People's Republic of China.

176 Wei Luo and Joan Liu, *A Complete Research Guide to the Laws of the People's Republic of China (PRC)* (2003) Law Library Resource Xchange <http://en.pkulaw.cn.ezproxy.leidenuniv.nl:2048/Article/Article1.aspx> accessed 12 September 2017.

177 Schmiegelow 2014 (n 142) 334; Lei Chen, 'Availability of Specific Remedies in Chinese Contract Law' in Chen-Wishart, Loke and Ong 2016 (n 156) 26.

178 Zhang 2006 (n 41) 31; Lei Chen, 'Availability of Specific Remedies in Chinese Contract Law' in Chen-Wishart, Loke and Ong 2016 (n 156) 26.

179 <https://www.cisg.law.pace.edu/cisg/countries/cntries-China.html> accessed on 4 August 2017.

180 Arts 1(1)(b), 95 CISG.

181 EH Hondius in C Mak in Schelhaas 2002 (n 19) 20, 21, Shenoy and Loo 2013 (n 13) para 2.35 and <http://www.singaporelaw.sg/sglaw/laws-of-singapore/overview/chapter-1/> accessed on 19 October 2015.

182 EH Hondius in C Mak in Schelhaas 2002 (n 19) 20, 21.

albeit certain elements have been kept in place. The same applies to the contract law of Singapore, which inherited English common law principles, but in 1994 started to reform its legal framework. The reformation of the Singapore legal system is based on the premise that future Singapore law should align with the country's domestic, social and economic fundamentals. Further, it is held that ambitions to customise the Singapore law system stem from the growing maturity and international standing of Singapore's legal system and the historical links between Britain and the European Union, which could make English law incompatible with Singapore's local developments and aspirations,[183] although Singapore's suppositions pre-date the outcome of the recent 'Brexit' referendum. China started its reforms a couple of years earlier with the introduction of the ECL (1981), but the complete transformation of the law on contracts only commenced in 1990 and resulted in the enactment of the Contract Law of the People's Republic of China in 1999. The contract law of China transplanted principles from the German civil law tradition, the CISG,[184] as well as the PICC.[185] It is the case, therefore, that the contract law of China shows an interesting combination of civil and common law elements.

33. It is obvious that the Netherlands, Singapore and China have been actively working on structuring a legal framework which is appropriate in light of their historical roots, but which also facilitates the evolving different interests in a balanced contract law mechanism. It may also seem fair to say that the three investigated jurisdictions have overcome significant barriers for commercial businesses involved in cross-border trade by becoming a signatory to the CISG. This international treaty for commercial sales, however, entails a significant exception to the rules on the enforceability of non-monetary obligations under a commercial sales contract, which reveals the dangers of relying on the efforts of the drafters to bridge the gap between the civil and common law traditions. This applies directly to the contract law of the Netherlands, Singapore and China as these legal frameworks have strong roots in the two major legal traditions, although influenced by domestic notions of the law. Nonetheless, on a general note, it may be said that the contract law of the Netherlands and China transplanted principles from the French and German civil law legal families respectively. The contract law of Singapore is, in essence, a codification of English law, although its principles are subject to revision by Singapore courts where this

183 Shenoy and Loo 2013 (n 13) para 2.35 and <http://www.singaporelaw.sg/sglaw/laws-of-singapore/overview/chapter-1/> accessed on 19 October 2015.

184 See United Nations Convention on Contracts for the International Sale of Goods, 11 April 1980, 1489 UNTS 3 (entered into force 1 January 1988) <http://www.uncitral.org/pdf/english/texts/sales/cisg/V1056997-CISG-e-book.pdf> accessed on 10 May 2016.

185 International Institute for the Unification of Private Law (UNIDROIT), Principles of International Commercial Contracts (2010 ed), <http://www.unidroit.org/english/principles/contracts/main.htm> accessed on 10 May 2016; Xu 2004 (n 142) 633; Schmiegelow 2014 (n 142) 58.

is appropriate in view of the domestic circumstances. These historical roots explain (partially) the marked differences between the thresholds to enforced performance of non-monetary obligations under a commercial sales contract, as discussed in the following chapters.

3 Ambit of a commercial sales contract

3.1 Introduction

34. This chapter analyses and compares three specific elements of establishing an enforceable commercial sales contract under the contract law of the Netherlands, Singapore and China. The investigated matters are: the concept of sale (section 3.2), the goods subject to the sales law principles (section 3.3), and the fundamental principles and requirements (from a comparative perspective) for bringing about enforceable obligations under a commercial sales contract (section 3.4). The findings are evaluated against the rules laid down in the CISG, PICC, PECL and DCFR, where relevant. The draft PACL does not include rules on formation of a contract and is, therefore, not taken into account.

There is a theoretical and practical reason for discussing the above-mentioned elements in the context of determining the availability of enforced performance of contractual rights arising under a commercial sales contract. The first reason is to bring about more in-depth insights in the doctrinal differences between the applicable concepts and, subsequently, to enhance the understanding of the impact of the different approaches on determining the actually enforceability of contractual rights. The second reason is to demystify the intricacies of the approaches taken by the discussed legal systems, which may give contracting parties false comfort and could result in a situation where they fall foul of unexpected consequences.

3.2 Concept of a sales contract

35. *Preliminary* – The following analysis focusses on the distinction between a sales contract seen as a type of juridical act, and performance of the obligations resulting therefrom.[186] The structural division between the concept of a sales contract seen as a juridical act, and the obligations resulting thereform is inspired by the purpose of the DCFR to make a clear distinction between the concept of 'contract' and 'obligations'.[187] An analysis of this approach is particularly helpful for enhancing the understanding of the notion of the juridical outcome of the conclusion of a sales contract and the legal relationship (consisting of obligations and rights) to which it gives rise at the national and international levels.

186 *E.g.*, art II.-1:101 Comments A DCFR.
187 *Ibid.*

The following discussion reveals that this undertaking is indispensable when comparing civil law and common law principles, such as in the present comparative study. This is because the two major legal traditions have adopted significantly different dogmatic approaches towards the concept of a sales contract (*i.e.* the juridical act) and the concept of sale (*i.e.* execution of the contractual obligations). It may appear that this discussion is not of any relevance for commercial practice. Nonetheless, understanding the differences is of significant importance for determining the moment a contractual right becomes enforceable.

> *Illustration* – On 1 September 2018, an exporter of spices and a wholesaler conclude a sales contract for the purchase and delivery of a certain quantity and quality of freshly produced vanilla pods from Madagascar, to be delivered by the seller at the warehouse of the buyer before 14 March 2019. However, unknown to both parties at the conclusion of the sales contract, the vanilla pods, which were on board of a ship in transit, had already been legitimately disposed of at sea because they were affected by a plant disease which endangered the other products on the ship.[188] In other words, the goods had already perished at the moment when the parties concluded the sales contract. A comparative review of this situation, where the goods have perished before the contractual obligations are due and the risk in the goods has not yet passed to the buyer, aims to highlight the divergence between the function and impact of the juridical act of concluding a sales contract and performance of the obligations deriving therefrom (*i.e.* bringing about the actual sale from a common law perspective).

36. *Domestic approaches* – Dutch contract law considers a commercial sales contract as a type of agreement which entails a set of reciprocal obligations and rights. This juridical act directly brings about the sale of the goods. In other words, the concept of a sales contract is the counterpart of the concept of sale. The latter should not be confused with performance of the obligations resulting from the juridical act of concluding a sales contract. An important consequence resulting from this approach is that, under Dutch contract law, the juridical act of concluding a sales contract (and thus bringing about a sale) springs from the promise of one party to deliver (existing or future) goods and the other party's promise to pay the price thereof.[189] The obligations deriving from the juridical act of concluding a sales contract are defined as the transfer (*overdracht*) of ownership of the goods sold with their accessories and delivery (*levering*) of the goods in accordance with the stipulated features, in return for payment of the purchase price. This interpretation of a sales contract (and thus a sale) reveals that an agreement entailing an exchange of goods

188 For a similar example under English law, see *Couturier v Hastie* [1856] 5 HL Cas 673, 10 E.R. 1065.
189 Art 7.1 DCC.

(*i.e.* a barter contract) for goods does not constitute a sales contract.[190] Nonetheless, the statutory provisions regarding the sale of goods apply *mutatis mutandis*.[191] However, there are differing opinions on the qualification of barter contracts in other jurisdictions and at the international level.[192]

Under Dutch contract law, the obligation to deliver the goods means giving possession of the thing, or, on a sale subject to reservation of title, control over it.[193] The obligation to deliver the goods and the transfer of property of the goods may coincide if it follows from the nature of the goods that physical possession suffices. In other words, for goods which are not subject to registration (as almost all movable goods are),[194] the ownership and possession of the goods may transfer on conclusion of the sales contract.[195] As well as already existing goods, a sales contract (and thus a sale) can also comprise future or ascertainable goods,[196] because the juridical act of sale only requires a commitment to deliver goods in return for payment of a certain sum.[197] For example, a manufacturer and rental company may bring about a sales contract (and thus a sale) on the basis of the promise of the former to deliver 10,000 bicycles in return for the agreed purchase price when the bicycles have not yet been manufactured.[198] It is not relevant that the bicycles do not exist at the moment of conclusion of the sales contract, because the contract law of the Netherlands does not require that the subject matter actually exists in order to bring about the juridical act of a sales contract, and thus the sale of the goods. It is only required that the parties intend to produce the juridical effects manifested by the sales contract,[199] and that the goods are determinable.[200] The above-described approach taken by Dutch contract law does not mean that a sale of future goods brings about the actual delivery and transfer of the ownership of the goods.[201] This is because delivery and transfer are merely

190 Art 7:49 DCC.
191 Art 7:50 DCC.
192 Schwenzer, Hachem and Kee 2012 (n 13) para 8.18.
193 Arts 7:1; 7:9(1)(2); 7:26(1) DCC.
194 *E.g.*, large vessels and aircrafts are subject to registration; see for an overview of the things subject to registration SE Bartels and AIM van Mierlo, *Mr. C. Assers Handleiding tot de beoefening van het Nederlands Burgerlijk Recht. 3. Vermogensrecht algemeen. Deel IV. Algemeen goederenrecht* (Kluwer 2013) 327; GT de Jong, HB Krans and MH Wissink, *Verbintenissenrecht algemeen* (Studiereeks Burgerlijk Recht, 5th edn, Wolters Kluwer 2018) 11.
195 Arts 3:84(1), 3:90 DCC.
196 *I.e.*, goods which can be defined at a later point in time.
197 Hartkamp 2011 (n 80) para 243.
198 Art 3:97(1) DCC; JFM Janssen, 'De levering bij voorbaat van toekomstige goederen' (2006) 6685 WPNR 745.
199 Arts 6:217, 3:33 DDC.
200 Art 6:227 DCC.
201 Janssen 2016 (n 198) 745, 746.

an execution of the obligations arising from the sale of the goods (*i.e.* concluding a sales contract).[202]

For determining the enforceability of the obligations arising from the sale of the goods, the preliminary assessment entails the question as to whether the subject matter is sufficiently determined, or determinable, to constitute a valid sales contract (*i.e.* a legal title for delivery and for the actual delivery). The thresholds for bringing about enforceable obligations are not set too high as a broad interpretation of the requirement of determinability of the obligations is commonly adopted by the courts,[203] applying the standards of reasonableness and fairness.[204] Nonetheless, if the goods did not exist or had already perished at the time when the parties entered into a sales contract, an order for enforced performance is generally not available due to the operation of the fundamental prerequisite of sufficient interest in obtaining a judicial order for enforced performance.[205] A seller may also defeat a claim for enforced performance where it can be shown that it is impossible to deliver the very thing the parties bargained for,[206] albeit the substantive right to performance does not cease to exist.[207] In practice, the aggrieved party may seek recourse to other judicial actions, such as a claim for monetary compensation.[208] Here, the main point is that the non-existence or perishing of the goods at or after the conclusion of the sales contract does not affect the existence of the contract, unless the sale is annulled on the basis of, for example, duress, fraud or undue influence.[209]

37. The contract law of Singapore starts with the principle that an agreement to sell future, or ascertainable goods and an agreement of sale brings about a juridical act in the form of a sales contract.[210] An important feature of the juridical act of concluding a sales contract under Singapore contract law is that it results in an obligation of the seller to transfer the

202 *Ibid.*

203 CH Sieburgh, *Mr. C. Assers Handleiding tot de beoefening van het Nederlands Burgerlijk Recht. 6. Verbintenissenrecht. Deel III. Algemeen overeenkomstenrecht* (Wolters Kluwer 2018) 285; Hijma, *Asser Koop en ruil* 7-I* 2013 (n 48) 200; MAMC van den Berg, *Mr. C. Assers Handleiding tot de beoefening van het Nederlands Burgerlijk Recht. 7. Bijzondere overeenkomsten. Deel VI. Aanneming van werk* (Wolters Kluwer 2017) 183; Hofmann 1976 (n 84) 14.

204 Art 6:248(1) DCC; Dutch Parliamentary History Book 3 (Kluwer 1981) 1123.

205 Art 3:303 DCC; The time for performance does not necessarily have to be due when a claim for enforced performance is initiated, see para 86.

206 D Haas, 'De grenzen van het recht op nakoming' (Dphil thesis, Vrije Universiteit Amsterdam 2009) 244; De Jong, Krans and Wissink 2018 (n 194) 76.

207 GJP de Vries 1984, *Recht op nakoming en schadevergoeding, excepties en ontbinding volgens NBW en BW* (Studiepockets privaatrecht nr 32, Tjeenk Willink 1984) 21; Dutch Parliamentary History Book 6 (Kluwer 1981) 488–489.

208 Hofmann 1976 (n 84) 16, 17.

209 Art 3:44(1) DCC.

210 SGA, s 2(1); Hunter 2017 (n 7) para 3.11; Chong et al 2016 (n 125) 10.2.13.

ownership or title of property in the goods to the buyer[211] and to deliver the goods, at a later point in time or directly.[212] In return, the buyer is obliged to take delivery and pay the agreed price.[213] Thus, the contract law of Singapore acts on the notion that a promise to deliver goods in return for payment of money constitutes a sales contract. Hence, an exchange of goods for goods (*i.e.* barter contracts) does not qualify as a sales contract and is, therefore, not governed by the sales law provisions.

As for the distinction between a sales contract and the concept of sale, Singapore contract law acts on the notion that where a sales contract derives from an agreement to sell, an additional juridical act (*i.e.* transfer of property in the goods) is required to bring about a sale.[214] In other words, only the execution of the obligation of the seller to transfer the property in the goods under a sales contract constitutes the sale.[215] It depends, however, on the specific characteristics of a sales contract whether the transfer of property comprises conveyance of property or merely the passing of risk.[216] The latter may occur when Incoterms® apply. Thus, under the contract law of Singapore, future goods can be subject to a sales contract entailing an agreement to sell, but this only becomes a sale when the property in the goods is transferred.[217] This notion is also laid down in the statutory principle that when in a sales contract the seller purports to effect a present sale of future goods, the sales contract is operating as an agreement to sell the goods.[218]

As for the determinability of the obligations, a sales contract may entail an agreement to sell unascertained goods; but to bring about a sale (by transfer of property) the goods must be ascertained.[219] If the goods form part of an identified bulk,[220] the sale entails a transfer of the property in an undivided share in a bulk of identified goods.[221] This distinction between the agreement to sell and the actual sale also causes a distinction in effect when the goods perish before or after contract formation. The general starting point is that where there is a sales contract which entails an agreement to sell specific goods, and without the knowledge of the seller the goods have perished at the time when the contract is made, the contract is void.[222] In cases where the goods have perished after the conclusion

211 SGA, s 2(1); Shenoy and Loo 2013 (n 13) para 22.61; Chong et al 2016 (n 125) para 10.2.13.
212 SGA, s 27.
213 SGA, s 27; Hunter 2017 (n 7) para 7.2.
214 SGA, s 2(1).
215 Chong et al 2016 (n 125) para 10.2.13.
216 Shenoy and Loo 2013 (n 13) para 22.61; Hunter 2017 (n 7) paras 4.1, 4.2, 5.5.
217 Hunter 2017 (n 7) para 3.10.
218 SGA, s 5(3).
219 SGA, s 16.
220 SGA, ss 20A(1)(2).
221 Chong et al 2016 (n 125) para 10.4.18.
222 SGA, s 6; Hunter 2017 (n 7) para 3.11.

of the sales contract but before the occurrence of the actual sale, a sales contract is voidable.[223]

38. The contract law of China entails the principle that a sales contract between two commercial parties with equal standing, comprises an undertaking whereby the seller promises to deliver the goods and to transfer the title to the buyer by providing the necessary documents, and the buyer promises to pay the purchase price.[224] An important feature of the juridical act of concluding a sales contract is that it also constitutes the actual sale of the goods. This means in effect, that the obligations of the parties to deliver the goods and to pay the purchase price arise from the juridical act of concluding a contract (and thus a sale). Nonetheless, it should be mentioned that where the agreement entails an exchange of goods (*i.e.* barter contract), the contract is governed by the provisions on sales contracts.[225]

Where a sales contract entails future goods, the obligation to transfer the property and delivery of the goods is postponed.[226] Put differently; it is not required that the goods already exist to constitute a sales contract (and thus a sale).[227] Consequently, a sales contract could include a transaction where the goods and the purchase price are immediately exchanged, and where parties agree to exchange the goods and the purchase price at a future specified place and date. The act of concluding a sales contract for the sale of existing, future and ascertainable goods should be distinguished from determining the effectiveness (*i.e.* validity) of the contract. In other words, parties may have concluded a sales contract, but this does not necessarily mean that the contract obtained effectiveness.[228] Consequently, the time of conclusion of a sales contract does not automatically coincide with the moment the obligations of the parties become effective (*i.e.* the moment at which the contract is legally valid and thus renders binding obligations).[229]

In order to establish an effective sales contract, the parties must comply with specific mandatory law provisions which have the function to prevent any undertaking that significantly harms the public interest.[230] A sales contract which is formed in accordance with these mandatory statutory requirements is directly effective (and thus establishes a

223 SGA, s 7; Hunter 2017 (n 7) para 3.11.

224 Art 130, 133, 135 CCL; Wang Liming, *Contract Law of China* (China Law & Society Library, William S Hein & Co., Inc 2016) 271.

225 Art 175 CCL.

226 Yuanshi Bu (ed), *Chinese Civil Law* (Beck and Hart Publishing 2013) 274.

227 Bu 2013 (n 226) 274.

228 Art 14(1) CCL.

229 Bing Ling, *Contract Law in China* (Sweet & Maxwell Asia 2002) paras 3.002, 3.003; Yi Wang, 'Prospect of Validity in Chinese Contract Law' in DiMatteo and Chen 2017 (n 19) 216, 223.

230 Read art 58 GPCL in conjunction with art 52 CCL; Liming 2016 (n 224) 84; Yi Wang, 'Prospect of Validity in Chinese Contract Law' in DiMatteo and Chen 2017 (n 19) 216.

sale) unless the sales contract is subject to specific conditions and where government approval or registration is required.[231] Where the sales contract does not comply with the laws and regulations for effective obligations, the sales contract has no binding effect on the parties (*i.e.* void *ab initio*).[232] Where the mandatory regulations on effectiveness are fulfilled, an effective sales contract may be revoked (*i.e.* voidable) on the basis of mandatory provisions of regulation where there is an infringement of the public order.[233]

In light of the thresholds above for establishing enforceable obligations under a sales contract, it is also important to bear in mind that the quantity and quality of the goods are sufficiently determined.[234] This statutory requirement not only requires conformity with the standards agreed by the parties; it also includes minimum quality requirements imposed by, for example, the state food and drug administration.[235] In addition, the contractually agreed quality standards need to be on par or higher in order to establish a sales contract.[236] That said, where the goods do not exist or have perished, the bindingness of the sales contract is not affected. In these instances, a claim for enforced performance shall be refused by the court on application of the statutory principle that an aggrieved party is not entitled to demand performance where performance is factually impossible.[237]

39. Figure 2 and Figure 3 are diagrammatic representations of the discussed principles in light of the case described under paragraph 35.

231 Art 44 GPCL; Bing Ling 2002 (n 229) para 4.004.

232 Mindy Chen-Whishart, 'Invalidity of Contract in Chinese and English Contract Law' in DiMatteo and Chen 2017 (n 19) 240.

233 Art 54 CCL; An aggrieved party may request the court to modify or revoke a contract where the undertaking is a result of a significant misconception, where the contract is obviously unfair at the moment of conclusion, and where the contract is concluded on the basis of fraud, coercion, or exploitation of the aggrieved party's unfavourable position; Yi Wang, 'Prospect of Validity in Chinese Contract Law' in DiMatteo and Chen 2017 (n 19) 217, 223.

234 Arts 12 (3), (4) CCL; Bing Ling 2002 (n 229) para 3.009; Bu 2013 (n 226) 274.

235 Zhang 2006 (n 41) 125.

236 *Ibid.*

237 Art 110 (1) CCL; Bing Ling 2002 (n 229) para 8.072.

Figure 2 The concept of a sales contract and sale

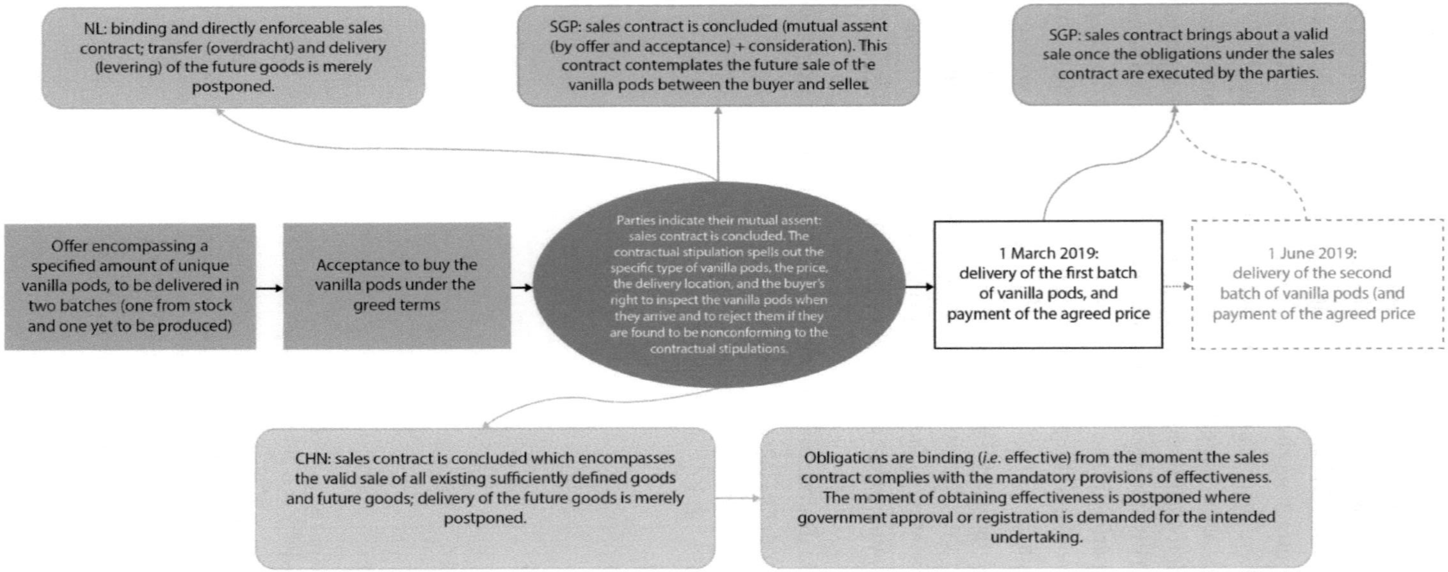

Figure 3 Goods perishing before making the contract / Goods perishing before sale but after conclusion of the contract

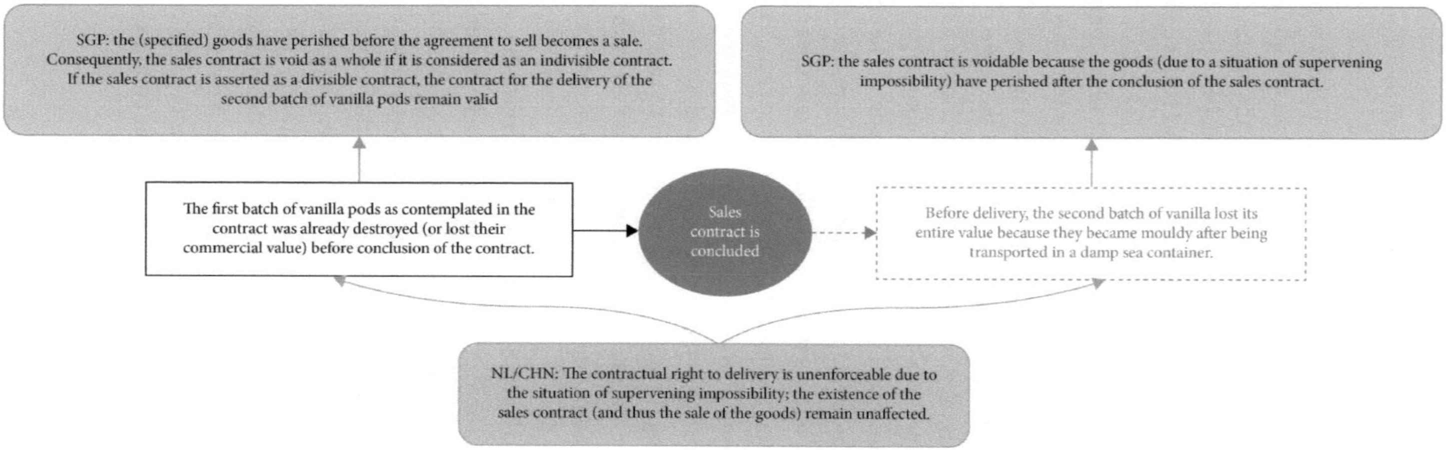

40. *Comparative analysis* – Aside from formation formalities,[238] it is unanimously agreed by the three investigated jurisdictions that the juridical act of an agreement to sell (existing, future and ascertainable) goods in return for payment of a certain sum creates a sales contract. The reciprocal element of payment of the purchase price follows a narrow interpretation in the sense that a mere exchange of goods for goods does not qualify as a sales contract, although Dutch and Chinese contract law have taken the approach that such contracts (*i.e.* barter contracts) are governed by the statutory sales law provisions. This point is of significant importance for those involved in international barter contracts, as it is not clear whether such contracts are governed by the CISG.

More importantly for the present study, there is a crucial difference when comparing the substantive requirements to bring about the actual sale. The contract law of the Netherlands and China start with the notion that the concept of sale is equated with the juridical act of concluding a sales contract, regardless of the nature of the subject matter (*i.e.* existing, future or ascertainable goods). A similar position is attained by the CISG and DCFR, which means that the juridical act of a sales contract is the counterpart of the concept of sale, which may concern a transfer of existing and future goods.[239] The contract law of Singapore adopted the common law structure which is the exact opposite of that of the viewpoint mentioned above; that is, it starts from the juridical act of a sales contract which is available for existing, future and ascertainable goods, but performance of the obligations deriving therefrom (*i.e.* transfer of property in the goods) is required to bring about the actual sale. This divergence between the notion of a juridical act of sale is of significant importance when determining the status of a sales contract in case the goods did not exist or perished at the time of the conclusion of the contract, and where the goods perish after conclusion of the contract but before the due date of the obligations and the transfer of property.

Insofar as the contract law of the Netherlands and China is concerned, the equation of the juridical act of concluding a sales contract with the concept of sale explains that a sales contract (and thus a sale) may concern existing as well as future goods. Furthermore, as the goods are regarded as sold once the contract is concluded, it is not relevant to have a separate discussion about the impediments for enforcement (or the impact on the contract) where the goods did not exist or have perished at the moment a sales contract is concluded. The key point is that the very existence of a sales contract is not affected unless there is a special cause for the court to invalidate the contract. By contrast, when considering the position of the contract law of Singapore, the example mentioned under paragraph 35 requires primarily an assessment of the question whether the sales contract is void (the goods did not exist or have perished before formation of the contract) or may

238 S 3.4.

239 Art 4(a) CISG; Arts IV.A.-1:201, IV.A.-1:202 Comment A DCFR.

be avoided (the goods perished after formation).[240] For those involved in commercial sales across the borders of the investigated jurisdictions, and national legislators aiming to remove legal barriers to international trade, it is of paramount importance to take note of the discussed differences, as validity matters are not governed by the CISG.[241]

3.3 Goods subject to sales law

41. *Preliminary* – This section examines the type of goods which fall under the application of the Dutch, Singapore and Chinese sales law provisions, and to what extent their approaches are in line with the definition of goods in the CISG and the type of goods subject to the sales law provisions of the DCFR.[242] The PICC, PECL and the draft PACL do not include specific provisions on sales contracts and are, therefore, not taken into account. The investigated legal systems show two different methods of defining goods. The first way is a general definition of goods. The second is more negative because it only clarifies which goods are not subject to the sales law provisions. In an ideal world, the outcome of both ways of defining goods should be reviewed on an annual basis because of the ongoing expansion of goods subject to sales transactions.

That having been said, the practical aim of the present undertaking, of determining the type of goods which can be the subject of a sales contract, is to reveal the common core and dissimilarities between the subject legal systems in order to provide clarity about the scope of the investigated sales law principles. The present section is also an attempt to enhance the understanding of the issues arising from the exclusion of certain goods from the CISG, which have thus far not received sufficient attention. The high-level aim of the undertaking of determining the goods subject to sales law is to disclose the underlying reasons for the divergence, which is helpful for obtaining a better understanding of the general availability of enforced performance of non-monetary obligations arising from a commercial sales contract. In particular, this is true for contemporary issues arising from the increasing sale of incorporeal goods in a commercial context.

> *Illustration* – A, a software developer, and company B which integrates digital information, located in different jurisdictions, enter into a software licence agreement for the usage of a specific software product not limited in time. The purchase price was paid on one single occasion and not through monthly instalments. As the software developer refuses to transfer the software to company B, the latter brings an action

240 SGA, s 7; Hunter 2017 (n 7) para 3.11.

241 Schwenzer 2016 (n 91) art 4 para 31.

242 The PICC, PECL and draft PACL are not taken into account as these unification instruments do not include specific rules on sales contracts.

against it alleging a failure in the performance of the licence agreement terms and conditions. In this situation, the contract brings about the problematic question – when dealing with parties across civil and common law borders – whether software can be the object of a sales contract, and thus subject to, for example, quality standards and performance remedies as laid down in the national sales law provisions.

42. The process of examining which goods are subject to the sales law provisions is merely a preliminary step for ascertaining the availability of enforced performance of non-monetary obligations arising from a commercial sales contract. The rationale is that in most civil and common law jurisdictions a transaction between two commercial parties is governed by the general contract law principles and, where the subject matter is regarded as a good subject to sales law, also by the applicable statutory provisions for sales contracts. It is, therefore, of paramount importance to assess the entire contract law framework in order to determine the enforceability of non-monetary obligations under a commercial sales contract. The following diagram may be helpful to clarify this point.

Figure 4 The rules governing the exchange of performances by commercial parties

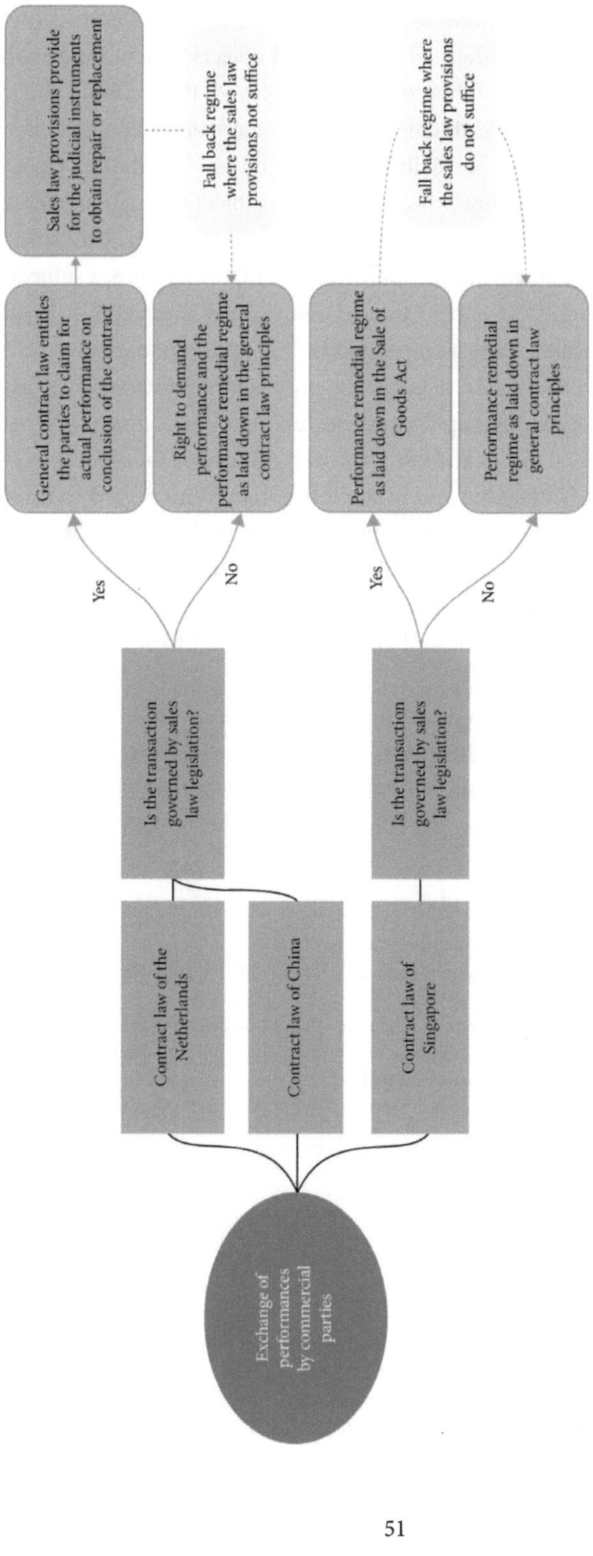

43. *Domestic approaches* – The general sales law provisions of the Dutch contract law convey the word 'things', which is defined as corporeal objects which can be subject to human control.[243] A broad notion of this concept is employed. For example, the sale of a share in an undivided bulk, provided that the goods are described in a sufficiently precise manner at the moment the goods are delivered to the buyer.[244] Although electricity is generally not recognised as something which can be the subject of a sales agreement, the specific statutory provisions for sales contracts stipulate that in the area of consumer sales, electricity, heating, cooling and gas are movable things and,[245] therefore, a subject matter of consumer sales legislation.[246] It is held that in commercial transactions, by analogy, electricity should also be dealt with as a sale of goods.[247] In addition to existing and future goods, a sales contract can also relate to property, proprietary rights and interests.[248] In such a case, the sales law legislation applies to the extent that this conforms to the nature of the right.[249] Thus, corporeal things and patrimonial rights can be the object of a contract of sale,[250] or, in other words, tangible and intangible goods. With regard to immovable goods, the Dutch sales law provisions are supplemented with specific provisions for registration.[251] Specifically designated movable goods can also be subject to registration duties, which need to be fulfilled in order to transfer the property in the subject matter of the contract. For instance, large vessels and aircrafts are subject to a duty of registration despite their movable nature.[252]

A wide interpretation of the concept of things subject to a commercial sales contracts is also seen in recent case law. In 2012, the Dutch Supreme Court considered in *De Beeldbrigade/Hulskamp* and *Hulskamp/Bell Microproducts* that the sale and purchase of software are in principle subject to the sales law provisions.[253] On the basis of both court

243 Arts 7:1, 3:2 DCC; Dutch Parliamentary History Book 3 (n 204) 64.

244 Arts 3:84(2), 6:227 DCC; Hartkamp 2011 (n 80) para 243; Janssen 2016 (n 198); Hijma, *Asser Koop en ruil* 7-I* 2013 (n 48) 195, 196, 200.

245 Art 7:5(5) DCC; The provisions with regard to a consumer sale apply to deliveries to a natural person (acting for purposes outside his commercial, business, craft or professional activities) of electricity, heating, cooling and gas, to the extent these are not packaged for sale in a limited volume or in a fixed quantity; of district heating and of digital content which is not delivered on fixed physical media but which is individualised and over which the consumer can exercise actual control.

246 Art 7:5(1) DCC.

247 Hijma, *Asser Koop en ruil* 7-I* 2013 (n 48) 196.

248 Arts 7:2, 7:46, 7:47, 3:6 DCC; J Hijma and MM Olthof, *Compendium van het Nederlands vermogensrecht* (13th edn, Wolters Kluwer 2017) 33; Hijma, *Asser Koop en ruil* 7-I* 2013 (n 48) 197.

249 Art 7:47 DCC.

250 Hartkamp 2011 (n 80) para 243.

251 *E.g.*, arts 7:2, 7:3, 7:8, 7:17(6), 7:26(4, 5) DCC.

252 Hijma, *Asser Koop en ruil* 7-I* 2013 (n 48) 75a; Bartels and Van Mierlo, *Asser* 3-VI 2013 (n 194) 274.

253 *De Beeldbrigade v Hulskamp* Dutch Supreme Court 27 April 2012, ECLI:NL:HR:2012:BV1301, NJ 2012, 293 paras 3.4, 3.5; *X v Bell Microproducts* Dutch Supreme Court 27 April 2012, ECLI:NL:HR:2012:BV1299, NJ 2012, 294 para 3.3; Hijma, *Asser Koop en ruil* 7-I* 2013 (n 48) 203a.

rulings, it may be assumed that the sale of embedded software (*i.e.* software which is a part of device) and downloadable software are considered as matters subject to the sales law provisions. It may therefore come as little surprise that stocks and shares may also be subject to a sales contract, despite their intangible nature.[254]

44. The sales law of Singapore stipulates that goods include personal chattels other than things in action and money; and in particular 'goods' includes emblements, industrial growing crops, and things attached to or forming part of the land which are agreed to be severed before sale or under the contract of sale and include an undivided share in goods.[255] This definition is based on the traditional English common law understanding of the concept of goods. This means in effect that the sales law of Singapore only applies for existing and future tangibles.[256] The tangible nature of aircrafts, ships and other vessels has the consequence that transactions of these goods are governed by Singapore sales law. The focus on the tangible nature of the things sold also explains that transactions of intellectual property rights, stocks and shares are excluded from the definition of goods.[257] The narrow definition of goods is demonstrated in the Singapore High Court case *Kong Swee Eng v Rolles Rudolf Jurgen August* where it was considered that goods do not include shares.[258] Despite the traditional notion that only tangibles are a part of the concept of goods, Singapore courts have not formed a legal precedent regarding software.[259] Nonetheless, in view of the concept of goods conveyed by English sales law and doctrine,[260] it is held that a distinction should be made between the physical (tangible) disk and the program itself (intangible). It should be mentioned that English (case) law is not binding on the Singapore courts since 1993,[261] although commercial decisions were traditionally regarded as a persuasive authority.[262] It appears, however, that Singapore courts are increasingly looking at local circumstances, which sometimes results in a deviation from

254 Arts 7:1, 3:1 DCC; Hijma and Olthof 2017 (n 248) para 537; *Poot v ABP* Dutch Supreme Court 2 December 1994 para 3.4.3, ECLI:NL:HR:1994:ZC1564, NJ 1995, 288; District Court Arnhem 4 March 1999, ECLI:NL:RBARN:1999:BP4960; Hijma, *Asser Koop en ruil* 7-I* 2013 (n 48) 128, 371.

255 SGA, s 61; Chong et al 2016 (n 125) paras 10.2.6, 10.2.7.

256 SGA, ss 5, 16; Halsbury's Laws of Singapore (Commercial Law 2014) vol 5(2) para 60.108; Chong et al 2016 (n 125) para 10.2.8; The distinction between specific, ascertainable and unascertained goods is discussed in s 4.4.3.

257 Hunter 2017 (n 7) para 2.3; Shenoy and Loo 2013 (n 13) para 22.9; Chong et al 2016 (n 125) para 10.2.6., 10.2.7.

258 [2011] SGHC 300, (2010) 1 SLR 873; Halsbury's Laws of Singapore (Commercial Law 2014) vol 5(2) para 60.108.

259 Chong et al 2016 (n 125) paras 10.2.11–10.2.12.

260 *St Albans City and District Council v International Computers Ltd* [1996] 4 All ER 481 at 493; Halsbury's Laws of Singapore (Commercial Law 2014) vol 5(2) para 60.109; Shenoy and Loo 2013 (n 13) para 22.9.

261 Statutes of the Republic of Singapore, Application of English Law Act (Cap 7A Rev Ed 1994).

262 Paul S Davies and James Penner, *Equity, Trusts and Commerce* (vol 24 Hart studies in private law, Hart Publishing 2017) 52.

the English position.[263] In this light, it is said that if the software in an electronic device fails to perform in accordance with the specifications set out in the contract, the remedial regime of Singapore sales law should apply.[264] This viewpoint is supported by a number of court rulings. For example, in *Management Corporation Strata Title Plan No 1166 v Chubb Singapore Pte Ltd* the Singapore High Court applied the sales law principles to a contract entailing the sale, installation, testing and commissioning of a security and communication system.[265] In *Computer-Aided Design (Asia) Pte Ltd v Sime Darby Singapore Ltd t/a Sime Darby Systems,* the purchase of computer equipment including software was characterised by the Singapore High Court as a transaction under the Singapore Sale of Goods Act.[266] In a similar vein, in *Fujifilm (Singapore) Pte Ltd (Formerly Known As Fuji Photo Film (Singapore) Pte Ltd) v Ultimate Packaging Pte Ltd*, a professional printer (the machine itself) was treated as a good under Singapore sales law.[267] However, if a contract solely considers a licence to use software, the sales law provisions do not apply.[268] Turning to another undetermined subject, electricity. At the moment, it is unclear whether a transaction of electricity can be the object of a sales contract which is governed by Singapore sales law.[269]

45. The contract law of China entails a specific set of principles to determine the rights and obligations of parties who are engaged in a sale of (existing or future) movable and immovable goods.[270] Considering movable goods, a sales contract may entail the transaction of an undivided share in a bulk, if the unit of measure and quality is sufficiently specified in the contract and where the parties agree that the quantity shall be determined in the future.[271] Considering the sale of special movables, such as vessels, aircrafts and vehicles, the agreements could be categorised as either a sale of goods or the delivery of a certain work, depending on the agreed terms of the contract. That said, it is already clear that a shipbuilding contract is regarded as a work by Chinese contract law and, therefore, not subject to the sales law provisions. The sale of rights is covered by other sections of the contract law principles and by specific statutory provisions.[272] In other words, stocks and shares are excluded from the specific provisions for the purchase and the sale of goods.

263 Davies and Penner 2017 (n 262) 53.
264 Hunter 2017 (n 7) paras 2.8, 2.10–2.14.
265 [1999] SGHC 192 [852], (1999) SLR(R) 1035.
266 [1993] SGHC 195.
267 [2012] SGDC 468 [39].
268 Chong et al 2016 (n 125) para 10.2.12; Compare *London Borough of Southwark v IBM UK Ltd* [2011] EWHC 549, TCC para 97.
269 Hunter 2017 (n 7) para 2.16; Halsbury's Laws of Singapore (Commercial Law 2014) vol 5(2) para 60.108.
270 Bu 2013 (n 226) 89, 274.
271 Bu 2013 (n 226) 274.
272 Bu 2013 (n 226) 89.

Any other non-gratuitous contract is required to comply with laws containing applicable provisions, and in the absence of such provisions, these transactions need to be handled with reference to the provisions governing purchase and sales contracts. Contracts concerning the supply of water, gas and heat in return for electricity fees are not governed by the sales law provisions. Instead, the contract law of China comprises a specific set of principles for supply contracts.

The sales law provisions entail the rule that where the contract includes the sale of intellectual property rights, such as computer software, these rights do not belong to the buyer,[273] and, hence, cannot be subject of a claim for enforced performance, unless the applicable laws or contractual stipulations provide otherwise. The treatment of software under the specific provisions of sales contracts indicates that software falls within the sphere of the sales law provisions. This view is also taken by the Supreme People's Court which provided an interpretation of the delivery and transfer of ownership of electronic goods.[274] That said, the transfer of technology is not subject to the sales law provisions. For these transactions, a separate set of statutory principles applies.[275]

46. *International level* – At the international level, there is a significant divergence between the coverage of the CISG and the DCFR. To start with the key instrument for international commercial sales, the CISG does not include a definition for 'goods', but it is undisputed that only existing and future movable, tangible objects can be the object of a sales contract.[276] It is not required that the goods are corporeal at the moment of contracting; it is sufficient that the goods are movable at the moment of delivery[277] – for example, materials which become movable after the demolition of a building. Aside from this general starting point, the CISG takes a negative approach by describing the categories which are excluded.[278] The CISG does not apply to sales contracts including goods bought for personal, family or household use, unless the seller, at any time before or at the conclusion of the contract, neither knew nor ought to have known that the goods were bought for any such use.[279] Thus, consumer sales are excluded.[280] The CISG also excludes sales by auction, sales on execution or otherwise by authority of law, sales of stocks, shares, investment securities, negotiable instruments or money, sales of ships, vessels, hovercrafts or aircrafts and sales of electricity.[281] In addition, and in deviation from the approach taken by civil law-based

273 Art 137 CCL.
274 Art 5 Judicial Interpretation of Sales Contracts (n 174).
275 Ch 18 CCL.
276 Schwenzer 2016 (n 91) 33; Schwenzer, Hachem and Kee 2012 (n 13) para 7.06, 7.16.
277 Schwenzer 2016 (n 91) 34.
278 Art 2 CISG.
279 Art 2(a) CISG.
280 Schwenzer 2016 (n 91) 48.
281 Art 2(b-f) CISG.

jurisdictions, it is stipulated that contracts for the supply of goods to be manufactured or produced are governed by the CISG unless the party who orders the goods undertakes to supply a substantial part of the materials necessary for such manufacture or production.[282] This test for goods to be manufactured is also used to ascertain whether software can be regarded as the purchase of a good to be manufactured.[283] This would be the case if the buyer did not contribute to the development of the software.[284] This situation needs to be distinguished from agreements for temporary use of the software which is not perceived as a sales contract for the purpose of the CISG.[285] In the case of bulk goods, such as rice and salt, a part of the quantity stored can be sold. These transactions of an undivided share in a bulk are said to be regarded as contracts of sale of goods.[286] The only issue which could emerge is whether the identification requirements for the passing of risk can be satisfied.[287] Concerning 'goods' or 'things' of which it is unclear if they can be the object of a sales contract, it is recommended to assess whether the domestic sale of goods provisions offers suitable remedies.[288] The approach taken by the DCFR is much broader. This means in effect that although goods are defined as corporeal movables (including large vessels and aircrafts),[289] the DCFR rules on sales (with appropriate adaption) also apply to contracts for the sale of electricity, software, stocks, shares and an undivided share in a bulk.[290]

47. The following table outlines the goods which can be the object of a sales contract in the investigated legal systems.

282 Art 3(1) CISG.

283 Schwenzer, Hachem and Kee 2012 (n 13) para 7.29.

284 Schwenzer, Hachem and Kee 2012 (n 13) para 7.29.

285 Schwenzer 2016 (n 91) 34.

286 John O Honnold, *Uniform Law for International Sales under the 1980 United Nations Convention* (3rd edn, Kluwer Law International 1999) 46–55.

287 Arts 67(1), 69(3) CISG; Honnold 1999 (n 286) 46–55.

288 Schwenzer, Hachem and Kee 2012 (n 13) para 7.05; Schwenzer 2016 (n 91) 33.

289 Art IV.A.–1:201 Comment A DCFR.

290 Art IV.A.–1:101 Comment A-C DCFR.

Figure 5 Goods subject to sales law

	Software	Stock, Shares	Undivided share in a bulk	Electricity	Large vessels	Aircrafts
Dutch Civil Code	Subject to sales law provisions	Subject to sales law provisions	Subject to sales law provisions	Subject to sales law provisions	Subject to sales law provisions	Subject to sales law provisions
SGA Singapore	Excluded (the program itself)	Excluded	Subject to sales law provisions	Unclear	Subject to sales law provisions	Subject to sales law provisions
Contract Law of China	Subject to sales law provisions	Excluded	Subject to sales law provisions	Excluded	Subject to sales law provisions	Subject to sales law provisions
CISG	Object of a sales contract if the buyer did not substantially contribute to the development	Excluded	Subject to sales law provisions	Excluded	Excluded	Excluded
DCFR	Subject to sales law provisions	Subject to sales law provisions	Subject to sales law provisions	Subject to sales law provisions	Subject to sales law provisions	Subject to sales law provisions

48. Considering the example provided at the beginning of this section, the adjudicating court first has to decide whether the licence agreement is governed by the CISG. Suppose that the CISG is not applicable and, according to the principles of international private law, the substantive elements of the contract are subject to Dutch, Chinese or Singapore contract law (the relevance of the description of the contract versus the intention of parties is not examined in this section). To start with the present approach of Dutch contract law, the purchase of software is subject to sales law principles, albeit that software, in general, is not expressly categorised as a thing which by law is subject to the provisions for sales contracts.[291] Nonetheless, it is generally assumed that an action for the delivery of software in accordance with the agreed terms is subject to the sales law principles. The contract law of China takes a similar stance in the sense that the sale of software, as above described, is subject to the specific provisions for sales contracts. Interestingly, however, the enforcement of the actual performance of the sale of software is excluded on the notion that the rights are not transferable. If the contract law of Singapore applies, it is important to take into account the focus of the sales law principles on tangible versus intangibles when considering if the subject matter of the present contract should be considered as a sale of goods. In Singapore, the sale of software is subject to the sales law legislation if the product is a part of a tangible medium such as DVDs, CDs or USB flash drive. Consequently, it may be assumed that the contract, comprising the mere sale of an intangible digital product, is considered a service contract rather than a sales contract. In case the companies are located in countries which are parties to the CISG, the court is obliged to solve the problem of categorisation of software without consideration of the domestic definition of goods as adopted by domestic sales law legislation. Considering the available case law and the viewpoint reflected in literature, it may be assumed that in the present case the subject of the software licence agreement is to be regarded as 'goods' within the meaning of the CISG.[292] The key factors to take into consideration are the aim of the CISG to provide uniform rules, the intention of parties, the understanding of a reasonable person with regard to the contract,[293] the lack of limitation in time and the payment of the purchase price in one instalment.[294]

---

291 *Beeldbrigade v Hulskamp* (n 253); Hijma and Olthof 2017 (n 248) para 537.

292 Schwenzer, Hachem and Kee 2012 (n 13) paras 7.05, 7.24; Schwenzer 2016 (n 91) art 1 para 16; *Corporate Web Solutions v Dutch company and Vendorlink BV* Court of first instance Midden-Nederland 25 March 2015, ECLI:NL:RBMNE:2015:1096; Germany: Oberlandesgericht Koblenz nr 2, 17 September 1993 U 1230/91; Landgericht München nr 8, 8 February 1995 HKO 24667/93; Oberlandesgericht München nr 23, 22 September 1995 U 3750; Austria: Oberster Gerichtshof nr 5, 21 June 2005 Ob 45/05m.

293 The CISG only allows for interpretation of individual statements made by and other conduct of the parties to a commercial sales contract along the lines of the standard of reasonableness (art 8(2) CISG). The CISG does not permit the usage of the good faith principle (art 7(1) CISG) for interpretation of the contract, to strike out unfair terms or penalty clauses; Schwenzer 2016 (n 91) art 8 para 31.

294 Schwenzer 2016 (n 91) art 1 para 18.

49. *Comparative analysis* – This section examined the type of goods which can be the object of a commercial sales contract. This undertaking reveals that the three investigated jurisdictions have not adopted a comprehensive list of goods which are governed by the domestic sales law provisions. This means in effect that the type of goods governed by Dutch, Singapore and Chinese sales law must be established on the basis of general principles. The starting point in this regard is that the Chinese contract law adopted the least restricted scope of transactions governed by sales law provisions. The language of the Dutch contract law appears to be slightly more restrictive due to the notion that things are corporeal objects which can be subject to human control. Nonetheless, a closer examination of both approaches suggests that there is not a significant difference in the scope of the Dutch and Chinese sales law provisions. It seems that Singapore sales law employs the most narrow understanding of the term goods, due to the understanding that goods must be tangible.[295] The CISG and DCFR have taken a completely different approach. Whereas the CISG excludes specific items (*i.e.* negative definition of goods excluded from the CISG), the DCFR governs the sale of corporeal movables and stipulates that (with appropriate adaptions) its principles may be applied to a number of incorporeal and intangible goods. That having been said, the three investigated jurisdictions, as well as the CISG and DCFR encompass an important common denominator in the sense that they do not provide an exhaustive list of goods covered by sales law provisions. This allows the courts to evolve the concept of goods which can be the object of a sales contract by challenging the boundaries of, for example, the notion of 'human control' under Dutch contact law and the notion of tangible versus intangible under Singapore contract law. This proposition entails the suggestion that there is a certain degree of flexibility for the courts (where this is appropriate) to deviate from the historical notion of goods conveyed by the civil and common law traditions. Nonetheless, it cannot be said that the subject legal systems have adopted a unanimous notion of goods which can be the object of a sales contract. The divergence may cause significant issues where a legal system excludes the sale of ships, vessels and aircrafts.[296] For parties who supply component parts of ships, vessels and aircrafts to the final manufacturer, and contract under Singapore law or the CISG, it is of paramount importance to take note of this point. To remove any uncertainty about the question as to whether the sales law provisions apply, contracting parties may draw inspiration from the CISG, which excludes the transaction of ships, vessels and aircrafts, but takes the approach that the sale of component parts can be governed by the Convention.[297] In this regard, particular attention must be paid to the situation where component parts are manufactured by different companies from the main manufacturer

295 This approach is in line with the concept of goods conveyed by traditional English law.
296 See Figure 5.
297 Schwenzer 2016 (n 91) art 2 para 33.

who is also responsible for attaching the component parts to the vessel or aircraft.[298] It is said that in these instances the exclusion of the sale of ships, vessels and aircrafts under the CISG may apply to the sale of the component parts where they are related to the sale (by the manufacturer) of the vessel or aircraft for which the component is used.[299] Aside from these complexities, it seems that qualification issues arising from the increasing variety in transactions concerning an exchange of money against (currently) undefined 'things' can be solved by the national courts irrespective of their domestic notion of goods subject to sales law. This approach is in line with the open-ended definition of goods adopted by the DCFR, although it may require more awareness in the present-day realities of the transfer of money for the delivery of digital (intangible) products between commercial parties (*e.g.* the unprecedented explosion of contracts encompassing the sale of digital products to ensure compliance with the new GDPR).

3.4 Formation of an enforceable commercial sales contract

3.4.1 *Introduction*

50. This section is structured around the proposition that the divergence between the thresholds for contract formation in the two major legal traditions (*i.e.* civil and common law) are inextricably linked with their attitude towards the enforceability of contractual rights to performance. For example, it appears that where a legal system adopted strict rules on contract formation, enforced performance is only available in exceptional situations. This seems to follow from a need to limit the type of promises which require legal protection by enforcement measures. By contrast, legal systems familiar with a more liberal approach towards the rules on contract formation, generally assume that the parties have a right to enforced performance. In view of these considerations, the following discussion aims to reveal the most fundamental differences between the primary requirements for bringing about an enforceable commercial sales contract under the contract law of the Netherlands, Singapore and China in view of the approaches taken by the CISG, PICC, PECL and DCFR (the draft PACL does not contain articles on contract

298 Mark Kantor, 'The Convention on Contracts for the International Sale of Goods: An International Sales Law', 1 International Law Practicum (NYS Bar Assoc. Autumn 1988) 11; Peter Winship, 'Aircraft and the International Sales Convention', 50 Journal Air Law & Commerce (1985) 1059; Annotated text of CISG, Art 2 words and phrases, ed. Albert H Kritzer <https://cisgw3.law.pace.edu/cisg/text/commentary 2.html#f8> accessed on 2 March 2019.

299 John P McMahon, 'Review' (1990) 21 Journal of Maritime Law and Commerce 306; Annotated text of CISG, Art 2 words and phrases <https://cisgw3.law.pace.edu/cisg/text/commentary2.html#f8> accessed on 2 March 2019.

formation and is, therefore, not taken into consideration). The findings of this assessment (in conjunction with the considerations provided in the previous sections) are ultimately used to determine the underlying reasons for the differences in the availability of enforced performance in the three investigated jurisdictions and to what extent they are related to the availability of enforced performance when a contract is concluded. In the long run, the result of this undertaking may be used at the international level to further the bridging of the gap between the civil and common law contract law principles. This is because a holistic analysis of the larger framework of legal principles provides more insights than a discussion which is only focussed on specific provisions.

51. In view of the foregoing, the first step entails an assessment of the methods of contract formation, and how the required intention to be bound is determined when considering the traditional offer and acceptance model (section 3.4.2). Following this discussion, the second step focuses on the most intractable difficulties which may arise, for example, where a commercial offer does not stipulate the purchase price or a formula to calculate the amount owed by the buyer (section 3.4.3). The main issue boils down to fundamental differences between the civil and common law approach to the interpretation of the words of an offer (*i.e.* statement of one party) and representations not incorporated into the offer.[300] This assessment should be viewed in light of well established differences between the principles and rules for contractual interpretation in civil and common law jurisdictions.[301] Firstly, whereas civil law courts may rely on the rules on the usage of the general notion of good faith to deal with unclear or ambiguous stipulations in an offer, common law courts may appeal to the institution of implied terms in such a situation. In other words, there is a crucial role to play for civil and common law courts when interpretation of the stipulations in an offer is required to determine as to whether enforceable obligations are established. Secondly, civil law jurisdictions would allow a court to take into consideration extrinsic evidence (*i.e.* oral and written representations) for the interpretation of an offer regarding, for example, the quality and price of the goods. By contrast, a strict application of the common law parol evidence rule would bar the court from taking into account contextual factors deriving from representations not recorded in the terms of the offer which, upon acceptance, represent the whole contract (albeit that exceptions apply, such as extrinsic evidence of trade usage or custom). Taking into account the diametrically opposing viewpoints mentioned above and the fiercely disputed approach taken by the CISG for commercial sales contracts entailing an indefinite price, the above

300 Schwenzer, Hachem and Kee 2012 (n 13) paras 26.44–26.50.

301 Catherine Valcke, 'Contractual Interpretation at Common Law and Civil Law: An Exercise in Comparative Legal Rhetoric' in Jason W. Neyers, Richard Bronaugh and Stephan G.A. Pitel (eds), *Exploring Contract Law* (Hart Publishing 2009), 77.

mentioned sections assess the position taken by the investigated jurisdictions and whether their approach resonates with the daily reality of cross-border sales transactions.

The third step deals with another potential enforcement conflict deriving from the seemingly irreconcilable principles in civil and common law jurisdictions arising from the bindingness of an offer and the promise to keep the offer open for a specific period, in relation to the effectiveness and time for acceptance (section 3.4.4). The substantive issue in question is whether the obligor is bound to perform (a) once the offer is received, or (b) when the acceptance is dispatched, or (c) when the acceptance is received within the statutory or contractual time limit. The crucial divergence in enforceability arising in this context derives from the applicable civil and common law principles when an offer is made via instantaneous communications or via post. Further enforcement challenges may arise if the promisor revokes the offer despite the promise to keep the offer open for a certain period. Whereas the civil law tradition would find such a promise binding, the common law viewpoint is quite the opposite. This leads to the last step, which examines enforcement conflicts arising in cases where it is held that the agreement does not contain a (sufficient) reciprocal promise (section 3.4.5). The key concern it raises is the impact of the distinction between the civil law requirement of synallagmatic promises to establish an enforceable sales contract and the common law bargain principle which is not easily overcome by the use of boilerplate language in a consideration recital.[302]

3.4.2 *Offer and acceptance model*

52. *Preliminary* – At the international level, the CISG adopted the notion that a proposal constitutes an offer when it indicates the intention of the offeror to be bound on acceptance.[303] The required intention to be bound may derive from the wording used in a document, such as 'order', 'we order' and 'immediate delivery' and also from the statements made during a conference call. As a result, the court adjudicating the dispute may infer that an enforceable contract is formed if the elements of offer and acceptance are found, which both show an intention of the parties to be bound by their promises.[304] Where the court does not find such an intention, only non-enforceable contractual commitments are made which may qualify as an invitation to treat. Aside from the legal, technical difficulties arising from this two-step approach, the line between an intention to

302 Where a recital consideration is included in the contracts, it is recommended to explicitly describe the fundaments of the bargain underlying the consideration of the parties in order to prove that the parties undertook a true risk.

303 Art 14 (1) CISG; see also art 2.1.2 PICC.

304 Consult: Tribunal Supremo 1 Juli 2013 (Spain) <http://www.unilex.info/case.cfm?id=1823> accessed on 3 October 2018 and Handelsgericht St. Gallen 5 December 1995, HG 45/1994 (Switzerland) <www.unilex.info/case.cfm?id=190> accessed on 22 August 2018.

be bound on acceptance and an invitation to treat is also not easy to draw due to various business values across jurisdictions. The complexity of the undertaking to distinguish an offer from an invitation to treat is exacerbated by the present-day extensive methods of communication.

In an attempt to ascertain whether the Dutch, Singapore and Chinese contract law are capable of accommodating the formation of commercial sales transactions across these jurisdictions, the following discusses first to what extent the subject legal systems have adopted the traditional mechanism of offer and acceptance to bring about an enforceable sales contract and whether other means of contract formation are accepted. The second step entails an assessment of the requirement that parties show their assent with an intention to establish legally binding obligations and the rules for determining the intentions of parties. This undertaking is most relevant for commercial sales contracts encompassing an exchange of transactions which are not performed at the same time. The rationale is that where there is an immediate and direct exchange of goods and payment of the purchase price (*e.g.* sale of a coffee to go), parties are not primarily concerned with establishing a legally binding contract entailing subsequent obligations. The DCFR is the only supranational contract law instrument which acknowledges the relevance of this distinction by stipulating that offer and acceptance (as unilateral acts) requires that the party doing the act intends to be legally bound or to achieve the relevant legal effect.[305]

> *Illustration* – A manufacturer of cereals, located in country A, sent a fax to a producer of wheat, located in country B. The fax contains an order for delivery of a specific amount of wheat, which is a standardized business usage for ordering goods in this specific sector. The producer asks the manufacturer by email to clarify certain details of its request. The parties proceed with their discussion through a conference call, and the manufacturer believes that the details of the transaction are fully worked out. Nonetheless, despite numerous requests of the manufacturer, the producer refuses to deliver the wheat as described in the fax. In response to this, the manufacturer commenced an action against the producer for delivery of the wheat. In this situation, the question arises whether the producer is subject to an enforceable obligation to deliver the wheat.

53. *Domestic approaches* – Dutch contract law acts on the assumption that a sales contract is formed on the basis of the offer and acceptance model.[306] It is, however, held that this statutory offer-acceptance model does not accommodate situations which typically occur

305 Art II.-4:301(a) DCFR; Nils Jansen and Reinhard Zimmerman (eds), *Commentaries on European Contract Law* (Oxford University Press 2018).

306 Art 6:217 DCC.

between those involved in complex international trade transactions. For example, when prolonged negotiations make it difficult to ascertain the actual offer,[307] where a proposal of a third party (*e.g.* a broker in wheat) is accepted by the buyer and the seller, and situations where parties tacitly 'renew' an expired contract.[308] It is said that in these instances, conduct, as an alternative to the traditional offer and acceptance model, may also suffice as a legal basis to constitute an enforceable sales contract.[309] In any case, the declarations of the parties (orally, written or conduct) must show an intention to constitute an enforceable sales contract. This requires an assessment of the thing parties have declared, the meaning the parties have mutually attached to the stipulations, the sense the parties could have reasonably attached in the present circumstances, and that which they could reasonably expect from each other in this regard.[310] This means in effect that statements and conduct are relevant in determining the intention of the parties to be bound, even if the circumstances justify great significance being given to a purely objective interpretation of the wording chosen in an oral or written offer.[311] Thus the requirement of an intention to be bound must be ascertained by a subjective-objective interpretation of intrinsic and extrinsic evidence in the form of written declarations, word of mouth (statements) or conduct.[312] The aforementioned considerations should be viewed in light of the statutory rule that an absence of an intention to be bound cannot be invoked against a person who interpreted another's declaration or conduct in conformity with the sense which he could

307 *Polak v Zwolsman* Dutch Supreme Court 14 June 1968, ECLI:NL:PHR:1968:AC3608, NJ 1968, 331; Dutch Court of Appeal Arnhem 4 January 1972, ECLI:NL:GHARN:1972:AB6792, NJ 1973, 207; *Van Beers v Van Daalen* Dutch Supreme Court 21 December 2001, ECLI:NL:HR:2001:AD5352, NJ 2002, 60; *Batavus v Vriend's Tweewielercentrum* Dutch Supreme Court 16 September 2011, ECLI:NL:HR:2011:BQ2213, NJ 2011, 572.

308 Dutch Parliamentary History Book 6 (n 207) 879.

309 Consult art 2.1.1 PICC; Dutch Parliamentary History Book 6 (n 207) 879; Sieburgh, *Asser 6-III* 2018 (n 203) 189; Hijma, *Asser* 7-I* 2013 (n 48); Hijma and Olthof 2017 (n 248) 465; *Batavus v Vriend's Tweewielercentrum* (n 307) para 3.4; *Lundiform v Mexx Europe BV* Dutch Supreme Court 5 April 2013, ECLI:NL:HR:2013:BY8101, NJ 2013, 214 (applicability of Haviltex principle to commerical contracts (n 310 below)); Tjittes 2018 (n 2) 70.

310 *Haviltex* Dutch Supreme Court 13 March 1981, ECLI:NL:HR:1981:AG4158, NJ 1981, 635; *Batavus v Vriend's Tweewielercentrum* (n 307) para 3.4; *Van Beers v Van Daalen* (n 307); see for the general standard of reasonableness and fairness under Dutch contract law: arts 6:2, 6:248 DCC; Hartkamp 2011 (n 80) para 117; Tjittes 2018 (n 2) 70, 265; The standard for determining whether the parties have concluded a contract is equated with the principles for interpretation of the contract.

311 *Batavus v Vriend's Tweewielercentrum* (n 307) para 3.4; *Van Beers v Van Daalen* (n 307); *Lundiform v Mex* (n 309).

312 Art 3:37 paragraph 1 DCC; *Bunde v Erckens* Dutch Supreme Court 17 December 1976, ECLI:NL:PHR:1976:AC5835, NJ 1977, 241; *Van Beers v Van Daalen* (n 307); *Batavus v Vriend's Tweewielercentrum* (n 307); YG Blei Weissmann, 'commentaar op artikel 127 Boek 6 BW' para 1.8.1 in RJQ Klomp and HN Schelhaas (eds), *Groene Serie Verbintenissenrecht* (Wolters Kluwer 2018); M Vriend, 'commentaar op artikel 248 Boek 6' para 2.10 in RJQ Klomp and HN Schelhaas (eds), *Groene Serie Verbintenissenrecht* (Wolters Kluwer 2018); Sieburgh, *Asser 6-III* 2018 (see n 203) 372; Tjittes 2018 (n 2) 267–269; De Jong, Krans and Wissink 2018 (n 194) 26–33.

reasonably attribute to it in the circumstances as a declaration of a particular implication made to him by that other person.[313] As a consequence, the court may find that an enforceable contract is established if the buyer has justifiable reasons to place reliance on the offer. Thus, where a buyer knows that the offer entails an essential mistake, the former may not assume that the requirement of an intention is fulfilled. Where the buyer could assume that the offeror intended to be bound, the latter may argue that, considering the circumstances of the case, the buyer was obliged to investigate whether the declaration represented the actual intent of the seller to be bound.[314] For example, in cases where the alleged obligation to deliver something imposes a strong negative impact on the seller, the buyer can be burdened with the obligation to examine whether the offer reflects the actual intention of the seller.[315] This also applies to the situation where the language of the contract is not fully understood by the buyer.[316] That said, Dutch courts attribute significant weight to the express language of a juridical act (*e.g.* offer and acceptance) in a commercial context.[317] In other words, it is crucial to take into account the capacity of parties when determining the appropriate test for the intention to be bound to an offer.

54. The contract law of Singapore acts on the presumption that the offer and acceptance model is the primary instrument to form an enforceable commercial sales contract.[318] It is, however, also suggested that this archaic mechanism is not absolute, which implies that conduct could also suffice to assume the conclusion of an enforceable contract.[319] When considering the traditional model, the undertaking of an offer and the expression of acceptances (both made expressly or by conduct) requires an intention to be legally bound, which have to be objectively ascertained.[320] This encompasses the assessment of whether a reasonable person (the promisee) could have assumed that the promisor intended to be bound.[321] This approach shows that the question of whether an offer includes an intention

---

313 Art 3:35 DCC; Hijma and Olthof 2017 (n 248) paras 32, 37.

314 Hartkamp 2011 (n 80) para 46.

315 *Coolwijk v Kroes* Dutch Supreme Court 28 May 1982, ECLI:NL:PHR:1982:AG4391, NJ 1983, 2.

316 *E.g., Hajzian* Dutch Supreme Court 14 January 1983, ECLI:NL:HR:1983:AG4523, NJ 1983, 457; *Petermann v Frans Maas* Dutch Supreme Court 2 February 2001, ECLI:NL:PHR:2001:AA9767, NJ 2001, 200.

317 *Haviltex* (n 310); *Meyer Europe v Pont Meyer* Dutch Supreme Court 19 January 2007, ECLI:NL:HR:2007:AZ3178, NJ 2007, 575; *Lundiform v Mexx* (n 309); Tjittes 2018 (n 2) 21.

318 Chong et al 2016 (n 125) para 10.2.16; Phang et al 2012 (n 112) para 03.001; Andrew Phang Boon Leong and Goh Yihan, *Contract Law in Singapore* (Wolters Kluwer 2012) para 85; The same applies to implied contracts: *Cooperative Centrale Raiffeisen-Boerenleenbank BA (Trading as Rabobank International), Singapore Branch v Motorola Electronics Pte Ltd* [2011] 2 SLR 63 [46] and [50] (SGCA).

319 <http://www.singaporelaw.sg/sglaw/laws-of-singapore/commercial-law/chapter-8/> accessed 14 August 2018.

320 Phang and Goh 2012 (n 318) paras 86, 143; Phang et al 2012 (n 112) paras 3.026, 3.027; *Bakery Mart Pte Ltd (in receivership) v Sincere Watch Ltd* [2003] 3 SLR(R) 462 (SGCA).

321 Phang and Goh 2012 (n 318) para 95; *Ong Chay Tong & Sons (Pte) Ltd v Ong Hoo Eng* [2009] 1 SLR(R) 305 (SGCA).

to be bound is to be ascertained from the viewpoint of a reasonable person in the position of the recipient.[322] Thus, the subjective intention of the person who received the proposal is not relevant.[323] The requirement of an intention to be bound is not fulfilled where a buyer knows that the seller has made a mistake in the offer, and where it is unclear for the buyer whether the seller has made objective manifestations of an intention to be bound. Put differently, under the contract law of Singapore it is required that there is an intention on the part of both parties to establish a legally binding sales contract (*i.e.* to create legal relations). As mentioned earlier, the requirement of an intention to create legal relations is subject to an objective examination of the facts of the case.[324] An important indication of the existence of an intention to create a legal relation derives from the rebuttable presumption that parties in business and commercial contexts intend to create a legal relation on acceptance (Dutch contract law also recognises such a presumption).[325] It is held that a commercial context is missing where a party acts administratively and not in a commercial manner.[326] In determining the intention to create an enforceable contract, special problems may arise when commercial parties, who place a high value on the act of making a promise, did not adopt the Western, more formal, way of doing business. In these instances, the courts in Singapore may find it difficult to find an intention to establish a contract with legal effect on the basis of the Western inspired legal standards, as set out above.[327] It is, furthermore, important to note that the requirement of an intention to create legal relations also stands apart from the requirement of a valuable consideration to establish an enforceable contract.[328] The latter condition is satisfied where the buyer's consideration for the seller's obligation to deliver the goods is the purchase price to be paid to the seller, and the seller's consideration for payment of the purchase price is the delivery of goods by the seller (section 3.4.5).

---

322 *SAL Industrial Leasing Ltd v Teck Koon (Motor) Trading* [1998] 1 SLR(R) 501 (SGCA); *Cooperative Centrale Raiffeisen-Boerenleenbank BA (Trading as Rabobank International), Singapore Branch v Motorola Electronics Pte Ltd* (nr 318); *Norwest Holdings Pte Ltd (in liquidation) v Newport Mining Ltd* [2010] 3 SLR 956 [37] (SGHC); Phang and Goh 2012 (n 318) paras 302–304; Phang et al 2012 (n 112) paras 3.024, 3.024; Shenoy and Loo 2013 (n 13) para 7.10; Chong et al 2016 (n 125) para 10.2.17.

323 Phang et al 2012 (n 112) paras 3.024, 3.025.

324 Phang and Goh 2012 (n 318) para 304; *Norwest Holdings Pte Ltd (in liquidation) v Newport Mining Ltd* (n 322); *Gay Choon Ing v Loh Sze Ti Terence Peter* [2009] 2 SLR(R) 332 [72].

325 *Chua Kim Leng (Cai Jinling) v Philip Securities Pte Ltd* [2006] SGHC 221; Phang and Goh 2012 (n 318) para 316.

326 Singapore Court of Appeal in *Management Corporation Strata Title Plan No 473 v De Beers Jewellery Pte Ltd* [2002] 1 SLR (R) 418 [10]; Phang and Goh 2012 (n 318) para 317.

327 Consult the Malaysian decision in *MN Guha Majumder v RE Donoughare* [1974] 2 MLJ 114, 117; Phang and Goh 2012 (n 318) paras 302–304.

328 *E.g., Gay Choon Ing v Loh Sze Ti Terence Peter* (n 324) [71]; Phang and Goh 2012 (n 318) para 306.

55. The contract law of China requires that the parties have made concordant declarations of intention in order to form a contract (the requirements for formation of a contract should be distinguished from the question whether the contract is effective; that is, a contract only becomes effective once the applicable requirements of government approval or registration are fulfilled). The formation of the declarations of intentions can be reached by means of the offer and acceptance model,[329] although this undertaking as a means to bring about a contract was previously not acknowledged by the three predecessors of the current contract law of China. In China's Economic Contract Law it was stipulated that a contract shall be in writing and it is formed as soon as the parties to the contract achieved agreement (unanimity) on the principal clauses of the contract through consultation in accordance with the law.[330]

It is said that the offer and acceptance model is not the only mechanism by which a contract can be concluded (*e.g.* instances of prolonged negotiations which make it difficult to determine the juridical act of an offer and acceptance).[331] Nonetheless, the offer and acceptance model is the most common basis for finding a sales contract. Where offer and acceptance are not clearly identifiable, it is required that declarations or conduct of parties show an intention to be bound in order to constitute a contract.[332] In any case, the intention of the party making the declaration may be inferred from an express declaration (in writing, by word of mouth or conduct) but also from all the circumstances of the case.[333] For determining the intent of the parties to be legally bound, there are two conflicting viewpoints. First, it is argued that the subjective test applies.[334] However, it is also suggested that only the objective intention of the party making the declaration is relevant and not what the recipient may have reasonably believed.[335] The notion that the subjective approach prevails follows from the reasoning that the contract law of China focusses on the requirement of the desire of the promisor to enter into a contract,[336] which suggests that the actual intent of the promisor is required to constitute an offer.[337] With regard to the idea that the contract law of China follows an objective approach, a leading commentator holds a view more in line with the PICC by focussing on the outward expressions of the

329 Art 13 CCL; Bing Ling 2002 (n 229) paras 3.006, 3.007.

330 Art 3, 9 ECL; Jianfu Chen, *Chinese Law, Towards an Understanding of Chinese Law, Its Nature and Development* (The London-Leiden Series on Law, Administration and Development, v 3, Kluwer Law International 1999).

331 Bing Ling 2002 (n 229) 3.0070; Art 2.1.1 PICC stipulates that a contract may be concluded either by the acceptance of an offer or by conduct of the parties that is sufficient to show agreement.

332 Arts 13, 14 CCL; Zhang 2006 (n 41) 97; Liming 2016 (n 224) 23, 24; Bing Ling 2002 (n 229) paras 1.010, 3.006.

333 Bing Ling 2002 (n 229) paras 1.010, 3.012; Liming 2016 (n 224) 28, Zhang 2006 (n 41) 92.

334 Zhang 2006 (n 41) 92.

335 Zhang 2006 (n 41) 92; Liming 2016 (n 224) 25; Fu 2011 (n 169) 80, 81.

336 Zhang 2006 (n 41) 92.

337 Zhang 2006 (n 41) 92.

parties, which should also apply when determining whether the requirement of an intention to be bound is fulfilled.[338] This approach encompasses an examination of what a reasonable person could have understood having all the background knowledge which would reasonably have been available to the parties in the situation in which they were at the time of the contract.[339] Due to this factual approach, the question whether the intention to be bound is voluntary or genuine is not essential to the assessment of whether the parties have formed a contract.[340] This undertaking becomes relevant when establishing the effectiveness and thus the enforceability of the obligations arising from the contract.

56. *Comparative analysis* – The present section entails an examination of the traditional mechanism of offer and acceptance, the possibility of inferring a commercial sales contract from conduct and the impact of the most crucial differences between the discussed approaches. The findings reveal an obvious but also very important common denominator, that is, the three investigated legal systems, as well as the CISG, PICC, PECL and DCFR,[341] have all adopted the notion that a sales contract is formed on acceptance of an offer, provided that the requirements attached to both actions are fulfilled. It appears that the Netherlands and China have adopted the most liberal approach towards alternative means of bringing about a commercial sales contract in the absence of a clearly identifiable offer and acceptance. The notion that the traditional offer and acceptance model is not absolute, is in line with the PICC, PECL and DCFR, because they expressly acknowledge that the existence of a contract may also be inferred from conduct by the parties that is sufficient to show agreement.[342] Although the contract law principles of Singapore make no express reference to conduct sufficient to show agreement as a starting point for the formation of a contract, it is suggested that this ground may be used by the courts to find a contract. Nonetheless, it appears that Singapore courts are more hesitant to recognise other forms of expression (other than offer and acceptance) as a method of contract formation. A similar conservative approach is taken by the CISG. The Convention allows parties to be bound by an explicit and implicit trade usage, although it seems unlikely that this principle shall lead to the conclusion of a CISG-contract because the thresholds for finding consensus and the minimum content are very high.[343] That having been said, there are justifiable reasons to recognise other methods of contract formation for specific instances in modern sales transactions where it is not possible to discern an offer and acceptance. This may

338 Bing Ling 2002 (n 229) paras 3.002; 3.012. 5.005.

339 Bing Ling 2002 (n 229) paras 3.002, 3.012.

340 Bing Ling 2002 (n 229) para 3.008.

341 NL arts 6:217(1), 7:1 DCC; SGA, s 2(1) (Singapore follows the English principle that offer and acceptance constitues a contract); CHN Art 13 CCL; Arts 14, 23 CISG; Art 2.1.1 PICC.

342 Art 2.1.1 PICC; Art 2:101(1) PECL; Art II.-4:101 DCFR.

343 Schwenzer 2016 (n 91) 248, paras 47–49.

occur, for example, in the case where prolonged (point-by-point) negotiations (or a lengthy exchange of correspondence) between commercial parties located in different jurisdictions have allegedly led to the reaching of an agreement, or where a party has justifiable grounds to consider silence of the other party as a consent on the basis of international trade usage or a practice that has been developed between the parties. However, where a commercial party argues that an enforceable sales contract is formed, the adjudicating court should not refrain from the principle of consensus, and the principle that the minimum content of the performance must be identifiable.[344]

57. The aforementioned suggestions should be viewed in light of the requirement of an intention to be bound which (though embedded in different legal rules and concepts) is adopted by the three investigated jurisdictions as an important feature of all methods of contract formation.[345] They do, however, place different weights on the objective and subjective intention of the parties in order to assess what the parties may have understood from their respective perspectives. In other words, there is a sliding scale from a purely objective meaning of the declaration to a subjective intention of the promisor. The contract law of Singapore seems to place the most emphasis on the objective meaning of the declaration by adopting the principle that the intention to be bound follows from an assessment of that which the conduct and words of the promisor amount to when reasonably construed by a person in the position of the promisee.[346] The contract law of the Netherlands appears to rely less on the objective meaning of a declaration by allowing the courts to set aside the wording used in the declarations by giving due weight to the interpretation of statements and conduct of the parties. Nonetheless, both legal systems attach considerable weight to the objective meaning of the express wording of an offer where this concerns commercial parties. It appears that the contract law of China adopted the least strict approach by placing more prominence on the actual intent of the parties, although it is also said that the objective approach prevails. This would mean that the intention to be bound has to be found in outward expressions. Despite these differences, the three investigated legal systems are all in line with the approach taken by the CISG, PICC, PECL and the DCFR, to the extent that they acknowledge that where there is a discrepancy between the objective meaning of the declaration and the subjective intention of the promisor, the courts should take into account the understanding a reasonable person

344 Schwenzer 2016 (n 91) 248, para 49.

345 It should be noted that the DCFR also acknowledges that, aside from an intention to establish a legally binding contract, a contract may be concluded on an intention to bring about some other legal effect. See in this regard art II.-4:101(a) DCFR.

346 *Chia Ee Lin Evelyn v Teh Guek Ngor Engelin née Tan* [2004] 4 SLR (R) 330 [43] (SGHC); affirmed *Teh Guek Ngor Engelin née Tan v Chia Ee Lin Evelyn* [2005] 3 SLR (R) 22 SGCA; Phang et al 2012 (n 112) para 03.012.

(the promisee) would have in the same circumstances.[347] Notwithstanding this common viewpoint and the fact that the assessment of the intention to be bound is to be judged exclusively according to the standards of the CISG, it is of paramount importance to take note of differences when dealing with the intricacies of commercial sales transactions across civil and common law jurisdictions which are a member state to the Convention because the domestic principles on defects in intention (and mistake) may be used by national courts to determine that the alleged agreement between the parties did not amount to a valid and enforceable sales contract.[348]

From a comparative perspective, the considerations above demonstrate that the rules surrounding the traditional offer and acceptance model are not absolute. This means in effect that there is no simple answer to the example mentioned under paragraph 52. Nonetheless, it is submitted here that the subject legal systems may allow for a commercial sales contract to be made without an explicit offer and acceptance, provided that the agreement between parties can be sufficiently inferred from declarations and conduct. In other words, the fax and emails exchanged by the parties and the content of the conference call may suffice to establish a commercial sales contract, although these 'declarations' do not qualify as an express offer and acceptance. Such a mechanism should, however, not easily be applied in the realm of international commercial sales transactions considering the far-reaching consequences of the availability of a claim for enforced performance under domestic law which does not (fully) account for the intricacies of the complexities of cross-border trade.

3.4.3 *Definiteness of the obligations assumed in an offer*

58. *Preliminary* – The domestic and international sales law principles concerning the definitiveness of an offer to sell in order to constitute an enforceable sales contract may cause significant enforcement issues when dealing with a sales transaction across civil and common law borders.[349] This is particularly true with regard to situations where the applicable law does not provide guidance to the minimum content, where the offer does not stipulate the purchase price or lacks a mechanism to determine a price. For commercial sales transactions between parties from the three investigated jurisdictions, it all starts with the CISG because the countries are signatory states.[350] The starting point under the

347 Arts 14(1), 8(1–3) CISG; Arts 2.1.2, 1.8 PICC; Art 2.102(1)(a) PECL; Art II.-4:102 DCFR; Schwenzer 2016 (n 91) para 26; Vogenauer 2015 (n 19) art 2.1.2 para 3.

348 Schwenzer 2016 (n 91) para 26.

349 The intricacies of the requirement of sufficient definiteness for an offer made to the public is not discussed. See for this issue: Vogenauer 2015 (n 19) art 2.1.2 para 4.

350 <http://iicl.law.pace.edu/cisg/page/cisg-list-contracting-states>.

Convention is that an offer can only amount to an enforceable sales contract if it indicates the goods and expressly or implicitly fixes or makes provision for determining the quantity and the price.[351] This principle appears to contradict with the open-price principle which serves as a safeguard to long-term commercial sales contracts and where the controlling mechanism is required to deal with rapidly changing market prices.[352] It follows from the open-price provision that a commercial sales contract may come into being where the offer does not expressly or implicitly fix or make provision for determining the price.[353] In these instances of an open-price sales contract, the buyer owes the price usually charged at the time of the conclusion of the sales contract for such goods sold under comparable circumstances in the trade concerned (*i.e.* objective test).[354] This rule reflects two schools of thought when a price is not fixed: the buyer owes the market price (this is approach is adopted by a number of civil law jurisdictions),[355] or the buyer must pay a reasonable price (this approach is adopted by UK and US common law and certain civil law jurisdictions).[356] Despite authoritative opinions on the matter,[357] the relation between the above-described principles is not clarified. Although this is more a theoretical than a practical problem, the same cannot be said for the issue that some courts are inclined to allow open-price offers only when they fulfil the prerequisites for the formation of a contract, that is, the offer expressly or implicitly fixes or makes provision for determining the price.[358] The complexity of the issue is further exacerbated where the parties located in one of the investigated jurisdictions are dealing with commercial parties with a place of business in a CISG signatory state, which did not adopt the requirements for the formation of an enforceable sales contract (including the principle that an implicit fixation of the price suffices), and the applicable domestic law does not allow the formation of a sales contract on the basis of an offer which does not fix a price or entails a mechanism for determining the price.[359] For an illustration of possible approaches in instances of an indefinite offer, see Figure 6.

351 Art 14(1) CISG.

352 Amalina Ahmad Tajudin, 'Article 55 on Open-Price Contract: A Wider Interpretation Necessary?' (2014) 3(3) Journal of Arts and Humanities 38.

353 Art 55 CISG.

354 Art 55 CISG; Schwenzer 2016 (n 91) art 55 para 14.

355 Schwenzer, Hachem and Kee 2012 (n 13) para 10.14.

356 UK: SGA 1979, s 8(2); US: § 2-305(1) UCC; Schwenzer 2016 (n 91) art 55, para 14.

357 Schwenzer, Hachem and Kee 2012 (n 13) para 10.18; Schwenzer 2016 (n 91) art 14 para 21.

358 Art 14(1) CISG.

359 Schwenzer, Hachem and Kee 2012 (n 13) paras 10.17–10.18.

Figure 6 Offers (subject to the CISG) which do not stipulate the purchase price nor encompasses a mechanism to determine the purchase price

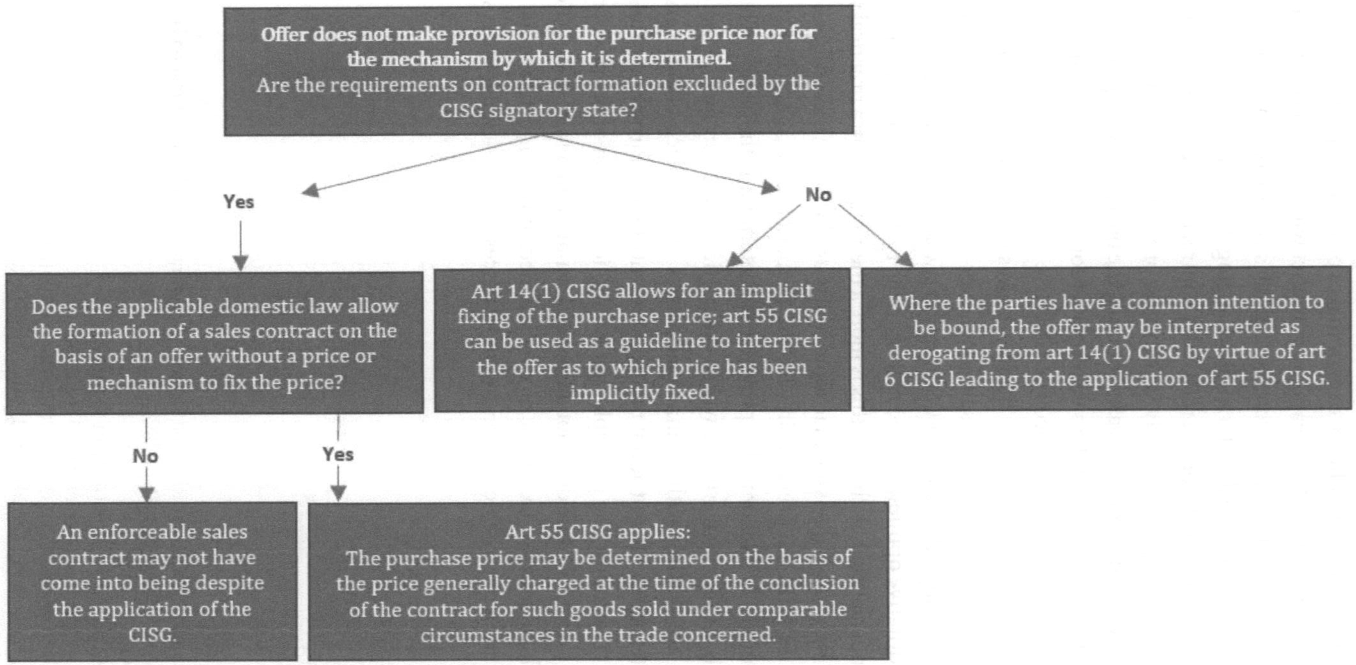

59. Considering the above, the present section analyses whether and to what extent an indefinite offer suffices to constitute an enforceable sales contract in the three investigated legal systems. The aim is to develop a better understanding of the various scenarios and their implications for the ability of commercial parties to conclude an enforceable sales contract. Important elements to consider in this context are the civil law notion of good faith and the common law institution of implied terms. These legal concepts can be used by the courts in order to establish whether the stipulations in an offer are sufficiently clear to bring about enforceable obligations. Considering the far-reaching impact of law of evidence in this regard,[360] special attention is paid to the role of extrinsic elements (*i.e.* statements, agreements and conduct) where contractual stipulations are clear but the parties disagree as to the actual meaning of the agreed terms.

> *Illustration* – A producer of tomatoes, located in country X, informs a trader of fruits and vegetables, located in country Y, that it will sell 'the entire harvest of organic produced cherry tomatoes for the following three crop years' with their price fixed during the season. On completion of an oral discussion, the producer confirmed via a letter that the deliveries would take place each year between June and August, and payments were to be made within 30 days of each invoice. The trader then places an order for the delivery of the first batch of cherry tomatoes at a price of EUR 2.00 per kg. The subsequent year, the seller sent the buyer a second letter to confirm the delivery of the cherry tomatoes at a price of EUR 2.50. The trader, however, insists that there is no valid contract of sale of cherry tomatoes at the price of EUR 2.50, alleging that the first and second letter are neither to be regarded as offers or commercial confirmation letters.[361]

60. *Domestic approaches* – The contract law of the Netherlands requires that obligations assumed in the offer must be determinable to form an enforceable contract on acceptance.[362] This requirement of determinability can be fulfilled at the moment of concluding the contract or at a later moment by contracting parties or third parties, the court or by other circumstances.[363] Where an offer is not sufficiently determinable in view of the statutory

---

360 Attention will be paid in particular to the common law parol evidence rule; Tjittes 2018 (n 2) 372–374; J Beaton, A Burrows and J Cartwright, *Anson's Law of Contract* (30th edn, Oxford University Press 2016) 146–148.

361 This example is based on the *Pitted Sour Cherries case*, see <http://cisgw3.law.pace.edu/cases/050803g1.html> accessed on 16 December 2018.

362 Arts 6:217, 6:227 DCC; Dutch Supreme Court 27 February 1980, ECLI:NL:HR:1980:AC6832, NJ 1980, 352.

363 CH Sieburgh, *Mr. C. Assers Handleiding tot de beoefening van het Nederlands Burgerlijk Recht. 6. Verbintenissenrecht. Deel I. De verbintenis in het algemeen, eerste gedeelte* (Wolters Kluwer 2016) 23; Sieburgh, *Asser 6-III* 2018 (n 203) 285.

requirements, an enforceable sales contract cannot be formed.[364] It must be noted in this regard that Dutch courts are not given the discretionary power to deviate from the statutory right to enforced performance,[365] the reason being that court rulings, which declare that an offer is not sufficiently determinable and therefore do not constitute an enforceable contract, are scarce.[366] That having been said, the starting point is that a valid offer contains the essential, and sufficiently determinable, elements of a promise to give a thing in return for a price in money.[367] Where an offer is not in accordance with these requirements, the general contract law provisions may apply along with any other statutory provisions appropriate on account of the particularities of the assumed performances. Hence, an indefinite purchase price is not necessarily a barrier for establishing an enforceable sales contract where the parties do not consider the price as an essential feature of the transaction. In instances of an indefinite price,[368] the buyer owes a reasonable price.[369] In determining that price, the prices usually stipulated by the seller at the time the contract is entered into are taken into account.[370] Where this indicator is missing or does not suffice to establish the price (*e.g.* unique goods), the adjudicating court may also seek recourse to general business usage and the requirements of reasonableness and fairness to determine the price owed by the buyer.[371] Thus, a Dutch court may look beyond the four corners of a contract and the benchmark of 'usually stipulated prices by the seller' to establish a reasonable price. It may, therefore, be said that under the Dutch Civil Code extrinsic indicators may be used to determine the price owed by the buyer in the absence of contractual stipulations.

61. To bring about an enforceable commercial sales contract in Singapore, it is also required that the parties specify their reciprocally binding performances by means of an offer and acceptance (in writing, by word of mouth or conduct),[372] which fulfil the requirements for

---

364 Sieburgh, *Asser 6-I* (n 363) para 23.

365 AC van Schaick, *Mr. C. Assers Handleiding tot de beoefening van het Nederlands Burgerlijk Recht. Procesrecht. 2. Eerste aanleg* (Wolters Kluwer 2016) paras 62, 263; *Claas v Van Tongeren* Dutch Supreme Court 28 June 1985, ECLI:NL:PHR:1985:AC8976, NJ 1986, 356. However, it is at the discretion of the judge, hearing applications for interim measures, to render an immediate provisionally enforceable decision including an order for performance of the contract in return for a satisfactory security.

366 Sieburgh, *Asser 6-III* 2018 (n 203) 285.

367 Arts 6:217, 6:22, 7:1 DCC.

368 District Court Utrecht 23 September 2009, ECLI:NL:RBUTR:2009:BJ8421, NJF 2010, 44; District Court Noord Holland 6 March 2013, ECLI:NL:RBNHO:2013:BZ5985 para 4.6; B Wessels, *Koop: algemeen* (Monografieën BW B65a, Kluwer 2015) para 45.

369 Art 7:4 DCC; Hijma, *Asser Koop en ruil* 7-I* 2013 (n 48) 214, 216; Schwenzer, Hachem and Kee 2012 (n 13) para 10.14 (footnote 28) mistakenly assume that the market price is to be paid under Dutch law.

370 Art 7:4 DCC.

371 Arts 6:227, 6:248(2) DCC.

372 SGA, s 4(1).

certainty as to the promised performance and completeness.[373] In other words, an offer must contain all essential elements of the envisaged transaction.[374] In answering the question as to whether the stipulations of an offer (upon its acceptance) brings about an enforceable contract and, subsequently, to determine the scope of the assumed obligations, Singapore courts may seek recourse, where necessary, to the below discussed institution of implied terms and the exceptions to the parol evidence rule. As for the former, it is observed by the Singapore Court of Appeal that the good faith principle (on the basis of the intentions of the parties) might fall under the narrow category of terms implied in fact [163].

Concerning a commercial sales contract, the starting point is that an offer is considered sufficiently definite when it encompasses the reciprocal promise to exchange goods in return for paying the price in money thereof.[375] It is, however, important to note that even when a sales contract comes into being under the Singapore Sale of Goods Act because the offer is in full compliance with the applicable requirements, the enforceability of a promise to deliver certain goods depends to a great extent on other specific common law barriers, such as the adequacy of damages test.[376] This is in stark contrast with the primary right of the seller to enforce payment of an implicitly or expressly agreed purchase price. In this regard, an offer may suffice, after acceptance thereof, to constitute an enforceable contract if the purchase price can be determined via a stipulated mechanism or by the course of dealing between the parties. Where both indicators are absent, the buyer owes a reasonable price, which is a question of fact dependent on the circumstances of each particular case.[377] From a practical point of view, the market price and experts are possible sources to determine a reasonable price,[378] but the imposition of a narrow interpretation of the common law statutory parol evidence principle would restrict the court to the language of the contract to be determined from the viewpoint of a reasonable observer (abstract viewpoint).[379] The operative effect of this rule is that extrinsic evidence cannot be used to add to, vary or contradict the terms of a written instrument (*e.g.* an offer) when

---

373 See the English case *Foley v Classique Coaches Ltd* [1934] 2 KB 1 at 13 affirmed for Singapore in *Grossner Jens v Raffles Holdings Ltd* [2004] 1 SLR (R) 202 [14]. See also the Singapore case *T2 Networks Pte Ltd v Nasioncom v Nasioncom Sdn Bhd* [2008] 2 SLR (R) 1; Phang et al 2012 (n 112) para 03.146.

374 The Contract and Sales Law in Singapore only allows an offer and acceptance as a legal basis to constitute a contract; Phang and Goh 2012 (n 318) para 85; Shenoy and Loo 2013 (n 13) para 7.6; Phang et al 2012 (n 112) para 03.003.

375 SGA, s 2(1).

376 *Yeo Long Seng v Lucky Park (Pte) Ltd* [1968–1970] SGHC 20 [20], [21], [32], (1970) SLR(R) 859.

377 SGA, s 8 (1)(2)(3); Where the SGA does not apply, a term that a reasonable price (objective norm) is to be owed may be implied by Singapore courts. See *Gold Coin Ltd v Tay Kim Wee* [1985–1986] SLR(R) 575; *Rabiah Bee bte Mohamed Ibrahim v Salem Ibrahim* [2007] 2 SLR(R) 655; Phang et al 2012 (n 112) para 23.344. See the English case *Foley v Classsique Coaches Ltd* (n 373); SGA 1979 (UK) s 8; Supply of Goods and Services (UK) s 15.

378 Hunter 2017 (n 7) paras 3.37, 3.29; Chong et al 2016 (n 125) para 10.2.26; Halsbury's Laws of Singapore (Commercial Law 2014) vol 5(2) para 60.110; *Hock Hin & Co v Allwie & Co Ltd* [1961] MLJ 232.

379 Evidence Act 1997, ss 93–97; Hunter 2017 (n 7) para 3.31.

the stipulations are unambiguous and complete, and (upon acceptance) represent the whole contract.[380] It must be noted that in Singapore, in contrast to England, the principles surrounding the parol evidence rule are codified in a statute.[381] The present comparative work shall not discuss the details of this Act. It is only noted that, as a starting principle, a Singapore court shall refuse the usage of extrinsic evidence (*e.g.* expert statements) to determine the price owed by the buyer on application of the parol evidence rule where the parties disagree as to the meaning of the contractual stipulations which are not ambiguous or incomplete, unless one of the exceptions apply (*e.g.* any fact may be proved which would invalidate a contract due to a failure in consideration).[382] Despite the historical common law fundaments of the contract law of Singapore, the courts of Singapore have not turned a blind eye to the dynamics of modern trade by allowing a more contextual approach for matters not governed by a commercial contract.[383] Hence, the enforceability of an agreement entailing an indefinite purchase price may be successfully challenged when the court ascertains that a conclusive payment term was essential to establish a valid sales contract.[384]

62. Where a sales contract is subject to the contract law of China, it is of paramount importance to make a distinction between the thresholds for the formation of a sales contract and the requirements for obtaining effectiveness.[385] The latter concern issues of legality, defect in capacity and possibility of performance.[386] The question of whether an offer suffices to constitute an enforceable sales contract is a matter of formation.[387] Consequently, when the offer complies with the conditions set out below, a contract may have been formed even if the contract did not obtain effectiveness yet (*e.g.* when the required government approval is not (yet) provided).[388] To bring about a sales contract, an offer

380 Anson's Law of Contract (n 360) 146–148; the most significant exceptions are rectification, partly oral and partly written contracts and terms implied through trade usage or custom.

381 Evidence Act 1997, ss 93, 94; Phang and Goh 2012 (n 318) para 995.

382 Evidence Act 1997, ss 93, 94; Hunter 2017 (n 7) para 3.34; see the English case *Chartbook Ltd v Persimmon Homes Ltd* [2009] 1 AC 1101 at 1119–1120, [39].

383 *R1 International Pte Ltd v Lonstroff* AG [2014] SGCA 56, (2015) 1 SLR 521; *Zurich Insurance (Singapore) Pte Ltd v B-Gold Interior Design & Construction Pte Ltd* [2008] SGCA 27, (2008) 3 SLR(R) 1029 [132]; *Goh Guan v AspenTech, Inc* [2009] 3 SLR(R) 590; *Straits Advisors Pte Ltd v Behringer Holdings (Pte) Ltd* [2010] 1 SLR 760; Hunter 2017 (n 7) paras 3.37, 3.38, 11.10.

384 Chong et al 2016 (n 125) para 10.2.27.

385 Bing Ling 2002 (n 229) para 3.009.

386 Bing Ling 2002 (n 229) paras 3.002, 3.009.

387 The Contract Law of China only recognises offer and acceptance as a basis to show that parties constituted a contract; Larry A DiMatteo and Jingen Wang, 'CCL and CISG: A Comparative Analysis of Formation, Performance, and Breach' in DiMatteo and Chen 2017 (n 19) 470.

388 Bing Ling 2002 (n 229) paras 3.003, 3.066; The importance of distinguishing contract formation and obtaining effectiveness follows from the principle that where approval is required for effectiveness, a contract can be concluded. However, where approval affects the formation of a contract, the contract only comes into being upon approval.

must include the parties (although appropriate capacity is not required to form a contract), an intention to be bound, and the object.[389] It is debated whether the requirement of certainty and definitiveness of the object is an element of the formation of a contract, or a matter of effectiveness.[390] That said, it appears that an offer must sufficiently define the goods transferred by the seller and the price owed by the buyer.[391] With respect to the level of definitiveness of the purchase price to bring about a sales contract,[392] it is not required that an offer makes provision for the purchase price or encompasses a mechanism to determine the price.[393] This also follows from the announcement of the Supreme People's Court which clarifies that a contract is formed, if the court is able to, generally, determine the names of the parties, subject matter and quantity, unless it is otherwise provided for by law or agreed on by the parties.[394] As a result, an open-price sales contract may be used as a basis to constitute a sales contract. Where the parties fail to reach an agreement on the purchase price, the purchase price shall be determined according to the words and sentences used in the contract, the relevant contractual stipulations, the purpose of the contract, the transaction practices and the principle of good faith.[395] This shows that under the contract law of China parties may rely on extrinsic (ancillary) evidence when they are confronted with an indefinite price.[396] Where the price is not clear (which should be distinguished from gap-filling), the People's Court is entitled to determine the purchase price in accordance with the prevailing market price at the place of performance at the time the contract was concluded. However, in a significant divergence from these principles, the contract law of China also stipulates that if adoption of a price commissioned by the government or based on government-issued pricing guidelines is required by law, such requirement applies.[397] It is argued that this remainder of the previously planned economy should be replaced by a 'reasonable-test'.[398]

63. *Comparative analysis.* – The contract law of the Netherlands, Singapore and China act on the internationally accepted principle that a sales contract is formed on the basis of a

389 Art 14(1) CCL; Bing Ling 2002 (n 229) paras 3.004, 3.009.
390 Bing Ling 2002 (n 229) paras 3.009.
391 Arts 130, 14(1) CCL.
392 Art 12 CCL.
393 Larry A DiMatteo and Jingen Wang, 'CCL and CISG: A Comparative Analysis of Formation, Performance, and Breach' in DiMatteo and Chen 2017 (n 19) 478; Liming 2016 (n 224) 23; Bing Ling 2002 (n 229) paras 3.009, 5.035.
394 Art 1 Judicial Interpretation (I) Contract Law (n 173).
395 Art 125 CCL; Zhang 2006 (n 41) 134–136.
396 Zhang 2006 (n 41) 137.
397 Art 62 (2) CCL; Zhang 2006 (n 41) 132, 133.
398 Larry A DiMatteo and Jingen Wang, 'CCL and CISG: A Comparative Analysis of Formation, Performance, and Breach' in DiMatteo and Chen 2017 (n 19) 479.

sufficiently definitive offer.[399] It appears that the Netherlands and China adopted the broadest approach to the concept of definiteness of an offer. However, when comparing these two jurisdictions, the process of determining whether an offer resulted in an enforceable sales contract under the law of China may seem puzzling from a Western perspective due to the complexity of the distinction between the requirements for the formation of a contract (introducing civil liability) and the thresholds for establishing an effective commercial sales contract. In other words, where the requirements for the formation of an enforceable sales contract are fulfilled, it may not be tacitly assumed that the contract is effective. Should there be a desire to advance international sales law which recognises non-Western principles, it is suggested here to address this specific characteristic of the world's largest exporting country at the level of international sales and contract law principles in order to improve the understanding of non-Western cultural notions and legal traditions.

Another point to take into consideration is the potential restrictive effect of the previously discussed common law parol evidence rule, which necessitates that an offeror must be more specific in its offer to bring about a valid sales contract on acceptance, in comparison to parties subject to Dutch or Chinese contract law. This is because the common law parol evidence rule does not allow contracting parties to seek recourse to manifestations which emerged during the negotiation process when the terms of the agreement are not ambiguous or incomplete and represent the whole contract (albeit that exceptions apply). The CISG adopted for the most part the civil law tradition and rejected the application of the parol evidence rule by acknowledging that due consideration is to be given to all circumstances of the case, including negotiations,[400] although the Convention demands a higher level of definitiveness by requiring that an offer must indicate the goods and expressly or implicitly fixes or makes provision for determining the quantity and price in order to constitute an enforceable sales contract.[401] That said, an indefinite purchase price (open-price contract) is not necessarily a barrier for establishing an enforceable sales contract in the three investigated jurisdictions and the CISG.[402] It appears therefore that the courts may come to the same conclusion when dealing with a commercial sales contract which is governed by Dutch, Singapore or Chinese law or the CISG and the written document does not provide for the price of the goods. The notion that an enforceable commercial sales contract does not necessarily require a price for the goods is in accordance with the approach taken by the PICC, the PECL and DCFR, which embraced the notion

399 Art 14 CISG; Art 2.1.2 PICC.
400 *Vide* arts 8, 9, 11 CISG; Hunter 2017 (n 7) para 11.10.
401 Art 14(1) CISG.
402 Arts 14(1), 55 CISG.

that essential terms may be left undetermined in the offer without necessarily making it insufficiently definite.[403]

Despite the low thresholds in the aforementioned legal systems for sufficient definiteness, the legal concept of an offer still requires close attention when a proposal encompassing an international sales transaction does not make a specific provision for the purchase price or a mechanism to determine the price. The main divergence follows from the principle that the buyer owes the prevailling market price under Chinese contract law, and a reasonable price under Dutch and Singapore contract law. Although the three investigated jurisdictions have not adopted the principle of *pretium certum* (*i.e.* it is not required that the parties have determined the purchase price or rules for determining the price),[404] the aforementioned different approaches may result in major difficulties in practice where a sales contract does not sufficiently make provision for fixing the price. It is therefore of paramount importance that in commercial sales contracts across the borders of the three investigated jurisdictions (and civil and common law borders in general), contractual stipulations provide for the basis of the price owed for the goods. This recommendation should be viewed in light of the principle that an enforceable commercial sales contract does not come into being if the price is essential to the agreement between the parties, but the court is not able to determine the price according to the mechanisms to fill the gap (*i.e.* reasonable price *versus* market price). As mentioned earlier, the contract law of Singapore entails the most restrictive approach in the situation where the parties disagree as to the price to be paid for the goods and the contract is not incomplete or ambiguous on the matter. This, in effect, means that the court is not entitled to rely on declarations made during the negotiations to determine the price to be paid by the buyer when the language of the contract is clear on the matter. In spite of this doctrinal barrier with a significant impact in practice, it is suggested that, within the limitations laid down in the Evidence Act, the courts in Singapore are willing to take a more lenient approach towards the parol evidence rule by taking into consideration the contextual surroundings in determining the price owed for the goods.

The considerations above allow for the conclusion that similar results can be expected if the courts in the three investigated jurisdictions are confronted with the question as to whether a valid commercial sales contract is concluded in the example mentioned under paragraph 59. This case concerns an offer which does not make provision for determination of the goods (*i.e.* entire harvest of three years) and the price. However, commercial parties entering into a commercial sales contract across civil and common law borders, with the genuine expectation that their performance interest shall be honoured, should take note

403 Vogenauer 2015 (n 19) art 2.1.2 para 2; Art 2:201(1)(b) PECL; Art II.-4:201(1)(b)DCFR.

404 See for a detailed discussion about the French civil law principle of *pretium certum* Schwenzer, Hachem and Kee 2012 (n 13) paras 10.15, 10.16.

of the fact that there is no consensus on the requirements for the determinability of the goods and the price. This matters when the language of the contractual stipulations is not in accordance with the initial intentions of the parties.

3.4.4 *Binding effect of offer and acceptance*

64. *Preliminary* – The present section deals with one of the most pronounced differences between the civil and common law traditions when considering the threshold for determining whether the parties have formed an enforceable sales contract. That is the matter of effect and effectiveness of the undertaking of offer and acceptance. The primary issues are the revocability of an offer and the divergence in the way the different legal systems deal with acceptance in the case of instantaneous communication and where the parties communicate *inter absentes*. The latter is most relevant for international commercial sales contracts and, unfortunately, is also the point where a dramatic difference arises.

> *Illustration* – A producer of women's garments, located in country A, solicits an offer from a fabric manufacturer, located in country B, for different types of fabrics for next season's production. The manufacturer submits its offer on 1 October 2018 which entails a period of ten days for acceptance. The producer relies on the offer when calculating its prices. The producer dispatches its acceptance of the offer on 3 October. The manufacturer sends a communication to the producer revoking its offer on the same day. The key question here is whether the offer is validly revoked or that an enforceable sales contract came into being which obliges the manufacturer to deliver the fabrics as stipulated in the offer.

65. *Domestic approaches* – Dutch contract law entails the principle that an enforceable sales contract comes into being where the parties have provided two declarations (oral or written declaration or conduct), namely, offer and acceptance.[405] The first interesting point from a comparative perspective is that an offer under Dutch law becomes effective when it reaches the promisee,[406] but it only brings about an enforceable contract on the receipt of acceptance.[407] Aside from the ability of the promisor to make an offer binding (for a certain time period) before acceptance, the court may assume the formation of an enforceable sales contract when the offeror did not receive the acceptance of the offer (in time) due to an act of the offeror, or by persons for whom the offeror is responsible, or due to other circumstances which are personal to the offeror and justify the detrimental

405 Art 6:217(1) DCC.
406 Art 3:37(3) DCC.
407 Art 3:37(3) DCC.

effect imposed by the constitution of an enforceable contract between parties.[408] From the rule that acceptance, in order to be effective, has to reach the promisor, it follows that it is not required that the promisor has actually taken note of the acceptance.[409] In contrast to the below discussed contract law of Singapore, the above-mentioned principles apply equally in instances of instantaneous and *inter absentes* communication. The promisor could prevent a sales contract from coming into being on receipt of the acceptance by sending a notice of withdrawal which must have reached the promisee before or at the same time as the offer.[410] It may be assumed that a promisor is entitled to withdraw revocable offers and offers which provide for their irrevocability (only effective offers are subject to revocability). In instances of a successful withdrawal, the offer does not become effective. Once an offer is effective, the promisor may revoke its offer as long as the offer has not been accepted and a communication accepting the offer has not been sent.[411] Revocation does not have a legal effect where the offer includes a period for acceptance, or it otherwise provides for its irrevocability.[412] Furthermore, the offeror is not able to revoke its offer where it promised to keep the offer open for a certain period.[413]

66. The contract law of Singapore entails the principle that an enforceable contract comes into being by the acceptance of a sufficiently definitive offer, provided that the requirement of a valuable consideration (*i.e.* something of value is given in exchange), and an objective intention to be bound is present. To determine the impact of the offer and acceptance model as a starting point for contract formation, it is important to take into account the distinction in Singapore between the common law rules on the constitution of a contract via instantaneous communication and *inter absentes* (*i.e.* by post).[414] Where the acceptance is made through instantaneous communication, the general rule applies that an enforceable contract is concluded once the acceptance is actually received by the promisor in the form of a written or oral declaration or by conduct.[415] This principle applies where commercial parties communicate face-to-face, or via telephone or fax. It appears that email and text messages (*e.g.* WhatsApp, WeChat) in most cases also qualify as instantaneous communication. There is, however, an exception in common law, which is referred to as

408 Art 3:37(3) DCC.
409 Hartkamp 2011 (n 80) para 38.
410 Art 3:37(5) DCC.
411 Art 6:219(1, 2) DCC.
412 Art 6:219(1, 2) DCC.
413 Hartkamp 2011 (n 80) para 40.
414 Examples of instantaneous communication are provided below.
415 Shenoy and Loo 2013 (n 13) paras 7.57, 7.58; Phang et al 2012 (n 112) para 03.116; Phang and Goh 2012 (n 318) para 152.

the 'postal acceptance' or 'mail box' rule.[416] From this rule it follows that acceptance sent by post (*i.e.* acceptance *inter absentes*) becomes effective, and thus brings about an enforceable contract, at the moment the acceptance is dispatched. It should, however, be noted that Singapore courts may take other factors into account to determine whether an enforceable contract came into being.[417] Nonetheless, the common law postal acceptance rule continues to hold a strong position in Singapore.[418] The aforementioned distinction between instantaneous and *inter absentes* communication should be taken into account when considering the instrument of revocation which allows the promisor to revoke its offer before acceptance, even if a time for acceptance is fixed by the promisor. This notion of free revocability of an offer holds the explanation that the law of Singapore is not familiar with the instrument of withdrawal. The effect of the revocation rule under the contract law of Singapore is that any action to revoke (or any attempt to terminate) an offer which has been accepted (and which therefore brings about an enforceable sales contract when consideration is provided) results in a breach of contract. Considering instances of offers *inter absentes,* the promisor is entitled to revoke its offer until the dispatch of the acceptance by the buyer. It may, however, be impossible for the promisor to determine the timeframe within which the offer can be revoked because the latter does not necessarily know when the acceptance is dispatched.[419] An offer made by instantaneous communication may also be revoked at any time before acceptance,[420] even if the offeror promised to keep the offer open.[421] However, in instances of instantaneous communication, the revocation becomes effective once it has actually been communicated (in writing, by word of mouth, or conduct) to the promisee; a mere mental assent is not sufficient. This principle contrasts to the rule that acceptance of an offer *inter absentes* must not necessarily have reached the promisor.[422]

67. The contract law of China act on the principle that a sales contract comes into being when the promisor receives the notice of acceptance of its offer (arrival rule).[423] It may,

416 This English common law rule was adopted in Singapore by the Straits Settlement Court in *Lee Seng Heng and others v Guardian Assurance Co Ltd* [1932] SSLR 110.

417 Phang and Goh 2012 (n 318) para 160.

418 Phang and Goh 2012 (n 318) para 159.

419 Hunter 2017 (n 7) para 3.14.

420 *E.g., Overseas Union Insurance Ltd v Turegum Insurance Co* [2001] 3 SLR 330 (SGHC); Phang and Goh 2012 (n 318) paras 126, 127; Shenoy and Loo 2013 (n 13) paras 7.34–7.38; Phang et al 2012 (n 112) paras 03.078, 03.080.

421 *E.g., Overseas Union Insurance Ltd* (n 420); Phang and Goh 2012 (n 318) paras 126, 127; Shenoy and Loo 2013 (n 13) paras 7.34–7.38; Phang et al 2012 (n 112) paras 03.078, 03.080.

422 See the English cases: *Routledge v Grant* [1828] 4 Bing 653; *Dickson v Dodds* [1876] 2 Ch D 463 at 472 and 474; *Mountford v Scott* [1975] 1 All ER 198; Shenoy and Loo 2013 (n 13) para 7.39; Phang et al 2012 (n 112) para 03.095.

423 Art 26 CCL; Larry A DiMatteo and Jingen Wang, 'CCL and CISG: A Comparative Analysis of Formation, Performance, and Breach' in DiMatteo and Chen 2017 (n 19) 470.

however, not be assumed that an offer (after dispatch but before acceptance) can be freely withdrawn or revoked by the promisor. By contrast, the specific rules on withdrawal and revocation drastically mitigate the sometimes perceived noncommittal nature of an offer.[424] A withdrawal notice must have reached the promisee (the recipient of the offer) before or at the same time as the latter receives the offer.[425] It is said that this rule applies to revocable and irrevocable offers.[426] Once an offer is received by the promisee it may only be revoked by the promisor before the notice of acceptance has been dispatched. This shows that a promisee can be rest assured that a sales contract comes into being by dispatching its acceptance, although a promisee may withdraw its acceptance before it reaches the promisor.[427] The aforementioned right of revocation is not unrestricted. An offer is irrevocable where it indicates a time for acceptance or otherwise explicitly states that the offer is irrevocable, or the promisee has reasons to believe that the offer is irrevocable and has already made preparations for the performance of the contract.[428] In this light, it is important to take note of the rule that acceptance of an offer must reach the promisor within the time limit as stated in the offer or, if no time is fixed, the acceptance has to reach the promisor within a reasonable time.[429] The promisee bears the risk of acceptance being delayed or getting lost. This risk is obsolete in instances of instantaneous communication because in these cases an offer has to be accepted immediately unless the parties agree otherwise.[430] If the promisee has no excuse for an overdue acceptance, the act of acceptance only constitutes a new offer, unless the promisor notifies the promisee in time that the acceptance is effective.[431] If an offer is accepted within the fixed time limit or within a reasonable time (if the offer did not entail a time limit for acceptance), but it reaches the promisor beyond the time limit due to reasons not attributable to the latter, the offer is regarded as accepted and an effective contract is concluded unless the promisor notifies the promisee in time that the acceptance is denied due to its delayed arrival.[432] This notification only gains effect if it has reached the promisee.[433] The premise that the receipt of acceptance after a fixed or a reasonable time may constitute a legally binding contract aligns with the value accorded to the act of promise making, which is reflected in the strict-liability principle discussed later. It also demonstrates the emphasis of the contract

424 Art 17–19 CCL.
425 Art 17 CCL.
426 The rules on revocable offers are laid down in arts 18, 19 CCL.
427 Art 27 CCL; Bing Ling 2002 (n 229) para 3.024.
428 Art 29 CCL; see also art 16(2) CISG and art 2.4(2) PICC.
429 Art 23 (2) CCL; Liming 2016 (n 224) 37.
430 Art 23 (1) CCL; Liming 2016 (n 224) 37.
431 Art 28 CCL; Liming 2016 (n 224) 39 and 40.
432 Art 29 CCL; Liming 2016 (n 224) 38, 39.
433 Liming 2016 (n 224) 40.

law of China on the progressive stance towards the conclusion of contracts.[434] It is therefore understandable that it is stipulated that if an acceptance needs no notice, an effective contract is concluded when an act of acceptance is performed in light of trade practices or as indicated by the offer.[435] This form of implied acceptance also shows the positive approach of the contract law of China regarding trade transactions.

68. See Figure 7 following for the impact of the differences between the three investigated jurisdictions in view of the case mentioned under paragraph 64.

434 Liming 2016 (n 224) 41.
435 Art 26 CCL; Liming 2016 (n 224) 41.

Figure 7 Binding effect of offer and acceptance in light of the revocability of an offer

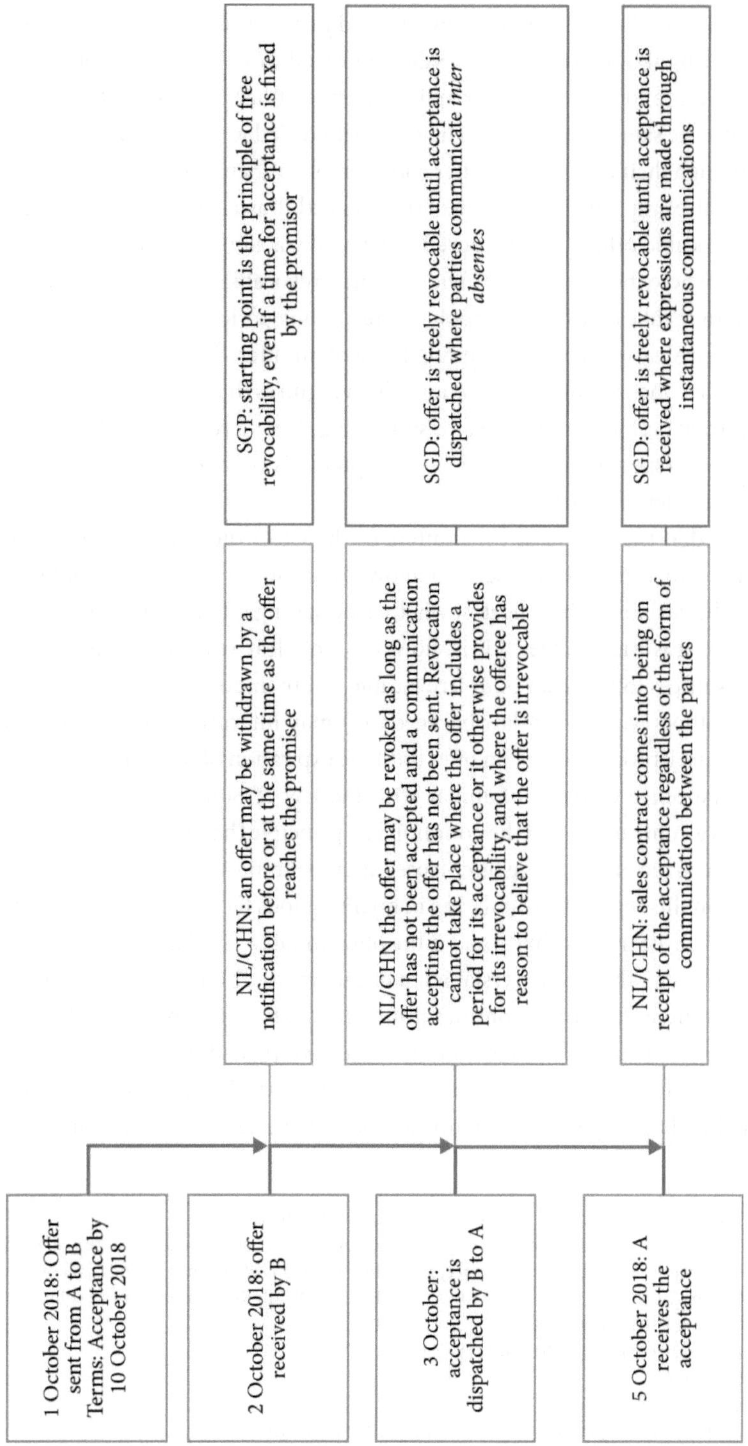

69. *Comparative analysis* – The three investigated jurisdictions all act on the notion that an offer may bring about an enforceable sales contract the moment its acceptance becomes effective (Singapore contract law also requires consideration). The unification instruments identified take the same approach.[436] They also acknowledge the noncommittal nature of an offer, although their approaches differ considerably. Where the Dutch and Chinese law adopted several exemptions in the form of rules on withdrawal and revocation and provide rules for irrevocable offers,[437] Singapore law generally acknowledges free revocability of an offer, even where the offer itself provides for its irrevocability. This means in effect that the freedom to revoke an offer also applies when a time period for acceptance is fixed by the promisor, which weakens the binding force of an offer. This principle derives from the common law doctrine of consideration which requires that a promise to keep an offer open for a certain period is exchanged for something else as a result of the bargain.[438] From a common law perspective, a fixed time for acceptance is generally interpreted as a period after which the offer merely lapses.

It appears that the efforts of the drafters of the CISG did not result in a successful merger of the two approaches described above. It follows from the Convention that an offer cannot be revoked if it indicates, whether by stating a fixed time for acceptance or otherwise, that it is irrevocable.[439] It is, however, not clear whether the mere fixing of a time period suffices to make an offer irrevocable. More importantly, Dutch and Chinese parties (and others with a civil law background) may interpret this provision as a rule providing for the irrevocability of an offer until the expiration of the time fixed in the offer. From the perspective of parties familiar with the law of Singapore, this rule could be interpreted as a confirmation of the common law principle that an offer must be accepted within the time fixed and that the offer lapses after expiration of this period. The PECL is much clearer in this regard by stipulating in unambiguous terms that an offer is revocable unless it indicates its irrevocability and if the offer entails a fixed time for acceptance.[440]

Notwithstanding the controversial issue of the irrevocability of an offer, it must also be noted that where the parties communicate *inter absentes* (*i.e.* by post), the timeframe for revocation of an offer is the same in the three investigated jurisdictions, as well as at the international level (*i.e.* an offer may be revoked before dispatch of acceptance).[441] As for the situation that the parties communicate via instantaneous communication methods

436 Art 23 CISG; Arts 2.1.1, 2.1.6 PICC; Art 2:205 PECL; Art II.4:205 DCFR.

437 In general, the rules on revocation of an offer apply where an offer has reached the promisee. An offer may be witdrawn before it reaches the promisee, *i.e.*, before it obtains effectivess; Withdrawal of an offer: art 15(2) CISG, art 2.1.3 PICC, art 1:303(5) PECL; Art II.-5:101 DCFR; Revocation of an offer art 16 CISG, art 2.1.4 PICC, arts 1:303(2)(6), 2:202 PECL; Art II.-4:202 DCFR.

438 Schwenzer, Hachem and Kee 2012 (n 13) paras 9.16, 10.26.

439 Art 16(2)(a) CISG.

440 Art 2:202(3)(a)(b) PECL.

441 Art 16(1) CISG; Art 2.1.4 PICC; Art 2:202(1) PECL; Art II.-4:202(1) DCFR.

(*e.g.* telephone, fax and electronic messages) there is, however, still a significant difference between the three investigated legal systems. In this situation, Singapore law acts on the notion that an offer may be revoked until its acceptance is received, rather than the moment the buyer dispatches its acceptance, as is the case under the contract law of the Netherlands and China, as well as the unification instruments. In other words, the contract law of Singapore strikes a different balance in cases of instantaneous communication by adopting the principle that offers are freely revocable, until the moment the notice of acceptance is received. That having been said, on an overall assessment, the discussed controversial issue of the irrevocability of an offer, and the divergence between the principles on the effectiveness of acceptance where the parties communicate via instantaneous communication methods, require more clarity for those involved in commercial sales contracts across civil and common law borders. This is particularly relevant for parties who are communicating via electronic messages. The international commercial courts in the three investigated jurisdictions may consider taking the lead in this regard by providing guidelines (on a case-by-case basis) when confronted with an enforcement dispute arising from the issues mentioned above.

3.4.5 *Synallagmatic performances, cause or valuable consideration*

70. *Preliminary* – One of the most fundamental differences between the investigated jurisdictions which is of paramount importance from the standpoint of parties involved in international commercial sales across civil and common law borders follows from the civil law concept of synallagmatic (reciprocal) promises, *cause* and the common law doctrine of consideration. From the perspective of the traditional common law viewpoint, the court would not find enforceable obligations where a benefit or detriment (*i.e.* consideration) is not exchanged by way of bargain, and where the promised performance is related to past performance of the promisee or where the reciprocal promise is illusionary in nature (see the example below). This means in effect that mutual assent arising from an offer and acceptance does not suffice. Put differently, the mutual assent only amounts to enforceable obligations if consideration is provided, although it is generally not taken into account whether the value of the promises is comparable or fair.[442] It is only required that the value of the promises are commercially measurable.[443] The requirement of consideration also

442 JF Burrows, J Finn and S Todd, *Law of Contract in New Zealand* (8th edn, Butterworths 1997) 103.

443 Petra Butler, 'The Doctrines of Parol Evidence Rule and Consideration -- A Deterrence to the Common Law Lawyer?' in *Celebrating Success: 25 Years United Nations Convention on Contracts for the International Sale of Goods* (Collation of Papers at UNCITRAL, SIAC Conference 22–23 September 2005, Singapore) <https://www.cisg.law.pace.edu/cisg/biblio/butler4.html#46> accessed 3 November 217.

applies to warranties made after the conclusion of the contract, and further arrangements regarding gaps in the initial contractual stipulations.

Generally, civil law jurisdictions take the approach that obligations assumed in the terms of the agreement may constitute a direct exchange of corresponding promises (synallagmatic). For example, the duty of the buyer to pay the sales price upon delivery of the goods by the seller. There are, however, also situations where the assumed obligations would not necessarily be characterized as synallagmatic. For example, where the terms of the agreement stipulate that the buyer is obliged to pay the purchase price if certain marketing targets of the seller are met. Although this obligation does not follow from a direct exchange of interrelated promises, the obligation is enforceable. The traditional civil law understanding even entails the notion that unilateral offers may suffice to constitute enforceable obligations. That said, certain jurisdictions which have historically drawn inspiration from French law are familiar with the requirement of cause (*e.g.* the Quebec Civil Code and the Italian Civil Code), to bring about an enforceable contract. The condition of a cause entails the notion that a contract is only valid if it has a cause and that cause is lawful. In the realm of sales contracts this means that the cause of the seller is payment of the purchase price and the cause of the buyer is to obtain ownership of the goods. However, the interests of a seller to a commercial sales contract can be severely affected when the court uses the absence of a cause to strike down an exemption or limitation clause. In 2016, the requirement of cause was removed from the French Civil Code because it was frequently used to interfere with contracts and, by doing so, causing uncertainty and controversy.[444]

The divergence between the required degree of reciprocity in civil and common law jurisdictions which suffices to constitute an enforceable obligation may cause significant difficulties for those doing business across civil and common law borders. Simply put, at one end of the spectrum, it is not compulsory that the assumed obligations are reciprocally binding. At the other end of the spectrum, it is required that the assumed obligations on either side are the counterparts and that consideration is given for each other. It appears that the drafters of the unification instruments have not managed to narrow the gap between the two viewpoints, and this thus remains an important legal barrier to international trade between parties from the two major legal families. Taking this into consideration, the present section discusses the direction in which the investigated jurisdictions have developed their legal principles in this regard and to what extent they are aligned with the unification instruments. The objective of this assessment is to determine whether the diversity between

444 Soléne Rowan, 'The new French law of contract' (2017) International & Comparative Law Quarterly; The requirement of consideration, which is not demanded by civil law, has led to many disputes involving sales that cross civil and common law jurisdictions; Mark B Wessman, 'Should We Fire the Gatekeeper? An Examination of the Doctrine of Consideration' (1993) 48 U. Miami L. Rev 48; Kevin J Fandl, 'Cross-Border Commercial Contracts and Consideration' (2016) 34 Berkeley J. Int'l Law 1, 3, 18; Treitel 1998 (n 55) 246; HW Ballantine, 'Mutuality and Consideration' (1914) 28(2) I, Harvard Law Review 121–134.

the rules on bringing about an enforceable commercial sales contract calls for closer attention in order to advance a legal climate which actually corresponds with the ambitions of the three investigated jurisdictions (chapter 1).

Illustration – A manufacturer of electric vehicles, located in country A, sends a proposal encompassing a letter of support to a ridesharing taxi company, located in country B, indicating that it is able to supply ten electric self-driving cars when government approval is granted. After submission of the support letter, the local authorities provide the required licence for the usage, but the manufacturer refuses to deliver the cars on the basis of the argument that a recent merger of the taxi company resulted in a monopsony, because they will be in complete control of the market for the purchase of electric cars (for commercial usage) in country B. This position enables the ridesharing company to dictate the purchase prices of the cars for its fleet. As a result, it shall be most likely impossible for the manufacturer to make up for the losses incurred by investing in the pilot of the ridesharing company. In response to this declaration, the taxi company claims for the delivery of the electric cars under the terms as stipulated in the initial proposal. The manufacturer counterclaims that nothing in return was promised for the submission of the support letter and is, therefore, not obliged to deliver the electric cars.

71. *Domestic approaches* – The contract law of the Netherlands only requires a bilateral undertaking whereby one or more parties assume an obligation towards one or more other parties,[445] that is, each party has to undertake an obligation with the intention to produce juridical effects.[446] It is not required that the promises are synallagmatic – that is, the promised performance by one party does not have to be an exchange of a corresponding promise by the other party.[447] This approach follows from the notion that 'a promise against a promise' by nature provides the parties with an action on the case,[448] and it holds the explanation that the promises made by the parties do not have to reflect an inextricably linked exchange of benefit or detriment. However, where a contract does not include any benefit for the party who is obliged to act, the principle of reasonableness and fairness could result in a rejection of a claim for enforced performance if enforcement would be

445 Art 6:216(1) DCC; Hofmann 1976 (n 84) 5; De Jong, Krans and Wissink 2018 (n 194) 262; Hijma and Olthof 2017 (n 248) para 453.

446 Arts 3:33, 6:213(1) DCC; The required undertaking to assume an obligation explains why certain unilateral acts not comprising an obligation, such as as a notice of termination of a contract, notice of default and notice of liability, are not qualified as a contract.

447 De Jong, Krans and Wissink 2018 (n 194) 262; Hijma and Olthof 2017 (n 248) 453.

448 See the English case *Strangborough and Warner's Case* [1589] 4 Leo. 3; 74 E.R. 686; WJ Zwalve, *C.Æ. Uniken Venema's Common Law & Civil Law: Inleiding tot het Anglo-Amerikaanse vermogensrecht* (Boom Juridische uitgevers 2008) 503; Hartkamp 2011 (n 80) para 46.

unacceptable in the given circumstances.[449] It is however of paramount importance to note that the derogatory function of the standard of reasonableness and fairness is not easily applied and entails a significantly higher barrier than the supplementing function of the standard of reasonableness and fairness. In a similar vein, Dutch contract law entails the principle that a promisor cannot exercise its right to performance to the extent that it constitutes an abuse.[450] This suggests that where the promisee brings an action to court for enforced performance, the court may indirectly require a *cause* (*i.e.* the civil law equivalent of consideration) via administering the derogative function of the standard of reasonableness and fairness (which requires a manifestly unacceptable impact), and the rules on abuse of rights.[451] It is worth bearing in mind that the absence of a reciprocal promise in the aforementioned situations does not affect the existence of the obligation.[452] To resolve the legal impasse arising therefrom, the parties could alter the terms of their agreement on the basis of mutual consent.[453] However, the creation of an enforceable contract does not necessarily mean that the statutory sales law provisions apply.[454] Put differently: an enforceable contract is only subject to the rules on sales when it comprises an undertaking of one person to give a 'thing' in return for the promise of the other party to pay the price in money.[455] As shown in section 3.4.3, it is not required that the parties already agree on the details of the transaction, for example, the amount of money which is exchanged for the goods.[456] Nonetheless, a sales contract does not come into existence in the case of a fictitious purchase.[457]

72. The contract law of Singapore requires a valuable consideration for the formation of legally enforceable obligations.[458] In other words, whether consideration has been provided by the parties is one of the fundamental steps in determining the enforceability of

---

449 Arts 6:2(2), 6:248(2) DCC; Hartkamp 2011 (n 80) paras 33, 46.

450 Art 3:13(1) DCC.

451 HC Schoordijk, *Het algemeen gedeelte van het verbintenissenrecht naar het nieuw burgerlijk wetboek* (Kluwer 1979) 464.

452 This concerns cases where a valid contract has come into being, but enforced performance is not available by application of the derogative effect of the standard of reasonableness and fairness (which entails a significantly high threshold in the form of a manifestly unacceptable impact), and the rules on abuse of rights.

453 Hartkamp 2011 (n 80) paras 49, 173.

454 Wessels (n 368) 1, 2.

455 Art 7:1 DCC.

456 Art 7:4 DCC; the buyer owes a reasonable price; in determining that price, the prices stipulated by the seller at the time the contract was entered into are usually taken into account; See s 3.4.3.

457 Hijma, *Asser Koop en ruil* 7-I* 2013 (n 48) 208.

458 Phang et al 2012 (n 112) 195, 199; <http://www.singaporelaw.sg/sglaw/laws-of-singapore/commercial-law/chapter-8> acccessed on 31 October 2017; *Bankers & Traders Insurance Co Ltd v Insurance Services* [1968–1970] SLR (R) 360; Phang et al 2012 (n 112) paras 04.002, 04.004; Goh Yihan and Yip Man, 'Past Consideration or Unconnected Consideration?' (2012) SAL Ann Rev 553.

contractual obligations. The requirement of a valuable consideration entails the notion that a sales contract must be the result of a situation where two parties expressly or implicitly undertake an obligation to exchange something of economic value for the performance of the other party (consideration does not need to be adequate).[459] The most common and straightforward type of consideration is that where a seller undertakes the obligation to deliver goods for a fixed sum which the buyer undertakes to pay.[460] In Singapore, the required valuable consideration for the formation of an enforceable contract is absent if the contract does not confer a benefit on the other party,[461] the promised performance is illusionary,[462] and where the contractual promise is solely the result of appreciation for previous performance(s) of the other contracting party.[463] For example, if parties to a cross-border sales contract agree on different quality standards for a certain product by modification of the original contract or by entering into a subsequent agreement, the promises of both parties must fulfil the requirements set out above. This means, in effect, that it does not suffice to refer to the obligations which already exist under the initial contract. It is important to note that the traditional usage of the past consideration principle is questioned in Singapore, as it is not uncommon for commercial parties to conclude a contract which, in essence, is inextricably linked with the previous performance of the other party.[464] For example, a manufacturer and a wholesaler conclude a sales contract which entails the promise of the manufacturer to reimburse a percentage of the sums paid by the wholesaler, but the provision does not refer to a specific period for which the discount is granted. After a year, the parties agree on the exact formula to calculate the amount recoverable by the wholesaler. From a traditional common law viewpoint, this subsequent agreement may be unenforceable by application of the past consideration rule.[465] However, the current viewpoint in Singapore case law suggests that the subsequent agreement entailing the formula to calculate the remuneration cannot be isolated from the original

459 For the assessment whether the considerations are exchanged, the court may rely on the core provisions of the contract (in conjunction with a recital) and consideration may be implied from other terms of the contract of conduct of the parties.

460 Treitel 1998 (n 55) para 189; Phang and Goh 2012 (n 318) para 205; Phang et al 2012 (n 112) para 04.001.

461 Where the sale entails a transaction of future goods, the parties only established an agreement to sell the goods (SGA, s 5(3)). An agreement to sell becomes a sale when the goods come into existence (SGA, s 2(6)).

462 *E.g.*, A agrees to pay B S$ 1 in exchange for B's promise to deliver 10 laptops. An enforceable contract is not established if these promises are not the result of an actually undertaking of the parties to commit to a certain risk.

463 In *Rainforest Trading Ltd v State Bank of India Singapore* [2012] 2 SLR 713 [at 34, 35, 36] the past consideration rule was affirmed and further clarified; Phang et al 2012 (n 112) para 04.011; Phang et al 2012 (n 112) 195, 199; Phang and Goh 2012 (n 318) para 213.

464 *Foo Song Mee v Ho Kiau Seng* [2011] SGCA 45; see Goh and Yip (n 458) 558 for a discussion about the English law cases *Dent v Bennett* [1839] 41 E.R. 105 and *Eastwood v Kenyon* [1840] 113 E.R. 482, which each underpin the view of the author that it does not matter if the consideration is past, but 'whether the promisor intended the consideration to be in exchange for the given promise'.

465 *Foo song Mee* (n 464) SGCA 45 [14].

sales contract.[466] It may be held that the sales contract, where no formula for the discount was inserted, is replaced by the agreement which stipulates the basis for a precise amount payable by the producer.[467] Based on this reasoning it may be held that in Singapore the traditional English rule of past consideration has evolved into a requirement of connectivity (*i.e.* connected considerations),[468] which better reflects the dynamics of commercial transactions. The willingness of Singapore to modernise certain legal common law doctrines is also reflected in the principle that the absence of a valuable consideration in an agreement between parties from different legal systems does not necessarily affect the enforceability of the promises made by the parties.[469]

73. According to the contract law of China, a contract requires an agreement between two equal parties comprising an undertaking to establish one or more rights and obligations.[470] It is not required that the performance promised by one party is to be exchanged for that of the other. Hence, the common law concept of consideration does not apply to contracts subject to the contract law of China.[471] In view of the above it appears that unilateral and bilateral promises suffice to establish an enforceable contract if all other requirements for the undertaking of offer and acceptance are fulfilled (*e.g.* the notice of acceptance has reached the promisor).[472] This clarifies why a promise to deliver a certain product or to perform a service without receiving an enforceable obligation in return may bring about a valid contract.[473] This situation occurs where parties enter into a loan, deposit, carriage and gift contract.[474] For example, A agrees to sell a number of large tents and accessories to B. In a subsequent agreement the parties stipulate that B may use the lorries of A to transport the goods to the airport. Two months prior to shipment, A informs B that the lorries are not available. B claims for enforced performance of the promise that the lorries can be used to transport the goods to the airport, and A argues that the subsequent agreement is not enforceable because B offered nothing of value in return. Assuming that the initial agreement is subject to the contract law of China, the undertaking of A to provide the lorries qualifies as an enforceable contractual obligation. Consequently, A is entitled to bring an action to court for enforced performance under the general contract law

466 *Foo song Mee* (n 464) SGCA 45 [20].
467 *Foo song Mee* (n 464) SGCA 45 [20].
468 Goh and Yip (n 458) 560, 564.
469 <http://www.singaporelaw.sg/sglaw/laws-of-singapore/commercial-law/chapter-8> accessed on 16 July 2018.
470 Liming 2016 (n 224) 3; Zhang 2006 (n 41) 70, 91.
471 Chuan Feng 2016 (n 38) 131.
472 Arts 25, 26 CCL; Liming 2016 (n 224) 3.
473 Arts 4, 8 CCL; Martin Hogg, 'A Scottish Perspective' in DiMatteo and Chen 2017 (n 19) 118; Zhang 2006 (n 41) 70; Bing Ling 2002 (n 229) paras 1.004, 1.005.
474 Bing Ling 2002 (n 229) paras 3.045–3.050.

principles. That said, for application of the sale law principles, reciprocity is required, in the sense that the agreement between the parties must entail the mutual consent concerning the promise of the seller to transfer the goods and the promised performance of the buyer to pay the agreed price.[475] This means in effect that where the aforementioned level of reciprocity is missing, the specific sales law provisions are not applicable, but it does not detract in any way from the result that a valid and enforceable contract is concluded which is subject to the general contract law principles. Nonetheless, it is submitted that the courts may avoid a commercial sales contract where the stipulated price is inadequate to provide the seller the very thing it bargained for.

74. *Comparative analysis* – The distinct view of the investigated legal systems on the required degree of reciprocity for establishing an enforceable sales contract may give rise to significant risks in international trade. In particular, when a party is located in a civil law jurisdiction which did not adopt the legal concept of cause,[476] such as the Netherlands and China, enter into a contract with a party from a common law system, such as Singapore.[477] The difficult issue of the divergence in the required degree of reciprocity appears to be 'fixed' by the unification instruments by excluding the common law requirement of consideration, and the French civil law requirement of a (licit) *cause*,[478] for establishing an enforceable contract.[479]

The CISG has taken the approach that a contract is concluded at the moment of an effective acceptance of an offer, which is sufficiently definite and indicates the intention of the promisor to be bound.[480] A form of cause or consideration is not required. The other unification instruments circumvent the issue of cause and consideration in a similar way

475 Art 130 CCL; Zhang 2006 (n 41) 36, 68; Bing Ling 2002 (n 229) para 1.004, para 3.002, para 3.006; Art 324 (3) CCL prescribes that essential terms that must be included in a technology contract; Compare art 5(2) of the Regulation on the Administration of Contract for the Import of Technology.

476 As mentioned earlier, the French civil law inspired requirement of cause is the equivalent of the common law doctrine of consideration to the extent that the contract is based on a legally valid reason. The French civil law concept of subjective cause is, however, different from the common law concept of consideration in the sense that the reason of a commercial party to bind themselves need not be to obtain something in return. The concept of objective consideration (*i.e.* acquisition of ownership and payment of the purchase) displays greater similarities with the common law concept of consideration.

477 N 444 above.

478 The term cause refers to the expected counter performance. In the French civil law tradition, a distinction is made between the objective cause (*e.g.* acquisition of ownership and payment of the price) and the subjective cause. The subjective cause differs per situation. It is noteworthy that the French Civil Code abandoned the concept of cause as from 1 October 2018; Vogenauer 2015 (n 19) Art 3.1.2, para 5. The contract law of the Netherlands and China follows the Germanic view on contracts, with no requirement of *cause*, nor are the jurisdictions familiar with the concept of consideration.

479 Schwenzer 2016 (n 91) art 11, para 13; Vogenauer 2015 (n 19) art 3.2.1 paras 1–8; Schwenzer, Hachem and Kee 2012 (n 13) para 9.05; Dimitar Stoyanov, 'Causa and Consideration – A Comparative Overview' (2016) 23 Lex ET Scientia Int'l J. 14, 30.

480 Arts 14(1), 23 CISG.

by adopting minimum substantive requirements for bringing about a commercial contract.[481] It is submitted here that this simple, clear and uniform approach taken by the unification instruments has removed any potential legal barrier for international trade following from the distinct requirement of cause and its functional common law equivalent in the form of the requirement of consideration.[482] This means in effect that where the unification instruments apply, commercial parties may assume that an enforceable sales contract is concluded if the relevant requirements are fulfilled, even if there is no cause or consideration. These domestic validity rules are pre-empted in the unification instruments by the rules on contract formation.[483]

That having been said, it seems that the gap is also narrowed at the national level; that is, it appears that Singapore courts have adopted a less restricted view on the traditional common law requirement that the reciprocal promises of the parties must arise from a real bargain, which is not related to a previous performance. This more open approach has narrowed the gap with civil law jurisdictions, which do not require that the promises made by the parties are supported by a cause, such as the Netherlands and China. However, it must be stressed that the investigated legal systems still have a diametrically opposed view on the enforceability of gratuitous promises. For example, a unilateral undertaking of a commercial party, such as a gratuitous promise to deliver ten electric cars to a ridesharing company for an innovative pilot project entailing the usage of these cars on public roads (see the example mentioned under paragraph 70) may have no binding effect in common law because nothing of value is provided in return. Another striking example is a promise of the seller to reimburse a percentage of the invoices paid over a designated year. In contrast to the Netherlands and China, these (sometimes entirely commercially sensible) unilateral promises are not enforceable in Singapore due to the requirement of reciprocity, which means that the contract must comprise an exchange of risks. Taking this into account along with the far-reaching impact of the common law doctrine of a valuable consideration, a sales contracts involving parties from the three investigated jurisdictions may induce serious enforcement risks which are not countered by the CISG. That being the case, the modern viewpoint of the Singapore courts has paved the way to bridging the gap between the thresholds for establishing an enforceable reciprocal sales contract by parties involving both Singapore and civil law jurisdictions, such as the Netherlands and China.

481 Art 3.2.1 PICC; Art 2:101(1) PECL; Art II.-4:101 DCFR.

482 Schwenzer 2016 (n 91) art 11 para 13, intro to arts 14–24 para 3; Vogenauer 2015 (n 19) art 3.2.1 para 6, 9; Schwenzer, Hachem and Kee 2012 (n 13) paras 9.03, 9.07, 9.11, 9.12, 9.13–9.25; Stoyanov (n 479) 14, 30.

483 Schwenzer 2016 (n 91) art 11, para 13, intro to arts 14–24, para 3; Vogenauer 2015 (n 19) art 3.2.1 para 6, 9.

3.4.6 *Conclusions*

75. The contract law of the Netherlands, Singapore and China are familiar with rules on contract formation, although a comparison of the fundamental steps in determining the legally enforceability of a contract reveals important differences between the thresholds for bringing about enforceable obligations. Before diving into a comparative analysis of the disagreement between the subject legal systems, Figure 8 below presents the interplay between the discussed principles. This illustration is particularly useful where there is a disagreement about the existence of an intention to be bound and the understanding of the promised performance. For example, A offers in writing to sell a recycling line for plastic for €100,000 or €500,000. B accepts in writing the offer, but (at the same time) A revokes the offer. In this situation, it is important to take into account that there are significant differences when considering the rules on offer and acceptance (see Figure 7), and the principles for determining the intention and understanding of parties (Figure 8). The civil law notion of good faith, the common law institution of implied terms, and law of evidence play an important role in determining as to whether the offer (upon its acceptance) suffices to establish an enforceable contract and the scope of the assumed obligations. It is therefore, that Figure 8 below also reveals a difference between the contract law of the Netherlands and China, which allows for a holistic assessment of the requirements for contract formation and interpretation of contractual terms, and the Singapore contract law approach which is primarily concerned with the objective expressions of the parties.

Figure 8 Principles for determining the intention and understanding of parties

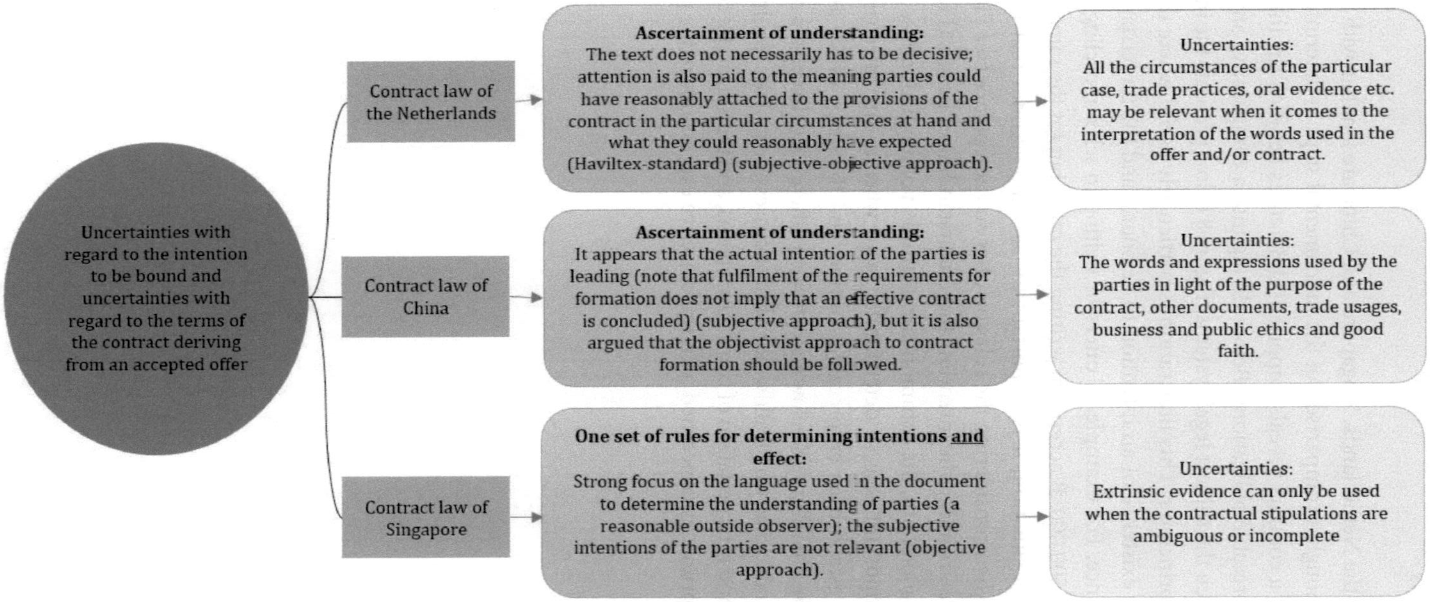

76. The discussion in this section shows that the unification instruments identified do not provide solutions which bridge the gap between the identified opposing viewpoints. There are four important issues in this regard, which (as later shown) are directly linked with the availability of enforced performance in the three investigated jurisdictions. The first issue concerns the methods of contract formation. The contract law of the Netherlands and China (in line with the PICC, PECL and DCFR) appear to have adopted the most liberal approach towards the notion that a contract can be inferred from an offer and acceptance, but also from conduct that is sufficient to show agreement. It seems that the courts of Singapore are more hesitant to recognise alternative methods of contract formation where there are not clearly identifiable elements of offer and acceptance. This approach is in line with the CISG, which (as shown by the drafting history) requires that the courts take great care in evaluating if it is possible to discern from other sources consensus of the parties and the minimum content required for a contract. As for the required consensus of parties (including the intention to be bound), the analysis of the approaches taken by the investigated legal systems reveals a sliding scale from the requirement of objective intentions to be bound to subjective intentions. As a general proposition, it can be said that the contract law of Singapore and China have adopted a more absolute approach as they show a strong preference for objective and subjective intentions respectively (it should be recalled that it is also argued that the objectivist approach prevails under Chinese contract law). The Dutch contract law holds a middle-ground position in this regard. These findings display that the investigated legal systems mark the border between non-binding promises and an enforceable contract quite differently, although there is an important common denominator in the form of the benchmark of a reasonable person, a basic principle which is also acknowledged by the unification instruments identified.

The analysis of the required level of minimum content, which applies to all methods of contract formation, reveals a second important difference between rules on contract formation, in particular when there is no provision for the purchase price or a method for determining the price. The common core is that the investigated legal systems allow for the formation of a commercial sales contract in this situation, although where the buyer is obliged to pay the market price under the contract law of China, the contract law of the Netherlands and Singapore demands that the buyer pays a reasonable price. That having been said, the three investigated jurisdictions, as well as the unification instruments, accept that a commercial sales contract may come into existence where a price had not been fixed. The danger lies more in the means for determining whether the required level of determinability of the *essentialia negotii* is present. When considering the impact of the parol evidence rule in this regard, which is of significant importance in the contract law of Singapore, it appears that a more liberal approach is adopted by the contract law of the Netherlands and China. The aforementioned considerations show that the latter two jurisdictions allow for a quite flexible interpretation of legal principles when taking into account the limitations of the discussed common law doctrines.

The impact of the above-described distinction is most apparent when considering the third difference, which is caused by distinct notions of the bindingness of an offer and acceptance. Where the applicable rules under the contract law of the Netherlands and China favour the position of the promisee, the contract law of Singapore generally protects the interest of the promisor. The unification instruments give consideration to both approaches by adopting a general rule of free revocability, although the instruments vary considerably in the way they have limited the impact of this rule.

The fourth and last identified issue is closely connected with the previous points. In essence, where the contract law of the Netherlands and China allows for a flexible interpretation of legal principles within the boundaries provided by the law, the contract law of Singapore follows the common law more conservative approach towards the interpretation of applicable rules and doctrines, although it allows for a significant degree of judicial control. This point is clearly reflected in the common law concept of consideration which requires that parties exchange a benefit and detriment (not related to a past performance). Where the agreement does not display an exchange of value, a valid and thus enforceable contract does not come into being. Moreover, the concept of consideration, as an important pillar of the contract law of Singapore, provides the court a significant level of control over the formation of an enforceable contract. In this regard, the unification instruments are completely in line with the contract law of the Netherlands and China as they are not familiar with the concepts of cause and consideration. It is submitted here that a new approach may be considered at the international level, which, at the very least, reflects the legal traditions described above (harmonising seems impossible). This undertaking must be carried out in view of the fact that the previously discussed domestic thresholds for the formation of a commercial sales contract are closely related to the availability of the actual enforcement of a contract.[484] This is because legal principles in the realm of commercial sales contracts are in essence the result of favouring the protection of the buyer's or seller's interest.[485]

3.5 Conclusions

77. The present chapter aims to define the ambit of a commercial sales contract to disclose the underlying principles for the boundaries set out in the three investigated jurisdictions, and to identify where there are differences or difficulties in view of the approaches taken

484 Ch 4.
485 S 4.2, 4.3, 4.4.

by the unification instruments identified. On an overall assessment, it appears that the investigated legal systems can be divided into two groups. The first group equates the concept of a sale with the juridical act of the conclusion of a sales contract, allow for a broad interpretation of the goods which may be the object of a sales contract and employ a liberal attitude towards the rules on contract formation. The contract law of the Netherlands and China fall into this category. Nonetheless, there are significant differences in the power of the courts to limit the impact of the obligations assumed in an offer. In the case where the contract law of the Netherlands applies and the aggrieved party argues that the offer demonstrates a gross disparity between the purchase price and the value of the goods and therefore a valid contract has not come into existence, a court may only act in exceptional situations. The thresholds for doing so are significantly lower under the contract law of China due to the principle that courts may interfere where adoption of a price is commissioned by the government or based on government-issued pricing guidelines is required by law.

The second group utilises a narrower definition of goods which may be subject to a sales contract, and the parties are generally not allowed to go beyond the applicable legal doctrines for contract formation. That is, the conclusion of a contract on the basis of alternative methods of contract formation (other than offer and acceptance) is only allowed in exceptional situations, the rules on the required consensus of the parties and the minimum content of their agreement are very strict, and the bargain has to reflect an exchange of a benefit and detriment (not related to a past performance). The contract law of Singapore falls into the second category.

The different approaches discussed above require that commercial parties pay careful consideration to the principles and rules for determining the scope of the buyer's and seller's performance obligations assumed in the offer which intend to bring about a commercial sales contract across civil and common law borders, more precisely when it concerns parties from the three investigated jurisdictions. This, in effect, means that commercial parties accustomed to the protective nature of the civil law tradition should be specifically aware of the implications of the ability of common law courts to seek recourse to the instrument of implied terms, the common law parol evidence rule and the doctrine of valuable consideration under Singapore contract law.[486] By contrast, commercial parties more familiar with the common law tradition may take note of the general civil law notion of good faith and the inextricably linked power of the courts in the Netherlands and China

486 The common law parol evidence rule brings about that evidence arising from the negotiations between the parties is not allowed for determining the extent of the performance of the parties when the terms of agreement are clear on the matter and represent the whole contract (s 3.4.3). In this regard it should also be noted that the doctrine of a valuable consideration is generally not concerned with a gross disparity between the assumed obligations (s 3.4.5).

to interfere with the obligations of the parties deriving from the accepted offer, although it should be noted that the thresholds differ significantly.

The distinction between the first and second group seems to be driven by the need of the discussed principles to protect different interests, which can be traced back to the civil and common law origin of the three investigated jurisdictions. This means in effect that although the contract law principles of the Netherlands and China are quite different in the way they operate, their shared civil law roots display an open attitude towards the promises which are provided legal protection. By contrast, the common law origin of the contract law of Singapore reveals a more protective approach arising from a need to clearly define the scope of the promises which deserve legal protection. The extent to which these considerations are correlated to the availability of enforced performance of non-monetary obligations arising under a commercial sales contact is presented in the final conclusion.[487] However, it should already be noted at this point that the unification instruments identified display a strong preference in this regard for certain elements of the civil law approach, which can also be found in the contract law of the Netherlands and China. Without calling into question the justifications for the choices made, it seems fair to say that this one-sided approach is a major bottleneck for bridging the gap between the civil and common law traditions at the international level. That said, the modern approach taken by Singapore courts may provide inspiration for consolidation of the domestic viewpoints at the international level.

487 Ch 9.

4 General availability of enforced performance

4.1 Introduction

78. Dutch, Singapore and Chinese contract law each act on the notion that the promise of a commercial party should be performed in accordance with the terms of the contract (*pacta sunt servanda*). These legal systems, however, differ greatly in their approach to the judicial instruments available to make parties to a commercial sales contract indifferent between the voluntary performance of the obligations arising from the contract and the availability of enforced performance (indifference principle).[488] This issue traditionally results in a comparison between the impact of enforced performance and monetary compensation which, however, until now has provided unsatisfactory answers because one cannot compare apples and oranges. The rationale of the proposition advanced here is that a judicial action for enforcement of performance and damages have a completely different objective. To put this in the context of commercial trade transactions: enforced performance aims to give the buyer the goods for which it bargained. The objective of monetary compensation is to put the buyer into the same financial position as it would have been in had the seller delivered the goods in accordance with the contract, and applicable legal rules and principles. A frequently discussed issue is that the two major legal families have adopted diametrically opposed views on whether the aggrieved party is entitled to performance or merely the remedy of damages. By moving away from this typical divergence between the civil and common law traditions, and analysing the way the idea of *pacta sunt servanda* operates, and the indifference principle in performance remedy schemes, the present section provides an opportunity to take stock of new insights and the achievements to date by lawmakers in the realm of commercial sales law.

79. The question regarding whether the availability of enforced performance is in accordance with the idea of *pacta sunt servanda* and the indifference principle is best ascertained in light of non-monetary obligations of contracting parties due to the absence of a distinguishable difference between voluntary performance of an obligation to pay money

488 As a practical matter, it should be noted that the costs of litigation and the distribution of these costs between the parties is not taken into account. This topic is more closely related with a comparison between the ability to claim actual performance and to obtain damages.

and a judicial decree for payment of the agreed purchase price.[489] By contrast, non-performance of non-monetary obligations can be remedied via a variation of performance remedies (and damages). As the most pronounced issues for commercial parties follow from distinguishing between the voluntary performance of a non-monetary obligation under a sales contract and a judicial decree to enforce performance, section 4.3 only briefly touches on the intricacies of the ability to obtain actual performance of monetary obligations. Section 4.4 provides a more in-depth examination of the availability of enforced performance of non-monetary obligations and the extent to which this is consistent with the broadly accepted legal concept that contracting parties should comply with promises they have made and the view of the subject legal systems concerning the indifference principle.

80. A commercial sales contract may also bring forth non-monetary obligations on the basis of the idea that parties should behave in accordance with the notion of good faith and best efforts. The central issue is that most civil and common law jurisdictions have a completely different view on the scope and ability to claim for the actual performance of ancillary duties arising from the notion of good faith, best efforts or a variation of it. Nonetheless, these typical legal sources for ancillary non-monetary duties are frequently used in international commercial contracts due to their flexibility.[490] Therefore, the principle of good faith and best efforts are analysed and contrasted against the rules adopted by the unification instruments in order to improve understanding of the different approaches (section 4.5).

4.2 Historical and contemporary underpinnings of enforced performance

4.2.1 *Introduction*

81. The present section seeks to lay out the historical and contemporary underlying principles of the availability of a claim for enforced performance of obligations arising from a commercial sales contract subject to the contract law of the Netherlands, Singapore and China and how the approaches taken by these legal systems relate to the nature of enforced performance in the unifications instruments. The premise advanced here is that the conceptual differences underlying the availability of enforced performance in the subject legal systems may be summarised, albeit in an oversimplified manner, as a basic

489 The costs of litigation are not taken into account.

490 *E.g.*, transboundary oil and gas industry and infrastructure contracts.

right to enforced performance on one hand (civil law), and on the other hand as a remedy (common law). The common assumption is that the dogmatic divergence between the two major legal traditions is caused by the distinct valuations of a contractual promise, which result in opposing viewpoints on the most suitable action to achieve the objective (*i.e.* purpose) of a contract. The following analysis of the approaches taken by the three subject jurisdictions demonstrates, however, that the ideological, statutory and practical differences are in reality multi-faceted.

4.2.2 *Primary status of performance in the Netherlands*

82. In 1798, preparation for the Civil Code in the Batavian Republic commenced with the establishment of a 'Committee of Twelve'.[491] Johannes Lodewijk Farjon (1766–1824) was appointed to prepare the general part of the Law of Obligations.[492] In his draft, Farjon followed the Early Modern Natural Law principle that all obligations should be performed.[493] Therefore, Farjon's draft stated that in the case of a failure in performance of a contractual promise, the aggrieved party was entitled to enforced performance or to set the contract aside; which consequently meant that the aggrieved party was not entitled to claim damages and thus basically forced to claim enforced performance.[494] In the case where the aggrieved party decided to set aside the contract, all actions had to be undertaken to restore the situation to as it was before the parties entered into the contract.[495] Farjon also held the view that a party in default was entitled to a second chance and therefore, an aggrieved party, choosing to set aside the contract rather than claiming enforced performance of the contract, was obliged to inform the non-performing party about its decision by means of a notarial writ.[496] On receipt of the writ, the party who failed to fulfil its obligations was entitled to undertake performance on the condition that the obligations must be performed

491 Oosterhuis 2011 (n 80) 199.

492 Oosterhuis 2011 (n 80) 199.

493 Oosterhuis 2011 (n 80) 221, 222.

494 Oosterhuis 2011 (n 80) 199, 222. In contrast to Oosterhuis, this author uses the term 'setting aside of a contract' instead of rescission, because of the common law view on the term rescission. The principal remedy for misrepresentation is rescission, which involves setting the contract aside an restoring the parties to the pre-contractual position. Instances where the representation is made fraudently, the aggrieved party could also opt to claim damages at common law for the tort of deceit (fraudulent misrepresentation). Rescission differs significantly from the process of termination of a contract for repudiatory breach.

495 Oosterhuis 2011 (n 80) 199; This principle is still present in art 6:271 DCC which states that in case a promisee chooses to set aside the contract, because his counterparty is in default, an obligation arises to reverse the performance of the obligations which contracting parties have already received.

496 Oosterhuis 2011 (n 80) 199.

within the shortest time possible and providing compensation for any damages incurred by the aggrieved party.[497]

83. In 1806, after the transfer of power over the Batavian Republic to the brother of Napoléon, the preparation of the Law of Obligations by Farjon was continued by Van der Linden, who held the view that in the case of a failure in performance of a contractual promise, the aggrieved party was entitled to enforced performance or to claim damages.[498] Importantly, Van der Linden held the view that a non-performing seller must be provided with a second chance to deliver the goods before a sales contract can be set aside by the aggrieved buyer. In the case of a personal act, Van der Linden followed an approach that for true personal obligations, such as an engagement, and for obligations not to do something, the Code Civil and English common law approach *nemo ad factum praecise cogi potest* applied, meaning that no one could be forced to perform such obligations against their will. This humanistic approach, that no one can be forced to perform, stems from the concept that the freedom of an individual is primary and therefore, a non-performing party cannot and should not be actually forced to perform.[499] Based on this viewpoint, Van der Linden upheld the opinion that in the case of non-performance of an obligation not to do something, the aggrieved party was only entitled to claim damages, while the use of civil custody and imprisonment was rejected.[500]

84. In 1809, the efforts to develop a Dutch Civil Code resulted in the promulgation of the Code (*wetboek*) Napoleon for the Kingdom of Holland, which significantly differed from the principles of Farjon and Van der Linden since it stipulated that the object of obligations could be an act or a good, and that all obligations had to represent a monetary value.[501] Therefore, it can be said that in 1809 the Kingdom of Holland upheld a view on non-performance, which is similar to the general principle in English common law and the current Singapore common law-based system – being that damages are the preferred remedy.[502] The Code Napoleon included a contradictory principle, since it stated that in the case of a failure in performance of a reciprocal agreement the aggrieved party was

497 Oosterhuis 2011 (n 80) 199; In the current Dutch Civil Code, the principle of a second change, and as such the preference for specific performance as a primary remedy for a breach of contract, can be found in art 6:81(1) 1 DCC providing the conditions for default of a party in breach.

498 Oosterhuis 2011 (n 80) 222.

499 Oosterhuis 2011 (n 80) 203, 222.

500 Oosterhuis 2011 (n 80) 227; Art 3:296(1) DCC stipulates that the right to bring claim to court for enforced performance can be excluded if this flows from the nature of the obligation. It follows that true personal obligations cannot be enforced.

501 Oosterhuis 2011 (n 80) 204.

502 See the English case *Cassell & Co Ltd v Broome* [1972] AC 1027 at 1070E; JD Mayne and H McGregor, *Mayne and McGregor on Damages* (18th edn, Sweet & Maxwell, 2009) paras 1–1001; Phang et al 2012 (n 112) paras 20.049, 20.050.

entitled to enforced performance or to set aside the agreement and to claim for damages.[503] It was also remarkable that the Code Napoleon adopted the Civil Code principle that a buyer is entitled to setting aside of the contract and to claim enforced performance if the seller fails to deliver the goods within the agreed time.[504] Interestingly, the principle that a promisor could not be physically compelled to do something did not apply to certain highly personal obligations.

In 1810, the Kingdom of Holland became a part of the French Empire, resulting in 1811 in the promulgation of the Code Civil in the Kingdom of the Netherlands and the introduction of the principle that in situations of non-performance of the seller's delivery obligation, the aggrieved buyer was entitled to choose between enforced performance, setting aside of the contract and to claim damages.[505] In the period 1811–1838, however, case law shows that enforced performance was seen by the courts as the primary remedy for non-performance of a contract.[506] With regard to determining the status of a claim for enforced performance under the subsequent Dutch Civil Code 1838; all obligations to do something or not to do something could be conferred into an obligation to compensate costs, damages and interest (article 1275 DCC 1838).[507] In this respect, it is noteworthy that, prior to 1870, it was believed that an obligation to pay damages could not be seen as the object of the contract, but merely as a substitute for the initially agreed performance. Therefore, damages could only be awarded on a subsidiary claim.[508] It may, therefore, not come as surprise that a promisee was primarily entitled to enforced performance or to bring a claim to court for termination of the contract.[509] In contrast to enforced performance, a request for termination of the contract could be combined with a claim for compensation of costs, damages, and interest.[510] The enforced performance of an obligation and termination of a contract, including a claim for damages, were regarded as

503 Oosterhuis 2011 (n 80) 205, 206.

504 It was believed impossible to force an unwilling promisor to physically do something. Oosterhuis 2011 (n 80) 207, 208.

505 Oosterhuis 2011 (n 80) 208, 216, 381.

506 Oosterhuis 2011 (n 80) 216, 218, 219, 381.

507 Art 1275 DCC 1838: *Alle verbintenissen om iets te doen, of niet te doen, worden opgelost in vergoeding van kosten, schade en interessen, ingeval de schuldenaar niet aan zijne verpligting voldoet.*

508 Oosterhuis 2011 (n 80) 450; District Court Amsterdam 20 June 1876, W. 4212; Dutch Court of Appeal Amsterdam 19 October 1877, W. 4200.

509 Art 1276 DCC 1838 stipulated that, in addition to a primary claim for specific performance, a promisee was entitled to claim termination of the contract in combination with a claim for compensation of costs, damages and interest (art 1276 DCC 1838). Art 1276 DCC 1838: *Niettemin heeft de schuldeiser het regt om de vernietiging te vorderen van hetgeen strijdig met de verbindtenis verrigt is, en hij kan zich door den regter doen magtigen om, ten koste van den schuldenaar, het gedane te doen vernietigen; onverminderd de vergoeding van kosten, schaden en interessen, indien daartoe gronden bestaan.*

510 Art 1308 DCC 1838: *Degene te wiens opzigte de verbindtenis niet is nagekomen, heeft de keus om of de andere partij, indien zulks mogelijk is, tot de nakoming der overeenkomst te noodzaken, of derzelver ontbinding te vorderen, met vergoeding van kosten, schaden en interessen.*

exclusive legal instruments.[511] These legal instruments had the awkward effect that, for example, a claim for the payment of arrears (enforced performance) or non-performance of long-term contracts could not be combined with a claim for termination of the contract for the future, including compensation of costs, damages, and interests.[512] Subsequently, interest over arrears could only be claimed if the promisor chose to claim for termination of the contract including a claim for damages.

85. After 1870, the Dutch Supreme Court held the view that the Dutch Civil Code of 1838 did not exclude a primary claim for damages or that a claim for damages had to be accompanied by a claim for termination of the contract.[513] Further, it was explicitly held that enforced performance could be combined with a claim for damages.[514] It was also considered that a claim for compensation of costs, damages, and interest could only be awarded if the promisor did not perform his obligation after he became in default (art 1274 DCC 1838),[515] if performance was impossible or in case of non-performance of an obligation not to act (art 1279 DCC 1838).[516] In this respect, it is relevant to note that the non-performance of an obligation was regarded as an implicit or explicit (inserted into the contract) resolutive condition which could not automatically lead to termination of the contract.[517] This principle was substantiated by the argument that contracting parties entered into a contract under the assumption that the other party would perform his part of the agreement.[518] In contrast to the current Dutch Civil Code, termination of a contract required a lawsuit,[519] even if the terms of the contract stipulated that non-performance was penalised with the termination of the contract.[520] Further, in the case of

511 Oosterhuis 2011 (n 80) 484.

512 Oosterhuis 2011 (n 80) 483, 484.

513 Art 1303 of the DCC 1838.

514 Oosterhuis 2011 (n 80) 496.

515 Art 1274 DCC 1838: *De schuldenaar wordt in gebreke gesteld, het zij door een bevel of andere soortgelijke akte, hetzij uit kracht der verbintenis zelve, wanneer deze meebrengt dat de schuldenaar in gebreke zal zijn, door het enkel verloop van een bepaalde termijn.*

516 Art 1279 DCC 1838: *Vergoeding van kosten, schaden en interessen, voortspruitende uit het niet nakomen eener verbindtenis, is dan eerst verschuldigd, wanneer de schuldenaar, na ingebreke te zijn gesteld, nalatig blijft om die verbindtenis te vervullen, of indien hetgeen de schuldenaar verpligt was te geven of te doen, slechts kon gegeven of gedaan worden binnen zekeren tijd, welken hij heeft laten voorbij gaan.*

517 Art 1302 Dutch Civil Code 1838; Oosterhuis 2011 (n 80) 214.

518 CL Schüller, *Het Burgerlijk Wetboek, met Aanteekeningen* (Utrecht, Schultze en Voerman 1841) 279.

519 Art 6:267(1)(2) DCC entails the principle that the termination of a contract shall be effected by a written declaration of the person entitled to do so, or via electronic means if the contract is concluded by electronic means. Further, termination of the contract may also be pronounced by the court on the demand of such person.

520 Art 1302 DCC 1838: *De ontbindende voorwaarde wordt altijd verondersteld in wederkeerige overeenkomsten plaats te grijpen, in geval eene der partijen aan hare verpligting niet voldoet. In dat geval, is de overeenkomst niet van regtswege ontbonden, maar moet de ontbinding in regten gevraagd worden. Deze aanvraag moet ook plaats hebben, zelfs indien de ontbindende voorwaarde wegens het niet nakomen der verpligting in de*

non-performance of an obligation to not act, the promisee could only claim compensation for costs, damages, and interest.[521] However, an exception was made for certain obligations, such as an obligation of non-disclosure.[522] The provisions of the Dutch Civil Code 1838 mentioned above were founded on the principle that all obligations should be performed. Therefore, a claim for termination of a contract and damages, contrary to enforced performance, could only be awarded if the party in breach was in default,[523] or performance was impossible, and the non-performance was attributable.[524] Another indication that enforced performance under the former Dutch Civil Code was regarded as the primary legal instrument to remedy a non-performance follows from the principle that it was at the discretion of the court to award an additional period if the promisor failed to deliver the goods in time.[525]

The flowchart below provides an overview of the position of the right to enforced performance in relation to remedies for non-performance under the Dutch Civil Code 1838. This overview shows that before and after 1870 the Dutch Civil Code upheld the principle that all obligations must be performed, but it also shows that after 1870, important doctrinal principles were imported to overcome certain injustices and omissions which negatively affected contractual relationships. For instance, it became possible to claim damages solely or to combine a claim for damages with a claim for enforced performance.[526] Nevertheless, it may be said that the core civil law principle that all obligations must be performed remained the primary overriding view since a claim for damages and termination of a contract was subject to the overall barrier of default and the inextricably linked second chance concept. In other words, under the Dutch Civil Code 1838, a contractual promise was primarily valued as an absolute obligation to perform and only after preconditions were met and barriers overcome, could the contract be set aside and damages awarded.

overeenkomst mogt zijn uitgedrukt. Indien de ontbindende voorwaarde niet in de overeenkomst is uitgedrukt, staat het den regter vrij om, naar gelang der omstandigheden, aan den vervreemder, op deszelfs verzoek, eenen termijn te gunnen om alsnog aan zijne verpligting te voldoen, welke termijn echter den tijd van ééne maand niet mag te boven gaan.

521 Art 1278 DCC 1838: *Indien de verbindtenis bestaat in iets niet te doen, is degene die daartegen handelt, uit hoofde van die overtreding alleen, gehouden tot vergoeding van kosten, schaden en interessen.*

522 Schüller (n 518) 274.

523 Oosterhuis 2011 (n 80) 346.

524 Dutch Parliamentary History Book 6, 1002; The Dutch Civil Code does not require attributability for awarding a claim for non-performance; Art 6:265 paragraph 1 DCC.

525 Art 1303 DCC 1838.

526 Oosterhuis 2011 (n 80) 481–484.

Figure 9 Historical underpinnings of enforced performance in the Netherlands

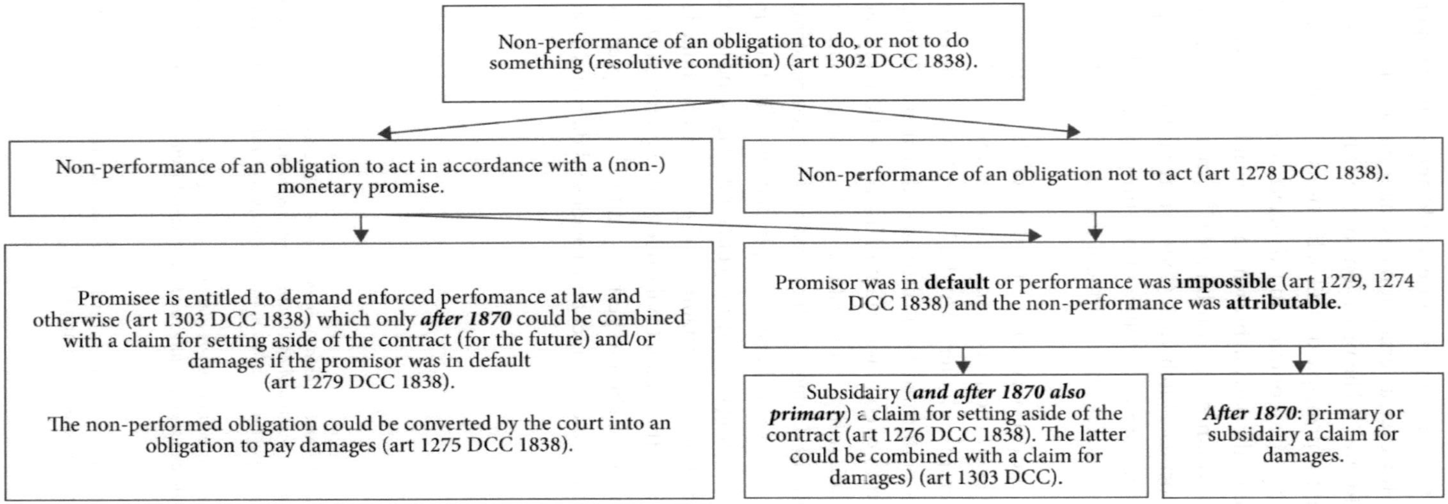

86. In the current Dutch Civil Code (hereafter Dutch contract law), the civil law principle of *pacta sunt servanda* prevails,[527] encompassing the view that by the act of promise making, contracting parties have voluntarily given up a part of their freedom and they are, therefore, bound to provide the actual performance.[528] Accordingly, it is considered that the substantive right to enforced performance of a contractual promise stems directly from the nature of the bindingness of a contractual promise,[529] and does not stem from the wrongdoing of a promisor.[530] These principles are laid down in the statutory right to demand enforced performance.[531] The only substantive requirements are sufficient interest of the promisor in obtaining an order for enforced performance and that performance is due (*i.e.* 'opeisbaar') according to the contractual stipulations.[532] In instances where the performance is not yet due and the contractual stipulations are clear about the time for performance, the court may order performance subject to the condition that actual enforcement is only available when the obligation is due and the promisee has sufficient interest in obtaining an order for enforced performance.[533] These considerations reveal that the time for performance does not necessarily have to be due when a claim for enforced performance is initiated. The above portrayed favourable look on the right to enforced performance is strengthened by specific requirements for damages. That is to say, Dutch contract law act upon the notion that establishing the civil liability of a non-performing party to pay damages demands additional legal justification. For example, the right to claim damages is only available in the case of an attributable failure in performance, or if the promisee has good reasons to fear that the promisor will fail in its performance and such an anticipatory failure is attributable to the latter.[534] For the liability of the promisor, it is important to take into account that the latter is only obliged to repair the damage for delay in performance for the time that it has been in default.[535]

527 V Mak, *Performance-Oriented Remedies in European Sale of Goods Law* (Studies of the Oxford Institute of European and Comparative Law, Hart Publishing 2009) 8.

528 Sieburgh, *Asser 6-III* 2018 (n 203) 41; Mak (n 527) 30.

529 Sieburgh, *Asser 6-III* 2018 (n 203) 43; Sieburgh, *Asser 6-I* (n 363) paras 322, 380; Mak (n 527) 8.

530 AW Jongbloed, 'commentaar op artikel 296 Boek 3 BW' para 3 in J Hijma (ed), *Groene Serie Vermogensrecht* (Wolters Kluwer 2018).

531 Art 3:296 DCC.

532 Arts 3:296(1), 3:303, 6:39 DCC; CH Sieburgh, *Mr. C. Assers Handleiding tot de beoefening van het Nederlands Burgerlijk Recht. 6. Verbintenissenrecht. Deel II. De verbintenis in het algemeen, tweede gedeelte* (Wolters Kluwer 2017) para 343.

533 Art 3:296(2) DCC; Sieburgh, *Asser 6-II* (n 532); Sieburgh, *Asser 6-I* (n 363) paras 32, 246; Mak (n 527) 31; Books 3 and 6 of the DCC include the general part of the law of obligations and separate provisions for torts and breach of contract. Book 7 of the DCC provides separate provisions for specific contracts. A claim for specific performance shall not be awarded for non-performance of obligations with a personal character and if performance has become impossible.

534 Arts 6:74(1), 6:80(1)(c) DCC.

535 Art 6:85 DCC; see also arts 6:74(2), 6:81 *ff* DCC; In general, default commences when the promisor is given written notice of default granting the latter a reasonable period for the performance and there is no

87. The considerations above presuppose that the Dutch Civil Code places great emphasis on the importance of actual performance of obligations by making a claim for enforced performance readily available.[536] The requirements for damages and setting aside of the contract, as well as the statutory provision for a situation of *force majeure* supports this view. The latter stipulates that the promisee is entitled to obtain what is due to him or her by execution or termination of the contract, even if the performance of the contractual promise is prevented by a cause not attributable to the promisor.[537] Another argument to substantiate the presumption that actual performance of the contract is primarily encouraged under Dutch law by the measure of enforced performance derives from the cases *Verheijen Seeds v Rijk Zwaan* (1990) and *Intres v Walt Disney Company* (1995).[538] In both judicial proceedings, the Dutch Supreme Court considered that, although the infringement of an intellectual property right was stopped, the aggrieved party remained entitled to claim the performance of the contract in the form of an infringement injunction under pain of a financial penalty. Besides these arguments, there is also the statutory right of the promisee to convert the right to performance into an obligation of the promisor to pay damages. This principle demonstrates that the right to enforced performance is the starting point and that it can be converted in damages upon the demand of the aggrieved party.[539]

88. The strong focus of Dutch contract law on the importance of performance of the contract by the promisor is also reflected in the statutory provision that the right to substantive damages and termination of a contract is secondary to a reasonable offer by the promisor (made by the promisor after the commencement of his or her default) to

---

performance within such period (art 6:82(1) DCC); Where performance is temporarily unavailable, or it is evident from the behaviour of the promisor that a warning notice would serve no purpose, the promisor may be put in default by a mere written liability notice (art 6:81(2) DCC); Default commences without the formality of putting in default in instances of the expiration of time limits, where the obligation arises from tort or relates to reparation of damages and the obligation is not immediately performed, and where the promisee may assume that the promisor will fail to perform (art 6:83 DCC).

536 MM Stolp 2007, 'Ontbinding, schadevergoeding en nakoming. De remedies voor wanprestatie in het licht van de beginselen van subsidiariteit en proportionaliteit' (DPhil thesis Radboud University Nijmegen 2007) 263 *ff.*

537 Art 6:79 DCC; Jongbloed (n 530) para 5.

538 *Verheijen Seed v Rijk Zwaan* Dutch Supreme Court 23 Februari 1990, ECLI:NL:PHR:1990:AD104, NJ 1990, 663; *Intres v Walt Disney Company* Dutch Supreme Court 1 December 1995, ECLI:NL:HR:1995:ZC1899, NJ 1996, 510.

539 Art 6:87(1) DCC entitles the promisor to convert his primary right to performance of a contractual obligation into a secondary legal obligation of the promisor to repair the monetary damages of the promisee; The following high thresholds apply when demanding damages instead of actual performance of a contractual promise: (i) promisor is in default; (ii) parties are connected through a continuing contract; (iii) it is not in the interest of the promisee to perform his obligation; (iv) the failure relates to the primary obligation of the promisor; (v) the failure in performance does not justify termination of the contract but is serious enough to justify conversion.

perform the contractual obligations and where applicable, to pay any additional damages and costs which in the meantime become due.[540] This shows that the Dutch Civil Code is primarily focussed on promises made by contracting parties and the certainty that the act of promise making results in an enforceable contract.[541] This approach aligns with the principle that a promise is binding because parties have commenced in the act of promise making which is believed to invoke expectations and trust.[542] Following this line of thinking, it is said that a contractual promise imposes an obligation on the promisor not to compromise the right of the promisee to enforced performance of the contract.[543] In view of these considerations, it is important to note that a claim for enforced performance can be brought to court for unilateral and reciprocal obligations deriving from private law (*e.g.* [intellectual] property law), public law (*e.g.* criminal law,) and, less obviously, obligations which are based on unwritten law such as the obligation to cooperate with a paternity test if it is likely that the person in question is the father of an unborn child.[544] A claim to progress negotiations can also be brought to court in the form of a claim for enforced performance by the promisee if there is no justification on the side of the counterparty of the aggrieved party to terminate the negotiations.[545] Moreover, obligations to which the Dutch government is a contracting party can be subject to a claim for enforced performance. Hence, the action for enforced performance covers a wide range of applications.

89. It appears that under Dutch contract law, the Dutch courts are entitled to enforce the promisor, on the demand of the promisee, to do exactly what it promised to do because,

540 Arts 6:86, 6:58, 6:61(1), 6:266(1), 6:265 DCC; In a recent case about the right of a supplier of clothes to remedy its failure in performance (*i.e.* delayed delivery), the Dutch Supreme Court considered that a refusal of the buyer to accept the seller's offer to deliver the goods with a discount, did not entitle the seller to unilateral terminate the contract, Dutch Supreme Court 7 December 2018, ECLI:NL:PHR:2018:692, NJB 2018, 2302; AJ Feenstra, 'Het aanbod tot betaling van schadevergoeding en kosten in art 6:86: harmonie- of conflictmodel?' (1998) WPNR 6319; Stolp (n 536) 122 *ff.*

541 This reflects the so-called 'promise-principle'; Charles Fried, *Contract as Promise: A Theory of Contractual Obligation* (Oxford University Press 2015).

542 Fried (n 541); Dori Kimel, 'Neutrality, Autonomy, and Freedom in Contract' (2001) 21 OJLS 473; Dori Kimel, *From Promise to Contract: towards a liberal theory of contract theory of contract* (Hart Publishing 2003).

543 Mak (n 527) 59.

544 *Vaderschapsactie* Dutch Supreme Court 22 September 2000, ECLI:NL:HR:2000:AA7204, NJ 2001, 647.

545 *Baris v Riezenkamp* Dutch Supreme Court 15 November 1957, ECLI:NL:PHR:1957:AG2023, NJ 1958, 67; *Van Oosterom v Majoor* Dutch Supreme Court 16 January 1981, ECLI:NL:PHR:1981:AG4132, NJ 1981, 426; *Stuyvers' Beheer v Eugster* Dutch Supreme Court 15 May 1981, ECLI:NL:HR:1981:AG4190, NJ 1982, 85; *Plas v Valburg* Dutch Supreme Court 18 June 1982, ECLI:NL:PHR:1982:AG4405, NJ 1983, 723; *VSH v Shell* Dutch Supreme Court 23 October 1987, ECLI:NL:PHR:1987:AD0018, NJ 1988, 1017; *Vogelaar v Skil* Dutch Supreme Court 31 May 1991, ECLI:NL:HR:1991:ZC0255, NJ 1991, 647; *Beliën v provincie Noord-Brabant* Dutch Supreme Court 24 March 1995, ECLI:NL:HR:1995:ZC1674, NJ 1995, 569; *ABB v Staat* Dutch Supreme Court 4 October 1996, ECLI:NL:HR:1996:ZC2158, NJ 1997, 65; *De Ruijterij v MBO Ruiters* Dutch Supreme Court 14 June 1996, ECLI:NL:HR:1996:ZC2105, NJ 1997, 481; *CBB v JPO Projecten* Dutch Supreme Court 12 August 2005, ECLI:NL:HR:2005:AT7337, NJ 2005, 467.

amongst other elements, a failure in performance is not required for granting a claim for enforced performance. This proposition accords with the statutory principle that voluntary performance of a contractual promise and an enforced performance have the same juridical effect (*i.e.* ownership is transferred and the buyer obtains possession of the thing sold).[546] However, it may also be said that in certain cases it is not possible for the courts to deliver a judgement for enforced performance which would provide the aggrieved party exactly what it bargained for because, for example, materials are no longer available, or the promisor can only be forced to repair the defects.[547] Further, the nature of the obligation can make it impossible for a court to provide an order for enforced performance of the initially agreed obligations.[548] Moreover, any such order can include a sanction for non-compliance, although this obligation was initially not a part of the contract. Based on these arguments it may be said that an order for enforced performance may not, in every circumstance, compel the promisor to perform exactly what it promised to do, and in these situations it is, therefore, merely a substitute for the initial promise – like damages, repair, and replacement.

90. An action to persuade enforced performance of a contractual promise in the civil law system of the Netherlands is regarded as a positive security measure to ensure the performance of contractual promises. Therefore, the statutory actions discussed below to enforce performance of a contract are based on the promises made by the contracting parties, in contrast to remedies of damages and (extra)judicial termination of a contract, which are regarded as remedies for failure in performance of a contractual promise in Dutch contract law.[549] For that reason, it is not unsurprising that in the layered structure of the Dutch Civil Code, the right of action to obtain enforced performance precedes the provisions for damages and termination of a contract. To put this into context: the action to obtain enforced performance of a contractual promise by the promisor is a statutory principle which follows from the General Provisions on Patrimonial Law,[550] applying to all legal duties to bring about a certain effect, such as the seller's and buyer's non-monetary obligations and rights resulting from the act of concluding a commercial sales contract.[551] The statutory provision for the right of action entails the rule that the person obliged to give, to do or not to do something, may be subject to an order for enforced performance, on demand by the person to whom the obligation is owed, in accordance with the agreed

546 Art 3:297 DCC.

547 *E.g.*, contracts entailing the sale of goods or construction of works.

548 *E.g.*, obligations with a personal character.

549 Haas 2009 (n 206); Floris Bakels, 'Ontbinding van wederkerige overeenkomsten' (Dphil thesis, Leiden University 1994) 27–28.

550 Book 3 Patrimonial Law in General.

551 S 3.2.

terms.[552] A claim for enforcement of a contractual promise, entailing the obligation to perform a positive or negative act,[553] may be combined with a *lex specialis* if applicable, which can be found in subsequent chapters of the Dutch Civil Code. In addition, the earlier mentioned General Provisions on Patrimonial Law, preceding the *lex specialis*, entail the instrument of authorisation of the promisee by the court to perform the thing the promisor promised to do (section 7.3).[554] The second instrument is the replacement of the promised act by a decision of the court or by the act of a court-appointed representative.[555] The aforementioned instruments replace the act of the promisor with the objective to provide the promisee with the thing which would have resulted from the performance. However, as shown below, these instruments are not available as of right to the promisee and, moreover, the judicial instrument of authorisation of the promisee is only available after a failure in performance by the promisor.

91. The primary focus on the right to performance of a contractual promise under the contract law of the Netherlands is reflected in the statutory provision that it is not at the discretion of the court to deny a claim for enforced performance unless it otherwise follows from the law, the nature of the obligation (*e.g.* a personal obligation), and a juridical act (*e.g.* derogatory agreements).[556] In other words, the court must award a claim for enforced performance except where one of the exceptions (*i.e.* non-actionable obligations) applies.[557] As mentioned earlier, for situations where an enforceable obligation is not yet due, the court may order its performance subject to the condition that enforcement is allowed only after lapse of the time of performance and the promisor failed to act in accordance with this stipulation.[558] These statutory provisions result from the notion that contractual promises are binding. This favourable view to protecting performance interest is also embedded in the principle that damages is only available when the non-performance is caused by an attributable failure in performance by the promisor, and the latter is in default.[559] Setting aside of the contract requires a simple failure in performance, and default if performance is not permanently or temporarily impossible. It follows from the rules on

552 Art 3:296(1) DCC; one example of an order not to do something can be found in the provisions for misleading and comparative advertising, which entails the right of the promisee to demand the promisor to cease making such information public or from causing it to be made public and also, if appropriate, to order the promisor to publish a correction of the unpermitted advertising (read art 3:296(1) DCC in conjunction with arts 6:194,6:196 of the DCC).

553 Sieburgh, *Asser 6-I* (n 363) para 21.

554 Art 3:299(1)(2) DCC; Sieburgh, *Asser 6-I* (n 363) para 20.

555 Art 3:300(1) DCC; Sieburgh, *Asser 6-I* (n 363) para 20.

556 Art 3:296(1) DCC.

557 De Jong, Krans and Wissink 2018 (n 194) 9, 12.

558 Arts 3:296(2), 6:39(1) DCC; De Jong, Krans and Wissink 2018 (n 194) 222; Sieburgh, *Asser 6-I* (n 363) para 246.

559 Arts 6:74(2), 6: 87(1) DCC.

default and inextricably linked statutory limitations that damages and setting aside of the contract are subject to specific thresholds.[560] This does not mean that a promisee is forced to opt first for enforced performance. Initially, it may claim for other judicial actions, such as damages and setting aside of the contract, provided that the applicable requirements are fulfilled. Nonetheless, the preference for performance of obligations is embedded in various principles such as the statutory right to demand performance (within a reasonable time) of a contractual performance in the case no term has been set for performance,[561] and the provision that an aggrieved party may refuse performance offered by the promisor after commencement of its default when the offer does not include payment of damages.[562] It may, therefore, be said that the notion of performance as the preferred remedy for a failed performance goes both ways. There are, however, numerous exceptions which considerably affect the status of enforced performance, and hence also the right of the aggrieved party to choose enforced performance over damages and termination of the contract. It may be said that these exceptions are based on the principle of adequacy, in the sense that an order for enforced performance is not available if this instrument is not capable of curing the non-performance.[563] This may occur, for example, when performance is impossible in law or fact when it is evident from the attitude or notice of the promisor that it will not perform, and where a contractual or statutory time limit for performance has expired.[564] A court may also refuse a claim for enforced performance when enforcement would result in a disproportionate burden.[565] The proportionality principle may be invoked on the account of the statutory principle that an aggrieved party is not entitled to exercise its right to require enforced performance to the extent that its exercise constitutes an abuse,[566] and on the basis of the statutory principle that parties are bound to act in accordance with the requirement of reasonableness and fairness.[567] Case law has interpreted the latter as an obligation of the aggrieved party to take into account the justified interest of the promisor when selecting the appropriate judicial action.[568] This effectively means that the freedom of the aggrieved promisee to choose for a remedy can be limited to damages. From the interplay between the principle of abuse of right, the standard of

560 Read arts 6:74(2), 6:265(2) in conjunction with art 6:81 DCC *ff*; Stolp (n 536) 263; See n 535 for the rules on the promisor's default.

561 Dutch Parliamentary History Book 6 (n 207) 170; Art 6:38 DCC.

562 Art 6:86 DCC.

563 Stolp (n 536) 264.

564 Ss 7.2.2 and 7.2.3.

565 S 7.2.3.

566 Art 3:13(1) DCC.

567 Arts 6:2(1), 6:248(1) DCC.

568 *Baris v Riezenkamp* (n 545); *Mulitvastgoed v Nethou* Dutch Supreme Court 5 January 2001, ECLI:NL:PHR:2001:AA9311, NJ 2001, 79, para 3.5; MBM Loos in Schelhaas 2002 (n 19) 355; MAMC van den Berg, 'De keuze tussen nakoming, schadevergoeding of ontbinding en de belangen van de crediteur' (2001) 6439 WPNR 299; M Veldman, 'Grenzen aan het recht op nakoming' (2001) 6455 WPNR 736.

reasonableness and fairness, and the applicable case law, it follows that the performance interest of the promisee must be balanced against the seriousness of the failure of performance, the availability of guarantees and the possibility that a less far-reaching remedial measure could also serve the purpose of the contract.[569] As a consequence, a claim for enforced performance may be refused if judicial enforcement would impose an unreasonable burden on the promisor and enforced performance is not more beneficial to the aggrieved party than another remedial measure. However, due consideration should be given to the principle that consent of the aggrieved party is required for an alternative method of performance, even where the offered alternative is equal or even greater in value than the initially agreed performance.[570] In this light, a promisor cannot ignore the performance interest of the aggrieved party by paying mere damages instead of performing the contract.[571] Based on the findings above, it may be said that the difference in impact between the right to require performance in the civil law system of the Netherlands, and the exceptional nature of an order for enforced performance in common law jurisdictions is lessened by the interplay in the Dutch contract law system between the numerous statutory limitations on the right to require performance and the reciprocal basis of the freedom of both parties to select specific remedial measures to cure a failed performance.[572] It must be added that the latter should be considered in light of the restricted discretionary power of Dutch judicature which does not allow the court to determine on its own motion the appropriateness of a judicial action in a given situation.[573]

As for the internal hierarchy between the available performance remedies for commercial sales, the contract law of the Netherlands adopted the principle that where the thing delivered does not conform to the contract, the aggrieved buyer may require delivery of that which is missing, repair of the thing delivered, provided that the seller can reasonably comply therewith, and replacement unless the variance from that which was agreed is too insignificant to justify this.[574] This statutory provision may be seen as an application of the principle of proportionality, in the sense that it requires a balancing of costs and benefits of the selected performance remedy. Moreover, it appears that the overarching subsidiarity principle applies to the extent that it requires a balancing of the impact of the entire remedial arsenal in this context, that is: repair, replacement and damages.

569 Sieburgh, *Asser 6-I* (n 363) para 240 in conjunction with the considerations T Hartlief and RPJL Tjittes, 'Kroniek van het vermogensrecht' (2001) v 76 Nederlands Juristenblad 1459, 1464; Mak (n 527) 94.

570 Art 6:45 DCC; District Court Gelderland 18 December 2015, ECLI:NL:RBGEL:2015:8280.

571 *Meegdes v Meegdes* Dutch Supreme Court 21 December 1956, NJ 1957, 126; Mak (n 527) 92.

572 See for support of this view Hartlief and Tjittes (n 569) 1464.

573 *Mol v Meijer* Dutch Supreme Court 4 February 2000, ECLI:NL:PHR:2000:AA4728, NJ 2000, 562 para 6.c annotation JBM Vranken.

574 Art 7:21(1) DCC.

4.2.3 Exceptional nature of enforced performance in Singapore

92. This section attempts to unravel the complexities surrounding an action for enforced performance of an obligation (monetary and non-monetary) arising from a commercial sales contract governed by the contract law of Singapore. The starting point is an introductory discussion of the underpinnings of the approach taken by the English common law system, because this is the foundation of Singapore contract law. The history of English contract law starts with the development of a *writ of covenant* which was only available for specific contractual obligations laid down in a deed (*e.g.* obligations concerning the conveyance of real property).[575] This ancient document was the source for an action to enforce performance and not the act of promise making, which explains that even today a grant or gift agreement must be laid down in a deed. Aside from the writ of covenant, common law also acknowledged a *writ of debt* which was used to enforce payment of a monetary debt and the delivery of designated goods if an action for a *writ of debt* was brought to court.[576] However, this would not lead to enforcement of a non-monetary obligation as the common law courts followed the adage that a party in breach might lose his property, but not his liberty.[577] Thus, if a promisor did not obey an order to deliver the goods, the common law court would order the sale of the goods instead of enforcement of the contract. For this reason, it is said that the maxim in civil law jurisdictions, *nemo ad factum praecise cogi potest*, which means nobody can be forced to a specific act, is similar to the English common law principle that a non-performing party might lose his property, but not his liberty.[578] Due to procedural and practical issues with a writ of debt, the writ of *assumpsit* (founded on the writ of trespass), as a measure for an unlawful act, became the foundation of an action to claim damages for failure in performance of a contractual promise.[579] The nature of this instrument explains that default and a second chance for performance are not required when seeking relief for failure in performance of a contract (the gist of the action being tort, and not breach of contract).

93. In time, the common law courts came to be seen to be too strict when concerned with disputes regarding a breach of a contractual obligation not laid down in a deed because they did not take into account the specific circumstances of the cases in question and could

575 Zwalve (n 448) 481.

576 F Pollock and FW Maitland, *The History of English Law before the Time of Edward I* (2nd edn, Liberty Fund 2010) 79; JH Baker, *Introduction to English Legal History* (4th edn, Oxford University Press 2007) 18; Mercantile Law Amendment 1856; HS Bowen, *Outlines of Specific Performance* (HeinOnline legal classics library, William S. Hein & Company 2018); Zwalve (n 448) 487.

577 *Hill v CA Parsons Ltd* [1971] 3 All ER 1345 at 1359.

578 Sir Fry Edward, *A Treatise on the Specific Performance of Contracts, Including Those of Public Companies* (2nd edn, W.C. Little 1861) 572.

579 Zwalve (n 448) 493 *ff.*

not order enforced performance of non-monetary obligations.[580] As a result, the Court of Chancery became concerned with individual cases to correct injustice and to soften and reduce the extremity of the law by providing equitable remedies, such as specific performance (enforcement of non-monetary performance obligations) and injunction orders (to refrain from doing something).[581] However, equitable remedies only fulfilled a supplementary or a corrective role when it was determined necessary.[582] It was recognised that this line of thought could lead to inequality if no consistent rules were followed. Therefore, a system of principles for awarding equitable remedies was developed.[583] In the nineteenth century, the work of the Court of the Chancery and the courts of Common Law overlapped to a great extent, eventually leading to the consolidation of these courts, by the Judiciary Act of 1873, into the Supreme Court of Judicature.[584] With the abolition of the Chancery and the common law courts, the Supreme Court became empowered to administer law and equity.[585] A Chancery Division of the High Court was empowered to handle contracts relating to land; even if the plaintiff claimed damages in the Common Law court and the defendant brought a counterclaim to this court for enforcement of a non-monetary obligation under a contract of lease, the whole procedure could be transferred to the Chancery Division.[586] However, in the overall framework of English contract law, a claim for enforcement of non-monetary contractual obligations remained a secondary remedy for non-performance due to the notion that such a claim is not available where damages are adequate.[587]

94. Singapore courts are only entitled to grant or deny a claim for enforced performance of non-monetary obligations within the boundaries of precedent and the applicable principles.[588] Despite these boundaries, the Singapore Court of Appeal considered in *Tay Ah Poon and another v Chionh Hai Guan and another* that the right of the court to award or deny a claim for enforced performance of non-monetary obligations exists independently of any contractual provision because it is at the discretion of the court to decide whether such a claim should be awarded or not.[589] As said before, this discretion is limited by

580 Zwalve (n 448) 617.
581 Baker (n 576) 106.
582 Zwalve (n 448) 48.
583 Baker (n 576) 106, 109–111.
584 Supreme Court Judicature Act 1873 36 & 37 Vict c. 66. Also, note that the Supreme Court of Judicature was subdivided into the High Court of Justice and the Court of Appeal.
585 Baker (n 576) 114–115.
586 *Ibid.*
587 Fry (n 578) 572; Peter Birks, 'Rights, Wrongs, and Remedies' (2000) 20(1) Oxford Journal of Legal Studies 20.
588 Phang et al 2012 (n 112) para 20.005; It is also suggested that the Court of Appeal is not bound by precedent, judicial custom and decorum, as well as the practical impact of an all too regular disregard of prior precedent.
589 *Tay Ah Poon and another v Chionh Hai Guan and another* [1997] 1 SLR(R) 596 [13] (SGCA).

existing rules and principles, and[590] therefore it may be said that – as with the English common law system – in Singapore also the discretion of the court to award a claim for enforced performance of non-monetary obligations is a weak one.[591] For the sake of efficiency, the flowchart in Figure 10 below provides a brief summary of the discussed historical foundations.

590 *Koek Tiang Kung v Antara Bumi Sdn Bhd* [2005] 4 MLJ 525 [16].

591 *Lee Chee Wei v Tan Hor Peow Victor* [2007] SGCA 22, (2007) 3 SLR(R) 537 [52]-[53].

Figure 10 Historical underpinnings of specific remedies in Singapore

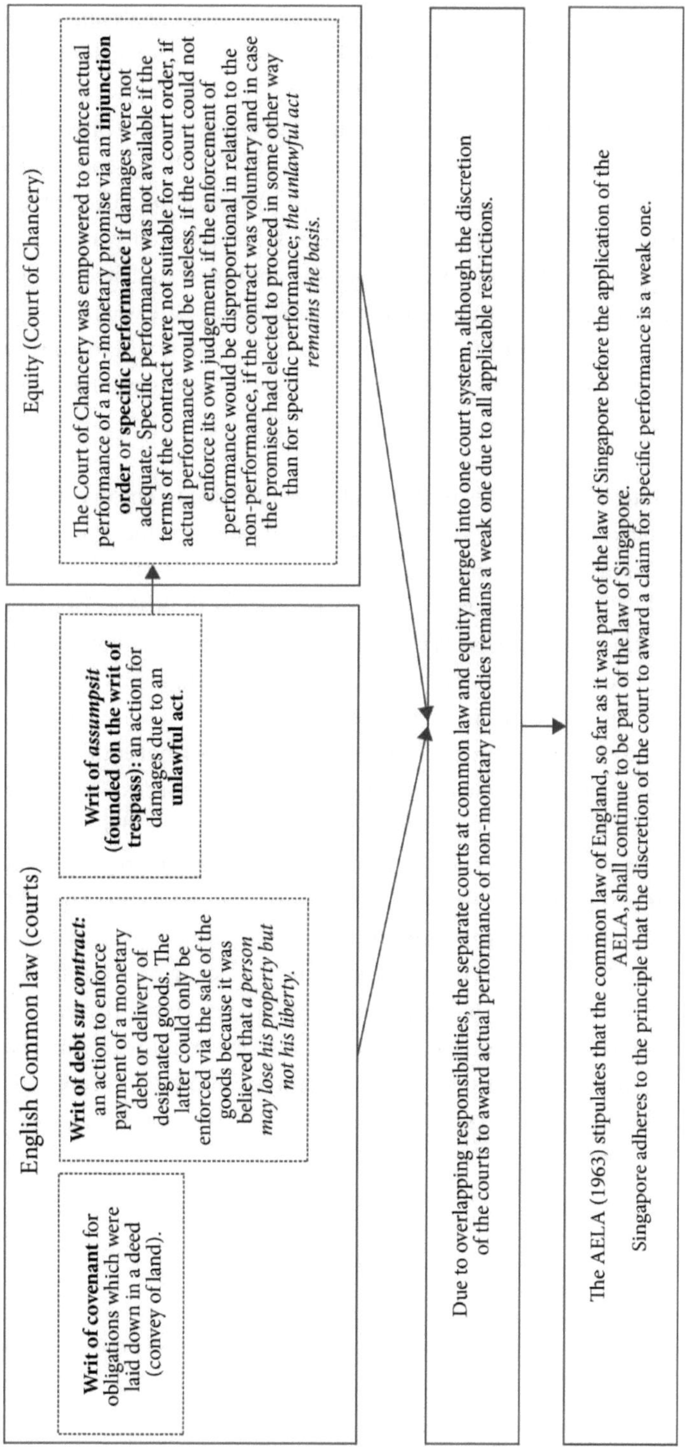

95. The following builds further on the findings set out above by analysing the modern view of the contract law of Singapore on the ability of commercial parties to enforce a contractual promise by means of specific remedies, entailing an action for an agreed sum (common law measure) and the discretionary (equitable) instrument to provide an order for enforced performance of a non-monetary promise.[592] The latter encompasses the judicial action of specific performance and (mandatory) injunction. The term specific performance applies where the aggrieved party claims for enforced performance of a non-monetary act to do something – for example, the obligation to deliver the goods in accordance with the agreed terms. An injunction order is appropriate where the aggrieved party brings an action to court for the obligation of the other party not to do something (*e.g.* a supplier of commodity goods is ordered to not cease supplying the goods it has promised [148]).

96. Before tapping into the intricacies of the legal tools available to enforce performance of non-monetary obligations arising from a commercial sales contract governed by the contract law of Singapore, the relationship between a contractual promise and specific remedies shall first be discussed. In the English case (which is to this day of influence in Singapore) *Photo Production Ltd v Securicor Transport Ltd* it was held by Lord Diplock that a commercial sales contract 'is the source of primary legal obligations upon each party to it to procure whatever he has promised will be done is done'.[593] It was further held that contractual promises are regarded as morally binding,[594] but they do not entitle the promisee to enforce performance of the contract.[595] This notion is also embedded in the principle of *neminem laede.* This so-called harm principle represents the view that the state is not entitled to restrict the personal freedom of contracting parties if there is no (expected) failure in performance of a contractual promise.[596] The mere infringement of the obligation not to harm the other contracting party does not entitle the aggrieved party to claim for enforced performance, but the aggrieved party may sue for damages or specific remedies to remedy the harm caused by the behaviour of the non-performing party,[597] provided that applicable preconditions are fulfilled.[598] Importantly, only a non-excusable failure in performance (in common law terms: a breach of contract) allows the promisee to seek protection of its performance interest by means of a judicial claim for damages or specific

592 Phang et al 2012 (n 112) para 23.002.
593 [1980] AC 848 (HL).
594 *Ibid.*
595 Fried (n 541) 17; Kimel 2003 (n 542) 22 *ff, 30*; Mak (n 527) 48.
596 SA Smith, *Contract Theory* (Oxford University Press 2004) 69; J Raz, *The Morality of Freedom* (Clarendon Press, 1986) 400–401.
597 Mak (n 527) 51.
598 S 4.3.3 for monetary obligations and s 4.4.3 for non-monetary obligations.

remedies.[599] A failure in performance may be lawfully excused where performance is frustrated, where a contractual *force majeure clause* applies,[600] or on the basis of a subsequent agreement between the parties.[601] Thus, an action for a specific remedy may be invoked on a non-excused failure in performance of a contractual obligation.[602] As presented earlier, this approach historically originates in the English common law writ of trespass, which is basically an action for an unlawful act.

97. Furthermore, it should be observed that under the contract law of Singapore, a contractual promise can entail promissory and contingent obligations, which are reflected in the terms of a contract. A term of the contract is qualified as contingent if it stipulates that a certain event must arise before the contracting parties are obliged to perform their obligations under the contract.[603] For example, the obligation to acquire the approval of a third party before the parties become obliged to enforced performance of their contractual promises.[604] A contractual term is also considered as contingent if the clause stipulates that the obligations of the contracting parties, which arise from their promises, end at the moment the described situation occurs.[605] The aforementioned conditions precedent or subsequent to the initially agreed contractual promises cannot be breached under Singapore contract law and are, therefore, not subject to an action for enforced performance, damages, or termination.[606] In contrast, where parties fail to perform the promissory terms of a contract, the aggrieved party may bring an action to court for damages or, where appropriate, for specific remedies.[607] Aside from a failure in performance of a promissory term, renunciation of a contract, before or after the due date,[608] may also invoke an action for relief by means of damages or specific remedies. A situation of renunciation arises in

599 D Neo, 'Specific Remedies and the Performance Interest in Singapore Contract Law' in Chen-Wishart, Loke and Ong 2016 (n 156) 193, 201; Phang et al 2012 (n 112) para 17.003.

600 See s 6.2 for an in-depth discussion about the distinction between the doctrine of *force majeure* and the doctrine of frustration; see for the application of a clause of *force majeure Magenta Resources (S) Pte Ltd v China Resources (S) Pte Ltd* [1996] 2 SLR (R) 316 [60] (SGHC), affirmed in *China resources (S) Pte Ltd v Magenta Resources (S) Pte Ltd* [1997] 1 SLR (R) 103 (SGCA); *RDC Concrete Pte Ltd v Sato Kogyo (S) Pte Ltd* [2007] 4 SLR (R) 413 [53], [54] (SGCA); Phang et al 2012 (n 112) paras 18.004, 18.005.

601 Phang et al 2012 (n 112) paras 17.002, 18.001 *ff*, 18.042 *ff*.

602 See the English cases *Scott v Corp of Liverpool* [1885] 1 Giff 216, 65 E.R. 851, affirmed in *Scott v Corp of Liverpool* [1885] 3 De G & J 334, 44 E.R. 1297; *Abbot v Blair* [1860] 8 WR 672 and *Douglas v Sidmouth Rly & Harbour Co* [1866] 14 WR 361; this position is affirmed for Singapore in Phang et al 2012 (n 112) para 23.070.

603 Phang et al 2012 (n 112) paras 17.084, 17.085.

604 *Chiang Hong (Pte) Ltd v Ong Boon Pok Realty (Pte) Ltd* [1983–1984] SLR (R) 481 [17] (SGCA); Phang et al 2012 (n 112) para 17.085.

605 *Loh Wee Tin v Transvic Investment Pte Ltd* [1995] 2 SLR (R) 251 [15], [16]; Phang et al 2012 (n 112) para 17.085.

606 Phang et al 2012 (n 112) para 17.004.

607 Phang et al 2012 (n 112) paras 17.004, 17.087.

608 Phang et al 2012 (n 112) para 17.005.

the event the promisor expressly or implicitly states that it is not willing to (fully) perform the contract in accordance with the agreed terms.[609] In a situation where the promisor fails to perform a contractual obligation on the basis of alleged financial impossibility, the aggrieved party may also seek recourse to specific remedies.[610] It may, however, not be tacitly assumed that an action for enforced performance of non-monetary obligations (*i.e.* specific remedy/performance) is readily available in the aforementioned situations – in fact quite the opposite; an order of enforced performance of non-monetary obligations is only available as a subsidiary remedy in relation to damages. See section 4.4.3 for an in-depth discussion about this barrier for obtaining enforced performance of non-monetary obligations to do something under a commercial (sales) contract.

98. In the case of a failure in performance of a contractual obligation arising from a commercial sales contract, the aggrieved party may choose between an action for a specific remedy (provided that the preconditions are met) and damages and/or setting aside of the entire contract. The fundamental notion is that the aggrieved party may claim for enforced performance at the outset and during the procedure. This means in effect that where the aggrieved party selects a remedy at the commencement of the judicial proceeding,[611] the court is obliged to give leave if the promisee first demanded enforcement of performance and subsequently terminates the contract and claims damages.[612] By contrast, if the promisee makes an unmistakable choice for termination of the contract because of a failure in performance, it loses the right to bring a claim to court for enforced performance and is, accordingly, only entitled to damages.[613] For example, in a case where a contract had been brought to an end by one of the contracting parties, the Singapore Court of Appeal considered that the contracting parties could not thereafter insist on enforced performance of the contract.[614] Having said that, the argument of the promisor that the promisee has terminated the contract and is, therefore, only entitled to damages, is not easily accepted; it has to be ascertained that the promisee has made an unequivocal choice.[615] In the Singapore High Court case, *Lim Beng Cheng v Lim Ngee Sing* it was argued that an order for enforced performance could not be provided because the plaintiff demanded, before

609 Phang et al 2012 (n 112) para 17.005.

610 See s 4.3.3 for monetary obligations and s 4.4.3 for non-monetary obligations.

611 *Indian Overseas Bank v Cheng Lai Geok* [1991] 2 SLR (R) 574 [54] (SGHC), affirmed in part in *Indian Overseas Bank v Cheng Lai Geok* [1993] 1 SLR (R) 32 (SGCA) and *Lee Chee Wei* 2007 (n 591) SLR (R) 537 [66]; See the English case *Johnson v Agnew* [1980] AC 367 at 392–394.

612 Phang et al 2012 (n 112) paras 23.078 (footnote 135), 23.079.

613 In the absence of any contradicting Singapore rulings, it is believed that this English common law principle applies in Singapore. See Phang et al 2012 (n 112) para 23.079 and the English case *Johnson v Agnew* (n 611).

614 *Lee Christina v Lee Eunice and another (executors of the estate of Lee Teck Soon, deceased)* [1993] SGCA 56, 2 SLR(R) 644; [1993]; see also the English case *Johnson v Agnew* (n 611) AC 367 [392].

615 *Lim Beng Cheng v Lim Ngee Sing* [2016] SGHC 282, (2015) 1 SLR 524.

the commencement of the trial, via email, SGD $200,000 plus losses. The court did not adopt this view and considered that the plaintiff was at wit's end and just wanted to settle the dispute. As a result, the court considered that the plaintiff did not unequivocally choose to waive his rights to claim enforced performance of the contract.[616] In contrast, in *Meng Leong Development Pte Ltd v Jip Hong Trading Co Pte Ltd* the buyer brought a claim to court for enforced performance. However, the court granted damages in lieu of an order for enforced performance because the property was already sold to a third party. The parties agreed that the seller was obliged to deposit the damages pending the appeal. The court considered that by demanding and accepting the deposit of damages, the buyer elected to be relieved via damages.[617] Subsequently, the buyer was precluded from claiming enforced performance.[618] The election for damages could not be reversed by an appeal against the court order for monetary compensation without causing any injustice to the sellers.[619] Having said that, a dissenting judge held, briefly put, that it was difficult to see any firm basis for the conclusion that insisting on the deposit had induced the seller to believe that the buyer had relinquished its claim to enforced performance of the contract.[620]

99. Since the contract law of Singapore makes a fundamental distinction between an action for enforcement of specific remedies and damages, it is interesting to look at the preconditions for the freedom to choose between the available judicial actions. The starting point is the principle that a promisee has a right to choose between the termination of the contract and damages or to insist on performance and claim the agreed sum.[621] This principle is developed in the English case *White and Carter (Councils) Ltd v McGregor*,[622] which equally applies in Singapore contract law.[623] This case concerned a contract for advertisements on litter bins. The plaintiffs sold advertising on litter bins, and the defendant was a garage who agreed to an advertisement contract for three years. The same day the contract was drawn up, the garage terminated the contract, which made it an anticipatory breach. The advertiser did not accept the termination and affirmed the contract (if the advertiser had accepted the breach, all outstanding obligations would have been discharged and, as a result, the advertiser was only entitled to nominal damages).[624] After three years, the advertiser had fulfilled its part of the contract and claimed the price. The court ruled

---

616 *Ibid.*

617 *Meng Leong Development Pte Ltd v Jip Hong Trading Co Pte Ltd* [1983-1984] SGCA (Privacy Council) 24 [20, 21 28, 29, 33], (1984) 6 SLR (R) 668.

618 *Meng Leong Development* (n 617) SGCA 24 [21, 33].

619 *Ibid.*

620 *Ibid* [37, 39].

621 See the English case *White and Carter (Councils) Ltd v McGregor* [1962] AC 413 (HL).

622 *Ibid.*

623 *MP Bilt Pte Ltd v Oey Widarto* [1999] 1 SLR(R) 908 (SGHC); Phang et al 2012 (n 112) paras 17.234 - 17.241.

624 Phang et al 2012 (n 112) para 17.229.

that the garage has breached a conditional term, and therefore, the advertiser was allowed to terminate the contract and claim damages or to insist on performance and claim the agreed price for its performance.[625] In addition, the court considered that the advertiser was not obliged to mitigate its losses because it claimed the performance of the contract instead of damages.

100. What is noteworthy and consistent with civilian law systems is that this case shows a strong focus on protection of the performance interest.[626] Another interesting aspect of this case is that the advertiser was not obliged to mitigate its losses, and could affirm the contract. It was further considered that the garage could not force the advertiser to accept its breach; that the advertiser was entitled to perform the contract and claim the price at the end of the contractual period as long as the advertiser fulfilled its obligations. The controversy, in this case, was that performance of the contract made no commercial sense and, therefore, was considered a waste of time and money because the advertiser knew from the beginning of the contract that the garage did not want to be a part of the contract and that it was not willing to pay the agreed price. To mitigate this side-effect of the right to claim the price of the contract, the following three limitations were formulated. First, a claim for a contractual price can only be awarded if the plaintiff has a legitimate interest in the performance of the contract.[627] Secondly, that a promisee is only entitled to claim the price of the contract or damages if the promisor can render its performance without cooperation of his counterpart. The final requirement for the assertion of the right to claim the contractual price by the promisee follows from the so-called doctrine of reciprocity, which can be used by the courts to deny a claim for enforced performance of non-monetary obligations. The doctrine of reciprocity entails the principle that the court shall not order the promisor to do what the latter had promised under the contract if the counterparty did not, cannot, or will not, render performance of its own obligations.[628] This means that the latter is obliged to show that it shall perform its part of the contract. The first two

625 See in the same vein, JW Carter, Andrew Phang and Sock-Yong Phang, 'Performance Following Repudiation: Legal and Economic Interests' (1999) 15(2) The Journal of Contract Law 97, 99.

626 Lei Chen, 'Availability of Specific Remedies in Chinese Contract Law' in Chen-Wishart, Loke and Ong 2016 (n 156) 13.

627 However, a commercial interest can already be enough to be qualified as legitimate interest. In comparison, under Dutch law, the promisee is obliged to show that it has sufficient interest in claiming specific performance if the contractual obligation is not yet due.

628 *Indulge Food Pte Ltd v Torabi Marashi Bahram* [2010] 2 SLR 540 (SGHC); Compare art 6:263(1) DCC stipulating that the party who is obliged to perform first, is nevertheless entitled to protect its interest by suspension of performance if, after entering the contract, circumstances occur which give rise to the suspicion that the other party will not perform its part of the bargain. Art 6:52(1) DCC is the lex generalis of aforementioned art 6:262 DCC. The former entails the basic right of a promisee to suspend an obligation, which is exigible against the promisor, until the latter has performed his obligation. The promisee is only entitled to suspension if there is sufficient connection between the claim and the obligation.

requirements are said to impose very limited restrictions on the right to claim the contractual price (enforced performance) and therefore,[629] it could be held that the strong focus on performance interest of monetary obligations remains unaffected. Nonetheless, the case *White and Cartner* demonstrates a balancing of interests of contracting parties by taking into account the legitimate interest of the aggrieved party in obtaining an order for enforcement versus the fairness of subjecting the non-performing party to unnecessary losses or burdens. Although *White and Cartner* concerned a claim for the agreed price, the courts may draw inspiration from the aforementioned balancing of interest of contracting parties when confronted with a claim for enforced performance of non-monetary obligations deriving from a commercial sales contract. However, on account of the case law today it is not possible to assess the restrictive implications of this premise.

4.2.4 A compromise of principles in China

101. The development of the right to claim enforced performance of a sales contract under Chinese contract law can be divided into three distinct stages. Firstly, the introduction of the civil law in ancient China due to the pressure from western countries. Secondly, the extreme emphasis on performance of a contract under the centrally planned economy and, thirdly, the gradual movement towards a market economy and with it a more balanced approach towards the right to actual performance of a contract.

From 1929 until 1949, the Civil Code of the Republic of China (CCRC) was in force in Mainland China. This civil code stipulated, in line with the civil law adage that a contractual promise is binding, that every person is bound to perform his obligations and that the promisor is responsible for his acts, even if they are unintentional or due to its fault.[630] To enforce this obligation, the CCRC stipulated that execution of actual performance and additional damages could be claimed by the promisee if the promisor fully or partially failed to perform his obligation. In line with the civil code tradition, the promisor had to be in default before the promisee could enforce these rights.[631] In 1949, after the CCRC was discarded, a period of contractual legal nihilism followed due to China's objective of establishing a planned economy [30]. Nonetheless, from 1949 until 1959 a number of contractual regulations were still in force due to the gradual implementation of a planned economy framework. In the 1950s, for example, the Trade Ministry of the Central People's Government introduced a rule that in certain situations of non-performance, damages are

629 D Neo, 'Specific Remedies and the Performance Interest in Singapore Contract Law' in Chen-Wishart, Loke and Ong 2016 (n 156).

630 Arts 219 and 220 Civil Code of the Republic of China (1929).

631 Art 229 Civil Code of the Republic of China (1929) *ff.*

available to the promisee.[632] Further, contracting parties were entitled to modify and terminate a contract, and moreover, the promisee had the right to reject the entire performance of a supplier.[633] From 1956 onwards, more emphasis was put on developing a centrally planned economy which encompassed the belief that all contracts should serve, and were a part of, the overarching plan of the state.[634] This meant that contracting parties were obliged to perform the contract, even if damages were paid, and the contract could not be modified or terminated without the permission of the authority.[635] The former also applied if the state plan was no longer in line with the purpose of the contract.[636]

102. In the centrally planned economy, there was also no need for an award for damages because there was no market where an alternative could be purchased,[637] which meant that the promisee could not be placed in the position it would have been in if the contract was properly performed.[638] From 1978 onwards, this system of extreme emphasis on the performance of a contract gradually changed due to economic reforms. In 1982, this led to the promulgation of the Economic Contract Law of China (ECL), which was introduced to regulate domestic contracts.[639] In 1985, the Law of the People's Republic of China on Economic Contracts involving Foreign Interest came into force (FECL).[640] In 1986, the General Principles of Civil Law (GPCL) came into force, which governed contracts which were not subject to these special regulations, such as civil contracts.[641] The introduction of the ECL, FECL and GPCL led to a distinction between economic and civil contracts, whereby economic contracts were said to serve the state plan, and therefore, more emphasis

---

632 Trade Ministry of the Central People's Government, *The Decision on the Careful Signing and Strict Enforcement of Contract,* 13 October 1950.

633 Corporation of China, *The Common Terms of Supply Contract in General Merchandise,* 1 July 1960.

634 Kimel 2016 (n 224) 18, 19; Bing Ling 2002 (n 229) para 8.065.

635 Han Shiyuan, 'The Performance Interest in Chinese Contract Law' in Chen-Wishart, Loke and Ong 2016 (n 156) 23; Liming 2016 (n 224) 18, 19; Heavy Industry Ministry, *Interim Basic Stipulations of Contract on Supply Goods;* Art 2 *The Notice about Strictly Following the Procedure of Project Contract and Strict Enforcement for Economic Contract,* issued on 10 December 1960.

636 Wang Liming, 'Specific Performance in Chinese Contract Law: An East-West Comparison' (1992) 1(2) Asia Pacific Law Review 18, 19; State Planning Committee, State Economic Committee, The First Industrial Ministry, *Decree No 985,* 8 June 1962. See State Planning Committee and State Economic Committee *Decree No 1204,* 29 June 1962 and State Economic Committee *Provisional Regulations Concerning the Basic Provision of Contract for the Ordering of Factory and Mining Goods,* 30 August 1963.

637 Liming 1992 (n 636) 19.

638 Han Shiyuan, 'The Performance Interest in Chinese Contract Law' in Chen-Wishart, Loke and Ong 2016 (n 156) 23.

639 (n 159).

640 (n 160).

641 (n 163).

was put on the performance of these contracts.[642] In 1999, the Contract Law of the People's Republic of China replaced the ECL and the FECL.[643]

103. Under the ECL, a distinction was made between contracts subject to mandatory and to instructive (guidance) State plans. A contract which was subject to a mandatory plan and/or included important productive means had to be performed.[644] However, if a contract was subject to an instructive plan (a so-called economic contract) the aggrieved party was entitled to choose to sue for actual performance or damages, or both.[645] The mandatory provision in the ECL stipulated that when a party fails to perform an economic contract, it is obliged to pay the liquidated damages and if the monetary loss exceeds the liquidated damages, it is also obliged to pay the excess. However, if the aggrieved party demanded actual performance of the contract, the latter was obliged to perform in accordance with the contract.[646] The right to request actual performance was basically unrestricted.[647] Consequently, the later discussed obstacles in the form of impossibility at law or in fact, the suitability of the subject matter of the contract, costs of performance and the time within which the aggrieved party has requested performance, were not present in the ECL.[648] This lack of restrictions for claiming actual performance of an economic contract is also reflected in the Supreme People's Court Opinion on the Implementation of the ECL, which indicates that payment of (liquidated) damages does not remove the right to claim delivery of the goods (or services) in accordance with the terms of the contract.[649]

The emphasis on the right to demand actual performance under the ECL is also expressed in the principle that an economic contract could only be terminated if it did not harm the interest of the state or the public if *force majeure* made performance impossible and if the contract was not performed within the agreed time limit.[650] Also, the Civil Procedure Law shows the preference of China for the actual performance of a contract. The principles described above reflect the idea, which prevailed under the previous policy of the centrally planned economy, that monetary compensation is an inadequate remedy if the availability of alternatives is limited and,[651] moreover, that a failure in performance

642 Liming 1992 (n 636) 21.
643 N 167.
644 Art 11 ECL; Liming 1992 (n 636) 26.
645 Art 31 ECL; Shen 1996 (n 140) 253–306.
646 Zheng Xiaochuan and Lei Mingguang, 'Reconsideration of Continuous Performance' (2003) iss 3 Habei Law Science 67 (郑小川， 雷明光. 对"继续履行"的再思考. 河北法学).
647 *Ibid.*
648 Art 110 CCL introduces these restrictions; Zheng and Lei (n 646).
649 Opinions of the Supreme People's Court on Several Issues Concerning the Implementation of the Civil Procedure Law in Economic Trials (最高人民法院关于在经济审判工).
650 Art 26 (1) – (3) ECL.
651 Liang HuiXing, 'On Contract Liability' (1982) 1 Study and Inquiry 62.

of an economic contract could affect the state plan and should, therefore, be restricted.[652] The former is explicitly recognised in the ECL for construction contracts and in the provision for the delivery of defective goods due to the lack of a mature market economy which provides adequate alternatives.[653]

Nonetheless, it is argued that damages were the preferred remedy for economic contracts because the ECL made it simple to determine the loss and, moreover, to execute a court order for damages since the courts and arbitrators were entitled to issue a notice to the promisor's bank, including directions that the sum of awarded monetary damages must be transferred from the account of the promisor to the account of the promisee.[654]

The discretion of the court to award damages instead of enforcing performance played an increasing role when it became easier for contracting parties to obtain an adequate alternative on the market.[655] Yet, it is also held that the courts and arbitrators were willing to deviate from the judicial measures of the ECL if this was required by the circumstances of the case. For example, if the state-prices were significantly higher or lower than the actual market price.[656] Based on all the considerations above, it could be said that under the ECL, the civil law principle of *pacta sunt servanda* remained of great importance for economic contracts because of the impact on the state planned economy.

104. The FECL governed contracts concluded between domestic and foreign companies. The FECL does not include a verbatim principle which entitles the promisee to claim the actual performance of the contract.[657] In the Judicial Interpretation on the FECL it was even stipulated that, apart from actual performance, the non-performing party shall compensate the suffered monetary damages, as well as the benefits which could have been received if the contract was properly performed (*e.g.* the interest in the case of an international sales transaction involving commodity goods).[658] This could point in the

652 Bing Ling 2002 (n 229) para 8.065; Gu Ming, vice-chairman of the NPCSC Legal Affairs Commission stated about the 4th sessions of the 5th NPC: '*Compensatory damages cannot be substituted for performance of contract. To have such a provision is mainly for the purpose of ensuring the implementation of state plans. As many economic contracts in our country are concluded in accordance with state plans, non-performance of economic contracts will affect the fulfilment of state plans. This principle of performance in kind is an important characteristic that distinguishes the socialist economic contract law from the capitalist economic contract law*'.

653 Liming 1992 (n 636) 25, 26.

654 Opinions of the Supreme People's Court on Several Issues Concerning the Implementation of the Civil Procedure Law in Economic Trials (see the Opinion under six) (最高人民法院关于在经济审判工); Liming 1992 (n 636) 23.

655 Liming 1992 (n 636) 31.

656 Liming 1992 (n 636) 23, 24, 26, 27; Liang HuiXing, 'Problems on Changes of Circumstance in Contract Law' (1988) in 6 Studies in Law 40.

657 Shen 1996 (n 140); Zhen and Lei (n 646).

658 Response of the Supreme People's Court to Certain Questions Concerning the Application of the Foreign Economic Law [Expired], Effective date: 19 October 1987.

direction that the Chinese government weighted the bindingness of contractual promises between foreign and Chinese parties significantly differently from that of contracts between domestic parties with their place of business in China. Nevertheless, article 18 of the FECL left an opening for contracting parties to demand actual performance of a contractual obligation by stipulating that, in a case of failure in performance of the contract, the promisee will have the right to ask the promisor to compensate for damages or to take other remedial measures.[659] It is held that the latter refers to the right of the promisee to claim the actual performance of a contractual obligation.[660] The view that the FECL recognised the right to claim actual performance also followed from the statutory principle under the FECL that a contract is binding and that the parties are obliged to fulfil their obligations.[661] In addition, it was stipulated that neither party shall make unauthorised changes to or terminate the contract.[662] In this respect, it is argued that performance was a statutory obligation under the FECL,[663] which, in turn, indicates that a promisee was primarily entitled to claim actual performance.

Nonetheless, it is said that the unrestricted choice for damages and actual performance under the FECL followed from the idea that the sole purpose of foreign entities is to obtain monetary profit and, therefore, in all cases, damages can provide complete relief.[664] In other words, non-performance was believed not to affect the implementation of the state's plan and, therefore, there was no need to prescribe actual performance as a mandatory default remedy.

105. In the framework of the GPCL, the civil law concept that a contractual promise provides contracting parties a substantive right to performance is reflected in the principle that if a party fails to fulfil its contractual obligations or fails to perform in accordance with the terms of a contract, the promisee shall have the right to demand performance of the contract or remedial measures and to claim compensation for its losses.[665] This freedom of the promisee to choose between a claim for the actual performance of the contract and damages derived from the idea that civil contracts were not a part of the planned economy, and therefore more leeway was provided to contracting parties.[666] Nevertheless, it is held

659 Art 18 FECL; Shen 1996 (n 140).
660 Shen 1996 (n 140).
661 Art 16 FECL.
662 *Ibid.*
663 Shen 1996 (n 140).
664 Zheng and Lei (n 646).
665 Arts 111, 134 GPCL.
666 Liming 1992 (n 636) 30; Bing Ling 2002 (n 229) para 8.065.

that enforced performance was always available to the promisee if the subject of the contract was ascertained as a specific thing,[667] such as a contract involving the purchase of a house.[668]

Overall, it could be said that the development of the instrument of enforced performance under the ECL, FECL and GPCL is inextricably linked with the state plan policy of China to the extent that a contract is regarded as an instrument to serve the overarching plan. However, the ECL's predominant role of enforced performance was weakened by the shift towards a market economy, which provided plentiful alternatives to buy on the market.[669] Further, the provisions under the ECL, FECL and GPCL suggest that a claim for actual performance is only available to the promisee in the event of non-performance, albeit that the Chinese law also indicates that contractual promises are legally binding.

106. As mentioned previously [102], in 1999, the ECL and the FECL were replaced by the currently applicable Contract Law provisions of China, which, under the influence of the CISG and the PICC, continue to follow the principle that the right to demand the actual performance of a contract derives from a failure in the performance of contractual obligations.[670] Returning to the historical underpinnings, the flowchart presented in Figure 11 below provides a summary of the introduction of the instrument of enforced performance in Chinese law.

667 Liming 1992 (n 636) 29; Wang ZhuoDang, *Textbook of Chinese Civil Law* (1982) 226.

668 Liming 1992 (n 636) 29; The Educational Central of High Judges, *The Collection of Civil Cases* (1989) [1] 12.

669 Bing Ling 2002 (n 229) para 8.065.

670 Art 107 CCL.

Figure 11 Historical underpinnings of the right to demand continuance of performance in China

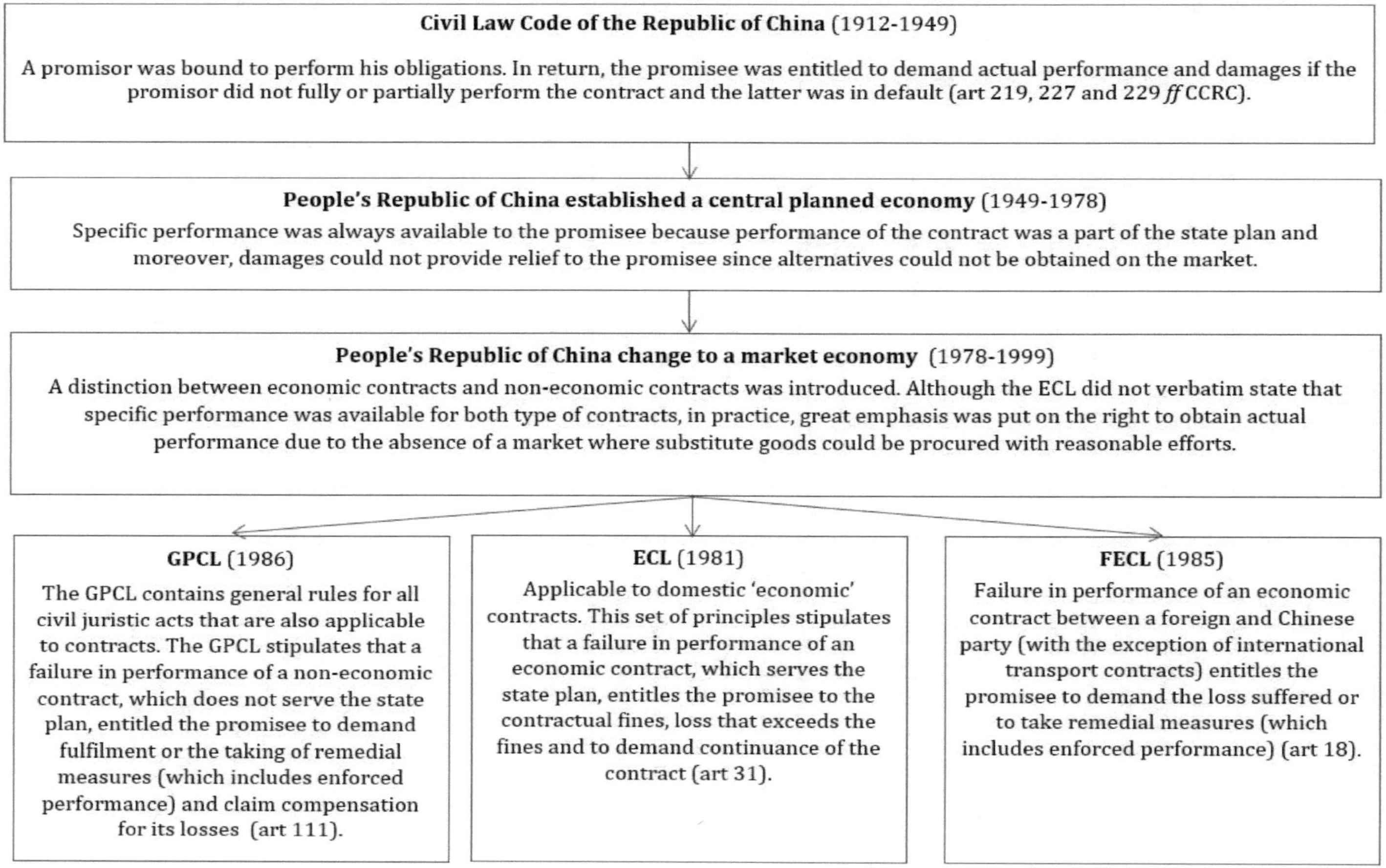

107. Under the contract law of China, a failure in performance of a contractual obligation can lead to a claim for termination of the contract,[671] substitute or compensatory damages,[672] or a demand for enforced performance by means of a claim for continuance of the contractual promise, executed by the promisee or a third party.[673] The right to demand continuance of performance of a contractual promise is basically a judicial measure to obtain actual performance of a non-monetary positive or negative obligation or performance of a monetary obligation, which in practice also qualifies as *specific performance*.[674] However, the term specific performance is in common law jurisdictions only used to address non-monetary obligations. In this work, the right to claim continuance of performance is referred to as a claim for the actual performance of a contract for sales in a commercial setting. These contracts are, for the vast majority, subject to the provisions of the contract law of China, but it may be noted that additional specific statutory terms can apply for certain agreements,[675] regardless of the premise that state intervention by imposing punitive measures is not in accordance with the private law character of the contract law of China.[676]

108. Before exploring the different aspects of judicial measures to obtain actual performance of (non-) monetary contractual obligations, it is important to take note of the impact of an act of promise making and of voluntarily concluding a reciprocal agreement under the contract law of China. It is held that a promise and a subsequent contractual agreement are embedded in a social institution, albeit that only legally enforceable contractual agreements are protected by statutory provisions.[677] This section shows that under the current contract law of China, provisions to enforce a contractual promise are no longer an instrument to ensure implementation of the state plan and,[678] moreover, that the system has moved towards a combination of civil and common law concepts on a substantive level.

671 Art 94 CCL.

672 Art 112 CCL.

673 Art 107, 108 CCL; Bing Ling 2002 (n 229) para 8.009; Lei Chen, 'Availability of Specific Remedies in Chinese Contract Law' in Chen-Wishart, Loke and Ong 2016 (n 156) 21–22, 24; the right to claim judicial remedies in the case of an anticipatory failure in performance is said to derive from the common law perspective on a failure in performance of a contractual obligation; compare Bu 2013 (n 226) 70; the burden of proof of the non-performance lies with the claimant; A claim for continuance of a contract is also known as enforced performance.

674 Arts 107, 109–110 CCL; Lei Chen, 'Availability of Specific Remedies in Chinese Contract Law' in Chen-Wishart, Loke and Ong 2016 (n 156) 21.

675 Bing Ling 2002 (n 229) para 8.010.

676 Bing Ling 2002 (n 229) para 8.003.

677 Zhang 2006 (n 41) 67.

678 It is held that the Chinese shifted towards a social-market economy; Han Shiyuan, 'The Performance Interest in Chinese Contract Law: Monetary Awards' in Chen-Wishart, Loke and Ong 2016 (n 156) 41.

109. The main principle under the contract law of China is that a promisor is obliged to perform an effective contractual promise in accordance with the agreed terms of the contract.[679] Therefore, the statutory right to claim continuance of a contract for (anticipatory) non-performance serves the (expectation) interest of a promisee by placing the latter in the position as if the contract was properly performed.[680] This premise should be viewed in light of the statutory principle that a legitimate contract has a legal binding force on the parties, which brings about that contracting parties are obliged to fulfil their promise in accordance with their agreement.[681] These statutory provisions are based on the premise that a legally binding and effective contractual promise reflects the primary duty of contracting parties to fully perform their promises in accordance with the terms of the contract and not a duty to compensate the damages of the promisee.[682] This premise is further substantiated with the argument that substitute products and compensatory monetary damages do not always achieve the same result.[683] For example, promisees may not be able to obtain similar substitute products from alternative suppliers.[684] For that reason, it is held that the duty to fully perform a contractual promise is not interchangeable with monetary damages if the contractual promise is not completely performed.[685] This means that an agreement between parties concerning the payment of damages by the promisor does not automatically have the effect of a waiver of the promisee to claim continuance of the contract.[686]

110. The aforementioned considerations demonstrate that the contract law of China adopts the civil law principle of *pacta sunt servanda*,[687] in the sense that a promisee is primarily entitled to claim for enforced performance of a contractual promise without the occurrence of an actual failure.[688] Yet, the contract law provisions appear to act on the notion that a

679 Bing Ling 2002 (n 229) para 8.079.

680 Bing Ling 2002 (n 229) paras 8.002, 8.064; Lei Chen, 'Availability of Specific Remedies in Chinese Contract Law' in Chen-Wishart, Loke and Ong 2016 (n 156) 21.

681 Arts 8, 60 CCL.

682 Bing Ling 2002 (n 229) paras 8.064, 8.065; Zhang 2006 (n 41) 200.

683 Bing Ling 2002 (n 229) para 8.064; Lei Chen, 'Availability of Specific Remedies in Chinese Contract Law' in Chen-Wishart, Loke and Ong 2016 (n 156) 27.

684 Bing Ling 2002 (n 229) paras 8.064, 8.065; Lei Chen, 'Availability of Specific Remedies in Chinese Contract Law' in Chen-Wishart, Loke and Ong 2016 (n 156) 27.

685 Bing Ling 2002 (n 229) para 8.064; Lei Chen, 'Availability of Specific Remedies in Chinese Contract Law' in Chen-Wishart, Loke and Ong 2016 (n 156) 23.

686 Lei Chen, 'Availability of Specific Remedies in Chinese Contract Law' in Chen-Wishart, Loke and Ong 2016 (n 156) 23; However, it should be noted that the CCL does not indicate any hierarchal order between the right to claim actual performance of a contract and damages.

687 Bing Ling 2002 (n 229) para 2.030.

688 In this respect reference is made to an official comment to the Uniform Commercial Code of the United States of America, which states: '*(...) the fact that the essential purpose of a contract between commercial men is actual performance and they do not bargain merely for a promise, or for a promise plus the right to*

claim for enforced performance can only be brought to court in the event of a failure in performance.[689] On the basis of this more or less common law approach, it is argued that enforced performance of a non-monetary obligation is only available to contracting parties if damages are assessed by the court as an inadequate measure.[690] Furthermore, the qualification as a remedy is justified by the argument that continuance of a contract compels the non-performing party to perform his or her contractual promises instead of voluntary compliance and, therefore, demand for the continuance of performance is qualified as a remedy.[691] However, one important and insurmountable difference with the discretionary common law remedy of specific performance remains. That is, the right to enforced performance is protected by law,[692] and may not, therefore, be characterised as a remedy which is left at the discretion of the court.[693] This means in effect that a Chinese court must substantiate a denial of a claim for enforced performance with justifiable reasons.[694] Moreover, intentional interference with a contractual promise can be regarded by the court as a tortious act.[695] Thus, contracting parties have a right to claim for enforced performance before any breach of contract has occurred. However, if the obligation is not yet due, the court shall only provide an order which entails a judicial recognition of the right to performance.[696]

111. It is important to highlight that the contract law of China stipulates that a promisor is liable for a failure in performance and, therefore, the promisee is entitled to choose between a claim for enforced performance, other remedial measures, and/or damages.[697] The option to choose enforced performance and other remedies is, however, barred by law, if performance is legally or practically impossible, the agreed performance is unsuitable for an order for enforced performance, performance is too expensive, or performance is

---

win a lawsuit and that a continuing sense of reliance and security that the promised performance will be forthcoming when due, is an important feature of the bargain.' UCC § 2–609, Official Comment 1.

689 Arts 107, 108 CCL; Lei Chen, 'Availability of Specific Remedies in Chinese Contract Law' in Chen-Wishart, Loke and Ong 2016 (n 156) 21, 22; Bu 2013 (n 226) 70 (Bu states that art 108 CCL is adopted from common law).

690 Zhang 2006 (n 41) 299; In contrast, it is held by Lei Chen that the right to continuance of the contract (qualified as specific performance) is regarded as a right of the promisee.

691 Zhang 2006 (n 41) 297.

692 Art 8 (2) CCL; Bing Ling 2002 (n 229) para 2.031.

693 Zhang 2006 (n 41) 297.

694 Lei Chen, 'Availability of Specific Remedies in Chinese Contract Law' in Chen-Wishart, Loke and Ong 2016 (n 156) 22.

695 Art 106 (2) GPCL; Bing Ling 2002 (n 229) para 2.031.

696 Clarisse von Wunschheim, Pierre Tercier and Gianmaria Ajani, *Enforcement of Commercial Arbitral Awards in China: business laws of China* (West 2017) § 4:22 and § 4:3 accessed Westlaw China on 31 January 2017.

697 Art 107 CCL is based on CISG, PICC and PECL; Han Shiyuan, 'The Performance Interest in Chinese Contract Law: Monetary Award' in Chen-Wishart, Loke and Ong 2016 (n 156) 41.

not demanded within a reasonable time.[698] Aside from these situations, the premises that a contracting party is free to choose between enforced performance, other remedial measures and damages imply that there is no hierarchy between the judicial instruments mentioned above.[699] This alleged lack of hierarchy indicates that in the current timeframe not all contracts are a part of the political agenda of China and for that reason, it could be held that the right of contracting parties to enforced performance is disconnected from the state plan.[700] However, it is also argued that the right to enforced performance remains the preferred remedy under the Chinese contract law since the termination of a contract and damages are only available to the contracting parties in specific statutorily defined situations and if particular requirements are met.[701] Having said that, where a contracting party remedies its failure by performing the agreed obligation, the initially aggrieved party remains entitled to claim losses incurred due to the failed performance, such as interest during the delay in the event of a failure in performance of a monetary obligation.[702] Aside from occurred losses, other forms of damages cannot be claimed if the aggrieved party decides to claim for enforced performance.[703]

112. To support comparisons, it is noted that Chinese contract law does not include a judicial instrument to request the court to authorise the aggrieved party to procure that which would have resulted from the contract or to undo what has been done in breach of the contract.[704] In the event a claim for enforced performance is awarded by the court, it is at the discretion of the court to appoint a third party to perform the obligations of the non-performing party, at the expense of the latter.[705]

113. In Chinese contract law, the right to enforced performance is a matter of strict liability.[706] This means that an aggrieved party is entitled to enforced performance of a

698 Art 110 CCL; See Ch 6.

699 Bing Ling 2002 (n 229) para 8.080; Lei Chen, 'Availability of Specific Remedies in Chinese Contract Law' in Chen-Wishart, Loke and Ong 2016 (n 156) 24; Han Shiyuan, 'The Performance Interest in Chinese Contract Law: Monetary Award' in Chen-Wishart, Loke and Ong 2016 (n 156) 40, 41, 53; Zhang 2006 (n 41) 296; before the enactment of the CCL, it was argued that a promisor was obliged to perform its promises unless an exception applied based on statutory provisions or the doctrine of economic contract.

700 Zhang 2006 (n 41) 297; Han Shiyuan, 'The Performance Interest in Chinese Contract Law: Monetary Award' in Chen-Wishart, Loke and Ong 2016 (n 156) 41.

701 Lei Chen, 'Availability of Specific Remedies in Chinese Contract Law' in Chen-Wishart, Loke and Ong 2016 (n 156) 24; Art 94 CCL.

702 Art 112 CCL; Bing Ling 2002 (n 229) para 8.080.

703 Bing Ling 2002 (n 229) para 8.080.

704 In contrast, the right to request for authorisation is a substantative right in the Dutch law of obligations and a direct judicial measure to obtain actual performance of a contractual promise (art 3:299(1)(2) DCC).

705 Civil Procedure Law of the People's Republic of China (2017 Revision); Bing Ling 2002 (n 229) para 8.801.

706 Art 107 CCL; Bing Ling 2002 (n 229) paras 8.009, 8.032; Bu 2013 (n 226) 70.

contract in the event of a (non-) attributable failure in performance,[707] even if the non-performance is caused by a third party.[708] Thus, the fault of the non-performing party is not required.[709] Nonetheless, a claim for enforced performance of a contractual obligation shall not be awarded in the event of a lawfully excused non-performance.[710] For example, parties have excluded the right to claim for enforced performance (or other judicial measures) in the terms of their contract,[711] the non-performance is caused by the conduct of a third party which amounts to – or results from – a situation of *force majeure*,[712] the promisor can bring a defence to court, which it also has against the third party (in the case of assignment of contractual rights),[713] if the non-performance of an indirect agent towards its principal is caused by a third party and the principal chooses to bring a claim to court against the third party.[714] Non-performance is also regarded as excused in the event of a valid defence of, for example, a situation of *force majeure*,[715] if the conduct of the promisor is by law not qualified as unlawful and if the non-performance is caused by an act of the promisee.[716]

114. The above-described approach of the right to obtain actual performance of a contractual promise under the contract law of China shows similarities with the common law perspective on the primary source of judicial measures to obtain actual performance.[717] The Chinese perspective on the right to demand continuance of a contract under the contract law of China is also reflected in the statutory provisions for failure in performance of monetary obligations, which in short stipulate that the promisee may demand payment

707 Bing Ling 2002 (n 229) para 8.032.

708 Art 121 CCL; Bing Ling 2002 (n 229) paras 8.009, 8.033, 8.039; Bu 2013 (n 226) 71, para 9; liability issues between the promisor and the third party are regulated by other statutory provision, such as art 254 of the PRC Contract Law for Work contracts, arts 123(1), 125(4)(2), 126, 132 Civil Aviation Law; arts 51(1)(12), 60(1), 70(1), 114 Maritime Law.

709 Art 121 CCL; Bing Ling 2002 (n 229) para 8.033; Bu 2013 (n 226) 70.

710 *E.g.*, art 110 CCL stipulates that the right to continuance of performance is not available to the promise in the event performance is legally or practically impossible, if performance is unsuitable or too expesive or continuance of performance is not required within a reasonable time.

711 Art 121 CCL can be subject to exemption; Bing Ling 2002 (n 229) para 8.034.

712 Bing Ling 2002 (n 229) para 8.035; in the event the act of the third party is caused by a situation of *force majeure*, the promisor may escape a claim for continuance of performace (or other judicial measures) in certain circumstances.

713 Bing Ling 2002 (n 229) para 8.036.

714 It follows from art 403 CCL that if a contract is concluded by an agent (mandatary) in the agent's name with a third party, who is not aware that the agent works as a proxy (representative/mandator) for another party (a principal), and the non-performance of the agent towards the principal is caused by this third party, the agent is obliged to disclose the third party name to the principal, and the principal may then exercise its rights of the agent against the third party, unless the third party would not have entered the contract if it was aware of the existence of the principal; Bing Ling 2002 (n 229) para 8.037.

715 Art 117(1) CCL; Bu 2013 (n 226) 70.

716 Bing Ling 2002 (n 229) para 8.010.

717 Bu 2013 (n 226) 70.

(performance) if the promisor fails to fulfil his or her monetary obligation.[718] However, from a doctrinal perspective, it is argued that a promisee is primarily entitled to demand continuance of a contractual promise[719] before any issue of non-performance arises because the right to performance of a contractual promise is said to derive from the bindingness of a contractual promise.[720] As to whether a Chinese court is actually prepared to follow this academic reasoning is doubtful because of the closed system of statutory provisions for the right to demand continuance of a contract in the contract law of China and due to unanswered questions in practice, on the matter of enforceability.[721]

115. The interim conclusion that a (non-)attributable failure in performance is required for the award of a claim for the actual performance of a contractual obligation can be derived from the considerations above, although article 8 of the contract law of China states that a contract is binding on parties. In this respect, it is argued that the civil law principle *pacta sunt servanda* still applies in China as one of its fundamental principles,[722] and therefore, that enforcement of actual performance can be demanded before any (expected) failure in performance.[723] Awarding such a claim, however, is solely regarded as a confirmation of liability of the promisor for continuance of performance of his or her contractual obligations.[724] From this perspective, it is understandable that Chen Lei labelled the option to demand the actual performance of a contractual obligation as a remedial right.[725] The reference to remedies is probably based on the idea that the wording of article 107 of the contract law of China suggests that enforcement of actual performance is only available after a failure in performance of the contractual promise. The word 'right' presumably reflects the civil law principle that performance is available as of right. However, in contrast to the historical view in Chinese law,[726] the statutory obligation to act in good faith entails a number of grounds on which a claim for continuance of performance can

718 Art 109 CCL.

719 Bing Ling 2002 (n 229) para 8.004.

720 Bing Ling 2002 (n 229) para 8.001; Lei Chen, 'Availability of Specific Remedies in Chinese Contract Law' in Chen-Wishart, Loke and Ong 2016 (n 156) 22, 23, 27; Han Shiyuan, 'The Performance Interest in Chinese Contract Law: Monetary Award' in Chen-Wishart, Loke and Ong 2016 (n 156) 40, 41.

721 Zhang 2006 (n 41) 67 *ff.*

722 Bing Ling 2002 (n 229) para 8.001.

723 In the case the promisor explicitly expresses or indicates by act its intention not to perform its obligations under the contract, the promisee is entitled, before the expiration of the due date of the contract, to demand that the promisor bear the liability for breach of contract; see for this statutory provision about anticipatory breach art 108 CCL; Lei Chen, 'Availability of Specific Remedies in Chinese Contract Law' in Chen-Wishart, Loke and Ong 2016 (n 156) 27.

724 Lei Chen, 'Availability of Specific Remedies in Chinese Contract Law' in Chen-Wishart, Loke and Ong 2016 (n 156) 22, 23, 27.

725 Lei Chen, 'Availability of Specific Remedies in Chinese Contract Law' in Chen-Wishart, Loke and Ong 2016 (n 156) 23, 26.

726 Bing Ling 2002 (n 229) para 8.064.

be rejected by the court.[727] It is argued that these statutory restrictions on the right to continuance of a contractual non-monetary promise have resulted in a significant change of the view on the bindingness of a contractual promise, by stipulating that the right to continuance of a contract is not available to the promisee if performance is impossible, if awarding a claim for continuance of performance is unsuitable, the costs of enforcement are disproportional, or if the promisee fails to bring a claim to court for continuance of performance within a reasonable time.[728]

116. The contract law of China does not provide clear guidance for the question of whether parties are free to choose between statutory performance remedies. It is, therefore, first discussed whether the aggrieved party is free to choose between actual performance, remedial measures and damages. The second point is whether the aggrieved party is free to choose between the remedial measures of repair and replacement. Following this, an analysis of the debate concerning the right to change the initial choice for a certain performance remedy is provided.

A promisee may require actual performance, remedial measures and damages if the promisor does not perform its obligations,[729] unless the statutory requirements are not met, or certain statutory barriers apply.[730] It is held that the aforementioned order of remedies suggest that the contract law of China prioritises an action for actual performance over remedial measures and compensation of damages,[731] and that future legislation should follow the same sequence.[732] In this vein, it is also said that adoption of the idea that parties are free to choose between available remedies is not in accordance with the principle that contracting parties should adhere to their promises (which is said to promote the development of trade and the economy).[733] Nonetheless, in recent literature it is held that a promisee is free to choose between a claim for actual performance, damages and judicial

727 Arts 6, 110 CCL; Lei Chen, 'Availability of Specific Remedies in Chinese Contract Law' in Chen-Wishart, Loke and Ong 2016 (n 156) 28.

728 Arts 6, 110 CCL; Bing Ling 2002 (n 229) para 8.003; a more elaborate discussion about these restrictions on the right to claim continuance of a contractual promise is presented in Ch 6.

729 Art 107 CCL; Bing Ling 2002 (n 229) para 8.080; *Changchun Foreign Economic and Trade Co. v Changchun Chaouang Real Estate Development Co* Changchun Intermediate People's Court and Jilin High People's Court (1993) SCPC (1992–1996 Collection) 202; Lei Chen, 'Availability of Specific Remedies in Chinese Contract Law' in Chen-Wishart, Loke and Ong 2016 (n 156) 24; Han Shiyuan, 'The Performance Interest in Chinese Contract Law: Monetary Award' in Chen-Wishart, Loke and Ong 2016 (n 156) 53; Zhang 2006 (n 41) 296.

730 Arts 107, 110 CCL.

731 Hao Liyan (郝丽燕), 'On Delivery of Substitute Goods in the Case of Defective Performance of Sales of Specific Goods' (论特定物买卖瑕疵履行时的交付替代物), Jinan University School of Political Science and Law (济南大学政法学院) (2017) iss 9 Politics and Law 86.

732 *Ibid.*

733 *Ibid.*

measures for defective performance, or a combination of these remedies if appropriate.[734] For example, in the case *Sofa Frames*, a supplier of wooden products signed a contract for the sale and delivery of 500 sofa frames to be delivered in multiple batches, with the last delivery by 20 June.[735] The seller also concluded a contract with a third party for the sale and delivery of 800 wooden sofa frames, although its manufacturing capacity was not sufficient to perform both contracts in accordance with the agreed time for delivery.[736] In order to comply with the second contract, the seller failed to deliver the outstanding wooden sofa frames under the first contract.[737] As a result, the court ordered continuance of performance of the contract, payment of a judicial penalty and damages.[738] In another case,[739] a contract was signed for the sale and purchase of a ginseng farm (the roots of the ginseng plant are used in traditional Chinese medicine for a wide variety of health issues).[740] The buyer of the farm sold the first harvest but failed to pay the first instalment of the purchase price of the farm.[741] As a result, the aggrieved sellers seized the harvest and sold it to another party.[742] The court considered that the terms of the contract did not provide a legitimate ground for this action and, therefore, it ordered the sellers to complete the delivery of the ownership of the farm and to pay the damages incurred by the buyer.[743] Aside from the fact that the examples above demonstrates that a claim for actual performance, damages and judicial penalties can coexist, it is also suggested that the payment of damages does not remove the right of the promisee to claim actual performance.[744]

That said, the right of a promisee to terminate a contract, in the event of a fundamental breach or after a reasonable period to cure the failure has elapsed, is subject to higher barriers than a claim for actual performance of the contract,[745] which suggests that the contract law of China favours a claim for actual performance of a contract over

734 Lei Chen, 'Availability of Specific Remedies in Chinese Contract Law' in Chen-Wishart, Loke and Ong 2016 (n 156) 36; He Xu Xu (贺栩栩), 'Improvement of Rules on Continuous Performance in Sales Contracts' (论买卖合同法中继续履行规则的完善) (2016) iss 12 Political Science and Law 94 (政治与法律).

735 Shen 1996 (n 140).

736 *Ibid.*

737 *Ibid.*

738 *Ibid.*

739 *Ibid.*

740 US Department of Health and Human Services, National Center for Complementary and Integrative Health <https://nccih.nih.gov/health/asianginseng/ataglance.htm> accessed on 22 August 2017.

741 *Ibid.*

742 *Ibid.*

743 *Ibid.*

744 Shen 1996 (n 140).

745 Art 94 CCL; Lei Chen, 'Availability of Specific Remedies in Chinese Contract Law' in Chen-Wishart, Loke and Ong 2016 (n 156) 24.

termination.[746] Nevertheless, the freedom of the promisee to choose between the available remedies is unaffected even if the promisor offers to repair or to replace the defective performance,[747] unless the promisee is a consumer and the promisor offers to cure the defects within a reasonable time.[748] In this respect, it may be noted that the freedom to choose between an action for actual performance, repair, replacement or damages, may be limited by a contractual exemption clause, albeit that Chinese scholars differ about the effect of such a clause.[749]

At this point, it is relevant to make a link with the earlier example of an advertisement on litter bins and the subsequent question whether *wasteful performance* could interfere with the choice to claim the actual performance of a contractual obligation.[750] In the event wasteful performance is not avoided, the Chinese court could appraise that the claimant breached its obligation to act in good faith and, subsequently, could deny the claim for continuance of performance. Thus, if the non-performing party 'has acted in such a way as to lead a reasonable person to conclude that he does not intend to perform the contract',[751] the claim for continuance of performance shall probably be rejected, unless the claimant shows that it had justified reasons to perform the contract, such as a well-founded expectation that damages would not cover its losses or any inextricably linked contractual obligations with third parties, which exposes the defendant to additional lawsuits.[752] Having said that, the bindingness of a contractual promise is a statutory principle in the contract law of China,[753] which is reinforced by the statutory principle to act in good faith.[754] It is, therefore, not to be expected that the Chinese courts are willing to abandon these fundamental principles of Chinese contract law. This proposition is also supported by the view that the promisee is provided with the right for enforced performance to be enforced by the court, and that Chinese courts are entitled to order enforcement of performance 'as a matter of principle'.[755]

746 Lei Chen, 'Availability of Specific Remedies in Chinese Contract Law' in Chen-Wishart, Loke and Ong 2016 (n 156) 24.

747 Lei Chen, 'Availability of Specific Remedies in Chinese Contract Law' in Chen-Wishart, Loke and Ong 2016 (n 156) 36.

748 A rejection of the consumer of the offer of the promisor to remedy the defect, can exempt the promisor from liability for the defective goods; Lei Chen, 'Availability of Specific Remedies in Chinese Contract Law' in Chen-Wishart, Loke and Ong 2016 (n 156) 36; Bing Ling 2002 (n 229) para 8.088.

749 Ch 8.

750 S 4.2.3.

751 Lei Chen, 'Availability of Specific Remedies in Chinese Contract Law' in Chen-Wishart, Loke and Ong 2016 (n 156) 28.

752 *Ibid.*

753 Art 8 CCL.

754 Art 6 CCL; Bing Ling 2002 (n 229) para 2.041.

755 Lei Chen, 'Availability of Specific Remedies in Chinese Contract Law' in Chen-Wishart, Loke and Ong 2016 (n 156) 28.

Concerning the relation between an action for repair and replacement, the contract law of China stipulates that if the quality of the goods are not in accordance with the terms of the contract, and the contract does not encompass a remedial scheme to cure a non-performance, the promisee is entitled, in light of the nature of the goods and the degree of loss, to reasonably choose between the performance remedies of repair, replacement, returning the goods, or reducing the price.[756] First, it is argued that the courts prioritise a promisee's right to repair over replacement, even if the consequences have a severely detrimental impact on the promisor (*e.g.* the costs of repair are higher than the costs of delivery of substitute goods).[757] In this vein, it is argued that in case of a defective performance, the right of the promisee to choose between repair and replacement could result in a very unfavourable outcome for the promisor because the latter has to bear the financial consequences.[758] By contrast, it is argued that the promisor already benefits from the actual performance of the promisees obligations (payment of the purchase price) and, therefore, should not also be allowed to choose between the elimination of its flaws (repair) or payment of an alternative (replacement).[759] In this respect, it is also said that awarding a claim of a promisee for repair or replacement fulfils two roles.[760] The first is fulfilment of the subjective right of the promisee to protect its interest in performance of the contract, and the second is to give the promisor another chance, by providing an opportunity to perform its obligations in return for payment of the purchase price.[761] In this approach, protection of the interest of the promisor in performance and payment is guaranteed by the obligation of the promisee to provide the former with the opportunity to repair or replace its non-performance and, thus, to continue to perform the contract.[762] Another reason for giving the option to the promisee to choose between repair and replacement is that the latter is not exposed to the risk of (temporarily) losing the ability to use the purchased goods, if the promisor chooses to repair its non-performance instead of replacement.[763] Theoretically, the promisee could sue for damages for the loss of use, but it is held that the courts are typically not inclined to provide a plaintiff with a court order for alleged monetary damages due to a loss of use because the objective of the contract law of China is said to pursue the fulfilment of the purpose of a contract.[764]

---

756 Arts 107, 111, 155 CCL; Lei Chen, 'Availability of Specific Remedies in Chinese Contract Law' in Chen-Wishart, Loke and Ong 2016 (n 156) 35.
757 Hao 2017 (n 731) 86.
758 *Ibid.*
759 *Ibid.*
760 Hao (n 731) 86; Mario Schollmeyer and Alper Utlu, 'Die Nacherfüllung im Kauf' (2009) 31(10) JURA 721.
761 Hao (n 731) 86; Schollmeyer (n 760) 721.
762 Hao (n 731) 86; Schollmeyer (n 760) 721.
763 Hao (n 731) 86.
764 *Ibid.*

The interest of the promisee is said to be protected by its alleged right to choose between repair and replacement. Conversely, the interest of the promisor is protected by the proportionality principle, which means that the latter may refuse to provide a replacement if the financial costs for providing an alternative performance are too high (disproportionality between the purpose of the contract and the means to achieve this purpose).[765] This is reflected in the principle that the choice of the promisee for repair or replacement should be reasonable.[766] In addition, it is argued that the interest of the promisor is protected by the principle that the promisee is not entitled to change its choice for repair and replacement during the period it has provided the promisor with the opportunity to perform one of these remedies.[767] This principle is based on the view that the choice of the promisee generates trust in the promisor and, therefore, the former may not be allowed to change its choice for repair or replacement.[768]

Turning briefly to the discussion about the right to revoke a choice for a certain performance remedy, the contract law of China only stipulates that the promisee is entitled to reasonably choose between the available remedies if the promisor fails to deliver the goods in accordance with the terms of the contract.[769] It does not provide any guidance for answering the question of whether the promisee is entitled to revoke its choice.[770] Nonetheless, it is held that the promisee is obliged to take into account the interests of the promisor and, therefore, may not arbitrarily change its choice (see the considerations above).[771] There is one exception. In unforeseen circumstances arising after the initial failure in performance, the promisee is allowed to change its choice, unless the promisor has already started with the necessary activities to repair or replace the goods.[772] All told, however, these viewpoints are currently not supported by statutory principles.

Another interesting point to take into consideration is that a promisee is not required to select one of the available performance remedies within a reasonable time.[773] This, ultimately, may result in a long period of legal uncertainty of the promisor, therefore, it is held that the contract law of China provides insufficient protection of the interest of a promisor to a sales contract.[774] The absence of an obligation to choose between the available remedies within a certain time limit is said to be in line with the contract law of China,

765 *Ibid.*
766 Art 111 CCL.
767 Hao (n 731) 86.
768 Hao (n 731) 86; He 2016 (n 734) 95 footnote 4.
769 Arts 111, 155 CCL.
770 He 2016 (n 734) 94.
771 *Ibid.*
772 *Ibid.*
773 *E.g.*, in No. 1 Intermediate People's Court of Beijing Municipality (2015), No. 03857 and No. 1 Intermediate People's Court of Beijing Municipality (2005), No. 51 the court awarded a claim for (continuance) of performance, even though a long period had elapsed after the non-performance.
774 He 2016 (n 734) 94.

which places great emphasis on the right to performance.[775] However, the lack of a deadline could also amount to a lack of incentive to fulfil the purpose of the contract,[776] and it contradicts with the preference of the contract law of China for the fulfilment of a contract (as soon as possible). Therefore, it is suggested to apply the following principles:[777] where there is no time limit set for demanding delivery, the seller may perform, and the promisee may require performance, at any time, provided that the other party shall be given the time required for preparation.[778] In case the remedy cannot be performed by the promisor due to any reasons attributable to the promisee, the latter is liable for damages.[779] Adoption of these principles would mean that the promisee is encouraged not to wait to inform the seller about its choice for a performance remedy.[780] Another suggestion which has been made is to adopt the principle that the aggrieved party is obliged to choose a performance remedy within a reasonable time on pain of expiration of its rights under the contract.[781] This option may positively affect the contractual relationship since it provides the promisee with the necessary time to consider which remedy would be most effective to cure the failed performance.

4.2.5 Conclusions

117. This section aims to determine the historical and contemporary foundation of the availability of a claim for enforced performance in order to enhance the understanding of the fundamental differences in approaches taken by the subject legal systems. As a preliminary note, the usage of the term enforced performance herein refers to a judicial action for obtaining the very thing parties bargained for under a commercial sales contract, that is, delivery of the goods and payment of the purchase price. In looking at the theoretical underpinnings of the availability of enforced performance of these obligations in the subject jurisdictions, there are three dogmatic common denominators, albeit with a completely different effect on the availability of enforced performance. First, the contract law of the Netherlands, Singapore and China each distinguish between legal rights deriving from the law governing the contract and the contractual stipulations, and the judicial instruments to protect these rights.[782] This means in effect that the rules for determining the availability

775 Art 107 CCL.

776 He 2016 (n 734) 94.

777 *Ibid.*

778 Application, by analogy, of art 139, 62(4) CCL.

779 Application, by analogy, of art 143 CCL.

780 He 2016 (n 734) 94.

781 *Ibid.*

782 As shown below, the nature of the legal rights of contracting parties are (in civil and common law traditions) not necessarily reflected in the available judicial actions.

of a claim for enforced performance are generally discussed after the definition of the legal rights of contracting parties.[783] The unification instruments are structured in a similar way.[784] It appears, therefore, that the legal structure adopted by the subject legal systems qualifies as a 'right-action model'.[785] In this model, the availability of enforced performance and its limits depends on the nature of the legal right which needs protection and the circumstances of the case.[786] This brings about the premise that a legal right is not necessarily protected by a judicial action for enforced performance. Nonetheless, when enforced performance is not available, the contract law of the three subject jurisdictions do not deny the existence of a legal right deriving from the contract law principles and contractual stipulations.[787] The influence of the nature of the legal right on the availability of enforced performance returns in the discussion about the third common denominator. In view of the controversy about enforced performance in the common law tradition, it is briefly noted here that Singapore contract law has taken an approach where enforced performance is not available if the nature of the legal right concerns a non-monetary performance obligation (with the exception of specific cases).[788] This approach fits neatly into the 'right-action' model, as discussed above. It can, however, also be said that the Singapore common law system reflects some elements of the (contested) Friedmann's 'primacy of remedy model', entailing the notion that legal rights derive from the available judicial

783 NL: the obligations of the seller are laid down in arts 7:9 and 7:17 DCC and the special consequences of the non-performance in art 7:21 DCC. It should be noted that Dutch contract law has taken a unique position in comparison to the other investigated legal systems, in the sense that it acts on the assumption that the mere existence of an obligation brings about a right to enforced performance. Dutch contract law only confirms this right in the form of a statutory provision which stipulates that the person who is obliged to perform can be ordered to do so. See art 3:296(1) DCC; SGP: the duties of the seller and buyer are laid down in SGA, s 27 and the actions for non-performance in SGA, s 49 *ff.*; CHN: Ch 4 CCL provides for the obligations of contracting parties and Ch 7 CCL for the consequences of a failure.

784 *E.g.*, arts 30, 35 CISG provides for the obligations of the seller and art 45 CISG *ff* for the remedies for a failure in performance; PICC: Ch 6 entails the rules on performance and Ch 7 is concerned with the consequences of non-performance; PECL: Ch 7 deals with the required performance and Chps 8 and 9 with the remedies for non-performance; DCFR: Book III, Ch 2 encompases the principles on performance and Book III, Ch 3 the remedies for non-performance; PACL: the draft articles on performance precedes the draft articles on non-performance.

785 This notion is modelled on the right-remedy model described by Friedmann in Cohen and McKendrick (n 4) 8–10.

786 *E.g.*, a commercial contract which entails the sale of certain goods, and the production of these goods require personal work of the seller.

787 A striking example follows from S 27 of the Singapore SGA, which stipulates that it is the duty of the seller to deliver the goods. This duty is not affected by the principle that enforced performance is not available where it concerns non-delivery of commodities (and substitute goods are available at the marketplace).

788 This concerns situations where damages are inadequate to cure the consequences of a non-delivery of specific and ascertained goods, and where substitute goods are scarce and procurement of substitute goods is practically unobtainable. The availability of enforced performance in these situations is further limited by counter-exceptions, such as the common law clean hands doctrine and where an order for enforced performance requires constant supervision of the court.

instruments.[789] Taking into account the fact that the common law of Singapore does not encompass a general right of contract parties to enforced performance of non-monetary obligations, this would mean that parties to a commercial contract have no legal right to enforced performance. This consequence runs entirely counter to the exceptions to this basic rule,[790] which directly relate to the nature of the legal rights arising from a commercial contract. Moreover, the primacy of remedy model ignores that the availability of a remedial measure is merely a response to a wrongdoing. As mentioned previously, its availability depends on the nature of the legal rights and the assessment of the court as to the appropriateness of enforced performance.

118. The second common denominator is found in the notion within the three subject jurisdictions that a legal right of contracting parties derives from the adage *pacta sunt servanda*. This theoretical principle operates, however, completely different in the three jurisdictions. The underlying reason for this is that the civil law tradition entails the notion that the availability of enforced performance is a direct consequence of the principle of *pacta sunt servanda*.[791] As a result, the law provides measures to ensure that contracts are performed. In the common law tradition, the availability of enforced performance depends primarily on an infringement of a legal right which cannot be remedied by monetary compensation.[792] A detailed discussion about this issue will be returned to later in section 4.4. Here it is reiterated that the present section demonstrates that the contract law of the Netherlands and China approaches are rooted in the civil law tradition. As a result, both jurisdictions consider a claim for enforced performance as a judicial action which is interrelated with the legal right deriving from the act of promise making. This means in effect that a claim for enforced performance of a legal right can be brought to court prior to a failure in performance. This runs counter to the approach taken by the contract law of Singapore which is rooted in the common law tradition. Consequently, the contract law of Singapore acts on the notion that the legal rights of contracting parties follow from the act of contract making, but the fundamental question of whether the discretionary remedy of enforced performance is available arises first and foremost after a failure in

789 Friedmann in Cohen and McKendrick (n 4) 4–8; See also SA Smith, 'Duties, Liabilities, and Damages' (2012) 125 Harvard Law review 1727. In this article two ways of understanding damages awards are explored. The first is the duties view, which supposes that damages awards confirm existing legal duties to pay damages. According to this view, damage awards are structurally similar to awards that require defendants to do things such as deliver contractually promised goods. The second way of understanding damage awards is the liability view, which supposes duties are not confirmed, but created by damage awards. According to this view, damage awards are structurally similar to a monetary fine for a criminal wrongdoing.

790 S 4.4.3.

791 Schwenzer 2016 (n 91) art 28 para 1.

792 Schwenzer 2016 (n 91) art 28 para 2.

performance.[793] The unification instruments have adopted a balanced approach in this regard, in the sense that legal rights are protected by a general availability of enforced performance which only arises in the case of a non-performance.[794] As for non-monetary obligations arising from a commercial sales contract subject to the contract law of Singapore, the picture is, unfortunately, more complicated due to the later discussed adequacy of damages test and the fact that it always remains at the discretion of Singapore courts to assess whether enforced performance is the most appropriate measure. As for the impact of these elements on the availability of enforced performance, it should be noted that the courts are entitled to deviate from the traditional English common law interpretation of the principle *pacta sunt servanda* where this is required in view of local circumstances. Today, this point is of significant importance considering the increasing divergence between the roles of England and Singapore as regional and international trading hubs for commodities.[795]

119. As mentioned earlier, the nature of a legal right may affect the available judicial actions. This point brings about the third common denominator, *i.e.*, enforced performance is not available when the performance of an obligation arising from a commercial sales contract requires a 'personal' undertaking of the promisor. The subject legal systems, however, differ on the question as to what extent enforced performance is not available in these situations. Disagreement between the legal systems brings about the proposition that a legal right arising from a commercial sales contract can be categorised as a strong or weak right, depending on the law governing the contract. The Dutch and Chinese contract law, as well as most unification instruments, have taken the default approach that enforced performance is available, unless the nature of the subject matter of a sales contract is related to highly personal work,[796] although it appears that counter-exceptions are possible in exceptional cases.[797] This escape route in the form of counter-exceptions needs to be interpreted liberally as the civil law roots of both jurisdictions hold the fundamental notion that an aggrieved buyer should not be forced to settle for damages as a substitute for the promised performance.[798] The Singapore common law approach starts with the notion

793 Phang et al 2012 (n 112) para 23.074.

794 Art 45 CISG; Arts 7.2.1, 7.2.2 PICC; Art 8:101 PECL; Art III.-3:101 DCFR, Comment A; Arts 6, 7 Draft Articles on Non-Performance PACL.

795 <https://www.singstat.gov.sg/modules/infographics/economy> accessed on 28 January 2019.

796 The CISG is silent on the matter, but a similar result can be achieved by seeking recourse to the exemptions discussed in s 6.2; Art 7.2.2(d) PICC; Art 9:102(c) PECL; Art III.–3:302(3)(c) DCFR; Art 7(b) Amendment Draft on Non-Performance PACL.

797 The term counter-exceptions is used to refer to limitations on the availability of enforced performance of delivery of specific and ascertained goods to the contract, and where substitute goods are only obtainable on the market with great difficulty, if at all.

798 Schwenzer 2016 (n 91) art 28, par 2.

that enforced performance is not available if it would infringe the freedom of contracting parties by forcing them to carry out a positive act, unless monetary compensation is inadequate to provide the required relief. The distinct interpretation of the non-availability of enforced performance of performance obligations can be traced back to a broad interpretation of the concept of the 'bindingness' of a contractual promise by the Dutch and Chinese contract law, and the narrow interpretation adopted by Singapore contract law.[799] Taking the above into consideration, it may be said that under Dutch and Chinese contract law, a legal right related to an obligation to perform something other than payment of the purchase price is significantly stronger, when compared to similar rights under Singapore contract law. It appears that the approach taken by the unification instruments is more on par with the contract law of the Netherlands and China.

120. It is a basic tenet that commercial parties conclude a sales contract in order to obtain the very thing they bargained for. The performance interest of commercial parties in this regard is reflected in the commonly shared view of Dutch, Singapore and Chinese contract law, that contractual promises bring about legal rights. Nonetheless, the cultural notions and legal traditions of the subject jurisdictions have resulted in fundamental differences in approaches to the protection of the performance of monetary and non-monetary legal rights. An important disagreement is related to the influence of the nature of a legal right on the availability of obtaining judicial protection in the form of enforced performance, which causes a significant degree of legal uncertainty in the realm of international commercial sales contracts and where parties are not aware of the (impact of the) diametrically opposed approaches. Despite the fact that the CISG brings about a more balanced approach in this regard, it does not provide a solid solution for contracting parties from different legal backgrounds. This follows from the principle that the court adjudicating a claim for enforced performance of a CISG-contract may react in the same way as it would react to similar sales contracts according to its own law.[800] Contracting parties could also opt for the PICC or draw inspiration from the approach taken by the other unification instruments. Although on the mere basis that the unification instruments encompass a solution in the form of a general availability of enforced performance on a failure in performance, it cannot be assumed that the drafters removed the dividing line between the civil and common law view on the question of whether enforced performance of a commercial sales contract should be available. This requires a detailed analysis of the rules on enforced performance of the buyer's obligation to pay the purchase price, the seller's

799 O Remien, 'Enforced Performance in European Contract Law' in K Boele-Woelki, FW Grosheide and EH Hondius (red), *The Future of European Contract Law : Essays in honour of Ewoud Hondius to commemorate his retirement as professor of civil law at the University of Utrecht* (Kluwer Law International 2007) 321 *ff*; Mak (n 527) 54 *ff*.

800 Schwenzer 2016 (n 91) art 28 para 3.

obligation to deliver the goods and the enforceability of additional performance obligations, such as the handing over of essential documents and the availability and delivery of spare parts.

4.3 Payment of the agreed price

4.3.1 Introduction

121. This section analyses the availability of enforced performance regarding the buyer's obligation to fully pay the contracted price of the goods. The importance of this discussion derives from the fact that requirements and limitations for the enforcement of monetary obligations vary considerably between jurisdictions and under the identified unification instruments. The divergence becomes clearly visible when considering the situation where a buyer repudiates the contract, but the seller continues to perform and subsequently claims for payment of the purchase price. From a comparative and practical perspective, another interesting issue that arises is that where the buyer only performs its payment obligation in part. This raises the question as to whether the seller releases the buyer from its remaining obligations by accepting partial payment. The two examples below show that there are a number of other situations where enforcement of the buyer's obligation to pay the purchase price is not quite so certain.

> *Illustration 1* – A fashion brand, located in country X, and a retail chain, located in country Y, conclude a sales contract for the entire winter collection 2018. The sales contract entails a commitment of the fashion brand to deliver the clothing before 1 August 2018. However, the goods were only sent to the buyer by the end of October 2018. Therefore, the retail chain refuses to pay the agreed price due to the late delivery. Subsequently, the fashion brand demands payment from a third party (Company C) who promised to pay the agreed purchase price if the buyer failed to do so. Company C argues that the seller is in breach of its duty to act in good faith because activating the guarantee is not an ultimate measure. This situation raises the question of whether the seller's right to obtain payment from Company C can be removed by avoidance of an unreciprocal promise; that is, the guarantee to pay the purchase price. Although avoidance, guarantees and good faith are not subject to discussion in the present research, this example displays the potentially complex nature of establishing whether a claimant is entitled to enforced performance of a monetary obligation. The aforementioned situation is illustrated below.

Figure 12 Example of the complex nature of determining the enforceability of the obligation to pay the price in a commercial context

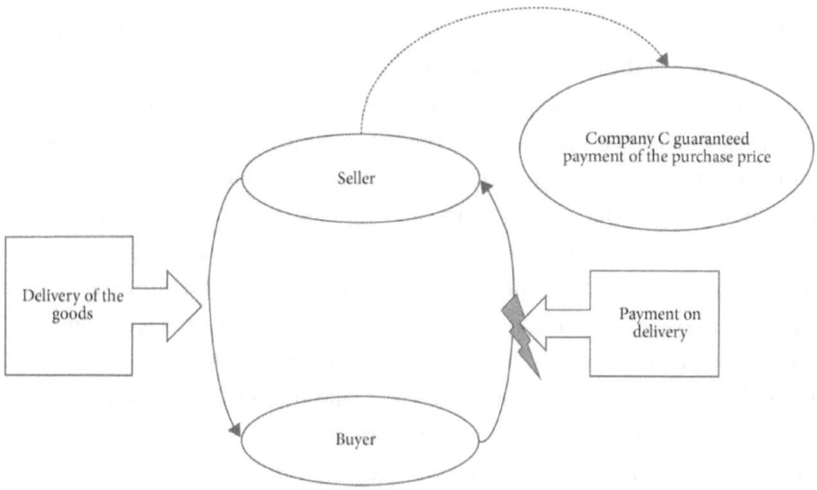

Illustration 2 – Suppose that a sales contract brings about the obligation of Company A (seller) to deliver two batches of a unique essential oil to the warehouse of Company B (buyer). The contract stipulates that the buyer can only be enforced to payment of the agreed purchase price for the second batch if the seller proves that it has sufficiently contributed to the joint effort to expand the business of the buyer. The contract further states that payment of the price for the goods only becomes due on delivery. Several months after delivery and payment of the first batch, the question arises as to whether the seller is entitled to payment of the second batch. In this situation, the buyer refuses to take delivery of the second batch and alleges that the seller did not show any commitment to support the expansion of the business of the buyer.

4.3.2 The right of action to obtain the agreed price in the Netherlands

122. Dutch contract law does not encompass an express right of the seller to recover the purchase price,[801] but it stipulates that the buyer is obliged to pay the full purchase price and that payment must be made at the stipulated time and place of delivery.[802] For situations where the buyer fails to pay the price in full, the seller can claim for payment of the outstanding amount under the overarching principle that the person obliged to give and

801 MBM Loos in C Mak in Schelhaas 2002 (n 19) 348; Sieburg, *Asser 6-II* (n 532).
802 Arts 6:29, 7:26(1)(2) DCC.

to do something may be ordered to do so by the court on the demand of the person to whom the obligation is owed.[803] This means in effect that a claim for enforcement of the buyer's obligation to pay the purchase price and enforcement of the seller's obligation to deliver the goods are subject to the same prerequisites. That is, limitations arising from the law, the nature of the obligation or a juridical act (*e.g.* the seller agrees to renounce its right to claim for the purchase price).[804] However, the aforementioned right to demand enforced performance (*i.e.* theoretically) does not require a failure in performance because it acts on the notion that the right to enforcement directly follows from the act of promise making. In principle, the court is therefore obliged to award a claim for enforced performance,[805] unless one of the previously mentioned limitations apply.

That having been said, the general consensus is that a claim for enforced performance of payment of the price shall only be awarded if the buyer's obligation is due and not (fully) fulfilled, although it is at the discretion of the court to order enforced performance on the condition that enforcement may only be carried out once the buyer's obligation becomes due.[806] Furthermore, a claim for enforced performance of the buyer's obligation may also be barred when the seller lacks sufficient interest,[807] when such a claim is manifestly unacceptable in view of the requirements of reasonableness and fairness,[808] and when a claim for enforcement constitutes an abuse of right.[809] This limitation may apply in the case where the buyer, for justifiable reasons, repudiates the contract before the seller's delivery obligation becomes due, but the latter decides to ignore the interest of the buyer by delivering the goods at the agreed place and time, and subsequently claims for the agreed price.

Enforcement issues may also arise when the buyer's obligation to pay the purchase price does not become due because it refuses to provide the necessary cooperation for delivery of the goods. There are some specific statutory provisions on the matter, but these are not in particularly helpful in this situation because Dutch contract law is simply not familiar with an overarching statutory duty to cooperate. For example, it follows from Dutch contract law that the buyer who demands delivery of the goods shall be in default where delivery is prevented because it does not provide the necessary cooperation.[810] It

803 Art 3:296(1) DCC.
804 Art 3:296(1) DCC.
805 S 4.2.2, 4.4.2.
806 Art 3:296(2) DCC; Sieburg, *Asser 6-II* (n 532) para 343; MBM Loos in C Mak in Schelhaas 2002 (n 19) 349.
807 Art 3:303 DCC.
808 Arts 3:12, 6:2(2), 6:248(2) DCC; This is the effect of the so-called derogatory effect of the standard of reasonableness and fairness, which means in effect that a contractual obligation to bring about a certain state of affairs is not enforceable to the extent that, in the given circumstances, this would be manifestly unacceptable according to the criteria of reasonableness and fairness; Hijma and Olthof 2017 (n 248) paras 300, 493.
809 Art 3:13 DCC.
810 Art 6:58 DCC

also follows from Dutch contract law that the buyer who demands delivery is in default where, for circumstances attributable to the buyer, the latter does not comply with an obligation owed on his part to the seller, who for that reason rightfully suspends delivery of the goods.[811] The court could discharge the seller from its obligation to deliver the goods if the buyer is in default.[812] All these principles do not have the effect that the buyer's obligation to pay the price becomes due in the example provided above. Nonetheless, where the court establishes that it follows from the requirements of reasonableness and fairness that the buyer is obliged to cooperate but failed to do so, the court could consider that the buyer's obligation to pay the price has become due and thus enforceable.

It should also be noted that there is a specific difference between the method of enforcement, in the sense that a failure in performance to pay a fixed sum may be enforced by direct execution. Put differently; it is possible to obtain payment without the cooperation of the non-performing party by means of a seizure and compulsory sale of goods owned by the latter.[813] For non-monetary obligations (*e.g.* the contractual obligation of the buyer to take delivery and the obligation of the seller to deliver the goods), the aggrieved party may claim for a court order for performance under pain of a judicial penalty (judicial penalties cannot be used to coerce performance of the obligation to pay the purchase price).[814]

4.3.3 *An action for the price in Singapore*

123. According to the sales law of Singapore, a buyer is obliged to make full payment of the purchase price for the goods, in accordance with the agreed time for payment.[815] An action for payment of the agreed sum is available as of right (in other words, at common law) to the seller,[816] once the contractual promise to pay the agreed price has become due and payable.[817] In contrast, a claim for the enforcement of a non-monetary obligation to bring about a certain state of affairs, and a claim for payment of a certain sum to a third

811 Art 6:59 DCC.

812 Art 6:60 DCC.

813 Arts 439 *ff*, 700 *ff* Dutch Code of Civil Procedure; Hijma, *Asser Koop en ruil* 7-I* 2013 (n 48) 589; Hartkamp 2011 (n 80) para 182.

814 Art 611a(1) Code of Civil Procedure; Hijma, *Asser Koop en ruil* 7-I* 2013 (n 48) 589.

815 SGA, s 27; Dora Neo, 'Specific Remedies and the Performance Interest in Singapore Contract Law' in Chen-Wishart, Loke and Ong 2016 (n 156) 194.

816 Phang et al 2012 (n 112) para 23.040; Dora Neo, 'Specific Remedies and the Performance Interest in Singapore Contract Law' in Chen-Wishart, Loke and Ong 2016 (n 156) 194.

817 *MP-Bilt Pte Ltd Oey Widarto* (n 623); Phang et al 2012 (n 112) paras 23.053, 23.088; Shenoy and Loo 2013 (n 13) para 18.82; Dora Neo, 'Specific Remedies and the Performance Interest in Singapore Contract Law' in Chen-Wishart, Loke and Ong 2016 (n 156) 194.

party is subject to the discretionary power of the courts.[818] Despite this distinction between actions for non-monetary and monetary obligations, it is held that enforcement of an obligation to pay the purchase price has the same effect as an order for enforced performance of a non-monetary promise, which, in essence, allows the promisee to obtain what it actually bargained for.[819] Considering the differences between the various monetary obligations, it is noted that an action for the agreed purchase price cannot be compared with a claim for (un)liquidated damages, because the former is considered a primary obligation arising from the contract, and the latter a secondary obligation enforced by law.[820] A claim for damages becomes relevant where the buyer wrongfully neglects or refuses to accept and pay for the goods.[821]

A seller is entitled to sue for payment of the outstanding purchase price if the property in the goods has passed to the buyer and the latter wrongfully neglects or refuses to pay for the goods according to the terms of the contract.[822] Aside from this obvious principle, it is important to focus on the occurrence of a partial payment in two situations. First, where the seller fails to deliver the goods and the buyer has already paid a part of the purchase price, the doctrine of a total failure of consideration prevents the seller to claim for the outstanding sum.[823] That is to say, the doctrine of consideration allows the buyer to ask for return of the sums paid. Secondly, in instances where the seller delivers the goods and accepts partial payment of the purchase price, the buyer could argue for application of the doctrine of promissory estoppel. This common law doctrine could (potentially) release the buyer from its obligation to pay the outstanding balance when the seller has led the buyer to believe that it will not enforce its legal right to full payment, the buyer relied on the seller's promise and the court establishes that it is inequitable for the seller to go back on its promise.[824] For the present comparative discussion, it is important to mention that these elements encompass moral considerations. For example, for the purpose of the doctrine of esptoppel the promisee should have acted in reliance on the promise in such a way as to make it inequitable to allow the promisor to act inconsistently with it.[825]

In instances where the property in the goods has not passed and the goods have not been appropriated to the contract, the seller also maintains an action for the purchase price

818 See the English case *Beswick v Beswick* [1968] AC 58, (1967) 2 All ER 1197; confirmed for Singapore contract law in Phang et al 2012 (n 112) para 23.038.

819 Shenoy and Loo 2013 (n 13) para 18.74; Hunter 2017 (n 7) para 8.5.

820 Phang et al 2012 (n 112) para 23.042.

821 SGA, s 50 (1); Phang et al 2012 (n 112) para 23.120 *ff*; Hunter 2017 (n 7) para 8.7.

822 SGA, s 49; Phang et al 2012 (n 112) para 23.120 *ff*; Hunter 2017 (n 7) para 8.6; Chong et al 2016 (n 125) para 10.7.14.

823 S 3.4.5.

824 Phang and Goh 2012 (n 318) para 275.

825 See *i.a., Abdul Jalil bin Ahmad bin Talib and others v A Formation Construction Pte Ltd* [2006] 4 SLR(R) 778 (SGHC); Phang and Goh 2012 (n 318) para 282.

if the price is payable on a certain day irrespective of delivery and the buyer wrongfully neglects or refuses to fulfil its monetary obligation.[826] Appropriation of goods means separation of the agreed quantity from the other goods. For example, Company A agrees to sell 1000 bags of jasmine brown rice to Company B out of 5000 bags available (the total harvest). Appropriation of the sold rice may be done by identifying the particular bags or by ((un)conditional) delivery of the bags. Appropriation of the goods is also present if the rice was filled by the seller into the bags supplied by the buyer. That being said, the seller is entitled to sue for the agreed price regardless of whether the property in the goods has passed; it is only required that the buyer factually or constructively has accepted the goods.[827] In the case the buyer argues that the accepted goods are not in accordance with the contract, the seller remains entitled to claim payment of the agreed price, albeit that the buyer may counterclaim for damages.[828]

The seller's right to enforced performance of the buyer's obligation to pay the purchase price is subject to two important prerequisites. That is, the seller has a legitimate interest in performance of the contract and delivery of the goods is possible without the cooperation of the buyer. The legitimate interest requirement is, however, of low significance as the seller is under no duty to mitigate its losses, and it does not apply if the seller is bound to the performance of other contracts based on the initial (repudiated) contract.[829] Furthermore, the requirement of the seller's legitimate interest in performance does not apply retrospectively for accrued obligations concerning payment of the purchase price, which can even be sued for after the seller accepted the buyer's repudiation of the contract.[830] In addition to the requirement of legitimate interest, Singapore contract law also requires a certain degree of reciprocity [100]. This effectively means that the buyer should be ready and willing to pay the purchase price and to be ready and willing to do everything to make delivery possible. In turn, the seller has to show it is willing to do all things on its part thereafter to be done.[831] The requirement of reciprocity, however, does not apply if the seller is not able to deliver the goods because the buyer refuses to cooperate (*e.g.* the buyer refuses to submit the required documents for shipment of the goods), and where the failure in performance does not affect the essence of the agreed performance.[832]

---

826 SGA, s 49; Phang et al 2012 (n 112) para 23.120 *ff*; Hunter 2017 (n 7) para 8.6; Chong et al 2016 (n 125) para 10.7.15.

827 Chong et al 2016 (n 125) para 10.7.16.

828 Chong et al 2016 (n 125) para 10.7.17.

829 See the English case *White and Carter* (n 621), applied and clarified for Singapore law in *MP Bilt Pte Ltd v Oey Widarto* (n 623); Dora Neo, 'Specific Remedies and the Performance Interest in Singapore Contract Law' in Chen-Wishart, Loke and Ong 2016 (n 156) 195.

830 *Ibid.*

831 *Indulge Food* (n 628) SGHC [53]; Dora Neo, 'Specific Remedies and the Performance Interest in Singapore Contract Law' in Chen-Wishart, Loke and Ong 2016 (n 156) 197.

832 *Indulge Food* (n 628) SGHC [61]; Dora Neo, 'Specific Remedies and the Performance Interest in Singapore Contract Law' in Chen-Wishart, Loke and Ong 2016 (n 156) 197.

4.3.4 *Right to demand payment in China*

124. The contract law of China acts on the notion that a right to enforced performance of the buyer's statutory obligation to pay the full purchase price arises from the act of promise making,[833] although the applicable statutory provisions reveal that actual enforcement is only available if the sales contract is effective, and the buyer did not pay the agreed price (regardless of its fault).[834] The same statutory prerequisites apply for enforced performance of non-monetary obligations, notwithstanding the fact that the limitations for obtaining an order for payment of the purchase price are less extensive.[835] This is because an action for payment of the price is not subject to specific statutory restrictions,[836] such as unsuitability or hardship of the buyer with the exception of unforeseen circumstances (see the considerations below).[837] In addition, enforced performance of payment of the outstanding amount does not have to be claimed within a reasonable time,[838] and it may not be excluded by contracting parties because of the highly replaceable character of money.[839] Only those general restrictions discussed hereafter are said to affect the seller's right to claim payment of the agreed price for the goods.

The overall principle is that contracting parties are obliged to act in good faith, and by not doing so, they are exposed to the risk that the court shall deny the claim for enforced performance of the obligation to the outstanding purchase price for the goods.[840] Furthermore, a claim for enforced performance of a monetary obligation is barred if the seller has not performed his or her own contractual obligations under the contract.[841] The seller may also be obliged to mitigate its losses (section 6.5), meaning that the seller has to cease all activities encompassing the preparation for delivery of the goods.[842] This applies in particular when the buyer has repudiated the contract, or where delivery of the goods

833 Arts 60, 159 CCL; Lei Chen, 'Availability of Specific Remedies in Chinese Contract Law' in Chen-Wishart, Loke and Ong 2016 (n 156) 23.

834 Arts 109, 130, 159–162 CCL; Lei Chen, 'Availability of Specific Remedies in Chinese Contract Law' in Chen-Wishart, Loke and Ong 2016 (n 156) 27; Peter Murray and Jiang Lin, *International Trade and Maritime Law in China* (Thomson Reuters 2017) § 4:68, accessed Westlaw China on 7 February 2017.

835 Art 109 CCL.

836 Bu 2013 (n 226) 72.

837 Bing Ling 2002 (n 229) para 8.066; In Zhang 2006 (n 41) 298 it is argued that a situation of *force majeure* is not a hurdle for awarding a claim of non-monetary obligation, which contradicts the suggestions in Bing Ling 2002 (n 229) para 8.069.

838 Art 109 CCL; Bing Ling 2002 (n 229) para 8.066.

839 Bing Ling 2002 (n 229) para 8.066; Zhang 2006 (n 41) 298.

840 Art 6 CCL; Lei Chen, 'Availability of Specific Remedies in Chinese Contract Law' in Chen-Wishart, Loke and Ong 2016 (n 156) 28.

841 Art 68 CCL; Bing Ling 2002 (n 229) para 8.067; Lei Chen, 'Availability of Specific Remedies in Chinese Contract Law' in Chen-Wishart, Loke and Ong 2016 (n 156) 27.

842 Arts 119(1), 6 CCL entails the obligation of contracting parties to act in good faith when exercising their rights and obligations under the contract; Bing Ling 2002 (n 229) para 8.067.

is contingent on the cooperation of the buyer.[843] If in such cases the goods are not delivered, the seller is not entitled to sue for payment of the agreed price, and is left with a claim for damages.[844]

In addition to the above-mentioned situations, the seller may not be entitled to claim for payment of the outstanding amount if performance of the contract objectively and subjectively impossible (section 6.2).[845] Further, a seller may also be deprived of its right to enforced performance of the buyer's obligation to pay the purchase price if government regulations or restrictions make it legally impossible to perform the contractual promise,[846] or in the event of a vital change in circumstances of the particular case, such as a significant decrease in the demand for offshore oil and gas services due to unexpected volatility of oil and gas prices.[847] In this respect, it may be noted that the court is entitled to take into account new circumstances (*i.e.* potential hardship of the buyer due to a change of circumstances) by altering the contractually agreed prices or to terminate the contract on a request of the promisor.[848] As a result, the initial contractual monetary obligations are amended or cease to exist.

4.3.5 Conclusions

125. The notion that the seller is entitled to enforced performance of the buyer's duty to pay the price for the goods when this obligation is due, is the common denominator between the investigated national and international legal systems. This rule is the result of the universally adopted principle of *pacta sunt servanda*,[849] which serves as the backbone for the protection of the seller's performance interest in receiving full payment of the purchase price. Nevertheless, an important difference between the three subject jurisdictions becomes apparent when considering a situation where the buyer's obligation to pay the

843 Art 119 (1) CCL; Bing Ling 2002 (n 229) para 8.067; A more elaborate discussion about the requirement to mitigate losses in relation to a claim for continuance is presented in s 6.5.

844 Bing Ling 2002 (n 229) para 8.067.

845 Bing Ling 2002 (n 229) para 8.068.

846 This principle is in line with art 62 of the CISG; Bing Ling 2002 (n 229) para 8.069.

847 Art 110(2) CCL should be applied by analogy in these cases; this particular article of the CCL is in accord with Art 245 of the German Civil Code and Art 402 paragraph 2 of the Japanese Civil Code. The latter is based on the German Civil Code; Bing Ling 2002 (n 229) paras 8.069, 8.070; Lei Chen, 'Availability of Specific Remedies in Chinese Contract Law' in Chen-Wishart, Loke and Ong 2016 (n 156) 31; A change of circumstances is not easily accepted as an excuse for non-performance. Any Chinese court that would like to apply the doctrine of a change of circumstances must have sought approval from a provincial high court or the Supreme Court. A more elaborate discussion about the barrier of change of circumstances is presented in s 6.2.

848 Bing Ling 2002 (n 229) para 8.079.

849 Arts 53, 62 CISG; Art 7.2.1 PICC; Art III.-3:301 DCFR; Art 9:101 PECL; Art 6 Amendment Draft on Non-performance PACL.

outstanding amount has not arisen because the seller has not yet delivered the goods, or where the agreed time for payment is not yet due. This brings about the important question how the subject legal systems react to a situation where the buyer refuses to provide the necessary cooperation to enable the seller to make delivery and subsequently refuses to pay the purchase price. The second example mentioned under paragraph 121 demonstrates that this situation is entirely conceivable in the realm of commercial sales. The enforceability of payment of the purchase price may also amount to difficulties where the buyer fails to act in accordance with its obligation to deliver (non-substantial) parts for the production of the goods, or to specify the goods to be delivered by the seller. The considerations in this section reveal that the three subject jurisdictions and the majority of unification instruments have not adopted a uniform legal solution for such cases. The same can be concluded when considering the situation where the buyer only pays a part of the purchase price. In view of this, the following aims to provide new insights in order to tackle potential enforcement issues in the situations mentioned above by those involved in international commercial sales contracts across the borders of the three subject jurisdictions. The following also aspires to enhance the understanding of the dogmatic divergence between the three subject legal systems and how the national interpretation of civil and common law concepts works out at the national level.

126. The starting point is that the differences between the approaches taken by the three investigated jurisdictions trace back to the dogmatic qualification of the judicial action to obtain payment of the price of the goods (*i.e.* basic right *vs* remedy).[850] To put this premise into context, the Dutch and Chinese contract law act on the notion that the seller's right to enforced performance of the buyer's obligation to pay the purchase price directly arises from the act of promise making (*i.e.* conclusion of the sales contract).[851] By contrast, the Singapore contract law has taken the approach that the right to enforced performance of a monetary obligation arises from a failure in performance. Hence, a claim for enforced performance of a monetary (and non-monetary) obligation is characterised as a remedial measure. It should, however, be noted that Chinese contract law also categorises a judicial action for enforced performance of (non-) monetary obligations as a remedial measure, although the statutory right to enforced performance emerges from the act of promise making.[852] The unification instruments identified adopt a similar theoretical qualification

850 S 4.2.

851 Sieburgh, *Asser 6-I* (n 363) para 412; Lei Chen, 'Availability of Specific Remedies in Chinese Contract Law' in Chen-Wishart, Loke and Ong 2016 (n 156) 23.

852 Arts 107, 109 CCL.

and structural approach by qualifying enforced performance as a right arising from the contract (*i.e.* the juridical act), which obtains operative effect on a failure in performance.[853]

127. The impact of the qualification of an action to obtain payment of the purchase price as a basic right or remedy becomes relevant when considering the situation where the monetary obligation is not yet due. With regard to situations where a commercial sales contract is subject to Dutch or Chinese contract law and the buyer is not yet obliged to pay the purchase price, the court could provide a judicial order for enforced performance (or a confirmation of the right to payment) on the condition that enforcement can be effectuated once the buyer's obligation is due. By contrast, the Singapore contract law, as well as the unification instruments, do not envisage the availability of an order to enforced performance before the monetary obligation is due. The PECL and DCFR, however, made a very important exception for situations where the buyer's obligation to pay the purchase price does not become due because it refuses to provide the necessary cooperation for delivery. In this situation, the PECL and DCFR adopt the principle that the seller may claim for enforced performance of the payment of the purchase price which is not yet due, provided that the buyer is unwilling to receive the reciprocal performance.[854] The CISG is not familiar with a similar principle, but it follows from the considerations in section 5.3 that the same result can be achieved by enforcement of the buyer's express duty to take delivery of the goods. This also applies for the PICC and the draft PACL which encompass an actionable obligation to provide the necessary cooperation for the fulfilment of the seller's obligation to deliver the goods.[855] If in these instances the enforcement order is carried out, the buyer's obligation to pay the purchase price becomes due and thus enforceable. Although this study contends that the three subject jurisdictions do not recognise an enforceable duty of the buyer to take delivery of the goods,[856] and are also not familiar with the solution offered by the PECL and DCFR, a similar result can be achieved under Dutch and Chinese contract law, where (theoretically) the availability of obtaining a judicial order for enforced performance of a monetary obligation is not related to the performance of the reciprocal obligation. However, Dutch contract law stipulates that payment of the price must be made at the time and place of delivery. The contract law of China brings about the rule that if the buyer fails to pay the price, the seller may claim

853 Art 46 CISG; Art 7.2.1 PICC; Art 9:10 PECL; Art III.-3:301 DCFR; Art 6 Amendment Draft on Non-Performance PACL.

854 Art 9:101(2) PECL; Art III.-3:301(2) DCFR.

855 The DCFR also adopted an enforceable obligation of the buyer to take delivery, but enforcement of this obligation is unnecessary in this situation considering the principle (art IV.A.–3:301 DCFR) that the seller is entitled to claim for enforced performance of a monetary obligation which is not yet due if the buyer is unwilling to take delivery.

856 S 5.3.

for payment. These provisions could be interpreted as a rule that payment of the price cannot be required if the duty to pay has not yet arisen, notwithstanding the dogmatic notion previously mentioned, that the right to payment arises from the act of promise making. Another option offered by both jurisdictions follows from the principle of good faith, which could potentially serve as a legal basis for demanding enforced performance of the buyer's obligation to pay the price for the goods because the latter is unwilling to cooperate to enable the seller to make delivery. Considering that the legal options described above bring about legal uncertainty, and the fact that Singapore contract law does not envisage payment of the purchase price before the due date, it is submitted here that the legislators of the three investigated jurisdictions, as well as the drafters of the CISG, PICC and the draft PACL, might draw inspiration from the approach taken by the PECL and DCFR.

128. Apart from the theoretical discussion above, consideration should also be given to the practical consequences of a situation where the seller accepts a partial payment. The starting point is that the contract law of the Netherlands, Singapore and China agree on the matter that the buyer is obliged to pay the outstanding amount where the seller rejects a partial payment. The same approach is adopted by the unification instruments.[857] Nonetheless, an important difference emerges when considering the situation where the buyer pays a lesser sum than agreed and this part performance is accepted by the seller.[858] Under Dutch and Chinese contract law, as well as the unification instruments, the obligation to pay the purchase price ceases to exist for the part which has been paid. The seller may claim for the remainder because the buyer is not released from its obligation to pay the outstanding amount. Only in extraordinary circumstances could the seller lose its right to claim for the remainder where the contract is governed by Dutch or Chinese contract law on the basis of the principle of reasonableness and fairness and the principle of good faith respectively (*e.g.* the buyer could reasonably rely on conduct or a declaration of the seller that partial payment releases the former from its obligation to pay the balance).[859] This approach stands in stark contrast to the solution provided for under the common law system of Singapore. As discussed earlier, the contract law of Singapore acts on the doctrine of a valuable consideration.[860] This, in effect, means that the buyer's obligation to make payment of the outstanding sum for the delivered goods is not affected by the seller's

857 Art 53 CISG; Schwenzer 2016 (n 91) para 23; Art 7.2.1 PICC; Art 9:101 PECL (full or partial non-performance of the buyer's payment obligation is not relevant, see art 1:301(4) PECL and MBM Loos in Schelhaas 2002 (n 19) 347); Arts III.-3:301, III.-3:101 DCFR; Art 1(c) Amendment Draft on Non-performance PACL; Lee 2016 (n 16) 193.

858 See for a general discussion about this matter Schwenzer, Hachem and Kee 2012 (n 13) paras 36.03–36.05.

859 NL: arts 6:248(2), 3:296 DCC; CHN: arts 6, 60, 109 CCL.

860 S 3.4.5.

acceptance of a part payment. The underlying rationale is that the seller's willingness to accept a lesser sum only amounts to a modification of the contract price when consideration for this adjustment is provided. That said, a claim for payment of the remainder can be refused by the court upon the doctrine of promissory estoppel. So, the main issue at hand is the requirement of a valuable consideration for the acceptance of the part payment and the doctrine of promissory estoppel, which is troubling for many businesses not familiar with the common law system. Interestingly, the principle of reasonableness and fairness, the principle of good faith and the doctrine of promissory estoppel all act on a moral level. Furthermore, the term 'waiver' of rights emerges in situations where these legal standards act as a barrier for the seller to obtain the outstanding amount on the basis of its own behaviour, which is a familiar concept under Dutch, Singapore and Chinese contract law, although the thresholds differ significantly. The difference between, on the one hand, the approach taken by Dutch and Chinese contract law, and on the other hand, the contract law of Singapore is that the common law doctrine of promissory estoppel can only be applied if certain elements are satisfied. Considering this divergence and that the different approaches are not consolidated in the unification instruments identified, explicit contractual stipulations for a situation of partial payment might prevent significant difficulties in the case of a commercial sales contract across the borders of the subject legal systems, and more generally when a sales contract concerns commercial parties from separate civil and common law jurisdictions. From a practical perspective, this means that parties to a commercial sales contract across civil and common law borders should be mindful of the Singapore common law rule that consideration is required if the buyer's obligation to pay the purchase price is varied in any way. So, for example, if the buyer agrees to pay 50% of the purchase price before the initially agreed time for payment and the seller in return promises to give the buyer more time to pay the balance or to reduce the total amount owed, there is consideration on both sides and the variation is contractually binding.[861] However, where the seller agrees to accept part payment of the purchase price (part payment is a unilateral variation) does not discharge the buyer to pay the remainder because the part payment is not good consideration.

861 Janet O'Sullivan and Jonathan Hilliard, *The Law of Contract* (6th edn, Oxford University Press 2014) para 6.56 *ff.*

4.4 Non-monetary obligations

4.4.1 *Introduction*

129. The purpose of the present section is to determine the basic degree of assurance that a contracting party is able to obtain the very thing it bargained for under a commercial sales contract. This is done by analysing the approaches taken by the contract law of the Netherlands, Singapore and China to the availability of enforced performance of non-monetary obligations in general and how these basic principles relate in substance with the approaches taken by the unification instruments. This comparative inquiry gives particular regard to the notion of non-monetary obligations in the realm of commercial sales transactions and the appropriateness of the domestic approaches in view of transactions involving generic and specific goods. In this section, enforced performance is understood as a judicial order to bring about the actual result of a commercial sales contract and does not encompass the ability of the aggrieved party to obtain the performance at the expense of the other party.[862] In other words, the discussion focusses on the obligation of the seller to deliver the goods in accordance with the terms of the contract and the availability of judicial enforcement in the case of, for example, non-delivery and delayed delivery.[863] It must also be noted that the considerations provided hereinafter should not be read in isolation when determining the flexibility of the judicial measures for enforced performance. By contrast, the findings presented in the subsequent chapters have a significant impact on the final conclusions.

> *Illustration* – A distributor, located in country A, entered into a contract with a trader, located in country B, for the purchase of reusable coffee cups from a manufacturer in country C. The parties agreed on the quantity, purchase price and method of payment, time for delivery and environmental standards for production. The seller threatens not to perform its contractual obligation and to sell the goods elsewhere if the buyer refuses to pay an additional surcharge to cover the costs of the seller. The buyer brings an action for an anticipatory failure in performance of the contract and enforced performance of the seller's delivery obligation.

862 Ch 7.

863 The availability of enforced performance in the form of replacement and repair is discussed in s 5.4.

4.4.2 Right to enforced performance in the Netherlands

130. Dutch contract law acts on the notion that the right to claim for enforced performance derives from the contractual rights of the parties.[864] In view of this, it is recalled that a failure in performance is not required for a judicial action to obtain an order for enforced performance of obligations to bring about a certain state of affairs.[865] Hence, the act of promise making is sufficient.[866] The privileged situation of the promisee is lessened by the obligation of the claimant to prove that it has sufficient interest in a court order for enforced performance before the due date.[867] The courts are given discretionary power to undertake the assessment of sufficient interest, and to restrict an award for enforced performance by requiring that enforcement is only available at the moment the obligation is due and claimable.[868] In this respect, the promisee is obliged to furnish the facts that the contractual promise becomes at one point due, and if the underpinnings of the request for enforcement are disputed by the promisor, to further substantiate its claim.[869]

131. The considerations above have to be seen in light of the key principle that an alleged impossibility of performance is not necessarily a barrier for granting a court order which confirms the right to performance of the promisee.[870] There is justified merit in keeping open the possibility of providing a judicial order for enforced performance. That is, the court could order that enforcement can only be carried out once the cause of the barrier to performance is lifted; the court could authorise the aggrieved party to obtain the very

864 S 4.2.2.

865 Art 3:296(1) DCC.

866 *Van der Gun v Farmex* Dutch Supreme Court 22 May 1981, ECLI:NL:PHR:1981:AG4192, NJ 1982, 59; Sieburg, *Asser 6-II* (n 532) para 343.

867 The Dutch word is *opeisbaar* which is best to be translated as claimable or enforceable; Mak (n 527) 91; CJJC van Nispen, *Sancties in het vermogensrecht* (serie Mon. NBW deel A11, Kluwer 2003) para 12; see for the requirement of sufficient interest art 3:303 DCC; Haas 2009 (n 206) 56; Sieburg, *Asser 6-II* (n 532) para 344; Sieburgh, *Asser 6-I* (n 363) para 166; AW Jongbloed, 'commentaar op artikel 296 Boek 3 BW' para 7 in J Hijma (ed), *Groene Serie Vermogensrecht* (Wolters Kluwer 2018) (n 530); AW Jongbloed and H Struik, 'Vooruilopen op tekortkoming bij niet-opeisbare verbintenissen volgens het NBW' (1983) *AA* 704; Compare art 150 of the Dutch Code of Civil Procedure, which stipulates that a plaintiff is burdened with the proof to the facts and rights such as the existence of a contractual obligation of the defendant to perform an obligation in favour of the plaintiff. The burden of proof of the plaintiff can be lessened, removed or shifted to the defendant if this follows from a special provision or the standards of reasonableness and fairness. A shift of the burden of proof is possible if the defendant has made it unreasonably burdensome for the plaintiff to prove the existence of the contractual obligation.

868 Art 3:296(2) 2 DCC brings about the principle that where the contractual promise is subject to a condition or term, the court is entitled to award a claim for enforced performance subject to that condition or term; Haas 2009 (n 206) 56; Hofmann 1976 (n 84) 136; De Vries 1984 (n 207); Dutch Supreme Court 21 October 1983, *NJ* 1984, 804; Sieburgh, *Asser 6-I* (n 363) paras, 14, 166, 246.

869 Haas 2009 (n 206) 56; Hofmann 1976 (n 84) 136; Jongbloed in *Groene Serie Vermogensrecht* (n 530) para 3.

870 Sieburgh, *Asser 6-I* (n 363) para 373; Dutch Parliamentary History Book 6 (n 207) 486–488.

thing it bargained for (section 7.3). It also prevents the non-performing party from suing for restitution if it finds a way to overcome the initial (practical) barrier to performance or just ignores a legal impediment and delivers the goods anyway.[871] In other words, impossibility of performance does not tacitly affect the right to performance. It should, however, be noted that even though the prerequisite of sufficient interest is satisfied, the right to enforced performance does not axiomatically result in a court order for enforced performance. For instance, the court shall not grant a claim for enforced performance of natural obligations,[872] nor is enforced performance available for obligations arising from moral promises (to be objectively determined).[873] In these cases, the parties are only subject to non-actionable duties (*i.e.* obliegenheiten).[874] An order for enforced performance is also not available if this is not appropriate considering the nature of the obligation, such as strictly personal obligations. In this vein, enforced performance is believed to be inappropriate for an obligation to give a speech, to write a manuscript and the moral obligation of the Dutch government to support homeless residents in finding a home by mediating between parties.[875]

132. In 2015, the aforementioned view on the availability of enforced performance of strictly personal obligations was shaken by a judgement of the District Court of Rotterdam.[876] This case came to the attention of the international press after the court ordered the artist Dahn Vo to perform his contractual obligation, which meant that he was obliged to produce a large and impressive artwork for the Dutch art collector Bert Kreuk for a price of US$350,000 on pain of a financial penalty.[877] In this case, the District Court established that a contract was concluded between Dahn Vo and Bert Kreuk and that the former failed to perform his contractual obligation.[878] The most logical subsequent reasoning would be that the nature of a contractual promise to produce an artwork entails a strict personal obligation and, therefore, the promisor cannot be forced to perform the contract. This line of thinking is based on the statutory principle that the person who is

871 Sieburgh, *Asser 6-I* (n 363) para 373; Hofmann 1976 (n 84) 126; Jan Smits, Daniel Haas and Geerte Hesen (eds), *Specific Performance in Contract Law: national and other perspectives* (Intersentia 2008) 19; Jongbloed *Groene Serie Vermogensrecht* (n 530) para 5.

872 Art 6:3 DCC; Sieburgh, *Asser 6-I* (n 363) para 14, 60 *ff*; Jongbloed in *Groene Serie Vermogensrecht* (n 530) para 6.

873 Consult Jongbloed in *Groene Serie Vermogensrecht* (n 530) para 6 for examples of various types of obligation which cannot be subject to a claim for enforced performance.

874 S 1.5.

875 *Lauppe v Lelystad* District Court Zwolle 27 maart 1985, KG 1985, 124; *Stichting Waterpakt v Staat* Dutch Supreme Court 21 March 2003, ECLI:NL:PHR:2003:AE8462, NJ 2003, 691.

876 District Court Rotterdam 24 June 2015, ECLI:NL:RBROT:2015:4417.

877 <https://artsbeat.blogs.nytimes.com/2015/12/02/danh-vo-and-bert-kreuk-settle-legal-dispute-over-artwork> accessed on 21 June 2017.

878 (n 876) para 2.17.

obliged to provide a certain work may be ordered to do so by the court on the demand of the person to whom the obligation is owed unless otherwise follows from the nature of the obligation.[879] This exception might be applicable in the case of an author who concluded a contract with a publisher to write a certain work. In case a claim for actual performance is not available to the promisor due to the nature of the obligation, the promisor is still entitled to claim damages.

133. The District Court of Rotterdam considered that the artistic nature of the contractual promise of Dahn Vo would only bar a court order to produce an artwork according to the initially agreed details.[880] Therefore, the judge stipulated that Dahn Vo was free to choose to adhere to the original assignment, but he was also free to deliver an artwork in accordance with the progress Dahn Vo had made as an artist.[881] In this respect, the court considered that contracting parties are professionals and, therefore, it could be expected that they would be able to reach a written agreement about the exact details of the work, which was to be large and impressive.[882] However, this well-argued practical solution of the court did not work out. In the following negotiations, Dahn Vo proposed to fulfil his contractual obligation by making a specific wall work for the amount of US$350,000 which would entail a line from the film *The Exorcist* that was said to represent Dahn Vo's inspiration of his latest body of work. It reads as follows: 'Shove it up your ass, you faggot'. Bert Kreuk did not accept the proposal of Dahn Vo but instead proposed the line 'From anger, hatred and all ill will', which was in turn rejected by Dahn Vo. Finally, the parties concluded that there was no solution to their dispute so the negotiations stopped and Dahn Vo has withdrawn his appeal.

134. Although it is not clear why the court did not apply the principle that a claim for actual performance is not available if this follows from the nature of the obligation, it could be that Dahn Vo did not, or did not sufficiently, argue that the performance of the initial agreement was impossible due to the nature of the obligation. Having said that, if the court ascertained that it was impossible for Dahn Vo to perform the contract, the alternative claim for damages could be allowed by the court. This may be the reason why Dahn Vo never argued that he was not able to perform his contractual obligation and that he agreed to negotiations about the fulfilment of the contract, albeit that it could be said that the earlier mentioned proposal of Dahn Vo shows that there was only an intention to frustrate and no desire to reach an agreement.

879 Art 3:296(1) DCC.
880 (n 876) para 2.21.
881 *Ibid.*
882 *Ibid.*

135. Although the considerations above suggest that the concept of enforced performance of an obligation to do or to give something has a very wide scope, a restriction follows from the principle that where a term for performance has been set, it is presumed to bar an earlier demand of performance.[883] Nonetheless, the impact of this principle is limited as the court is provided with the discretion to grant a claim for enforced performance on the condition that actual performance becomes available after lapse of the stipulated time for performance.[884] In other words, the focus lies on the right to enforced performance deriving from the act of promise making, rather than a decree for enforced performance deriving from a legal action.[885] Furthermore, the statutory principle embodying the right to claim for enforced performance is merely a general legal basis for specific actions to remedy a non-performance,[886] such as a demand for the removal of a charge or encumbrance,[887] a claim for delivery of what is missing,[888] and a claim for repair and replacement.[889] The Dutch contract law expressly requires a failure in performance for bringing about these specific forms of enforced performance of a sales contract. This is a fundamental departure from the general right to enforced performance, which (theoretically) does not require the occurrence of a non-performance.

4.4.3 *The discretionary remedy in Singapore*

136. In Singapore, the judicial remedy to obtain the actual performance of a positive non-monetary contractual promise on a failure in performance, is given at the discretion (the equitable jurisdiction) of the court.[890] Hence, the mere conclusion of a contract does not constitute a directly enforceable right to enforced performance of the non-monetary obligations arising therefrom.[891] In the case of a sale of goods, this means that it is at the discretion of the court, on the application of the aggrieved party, to order that the non-monetary contractual promise shall be performed specifically by the non-performing party.[892] It is, therefore, not the act of promise making but the failure in performance which entitles a contracting party to claim for enforced performance of the delivery of specific

883 Art 6:39(1) DCC.
884 Art 3:296(2) DDC.
885 De Jong, Krans and Wissink 2018 (n 194) 9.
886 Hijma and Olthof 2017 (n 248) paras 542–543.
887 Art 7:20 DCC.
888 Art 7:21(2) DCC.
889 Art 7:21(1)(b-c) DCC.
890 *Chung Khiaw Bank Ltd v Bajaj Textiles Ltd* [1968–1970] SLR(R) 78 [9] (SGHC); Halsbury's Laws of Singapore (Contract 2016) vol 7 paras 80.585, 80.588; Hunter 2017 (n 7) para 8.19; Phang and Goh 2012 (n 318) para 1552.
891 Halsbury's Laws of Singapore (Contract 2016) vol 7 para 80.585.
892 SGA, s 52(1).

and ascertained goods,[893] as well as the delivery of generic goods which are scarce, rendering the procurement of substitute goods practically unobtainable [138–149]. Starting from this principle, a claim for enforced performance can be brought to court if the dispute encompasses non-performance of designated contractual obligations,[894] unless the Singapore government is a contracting party.[895] Aside from this observation, the principle of priority of damages plays a central role in determining the enforceability of a non-monetary obligation.[896] This means in effect that a court order for enforced performance is only available 'when it will do more perfect and complete justice than an award of damages'.[897] This is said to be the case if the subject matter is not easy to quantify, or when the subject of the contract has an intrinsic value to the aggrieved party and, therefore, awarding a claim for damages cannot give the latter satisfactory relief.[898] It may be recalled that the adequacy of damages test derives from the competitiveness between the (abolished) courts of common law and equity (s 4.2.3), and the reluctance of the courts to enforce performance because disobedience could result in imprisonment following a contempt of court proceeding (s 6.6 and 7.4). It is also important to note at this point that a claim for the costs incurred in obtaining substitute goods is regarded as a form of damages instead of a consequence of enforced performance (s 7.3). Put differently, where an aggrieved buyer can obtain replacement goods from the market which provide the required satisfaction, a court order for enforced performance is not available. It, therefore, follows that an obligation to deliver generic goods is generally not enforced by a Singapore court.

137. The common law principle of priority of damages encompasses a two-step test. First, a claim for actual performance is only available where damages are not adequate to protect the performance interest of the aggrieved party (to be determined on the factual matrix of the case).[899] In the realm of commercial sales, this principle follows a subject approach,

---

893 *Ibid.*

894 Shenoy and Loo 2013 (n 13) para 18.3; *Excelsior Hotel Pte Ltd v Hiap Bee (Singapore) Pte Ltd (OCBC Finance (Singapore) Ltd, intervener)* [1989] SGHC 84 [12], (1989) 2 SLR(R) 322.

895 Government Proceedings Act (Cap 121, 1985 Rev Ed), s 27(1)(a); Shenoy and Loo 2013 (n 13) para 18.88; Halsbury's Laws of Singapore (Contract 2016) vol 7, para 80.587; *Bocotra Construction Pte Ltd and others v Attorney-General* [1995] SGCA 51 [7], [8], [25] – [38], (1995) 2 SLR(R) 282.

896 Halsbury's Laws of Singapore (Contract 2016) vol 7 para 80.586; Phang and Goh 2012 (n 318) para 1552.

897 Halsbury's Laws of Singapore (Contract 2016) vol 7 para 80.586.

898 Shenoy and Loo 2013 (n 13) para 18.87; Chow Kok Fong, *Law and Practice of Construction Contracts* (v 1, 4th edn, Sweet & Maxwell Asia 2004) para 4.35; *Coastland Properties Pte Ltd v Lin Geok Choo* [1999] SGHC 293 [2].

899 Shenoy and Loo 2013 (n 13) paras 18.3 and 18.89; Phang et al 2012 (n 112) para 23.071; Phang and Goh 2012 (n 318) paras 1552, 1553. In this respect it is noteworthy that awarding specific performance is a discretionary remedy of Singapore courts and therefore, an appellate court will only overrule a first instance judge on the basis that (i) the ruling was based on a misunderstanding of the law and evidence before him or her and if (ii) the appellate court ascertains that no reasonable judge would have reached such an order. See *EC Investment Holding Pte Ltd v Ridout Residence Pte Ltd and others and another appeal* [2012] SGCA

to the extent that the availability to claim for the actual performance of a non-monetary obligation is limited to situations where the seller fails to deliver specific or ascertained goods, and where the seller fails to deliver generic goods which are scarce, rendering the procurement of substitute goods practically unobtainable. Secondly, in instances of a failure to deliver specific or ascertained goods, the Sale of goods Act stipulates that enforcement can be awarded whether awarding a claim for actual performance is a just and appropriate remedy.[900] The two-step test discussed above is based on the premises that damages comply with the economic interest of contracting parties and the moral perspective that contracting parties should not be exposed to the risk of infringement of their liberty to act or not to act.[901] In this light, the following discusses whether a claim for damages and an order for enforced performance of a non-monetary obligation should be equally available to the aggrieved party because awarding a claim for damages is not in every situation in accordance with the justified performance interest of the latter.[902] The following arguments substantiate this view: (i) actual performance compels the promisor to do what it promised to do rather than leaving the promisee behind with only the financial equivalent, which was not that which parties initially contracted for;[903] (ii) the core obligation is performance, and therefore, first and foremost, the promisee should be entitled to enforce the promisor to perform his or her undertaking;[904] (iii) actual performance, in general, leads to a better result than substitutive damages, in certain situations, because the latter imposes the obligation on the parties to mitigate their losses.[905]

---

50 [76], (2012) 1 SLR 32; Confirming *Guan Chong Cocoa Manufacturer Sdn Bhd v Pratiwi Shipping SA* [2003] 1 SLR(R) 157, *The Vishva Apurva* [1992] 1 SLR(R) 912 and *Federal Computer Services Sdn Bhd v Ang Jee Hai Eric* [1991] 2 SLR(R) 427.

900 SGA, s 52; Singapore law adopted this principle as stated in the English case *Johnson v Agnew* (n 611); See the Singapore cases: *Indian Overseas Bank* [1991] (n 611); *Indian Overseas Bank* [1993] (n 611); *Lee Chee Wei* 2007 (n 591) 3 SLR (R) 537 [55], [66]; See also Phang et al 2012 (n 112) para 23.079 and the considerations in *E C Investment Holding Pte Ltd* (2012) (n 899) SGCA 50 [103]; Phang and Goh 2012 (n 318) para 1552.

901 *Lee Chee Wei* 2007 (n 591) SLR(R) 537, [52]; Phang and Goh 2012 (n 318) para 1552; Dora Neo, 'Specific Remedies and the Performance Interest in Singapore Contract Law' in Chen-Wishart, Loke and Ong 2016 (n 156) 201; This would mean, in a commercial context, that an order for actual performance is not available where this would force a party to run a business, see the English House of Lords decision in *Co-operative Insurance Society Ltd v Argyll Stores (Holdings) Ltd* [1997] 2 WLR 898; ABL Phang, 'Specific Performance – Exploring the Roots of "Settled Practice"' (1998) 61 Modern Law Review421, 423; Phang and Goh 2012 (n 318) para 1556.

902 O'Sullivan (n 861) para 18.3.

903 *Ibid.*

904 Kimel 2003 (n 542); Fried (n 541) 142; *Restatement (Second) of Contracts* §347 (1981).

905 Donald Harris, David Campbell and Roger Halson, *Remedies for Breach of Contract* (2nd edn, Cambridge University Press 2002); see the English case *British Westinghouse Electric and Manufacturing Co Ltd v Underground Electric Rlys Co of London Ltd* [1912] AC 673; see s 6.5 for the impact of a duty to mitigate.

138. Based on these arguments, it is said that a promisee should be equally entitled to claim for damages and enforced performance of an obligation to do or convey something.[906] In view of this, the courts in England and the United States have shown a tendency to move away from the 'adequacy of damages test' to an assessment of the appropriateness of enforced performance.[907] Put differently, enforced performance is available where goods are unique or ascertained, 'or in other proper circumstances'.[908] In this respect reference is made by the Singapore court to the English case *Argyll v Waddell* (1997), where the English House of Lords did not show any willingness to veer from the underlying principles of the adequacy test, and[909] the English case *Rainbow Estates v Tokenhold* (1999) where a more relaxed approach was shown.[910] From the perspective of a broader availability, enforced performance of a delivery obligation of generic goods could be ordered where the buyer cannot obtain substitute goods from another source (*e.g.* in instances where 'the petroleum market is in an unusual state in which a would-be buyer cannot go out into the market and contract with another seller, possibly at some sacrifice to the price').[911] In view of the foregoing, it may even be said that enforced performance is becoming the default remedy in certain situations.[912] As a consequence, the gap between the Anglo-American approach and the civil law tradition is starting to narrow.[913] It appears, however, that Singapore courts do not necessarily follow the trend in English and American case law of extending the availability of enforced performance because such a judicial order is still firmly believed to be an extensive interference with the liberty of the promisor.[914] The Singapore Court of Appeal reinforces this notion in *Chuan Hong Petrol Station Pte Ltd v Shell Singapore (Pte) Ltd.*[915] However, in this case, it was also considered by the court that the principle as mentioned above did not apply to an operating licence which entailed the obligations to conform to the rules and regulations of Shell because this was, in essence, a commercial contract between two independent contractors.[916] That being said, the key

906 O'Sullivan (n 861).

907 See the English cases *Bewick v Beswick* (818); *Tito v Waddell* (No 2) [1977] Ch 106 [1977] 3 All ER 129; Uniform Commercial Code (US) s 2-716(1); Treitel 1998 (n 55) para 63.

908 Treitel 1998 (n 55) para 63.

909 *Co-operative Insurance Society Ltd v Argyll Stores (Holdings) Ltd* [1998] AC 1, (1997) 3 All ER 297.

910 [1999] Ch 64, (1998) 2 All ER 860; See also *Beswick v Beswick* (nr 818) AC 58 at 88, 102; Treitel 1998 (n 55) para 63.

911 See the English case *Sky Petroleum Ltd v V.I.P. Petroleum Ltd* [1974] 1 WLR 576; Treitel 1998 (n 55) para 63.

912 Cohen and McKendrick (n 4) 232.

913 Cohen and McKendrick (n 4) 232.

914 Phang et al 2012 (n 112) para 23.080; *Lee Chee Wei* 2007 (n 591) SLR(R) 537 [52], [53]; O'Sullivan (n 861) paras 18.49, 18.50; See the English cases *Cud v Rutter* [1720] 1 P Wms 570, 24 E.R. 521; *Wilson v Northampton and Banbury Junction Rly Co* [1874] 9 Ch App 279 at 284; *Bankers Trust Co v PT Jakarta International Hotels & Development* [1999] 1 Lloyds's Rep 910 at 915; See also Dori Kimel 'Remedial Rights and Substantive Rights in Contract Law' (2002) 8 Legal Theory 313; Kimel 2003 (n 542).

915 *Chuan Hong Petrol Station Pte Ltd v Shell Singapore (Pte) Ltd* [1992] SGCA 35 [72], [75], (1992) 2 SLR(R) 1.

916 *Ibid.*

point is that, regardless the nature of the agreed performance and terms of the contract, it is at the discretion of a Singapore court to allow or deny a claim for enforced performance.

139. The notion of the concept of enforced performance described above, is also visible in the Singapore Court of Appeal case *Ng Lay Choo Marion v Lok Lai Oi* where it was held that the general threshold regarding whether damages are adequate is a fundamental element of the assessment of the court whether it is just and equitable to award a claim for enforced performance of a contract of sales.[917] The Singapore Court of Appeal case *Meng Leong Development Pte Ltd v Jip Hong Trading Co Pte Ltd* provides a clear example of the interpretation of Singapore courts of the adequacy of damages principle in view of protection of the buyer's performance interest.[918] It was considered by the court that an order for damages would have taken away the rights of the buyer's superior proprietary (*i.e.* ownership) rights in favour of the third parties involved and, therefore, the equities were assessed to be in the purchaser's favour, which meant that an order for enforced performance of the agreement was the most appropriate remedy.[919] The Singapore High Court case *Yeoh Wee Liat v Wong Lock Chee and another suit* offers another view on the assessment as to whether damages are an adequate remedy and the weight attached to the interest of the buyer in the actual performance of the contract.[920] In this case, the defendant did not fulfil its obligation to effect the necessary transfer of shares to the plaintiffs. The latter brought an action to court for enforced performance. The court considered that parties concluded an agreement for the two plaintiffs to hold 33% of the shares and the defendant the remaining 34%, which meant that parties had contracted to have nearly equal stakes, such that not one party would be the dominant shareholder, and not to be minority shareholders powerless to oppose a majority shareholder. Therefore, the court concluded that damages would not be an adequate remedy.[921]

140. Despite the considerations above, damages remain the preferred remedy in the realm of commercial sales. The favourable look on the appropriateness of a monetary remedy coincide with the argument that the purpose of contracting is to allocate future risks.[922] This consideration also operate alongside the 'harm principle',[923] which entails the idea that a *breach of promise* and a *breach of contract* should be distinguished.[924] The former

---

917 [1995] SGCA 67 [16], (1995) 3 SLR(R) 77; Phang et al 2012 (n 112) para 23.119.

918 *Meng Leong Development Pte Ltd v Jip Hong Trading Co Pte Ltd* (n 617).

919 *Meng Leong Development Pte Ltd v Jip Hong Trading Co Pte Ltd* (n 617) SGCA 24 [17].

920 *Yeoh Wee Liat v Wong Lock Chee and another suit* [2013] SGHC 153, (2013) 4 SLR 508.

921 *Yeoh Wee Liat v Wong Lock Chee and another suit* (n 920) SGHC 153 [54].

922 Fried (n 541) 142; Kimel 2002 (n 914); Kimel 2003 (n 542).

923 See the explanation of John Stuart's harm principle in Kimel 2003 (n 542).

924 C MacMillian, 'From Promise to Contract: towards a liberal theory of contract' (2004) 15(1) King's Law Journal 202; Kimel 2003 (n 542).

leads to abused trust and personal insult and the latter merely to a loss of benefits, which can be restored by (expectation) damages and only when the monetary hurt is not restored, enforced performance can be awarded.[925] From this perspective and simply put, it is understandable that in common law a contract can be breached on the basis that there is a better bargain available because the harm can be restored through substitute damages.[926] It seems, however, that the main reasons for Singapore courts to stick to the view that damages are the preferred remedy, is that the courts are reluctant to actually interfere with the liberty of a person to act or not to act if substitute damages could also cure the failed performance and because ignoring an order for enforced performance of a non-monetary obligation could lead to harsh measures, such as penal sanctions and imprisonment.[927]

141. A Singapore court may grant an order for enforced performance if the subject matter of a contract has a unique and intrinsic value. These elements must be assessed from the viewpoint of the purchaser claiming for enforced performance. In this vein, it was adjudicated by the Singapore High Court in *Lee Chee Wei v Tan Hor Peow Victor and Others* that in the case of shares of a private limited company the vendor's interest are strictly monetary (that is, payment of the purchase price) and, therefore, it would not be appropriate to provide an order for enforced performance of the sales contract in favour of the vendor of such shares.[928] Concerning the sale of real estate, the principle applied that no two pieces of land are the same and, therefore, it was axiomatic that the subject matter was unique and of intrinsic value to the buyer.[929] In *Tay Ah Poon and another v Chionh Hai Guan and another*, the Court of Appeal confirmed this principle by stipulating that a claim for enforced performance is almost invariably granted when seeking to enforce contracts for the purchase and sale of land, since the purchaser is entitled to get the very parcel bargained for and not to be forced to take an inexact substitute.[930]

142. In recent years, Singapore courts have considered that all circumstances are relevant in determining whether a claim for enforced performance should be awarded. This new

---

925 Macmillian (n 924) 205; Kimel 2003 (n 542); E Allan Farnsworth, 'Legal Remedies for Breach of Contract' (1970) 70 Columbia Law Review 1145; Charles Goetz and Robert Scott, 'Enforcing Promises: An Examination of the Basis of Contract' (1980) 80 Yale Law Journal 1261; See also for the preference for expectations damages Seana Valentine Shiffrin, 'The Divergence of Contract and Promise' (2007) 120 Harvard Law Review 708.

926 This is a reflection of the doctrine of 'economic breach'. According to economics, this doctrine shows that the common law entails more a hybrid of practical principles than morality; Macmillian (n 924) 206; Kimel 2003 (n 542); Fried (n 541) 143.

927 Dora Neo, 'Specific Remedies and the Performance Interest in Singapore Contract Law' in Chen-Wishart, Loke and Ong 2016 (n 156) 201; Shenoy and Loo 2013 (n 13) para 18.87.

928 *Lee Chee Wei v Tan Hor Peow Victor* [2006] SGHC 116 [9].

929 Halsbury's Laws of Singapore (Contract) vol 7 para 80.595.

930 *Tay Ah Poon and another v Chionh Hai Guan and another* (n 589).

approach has been adopted in a case where two parties claimed enforced performance of a contract of sale of a property which was based on an option to purchase the property.[931] The court considered that all the relevant facts and circumstances of the case should be taken into account to assess whether the party claiming for enforced performance had intended to buy the land for investment or for other reasons. In this case, the Singapore High Court refused a claim for enforced performance of a contract of sale of a property as the seller only had a financial interest in the subsequent execution of the sale of the premises.[932] In a similar vein, in *Lim Beng Cheng v Lim Ngee Sing* the Singapore High Court considered that damages were an adequate remedy as the plaintiff's interest in the property was primarily monetary in the form of an investment, the latter was, at some point, prepared to accept monetary compensation if it was right, and the property was also not a particularly unique piece of property.[933] In this case, the English common law default consideration that two pieces of land are not alike and damages do not provide the aggrieved party with an adequate remedy, did not apply.[934] However, a strict monetary interest in the initial performance of the contract does not necessarily rule out an order for enforced performance.[935] For example, in *Lee Chee Wei v Tan Hor Peow Victor* the court dealt with a failure in performance of a sale of shares of an unlisted company.[936] The court considered that a contractual promise to sell shares in an unlisted company could be specifically enforced because these shares are limited in number and not always available in the open market. Nonetheless, the court made use of its discretionary power to assess whether it would be just and appropriate to enforce performance of the contract.[937] In addition, the court considered that a claim for enforced performance would be impractical and required supervision of the court.[938] Based on these circumstances, the court denied the claim for enforced performance and ordered payment of nominal damages instead. The limitations of impracticality and constant supervision are further discussed in chapter 6. Other limiting aspects can also be taken into account. For example, the courts may consider the traditional common law concept of mutuality, which entails the principle that the court will not compel a defendant to perform its obligations specifically if it cannot at the same time ensure that any unperformed obligations of the plaintiff will be specifically performed, unless damages would be an adequate remedy to the defendant for any default on the

931 *EC Investment Holding Pte Ltd v Ridout Residence Pte Ltd & Anor (Orion Oil Limited & Anor, Interveners)* [2010] SGHC 270.

932 *New Dennis Arthur & Anor v Greesh Ghai Monty & Anor* [2012] SGHC 122; Singapore Academy of Law Annual Review of Singapore Cases (n 120) 12.136 *ff.*

933 *Lim Beng Cheng* (n 615) SGHC 282 [105], [107]-[110].

934 *New Dennis Arthur & Anor v Greesh Ghai Monty & Anor* (n 932).

935 *Lee Chee Wei* 2007 (n 591) SGCA 22 [54].

936 *Ibid.*

937 *Lee Chee Wei* 2007 (n 591) SGCA 22 [55].

938 *Lee Chee Wei* 2007 (n 591) SGCA 22 [56].

plaintiff's part.[939] The requirement of mutuality should be assessed in light of the requirement of reciprocity as set out in the Singapore case *Indulge Food Pte Ltd Torabi Marashi Bahram* [123]. In this case, the Singapore High Court reiterated the principle that enforcement of non-monetary obligations cannot be enforced when the claimant did not, cannot, or will not, render its own performance owed under the contract.[940]

143. An essential factor of the adequacy test is whether the subject matter is unique in the sense that there is no substitute performance available.[941] Thus, when answering the question as to whether enforced performance is available for sales contracts, it has to be assessed whether procurement of substitute goods is practically obtainable.[942] For example, a subsidiary of a Japanese construction company brought a claim to court against a sub-contractor with its principal business in Australia for enforced performance of the obligation to deliver building materials on site for the construction of several apartment blocks in Singapore. A part of the agreed price for these materials was paid in advance of delivery. Nonetheless, the sub-contractor refused to deliver the containers with the material which had already been paid for. It was held by the court that the non-delivery was unjustified and that the materials probably had no market value because the goods manufactured by the sub-contractor were specifically made for the project. Taking this into consideration, the court provided an order for enforced delivery of the containers with the materials at the worksite.[943]

144. The qualification of specific and ascertained goods requires some extra attention since this is one of the main thresholds for awarding a claim for enforced performance of a non-monetary promise under the Singapore Sale of Goods Act. Difficulties may arise, for example, in the earlier described situation of bulk goods.[944] In short, a sales contract with bulk goods may be subject to a claim for enforced performance if the agreement is clear about the quantity and other specifics of the goods.[945] For example, the sale of 500 metric tonnes of organically produced jasmine rice which is a part of a bulk of 2000 metric tonnes. It is, however, unclear as to whether the jasmine rice should be existing at the time of

---

939 *Co-operative Insurance Society* (n 909); *Price v Strange* [1978] Ch 337 [367-368]; Phang et al 2012 (n 112) para 23.136; Dora Neo, 'Specific Remedies and the Performance Interest in Singapore Contract Law' in Chen-Wishart, Loke and Ong 2016 (n 156) 206.

940 N 909; Dora Neo, 'Specific Remedies and the Performance Interest in Singapore Contract Law' in Chen-Wishart, Loke and Ong 2016 (n 156) 206.

941 Halsbury's Laws of Singapore (Contract 2016) vol 7, para 80.586; Hunter 2017 (n 7) para 8.18, 8.19.

942 SGA, s 52; Phang et al 2012 (n 112) para 23.109; Halsbury's Laws of Singapore (Contract 2016) vol 7, para 80.596; Hunter 2017 (n 7) para 4.3.

943 *Kajima Overseas Asia Pte Ltd v Glenn Industries Pty Ltd* [1997] SGHC 11.

944 S 3.3.

945 Hunter 2017 (n 7) para 4.4.

conclusion of the contract in order to be defined as specific goods.[946] This touches on the question of whether future goods could be subject to a claim for enforced performance. In *Simgood v MLC Shipbuilding* (2015) the Singapore High Court awarded a claim for enforced performance of a contractual promise to construct and deliver a vessel pursuant to section 52(1) of the Sale of Goods Act, which stipulates that in any action for breach of contract to deliver specific or ascertained goods, the court has the power, on the plaintiff's application, to provide an order for enforced performance of the contract, without giving the defendant the option of retaining the goods on payment of damages.[947] In order to provide an order for enforced performance, the court had to assess whether the thing sold was specific or ascertained. In accordance with section 61(1) of the Singapore Sales of Goods Act, the court considered that goods might only be qualified as specific if they exist at the moment parties concluded the contract. As the vessel was not in existence at the moment parties entered into the contract, the thing sold could not be qualified as a specific good. Nonetheless, the court assessed that the contracting parties had identified the vessel, without any doubt, as the thing sold under the contract and, therefore, the vessel was ascertained, which in turn, provided the court with the statutory power to award the claim for enforced performance of the contract. Thus, even if the things sold cannot be qualified as specific, the court remains entitled to award a claim for enforced performance of a non-monetary promise if contracting parties can identify the goods as the things to be delivered at a later stage. This could occur, for example, if the goods sold are still under construction.

145. In assessing whether the claim for enforced performance of the obligation to construct and deliver the ship should be allowed, it was also considered whether it would be just and fair in all circumstances for the court to exercise its equitable power to award enforced performance instead of damages. In this regard, it was also taken into account as to whether the thing sold was unique to the aggrieved party,[948] if the thing sold was needed for immediate use and if contingency plans were made for the use of other ships, whether it would be difficult for the aggrieved party to establish the purchase price and if the seller would be able to pay any damages awarded by the court. In this respect, the court held that a claim for damages is unlikely to be awarded if this would result in the insolvency of the seller because this would benefit the buyer over the other promisees.

146. The discretion of the court also entails the right to provide an order for enforced performance of the contract under a variation of the conditions as agreed by parties. In

---

946 Chong et al 2016 (n 125) para 10.2.10.

947 [2015] SGHC 303.

948 Halsbury's Laws of Singapore (Commercial Law 2014) vol 5(2) para 60.221.

Lee Cheng Kang and another v Lee Tian Kai, the Singapore Court of Appeal dealt with a case where an allegedly naïve seller sold his share in a property for less than the market price under the influence of his nephew, who was a real estate agent.[949] This situation entitled the court to provide an order for enforced performance under a different consideration than stipulated by parties (the agreed price).[950] That is, the buyers were ordered to pay the market value of the shares in the property based on an average of three values.[951] In the Singapore Court of Appeal case *Ng Lay Choo Marion v Lok Lai Oi* the court first established that it could not see any ground for denying the aggrieved party an order for enforced performance of the contract. Preceding this assessment, the court stated that it was relevant to consider what terms should be imposed in order to do justice to the parties.[952] This meant that the respondent was ordered to transfer the apartment in question on the terms that the appellant had to make payments on the loan and interests.[953]

147. Although the above considerations may imply that enforcement of the seller's delivery obligation is only available when the goods are deemed specific or ascertained and damages do not provide the aggrieved buyer with an adequate remedy, the Supreme Court of Judicature Act of Singapore states that the High Court has the power to grant all reliefs and remedies at law and in equity, including specific performance.[954] This suggests that Singapore courts retain the discretionay power to issue an order for enforced performance outside the Sale of Goods Act when justified by the particularities of the contract rendering damages an inadequate remedy.[955] For example, when the goods are ordinary articles of commerce with no special value or interest, but due to global trade war substitute goods are obtainable on the market only with great difficulty, if at all.[956] In this situation, damages are not an adequate remedy when the court establishes that non-delivery of the supplies impels the buyer towards insolvency, because the latter is not able to fulfil the outstanding purchase orders. This consideration should be viewed in light of the usage of the instrument of mandatory injunctions to specifically order the promisor to do what it had promised under the contract, even though the obligation cannot be enforced under the Sale of Goods

949 [1996] SGCA 4, (1996) 1 SLR(R) 87.

950 *Lee Cheng Kang and another v Lee Tian Kai* (n 949) SGCA 4 [24, 25].

951 *Lee Cheng Kang and another v Lee Tian Kai* (n 949) SGCA 4 [23].

952 *Ng Lay Choo Marion* (n 917) SGCA 67 [21].

953 *Ibid.*

954 Supreme Court Judicature Act (Cap 322, 2007 Ed) s 18(2), Sch 1 para 14 (as amended by the Supreme Court of Judicature (Amendment) Act (No 16/1993)).

955 Phang et al 2012 (n 112), para 23.119.

956 *Howard E Perry v British Rly Board* [1980] 1 WLR 1375 [1382-1383]; Phang et al 2012 (n 112), para 23.119.

Act because the goods are not specific or ascertained to the contract.[957] This way of protecting the parties' performance interest is described in more detail below.

148. In *Sky Petroleum Ltd v VIP Petroleum Ltd*, the buyer agreed to purchase at a fixed price its entire order (with a minimum annual quantity) of petrol and diesel fuel for its filling stations for the next ten years.[958] During the 1973 oil crisis, the seller terminated the contract and the buyer brought an action to court to restrain the seller from withholding its supplies. The court held that an injunction, under the circumstances would essentially be an order of specific performance of the contract to sell, which would normally be refused on the basis that damages would be sufficient. However, in the rare situation where the defendant was the only supplier and the only method which would enable the plaintiff to carry on their business, an interim mandatory injunction would be granted as damages would no longer be a sufficient remedy. Interestingly, the subject matter could not be qualified as specific or ascertained goods, but an indirect award for enforced performance in the form of an interim mandatory injunction was justified on the basis that it was uncertain as to whether the claimant could obtain an alternative supply.[959] This shows the far-reaching power of the courts to grand enforced performance by indirect means in cases where such an order normally is not available (unascertained goods). However, the availability of enforced performance outside the ambit of the Sale of Goods Act should not be overestimated due to various common law counter-exceptions, such as difficulty of supervision and want of mutuality.[960] It must also be mentioned that the contract in *Sky Petroleum Ltd v VIP Petroleum Ltd* did not qualify as a contract for the sale of goods, but it involved a long-term supply contract under which successive sales would arise if orders were placed and accepted.[961] Nonetheless, contracting parties should be aware of the discretionary power of the courts to issue a mandatory injunction in relation to contracts for the sale of goods which are neither specific nor ascertained.[962]

149. The aforementioned availability of a mandatory injunction order as an indirect form of the common law remedy of 'specific performance' (*i.e.* enforcement of non-monetary obligations to bring about a certain state of affairs) should be distinguished from a

957 Dora Neo, 'Specific Remedies and the Performance Interest in Singapore Contract Law' in Chen-Wishart, Loke and Ong 2016 (n 156) 193; Phang et al 2012 (n 112), para 23.119.

958 *Sky Petroleum Ltd* (n 911).

959 *Sky Petroleum Ltd* (n 911); Halsbury's Laws of Singapore (Contract 2016) vol 7 para 80.596; Anson's Law of Contract (n 360) 616. See also the English case *Metropolitan Electric Supply Co Ltd v Ginder* [1901] 2 Ch 799.

960 Dora Neo, 'Specific Remedies and the Performance Interest in Singapore Contract Law' in Chen-Wishart, Loke and Ong 2016 (n 156) 206; Phang et al 2012 (n 112), para 23.136.

961 Phang et al 2012 (n 112), para 23.119, footnote 246.

962 *Gatekeeper Inc v Wang Wensheng (t/a Hawkeye Technologies)* [2011] SGHC 239.

prohibitory injunction order.[963] This instrument may be used to order the promisor not to do something.[964] For example, an injunction to restrain the supplier to sell its products to other distributors in a certain territory. However, in situations where enforcement of a prohibitory injunction would come close to the common remedy of 'specific performance' Singapore courts, generally, will refuse such an order.[965]

Another interesting point in this context is that Singapore courts may consider an interim mandatory injunction as in indirect enforcement measure when there is a serious question to be tried with a real prospect of success, damages are inadequate and the risk of injustice to the promisee if the injunction were not granted is greater than the risk of injustice to the other party if the injunction were granted.[966] On whether there is a distinction between interim mandatory injunctions and prohibitory injunctions, the Singapore Court of Appeal held that the courts generally require a higher degree of assurance before they are willing to grant interim mandatory injunctions as opposed to interim prohibitory injunctions.[967] However, the Court held that this was "no more than a generalisation, albeit a useful one, of what courts normally do".[968]

4.4.4 Mixed approaches in China

150. The contract law of China stipulates that if a party fails to perform its non-monetary contractual obligations, it may be ordered, amongst other things, to continue to perform the contract.[969] It appears that the term 'enforced performance' is similar to the meaning of the term 'continues to perform'.[970] The aggrieved party to a commercial sale is generally

963 Dora Neo, 'Specific Remedies and the Performance Interest in Singapore Contract Law' in Chen-Wishart, Loke and Ong 2016 (n 156) 207, 208; Anson's Law of Contract (n 360) 615-619.

964 Dora Neo, 'Specific Remedies and the Performance Interest in Singapore Contract Law' in Chen-Wishart, Loke and Ong 2016 (n 156) 207; Anson's Law of Contract (n 360) 615.

965 Phang et al 2012 (n 112), para 23.174; Phang and Goh 2012 (n 318) para 1566; Dora Neo, 'Specific Remedies and the Performance Interest in Singapore Contract Law' in Chen-Wishart, Loke and Ong 2016 (n 156) 207, 208, 214; *Pub 1997 Pte Ltd v Scorpion [1994] 1 SLR(R) 437* [20]-[21], [25]; *Tomongo Shipping Co Ltd v Heng Holdings SEA (Pte) Ltd [*1997] 1 SLR(R) 263 (SGHC); *Chua Kwok Fun Kevin and another v Etons Management Consultants Pte Ltd and others* [1999] SGHC 84, (1999) 1 SLR(R) 1088 [956]; *Chuan Hong Petrol Station Pte Ltd v Shell Singapore (Pte) Ltd* (n 915) SGCA 35 [69].

966 *Singapore Press Holdings Ltd v Brown Noel Trading Pte Ltd and others* [1994] 3 SLR(R) 114; *American Cynamid Co. v Ethicon Ltd* [1975] AC 396.

967 *Chuan Hong Petrol Station v Shell Singapore Pte Ltd* (n 915).

968 *Ibid.*

969 Art 107 CCL.

970 Chen Lihu and Zhu Ping, 'On the Actual Performance System in International Contract Law' (2008) iss 1 Present-day Law Science 94 (陈立虎，朱萍．国际合同法上的实际履行制度研究．时代法学); Tan Ling, 'Actual Performance Responsibility and its Legal Application' (2000) 5 Modern Law 85 (谭玲．实际履行责任及其法律适用[J]. 现代法学); Zheng and Lei (n 646).

entitled to enforced performance, unless one of the statutory exemptions apply.[971] There are three main observations that need to be addressed in that regard. First, the contract law of China adopted the general structure of the PICC for actions to obtain performance of non-monetary obligations. This approach resulted in merging civil and common law principles. This means in effect that the contract law of China establishes the right to enforced performance in line with the civil law structure but then directly limits this right by means of various statutory limitations, which more resembles the common law approach. Second, the contract law of China embraces the common law approach in the sense that enforced performance is available if a party fails to perform its contractual obligations.[972] However, the systems are not identical as Chinese contract law does not confine the right to enforced performance of non-monetary obligations under commercial sales contracts to specific situations. By contrast, Chinese contract law has adopted the civil law distinction between a failure in performance of any obligation, and a failure to deliver in accordance with the agreed quality. In the case of the latter, the aggrieved party is entitled to claim repair and replacement, provided that the statutory requirements are fulfilled.[973] Lastly, the contract law of China comprises a statutory right to enforced performance of a non-monetary obligation where one party expresses explicitly or indicates by its conduct that it will not perform its obligations under a contract (*yugi huiye*).[974] The right to require performance in instances of a prospective failure in performance is based on the common law concept of anticipatory breach. The latter allows the aggrieved party to terminate the contract if, prior to the agreed date for performance, the other party repudiates the contract.[975]

151. A sales contract which is subject to the contract law of China entails by law transfer of the ownership of the goods on their delivery,[976] to deliver the goods within the time limit and place agreed,[977] and delivery in accordance with the agreed quality.[978] If a party fails to perform one of these obligations, it could be ordered by the court to perform its obligations or to take remedial measures.[979] The right to claim continuance of performance is also qualified as enforced performance and, in light of common law terms, as a remedial right or the broadly known term 'specific performance'.[980] The approach as mentioned

971 Art 110 CCL.
972 Art 107 CCL.
973 Art 111 CCL.
974 Art 108 CCL; Bing Ling 2002 (n 229) para 8.022; Zhang 2006 (n 41) 294.
975 Art 94(2) CCL; Bing Ling 2002 (n 229) paras 8.017–8.022; Zhang 2006 (n 41) 294.
976 Art 133 CCL.
977 Arts 136, 138, 141 CCL.
978 Art 155 CCL.
979 Art 107 CCL.
980 Chen-Wishart, Loke and Ong 2016 (n 156) 19.

above is similar to the view taken by the General Principles of Civil Law, which also provides an aggrieved party with a right to demand enforced performance.[981] Compared to the earlier mentioned ECL it is said that the principles of the contract law of China are a great step forward because the latter have introduced a number of restrictions on the right to claim enforced performance, albeit it is held that the scope of application is still too broad and[982] that the remaining emphasis on enforced performance of the contract hinders the economic development of China.[983] In this respect, it is argued that in the current market economy contracting parties should be encouraged by the law to focus on efficiency and to require compensation of the monetary benefits of a contract in the case of a failed performance, especially when there are alternatives readily available on the market.[984] However, the statutory maximum limit on damages suggests that enforced performance of a contractual obligation remains the preferred option.[985] Moreover, it is frequently repeated in case law that contracts should be performed.[986]

152. A court order for enforced performance of the contract means in effect that the aggrieved party is entitled to request the court to enforce the defaulting party to fulfil its contractual obligations. It is held that this right enables the aggrieved party to achieve the purpose of the contract,[987] and to do justice to the integrity of social life.[988] It is held that, on the face of it, an order for enforced performance would result in the fulfilment of the initial contractual obligations, because the scope of the obligations of the promisor remains unchanged.[989] In other words, the burden placed on the non-performing party by the contract does not increase and, therefore, it could be said to make promisees indifferent.[990] In view of the above, it is held that a claim for enforced performance does not arise from (the liability for) the non-performance, but from the act of promise making and, therefore, performance of a court order for enforced performance does not differ in nature from the results if, from the outset, the contract was correctly performed.[991] From this perspective

981 Art 111 GPCL.
982 Zheng and Lei (n 646).
983 Art 110 CCL; Zheng and Lei (n 646).
984 Zheng and Lei (n 646).
985 Art 113 CCL stipulates that the amount of damages shall be equivalent to the losses caused by the non-performance, but shall not exceed the amount that may be foreseen as a result of a failure in performance.
986 *E.g., Daqing Kaiming Wind Power Tower Manufacturing Co Ltd v Huarui Wind Power Technology (Group) Co Ltd* [2015] SPC Gazette 2015, issue 11.
987 Zheng and Lei (n 646).
988 Lu Chen, 'Specific Performance and Its Limits' (2007) iss 4 Journal of Comparative Law 98 (芦谌, . 履行请求权及其界限.比较法研究. 2007年. 期号 4. 页码 98).
989 Chen (Lihu) and Zhu (n 970).
990 Ye Changfu, 'On Judgment and Choice of the Value of Specific Performance of Contract' (2005) iss 2 Modern Law Science Xiandai Faxue 152 (叶昌富. 论强制实际履行合同中的价值判断与选择. 现代法学. 2005 年. 期号 2. 页码 152).
991 *Ibid.*

a claim for the continuance of performance is not regarded as a remedy for non-performance, but merely a right which arises from the act of concluding a contract.[992]

153. However, it is also argued that the fulfilment of a court order for enforced performance is different in nature compared to voluntary performance because the former takes place after the expiry of the agreed time for performance and thus amounting to a non-performance (negative behaviour), and interference of the coercive power of the state is required.[993] Based on this reasoning it is held that the right to claim enforced performance is a remedy deriving from the *civil liability* for the incorrect performance of a contractual promise.[994] The mandatory character of the statutory right to require performance of a contractual obligation is said to be reflected in the principle that payment of the incurred damages does not deprive the aggrieved party of its right to claim enforced performance.[995] These considerations are in line with the wordings of the provisions of the contract law of China, which clearly indicate that an aggrieved party to a contract is entitled to claim continuance of performance in the event the contract is not properly performed.[996] The strong emphasis on the right to performance of a contract is also reflected in the statutory principle that if the buyer is burdened with the risk of damages or loss of the goods, the right to claim enforced performance is not affected.[997] All told, however, an act of termination of the contract or an action to obtain other remedies is regarded as an implied waiver of the promisee of its right to claim enforced performance.[998] Based on the obligation of the promisee to act in good faith (section 4.5) it is also held that a change in circumstances and a failure in performance by the promisee to mitigate its losses, could limit the availability to claim enforced performance of the contract.[999] The relation between the obligation to mitigate losses and the right to claim enforced performance of a contract is discussed in section 6.5. Apart from the effect of the obligation to mitigate losses, contractual promises based on personal trust and confidence (a distinct form of the earlier mentioned barrier

992 Chen (Lihu) and Zhu (n 970); Wang Liming, *Breach of Contract Theory* (China University of Political Science and Law Press 2003) 430; Ye (n 990).

993 Chen (Lihu) and Zhu (n 970).

994 *Ibid.*

995 *Ibid.*

996 Lei Chen, 'Availability of Specific Remedies in Chinese Contract Law' in Chen-Wishart, Loke and Ong 2016 (n 156) 34.

997 Art 149 CCL.

998 Bing Ling 2002 (n 229) para 8.077; Han Shiyuan, 'The Performance Interest in Chinese Contract Law: Monetary Damages' in Chen-Wishart, Loke and Ong 2016 (n 156) 41.

999 Lei Chen, 'Availablity of Specific Remedies in Chinese Contract Law' in Chen-Wishart, Loke and Ong 2016 (n 156) 31; a more elaborate discussion about the relation between the right to actual performance and the duty to mitigate losses is presented in s 6.5.

of unsuitability), such as partnerships, are also said to restrict the ability to obtain the actual performance unless the obligations of contracting parties can be explicitly defined.[1000]

154. In addition to the arguments mentioned above, which show a strong preference for enforced performance as the primary remedy, it is argued that adoption of the common law preference for damages and, thus, abandonment of the primary right to enforced performance, would diminish the social benefits of the market economy in China (which are designed to, *i.a.*, increase employment opportunities).[1001] Furthermore, it is held that acceptance of the common law view that a contract merely represents a monetary bargain would be tantamount to a denial of the bindingness of a contractual promise and the protective nature of the contract law of China, in the sense that it is said to protect society against parties who engage in business activities, without any consideration of the interests of the other party.[1002]

4.4.5 Conclusions

155. The current divergence of views between the three jurisdictions can be traced back to their fundamental notions of the bindingness of a contractual promise and their perspective on the appropriate means to protect the interests in performance of contracting parties. The present section reveals in this regard that Dutch and Chinese contract law qualify enforced performance of non-monetary obligations as a right of contracting parties. By contrast, the contract law of Singapore adheres to the common law approach which deals with enforced performance of non-monetary obligations as a remedy. Consequently, Dutch and Chinese contract law act on the overarching principle that commercial parties are, by default, entitled to enforced performance of a non-monetary obligation, whereas the contract law of Singapore takes the view that the availability of enforced performance depends on the extent an infringement of the interest of the aggrieved party can be remedied by damages. In the realm of commercial sales, the assessment to be made also entails the question whether the goods are specific or ascertained. However, the considerations above reveal that Singapore courts may issue an order for enforced performance of goods which do not qualify as specific or ascertained to the contract and fall outside the ambit of the Sale of Goods Act. The discussed case law demonstrates that the courts may grant an order to enforced performance of the delivery of generic goods when substitute goods are only obtainable on the market with great difficulty. The remedy of a (interim) mandatory

1000 Bing Ling 2002 (n 229) para 8.074 ; Lei Chen, 'Availablity of Specific Remedies in Chinese Contract Law' in Chen-Wishart, Loke and Ong 2016 (n 156) 29.

1001 Ye Changfu 2005 (n 990).

1002 *Ibid.*

injunction can be used to achieve this result (*i.e.* to compel the positive performance of a contractual obligation), but this option is only available in very specific circumstances. Thus, it may be said that the buyer's contractual right to delivery of the stipulated goods is only protected in exceptional situations. Another approach is that the default remedy available for enforcement of the seller's delivery obligation (*i.e.* damages) does not reflect the nature of this obligation (*i.e.* non-monetary positive performance obligation to bring about a certain state of affairs). Nonetheless, on an overall assessment of the discussed viewpoints, it appears that the disagreement between the investigated jurisdictions is rooted in the central issue of whether a judicial award for enforced performance provides the most desirable relief in view of the subjective interests of the contracting parties and the factual situation. It is, however, not possible to provide a general statement as to the availability of enforced performance in the realm of commercial sales contracts other than the overarching notion that the desirability and adequacy of the measure is related to the nature of the subject matter. This is because the discussed legal developments demonstrate a significant degree of willingness of the national courts to re-examine their views on the extent to which enforced performance should be available. Special mention must be made here of the Dutch case Dahn Vo, the fact that enforced performance of a non-monetary obligation under a commercial sales contract is not confined to the narrow approach found in the sales law of Singapore and the flexibility of the rules on enforced performance under the contract law of China.

156. That having been said, the default availability of enforced performance of non-monetary obligations under the contract law of the Netherlands and China runs counter to the frequently advanced argument that commercial parties merely contract for economic reasons. On the other hand, the preference for damages in the contract law of Singapore given the dynamics of international trade, also do not appear to necessarily provide a satisfactory solution for commercial sales transactions. This is because, generally speaking, it is difficult to determine the exact monetary damages suffered by the aggrieved party. This holds especially true for the monetary investment in finding suitable substitutes, the additional costs arising from the negotiations of the terms of the transaction of substitute goods and the calculation of the potential costs of returning defective goods (*e.g.* in the case the port of destination lies in a developing country). Due to the complexities of international trade, the costs mentioned above are generally higher in comparison to standard domestic sales transactions. It is, therefore, submitted here that a court order for enforced performance of a non-monetary obligation is most appropriate for cross-border sales transactions as it will most likely provide full relief to the aggrieved party and, thus, make the promisee indifferent as to performance or legal relief. That said, when a significant monetary investment is required for the fulfilment of a court order for enforced performance, the interest of the non-performing party should not be ignored. This situation

typically occurs where a non-performing seller is required to deliver replacement goods. On top of the cost of providing a replacement, the seller is also exposed to the financial burden of reselling the goods if the latter is not able to find another buyer due to, for example, regulations of the port of destination or the perishable nature of the goods. Nevertheless, the financial burden could also be seen as a part of the responsibility of the seller for its non-performance.

157. It appears that the unification instruments attempt to balance the above-discussed right *versus* remedy approach by theoretically labelling enforced performance of non-monetary obligations as a right of contracting parties, although the legal instruments to obtain a judicial order for enforcement are dealt with as a remedy for a failure in performance.[1003] In practice, Dutch and Chinese contract law act on the same notion, as a claim for enforced performance only brings about a judicial confirmation of the right to performance where the obligation is not yet due. Furthermore, the understanding of enforced performance as a default right of contracting parties in a commercial context is in both jurisdictions counterbalanced by considerations of sufficient interest and good faith.[1004] See the illustration below for a simplified overview of the practical impact of the discussed principles.

1003 Art 46 CISG; Art 7.2.2 PICC; Art 9:102 PECL; Art III.–3:302 DCFR; Art 7 Draft Articles on Non-Performance PACL.

1004 S 4.2.

Figure 13 Operative effect of the rules on enforced performance of non-monetary obligations

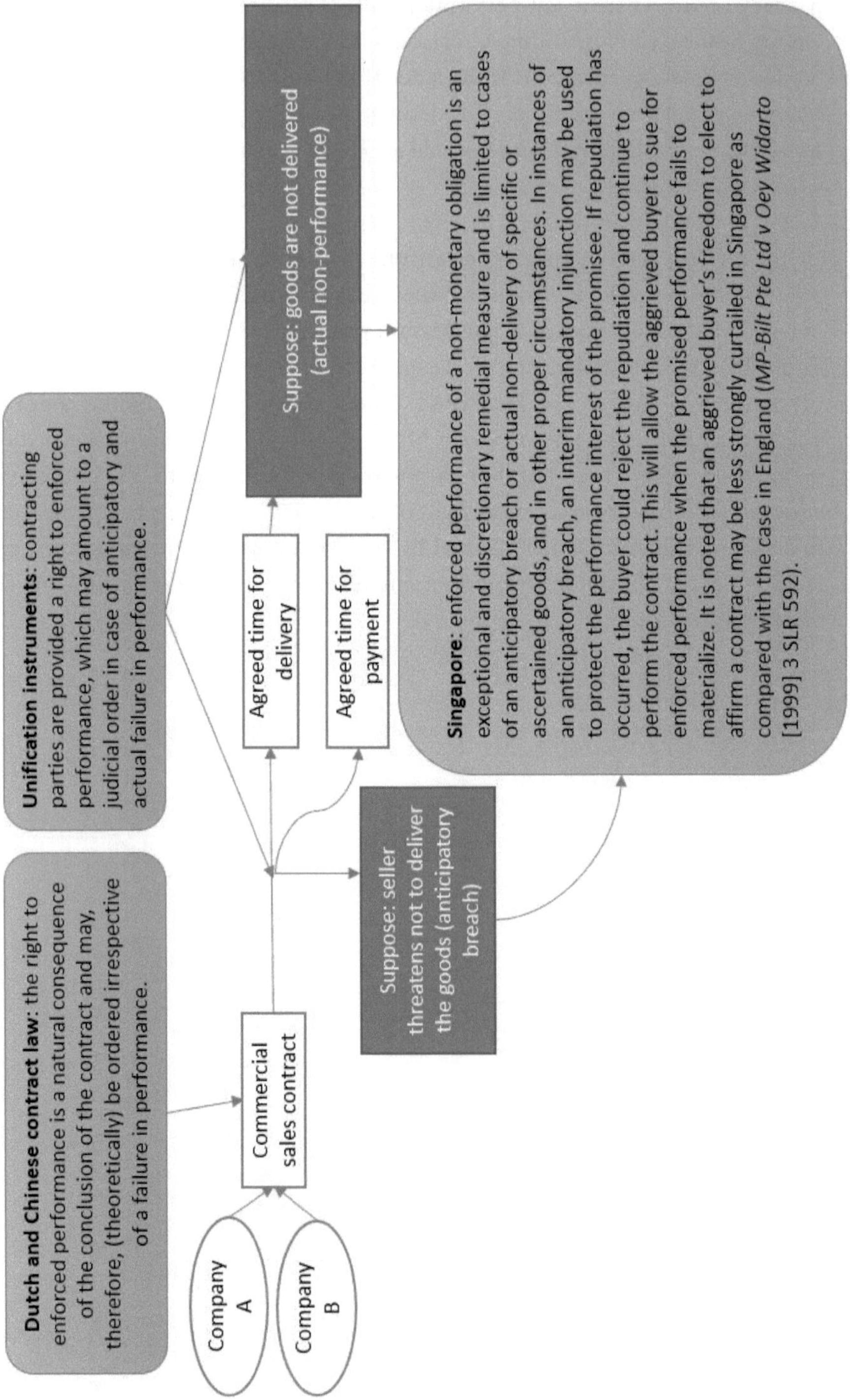

158. In light of the above, it is of little surprise that enforced performance of the seller's obligation to deliver the goods (generic and specific) is available as of right under Dutch and Chinese contract law. In other words, the buyer to a commercial sales contract is provided with the assurance that it can enforce what is expected under the contract, which can take the form of enforced delivery or a cure, either by repair or by replacement. A major drawback of the general availability of enforced performance in the contract law of the Netherlands and China is that it ignores the interests of commercial sellers involved in sales transactions of generic goods, as damages are usually believed to be the most sufficient form of relief for both parties to the contract. Nonetheless, the aggrieved buyer may insist on enforced performance in these instances, unless there are reasons to limit its right to performance. It appears that the approach taken by the contract law of Singapore (*i.e.* enforced performance is only available in exceptional circumstances) is more adequate in cases of generic goods, although it brings about a situation of legal uncertainty because it imposes the entire risk of non-performance on the aggrieved buyer. These considerations brings about the fundamental question of whether a legal system is capable of answering the question of which party is in need of protection by a judicial order for enforced performance. It is submitted here that this is virtually impossible because the buyer's interest in actual delivery of the goods in accordance with the contract is always subjective and dependent on the circumstances of the case (*i.e.* the actual availability to obtain substitute goods in light of the agreed parameters in the contract).

159. As mentioned above, it seems that the drafters of the CISG bridged the gap between the 'right *versus* remedy' approach by providing for the availability of enforced performance, although this was achieved by categorising the judicial action for obtaining an order for enforced performance as a cure for a failed performance and by adopting specific restrictions. An important limitation of common law descent is the requirement of a fundamental breach to demand replacement of non-conforming goods.[1005] However, this attempt to balance both approaches in a legal framework which reflects the civil and common law traditions has barely any significance for commercial sales contracts, as the CISG adopted the principle that a court is not bound to enter a judgement for enforced performance unless it would do so under its own law (*i.e.* it allows the court to follow domestic law if it so chooses).[1006] The PICC, PECL, DCFR and the draft PACL achieved a more successful solution by starting with the default availability of enforced performance of a non-monetary obligation, which cannot be circumvented by the application of the law of the court adjudicating the dispute (provided that the applicable domestic law accepts this). The solution offered entails the notion that enforced performance is available as of

1005 S 5.4.3.
1006 Art 28 CISG.

right, which is subject to various restrictions as present in the civil and common law tradition, such as impossibility of performance, hardship and notification duties.[1007] An important point to note is that the PICC, PECL, DCFR and draft PACL (expressly and implicitly) adopted the common law principle that enforced performance is not available if the buyer could have reasonably obtained the goods from another source (this requirement is generally not adopted by civil law jurisdictions).[1008] The common law system of Singapore is also familiar with this requirement, but it is absent in the contract law of the Netherlands and China. The complexity of the divergence between the subject legal systems can best be clarified by analysing the response of the court to the simplified example mentioned under paragraph 129. In this case the adjudicating court shall have to deal with the substantive issue of the alleged anticipatory breach of the contract by the seller. This follows from the threat of the seller not to deliver the coffee cups if the buyer does not pay a surcharge to cover an increase in production costs. According to the principles adopted by Dutch and Chinese contract law, as well as the CISG, a judicial order for enforced performance shall be available, even if the buyer could obtain the goods elsewhere (it should, however, be noted that where the buyer is obliged to mitigate the impact on the seller of enforced performance, the right to claim for enforced performance can be excluded by the court if the seller argues that the buyer could reasonably obtain substitute goods elswhere). This stands in stark contrast with the approach taken by the sales law of Singapore, as well as by the PICC, PECL, DCFR and the draft PACL, which have taken (indirectly) the approach that enforced performance is not available if the buyer could reasonably obtain the goods from another source.

160. This does not mean that the approach taken by the unification instruments suits the dynamics of commercial sales transactions best because this requires a significant level of adaptability of the applicable rules to changing needs and circumstances. It is therefore suggested that parties to a commercial sales contract across the borders of the three investigated jurisdictions carefully consider the most appropriate approach for their situation in view of the differences discussed in the following chapters. This time-consuming undertaking is required because contracting parties cannot overcome the divergence between the civil and common law tradition by simply relying on the CISG. Contracting parties could opt-out and agree to contractual stipulations which are in full accordance

---

1007 Chs 5, 6.

1008 Art 7.2.2(c) PICC adopted the restriction that enforced performance cannot be granted when the aggrieved party may reasonably obtain performance from another source; Art 9:102(2)(b) PECL and art III–3:302(3)(b) DCFR act on the notion that in deciding whether enforced performance would be unreasonably burdensome or expensive, it may be relevant to take into account whether the aggrieved part could easily obtain the goods from another source and claim the costs of doing so from the non-performing party (see Comment F); Art 7(d) Amendment Draft on Non-Performance PACL.

with their commercial needs. This option, however, ignores the restrictions on contractual modification of the available remedies for the situation where the seller fails to deliver the goods in accordance with the agreed terms.[1009] It is therefore of paramount importance to assess the considerations above in view of the analyses provided in the subsequent chapters in order to determine the actual flexibility with which the courts can act as regards to granting enforced performance of a commercial sales contract under the subject legal systems, the degree of protection against abuse and the extent the law can assure the promisee's interest in obtaining the actual thing it bargained for.[1010]

4.5 Ancillary performance obligations arising from the principle of good faith

161. *Preliminary* – The central question of the present section is the question of whether an actionable ancillary performance obligation can arise under a commercial sales contract by application of the behavioural standard of good faith.[1011] The aim of this section is to determine the extent to which this highly contested legal concept provides guidance in determining the degree of performance owed by parties to a commercial sales contract and if it may be used to assume ancillary enforceable obligations beyond the seller's obligation to deliver the goods and the buyer's obligation to pay the purchase price. This discussion is treacherous ground because the divergence between the legal systems on whether the principle of good faith could bring about actionable ancillary obligations under a commercial sales contract derives from strong cultural notions and legal traditions.

> *Illustration 1* – A manufacturer, located in country X, concludes a sales contract with a buyer, located in country Y. Under the sales contract, the manufacturer is obliged to hand over documents of title at the stipulated place of delivery in order to allow the buyer to take possession of the goods. Two weeks before delivery, country Y announces that it prohibits the import of goods from a number of designated countries with immediate effect. As a result, the buyer is obliged to submit a certificate of origin and a number of other administrative documents in order to obtain the goods once they have arrived. The contract and default provision of the applicable law is, however, silent on the question of whether the manufacturer is obliged to provide these documents.

1009 Ch 8.

1010 Ch 9.

1011 This section does not discuss ancillary protection duties because a failure in performance is generally governed by the rules on damages.

Illustration 2 – A seller, located in country X, and a buyer, located in country Y, conclude a sales contract for delivery of industrial equipment, which requires labour-intensive maintenance and frequent replacement of certain parts. For the delivery of the spare parts, the parties concluded separate sales contracts on an ad hoc basis. After two years, the seller stops the delivery of the spare parts needed for the operation of the equipment. The contract and default provisions of the applicable sales law are, however, silent on the question of whether the seller is subject to an ongoing obligation to ensure the availability of spare parts for a particular period.[1012]

162. *Domestic approaches* – The starting principle under Dutch contract law is that where enforced performance is demanded of an obligation which is not laid down in the express language of the contract and does not follow from the default provision of the law, the court shall first determine the meaning, and the juridical effects of the contract concluded by the parties.[1013] The above-described undertaking runs via the so-called *Haviltex*-formula, which means that the court assesses 'the sense the contracting parties could reasonably attach to the stipulations in the present circumstances and that which they could reasonably expect from each other in this regard'.[1014] As a second step, the court takes into consideration that contracting parties are obliged by law to act, between themselves, in accordance with the requirements of reasonableness and fairness.[1015] This principle is further set out in the statutory provision for reciprocal obligations that a contract not only has the juridical effects agreed to by the parties, but also those which, according to the nature of the contract, apply by virtue of law, usage or the requirement of reasonableness and fairness.[1016]

The mandatory legal standard of reasonableness and fairness derives from the *bona fides* principle as developed in Roman law.[1017] The principle that a contract include not only the things agreed on by contracting parties,[1018] but also the effects deriving from the principle of reasonableness and fairness, means in the realm of commercial trade relations

1012 ICC Arbitration Case n 8611 of 23 January 1997 (Industrial equipment case) <http://cisgw3.law.pace.edu/cases/978611i1.html> accessed on 19 December 2018; David Ramos Muñoz, 'The Rules on Communication of Defects in the CISG: Static Rules and Dynamic Environments. Different Scenarios for a Single Player' (2005) Pace essay <http://www.cisg.law.pace.edu/cisg/biblio/munoz.html#389> accessed on 19 December 2018.

1013 Hartkamp 2011 (n 80) para 116; Anne Hendrikx, 'Het aanvullen van een leemte in de overeenkomst naar Nederlands en Engels recht', *Een Kwart Eeuw : Privaatrechtelijke Opstellen, Aangeboden Aan Prof. Mr. H.J. Snijders Ter Gelegenheid Van Zijn Emeritaat* (Wolters Kluwer 2016) 155.

1014 *Haviltex* (nr 310).

1015 Art 6:2(1) DCC; *Haviltex* (nr 310).

1016 Arts 6:216, 6:248(1) DCC; Hartkamp 2011 (n 80) paras 32, 105; Hendrikx (n 1013) 155.

1017 Sieburgh, *Asser 6-III* (n 203) 380, 392.

1018 Sieburgh, *Asser 6-III* (n 203) 379.

that parties are obliged to observe the legitimate interest of the other party and,[1019] more specifically, to adhere to the reasonable commercial standards of fair dealing.[1020] The behaviour of contracting parties is *objectively* assessed by the court, meaning that the state of mind of the involved parties is not taken into account.[1021] In this regard, a court shall assess, in light of the nature of the agreement, whether, in the given circumstances, any commercial party could have reasonably expected that the contract included the alleged obligation. Thus, the standards of reasonableness and fairness may come into play as a basis for ancillary obligations if the contract, default provisions of the law and usage do not provide a solution for the shortcoming in the agreement of contracting parties. For example, the standard of reasonableness and fairness could impose an obligation on a company to a joint venture to provide its cooperation to maintain the daily operation of the joint venture by the continuation of the lease of the factory.[1022] In instances where the court assesses that an additional provision is necessary for effective performance, it is required to take into account the nature, purpose and intentions of the agreement, the legitimate interest of the parties and the law.[1023] For example, the standards of reasonableness and fairness would require a buyer, who already took delivery of 600 metric tonnes of goods, to also be obliged to take the remaining three metric tonnes in order to empty the ship.[1024]

163. Singapore contract law, generally, does not acknowledge the usage of the substantive legal principle of good faith in a commercial context.[1025] The main objections for not adopting the legal concept of good faith as a matter of law are the sanctity of contract, uncertainty, setting an unwanted precedent, the indeterminable scope of a duty of good

1019 Sieburgh, *Asser 6-III* (n 203) 392; *Baris v Riezenkamp* (545); *Vodafone v ETC Dutch Supreme Court* 19 October 2007, ECLI:NL:HR:2007:BA7024, NJ 2007, 565.

1020 *Baris v Riezenkamp* (n 545); *Vodafone* (n 1019); Sieburgh, *Asser 6-I* (n 363) para 55; Sieburgh, *Asser 6-III* (n 203) 392; Hartkamp 2011 (n 80) para 32.

1021 *Artist de Laboureur* Dutch Supreme Court 9 February 1923, ECLI:NL:HR:1923:175, NJ 1923, 676; Dutch Supreme Court 21 June 1957, NJ 1959, 91; Sieburgh, *Asser 6-III* (n 203) 394; Hartkamp 2011 (n 80) para 32.

1022 Dutch Supreme Court 19 December 1958, NJ 1959, 129; *Meegdes v Meegdes* (n 571); Dutch Parliamentary History Book 6 (n 207) art 6.5.3.1, 921.

1023 PJM von Schmidt auf Altenstadt, FE Vermeulen and BTM van der Wiel (eds), *Middelen voor Meijer. Liber amicorum mr. R.S. Meijer* (Boom Juridische Uitgevers 2013) 389 *ff.*; Sieburgh, *Asser 6-III* (n 203) 386, 403.

1024 Dutch Court of Appeal Amsterdam 14 April 1919, NJ 1919, 1101; Sieburgh, *Asser 6-III* (n 203) 403.

1025 *Hewlett-Packard Singapore (Sales) Pte Ltd v Chin Shu Hwa Corinna* [2016] SGCA 19, (2016) 2 SLR 1083; *The One Suites Pte Ltd v Pacific Motor Credit (Pte) Ltd* [2015] SGCA 21, (2015) 3 SLR 695; Ter Kah Leng, 'Good Faith in the Performance of Commercial Contracts Revisited' (2014) n 26 Singapore Academy of Law Journal 111; Hunter 2017 (n 7) paras 10.21, 10.30, 10.31, 10.39; Kim Shi Yin, 'All in Good Faith: Recognising the Doctrine of Good Faith in Singapore's International Sales Law' (2016) <http://www.singaporelawblog.sg/blog/article/168> accessed on 10 November 2016; By contrast, the legal doctrine of good faith applies in fudiciary relationships, such as agreements arising in equity, insurance and employment contracts.

faith and the current conception of academics that good faith is inherent in contract law.[1026] The latter is substantiated with the argument that protection of the reasonable expectations of contracting parties is already an accepted principle in contract law.[1027] In addition, it is said that the soft law application of *lex mercatoria* imposes a duty to act in good faith on contracting parties involved in international sales transactions.[1028] To date, it appears, however, that the concept of good faith cannot be implied as a matter of law, and can therefore not be used as a source to assume ancillary obligations of parties under a commercial sales contract.

That being said, it is discussed whether the principle of good faith can be implied in fact on the basis of the intentions of the parties (hence, the term implied 'in fact').[1029] In the view of the Singapore Court of Appeal this means that a good faith principle can be anchored in the express contractual language, the internal and external contexts of the contract and, more broadly speaking, the contractual purpose.[1030] In another case, it was observed that it is possible to incorporate the doctrine of good faith into a contract under the narrow category of terms implied in fact, albeit that this is not likely given (as mentioned above) the uncertain status of the doctrine of good faith.[1031] Nonetheless, it is pointed out that the court could examine the particular facts of the case in order to ascertain whether or not an obligation to act in good faith could be implied in fact.[1032] The actual test to imply a duty to act in good faith, as a matter of fact, comprises the so-called 'officious bystander test' and the below discussed 'business efficacy test'.[1033] The former entails the test as to whether any person would have expected that the alleged obligation was a part of the agreement. The latter reflects the assessment as to whether the alleged obligation is necessary to make the contract effective. In view of the considerations above, it is suggested that with

1026 *Ng Giap Hon v Westcomb Securities Pte Ltd* [2009] 3 SLR (R) 518.

1027 Jay M Feinman, 'Good Faith and Reasonable Expectations' (2013) Arkansas Law Review <http://media.law.uark.edu/arklawreview/files/2015/02/525-570-Feinman.pdf> accessed 28 April 2016.

1028 In Kim (n 1025) the *lex mercatoria* is defined as 'a set of legal norms, or a body of soft law that is neutral, capable of serving as the lex contractus, and independent of any domestic legal regime. Since they are not supported by any governmental authority, the principles of lex mercatoria have no binding character unless the contracting parties choose to bind themselves to them'. In this respect it is held that the lex mercatoria derive from a variations of sources, such as the CISG, the UNIDROIT Principles, the contractual terms stipulated by the parties, usage, et cetera.

1029 *Ng Giap Hon v Westcomb Securities Pte Ltd* (n 1026); in the case *The One Suites Pte Ltd v Pacific Motor Credit (Pte) Ltd* (n 1025) it was affirmed that 'the law in this particular sphere (viz, good faith) continues to be in a state of flux', yet refused to discuss the doctrine as it did not come directly for decision before the courts; Ter Kah Leng 2014 (n 1025) 111, 131; Hunter 2017 (n 7) para 10.31.

1030 *Hewlett-Packard Singapore (Sales) Pte Ltd v Chin Shu Hwa Corinna* (n 1025) SGCA 19 [53]; Hunter 2017 (n 7) para 10.36.

1031 *Ng Giap Hon* (n 1026) SLR (R) 518 [61].

1032 *Ng Giap Hon* (n 1026) SLR (R) 518 [34].

1033 *Foo Jong Peng and others v Phua Kiah Mai and another* [2012] SGCA 55; *Forefront Medical Technology (Pte) Ltd v Modern-Pak Pte Ltd* [2006] 1 SLR(R) 927 [29]–[31] affirmed in *Ng Giap Hon* (n 1026) SLR(R) 518 [36]); see in similar vein, the English case *Marks & Spencer plc BNP Paribas* [2015] UKSC 72.

two commercial parties, who have done multiple deals together, certain expectations of the performance of the contract may have developed.[1034] It is also advocated that Singapore law should follow the broadly accepted doctrine of good faith in commercial contracts due to its position as an international business hub.[1035] The most likely approach by Singapore courts to the accepted principle in international trade to act in good faith would be that contracting parties are 'expected to make a reasonable effort to fulfil the purposes of their agreement'.[1036] This suggests that a seller could be forced, for example, to hand over instructions for the usage of the equipment sold or to hand over a certificate of manufacturing compliance if this is required by local authorities. In spite of these considerations, the expressed language of a commercial sales contract retains priority under Singapore law in determining the obligations of the parties. Although this is a reflection of the justified responsibility of commercial parties to guard their own interests, it may also act as a legal barrier for international trade because it could be interpreted as a duty to write down all the necessary steps to fulfil the promises made by each party (which is factually impossible). Should there be a desire to lower this legal barrier, the courts could follow the argument that a commercial sales is, by default, based on the reciprocal expectation that each contracting party shall do everything in its power to provide the intended outcome of the contract. Consequently, non-compliance of the promisor with this self-imposed obligation could entitle the promisee to sue for enforced performance of an ancillary obligation arising from its 'justified' expectations.

164. Under the contract law of China, contracting parties are obliged to observe the principle of good faith in accordance with the nature and aims of the contract and trade practices.[1037] This means, for example, that the parties could also be subject to an obligation to notify, disclose material facts or acceptance of delivery of goods which exceed the agreed quantity if this does not result in unreasonable difficulties.[1038] In other words, the contract law of China acts on the notion that the express language of a contract does not always reflect all the commitments deriving from the contract.[1039] However, it is not clear as to whether there is a hierarchical order between the context for the interpretation of the good faith principle, that is, the nature of the contract and trade practices. That said, most notable is that the general principle mentioned above seems to treat trade practices not as a separate source to impose a duty on the parties, but as a framework for the assessment regarding

1034 Hunter 2017 (n 7) paras 10.34, 10.35.
1035 Kim (n 1025).
1036 Hunter 2017 (n 7) para 10.37.
1037 Arts 6, 61 CCL; The obligation to act in good faith is also laid down in specific regulations, such as art 4 GPCL, art 4 Consumer Rights and Interests Protection Law and art 2(1) Law against Unfair Competition.
1038 Liming 1992 (n 636) 16; Bu 2013 (n 226) 52 para 3.
1039 Bu 2013 (n 226) 52 para 3.

whether the legal concept of good faith could amount to an enforceable obligation which is not reflected in the express language of the contract. Nevertheless, the true meaning of the doctrine of good faith under the Civil Law Principles of China, as discussed below, reveals a different stance on this point.[1040]

The scope of application of the legal concept of good faith under Chinese contract law, as a basis for imposing additional duties on contracting parties, seems to be very restricted. This proposition derives from the fact that the contract law of China meticulously sets out the route for establishing the contractual obligations in case the express language falls short.[1041] The basic starting point is that in case contracting parties have not (sufficiently) stipulated the terms for quality, the purchase price or place of performance, the contractual obligations may be determined in accordance with the related clauses of the contract and trade practices.[1042] In the event these sources do not provide an adequate solution for the alleged shortfall in the agreement, it is stipulated which sources could also be used as a basis for ascertaining the required quality of the goods, price, place of performance, time limit for performance and method of performance. For example, it is prescribed by the contract law of China that in case contracting parties fail to determine the mode of performance, the parties are obliged to perform the contract in a manner conducive to the realisation of the aim of the contract.[1043] In case of unclear quality requirements, the parties are obliged to perform the contract in accordance with state standards or trade standards, or in the absence of such standards, in accordance with common standards or special standards conforming to the aim of the contract.[1044] However, the good faith principle is not specifically mentioned as a basis for the implication of obligations. This raises the question as to whether the application of the principle of good faith, as a basis for ancillary obligations, is self-evidentiary due to its prominent position in the contract law of China, or that it simply does not apply to obligations concerning the quality of the goods, price, place of performance, time limit for performance and method of performance. It is held that the legal concept of good faith may be used 'to fill in legislative and doctrinal gaps' where there are also shortfalls in the express language of the contract.[1045] Nonetheless, given the repeated emphasis in the contract law of China on the principle that the parties are obliged to act in accordance with the principle of good faith from the start of the

1040 Arts 61 and 62 (1)-(6) CCL.

1041 *Ibid.*

1042 Art 61 CCL.

1043 Art 62 (5) CCL; *Latex Gloves* [1999] China International Economic and Trade Arbitration Commission [CIETAC] 13 January 1999 <http://cisgw3.law.pace.edu/cases/990113c1.html>.

1044 Art 62 (1) CCL.

1045 Nadia Zayani, 'The Doctrine of Good Faith in China: A Tool to Correct the Contractual Behaviour or a Serious Restriction to the Freedom of the Contract and Individual Interests' (2016) 1(10) Dama International Journal of Researchers 13–19 <http://www.damaacademia.com/issue/volume1/issue10/DIJR-O-003.pdf> accessed 3 August 2017.

negotiations until the contract is discharged,[1046] it may be assumed that every commercial agreement may be supplemented by the court with collateral commitments on the basis of this open-ended legal concept. This assumption also follows from the statutory principle that, in the event that the parties argue about the understanding of a clause of the contract, the actual meaning of the clause shall be inferred and determined by the court on the basis of the words and sentences used in the contract, related clauses of the contract, aim of the contract, trade practices and the principle of good faith.[1047] Thus, it may be held that the obligations of contracting parties can arise from the language of the contract, the determination of the purpose of the contract, the trade usage and the principle of good faith.[1048] These sources may be addressed as the four corners of a contract which are subject to the contract law of China.

165. *Comparative analysis* – The usage of a general duty of good faith as a source for the imposition of ancillary obligations (*e.g.* packaging and handing over of documents) is a controversial concept in Dutch, Singapore and Chinese contract law. The key issue is that the contract law of the three jurisdictions differ with regard to the question of whether good faith may directly oblige commercial parties to bring about a certain state of affairs. Dutch and Chinese contract law adopt the broadest approach in the sense that commercial parties to a sales contract are subject to a general duty of good faith. The principle of good faith, as a general principle of contract law, could be used to identify ancillary performance duties under a commercial sales contract which may be subject to a judicial order for enforced performance. The approach taken by Singapore contract law is, for doctrinal reasons, significantly restrictive since the principle of good faith cannot be implied in law and thus may not be used as a source to find obligations outside the express language of the contract. That having been said, the discussed viewpoints on the possibility of implying the good faith principle, as a matter of fact, suggest that the Singapore courts are moving towards a more liberal approach for commercial contracts. This development is in line with a global trend towards an increasing role of the principle of good faith in global trade.[1049] Nonetheless, at the present juncture, it goes too far to assume that Singapore courts shall support a claim for enforced performance of an ancillary obligation on the basis of a duty of good faith implied as a matter of fact. This conservative view on the direct imposition of the principle of good faith in commercial contracts (*i.a.* as a source to assume

1046 Arts 6 (application of the good faith principle for fulfilment of obligations), 42 (3) (application of the good faith principle for the pre-contractual stage), 60 (application of the good faith principle for performance of the contract), 92 (application of the good faith principle after termination of the contract), and 125 (determining the actual meaning of a clause in light of the principle of good faith).

1047 Art 125 CCL.

1048 Fu (n 169) 79.

1049 Vogenauer 2015 (n 19) art 1.7 paras 1, 7–8.

ancillary obligations) matches the approach taken by the CISG which does not allow the courts to apply the good faith principle directly to the relationship between the parties.[1050] The idea that good faith cannot be applied directly to individual contracts runs counter to the (civil law inspired) standard of good faith as adopted by the PICC, PECL and DCFR which primarily addresses the good faith principle to the contracting parties.[1051] This means in effect that the duty of good faith could serve as a source to assume ancillary performance obligations of the seller or buyer which go beyond their obligations as provided by law and stipulated in the contract. This concept of good faith as a source for ancillary obligations is most in line with the approach taken by Dutch and Chinese contract law.[1052]

The liberal approach taken by the aforementioned legal systems needs to be offset against the CISG, which is (as previously mentioned) not familiar with the concept of good faith as an independent principle; the concept of good faith can only be used as a source for the duty of the courts to interpret the provisions of the Convention in light of its international character and the need to promote uniformity in its application and the observance of good faith in international trade.[1053] As for individual commercial sales contracts, a duty of good faith (as a source for ancillary obligations) can only be assumed where this follows from usages and practices established between the parties, such as on ongoing ancillary obligation to deliver spare parts.[1054] It is also suggested that that principle of good faith can be used in CISG-contracts via interpretation of the statements made by the parties to determine the degree of performance owed for the fulfilment of the buyer's and seller's obligations under the CISG.[1055] That having been said, it is suggested that where the courts are inclined or reluctant to impose a duty of good faith as a source for ancillary obligations under a CISG-contract, they may seek recourse to the general principles on which the Convention is based and where this fails, to the domestic rules determined by the private international law of the forum.[1056] This viewpoint is, however, contentious because parties to a CISG-contract simply cannot be subject to a general duty of good faith following from domestic law.[1057] Taking into consideration all the above, it is advocated here that the approach taken by Dutch and Chinese contract law, as well as the majority of the unification instruments, is most suitable for the complex reality of international trade which may require going beyond the express language of the contract and default

1050 Schwenzer 2016 (n 91) art 7 para 17; Vogenauer 2015 (n 19) art 1.7 para 2.

1051 Art 1.7 PICC; Art 1:201 PECL; Art III.-1:103 DCFR; Vogenauer 2015 (n 19) art 1.7 para 8.

1052 Vogenauer 2015 (n 19) art 1.7 para 24.

1053 Art 7(2) CISG; Schwenzer 2016 (n 91) 127 at para 17; Hunter 2017 (n 7) para 10.16.

1054 Art 9 CISG; Schwenzer 2016 (n 91) 127 at para 18.

1055 Schwenzer 2016 (n 91) art 7 para 17.

1056 Farnsworth (n 7) 227 at 231. Professor Farnsworth holds the view that art 7(2) CISG provides the court the option to apply the law that would govern the contract under the choice of law; Hunter 2017 (n 7) para 10.16; Schwenzer 2016 (n 91) art 8 para 27.

1057 Schwenzer 2016 (n 91) 127 at para 18.

provisions of the law to identify the obligations of the parties. That said, Singapore contract law is gradually diverging from the English common law reluctance to directly apply good faith to the contract, and therefore may follow suit where this is appropriate. This development is in line with the US and Canadian courts which are increasingly inclined to adopt a general duty of good faith.[1058] In the context of ancillary obligations of parties to a commercial sales contract, this development suggests that where the contract is silent, good faith could be used to assume an ancillary obligation. Should there be a desire at the international level to bring the CISG on par with the global trend to acknowledge the concept of good faith as a source for positive obligations, an important step would be the express recognition of good faith as a standard in commercial sales contracts. This suggestion should not be controversial, as the standard of good faith may already be used to determine the level of performance owed under a commercial sales contract.[1059] At a practical level, this would mean that the domestic courts could come to the same conclusion when adjudicating an enforcement dispute arising from the two examples mentioned under paragraph 161. This, in effect, would mean that the seller is subject to an enforceable obligation to furnish additional documents (where it is not already a part of the delivery obligation) and to continue the delivery of spare parts. The considerations above, however, also reveal that good faith is not a generally accepted source for ancillary obligations at the national and international levels. In order to prevent difficulties after conclusion of a contract, it is suggested here that those involved in commercial sales contracts across the borders of the subject legal systems pay sufficient attention to the tacitly assumed obligations they consider relevant to their agreement.

4.6 Conclusions

166. The comparative analysis provided in this chapter demonstrates a strong disagreement between the views of the subject legal systems on the question of whether a claim for enforced performance of the obligations under a commercial sales contract should be available. The divergence is caused by the influence of cultural notions and legal traditions on the structure of the law and the diametrically opposed interpretation of the universal adage *pacta sunt servanda*. The starting point of this proposition is that Dutch and Chinese law encompass an overarching structure with principles for legal obligations deriving from, for example, contractual rights. This legal approach is broken down into general rules on enforced performance of contractual obligations. Both legal systems also adopt more

1058 See the leading Canadian contract law case *Bhasin v Hrynew* [2014] SCC 71; See for the US: Vogenauer 2015 (n 19) art 1.7 para 7.
1059 Schwenzer 2016 (n 91) art 7 para 17.

detailed rules for specific contracts, such as sales contracts. These rules should be viewed in light of the civil law interpretation of the adage of *pacta sunt servanda*, which imposes a duty on the promisor to uphold its promise. This principle is the dogmatic backbone of the notion that enforced performance of monetary and non-monetary obligations arising from a commercial sales contract is available regardless of a failure in performance. In other words, the theoretical starting point in the contract law of the Netherlands and China is the default availability of enforced performance of the seller's delivery obligation and the buyer's obligation to pay the purchase price, even before the promised performance fails to materialize. This favourable consideration toward enforced performance is further strengthened by the imposition of additional requirements for a valid termination and for claiming damages in the case the promisor fails to perform its obligations. Nonetheless, the statutory provisions of the contract law of China have linked the availability of enforced performance to a failure in performance (attributability is not required). Although it may appear that this approach is of common law descent, it cannot be equated with the common law notion of a breach of contract. This is because the requirement of a failure in performance is the result of the influence of the CISG and PICC. It is also for this reason that the reference to a failure in performance does not preclude the right to claim for enforced performance prior to an (anticipatory) non-performance. In other words, the civil law tradition prevails in the rules on enforced performance in the contract law of China.

The availability of enforced performance without an (anticipatory) breach of the contract, is inconceivable under the contract law of Singapore because this common law legal system is based on the general framework of English contract law. This system developed in a more consecutive way in the sense that first the judicial framework for torts was developed and on this foundation came the principles of contract law.[1060] This provides the historical development of the fundamental requirement of a failure in performance for claiming enforced performance under the contract law of Singapore. Nonetheless, it should be recalled that the contract law of Singapore also adheres to the idea that promises are binding, although this principle only results in a default right to enforced performance of payment of the purchase price. The seller's delivery obligation must be assessed in light of the notion that a non-monetary promise is binding, although a failure in performance to bring about a certain state of afairs merely amounts to a legal obligation to pay damages. The default response of damages appears to derive from the notion that enforced performance may result in an unacceptable judicial interference with the liberty of contracting parties. Consequently, the contract law system of Singapore does not envisage enforced performance of non-monetary obligations as a remedy under a commercial sales

1060 Damages and the action for an agreed sum where developed in the courts of common law and later, specific performance in the courts of equity.

contract, unless it concerns non-delivery of specific or ascertained goods and damages are inadequate (restrictive interpretation). It appears that Singapore courts are also entitled to issue an (interlocutory) mandatory injuction to direct performance of contracts for the sale of goods of generic goods which are scarce, rendering the procurement of substitute goods unobtainable. However, enforced performance of the delivery of specific or ascertained goods, and delivery of generic goods in appropriate circumstances, is still subject to the courts reluctance to specifically enforce performance of a contract. In these cases the buyer may also apply to court to protect its performance interest in the delivery of the goods by means of an (interlocutory) mandatory injuction. However, the courts require a high degree of assurance that the question will be tried with a real prospect of success.

The aforementioned restrictive availability of enforced performance runs obviously counter, as discussed above, to the default availability of enforced performance of monetary and non-monetary obligations arising from a commercial sales contract under Dutch and Chinese law. The disagreement between the legal systems on the question of whether enforced performance is or should be available also brings about legal uncertainty when considering the possibility of ancillary performance obligations of contracting parties (*e.g.* packaging duties). It is important to recognise this option because commercial sales contracts and the default provisions of the law governing the contract nowadays may impose performance obligations besides the standard delivery and payment duties. For example, the obligation of the seller to ensure the availability of spare parts and the obligation of the buyer to provide the necessary information to enable the seller to make delivery and where it is not a part of the buyer's obligation to take delivery and/or to cooperate. Under Dutch and Chinese contract law, as well as the PICC, PECL and DCFR, ancillary obligations can be derived from the principle of good faith depending on the circumstances surrounding the contract. It appears, however, that the general duty of good faith as a source for ancillary duties does not exist in the contract law of Singapore. Consequently, the subject legal systems dramatically differ in their views on the scope of enforceable obligations arising from a commercial sales contract if the contract and the law are silent on matters such as the handing over of relevant documents to the seller or buyer, availability of spare parts, or other obligations other than delivery of the goods and payment of the price. This brings about considerable legal uncertainty for those involved in commercial trade across civil and common law borders. That said, the considerations above are, however, by no means sufficient to determine the actual availability of enforced performance, the degree of flexibility with which such a claim can be awarded, and the level of assurance provided for protection against abuse and protection of performance interest. This assessment completely depends on the limitations adopted by Dutch and Chinese contract law and the counter-exceptions found in the contract law of Singapore.[1061]

1061 Chs 5 and 6.

The legal options to give effect to a judicial order for enforced performance (outside enforcement proceedings) also play a key role in this regard.[1062]

167. It appears, at first glance, that the unification instruments identified provide a balanced enforcement regime for those involved in commercial sales contracts across civil and common law regimes. The solution adopted by the unification instruments provides the aggrieved party (buyer or seller) with the right to claim for enforced performance of monetary and non-monetary obligations, which can be brought to court when the obligation is due and not performed. In other words, the unification instruments bring about a theoretical merger of the civil law strict priority of the claim for enforced performance and the common law qualification of enforced performance as a remedial measure. This starting point applies to both forms of performance, monetary and non-monetary obligations, although a distinction is made between the primary limitations on enforced performance. Parties to a commercial sales contract should, however, not rely on the CISG if they are seeking a uniform law which bridges the gap between the fundamental differences in approaches taken by the civil and common law traditions, and more particularly where contract parties are seeking a solution for the disagreements between the three investigated jurisdictions. The reason is that the CISG entails the principle that enforced performance does not have to be awarded if the court adjudicating the dispute is not bound to enter a judgement for enforced performance of an action for the purchase price and delivery of goods if it would not do so under its own law in respect of similar contracts not governed by the Convention. Importantly, a careful assessment is required, even when those involved in commercial sales across civil and common law borders seek a compromise, drawing inspiration from the approach taken by the CISG or the other unification instruments (*i.e.* the PICC, PECL, DCFR and the draft PACL). This is because the remarkably different ways a claim for enforced performance for monetary and non-monetary obligations can be established. For example, whereas the CISG, PICC and the draft PACL set forth the basic obligation of the buyer to pay the purchase price, which is subject to general limitations, the PECL and DCFR have adopted an important exception to the requirement of a failure in performance. This exception allows a claim for enforced performance where the buyer's obligation to pay the purchase price becomes due on delivery of the goods, but the buyer refuses to provide the necessary cooperation for delivery. The contract law of Singapore is not familiar with such an exception, and the approach taken under Dutch and Chinese contract law, and the other unification instruments, only encompasses indirect solutions. Accordingly, it is suggested here that the national legislators of the three subject jurisdictions and the drafters of the CISG, PICC, and the draft PACL could take into consideration the solution offered by the PECL and DCFR.

1062 Ch 7.

It is however unlikely that there will be a universally acceptable solution for the discussed divergence in the foreseeable future. It is therefore suggested in the preceding chapters that those involved in commercial sales transactions across the borders of the subject legal systems (and more in general, where it concerns parties from civil and common law jurisdictions) focus on the possibility of contractual modification of the default availability of enforced performance under the law governing the contract. However, due consideration should also be given to the different thresholds for establishing or excluding enforced performance at the national and international levels.[1063]

1063 Ch 8.

5 Specific failures to bring about a certain state of affairs

5.1 Introduction

168. This chapter focusses on three different causes for a disturbance in the performance of a commercial sales contract and the extent to which the subject legal systems allow for enforced performance in these situations. The three scenarios are: non-delivery of the goods (section 5.2), refusal to take delivery of the goods and acceptance of the goods (section 5.3), and instances of defective delivery (section 5.4). These forms of disturbance in performance are selected on the factual basis that they go to the very root of performance obligations arising under a commercial sales contract on a practical level and because they are examples of the impact of the disagreement between traditional civil and common law approaches at the national and international levels.

Having said that, there are specific reasons for distinguishing the above-mentioned different kinds of non-performance. First, the specific focus on the various forms is rooted in a disagreement about the substance of the performance obligations arising under a commercial sales contract. For example, where the seller is required to bring about a physical or constructive delivery to comply with its delivery obligation (rather than making the goods available), the question arises as to whether the seller may claim for enforced performance where the buyer fails to take delivery. The second reason for the differentiation in causes of non-performance follows from the broadly accepted notion that non-conforming goods can be delivered. In such cases, the seller's delivery obligation can be fulfilled, despite the fact that the goods do not possess the features agreed in the contract. This premise indicates that the interest of the buyer is not protected by the rules on enforced performance of non-monetary obligations, but is structured in a different way. The third reason is of a dogmatic nature because it concerns the (traditionally) civil law distinction between the available performance remedies in case of the delivery of goods which are different in nature (*aliud*) and delivery of defective goods (*peius*).[1064]

169. Broadly speaking, in certain (generally civil law) jurisdictions, delivery of different goods qualifies as non-delivery, entitling the aggrieved buyer to sue for enforced performance of the seller's delivery obligation to comply with the contract. The remedies

1064 Ss 5.2, 5.4; See for legal systems which have not abandoned the distinction between the deliver of an *aliud* and *peius* Hachem and Kee 2012 (n 13) paras 29.10, 31.15.

of repair and replacement are available for defective goods provided that the applicable requirements are fulfilled. By way of contrast, the common law tradition is focussed primarily on the non-performance and the qualification of the goods, to wit, a sale for generic or specific goods. The type of non-performance, that is, non-delivery and non-conformity, are not an essential concern when determining the willingness of the courts to order enforcement of performance. The relevance of the contrasting viewpoints between civil and common law becomes particularly visible when a completely different product is delivered than initially agreed. From a civil law perspective, the delivery of a completely different product entitles the buyer to sue for actual performance on the basis that the seller failed to fulfil its delivery obligation. In the case of delivery of non-conforming goods, the obligation to deliver the goods is fulfilled, but the buyer may sue for repair or replacement. In general, this distinction between available performance remedies is not familiar to the common law system. In effect, in instances of non-delivery and non-conforming delivery of goods (be it *aliud* or *peius*) which qualify as specific or ascertained, the court may order actual performance if it thinks fit.[1065] This reasoning also applies in the case of the delivery of generic goods which are scarce, rendering the purchase of substitute goods practically unobtainable, and the court establishes that in this situation damages are not an adequate remedy [138–149].

170. Although the opposing doctrinal principles above are the pillars of the civil and common law remedial systems, this section shows that the courts of the investigated legal systems are, increasingly, developing an approach which is more in line with the commercial reality of a trading nation, by assessing, on a case-by-case basis, whether the aggrieved party is entitled to uphold the promises made under a sales contract. The domestic boundaries of this premise are discussed in this section.

5.2 Non-delivery of the goods

171. *Preliminary* – The present section deals with a failure in performance to legally deliver the goods, which is not due to an insurmountable obstacle,[1066] but for other reasons, which do not necessarily make delivery impossible. For example, if the seller does not feel any contractual pressure to comply with its duty to deliver the goods to a foreign buyer, the seller is a major overseas manufacturer and does not give priority to small orders, or if the seller pretends to be a factory but is actually a trading company which does not properly manage its supply chain. In view of this, this section discusses whether the seller is subject

1065 SGA, s 52(1).
1066 Ch 6.

to a statutory duty to deliver the goods, the substance of this obligation and whether the seller's delivery obligation is also fulfilled where the features of the goods deviate from the stipulations of the contract. The latter point is of immense importance in bringing about new insights for the potential consolidation of different viewpoints at the international level, and also from a practical perspective. This is because, where the handing over of non-conforming goods (*i.e.* delivery of an *aliud* or *peius*) does not amount to legal delivery, considerations about the availability of enforced performance in the case of non-delivery may suffice.[1067] When non-conforming goods can be legally delivered, the question arising is whether the aggrieved buyer may seek recourse to enforced performance which would require the seller to put the defect right by repair or by a fresh delivery.[1068]

172. Regarding the legal requirements for the fulfilment of the seller's delivery obligation, the following assesses whether the latter is only obliged to make the goods available to the buyer, or must also provide possession of the goods via physical delivery or by transfer of control over the goods (*i.e.* constructive delivery). Aside from physical and constructive delivery, it is important to note that certain jurisdictions are familiar with the instrument of deemed delivery. This may occur, for example, when the buyer fails to notify the buyer (within a reasonable time) that the goods have not arrived at the designated warehouse or when the buyer does not cooperate in a timely fashion. The different forms which might constitute legal delivery in the subject legal systems are illustrated below.[1069]

1067 Ss 5.2, 5.4

1068 See s 5.4 for the question as to whether the investigated legal systems envisage a claim for enforced performance in the form of cure by repair or replacement.

1069 See for a detailed discussion about various aspects of delivery Schwenzer, Hachem and Kee 2012 (n 13) Ch 29.

Figure 14 Different forms of legal delivery

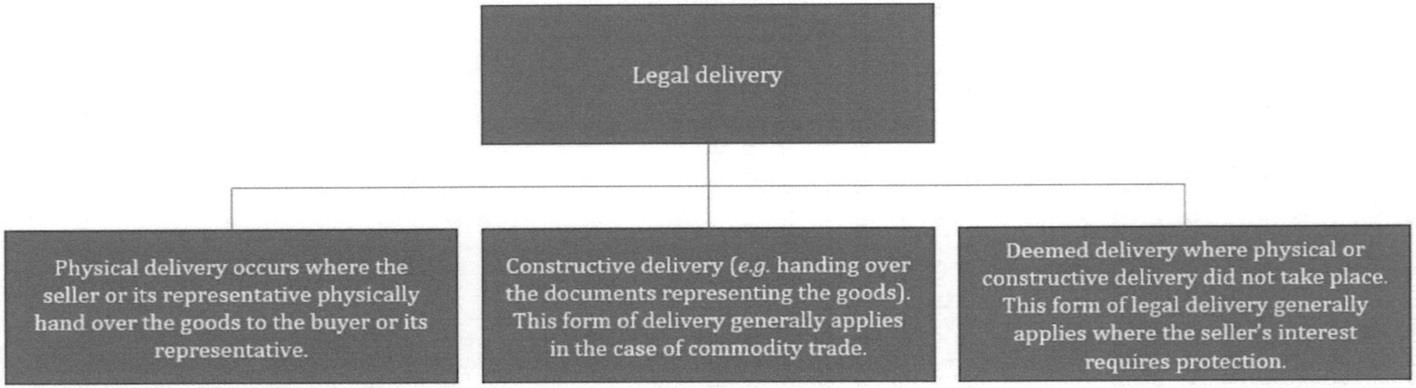

173. Considering the fact that the various forms of legal delivery requires that the buyer cooperates, section 5.3 discusses whether and to what extent a seller is able to force the buyer to take delivery of the goods. The following discusses the intricacies of a situation of non-delivery and whether the buyer is entitled to demand immediate delivery or whether it should give the seller a reasonable time to deliver the goods in cases where the parties have not fixed a time for delivery and where a time for delivery is not determinable from the contract.

> *Illustration* – A producer of fruit juices (buyer) concludes a contract with a corporation of farmers (sellers). The parties agree that the farmers are obliged to deliver their crop of Valencia oranges covering the 2017–2018 crop year once the harvest season has ended. The contract does not specify what the sellers must do in order to perform their delivery obligation. The sellers encounter various issues in delivery of the oranges and a dispute arises about the question as to whether the oranges are legally delivered by making them available to the buyer instead of providing physical possession.

174. *Domestic approaches* – Dutch contract law expressly stipulates that the seller is obliged to transfer ownership with its accessories, to deliver the goods and to deliver goods which conform to the contract.[1070] This distinction between the seller's obligations reveals that the delivery obligation can be fulfilled even if the seller delivers goods which do not possess the features as agreed in the contract. This is because the delivery and conformity questions are separate under Dutch contract law.[1071] The seller's obligation to delivery can be fulfilled by giving the buyer the actual or constructive control over the goods.[1072] This can be achieved by enabling the buyer to exercise such control over the goods as the seller was able to exercise over it.[1073] The seller can provide this degree of control by an actual or symbolic transfer (*tradition symbolica*) of the goods, or by means of a bilateral declaration.[1074] As for the latter, a bilateral declaration suffices where: (1) the seller possesses the goods and henceforth holds the goods for the buyer by virtue of a stipulation made at the time of delivery (delivery *constitutum possessorium*); where the buyer already held the

---

1070 Arts 6:38, 7:9(1)(2), 7:17 DCC; Hijma, *Asser Koop en ruil* 7-I* 2013 (n 48) 268, 289; HN Schelhaas, AJ Verheij and B Wessels, *Bijzondere overeenkomsten* (Studiereeks Burgerlijk Recht 4th edn, Wolters Kluwer 2016) para 25.

1071 An important point to note is that Dutch contract law does not make a distinction between the delivery of *aliud* or *peius*. Both situations are considered as non-conforming deliveries; See s 5.4.

1072 Arts 7:9 (2), 3:114 DCC.

1073 Art 3:114 DCC.

1074 Arts 3:112, 3:115 DCC; Hijma, *Asser Koop en ruil* 7-I* 2013 (n 48) 291; Dutch Parliamentary History Book 7 (Kluwer 1991) 96; AS Hartkamp, *Mr. C. Assers Handleiding tot de beoefening van het Nederlands Burgerlijk Recht. 3. Vermogensrecht algemeen. Deel I. Europees recht en Nederlands vermogensrecht* (Wolters Kluwer 2018) para 143; Schelhaas et al *Bijzondere overeenkomsten* (n 1070) para 28.

goods for the seller (delivery *brevi manu*); and where a third party held the goods for the seller and holds it for the buyer from the time of delivery (delivery *longa manu*). In this event, possession of the goods does not pass until the third party has acknowledged the transfer of the goods or has been notified of it by the seller or buyer. From the considerations above it follows that it is not enough to make the goods available to the buyer. As for a sale subject to reservation of title, delivery also means giving control over the goods to the buyer, although the seller remains the possessor of the goods.[1075]

In instances where the parties did not implicitly or explicitly agree on a time for delivery, and no time limit can be derived from practices established between the parties or trade usage and/or practice, delivery may be demanded immediately by the buyer.[1076] That said, standards of reasonableness and fairness generally oblige the buyer to provide the seller sufficient time to fulfil its obligations to deliver the goods.[1077] In the case a seller completely fails its obligation to deliver the goods, the aggrieved buyer is entitled to resort to a claim for enforced performance under the *lex generali* for obligations and the *lex specialis* for sales contracts.[1078] Although, where the sales contract stipulates a time for delivery, it is presumed to bar an earlier demand for performance.[1079] Nonetheless, the limiting effect of a stipulated time for performance is not significant as the court is entitled to grant a claim for enforced performance on the condition that actual enforcement of the court order is only available on lapse of the stipulated time for performance and the promisor fails to act in accordance with this stipulation.[1080]

175. Sales law of Singapore entails the duty of the seller to voluntarily tender delivery of the goods in accordance with the terms of the contract.[1081] The act of delivery of goods means that the seller must be ready and willing to give physical or constructive possession of the goods, unless otherwise agreed.[1082] Considering this, the question of whether it is for the seller to send the goods to the buyer depends in each case on the contract, expressed

---

1075 Art 7:9 DCC; Schelhaas et al *Bijzondere overeenkomsten* (n 1070) para 28.

1076 Art 6:38 DCC; Hijma, *Asser Koop en ruil* 7-I* 2013 (n 48) 312; De Jong, Krans and Wissink 2018 (n 194) 80.4

1077 Dutch Parliamentary History Book 6 (n 207) 170, 171; Compare Dutch Parliamentary History Book 3 (n 204) 162; Hijma, *Asser Koop en ruil* 7-I* 2013 (n 48) 312; De Jong, Krans and Wissink 2018 (n 194) 80.4; RMChM Koot, 'commentaar op artikel 38 Boek 6 BW' in RJQ Klomp and HN Schelhaas (eds), *Groene Serie Verbintenissenrecht* (Wolters Kluwer 2011); Dutch Court of Appeal's-Gravenhage 30 May 2000, ECLI:NL:GHSGR:2000:AK4304, S&S 2001/54.

1078 Arts 3:296(1) 7:9(1) DCC.

1079 Art 6:39(1) DCC; Hijma, *Asser Koop en ruil* 7-I* 2013 (n 48) 312; De Jong, Krans and Wissink 2018 (n 194) 80.4.

1080 Art 3:296(2) DCC; Dutch Parliamentary History Book 6 (n 207) 172; Sieburgh, *Asser 6-I* (n 363) para 246.

1081 SGA, s 27; *Export Services Singapore Pte Ltd v Idemitsu Chemicals Southeast Asia Pte Ltd* [1998] 1 SLR 93; Halsbury's Laws of Singapore (Commercial Law 2014) vol 5(2) para 60.172.

1082 SGA, s 25, 61(1); Shenoy and Loo 2013 (n 13) paras 22.26, 22.25.

or implied, between the parties.[1083] Where a contract of sales entails the obligation of the seller to send the goods to the buyer, delivery of the goods to a carrier is regarded as a delivery of the goods to the buyer.[1084] For a constructive delivery of goods, the goods may be regarded as delivered if the seller or another party holds the goods on the buyer's behalf after the sale, or in the event that the property was already in possession of the buyer before the sale, and the latter continues its possession.[1085] The delivery of the goods may take place by giving access to the warehouse or via a bill of lading.[1086] This obligation is also regarded as fulfilled if the goods are delivered to a carrier for the purpose of transmission to the buyer.[1087] Thus, Singapore contract law has taken the approach that the seller must make the goods available to the buyer in order to perform its delivery obligation.

Where a delivery obligation is assumed, a seller is obliged to deliver the goods in accordance with the agreed time.[1088] Where the time for delivery of the goods is not fixed in the contract, the seller is bound to deliver the goods within a reasonable time.[1089] The amount of time reasonably required follows from the circumstances of the case (*i.e.* a matter of fact).[1090] A demand of the buyer for delivery may be treated as ineffectual unless made at a reasonable hour, and what a reasonable hour is should be determined on the facts of the case.[1091] In *Ng Lay Choo Marion v Lok Lai Oi*, the Singapore Court of Appeal considered that when exercising its discretion to award a claim for enforced performance, it is relevant to consider what terms should be imposed in order to do justice to the parties.[1092] Considering the moment at which a buyer may claim for actual and constructive delivery, the sales law of Singapore has taken the approach that handing over the possession of the goods may only be required if the buyer is capable and willing to pay the agreed purchase price for the goods.[1093] The parties are entitled to agree on a different exchange moment, which (obviously) may affect the moment at which the buyer is entitled to claim for delivery. From the general rule that performance must be precise and exact (*e.g.* the seller's obligation to deliver the goods in accordance with the contractual stipulations), it follows that where the seller fails to perform its delivery obligation, the buyer may claim for a remedial measure (it is sufficient for the seller to place the goods in question in a

1083 SGA, s 29(1).

1084 SGA, s 32(1).

1085 SGA, s 29(4); Chong et al 2016 (n 125) para 10.5.8.

1086 See the English case *Hilton v Tucker* (1888) 39 Ch.D. 669 for fulfilment of the obligation to deliver the goods by handing over the keys of the warehouse; Shenoy and Loo 2013 (n 13) para 22.26.

1087 SGA, s 32 (1) SGA Singapore; Chong et al 2016 (n 125) para 10.5.15.

1088 SGA, s 27.

1089 SGA, ss 29(3), 61(1); Hunter 2017 (n 7) para 7.3.

1090 Shenoy and Loo 2013 (n 13) para 22.28; Chong et al 2016 (n 125) para 10.5.16.

1091 SGA, 29(5); Chong et al 2016 (n 125) para 10.5.16.

1092 *Ng Lay Choo Marion* (n 917) SGCA 67 [21], [23-25].

1093 SGA, s 28; Hunter 2017 (n 7) para 7.1; Halsbury's Laws of Singapore (Commercial Law 2014) vol 5(2) para 60.169.

deliverable state at the disposition of the buyer without any further act on the part of the seller).

176. The contract law of China stipulates that a sale amounts to an obligation of the seller to deliver the goods and to transfer the ownership of the goods.[1094] The obligation to transfer the ownership of the goods is said to be the foundation of the statutory obligation to deliver the goods by the agreed time limit.[1095] From the delivery obligation it derives that the seller is required to provide the buyer with actual or constructive possession of the goods. Constructive delivery (*i.e.* transfer of ownership) could involve the transfer of the actual title to the buyer which enables the latter to take possession of the goods.[1096] Thus, where tangible goods are in possession of a third party, the seller can fulfil its obligation to deliver the goods by transferring the right of restitution of the goods to the buyer.[1097] In the event the parties' only intent is to transfer ownership, they can agree that the seller remains holding physical possession of the goods.[1098] Where the sales contract entails a software product which does not require physical delivery, and the parties have not explicitly agreed on the delivery mode and the delivery mode also cannot be determined via the existing contract or business practices, delivery shall be deemed to occur when the buyer receives the agreed-on electronic product or a certification of rights.[1099]

Where a contracting party is subject to a delivery obligation, it is obliged to deliver the goods to the buyer by the agreed time.[1100] In the absence of an agreed time for delivery, the seller may deliver the goods, and the buyer may require delivery, at any time, provided that the other party shall be given the time required for preparation.[1101] It must also be noted that where a commercial sales contract is not clear on this matter and the parties are not able to reach an agreement, it is at the discretion of the court to determine an appropriate time of delivery in accordance with the existing contract or business practices.[1102] Considering the availability of enforced performance, the time for delivery should be due to constitute a delay in performance.[1103] Where the time for delivery has lapsed, the aggrieved buyer may claim for enforced performance.

1094 Art 130 CCL; Liming 2016 (n 224) 276–278.
1095 Art 138 CCL; Liming 2016 (n 224) 276–278.
1096 Liming 2016 (n 224) 277.
1097 *Ibid.*
1098 Bu 2013 (n 226) 90 para 12; Liming 2016 (n 224) 277.
1099 Art 5 Judicial Interpretation of Sales Contracts (n 174).
1100 Arts 135, 138 CCL.
1101 Arts 139, 62 (4) CCL.
1102 Arts 61(4), 139 CCL; Bing Ling 2002 (n 229) paras 8.082, 5.038; Bu 2013 (n 226) 91 para 15.
1103 Art 107 CCL; Lei Chen, 'Availablity of Specific Remedies in Chinese Contract Law' in Chen-Wishart, Loke and Ong 2016 (n 156) 24; Bing Ling 2002 (n 229) para 8.015.

177. *Comparative analysis* – This section deals with the question of whether the seller is subject to a statutory delivery obligation, and if so, what is required to fulfil the delivery obligation and whether non-delivery can be subject to a claim for enforced performance. The starting point for this discussion is an important common denominator. That is, the three investigated jurisdictions, together with the CISG and DCFR,[1104] encompass the obligation of the seller to deliver the goods.[1105] The legal systems, however, disagree on the question of what the seller must do in order to fulfil its delivery obligation. Whereas Dutch and Chinese contract law has taken the approach that legal delivery can take place by providing physical or constructive possession, the CISG and DCFR merely require that the seller dispatches the goods or put the goods at the buyer's disposal.[1106] The contract law of Singapore has taken a different approach by adopting the principle that the seller must be ready and willing to give possession of the goods, although the question whether it is for the buyer to take possession of the goods or the seller to send them to the buyer depends in each case on the contract, expressed or implied, between the parties. The difference between the investigated legal systems can be best observed by considering the situation where a contract requires a change in physical possession and the buyer refuses to take delivery. In such a case, Singapore may deem delivery to have occurred where the seller has made the goods available to the buyer. The CISG and DCFR have taken the approach that the obligation of the seller to deliver the goods, entails the mere requirement that the seller dispatches the goods or places them at the buyers disposal. By contrast, Dutch and Chinese contract law require a physical or constructive change of possession for the fulfilment of the seller's delivery obligation.[1107] This, in effect, means that under Dutch and Chinese contract law, the buyer could claim for enforced performance of the seller's delivery obligation in the example provided under paragraph 173 because the oranges have not actually reached the buyer. In the case the contract is governed by the sales law of Singapore or the CISG (or inspiration is drawn from the approach taken by the DCFR), and the court establishes that the oranges are made available (*e.g.* by handing over the oranges to the carrier) dispatched or placed at the buyers disposal, it appears that the farmers may have fulfilled their delivery obligation and the buyer therefore may no longer request for delivery.

Importantly, the aforementioned differences between the requirements for the fulfilment of the seller's delivery obligation reveals that the applicable rules under Dutch and Chinese contract law can be characterised as buyer friendly (*i.e.* the seller is responsible for actual

1104 The PICC, PECL and draft PACL are not familiar with specific sales law provisions.

1105 Art 30 CISG; Art IV.A.-2:101 DCFR.

1106 Arts 30, 31 CISG; Art IV.A.-2:201(1) DCFR.

1107 The latter approach is one of the reasons why s 5.3 discusses whether the buyer is subject to an obligation to take delivery of the goods, and if so, whether the subject legal systems envisage enforced performance of this obligation.

delivery, dispatching the goods or placing the goods at the sellers disposal) and the rules under a Singapore jurisdiction contract, the CISG and DCFR as seller-friendly (*i.e.* the seller is only responsible for making the goods available). An important interrelated effect of favouring one party over the other is that it creates a divergence in thresholds for claiming enforced performance of delivery of the goods. In other words, under Dutch and Chinese contracts, non-delivery occurs where the seller fails to deliver the goods by a physical or constructive change in possession. This is easier to prove for the buyer than the unwillingness of the seller to make the goods available.

178. Regarding the time for performance of the seller's delivery obligation, the three subject jurisdictions and the unification instruments identified adhere to the principle that a seller is obliged to perform its obligations at the time fixed by the parties.[1108] At first glance, it appears that this rule is not of significant importance for determining the availability of enforced performance under Dutch and Chinese contract law because the default regime of both jurisdictions (from a dogmatic perspective) allows such a claim to be brought, regardless of a failure in performance. A significant deviation from this dogmatic principle (rooted in the universal adage *pacta sunt servanda*) can be found in the Dutch contract law principle that a stipulated time for delivery is basically intended to protect the interest of the seller. It is the case, therefore, that the buyer is not entitled to enforced performance of the seller's delivery obligation before the stipulated time for delivery when the contract is governed by Dutch contract law. That said, the buyer is entitled to claim for enforced performance of the seller's delivery obligation, which can be granted by the court on the condition that execution can only take place after, for example, the time of delivery has lapsed and the goods are not delivered.

It can be said that the contract law of the Netherlands displays a position which most resembles the middle-ground solution offered by the unification instruments. This solution encompasses a right to enforced performance, which is only available on a non-delivery. A similar principle is reflected in the contract law of China, although it is also held that the dogmatic view is that a claim for enforced performance is available independent of a failure in performance. In view of the above, it is submitted here that the approach taken by the Dutch and Chinese contract law may cause confusion among those not familiar with the interaction between the provisions for sales contracts and the above-discussed doctrinal viewpoints. The legitimate question for national legislators is, therefore, whether the applicable statutory principles for the enforcement of the seller's delivery obligation should expressly stipulate that a claim for enforced performance is an exclusive remedial instrument. The mere assumption that this is already the case in practice (*i.e.* enforced

1108 Art 33(a) CISG; Art 6.1.1(a) PICC; Art 7:102(1) PECL; Art III.-2:102(1) DCFR; Art 5(1) Amendment Draft on Performance PACL, Lee 2016 (n 16) 111.

performance shall not be awarded without a failure in delivery)[1109] is not sufficient to remove the uncertainty arising from the dormant effect of the strict civil law interpretation of the principle of *pacta sunt servanda* in Dutch and Chinese contract law.

The viewpoints of the subject legal systems also differ considerably in the case where contracting parties have not agreed on a time for delivery. The Dutch and Chinese contract law, as well as the draft PACL, appear to have taken the strictest approach by entitling the aggrieved buyer to require immediate performance of the obligation to deliver the goods, although the seller should be given a time which is reasonably necessary for the delivery of the goods.[1110] It seems that Singapore sales law is less strict by 'merely' requiring delivery of the goods 'within a reasonable time'. The approach taken by Singapore is in line with the more flexible structure of the CISG, PICC, PECL and DCFR.[1111] In determining the start of a reasonable period for delivery, the aforementioned unification instruments follow the rule that a reasonable period starts to run following the conclusion of the contract.[1112] For Singapore, it may be assumed that the court shall establish – in light of the circumstances of the case – the moment at which the reasonable time for delivery of the goods starts.

179. For those involved in commercial sales transactions across the borders of the investigated legal systems, it is of immense legal and practical importance to fully grasp the scope of the above-described principles for the time at which delivery of the goods is to be performed (*e.g.* when the goods are placed at the disposal of the buyer, when the goods are loaded on the means of transport arranged by the buyer, when the goods are placed alongside ship). This is because the time of legal delivery may play a decisive role in determining when the risk of loss passes from the seller to the buyer.[1113] It should be

---

1109 In other words, enforced performance shall not be awarded without a failure in performance.

1110 Art 5(2) Amendment Draft on Performance PACL, Lee 2016 (n 16) 111.

1111 Art 33(c) CISG; Art 6.1.1(c) PICC; Art 7:102(3); Art III.-2:202(1) DCFR.

1112 Art 6.1.1(c) CISG; Art 33(c) PICC; Art 7:102(3) PECL; Art III.-2:102(1) DCFR.

1113 NL: the seller is subject to a statutory duty to transfer the title (*i.e.*, ownership) and to deliver the goods, see art 7:9(1) DCC. Art 7:10(1) DCC stipulates that the goods are at risk of the buyer from the time of legal delivery. The latter, however, does not necessarily bring about the transfer of title. This depends on the particularities of the case. If no term has been set for the obligation to transfer the title and to deliver the goods, these obligations may be performed as well as demanded immediately, art 6:83 DCC; SGP: unless otherwise agreeed, the risk of loss is related to the time of passage of property (transfer of ownership) to the buyer. The property in the goods normally passes when the goods are ascertained to the contract, and (in the case of specific and ascertained goods) at such time the parties to the contract intend it to be transferred. See for a detailed discussion Hunter 2017 (n 7) Chs 4, 5; CHN: arts 130, 133, 142 CCL. The seller is obliged to transfer the title (*i.e.*, ownership). The risk of loss passes and the ownership transfers at the time of delivery of the goods; An in-depth discussion about the transfer of risk and title is beyond the scope of this work because of the huge differences amongst national contract law systems at the national and international levels.

noted that the transfer of risk and title may not necessary coincide.[1114] Where an international sales contract involves transport by sea or inland waterway, commercial parties could circumvent potential difficulties in this regard by relying on the Incoterms® such as FAS (*i.e.* free alongside ship-(named port of shipment)) It must, however, be stressed that the moment of transfer of possession and property should be specifically arranged in the contractual stipulations. The same applies when parties opt for another Incoterms® rule. The practical relevance of enhancing the understanding of the rules on the time for legal delivery also follows from a potential relationship with the time for determining the market or a reasonable price owed for the goods and with the time for establishing whether the features of the goods are in accordance with the contractual stipulations (this is generally the case where legal delivery coincides with the time at which the risk passes).[1115] Furthermore, the time at which the risk passes is generally decisive for the impact of subsequently discussed subjective impediments for performance, altering the purpose or equilibrium of a commercial sales contract.[1116] Another important and practical point to bear in mind when considering the rules on the time for delivery of goods in international commercial sale transactions, is that the three investigated legal systems do not include specific rules for the interpretation of sales contracts with respect to time zones, 'business day' definitions, hour format and daylight saving rules. Only the PICC provides a clear-cut rule for time zones but is not concerned with hour format and daylight saving time rules. Considering the importance of cross-border sales in the Netherlands, Singapore and China, it may be worth the consideration of these jurisdictions to adopt a system which governs and defines time zones, hour format and daylight saving rules for international sales transactions. At a practical level, contracting parties may consider to specify which time zone applies to their respective obligations. For example, parties could stipulate that a reference to a time of day is a reference to China Standard Time (Beijing Time domestically).

5.3 Failure in taking delivery of the goods

180. *Preliminary* – This section deals with the situation where the buyer fails to take delivery of the goods. The concept of taking delivery must in this context be understood in a broad sense because legal delivery of the goods may occur in various forms (s 5.2).[1117] Where legal delivery brings about a transfer of risk and title, the act of taking delivery also requires that the buyer takes control and bears the responsibility for the risk of loss. The importance

1114 Ss 3.4, 4.3.
1115 *Ibid.*
1116 Ch 6.
1117 S 5.2.

of discussing the enforceability of the act of taking delivery of the goods becomes apparent when considering the complexity of international commercial sales transactions, in particular when it involves the carriage of goods and when the law or the contract requires that the seller (or its representative) is obliged to deliver the goods to the buyer's (or its representatives) premises. In these cases, numerous challenges may arise due to the potential involvement of third parties, long-range transboundary transport and the fact that the goods cannot be immediately exchanged against the price. The consequences of a failure to take delivery are also significant when the contract concerns the sale of perishable and/or hazardous goods, and the seller remains responsible for the goods until the time, for example, a third party has taken delivery of the goods at the port of destination. With this in mind, it is first discussed whether the investigated legal systems encompass a legal obligation of the buyer to take delivery which can be subject to a claim and subsequently a judicial order for enforced performance.

The second point of discussion concerns the situation where a legal system is not familiar with an express legal obligation of the buyer to take delivery of the goods, but, instead, acknowledges an obligation of the buyer to cooperate. The analysis of the two points above should be considered in view of the disagreement between the civil and common law traditions on the relationship between the factual act of taking delivery and the legal acceptance of the performance. It could be said that civil law jurisdictions make a distinction between the obligation to take delivery and the legal concept of acceptance while common law jurisdictions are more familiar with an overall obligation to accept the goods which encompasses a duty to take delivery.[1118] It should further be noted that the following discussion about consequences of failure in taking delivery draws attention to the distinction between enforceable obligations and an 'obliegenheit' (*i.e.* a non-actionable obligation which only serves as a limitation of the rights of the non-performing party).[1119]

Illustration – A supplier of building materials, located in country A, is the owner of 200,000 metric tons of iron ore. The supplier sells the iron ore to a company located in country B. The parties agree that the iron shall be delivered at a designated warehouse company. However, upon arrival of the iron ore, it becomes apparent that the buyer has failed to secure sufficient storage and to make arrangements for taking delivery of the iron ore in other ways.

1118 Schwenzer, Hachem and Kee 2012 (n 13) paras 35.03, 35.17, 37.01–37.06, 37.13, 37.12.
1119 S 1.5.

181. *Domestic approaches* – Dutch contract law is not familiar with a general obligation of the buyer to take delivery of the goods;[1120] the buyer is only subject to a non-actionable duty (*i.e.* obliegenheit) to provide the necessary cooperation to enable the seller to fulfil its obligation to deliver the goods.[1121] An important principle in this regard is that a promisee is considered to be in default where the performance of the obligation of the promisor is prevented because it does not cooperate where necessary, or another impediment arises on the part of the promisee, unless the cause cannot be attributed to the latter.[1122] Hence, if a company fails to provide the necessary cooperation, the company, as a promisee of the delivery obligation, can be considered to be in default on the basis of the aforementioned principle. Apart from an explicit duty to cooperate, a commercial party can be subject to a non-actionable obligation if the contract or the law requires that the latter specifies the goods. If the buyer fails to act in accordance with this obligation, the seller is entitled to proceed to do so on its own motion, taking into account the needs of the buyer of which the seller is aware.[1123] It is reiterated that a refusal of the buyer to cooperate does not allow the seller to claim for enforced performance. This situation only results in a *mora creditoris*[1124] which negatively affects the rights of the non-performing buyer and may give rise to the question of whether the seller is entitled to damages.[1125]

There are, however, important exceptions to the general rule that a buyer is not subject to an actionable duty to take delivery of the goods (*i.e.* to cooperate with delivery). For example, when the buyer intends to reject the delivered goods but is not obliged to pay for the goods, the buyer is required to physically take delivery (property in the goods is not transferred; aflevering maar geen ontvangstneming),[1126] unless taking delivery results in serious inconvenience or unreasonable costs or unless the seller or an authorised person is present to take delivery.[1127] Where the buyer is in default in taking delivery in the aforementioned situation, the seller is – in accordance with its obligation to mitigate losses – required to sell the goods in an appropriate manner (for the best possible price) if the

1120 This notion follows from the principle that a promisee is not obliged to accept performance; Dutch Parliamentary History Book 6 (n 207), 219, 230; See for sales contracts: Hijma, *Asser Koop en ruil* 7-I* 2013 (n 48) 575.

1121 Art 6:58 DCC; see for a detailed discussion about the concept of obliegenheit in Dutch law: De Jong, Krans and Wissink 2018 (n 194) 11, 157, 159. 170.

1122 Art 6:58 DCC.

1123 Art 7:31 DCC; Hijma, *Asser Koop en ruil* 7-I* 2013 (n 48) 575, 576.

1124 Art 6:58 DCC.

1125 Art 6:58 DCC.

1126 *E.g.*, a duty to take delivery of the goods does not arise in case of CIF contracts because the obligation of the buyer to pay the price arises at the moment the seller tenders the shipping documents and does not depend on an inspection of the goods or the arrival of the goods in the port destination; Filippo Lorenzon, Yvonne Baatz, C Nicoll and David Myer Sassoon, *C.I.F. and F.O.B. Contracts* (5th edn, Sweet & Maxwell 2012) paras 8–001.

1127 Art 7:29 (2) DCC; Hijma, *Asser Koop en ruil* 7-I* 2013 (n 48) 581, 584.

goods are subject to rapid loss or deterioration or if its safekeeping would cause serious inconvenience or unreasonable costs.[1128]

The buyer may also be obliged to take delivery of the goods on the basis of an express term or implied term by business usage or under the requirements of reasonableness and fairness in view of the interests of the seller.[1129] A crucial factor for recognising the existence of a duty to take delivery of the goods is the requirement that the seller has a justified interest in acceptance of the goods and that the rights of the latter are affected when the buyer defaults.[1130] For example, in the case where a supplier of gas concluded a contract for the sale of ammonia, which is a by-product from the production process, the buyer was not entitled to refuse the delivery of the ammonia.[1131] In this situation, the seller had a special interest in the buyer's act of taking delivery.

182. The contract law of Singapore expressly and implicitly imposes the duty to take delivery on the buyer.[1132] This fundamental obligation derives from the buyer's statutory obligation to accept the goods, which entails two elements, to wit: taking delivery of the goods and the legal acceptance of the goods.[1133] The aforementioned act of taking delivery of the goods does not automatically constitute an act of *legal* acceptance of the goods.[1134] The delivered goods are only deemed to be *legally* accepted if the buyer declares that it has accepted the goods, when the conduct of the buyer is inconsistent with the ownership of the seller (*e.g.* the buyer uses or resales the goods),[1135] and when after delivery of the goods, the buyer fails to notify the seller within a reasonable time that it has rejected them.[1136] Considering the principle that a buyer is subject to an express or implied duty to take delivery of the goods, the subsequent question arises whether an unjustified delay or refusal in performance

1128 Arts 7:30, 7:32 DCC.

1129 Art 6:248 (1) DCC; Hijma, *Asser Koop en ruil* 7-I* 2013 (n 48) 578; see for the interest of the promisor Dutch Parliamentary History Book 6 (n 207) 230; *E.g.*, District Court Breda 16 August 2006, ECLI:NL:RBBRE:2006:AY6407, NJF 2006, 444; District Court Rotterdam 10 January 1921, ECLI:NL:RBROT:1921:46, NJ 1921, 384; It is argued that a duty to accept performance follows from the obligation of the parties to take into account each other's justified interest. See MAMC van den Berg, 'Crediteursverzuim: relict van een verouderd rechtsdenken', in Gijs van Dijck, Rob van Gestel, Ivo Giesen and Fred Hammerstein (eds), *Cirkels. Een terugblik op een vooruitziende blik* (Kluwer 2013) 89–96; Van den Berg, Van Gulijk, *Asser 7-VI* 2017 (n 203) 77.

1130 Hijma, *Asser* 7-I* 2013 (n 48) 578; Sieburgh, *Asser* 6-I (n 363) para 291.

1131 Dutch Court of Appeal 's-Gravenhage 8 April 1921, NJ 1921, 1151; Hijma, *Asser* 7-I* 2013 (n 48) 578.

1132 SGA, ss 27, 29, 37(1); Hunter 2017 (n 7) para 7.1; Schwenzer, Hachem and Kee 2012 (n 13) para 35.17.

1133 Shenoy and Loo 2013 (n 13) para 22.57; Chong et al 2016 (n 125) para 10.6.15; Hunter 2017 (n 7) para 7.1.

1134 Shenoy and Loo 2013 (n 13) para 22.57.

1135 In *WBG Network (S) Pte Ltd v Sunny Daisy Ltd* [2007] SGCA 1 [2], (2007) 1 SLR(R) 1133 it was considered that the buyer had legally accepted the goods by selling them to its customers; SGA, s 35(1)(b).

1136 SGA, ss 6, 35(1)(2)(4); Chong et al 2016 (n 125) paras 10.6.10, 10.8.3; If the buyer has factually taken delivery, but rightfully rejected acceptance and has informed the seller about its refusal, the buyer is not obliged to return the goods; *Chuan Hiap Seng (1979) Pte Ltd v Progress Manufacturing Pte Ltd* [1995] SGHC 17 [11]-[15]), (2015) 1 SLR(R) 122.

of this obligation entitles the seller to claim for enforced performance. This question is answered in the negative as the equitable action of enforced performance of non-monetary obligations is only available for non-delivery of specific or ascertained goods,[1137] and in other proper circumstances [138, 149]. This means in effect that the aggrieved seller is only entitled to claim damages when the buyer wrongfully neglects or refuses to take the goods or when the latter causes unreasonable delays in taking delivery.[1138] It should also be noted that an express and implicit duty of the buyer to take delivery of the goods does not entail an enforceable ancillary duty of the buyer to provide the seller with the necessary cooperation to deliver the goods.[1139] Considering the comparative nature of this work, it should also be noted that the contract law of Singapore is not familiar with an overarching duty of commercial parties with equal bargaining power, to act in good faith. Consequently, it appears that there is no legal foundation to adopt a substantive duty of the buyer to cooperate where this is required for delivery. This might be different if the good faith principle is assessed in light of the purpose of the contract (*i.e.* transaction of goods) and the facts of the case (section 4.5), although this shall not result in an actionable duty due to the limited availability of enforced performance of non-monetary obligations under a commercial sales contract.

183. The contract law of China does not explicitly adopt an express obligation of the buyer to take delivery of the goods,[1140] but it appears that the statutory provisions for the sale of goods impose implicitly a non-actionable duty to take delivery of the goods on the buyer.[1141] In addition, note should be taken of the predecessor of the Chinese contract law, that is, the Economic Contract Law. This set of principles included an obligation of the buyer to accept delivery within the time fixed by the parties, which entails the element of taking delivery.[1142] The obligation to pay damages was the statutory remedy for failure in performance of this obligation.[1143] Despite the absence of an enforceable duty of the buyer to take delivery of the goods, the statutory obligation to act in good faith may impose such obligation on the buyer, unless there are justifiable reasons for refusal.[1144] In this context, the obligation to act in good faith may also bring about a duty of the buyer to cooperate,

1137 SGA, s 52(1).

1138 SGA, ss 37(1), 50; Chong et al 2016 (n 125) para 10.6.7; Halsbury's Laws of Singapore (Commercial Law 2014) vol 5(2) para 60.191; *Sunny Daisy Ltd WBG Network (Singapore) Pte Ltd* [2006] SGHC 130 affirmed in *WBG Network (S) Pte Ltd* (n 1135).

1139 Compare Hunter 2017 (n 7) para 7.30.

1140 Bing Ling 2002 (n 229) para 8.027; A different view is taken by S Han mentioned in Schwenzer, Hachem and Kee 2012 (n 13) para 37.01 footnote 1 and para 35.17 footnote 28.

1141 Art 143 CCL.

1142 Art 17(4) ECL.

1143 Art 33(2)(a) ECL.

1144 Bing Ling 2002 (n 229) para 8.027; Bu 2013 (n 226) para 7.

which could serve as a legal basis to establish the buyer's obligation to provide reasonably expected assistance by taking delivery of the goods.[1145] A failure in performance of the obligation to take delivery and/or to provide the necessary cooperation (on the basis of the obligation to act in good faith) is formally regarded as non-performance,[1146] although the buyer's duty to take delivery in this regard is also not actionable because it requires a personal act. Taking into account the consideration above, it is submitted here that a buyer could be subject to a duty to take delivery of the goods under Chinese contract law. However, in a similar vein as the Economic Contract Law principles, a failure in performance of this obligation only entitles the seller to sue for monetary non-performance remedies, such as damages or contractual fines.[1147] This applies equally to cases where the duty to take delivery and/or to provide the necessary cooperation arises from the principle of good faith. This is because obligations founded on the good faith principle are said to be unsuitable for enforced performance.[1148]

184. *Comparative analysis* – The contract law of the Netherlands and China draw a distinction between the general availability of enforced performance for a failure in delivery of the goods and the situation where the buyer fails to take delivery of the goods. The two jurisdictions act on the principle that, while the seller is obliged to deliver the goods, the buyer has no such express duty to take delivery of the goods. This may be different where the courts of the Netherlands and China see reason to implicitly impose an obligation to take delivery on the buyer, or to assume such an obligation (*e.g.* in the form of a duty to cooperate) in view of the standards of reasonableness and fairness and good faith respectively. It appears, however, that the default regimes of both jurisdictions do not envisage an actionable obligation of the buyer to take delivery. This is because a failure in performance of an obligation to take delivery on the grounds set out above merely results in a situation of *mora creditoris*. This qualification brings about certain consequences for safeguarding the seller against harm caused by the refusal to take delivery of the goods. Potential consequences are: the threshold for the duty of care of the seller is lowered, the seller may sell the goods, or claim for monetary compensation (not damages), or both when this is appropriate in view of the circumstances of the case.

The contract law of Singapore takes a different approach by expressly and implicitly imposing the obligation to take delivery on the buyer in view of its positive duty to accept the goods. Nonetheless, also under Singapore contract law, the applicable principles merely result in a non-actionable duty of the buyer. Moreover, there is no alternative legal route

---

1145 Bing Ling 2002 (n 229) paras 5.016, 8.027.

1146 Bing Ling 2002 (n 229) para 8.027.

1147 Art 33(2)(2), 34(2)(5) ECL; Bing Ling 2002 (n 229) para 8.028; s 7.5.

1148 Art 110(2) CCL; Bing Ling 2002 (n 229) para 8.028.

as the buyer is not subject to a general duty to cooperate. Hence, the three investigated jurisdictions all assume that the buyer to a commercial sales contract is subject to a non-actionable duty to take delivery of the goods. Consequently, it appears that the court adjudicating the case mentioned under paragraph 180 shall not grant the seller's claim to assist the latter with the modalities required for making delivery if the contract is covered by the contract law regime of any of the three investigated jurisdictions.

At a legal and practical level, it is also of immense importance to take note of potential gaps where a commercial sales contract entails the carriage/shipment of goods, while the payment of the purchase price becomes due during transit. In this situation, if the seller is not able to seek recourse to the civil law instrument of suspension of performance (*i.e.* delivery of the goods on arrival), and common law concepts of the seller's lien and right of *stoppage in transitu* (*e.g.* the seller looses its lien when the goods are delivered to the carrier),[1149] the seller may be left empty handed when the buyer refuses to pay the agreed purchase price and takes delivery of the goods upon arrival.

The non-actionable nature of the buyer's duty to take delivery has a significant impact where the buyer's obligation to pay the purchase price only becomes due after delivery of the goods and the buyer refuses to take delivery.[1150] Taking this into consideration, along with the fact that international trade is the backbone of the three subject jurisdictions, it is important to note that the CISG and DCFR have taken a completely opposite approach by adopting an express duty of the buyer to take delivery of the goods in conjunction with the notion that all obligations of the buyer are subject to the same remedies.[1151] This means in effect that an aggrieved seller is entitled to claim for enforced performance of the buyer's obligation to take delivery. A similar result may be achieved under the PICC, PECL and the draft PACL on the basis of the principle that the buyer is under an enforceable duty to cooperate, which means that the buyer can be required to engage in actions to facilitate the seller's obligation to deliver the goods.[1152] The aforementioned approaches may be used as a source of inspiration by the national legislators of the subject jurisdictions in order to develop a solution for the above-mentioned contingent obligations of the parties to a commercial sales contract.

1149 The concept of the seller's lien allows the unpaid seller to secure its right to payment by retaining possession regardless of the passing of title. The concept of *stoppage in transitu* is a form of suspension of performance after performance which is useful where the handing over of the goods brings about the legal delivery and the transfer of title (note that transfer of possession does not necessarily coincide with transfer of property). In this situation, the seller may prevent the physical handing over of the goods if specific requirements are fulfilled. The concept of *stoppage in transitu* is also adopted by the CISG in art 71(2).

1150 S 4.4, 5.3.

1151 Art 53, 60 CISG; Schwenzer 2016 (n 91) para 41; Arts IV.A.-3:101(b) Comment C, IV.A.-3:301 Comment A DCFR.

1152 Art 5.1.3 PICC; Vogenauer 2015 (n 19) Art 5.1.3 para 10; Arts 1:202, 8:101, 9:102 PECL; Art 1(2) draft on non-performance PACL, see Lee 2016 (n 16) 146, 193.

5.4 Discrepancy in quantity and quality

5.4.1 Introduction

185. The foregoing section shows that for a comparative analysis of the availability of enforced performance, a distinction must be made between a situation of non-delivery and where the seller delivers goods which do not conform to the contract. It is recalled that the fulfilment of the delivery obligation does not require that the goods possess the features as agreed in the contract. But this does not mean that the buyer has lost its performance interest. Therefore, this section will discuss whether the default regimes of the subject legal systems envisage the protection of the buyer's performance interest by means of enforced performance - which requires the seller to put the defect right by repair or by making a fresh delivery. Considering the contrasting doctrinal foundations under civil and common law of the availability of enforced performance,[1153] a sub-question that arises is whether these differences impact the ability of the buyer to compel the seller to cure a defect in the goods related to discrepancies in quantity and quality at an international level. A comparative discussion of solutions offered for a non-conforming delivery reveals an important divergence between the two major legal families. Generally, civil law jurisdictions follow the promissory theory which encompasses the notion that the seller, when entering into a sales contract, promises to deliver the goods of the agreed quality and quantity.[1154] This specific undertaking (promise) of the seller to deliver goods in accordance with the terms of the contract is usually codified in a statutory duty,[1155] which serves as the basis for the obligation of the seller to inform the buyer about a deviation of the promised features of the goods (*caveat venditor principle*). The seller's obligation to deliver the goods in accordance with the terms of the contract is also the basis for legal compulsion of the seller to cure a defective performance.[1156] By contrast, common law acts on the *caveat emptor* principle, which literally means 'let the buyer be aware'.[1157] It is, therefore, of little surprise that Singapore contract law is not familiar with a specific notification duty of the buyer as mentioned above. Another important point in this regard is that the contract law of Singapore acts on a system of guarantee liability.[1158] This means in effect that a seller may cure a defective performance in order to prevent liability in damages (*i.e.* the primary response to a failure in performance), but the buyer cannot rely

1153 Ch 4.
1154 NL: art 7:17(1)(3) DCC; CHN: arts 150, 153, 156 CCL.
1155 Hijma, *Asser Koop en ruil* 7-I* 2013 (n 48) para 328; Tjittes 2018 (n 2) 423.
1156 NL: art 7:21 DCC; CHN: arts 107, 111 CCL; See for the general distinction between civil and common law in this regard: Treitel 1998 (n 55) 44.
1157 Tjittes 2018 (n 2) 420.
1158 Treitel 1998 (n 55) 44.

on specific actions to demand cure of a defective delivery in a commercial sales context.[1159] These conflicting viewpoints require specific attention in the case of a commercial sales transaction across civil and common law countries which are members of the CISG, such as the Netherlands, Singapore and China. The rationale is that the law of the country where the buyer claims actual cure of goods may overrule the availability to cure a defective delivery where a sales contract is subject to the CISG.[1160]

186. Another main point of divergence surrounding the assessment of the availability of enforced performance in this study is more practical than dogmatic, but no less important. This concerns differences in the classification of cases of non-conformity and non-delivery and the legal consequences arising therefrom.[1161] For example, when a legal system classifies a discrepancy in quantity as a non-conformity, the availability of enforced performance is usually significantly stricter than legal systems which classify such a case as a non-delivery. This is because the rules on conforming delivery generally oblige the buyer to inspect the goods on delivery and to notify the seller of any defects discovered. That said, the discussion below demonstrates that a buyer could be subject to a notification duty, although a shortfall in goods is not considered as a non-conformity. Furthermore, the differences in classification also may result in a situation where a claim for outstanding goods in country X has a different limitation period when compared to the situation for a buyer located in country Y.

187. In light of the above, the analysis below reviews the availability of a claim for delivery of goods which are missing,[1162] repair and replacement under the contract law of the Netherlands, Singapore and China.[1163] It is also discussed whether there are specific constraints (*e.g.* reasonableness considerations); and if so, to what extent they influence the availability to enforce correction of a defective delivery. Furthermore, specific attention is given to the 'mere' duties of the buyer to examine the goods and to notify the seller about defects and to what extent non-performance of these duties affects the availability to claim for cure.[1164]

1159 Treitel 1998 (n 55) 44.

1160 Art 28 CISG; Treitel 1998 (n 55) 45.

1161 Schwenzer, Hachem and Kee 2012 (n 13) paras 31.09, 31.10.

1162 S 5.4.2.

1163 S 5.4.3.

1164 S 5.4.4.

5.4.2 Shortfall in goods

188. *Preliminary* – In a commercial sales contract, different quantitative values can be used to clarify the scope of the seller's delivery obligation. For example, specific parameters for the identification of a unique batch of premium olive oil. Also general phrases can be used, such as the sale of the entire crop of fruit in a designated year, or the sale of trees on a specified plot of land (*e.g.* a timber sales contract). Should the seller fail to deliver the goods in accordance with the agreed quantity parameters, the question arises whether the aggrieved buyer is entitled to claim for enforced performance of the delivery of the outstanding goods, and to what extent the availability of such a claim is influenced by the legal classification of the seller's non-performance. The following discussion reveals that three situations can be identified in this regard. First, legal systems which regulate discrepancies in quantity as cases of non-conformity and subject the buyer to a specific notification duty (in addition to the general exceptions for enforced performance). The second category consists of legal systems which equate under-delivery with cases of non-delivery, although it establishes specific notification duties where the seller fails to deliver the goods in conformity with the contractual stipulations. The third situation concerns legal systems which equate cases of non-performance (non-delivery) with a non-conforming performance, without any separate notification duty of the buyer.

> *Illustration* – In November 2018, a trader in cocoa contracts to sell a quantity of high quality organic cocoa to a party located in a different jurisdiction and to deliver this by 1 February 2019. However, the trader only delivers half of the ordered cocoa to the buyer and refuses to deliver the outstanding part due to other delivery obligations. Given the growing market demand for this product, the buyer is not able to obtain this type of cocoa from another supplier, although the initial seller still has a significant stock at its premises. In view of this, the question arises to what extent a claim for enforced performance of delivery of the outstanding goods is available.

189. *Domestic approaches* – Under Dutch contract law, a buyer is legally obliged to deliver the goods in accordance with the agreed quantity.[1165] A failure in performance of this obligation makes a case for non-conformity.[1166] Consequently, the aggrieved buyer is entitled to claim for the delivery of the missing goods (be they generic or specific),[1167] provided that the former acted in accordance with its duty to notify the seller in a timely

1165 Art 7:17(1)(3) DCC.
1166 Art 7:17(3) DCC.
1167 Art 7:21(1) DCC.

manner about the discrepancy in quantity.[1168] The buyer is, however, not bound to the limiting preconditions which apply to a claim for repair and replacement.[1169] This means in effect that a claim for enforced performance in the form of delivery of the outstanding goods is not subject to the principle of proportionality and subsidiarity. Nonetheless, it is suggested that the subsidiarity principle should apply in the exceptional situation that another legal measure is rendered a less far-reaching performance remedy.[1170] This viewpoint, however, contradicts the doctrinal principle that a buyer is free to opt for other judicial actions where appropriate.[1171] Moreover, it is submitted here that the absence of specific constraints on the action for a discrepancy in quantity fully accords with the fact that it is a simple failure in performance of a delivery obligation, which does not amount to specific difficulties such as the return transport of defective goods.[1172] Nonetheless, under the Dutch sales law regime, a claim for goods which are missing is constructed as a case of non-conformity and, therefore, differs from an action for enforced performance which (from a conceptual perspective) does not require a failure in performance. Nonetheless, a claim for enforced performance in the form of an order for delivery or cure by repair or replacement is in all instances rooted in the contractual and statutory right of the buyer to be provided with the goods in accordance with the contractual stipulations.

190. The sales law of Singapore follows the traditional common law approach by treating discrepancies in quantity as a failure of the seller's delivery obligation.[1173] In other words, the approach taken by the sales law of Singapore is to treat discrepancies in quantity as a partial failure to deliver the goods (*i.e.* partial delay in delivery), and not as a non-conformity. The consequence is that the buyer is not burdened with a notification duty in order to preserve the availability of obtaining an order for enforced performance.[1174] It also means that the standard process for enforced performance applies where the buyer decides to claim for delivery of missing goods. Hence, a court shall only grant a claim for the delivery of goods which are missing if the goods are specific or ascertained and if it is

1168 Art 7:23(1) DCC; See also art 6:89 DCC. This statuory provision entails a general notification duty for a defective performance.

1169 Hijma, *Asser Koop en ruil* 7-I* 2013 (n 48) 424, 425; see s 5.4.3 for a more detailed discussion about the requirements for preservation of a claim for repair and replacement.

1170 Stolp (n 536) 254.

1171 Dutch Parliamentary History Book 7 (n 1074) 141; Compare Hijma, *Asser Koop en ruil* 7-I* 2013 (n 48) 387.

1172 Schwenzer 2016 (n 91) art 46, para 21.

1173 SGA, s 27; Hunter 2017 (n 7) 7.1.

1174 Despite the non-bindingness of judicial precedent from other Commomwealth countries, reference is made to the Australian case *Castel Electronics Pty v Toshiba Singapore Pte Ltd* (2010) FCA 1028. It was considered that the domestic requirements for correct delivery are equated with art 35 CISG. Hence, a delivery may be regarded as defective where the goods do not correspond to the contract or the requirements set out in the CISG (*i.e.*, quality, quantity and packaging); Hunter 2017 (n 7) para 7.20.

appropriate and justified to do so.[1175] Enforced performance of the seller's obligation to delivery generic goods can also be granted when procurement of substitute goods is practically unobtainable, and the court establishes that damages are not an adequate remedy [138–149]. Aside from this narrow notion of the availability of enforced performance, a claim for the delivery of too few goods is further subject to the limitations discussed in chapter 6. Nonetheless, the aggrieved buyer is not left empty handed where the seller delivers a lesser quantity of commodity goods than it contracted to sell. In this situation, the buyer who does not deal as a consumer, may reject them in the event of a serious shortfall.[1176]

191. Chinese contract law provisions on conformity are largely based on the CISG.[1177] Unfortunately, the process of borrowing provisions from the Convention appears to have led to uncertainty in the qualification of cases concerning a shortfall in goods.[1178] The starting point under the contract law of China in this regard is the provision that a contract shall generally contain clauses on the quantity and quality of the subject matter of the contract.[1179] In contrast to clauses on the required quality of goods and the consequences where the delivered goods fail to satisfy the contract,[1180] the law does not specify a duty for the seller to deliver the goods in compliance with the agreed quantity nor the available performance remedies in cases of a shortfall in goods.[1181] This may suggest that Chinese contract law treats discrepancies in quantity as a non-delivery, and not as a case of non-conformity. Nonetheless, the aggrieved buyer is subject to a specific statutory duty to notify the seller about any non-compliance in quantity.[1182] This means in effect that where the buyer acts in accordance with the aforementioned notification duty, the buyer retains the right to claim for enforced performance of delivery of the outstanding goods.[1183] In other words, it appears that under-delivery of the goods makes a case of non-delivery under the contract law of China, although specific limitations apply where a claim for enforced performance is brought to court.

1175 SGA, s 52(1).

1176 SGA, s s30(1)(2A)(a); Shenoy and Loo 2013 (n 13) para 22.115.

1177 André Janssen and Samuel CK Chau, 'CCL and Unidroit Principles' in DiMatteo and Chen 2017 (n 19) 450, 466.

1178 *Ibid.*

1179 Art 12(3)(4) CCL.

1180 Arts 111, 153 CCL.

1181 Art 153 CCL; Art 5.1.6 PICC employs the concept of average quality, but this entails a different standard than the concept of conformity in art 35(1) CISG and art I V.A.–2:101, art IV.A.–2:301 DCFR Conformity with the contract.

1182 Art 158 CCL.

1183 Art 107 CCL; André Janssen and Samuel CK Chau, 'CCL and Unidroit Principles' in DiMatteo and Chen 2017 (n 19) 379; Bing Ling 2002 (n 229) para 8.082.

192. *Comparative analysis* – Although the three investigated jurisdictions, as well as the unification instruments, all adopt principles for a defective performance,[1184] there is a significant disparity when considering the qualification of cases of a shortfall in goods. The need to address this issue and to strive for a uniform approach derives from the far-reaching consequences following from the applicable thresholds for obtaining an order for delivery of the missing goods. In other words, the aggrieved buyer may lose its right to claim for outstanding goods when it does not realise that the law governing the contract classifies a shortfall in goods as a non-conformity and thus imposes a specific notification duty on the buyer. The same applies when the seller mistakenly assumes that a shortfall in goods is not subject to a notification duty because the statutory principles are merely concerned with remedies for discrepancies in quality. The overarching power of domestic rules in the realm of CISG-contracts is another risk factor which undermines the protection of the buyer's performance interest at the international level. The general rationale of a notification duty for a shortfall in goods is that the seller must be provided with an opportunity to restore its failure in performance.[1185] One could question if this reason aligns with the loss of a claim for a conforming performance upon the expiry of a limitation period, because an important aspect of this barrier to enforced performance is similar to the objective of the buyer's notification duty. That is, to protect the seller against stale claims. Nevertheless, a case could be made that the seller is negatively affected where the buyer claims for the outstanding goods after an unreasonably long period, but before the expiry of the applicable (relative) limitation period.

193. The approach to under-delivery found in Dutch contract law is to treat discrepancies in quantity as a non-conformity, which brings about a specific notification requirement for the buyer. This also means that a claim for enforced performance of delivery of the missing goods cannot be equated with the general availability of obtaining a claim for enforced performance, as the latter (theoretically) does not require a failure in performance.[1186] Nonetheless, in both situations (complete non-delivery and non-conforming delivery), the contractual right to performance is the source of the action for enforced performance. The situation under the contract law of China is less clear, although it is assumed that discrepancies in quantity classify as a non-delivery, which means that the general exceptions for enforced performance apply. Nonetheless, Chinese contract law establishes a specific notification duty for the buyer for situations of under-delivery. Another interesting point is that the classification of non-delivery does

1184 Art 35(1) CISG; Art 7.2.3 PICC; Art 9:102(1) PECL; Art III.-3:201 DCFR; Art 1 Draft Articles on Non-Performance PACL.

1185 Comment A under art III.-3:107 DCFR.

1186 Ss 4.2.2, 4.4.2.

not align with the dogmatic notion that a claim for enforced performance derives from the act of contract making and may, therefore, be brought to court before an infringement of a statutory or contractual right. The contract law of Singapore takes a similar approach in the sense that discrepancies in quantity are treated as non-delivery, although the aggrieved buyer is not subject to a (specific) notification duty.[1187] Hence, the aggrieved buyer is entitled to claim for enforced performance in the form of delivery of the outstanding goods, provided that the goods are specific or ascertained from the contract, and in other proper circumstances, and damages are inadequate.[1188] This, in effect, means that the cocoa trader in the example mentioned under paragraph 188 can be ordered by the court to deliver the outstanding amount of cocoa under the contract law of the investigated legal systems, provided that domestic prerequisites are fulfilled.[1189] That said, in view of the differing perspectives on the notification duty of the buyer, it is submitted here that the divergence in the dogmatic classification of discrepancies in quantity by the three subject jurisdictions results in a different degree of protection of the interests of the aggrieved buyer to obtain the very thing it bargained for.

194. From a theoretical perspective, the approaches taken at the international level also differ significantly. The most important instrument for commercial sales qualifies discrepancies as a non-conforming delivery and encompasses specific requirements and duties of contracting parties, such as the obligation to give notice of lack of conformity.[1190] Under the DCFR and the draft PACL, discrepancies in quantity qualify as a non-performance, but they each adopt a specific notification requirement where the goods delivered are not in accordance with the values set out in the contract.[1191] Although the PICC and PECL mention the occurrence of a defective performance, they also classify discrepancies in quantity (and quality) as a general failure in performance.[1192] Importantly, the language of the applicable principles suggests that the buyer is not subject to specific notification duties for a defective performance. Nevertheless, it is held that the PICC encompasses a duty for the buyer to give notice of defects within a reasonable time on loss

1187 See s 5.4.4 for a detailed discussion about the underpinnings of the absence of a notification duty in the contract law of Singapore.

1188 S 4.4.3.

1189 S 4.4; In the case where the type of cocoa qualifies as a commodity, enforced performance can be granted when it is practically unobtainable to purchase substitute goods at the market (paras 138, 149).

1190 Arts 35(1), 39 CISG.

1191 Art III.-3:107(1) DCFR entails a duty of the buyer to inform the seller about a non-conforming delivery, the right to claim for a conforming delivery is subject to the general rules on enforced performance as set out in art III.-3:302 DCFR; In a similar vein, art 3 Draft Articles on non-performance PACL bring about a notification duty. The other exceptions to claim for a conforming performance follow from the general rules on the availability of enforced performance as laid down in, *i.a.*, arts 1, 7 of the Draft Articles on Non-Performance PACL.

1192 Arts 7.2.2, 7.2.3 PICC; Art 1:301, 9:102(1) PECL; Art III.-3:201 DCFR.

of a claim for enforced performance.[1193] The considerations above expose a myriad of approaches, indicating that there is no general consensus on the issue of qualification of a scenario of discrepancies in quantity and the legal consequences deriving therefrom.

The proposition submitted here is that those involved in international commercial sales contracts looking for an alternative to bridge the gap between national perspectives must carefully assess the applicable principles under the unification instruments to find the most appropriate and acceptable outcome for both parties. When considering the objective of the present comparative research, it is maintained here that the interests of the parties to a commercial sales contract are best protected by the CISG (*i.e.* the seller's interest in being protected against abuse and the buyer's performance interest). This is because the parties can easily determine what is required due to the express reference to a situation of discrepancies in quantity, by regulating this scenario in a separate framework for non-conforming goods, and by setting out the legal consequences where one of the parties fails to act in accordance with the stipulated duties.[1194]

5.4.3 *Repair and replacement*

195. *Preliminary* – This section discusses the availability of enforced performance in the form of repair and replacement in cases where the quality of the goods delivered is not in conformity with the contract and the applicable law. An analysis of this topic is perilous due to the disagreement between the civil and common law traditions on whether an aggrieved party to a commercial sales contract should be entitled to enforced performance at all and, if so, to what extent limitations apply, or whether enforced performance is only available in exceptional situations (section 4.4). In order to bring more clarity to the matter, this section does not merely discuss the opposing viewpoints and whether they originate in the civil or common law traditions, but delves into the intricacies of the entire framework of the rules on non-conformity and the availability of enforced performance in the form of cure where the goods delivered deviate from the applicable conformity standards. This approach is justified by the absence of any balanced solution in the unification instruments identified and the potentially grave consequences where the parties are not aware of the discussed differences between the investigated legal systems. For example, certain civil law jurisdictions differentiate between the available judicial actions for defective goods (delivery of a *peius*) and delivery of different goods (delivery of an *aliud*). Difficulties from the distinction between cases of a non-conforming delivery and non-delivery may arise where the goods could be assessed as generic and specific (*e.g.* olive oil or coffee from a specific

1193 Vogenauer 2015 (n 19) art 7.2.2 para 58.

1194 The discussion in this section implies that the same can be said of Dutch contract law, as the latter has adopted similar provisions for a scenario where the seller fails to deliver the agreed quantity.

region or harvest year). In circumstances where such goods do not comply with the applicable conformity requirements, a case could be made for non-conformity, but it may also qualify as a non-delivery. Aside from determining the available remedies in both situations, understanding the approach taken by a legal system is also of paramount importance because different legal barriers apply to cases of non-delivery and non-conformity (*e.g.* examination and notice requirements, and limitation periods).

> *Illustration 1* – A vehicle manufacturer, located in country X, enters into a sales contract with an international transport company, located in country Y. The sales contract stipulates that the vehicle manufacturer is obliged to deliver 100 electric trucks. After delivery, the buyer notices that the manufacturer delivered hybrid trucks. This, in effect, means that the buyer shall not be able to lower the costs of petrol as envisaged and the buyer is not entitled to apply for specific governmental grants.

> *Illustration 2* – Company A (seller), located in country X, agrees to sell a specified amount of minerals, to Company B, located in country Y. Company A delivers the minerals with its accessories (*i.e.* documentary evidence of the conditions under which the minerals have been extracted), but inspection of the accessories shows that the minerals were not extracted from the designated source. The buyer argues that the minerals do not comply with the quality requirements and therefore claims for a substitute delivery, although the minerals were physically in conformity with the contract.

196. The discussion below focusses first on the characteristics of the conformity scheme and whether different standards apply to contracts which specify the quality of the goods and contracts which are silent on the matter. It then looks at the classification of judicial actions for repair and replacement, to what extent their availability is affected by specific constraints, and whether the availability of cure by replacement can be frustrated where the seller insists on repair of the goods.[1195] This comparative analysis is essential given that the solution offered by the CISG is not very effective due to the principle that domestic restrictions can be invoked against a claim for enforced performance of an obligation under a commercial sales contract which is subject to the Convention.[1196] The premise that this principle also applies in case of non-conformity follows from its position in the General Provisions of the CISG which governs the various (interrelated) forms of enforced performance of the seller's obligation.[1197]

1195 Treitel 1998 (n 55) para 376.

1196 See the preconditions in arts 46(1), 28 CISG; Schwenzer 2016 (n 91) art 46, para 17.

1197 Art 46 CISG shows that the drafters of the Convention adopted a broad notion of the concept of enforced performance. That is, enforced performance entails a general right to require performance of the selller's obligations, and in the case of non-conformity; a right to require delivery of substitute goods and repair.

Illustration 3 – A textile manufacturing company, located in country X, buys a specific and unique sustainable dyeing machine from a technology company, located in country Y. After four weeks, the machine can no longer be used due to an incurable defect. The buyer claims for enforced performance in the form of the installation of a replacement machine by the initial seller. The buyer substantiates the claim for enforced performance with the argument that its financial position is too limited to acquire a similar machine from another technology company.

Illustration 4 – A producer of machinery for the aerospace, energy and medical industry concludes a sales contract with a party in the commercial sector. The contract encompasses the sale of a specific and unique machine. After delivery, however, the buyer notices that the machine is inoperable and defective. In this situation, the buyer is not interested in returning the machine because uninstalling and dismantling the thing would cause great inconvenience. Taken together, the buyer claims for repair of the machine.

197. *Domestic approaches* – Dutch contract law differentiates between the conformity standards for commercial sales contracts which are silent on the matter and commercial sales contracts which specify the features and required quality of the goods to be delivered. The first situation may arise where commercial parties conclude a contract for the sale of generic goods (*e.g.* palm oil, rice or grain).[1198] Absent of a party agreement on the quality standards of the goods, recourse must be had to the principle that if the thing due is only determined as to kind and if there exists a difference of quality within the specified kind, the seller may not deliver goods of less than average good quality.[1199] With this statutory rule, the legitimate interests and reasonable expectations of the aggrieved buyer are the main sources to determine the conformity standards in the absence of a party agreement.[1200] Dutch contract law takes a different approach where a commercial contract encompasses the sale of specific goods and where the features of generic goods are specified in the contract.[1201] In these instances, the seller is obliged to deliver the goods in accordance with the specifications of the contract.[1202] It is assumed that the goods are not in conformity with the contract if they do not have the characteristics which the buyer is entitled to expect under the contract, taking into account the nature of the goods and the statements made

1198 De Jong, Krans and Wissink 2018 (n 194) 60, 81.

1199 Art 6:28 DCC; Sieburgh, *Asser 6-I* (n 363) para 236.

1200 Art 6:248(1) DCC; AC van Schaick in Schelhaas 2002 (n 19) 276.

1201 MM van Rossum, 'commentaar op artikel 17 Boek 7 BW' in CG Breedveld-de Voogd and SE Bartels (eds), *Groene Serie Bijzondere overeenkomsten* (Wolters Kluwer 2017); Hijma, *Asser Koop en ruil* 7-I* 2013 (n 48) 325.

1202 Art 7:17(1) DCC (based on arts 18 , 19(1) ULIS); see also art 35 CISG.

by the seller about them.[1203] In this regard, the buyer may expect that the goods have the characteristics necessary for normal use and the presence of such quality expectations the buyer had no reason to doubt, and that the goods have the characteristics for the particular use foreseen in the contract.[1204] The goods are also not in conformity with the contract where the seller delivers goods other than those agreed in the contract (delivery of an *aliud*).[1205] Hence, Dutch contract law has not adopted the traditional civil law distinction between the causes of non-conformity.[1206] This means in effect that where the seller supplies defective goods (*peius*) or something completely different (*aliud*) than stipulated in the contract, the rules on non-conformity apply. In these instances, the aggrieved buyer may sue for an order for enforced performance which may require the seller to put the defect right or to deliver substitute goods, provided that the applicable preconditions are fulfilled.

Where the contract (in)directly specifies the quality of the goods, an aggrieved buyer is entitled to demand performance in the form of an order for repair or replacement of the non-conforming goods. These actions are sometimes described as subforms of the right to obtain an order for enforced performance when non-conforming goods are delivered.[1207] This approach is understandable when considering the broad discretionary power of the buyer to make use of its right to claim enforced performance, and cure by repair and replacement. Nonetheless, the right to enforced performance of the delivery obligation follows directly from the act of promise making and should, therefore, not be equated with a right to claim for a cure by repair and replacement which is the statutory response to non-conformity. In this light, it is also unsurprising that the independent legal concept of repair and replacement is subject to specific restrictions and that these bring about specific duties for the buyer (section 5.4.4). The distinction between a claim for enforced performance and a claim for a cure also results in different limitation periods (section 6.4). As for the specific constraints on the buyer's right to cure, the latter is only entitled to claim repair provided that the seller technically and economically can reasonably comply therewith.[1208] Alternatively, a buyer could demand a replacement, unless the variance from what was agreed is too insignificant to justify this.[1209] The threefold assessment to be made is whether repair is possible, whether an order for repair or replacement would have an adverse impact on the seller (proportionality),[1210] and if there is a less far-reaching performance remedy which could also accomplish the objective of

1203 Art 7:17(1)(2) DCC.
1204 Art 7:17 (2) DCC.
1205 Art 7:17(3) DCC.
1206 Schwenzer, Hachem and Kee 2012 (n 13) para 31.15.
1207 Hijma, *Asser Koop en ruil* 7-I* 2013 (n 48) 380; Mak (n 527) 120; Stolp (n 536) 188.
1208 Art 7:21(1)(b) DCC, Hartkamp 2011 (n 80) para 256.
1209 Art 7:21 (1)(a)(b) DCC.
1210 Stolp (n 536) 189, 250; Dutch Parliamentary History Book 7 (n 1074) 136.

the contract (subsidiarity).[1211] If these requirements are met, the seller may be obliged to repair and replace the goods within a reasonable period, and without causing serious inconvenience to the buyer, taking into account the nature of the thing and the particular use of it specified in the contract.[1212] The discretionary power of the buyer to claim cure by replacement and repair is, however, restricted by the seller's right to cure a non-conformity (after the time for performance and regardless of the severity of the non-conformity) as long as the seller offers to compensate the aggrieved buyer's damages and costs and the performance obligation of the seller is not removed by, for example, avoidance of the contract.[1213]

198. The Singapore Sale of Goods Act is familiar with a number of rules related to the required quality of goods delivered under a commercial sales contract. These statutory provisions do so in a manner distinct from the two other subject jurisdictions due to the English common law origin of Singapore sales law. As a result, the rules on conformity are designated as express and implied warranties.[1214] In basic common law terminology, conformity standards stipulated in the contract are addressed as express warranties or conditions. Briefly put, a failure in performance in accordance with a condition gives the aggrieved party the right to terminate the contract, whereas a failure in performance in accordance with a warranty gives rise to a right to claim damages but not to end the contract. Another form is failure in performance of an innominate or intermediate term which entitles the aggrieved party to end the contract only if the non-performance is sufficiently serious. The starting point for the present discussion is that the goods supplied under a commercial sales contract are of satisfactory quality.[1215] Goods are of satisfactory quality if they meet the standard that a reasonable person would regard as satisfactory, taking account of any discretion of the goods, the price (if relevant) and all the other relevant circumstances.[1216] The aforementioned implied rules on the conformity of the goods apply

1211 Stolp (n 536) 192; Dutch Parliamentary History Book 7 (n 1074) 134, 135.

1212 Art 7:21(3) DCC.

1213 Art 6:86 DCC; See art 6:269 DCC for the situation where the seller insists on curing the non-conformity after the aggrieved buyer claimed for avoidance of the contract; Haas 2009 (n 206) 265, 266; De Jong, Krans and Wissink 2018 (n 194) 258; It is important to mention that Dutch contract law considers cure of non-performance by repair and replacement of the thing deliverd as a method of providing the seller the very thing it contracted for. A different approach is to consider cure by repair and replacement as a form of damages because the seller bears the incurred costs.

1214 SGA, s 53(3); Chong et al 2016 (n 125) paras 10.8.21–10.8.23; see also Hunter 2017 (n 7) para 6.1; Anson's Law of Contract (n 360) 152, 153; Adam M Giuliano, 'Nonconformity in the Sale of Goods between the United States and China: The New Chinese Contract Law, the Uniform Commercial Code, and the Convention on Contracts for the International Sale of Goods' (2006) 18(1) Florida Journal of International Law 331, 341–342.

1215 SGA, s 14(2); Chong et al 2016 (n 125) para 10.3.21.

1216 SGA, s 14(2A).

equally to generic and specific goods. Furthermore, no distinction is made between the delivery of an *aliud* and *peius* because the focus is on the occurrence of a failure in performance and not the exact cause (*e.g.* delivery of defective goods and delivery of different goods). Taking this into account, the express reference to non-delivery in the provision for specific performance, and the fact that damages are the default legal response to remedy a failure in performance of a commercial sales contract which does not involve consumers, (partially) explains why a Singapore court shall not make a decree for repair or replacement where the seller fails to deliver the goods in accordance with the express and implied conformity standards.[1217] This does not mean that the aggrieved buyer is not entitled to sue for enforced performance (which may require to repair the goods or to make a fresh delivery) where the seller delivers defective goods. This proposition will be discussed in more detail below.

As previously mentioned, the contract and sales law of Singapore is based on the common law system of England, which is not familiar with enforced performance in the form of repair and replacement for non-conforming delivery under a commercial sales contract. As for the latter, the present research does not concern the availability of repair and replacement where a 'business to business transaction' qualifies as a consumer sale [14].[1218] For the purposes of the present study, it suffices to note in this regard that a failure in performance of the applicable non-conformity standards arising from a commercial sales contract (*i.e.* express warranties or conditions) and from the law (*i.e.* implied warranties or conditions) only entitles a business purchasing goods to claim for performance in the form of damages when the purchaser does not qualify as a consumer in the specific transaction. It appears, however, that the discretionary power of Singapore courts (in the realm of commercial sales) to provide a decree for enforced performance is not restricted to cases of non-delivery of specific and ascertained goods.[1219] It is suggested that this statutory restriction does not affect the discretionary power of Singapore courts to grant an order for enforced performance in cases of non-delivery which fall outside the ambit of the Singapore Sale of Goods Act.[1220] This approach implies that Singapore courts may provide an order for enforced performance of non-delivery of generic goods, provided

1217 Phang et al 2012 (n 112) paras 23.124, 23.124; Hunter 2017 (n 7) para 6.4; Schwenzer, Hachem and Kee 2012 (n 13); Treitel 1998 (n 55) 44.

1218 Phang et al 2012 (n 112) paras 23.119, 23.124; Schwenzer, Hachem and Kee 2012 (n 13) para 6.23, 43.38; SGA, s 52(1); S 12C of the Consumer Protection (Fair Trading) Act (Chapter 52A) (Rev Ed 2009) allows a business purchasing goods to demand replacement of repair of non-conforming goods where it qualifies as a consumer under ss 12(1)(a) and (b) of the Unfair Contract Terms Act (Chapter 396) (Rev Ed 1994), see s 12A(2) the Consumer Protection (Fair Trading) Act (Chapter 52A) (Rev Ed 2009). In view of the principles set out in these statutory provisions, it is important to bear in mind that the Singapore Court of Appeal adopted a broad definition of situations (intended use of the goods) where a business purchasing goods may be regarded as a consumer and thus is entitled to claim for repair and replacement, see para 14.

1219 SGA, s 52(1); Phang et al 2012 (n 112) paras 23.119, 23.124.

1220 Phang et al 2012 (n 112) para 23.119; Anson's Law of Contract (n 360) 610.

that it is commercially impractical for the aggrieved buyer to obtain substitute goods and damages are inadequate.[1221] It appears, however, that the aforementioned extension of the discretionary power of the courts to cases which fall outside the ambit of section 52 of the Singapore Sale of Goods Act does not go so far as to allow the court to provide a decree for performance which requires the seller to put a defective delivery right by repair or replacement of the goods. As Singapore judges are entitled to deviate from the traditional English law position where appropriate, it is worth noting that in US case law a broader notion of the concept of enforced performance is adopted.[1222] For example, in exercising its discretion, a court adjudicating a dispute under the UCC reached the conclusion that forcing the seller to repair a malfunctioning machine is justified because the buyer already paid for the machine, and is unable to raise money to buy a substitute machine from another seller.[1223] Nonetheless, from a recent Singapore contract law treatise it follows that the concept of enforced performance does not include repair and replacement as special forms of performance for cases where the goods sold under a commercial sales contract deviate from the quality standards arising from express and implied warranties.[1224] It must be noted that the legislation for consumer sales has departed from this restricted approach as Singapore legislators made it clear that an aggrieved buyer may apply for repair or replacement if the goods which are delivered by a commercial seller deviate from the applicable conformity standards.[1225]

199. Chinese contract law has adopted an extensive scheme with rules on conformity of the goods supplied under a commercial sales contract. The starting point for determining the scope of these rules is the notion that the parties are obliged to deliver the goods in conformity with the terms of the contract.[1226] This principle is further articulated in the statutory provision that the seller is obliged to deliver the goods in compliance with the agreed quality standard.[1227] The assessment of whether the goods are in conformity to the contract should be made in view of the later discussed broad interpretation of the concept of non-conformity and defective goods as adopted by the CISG and PICC respectively. This is because the drafters of the contract law of China draw inspiration from the

1221 Phang et al 2012 (n 112) para 23.124; SGA, s 52(1).

1222 Shael Herman, 'Specific Performance: a Comparative Analysis' (2003) 7(1) Edinburgh Law Review 5; Shael Herman, 'Specific Performance: a Comparative Analysis' (2003) 7(2) Edinburgh Law Review 194.

1223 See the US case *Stephan's Machine & Tool Inc v D&H Machinery Consultants Inc* [1979] Ohio Ct App, (1979) 417 NE2d 579.

1224 In Dora Neo, 'Specific Remedies and the Performance Interest in Singapore Contract Law' in Chen-Wishart, Loke and Ong 2016 (n 156) 208 it is clearly stated that a claim for repair and replacement can only be brought to court under the CPFTA.

1225 Singapore Consumer Protection (Fair Trading) Act (Cap. 52A), s 12C; The so-called Lemon Laws are added to the aforementioned Consumer Protection Act, effective 1 September 2012.

1226 Art 8 CCL.

1227 Art 153 CCL.

unification instruments in this regard. It may, therefore, be assumed that delivery of defective goods (*peius*) and delivery of different goods (*aliud*) are governed by the non-conformity rules.[1228] In cases where the contract is silent on the matter or the provisions of the contract are not clear about the required features of the goods, Chinese contract law stipulates that the parties may agree on supplementary terms through negotiation; if a supplementary agreement cannot be reached, such terms shall be determined in accordance with the relevant provisions of the contract or transaction practices.[1229] Should it prove to be impossible to determine the quality requirement along the lines of the aforementioned principles, the seller is obliged to deliver the goods in accordance with the state standard or industry standard. In the absence of such standards, the quality of the goods must comply with customary standards or any particular standard consistent with the purpose of the contract.[1230] Unfortunately, the conformity standards arising from this three-step approach (*i.e.* (i) party agreement, (ii) business usage, (iii) specific standards) do not provide the same level of clarity as the CISG,[1231] which is one of the main sources of inspiration for the drafters of the Chinese contract law. As for the legal consequences of a deviation of the conformity standards (*e.g.* the goods are defective or different goods are delivered than agreed in the contract), the aggrieved buyer is entitled to sue for enforced performance by means of repair and replacement of the goods. In sum, the Chinese contract law does not differentiate between non-conformity of specific and generic goods, nor does it make a distinction between the classification of delivery of different goods and delivery of defective goods. Both situations appear to fall under the non-conformity rules.

Where the seller delivers non-conforming goods, the aggrieved buyer may, in light of the nature of the goods and the extent of its loss reasonably choose to request cure in the form of repair or replacement.[1232] The courts are given the discretionary power to grant these remedies for non-conformity if awarding an order for enforced (continued) performance of a delivery obligation is practically meaningless.[1233] As for the hierarchy between the remedies to cure a non-conformity, it is held that an aggrieved buyer is entitled to demand replacement only in the event of a serious or incurable defective performance.[1234] So, it appears that a claim for replacement is not available if the defects are insignificant

1228 Art 7.2.3 PICC acknowledge the availability of enforced performance by cure in the form of repair and replacement, but the PICC does not encompass separate rules for non-conformity.

1229 Art 61 CCL.

1230 Art 62(1) CCL.

1231 Art 35 CISG; Larry A DiMatteo and Jingen Wang, 'CCL and CISG: A Comparative Analysis of Formation, Performance, and Breach' in DiMatteo and Chen 2017 (n 19) 479.

1232 Arts 107, 111, 154 CCL; Bing Ling 2002 (n 229) paras 8.023, 8.024 8.026; Lei Chen, 'Availablity of Specific Remedies in Chinese Contract Law' in Chen-Wishart, Loke and Ong 2016 (n 156) 35.

1233 Art 15 the Interpretation of the Supreme People's Court on Several Issues concerning the Application of the Administrative Litigation Law of the People's Republic of China, as adopted at the 1,648th meeting of the Judicial Committee of the Supreme People's Court on April 20, 2015, effective from 1 May 2015.

1234 Bing Ling 2002 (n 229) paras 8.024, 8.084.

and can be repaired.[1235] This viewpoint derives from the notion that repair of defective goods is less burdensome for the seller than replacement.[1236] Aside from these considerations, it is said that the remedies of repair and replacement are a part of the concept of enforced performance,[1237] because they are able to place the buyer in the position as if the contract was properly performed.[1238] However, the premise that repair and replacement can be brought to court as a form of enforced performance is contested to the effect that – on a doctrinal level – the right to obtain an order for enforced performance arises from the act of promise making and the judicial measures of repair replacement from a defective performance.[1239] Lastly, it is important to mention that there is some controversy about the availability of the remedy of replacement for non-conformity.[1240] The starting point is that where the seller does not deliver the goods in compliance with the agreed quality standards, the aggrieved buyer may demand that the seller bears the liability for its non-performance in the form of delivery of replacement goods.[1241] However, it is argued that a sales contract concerning specific goods cannot be subject to a claim for replacement goods, because the delivery of an alternative, which also could satisfy the aggrieved buyer, is said to fall outside the scope of the contractual obligations of the seller.[1242]

The alternative view is, simply put, that if the claim entails substitute goods, which are of a comparable nature and represents an equal value compared to the goods as described in the contract, a claim for replacement could be awarded.[1243] The latter is justified with the reasoning that delivery of not entirely the same goods could also comply with the interest the parties have in the fulfilment of the contract.[1244] For example, a diving company purchases ten wetsuits, which were displayed by a manufacturer of diving gear at a trade fair in China. Although the subject matter of this sales transaction is specific, the purpose of the contract could also be fulfilled if the buyer receives substitute goods in the form of unboxed wetsuits. In light of the foregoing, it is held that the contract law of China leaves room to sue for replacement of goods which are not completely in accordance with the

---

1235 Bing Ling 2002 (n 229) para 8.084; Lei Chen, 'Availablity of Specific Remedies in Chinese Contract Law' in Chen-Wishart, Loke and Ong 2016 (n 156) 36.

1236 Bing Ling 2002 (n 229) para 8.084.

1237 Chen (Lihu) and Zhu (n 970); Zheng Xiaochuan and Lei Mingguang, 'On the "Continue to Fulfil" the Rethinking' (2003) iss 3 Hebei Law Science 67 (郑小川，雷明光．对"继续履行"的再思考[J]．河北法学).

1238 Lei Chen, 'Availablity of Specific Remedies in Chinese Contract Law' in Chen-Wishart, Loke and Ong 2016 (n 156) 35; Bing Ling 2002 (n 229) para 8.026.

1239 Lei Chen, 'Availablity of Specific Remedies in Chinese Contract Law' in Chen-Wishart, Loke and Ong 2016 (n 156) 36.

1240 Hao Liyan (n 731).

1241 Arts 111, 153, 155 CCL.

1242 Hao Liyan (n 731).

1243 *Ibid.*

1244 *Ibid.*

specifications of the goods as described in the contract.[1245] In this light, the court could consider whether the legal relief of replacement would make the buyer indifferent and if the effect of awarding a claim for replacement is within the limitations of the impairment rule.

200. *Comparative analysis* – The issue of repair and replacement plays a significant role in the present research as it goes to the very essence of the differences in availability of enforced performance of a commercial sales contract in the subject legal systems. In this regard, there are three key issues which deserve particular scrutiny because they may cause contention between contracting parties and they emphasise the importance of obtaining more uniformity in the field of conformity at the national and international levels. The first and main point of divergence arises from the scope and understanding of the concept of enforced performance. The most narrow notion of the concept of enforced performance in the realm of commercial sales is present in the legal system of Singapore, which restricts the discretionary power of the courts to provide a decree for enforced performance to cases of non-delivery of specific and ascertained goods, and generic goods which fall outside the ambit of the sales law of Singapore, and the court establishes that damages are not adequate. Thus, although a seller is obliged to undertake that the goods sold are in accordance with the quality standards arising from the contract and the law (*i.e.* express and implied warranties respectively) enforcement of this obligation generally takes the form of damages.[1246] The approach taken under Dutch and Chinese contract law completely departs from this restrictive notion of enforced performance by providing the aggrieved buyer with a right to require the seller to cure a non-conforming delivery by repair and replacement. Nonetheless, there is also a major conceptual difference between the two countries' legal systems. To fully grasp this distinction it must first be noted that under Dutch contract law the statutory right to demand enforced performance of obligations in general (*e.g.* gratuitous, unilateral and reciprocal obligations) stands on a different statutory footing than a claim for cure by repair or replacement which may be brought to court to cure a non-conforming delivery under a commercial sales contract. By contrast, the contract law of China acts on the notion that the default regime for enforced performance governs situations of non-delivery and non-conformity. In other words, a claim for enforced performance in response to the seller's failure to deliver the goods and a cure for defective delivery both arise from the same legal provision under the contract law of China. As a result, the preconditions for enforced performance directly apply to a claim for repair and replacement of non-conforming goods. This means in effect that such a claim (governed

1245 *Ibid.*

1246 Larry A DiMatteo and Jingen Wang, 'CCL and CISG: A Comparative Analysis of Formation, Performance, and Breach' in DiMatteo and Chen 2017 (n 19) 466.

by Chinese contract law) is subject to the general statutory limitations for enforced performance, that is, impossibility in law or in fact, where the subject matter of the contract is unfit for compulsory performance and where the aggrieved buyer does not require performance within a reasonable time.[1247]

The unification instruments identified encompass a similar understanding of the relation between enforced performance of the seller's delivery obligation and an order to cure a non-conforming delivery by means of repair and replacement.[1248] For example, the CISG adopted the principle that enforced performance is not available where the buyer has resorted to a remedy which is inconsistent with the application for enforced performance. This restriction also applies where the aggrieved buyer requires repair or replacement in response to a non-conformity in the goods delivered.[1249] Hence, a claim for enforced performance in response to a non-delivery and non-conformity under Dutch law stands on a different doctrinal footing than similar claims under Chinese contract law and CISG-contracts.

That said, there is a very practical common denominator between the Dutch and Chinese contract law, that is; the right to require the seller to replace the delivered goods is only available in severe cases of non-conformity. This limitation follows from the assumption that an order for replacement of defective goods will most likely have a greater financial impact on the seller than when the seller is only required to repair the goods. The PICC and DCFR adopted a similar approach by limiting the right to require replacement where such an undertaking is unreasonably burdensome or expensive.[1250] The CISG goes a step further by requiring that the non-conformity must represent a fundamental failure in performance. This restriction follows from the reasoning that the delivery of substitute goods in international trade is expected to generate excessive costs because the seller is required to bear the costs of providing substitute goods and the risk of transport.[1251] To put this into context, it may be assumed that in the example mentioned under paragraph 196 (illustration 3), Dutch and Chinese contract law, as well as the CISG and DCFR, allow the courts to provide the textile manufacturing company with a judicial order for replacement of the dyeing machine due to the incurable defect and the limited financial resources of the buyer to acquire a similar machine on the market within a short timeframe. The courts may come to similar conclusions when adjudicating the second example

1247 Art 111 CCL.

1248 Art 46 CISG; Schwenzer, Hachem and Kee 2012 (n 13) paras 43.08, 43.09; Arts 7.2.2, 7.2.3 PICC, Vogenauer 2015 (n 19) art 7.2.3 para 1; Arts 1:301, 9:102(1) PECL; Art III.-3:302 Comment C DCFR; Arts 1, 7 of the Amendment Draft on Non-performance PACL, see Lee 2016 (n 16) 193, 198.

1249 Schwenzer 2016 (n 91) art 46 paras 7, 17, 39.

1250 Arts 7.2.2(b), 7.2.3 PICC; Vogenauer 2015 (n 19) art 7.2.3 para 13; Art III.–3:302(3)(b) DCFR, Comment C clarifies that a conforming performance may be achieved by, *e.g.*, repair and delivery of a replacement.

1251 Art 46(2) CISG; Schwenzer 2016 (n 91) art 46, para 23.

(illustration 4), in the sense that the buyer may be granted an order for enforced performance which requires the seller to put the defect right by repair of the machine. In view of this, Dutch and Chinese contract law, as well as the unification instruments identified, are also on the same page when considering the most fundamental requirements. This means in effect that a claim for repair is merely subject to reasonableness and appropriateness considerations and the limitations discussed in section 5.4.4.[1252]

201. The second point of consideration is that the approach taken by Dutch contract law stands apart to a certain extent because it makes a distinction between the conformity standards for commercial sales contracts which specify the quality of the goods and contracts which concern a transaction of goods only determined as to kind. In the latter case, the law of obligations brings about the standard that the seller may not deliver goods of less than average quality of the specified kind.[1253] Nonetheless, in both situations, the aggrieved buyer is entitled to claim for repair or replacement under the sales law principles. This may cause confusion amongst those not familiar with the structure of Dutch contract law. Where a commercial sales contract does not provide for the features of the goods, the PICC also obliges a seller to deliver goods of a quality that is reasonable and not less than average. The major difference to Dutch contract law is that the PICC clarifies, in an overarching principle, that non-performance of this obligation entitles the aggrieved buyer to apply for enforced performance which includes repair and replacement.[1254]

Another issue that warrants particular attention in this regard is the ambiguous three-step approach adopted in the contract law of China for cases where a commercial sales contract is unclear or does not specify the features and required quality of the goods.[1255] That said, Dutch and Chinese contract law have reached a significant level of uniformity by abandoning the distinction between the rules on delivery of different goods (*aliud*) and delivery of purely defective goods (*peius*). The CISG and the DCFR also equate the two forms of non-performance.[1256] Adopting a broad definition of non-conformity allows the aggrieved buyer to apply for enforced performance by means of repair and replacement in similar cases. Although the PICC, PECL and the draft PACL have not adopted specific rules on sales contracts, their broad notion of non-conformity removes the necessity to

---

1252 Art 46(3) CISG; Schwenzer 2016 (n 91) art 46, para 40; Arts 7.2.2(b), 7.2.3 PICC, Vogenauer 2015 (n 19) art 7.2.3 para 10; Art 9:102(2) PECL; Art III.-3:302 DCFR; Arts 1, 7 Amendment Draft on Non-performance PACL, see Lee 2016 (n 16) 193, 198.

1253 Art 5.1.6 PICC.

1254 Arts 7.2.2, 7.2.3 PICC.

1255 *I.e.*, determining the quality standards by party agreement, and if this fails, by business usage. As last resort, the quality standard can be determined by having recourse to specific standards.

1256 Art 35 CISG; Schwenzer 2016 (n 91) art 35, para 4; Villy de Luca, 'The Conformity of the Goods to the Contract in International Sales' (2015) 27(1) Pace International Law Review 163; Art IV.-2:301, Comment E DCFR.

undertake an extensive assessment of the exact cause of a failure in performance in order to determine the availability of a cure for non-conforming goods.[1257] Taken together, it appears that under the legal systems mentioned above, the deviation of the agreed features of the goods in the two examples mentioned under paragraph 195 (*i.e.* delivery of hybrid cars instead of true electric cars and the delivery of minerals from a different origin than stipulated), allows for enforced performance which requires the seller to put the defect in performance right by making a fresh delivery. At a theoretical level, there is however an important drawback when looking more closely at the PECL, and the draft PACL as both unification instruments do not expressly stipulate whether a decree for performance may require the seller to set a defect right by delivery of substitute goods.[1258] It may, however, be argued that such a provision is unnecessary because repair and replacement are special forms of a performance order.[1259]

202. The third point of divergence becomes apparent when considering the constraints on the buyer's right to require replacement in the case of a severe form of non-conformity, although the seller claims that it is able to put the defect right by repair. The key point in this regard is that under Chinese contract law there is no concrete limitation on the buyer's freedom to choose for cure by replacement where the seller argues that it is able to cure a severe non-conformity by repair. The seller is only granted a right to cure in case of an early delivery.[1260] By contrast, where a commercial sales contract is subject to Dutch contract law, the seller is entitled to defeat a claim for replacement of the goods by offering cure by repair of (non-) fundamental non-conformity provided that the seller offers to pay damages and costs, and the contract is still in existence.[1261] The CISG operates along the same lines by limiting the right of the aggrieved buyer to claim for replacement if the seller insists on cure by repair.[1262] This limitation arises from the notion that where repair is possible, the requirement of a fundamental non-conformity for obtaining an order for replacement is not fulfilled.[1263] Although under different conditions, the PICC, PECL and DCFR also

1257 Arts 7.1.1, 7.2.2, 7.2.3 PICC, see Vogenauer 2015 (n 19) art 7.2.3 paras 1, 7, 13; Arts. 8:101, 9:102(2) PECL, JM Smits in Schelhaas 2002 (n 19) 325; Art 1 Amendment Draft on Non-Performance PACL, see Lee 2016 (n 16) 193.

1258 Art 9:102 PECL and art 7.2.3 PICC clarifies that the right to performance includes in appropriate cases the right to require repair, replacement or other cure of defective performance, unless the right to performance is excluded under art 7.2.2 PICC.

1259 Vogenauer 2015 (n 19) art 7.2.3 para 1.

1260 Arts 71, 72 CCL.

1261 Art 6:86 DCC.

1262 Arts 46(3), 48(1) CISG; Schwenzer 2016 (n 91) art 46 paras 32, 35 and art 48 para 20.

1263 Arts 46(3), 48(1) CISG; Schwenzer 2016 (n 91) art 46 paras 32, 35 and art 48 para 20.

restrict the aggrieved buyer's right to demand replacement where the non-performing seller insists on repair of the non-conforming goods.[1264]

203. On an overall assessment, the approach taken by the unification instruments towards the availability of enforced performance where the goods deviate from the conformity standards does not reflect a compromise between the approaches found in the three subject jurisdictions. By contrast, the availability of enforced performance in the form of repair and replacement under the unification instruments identified are completely unknown actions in the sales and contract law of Singapore. Nonetheless, the rules on conformity under the CISG reflect, to a certain extent, a merger of the basic principles underlying the availability of enforced performance in the investigated three jurisdictions. That is, the CISG grants the aggrieved buyer the remedy of requiring repair and replacement of non-conforming goods, but enforced performance in the form of repair is only available (contrary to the approach taken by Dutch and Chinese contract law) where the lack of conformity constitutes a fundamental failure. The regulation of the availability of obtaining a cure as remedies and the requirement of a fundamental failure reflects to a certain degree the common law tradition as present in the contract and sales law of Singapore. The traditional common law reluctance to adopt enforced performance is also satisfied to a certain extent by the principle that the aggrieved buyer is not entitled to force the seller to replace the non-conforming goods where the latter prefers cure by repair.

5.4.4 *Inspection and notification duties*

204. *Preliminary* – A potential limitation to the availability of requiring a performance remedy (*i.e.* delivery of missing goods, repair and delivery of replacement goods) may arise from the default rules on inspection and notification.[1265] In the present research, the analysis of the impact of a duty to inspect and to notify the seller in cases of a defective performance stands apart from the discussion about a duty of the buyer to request performance within a certain time limit.[1266] This is because the time limit for giving notice about any defects discovered and a request for a conforming performance do not necessarily coincide. For example, the CISG adopted an indirect duty of the buyer to notify the seller about any

1264 Art 7.1.4 PICC, see Vogenauer 2015 (n 19) art 7.1.4 para 5; Art 8:104 PECL; Arts III.-3-201 Comment A, IV.A.-2:203 DCFR.

1265 It should be noted that for international sales transactions different rules may apply for determining whether the buyer has a right or is subject to a duty to inspect the goods (generally decided by the law governing the contract), and the actual process of inspection. The latter may be governed by the law where the contract is performed, see Schwenzer, Hachem and Kee 2012 (n 13) paras 34.30–34.30.

1266 S 6.3.

defects discovered on pain of loss to rely on a non-conformity.[1267] As for the actual claim for a conforming performance, the aggrieved buyer may require repair and replacement in conjunction with a notification about the defects discovered or within a reasonable time thereafter.[1268] This means in effect that an aggrieved buyer may be required to take into account three time limits, that is, a time limit for inspection, a time limit for notification and a time limit for requesting a conforming performance. The importance of distinguishing a notification duty and the requirement of requesting enforced performance within a certain time limit also follows from the fact that the latter could be limited to cases where the buyer requests for repair and replacement.[1269] As for the following discussion on the intricacies of the rules on inspection and notification, specific consideration is given to three points: the legal sources of a potential duty to inspect the goods and to notify the seller about any defects discovered, the applicable time limits and the legal consequences.[1270] For the sake of clarity, it should be noted that the discussed inspection and notice requirements are only limitations on legal actions and are not actionable by the seller.

> *Illustration* – Company A, a wholesale dealer of outdoor garments, located in country X, buys a new range of jackets from a manufacturing company, located in country Y. On 30 December, the manufacturer delivered the jackets at the warehouse of the wholesale dealer, where labels were attached and the jackets were packed for distribution to various retail chains. After distribution on 26 January, the manufacturer receives the first complaints about the quality of the zippers. In this situation, the wholesale dealer failed to inspect the jackets directly on receipt. Only after a lapse of a significant period of time did the wholesaler inform the manufacturer about the discovered defects. It was, therefore, questioned whether the wholesale dealer had lost its right to claim for a conforming delivery.

205. *The (indirect) obligation to inspect the goods* – The contract law of the Netherlands is not familiar with a statutory duty on the buyer to examine the goods.[1271] Nonetheless, the obligation to notify the seller (promptly) after the buyer has, or reasonably should have

---

1267 Art 39(1) CISG.

1268 *E.g.*, art 46(2)(3) CISG.

1269 *E.g.*, art 46(2)(3) CISG, although s 6.3 will show that the contract law of the three investigated jurisdictions, as well as the PICC, PECL, DCFR and the draft PACL, all adopt the principle that the availability of enforced performance is affected where the buyer fails to request for performance within the applicable time limit.

1270 Other important questions concern the point in time at which the time limit for inspection and notification begins and whether inspection takes place before or after the delivery of the goods, although it goes beyond the scope of this study to discuss these issues.

1271 Where the seller has provided the buyer with a guarantee, the buyer is under no obligation to inspect the goods; *Van Dalfsen v Kampen* Dutch Supreme Court 14 November 2007, ECLI:NL:HR:2008:BF0407, NJ 2008, 588; Tjittes 2018 (n 2) 431, 451.

discovered the defect on pain of loss to rely on a non-conformity, presupposes a requirement to inspect the goods in order to preserve the right to obtain a conforming performance by delivery of the missing goods, repair or delivery of replacement goods.[1272] A similar conclusion can be drawn for the contract and sales law of Singapore, although it does not recognise a claim for repair or replacement in a commercial context. For commercial sales the starting point is a buyer's right to inspect the goods for the purpose of ascertaining whether the goods are in conformity with the contract.[1273] It may be said that the loss of the remedy to cure a defective performance (*i.e.* damages) where the buyer fails to inspect the goods, presupposes a duty on the buyer to make use of its right to inspect the goods.[1274] Hence, under the contract law of the Netherlands and Singapore, the obligation of the buyer to inspect the goods is indirect. The contract law of China provides more clarity on the matter by establishing a statutory duty of the buyer to inspect the goods on receipt.[1275] This approach is most in line with the CISG and the DCFR which include specific rules on the duty of the buyer to inspect the goods.[1276]

206. *Time limit for inspection of the goods* – Dutch contract law does not expressly establish a time limit for the inspection of goods delivered, but it follows from case law that the buyer is required to inspect the goods as soon as can reasonably be expected in the circumstances of the case upon loss of the right to claim for a cure.[1277] In this regard, the complexity of the investigation, and the nature and detectability of the defects are important factors for determining the time limit for inspection of the goods.[1278] Although the contract law of China entails a specific provision on inspection, it does not go further than stipulating that the buyer shall inspect the subject matter in a timely manner.[1279] That having been said, it is clear that both jurisdictions have adopted a flexible approach, although the approach taken by Dutch contract law and the use of the phrase 'timely' by the Chinese contract law indicate a shorter time limit than adopted by the contract law of Singapore.

1272 Arts 6:89, 7:23(1) DCC.

1273 SGA, s 34.

1274 SGA, s 35(4); Lee 2016 (n 16) 766.

1275 Art 157 CCL; Bing Ling 2002 (n 229) para 8.024; Larry A DiMatteo and Jingen Wang, 'CCL and CISG: A Comparative Analysis of Formation, Performance, and Breach' in DiMatteo and Chen 2017 (n 19) 488.

1276 Art 38(1) CISG; Art IV.A-4:301 DCFR; The PICC, PECL and draft PACL have not included specific provision on sales contract which explains the absence of detailed provision about inspection of the goods delivered and notification of any defects discovered.

1277 Arts 6:89, 7:23(1) DCC; Hijma, *Asser Koop en ruil* 7-I* 2013 (n 48) 544–557.

1278 *Pouw v Visser* Dutch Supreme Court 29 June 2007, ECLI:NL:HR:2007:AZ7617, NJ 2008, 606; *Ploum v Smeets II* Dutch Supreme Court 25 March 2011, ECLI:NL:HR:2011:BP8991, NJ 2013, 5; *Van de Steeg v Rabobank* Dutch Supreme Court 8 February 2013, ECLI:NL:HR:2013:BY4600, NJ 2014, 497; *Nieuwe Dam and Pereboomsloot v VVE et al* Dutch Supreme Court 19 November 2010, ECLI:NL:HR:2010:BN7084, NJB 2010, 2202.

1279 Art 157 CCL.

It appears that the latter favours a less restrictive (and thus more buyer-friendly) approach. This premise follows from the reasoning that the buyer is (indirectly) required to reject the goods within a reasonable time, which presupposes that a corresponding inspection of the delivered goods is performed by the buyer within that period.[1280]

The CISG also takes a more buyer-friendly approach towards the time limit for inspection of the goods because it expressly establishes that the buyer should inspect the goods within as short period as practicable in the circumstances.[1281] The approach taken by the DCFR also seems to qualify as more buyer-friendly as it adopts the principle that a buyer should examine the goods, or cause them to be examined, within as short a period as is reasonable in the circumstances.[1282] That having been said, the common denominator between the subject legal systems is that they all (implicitly) act on the notion that the precise time period for carrying out an inspection should be determined under consideration of the circumstances of the case.[1283]

207. *Notification of the seller about any non-conformities discovered* – The notice requirements in Dutch and Chinese contract law, as well as the CISG and DCFR, qualify as a non-actionable duty of the buyer. This means in effect that where the aggrieved buyer fails to notify the seller about any defects discovered, it loses the right to claim for enforced performance in the form of a fresh delivery or repair on the basis that the delivered goods do not conform to the contract.[1284] The contract law of Singapore does not expressly recognise such a duty of the buyer to notify the seller of defects.[1285] Nonetheless, the principle that the buyer is deemed to have accepted the goods where it does not reject them,[1286] presupposes that the rejection is made in conjunction with a notification of defects (though damages are the only remedy). That having been said, at a purely technical level the statutory requirement to actively reject the goods does not directly bring about a duty to inform the seller about the defects discovered. In practice, this divergence from the Dutch and Chinese contract law, as well as the CISG and DCFR, is most likely not of particular relevance because a claim for cure usually requires disclosure of the discovered defects.

1280 SGA, s 35(4).

1281 Art 38(1) CISG; Schwenzer 2016 (n 91) art 38 para 2.

1282 Art IV.A.-4:301 Comment A and B DCFR.

1283 NL: Schelhaas et al *Bijzondere overeenkomsten* (n 1070) para 48; SGP: Hunter 2017 (n 7) para 7.17 and *Sun Qi v Syscon Pte Ltd* [2013] SGHC 38; CHN: art 17 Judicial Interpretation of Sales Contracts (n 174); Lee 2016 (n 16) 316; Art 3(1) Draft Articles on Non-Performance PACL, see Lee 2016 (n 16) 193; Art 7.2.2(2) PICC, see Vogenauer 2015 (n 19) art 7.2.2 para 52–53.

1284 Arts 6:89, 7:23(1) DCC; Tjittes 2018 (n 2) 450; Art 158 CCL; Art 46(2)(3) CISG; Art IV.A.-4:301 Comment C DCFR.

1285 Art 158 CCL; SGA, s 35(4).

1286 SGA, s 35(4).

208. *Time for notification* – An important common denominator between the legal systems is that they do not stipulate a fixed period for notification, although there are significant differences between the statutorily defined timeframes. The contract law of the Netherlands and China have adopted the strictest approach. This proposition follows from the use of the phrase 'promptly' and 'timely' in Dutch and Chinese contract law respectively.[1287] This timeframe for notification of the seller is only relevant where the buyer is under a duty to inspect the goods,[1288] and for situations where the buyer discovers a defect. As the sales law of Singapore has taken a more buyer-friendly approach, it is not surprising that it expressly uses the phrase 'a reasonable time'. It must, however, be noted that the reasonable time relates to a notification of a rejection of the goods and does not clarify whether a different time limit applies for notifying the seller about the defects.[1289]

The CISG and the DCFR also establish a reasonable period, but this period is directly related to a notification of the lack of conformity.[1290] At the international level, the use of the phrase 'reasonable time' is rather unfortunate due to its open-ended nature and the divergence between the time limits at the national level. As a result, national courts can be inclined to interpret the reasonable time limit in view of their own domestic law.[1291] This situation runs counter to the ambition of the investigated jurisdictions to encourage cross-border trade by bringing about legal certainty in the realm of international commercial sales.

209. *Legal consequences* – It appears that Dutch and Chinese contract law adopt the strictest consequences when the buyer fails to notify the seller of any defect discovered. This means in effect that notification of the discovered defects is required to preserve all available remedies to cure a non-conforming delivery, such as the right to obtain a performance order for delivery of the missing goods, repair and replacement of non-conforming goods.[1292] Put differently, the buyer who fails to notify the seller about the discovered defect loses the right to claim for enforced performance in the aforementioned forms and to sue for damages to cure the monetary harm.

1287 Arts 6:89, 7:23(1) DCC; Art 158 CCL.

1288 In both jurisdictions, the buyer is not under an inspection duty where the seller provided information about the absence or presence of certain features of the goods. The notification duty of the seller about the features of the goods must also be noted.

1289 This consideration is of relevance as a second time limit is adopted by § 2–607(3)(a) UCC.

1290 Art 39(1) CISG; Art IV.A.-4:302 DCFR.

1291 Schwenzer, Hachem and Kee 2012 (n 13) paras 34.67, 34.68.

1292 NL: Arts 6:89 7:23(1) DCC; MBM Loos in Schelhaas 2002 (n 19) 357; SE Bartels and AA van Velten, *Mr. C. Assers Handleiding tot de beoefening van het Nederlands Burgerlijk Recht. 5. Zakenrecht, Eigendom en beperkte rechten* (Wolters Kluwer 2017) paras 548–549; De Jong, Krans and Wissink 2018 (n 194) 210; CHN: Arts 157, 158 CCL.

A similar approach is taken by the CISG and DCFR which obliges the buyer to give notice of a lack of conformity on pain of losing the right to require performance under the contract, to demand delivery of substitute goods, to effect repair and to claim damages.[1293] It may, therefore, be said that the notice requirement under Dutch and Chinese contract law, as well as by the CISG and DCFR, is a strong weapon of the seller to defeat a claim to cure the impact of a non-conforming delivery. The sales law of Singapore takes a completely different approach when considering the legal consequences of a failure to reject non-conforming goods (the buyer is not expressly required to notify the seller about the defects). This is because enforcement of the obligation to deliver goods free from certain defects generally takes the form of damages. Another reason is that the sales law of Singapore has taken the approach that the buyer has a right to inspect the goods and notify the seller in case of any non-conformity.[1294] Where the buyer fails to do so, the buyer is deemed to have accepted the goods, and it subsequently loses the right to avoid the contract; the right to claim damages is unaffected.[1295] This rule can be traced back to the previously mentioned *caveat emptor* principle.[1296] That having been said, in all the subject legal systems, a failure of the buyer to inspect the goods and to notify the seller only brings legal consequences for the buyer.

210. *Comparative analysis* – An important exception to the availability of a cure in case of a non-conformity is rooted in the rules on inspection of the goods and (timely) notification of the defects discovered. At the national and international levels, there is however a significant divergence between the imposition of the applicable rules and how they operate. Whereas the Dutch and Chinese contract law approach can be described as seller-friendly due to their restrictive time limits for inspection and notification, the CISG and DCFR clearly favour the buyer's side by adopting open-ended time limits. The same can be said from the approach taken by the contract law of Singapore, although the similarities are notably limited. This follows from the fact that under the Dutch and Chinese contract law, as well as the CISG and DCFR, the rules on inspection and notification arise in the context of the preservation of the buyer's right to enforced performance, which is counterbalanced by the principle that the buyer loses its right to claim for enforced performance and damages when it fails to (correctly) notify the seller about the discovered defects. By contrast, under the sales law of Singapore the concept of inspection and notification should be interpreted in a completely different context, that is, a buyer's right to inspect the goods and to reject them within a reasonable time. In other words, exercising (or failing to exercise) the right

1293 Art 39(1) CISG; Art IV.A.-4:302(2) DCFR.
1294 SGA, s 34.
1295 SGA, s 35(4).
1296 Para 185.

to inspect the goods and to notify the seller about defects are no part of the assessment of whether enforced performance should be granted. Taken together, these considerations reveal that the divergence between the three investigated legal systems is not resolved under the CISG. It is therefore of paramount importance for those involved in international sales contracts to pay close attention to the discussed differences (in conjunction with section 6.3) to strike the right balance between the buyer's and seller's interests. This is of particular relevance where the contract concerns the sale of perishable goods. Moreover, it must be borne in mind that under Dutch and Chinese contract law, as well as under the unification instruments, the overarching reasonableness and good faith standards may also preclude the buyer from obtaining an order for repair and replacement in the case of an unjustifiable failure to notify the seller about the discovered defects for an unwarranted period of time which seriously affect the interests of the seller. This, in effect, means that in the example mentioned under paragraph 204, the wholesaler most likely has lost its right to claim for a conforming delivery. The insights provided above are, however, merely helpful at a practical level and do not remove the legal barriers arising from the discussed differences between the rules on inspection and notification. It is, therefore, suggested here that the national legislators of the three investigated jurisdictions address this unresolved issue in due course in view of the findings set out above, their position as a trade hub and their commonly shared ambition to become an important hub for international commercial (sales) disputes.

5.4.5 Conclusions

211. The central issue of this section concerns the question of whether enforced performance (in the form of an order for delivery, repair or replacement) is available in the case the goods delivered by the seller do not conform to the contract in quantity or quality, and, if so, with which degree of flexibility this claim can be granted in order to protect the buyer's performance interest and to protect the seller against abuse. The analyses provided for in this section show that Dutch and Chinese contract law give the most protection at the national level, and the CISG and DCFR at the international level. Nonetheless, there are still blatant and subtle dogmatic and practical differences between the rules on conformity employed by these legal systems. This may cause significant legal uncertainty for those involved in international commercial sales transactions. In particular, when considering the diametrically opposed approach taken by the contract law of Singapore and the intermediate approaches found in the PICC, PECL and draft PACL, the impact of these differences makes a strong case for further harmonisation of the rules for discrepancies in quantity and quality of the goods. The most progress can be made by adopting a broad interpretation of the concept of non-conformity and enforced performance, in line with

clear and balanced rules on examination and notification, in particular for the applicable time periods.

In view of the above-described proposition, it is of paramount importance to first make note of the key common core of the contract law of the Netherlands and China, and the unification instruments identified in this section. That is, a claim for enforced performance is not subject to the *caveat emptor* principle.[1297] This in effect means that the legal systems mentioned above, do not assume that a buyer to a commercial sales contract purchases the goods as they are delivered, in the sense that the consequences of a deviation of the contractually agreed values are assigned to the buyer. Today, the question of whether enforced performance is available depends on the classification of cases where the goods do not conform with the contract and any specific requirements that apply.

With regard to cases where the seller has delivered less than agreed, there is an important common core of the subject legal systems, but there are also fundamental differences. The common core is that the default regime of the three investigated jurisdictions, as well as the unification instruments, envisage a claim for enforced performance in the form of the delivery of the outstanding goods, provided that such a claim is not barred by general limitations and counter-exceptions.[1298] Nevertheless, the approach found in the contract law of the Netherlands and China brings about that the aggrieved buyer is required to notify the seller where the delivered goods do not conform to the contractual stipulations, on pain of loss of the right to enforced performance and damages. This is notwithstanding the fact that the Dutch contract law explicitly categorises a discrepancy in quantity as a non-conforming delivery, which is contrary to the Chinese contract law approach of classifying such a scenario as non-delivery. The approach taken by the contract law of Singapore differs in that discrepancies in quantity are treated as a failure to comply with a delivery obligation, but it does not establish an explicit notification duty for the buyer as a prerequisite for the preservation of a claim for enforced performance. The buyer is merely provided with a right to inspect the goods and to notify the seller about any defects discovered on pain of loss of the right to reject the goods and to avoid the contract. The availability of enforced performance is, however, significantly limited under the contract law of Singapore in comparison to the Dutch and Chinese contract law.[1299] There are two main reasons for this proposition. First, the default contract law regime of Singapore does not envisage enforced performance of non-monetary obligations in the realm of commercial contracts, unless a special situation exists. The second reason derives from the narrow interpretation of the concept of enforced performance.[1300]

1297 Schwenzer, Hachem and Kee 2012 (n 13) paras 31.03–31.08.

1298 See Ch 6 for a detailed discussion about the barriers to enforced performance.

1299 S 4.4.3.

1300 S 5.4.3.

The issue of distinguishing non-conformity and non-delivery where the seller delivers goods less than agreed also returns at the international level. This is because the approaches taken by the unification instruments vary significantly in that regard, suggesting that there is no consensus on the matter. Nevertheless, the proposition here is that in cases of a shortfall in goods the CISG provides the most protection against abuse in view of the seller's interest, and protection of the performance interest of the buyer. This is because the CISG explicitly classifies a discrepancy in quantity as a non-conforming delivery and by regulating this scenario in an overall framework of clear rules for cases where the goods do not conform to the contract. The same could be said of Dutch contract law, although parties from a different legal tradition and not familiar with the Dutch cultural notions of contracting may not feel entirely comfortable with the broad scope of the sales law principles.[1301]

212. With regard to the availability of enforced performance where the features of the goods deviate from those required under the contract, there is a fundamental division between the investigated legal systems. This follows from the fact that the Dutch and Chinese contract law, as well as the CISG, DCFR and draft PACL, make a distinction between the applicable rules for two different causes of a failure in performance, that is, non-delivery and delivery of goods which are not in conformity with the contract. As for the latter, the Dutch and Chinese contract law are aligned with the unification instruments mentioned above in the sense that they employ a broad interpretation of the concept of conformity. This means in effect that delivery of defective goods (*peius*) and delivery of different goods (*aliud*) may invoke a claim for repair and replacement respectively. Acknowledging and understanding the aforementioned cause-oriented approach is of significant importance as the buyer is subject to a strict notification duty where the features of the goods deviate from those required under the contract. In other words, the aggrieved buyer loses its right to a judicial order for repair and replacement, and even damages, where it fails to notify the seller about the defects.[1302]

At the international level, the CISG, DCFR and draft PACL encompass a similar notification requirement, although they have taken a more buyer-friendly approach towards the applicable time periods. Another important point of divergence follows from the remarkable exemption adopted by the DCFR, which exempts the buyer's notification duty in the case of a discrepancy in quantity, and the buyer may reasonably assume that the seller shall deliver the outstanding goods.[1303] It appears that this principle is not necessary

1301 S 3.3.

1302 The buyer's duty to notify the seller, presupposes that examination must take place. This notion is laid down in arts 157, 158 CCL, Art 38 CISG; Art IV.A.-4:301 DCFR.

1303 Art IV.-4:303 DCFR.

as a similar result can be achieved by the general principle of good faith. It is noteworthy that the PICC and PECL also adopt a broad interpretation of the concept of enforced performance by recognising the aggrieved party's right to claim for enforced performance in the form of cure. Nonetheless, such actions are not subject to a specific notification requirement as described above. This is of little surprise as the two unification instruments are not familiar with the concept of non-conformity, although they allow for enforced performance in the form of cure by repair and replacement.

In contrast to the approach taken by the legal systems mentioned above, the contract law of Singapore does not distinguish between various forms of infringement of a legal right. This means in effect that where the seller fails to perform its contractual obligations, the default rules on the availability of enforced performance apply.[1304] These rules bring about that the contract law of Singapore does not recognise cure of a defective performance by repair and replacement for commercial sales. Moreover, when the aggrieved buyer claims for enforced performance of the seller's delivery obligations because the latter delivered something completely different than agreed,[1305] the buyer is not subject to an express notification duty.[1306] Nonetheless, the buyer may lose its right to claim for a remedial measure when it fails to inspect the goods and notify the seller about any defects discovered. Despite the diametrically opposite approach taken by Dutch and Chinese contract law when considering the available remedial measures to cure a defective performance, it may not be assumed that enforced performance of cure by repair and replacement is unrestrictedly available in the latter two jurisdictions. Rather, specific requirements apply, which favour repair over replacement as the latter is, in both jurisdictions, considered a more costly measure. Furthermore, the general limitations to enforced performance may play an essential role where, for example, a claim for cure by repair or replacement amounts to an abuse of rights.[1307] Consequently, for the assessment of the actual ability of the subject legal systems to protect the buyer's and seller's interest in obtaining a conforming delivery, the considerations in the following chapter are of significant importance.

213. The discussion above concerns the most pronounced dogmatic difference between the scope of the concept of enforced performance in the subject legal systems, but the

---

1304 S 4.4.3.

1305 The delivery of an *aliud* qualifies as a non-conforming delivery under Dutch and Chinese contract law, as well as the CISG. Consequently, a strict notice requirement applies for a claim for enforced performance of cure by replacement.

1306 SGA, s 34 provides the buyer a right to inspect the goods and to notify the seller of defect on loss of the right to reject the goods and to avoid the contract. In this situation, the buyer is merely subject to an indirect examination duty.

1307 See s 6.2.4 for a detailed analysis of the rules on hardship; See art 3:13(1) DCC and the principle of good faith under Chinese contract law for a situation where a claim for enforced performance of a cure amounts to an abuse of rights.

discussed divergence between the rules on non-conformity also brings about an important practical consequence. That is, the moment at which non-conformity of the goods needs to be ascertained. A discussion about this matter requires an understanding of the concept of legal delivery and to what extent this undertaking brings about a transfer of risk from the buyer to the seller.[1308] This is because the time for ascertaining whether the goods conform with the contractual stipulations and the risk passes to the buyer can be related to the time of legal delivery (*e.g.* physical or constructive transfer of possession, dispatching the goods or putting them at the buyer's disposal), but also to the passage of property. In this regard, Dutch and Chinese contract law have taken the approach that the moment of ascertaining the conformity of goods coincides with the transfer of risk (hence, the time of legal delivery of the goods).[1309] In a similar vein, it appears that the contract law of Singapore takes the approach that the time of ascertaining the conformity of the goods could coincide with the time of legal delivery because at that point in time the buyer is able to assess whether there are reasons to reject the delivered goods.[1310] When the parties are not aware of the time at which non-conformity must be established under the law governing the contract, they could be exposed to losing their right(s) to claim for cure for the non-conformity when they fail to examine the goods at the designated moment and it is not possible to establish whether a later detected defect falls under the responsibility of the seller or is caused by, for example, environmental factors in the warehouse of the buyer. That having been said, to answer the question as to when a non-conformity has become apparent to the aggrieved buyer, recourse must be made to the above-discussed differing viewpoints on the requirements of examination and notification.[1311]

5.5 CONCLUSIONS

214. The present chapter reveals a dramatic division between the perspectives of the investigated jurisdictions on the availability of enforced performance in three different situations of non-performance in the realm of international commercial sales contracts. The discussion shows that the underpinnings of the applicable principles are rooted in the traditional civil and common law views on the desirability of enforced performance. These historical roots and the inseparable preference for favouring the seller's or buyer's interests, bring about three significant dissimilarities which influence the overarching assessment

1308 S 5.2.

1309 NL: Hijma, *Asser Koop en ruil* 7-I* 2013 (n 48) 332, see for the obligation to delivery the goods art 7:10 DCC; CHN: arts 153–155 CCL; Art 36(1) CISG; Art IV.A.-2:308(1) DCFR.

1310 SGA, ss 16, 18, 20.

1311 S 5.4.4.

of the actual availability of enforced performance of non-monetary obligations under a commercial sales contract.

The first difference follows from a distinct view of the respective subject legal systems on the substance of the seller's delivery obligation and the objective of the applicable substantive rules for enforced performance. Thus, where the rules for enforced performance of the seller's delivery obligation are primarily focussed on protection of the buyer's performance interest in the contract law of the Netherlands and China, the protection of the seller's interest is prioritised in the contract law of Singapore and to a certain extent also under the unification instruments. Nonetheless, Dutch contract law's focus shifts to the protection of the seller's interest in the case where the buyer sues for delivery before the stipulated time for delivery. That having been said, the dormant strict interpretation of the adage *pacta sunt servanda* underlying the Dutch and Chinese default regimes on the availability of enforced performance legitimises a statutory clarification of the exclusive nature of the instrument of enforced performance in the case the seller entirely fails to deliver the goods (*i.e.* non-delivery). This situation should be distinguished from the later discussed situation of the delivery of *aliud* and *peius* which may give rise to enforced performance by means of making a fresh delivery or by repairing a defect.[1312] Apart from the dogmatic considerations above, enhancing the understanding of the effect of the principles on the time for delivery is also of significant legal and practical importance for establishing the full scope of the consequences of a failure to deliver the goods at the agreed time. This is because the time for delivery may play a critical role in determining the passage of risk, and the time for determining the conformity of the goods.[1313]

The second difference concerns a disagreement between, on one hand, the three investigated jurisdictions, and on the other hand, the unification instruments identified. The lack of consensus follows from differing perspectives on the ability of the seller to force the buyer to take delivery. On this point, the three investigated jurisdictions agree that the buyer is merely subject to a non-actionable duty to take delivery (or to cooperate). Although the Dutch and Chinese contract law provide the traditional civil law escape route in the form of the principle of reasonableness and fairness, and good faith respectively. It is advocated here that this open-ended legal principle is a crucial balancing instrument for Dutch and Chinese contract law considering their favourable perspective on the protection of the buyer's performance interest in the case of non-delivery. In other words, the earlier discussed Dutch and Chinese contract legal notion that the seller's delivery obligation requires a physical or constructive change of possession, is counterbalanced by

1312 S 5.4.

1313 Ss 5.2, 5.4; Internal consequences relate to the relationship between the seller and the buyer. The external consequences relate to the law applicable to the contract.

reasonableness and good faith considerations, which may allow the court to assume an enforceable obligation of the buyer to cooperate by taking delivery of the goods.

At a practical level, the differing approaches to the buyer's duty to take delivery may cause significant issues when the contract involves the carriage in goods. In this situation the unpaid seller may be exposed to a substantial financial risk where the dispatch of the goods does not bring about legal delivery and the buyer refuses to take delivery on arrival of the goods. It is therefore of paramount importance that parties to a commercial sales contracts involving the carriage of goods take full account of the understanding of the concept of delivery and the buyer's duty to take delivery under the law governing a potential dispute between the parties.

The last and most important point of divergence is the availability of different forms of enforced performance in the case the seller fails to comply with its obligation to deliver goods which possess the features as agreed in the contract. This division can also be traced back to the interpretation of the bindingness of a contractual promise and the ability of the buyer to obtain the very thing it bargained for. The contract law of Singapore has taken the strictest approach because the buyer to a commercial sales contract is not able to require enforced performance in the form of cure by repair and replacement. This stands in contrast with Dutch and Chinese contract law, which take a broader, more buyer-friendly approach by allowing for enforced performance in the form of cure by repair and replacement in the case the seller delivers an *aliud* or *peius*. This approach is counterbalanced by seller-friendly notification requirements (*i.e.* 'promptly' and 'timely'). The unification instruments are also familiar with a right to repair and replacement, but they balance the interests differently by adopting buyer-friendly notification requirements (*i.e.* notification within a reasonable time). In practice, this distinction is however not that clear due to innumerable factors affecting the performance of contractual rights arising under international sales contracts. In view of this, it is interesting to note that Singapore contract law (in line with most common law jurisdictions) also encompasses the concept of a reasonable period (for examination and rejection of the goods).[1314] Another important difference in this regard follows from the thresholds for requiring enforced performance in the form of cure by replacement. Whereas Dutch and Chinese contract law, as well as the PICC, PECL, DCFR and draft PACL, only allow this claim in severe cases of non-conformity, the CISG requires a fundamental failure in performance. The latter is clearly of common law descent. The differences between Dutch and Chinese contract law and the other unification instruments are negligible given the general nature of the earlier mentioned limitation on obtaining an order for replacement and the abstract nature of the present discussion.

1314 SGA, s 35; see also Schwenzer, Hachem and Kee 2012 (n 13) para 34.64.

At a practical level, however, commercial parties should take into account that the rules on conformity are not stand-alone principles, as this research reveals that they must be read in line with the domestic notion of the concept of a legal delivery. This is of particular importance for those involved in commercial sales contracts across the borders of the three investigated jurisdictions as these legal systems act on the principle that the time for ascertaining the conformity of the goods occurs at the same time as the transfer of risk of loss from the buyer to the seller. The time for ascertaining conformity may differ when the parties agreed to a different regime by adopting, for example, the Incoterms® FOB (Free on Board: the risk of loss or damage to the goods passes when the goods are on board the vessel) and FAS (Free Alongside Ship: the risk of loss of or damage to the goods passes when the goods are alongside the ship). The Incoterms® CFR (Cost and Freight) and CIF (Cost Insurance and Freight) also adopted the principle that the risk of loss or damage to the goods passes when the goods are on board the vessel. The parties to a commercial sales contract are allowed to include a regime which is more suitable for their situation. For example, the parties could agree that the risk passes after the goods are delivered and unloaded at a specific terminal. So, the moment of the passing of risk requires close attention as it does not necessarily coincide with the conclusion of the contract nor the transfer of title. Although a misunderstanding in this regard may negatively affect the availability of obtaining an order for enforced performance of the seller's obligation, it should not be confused with assessment of the time available for the non-conformity to become apparent to the buyer.

The analysis of the operative part of the national and international sales law provided above reveals that every principle protects a certain interest which is generally counterbalanced by another principle. This means in effect that any undertaking to consolidate the differing national approaches requires a careful examination of the interrelationships between the applicable principles. This suggestion goes a step further than the existing efforts to bridge the gap between the civil law notion that enforced performance is available as of right and the common law default regime which only envisages enforced performance in exceptional situations. Put differently, the discussion above demonstrates that stand-alone solutions to eliminate the most controversial divergence between the two major legal families are ineffectual in the realm of commercial sales contracts. It is, therefore, of paramount importance to take a holistic approach by looking at the general contract and sales law provisions when considering harmonisation of the differing viewpoints on the availability of enforced performance of non-monetary obligations under a commercial sales contract.

6 Barriers to the availability of enforced performance

6.1 Introduction

215. The contract law of the Netherlands, Singapore and China are all familiar with limitations on obtaining an order to enforced performance of the obligation to bring about a certain state of affairs under a commercial sales contract. Nonetheless, the respective distinct traditional understandings of rights and remedies make it necessary to distinguish two approaches. First, Dutch and Chinese contract law act on the notion that enforced performance of a contractual right is generally available, albeit that the legal right to enforced performance is subject to certain exceptions. The contract law of Singapore adopts the approach that enforced performance is a discretionary instrument of the court to force a promisor to comply with the contract, which is only available in specific circumstances when not affected by counter-exceptions. It is these distinct approaches which lend force to the preliminary premise that the Dutch and Chinese contract law systems seem to allow an order for enforced performance of a contractual right in more cases than under the contract law of Singapore. In the following, it is investigated whether this assumption is justified when taking into account the limitations on enforced performance under the contract law of the Netherlands and China, and the counter-exceptions under the contract law of Singapore (*i.e.* the limitations on enforcement of specific non-monetary obligations, which are traditionally considered suitable for enforced performance).

216. The interpretation and application of the limits on obtaining an order to enforced performance of a contractual right differ tremendously per jurisdiction, due to the aforementioned fundamental differences in approaches and specific domestic economic, social and legal developments. For example, the profound influence of the European Union on the ability to obtain an order to enforced performance of a sales contract subject to Dutch law, and the principle in Singapore that it is at the discretion of Singapore courts to adjust the requirements and bars for awarding a claim for actual performance if the conditions of modern life and economics have changed.[1315] In China, the problems with limits on obtaining an order to enforced performance appear to arise from the disconnection

1315 <http://www.singaporelaw.sg/sglaw/laws-of-singapore/overview/chapter-1>. accessed 27 March 2016.

between the domestic contract law principles and the interpretation in practice,[1316] political interference and the lack of up to date foreign business legal expertise.[1317] In view of this, it is said that the missing link is the proper implementation of the statutory principles in the entire judicial system together with a continuous process of quality control on decisions of the court.[1318]

217. This section starts with the most important and best known barrier to enforced performance of a contractual right, that is, impossibility of performance of actionable obligations (section 6.2). This barrier centres around external impediments rendering performance of a contractual right impossible, whether objective or subjective. There are, however, also important internal impediments deriving from a prolonged demand for enforced performance. Accordingly, section 6.3 discusses the legal consequences of a delayed request for delivery while section 6.4 focusses on the impact of specific limitation periods. In addition to these (external and internal) barriers to enforced performance, attention is also paid to two less known limiting factors, that is, a duty to mitigate damages in the form of a precautionary cover transaction and the argument of constant supervision on performance (section 6.5 and 6.6). Both impediments may have a significant impact in practice, where it concerns a commercial sales contract across the borders of the three investigated jurisdictions, and in general when a contract is concluded between parties from civil and common law backgrounds respectively. The discussion about a duty to mitigate and the constant supervision argument aims to enhance the understanding of the underlying principles and to reveal that they are reflected in different rules at the national and international levels.

6.2 Impediments

6.2.1 *Introduction*

The notion of impediments for enforced performance entails various legal concepts, such as objective and subjective impossibility, (fundamental, radical, exceptional and drastic) change of circumstances, frustration of purpose, hardship, disproportionality and commercial impracticalities. In order to clarify the role and function of these doctrinal

1316 Yin Lily Zheng, 'It's Not What Is on Paper, but What Is in Practice: China's New Labor Contract Law and the Enforcement Problem' (2009) 8(3) Washington University Global Studies Law Review 596.

1317 Jainfu Chen, *Chinese Law, Context and Transformation* (Martinus Nijhoff Publishers, 2008) 661 *ff*; Randall Peerenboom, *Judicial Independence in China: Common Myths and Unfounded Assumptions* (Cambridge University Press 2010) 69.

1318 Jainfu Chen 2008 (n 1317) 653.

formulas, three specific situations are discussed in this section. The first situation looks at the scenario where performance is impossible from the outset (section 6.2.2). This form of initial impossibility could occur when the goods have already perished at the time of contracting, or an already existing specific legal prohibition makes it impossible to perform the contract. To assess the availability of enforced performance once the impediment is removed or by an order for delivery of replacement goods, this section investigates the extent to which initial impossibility affects the validity of the contract.

219. Where initial impossibility does not affect the validity of a sales contract, it is discussed whether the consequences of initial impossibility are equated with the rules on non-performance occurring after the formation of the contract. Lastly, it is examined to what extent the availability of obtaining an order for enforced performance is affected by the knowledge of the seller – who was aware of the impediment to performance at the time of contracting. In view of this interrogative approach, special consideration is given to the difference between the situation where performance of a sales contract is impossible due to a legal prohibition (*e.g.* a national prohibition on the import or export of certain goods) and impossibility caused by a physical and practical barrier(s) for performance (*e.g.* the goods are lost during transition and recovery would require a large-scale operation). The reason being that invalidation of the contract due to initial impossibility removes the necessity to determine the enforceability of the contract by means of the rules on non-performance. More importantly, the examination of the legal response to initial impossibility *vis-à-vis* third-party rights reveals a prominent difference between the impact of civil and common law principles embedded in the three investigated legal systems.

220. The second situation considers subsequent impossibility of performance in light of various objective and subjective impediments for performance (section 6.2.3). Analysing these categories of impossibility is of significant relevance for situations where the aggrieved party is still interested in obtaining the goods once the physical or legal barrier for performance is lifted. In this light, it is investigated how cases of objective and subjective impossibility of performance are grouped. It is also examined whether a distinction is made between foreseeable and unforeseeable impossibility and between partial and temporarily impossibility.

221. The third situation involves cases where performance may still be possible, although with disastrous results for the party who is obliged to perform. It is, however, not always easy to draw a line between a situation where enforced performance should not be available due to an excessive change in the monetary equilibrium of the contract, and the situations mentioned above, of initial and subsequent impossibility (section 6.2.2 and 6.2.3). Where performance is totally impeded by impossibility, the obvious legal response is that an order

for enforced performance is not available. For commercial sales, the legal response should be different where the monetary equilibrium of the contract alters after the conclusion of the contract, in the sense that it results in a gross disparity between costs and benefits of the contract, or put differently, where performance becomes excessively onerous because of a (for the promisor unforeseen) change of circumstances. In such a case, issues of enforcement arise when the aggrieved party did not lose its interest in enforced performance of, for example, a delivery obligation or an obligation to take delivery. In this light, section 6.2.4 provides an analysis of the possible causes of a change in the monetary equilibrium of a commercial sales contract, their impact on availability of obtaining an order for enforced performance, and how these findings relate to the principle of *rebus sic stantibus* (*i.e.* enforcement of performance is not available because extraordinary circumstances arising after conclusion of the contract render performance literally or virtually impossible). It should be mentioned that the doctrines applicable in a situation where performance is rendered unreasonably burdensome or expensive or where enforcement of performance is impossible due to an insurmountable financial obstacle, to some extent shade into each other, since they both refer to a situation of a change of circumstances after the conclusion of the contract. However, when considering the impact on the availability to obtain an order for enforced performance, major differences arise, particularly in cases of temporary and partial impediments for performance.

6.2.2 *Initial impossibility*

222. *Preliminary* – In the present research, the concept of initial impossibility focusses on situations where performance of the seller's obligation to deliver the goods and the buyer's obligation to take delivery is objectively impossible for all time due to an uncontemplated impediment which was present at the time of the formation of the contract.[1319] Determining the enforceability of an obligation in these instances may be perceived as purposeless because performance is simply impossible. In certain situations, however, the aggrieved party may still be interested in upholding the contract and thus the delivery obligation, in order to acquire the goods once a temporary impediment (in fact or in law) is removed. This assessment is also of relevance for situations where the parties may be interested in enforcement of ancillary duties (see section 4.5) and situations where there are reasons to allow a claim for damages. In view of these considerations, the following aims to determine to what extent the investigated legal systems treat initial impossibility as a situation which only makes the performance unenforceable, or where the existence of the obligation retrospectively or prospectively ceases to exist. Particular attention is given to the question

1319 Where an initial impediment renders the performance of a contract more onerous is discussed in s 6.2.4.

of whether the seriousness of the misapprehension to the ability of performing the contract is of any relevance. This consideration is of significant importance in the situation where the non-performing party wishes to escape its obligation even though the misconception does not go to the core of the promises made by the parties. This form of initial impossibility is one of the most complicated areas of law to compare. As shown below, this is due to the various ways domestic and international law regulate issues on initial impossibility of fact and law.[1320]

> *Illustration* – An exporter of dairy products, located in country A, and a retail cooperation, located in country B, conclude a contract for the purchase and sale of milk powder under the general conditions for the international trade in dairy products (MPC). However, unknown to both parties, the moment they entered into the contract, a temporary import ban prohibits the import of milk powder. In addition, it is held by the exporter that both parties share the same misimpression concerning the availability of milk powder which satisfies the safety standards of country B. In this situation of initial impossibility in law and in fact, the question arises whether the delivery obligation ceases to exist which makes it impossible to obtain an order for enforced performance, or that this form of initial impossibility in fact and in law merely suspends performance until the impediments are removed.

223. *Domestic approaches* – Dutch contract law does not make a distinction between the situation where performance is impossible from the outset (initial impossibility) and after the conclusion of a contract (subsequent impossibility).[1321] In both situations, the same rules apply in determining whether the contractual right for performance is impeded to such an extent that a claim for enforced performance is not available to the aggrieved party. In general, Dutch contract law adopts a wide notion of the concept of impossibility, which means that a contractual right to performance is not protected by a statutory right to claim for enforced performance in the case of objective and subjective impossibility.[1322]

Where performance is classified as objectively impossible, this means that no one is able to perform the assumed obligation. Subjective impossibility involves situations where performance is rendered practically,[1323] morally or legally impossible for the party who is

1320 See also Schwenzer, Hachem and Kee 2012 (n 13) paras 17.01–17.03.

1321 De Jong, Krans and Wissink 2018 (n 194) 135; De Vries 1984 (n 207) 17; GT de Jong, *Niet-nakoming van verbintenissen* (Monografieën BW n B33, Kluwer 2017) s 9.1; Stolp (n 536) 235; Smits 2008 (n 871) 18.

1322 De Jong, Krans and Wissink 2018 (n 194) 135.

1323 *E.g.*, a Dutch trading company sells a number of antique designer dresses to a Chinese museum. However, the ship carrying the antique dresses is lost in a heavy storm. Despite the fact that the container is airtight and could be recoverd, this would require an unreasonable amount of effort of the seller. Therefore, enforced performance of the contract is regarded as practically impossible.

obliged to perform (someone else may be able to perform).[1324] Both forms of impossibility can be divided into final and temporary impossibility, and whole and partial impossibility.[1325]

As previously mentioned, judicial execution of a contractual right to performance is not available where performance is impeded. This may result in an impasse, which can be resolved by various legal principles. Where the impediment is caused by an attributable failure in performance of the promisor, a claim for damages is the most obvious remedy.[1326] In combination or as a stand-alone solution, the promisee could also opt (claim or counterclaim) for suspension as a stepping stone towards termination of the contract,[1327] and for avoidance of the contract on the basis of the argument that the contract is established under the influence of an error and it would not have been concluded had there been a correct assessment of the facts. A contract can be voided where: a fundamental mistake is caused by incorrect information – unless the defendant was entitled to rely on the information;[1328] the claimant, in view of what it knew or ought to have known regarding the misconception, should have informed the mistaken party;[1329] a contract is concluded on the basis of mutual and fundamental mistaken assumption (common mistake).[1330]

Where impossibility is caused by unforeseen circumstances the court may, on request of either of the parties, modify the effects of a contract or set it aside in whole or in part, if the impediment for performance is of such a nature that the other party, given those circumstances, cannot expect the unaltered contract to continue to be valid and enforceable in accordance with generally held standards of reasonableness and fairness.[1331] Where performance is permanently impeded due to unforeseen circumstances, only the contractual right to performance is not enforceable, the right itself does not cease to exist.[1332]

In addition to the case study provided under paragraph 222, the following example may also help to clarify the impact of this principle on the enforceability of a delivery obligation. A Dutch company (seller) and a Singapore company (buyer) conclude a contract for the sale and delivery of a batch of 250 bottles of exclusive red wine which was already on its way to Singapore when the parties started their negotiations. However, the day before

1324 De Vries 1984 (n 207) 18; De Jong 2017 (n 1321) s 9.3; Haas 2009 (n 206) 249; Sieburgh, *Asser 6-I* (n 363) paras 338 *ff*, 343, 355, 382; BJ Broekema-Engelen, 'commentaar op artikel 74 Boek 6 BW' para 2–4 in RJQ Klomp and HN Schelhaas (eds), *Groene Serie Verbintenissenrecht* (Wolters Kluwer 2011); Stolp (n 536) 236, 237; Smits 2008 (n 871) 18; De Jong, Krans and Wissink 2018 (n 194) 135.

1325 See for different classifications of impossibility <https://www.cisg.law.pace.edu/cisg/biblio/southerington.html> accessed on 3 March 2019.

1326 Art 6:74 DCC.

1327 Arts 6:264, 6:265 DCC; De Jong, Krans and Wissink 2018 (n 194) 135.

1328 Art 6:228(1) DCC.

1329 Art 6:228(2) DCC.

1330 Art 6:228(3) DCC.

1331 Art 6:258(1) DCC; Sieburgh, *Asser 6-I* (n 363) para 372; De Jong, Krans and Wissink 2018 (n 194) 133.

1332 Sieburgh, *Asser 6-I* (n 363) para 373.

the conclusion of the contract, the vessel lost the container with the bottles of wine, but the communication on this issue only reached the parties a week later. Under Dutch contract law, this situation of initial impossibility in fact (caused by non-existence of the goods) generally does not affect the existence of the delivery obligation, but it merely removes the right of the buyer to enforcement as long as delivery is impeded.[1333] Thus, if the seller produces red wine of the same quality the next year, the buyer may sue for enforced performance if this is permitted under the terms of the initial agreement.[1334] In view of the foregoing, it is important to note that where performance is only temporarily impeded, the court may grant a claim for enforced performance under the condition that actual execution is available once the impediment to performance is lifted.[1335]

Aside from misconceptions rendering a contractual right to performance permanently impossible (be it objective or subjective) from the start of the contract, there are other specific situations of initial impossibility in law which may invalidate the entire contract with the consequence that a contractual right ceases to exist. For example, if the obligations stipulated in a commercial sales contract are an infringement of the principle of good morals and public policy,[1336] or the agreed performances are contrary to other mandatory statutory provisions.[1337]

224. The starting point under the contract law of Singapore is that enforced performance is not available where the parties have reached an agreement (offer and acceptance coincide perfectly), but the delivery of the goods, as understood by both parties, is impossible in fact or law from the outset.[1338] In these instances, a commercial sales contract may be void under the law of Singapore due to a common mistake where the impediment to performance makes it impossible to fulfil the shared purpose of the contract, where neither party is at fault,[1339] and have undertaken the risk of non-performance.[1340] The doctrine of common mistake also requires that the alleged initial impediment to performance in fact or in law must render the subject matter of the contract fundamentally different from the thing the parties envisaged as the basis constituting their contract.[1341] There are two general principles

1333 MM van Rossum in Schelhaas 2002 (n 19) 197.

1334 Art 6:248(2) DCC.

1335 Art 3:296 DCC; De Jong, Krans and Wissink 2018 (n 194) 136; Sieburgh, *Asser 6-I* (n 363) 373.

1336 Art 3:40(1) DCC.

1337 Art 3:40(2) DCC.

1338 This concerns the requirement that the mistake must be shared by both parties and relate to facts or law before the contract was concluded; *Ho Seng Lee Construction Pte Ltd v Nian Chuan Construction Pte Ltd* [2001] 2 SLR(R) 184; *Wong Lai Keen v Allgreen Properties Ltd* [2009] 1 SLR (R) 148; Phang et al 2002 paras 10.008, 10.090–10.092, 10.102.

1339 *Ho Seng Lee Construction Pte Ltd* (n 1338); Phang et al 2002, para 10.100.

1340 *Ho Seng Lee Construction Pte Ltd* (n 1338); see also the English case *Associated Japanese Bank (International) Ltd v Crédit du Nord* [1989] 1 WLR 255; Phang et al 2012 (n 112) para 10.098.

1341 *Ho Seng Lee Construction Pte Ltd* (n 1338); Phang et al 2002s para 10.103.

underlying this narrow test. First, the courts are primarily concerned with the protection of the sanctity of a contract.[1342] Second, the doctrine of mistake only applies where an unexpected and exceptional mistake lies at the root of the contract.[1343] Aside from a situation of a common mistake, in circumstances where the goods have already perished at the time when the contract is made, the sales law of Singapore entails the principle that the contract is void.[1344] The considerations in *Chop Ngoh Seng v Esmail and Ahmad Bros* are illustrative in this regard.[1345] In this case, the parties had entered into a contract for the supply of fifty bales of gunny bags to be delivered in Singapore.[1346] When the ship, which in fact sailed from Calcutta the day after the contract was signed, arrived in Singapore, the fifty bales of gunny bags were not on board and never had been. Neither party to the contract was aware of the fact that the subject matter of the contract of sale did not exist at the time the contract was entered into. The court held that the contract was for the sale of specified goods on a specified ship arriving at Singapore on or about a specified date and as the goods were not on board the ship, performance was impossible from the outset rendering the contract void.[1347]

Considering a situation of initial legal impediment caused by a common mistake, the existence of the obligation could also be affected on application of the aforementioned principles. For example, a Singapore wholesaler (buyer) and a Dutch producer of meaty snacks (supplier) conclude a continuing sales contract for the delivery of Dutch croquettes without the required approval of the relevant authorities. In this situation, if approvals are not forthcoming, the contract is not frustrated,[1348] as is often presumed, but performance cannot be enforced due to initial legal impossibility.[1349] In other words, the law's response to common mistake of law and fact is similar, that is, the delivery obligation ceases to exist.

1342 *Ho Seng Lee Construction Pte Ltd* (n 1338) SLR(R) 184 [71]; Phang et al 2012 (n 112) para 10.094; this approach differs slightly from the approach of English common law, *i.e.*, a party should be entitled to rely on the doctrine of mistake only in exceptional circumstances. See the English cases *Associated Japanese Bank (International) Ltd* (n 1340); *Great Peace Shipping Ltd v Tsavliris Salvage (International) Ltd* [2003] QB 679 at 706 [86]; *Bell v Lever Brothers Ltd* [1932] AC 161 at 224; Anson's Law of Contract (n 360) 300 *ff*.

1343 *Adani Wilmar Ltd v Cooperative Centrale Raiffeisen-Boerenleenbank BA ("Rabobank Nederland")* [2002] 2 SLR (R) [52]; Phang et al 2012 (n 112) para 10.095.

1344 SGA, s 6. This Act was made applicable by the Application of English Law Act in Singapore on 12 November 1993 (Sale of Goods Act (Cap 393, 1994 Rev Ed). The AELA 1993 clarified the application of English law in Singapore. For sales contracts this meant that the UK Sale of Goods Act (which was first adopted in 1993 and modified in 1979) continued to be a part of the law of Singapore in the form of the Sale of Goods Act (Cap 393, 1994 Rev Ed). Before the AELA 1993, the reception of English commercial law appears to derive from section 5, Civil Law Act (Cap 43, 1988 Rev Ed). See also the comments in footnote 118.

1345 *Chop Ngoh Seng v Esmail And Ahmad Bros* [1948] 2 MLJ 93.

1346 *Ibid.*

1347 *Ibid.*

1348 Only where the impediment arises after the conclusion of the contract does the doctrine of frustration apply; Phang et 2012 (n 112) paras 10.072, 19.057.

1349 *Lim Xue Shan v Ong Kim Cheong* [1990] 2 SLR(R) 102.

Aside from a common mistake (in fact or in law) at common law, a situation of initial impossibility may also be governed under Singapore law by the doctrine of common mistake in equity.[1350] From the perspective of a temporarily initial impossibility in fact or in law following from a common mistake, the latter provides much more flexibility since it allows the courts to provide a judicial order on terms which are appropriate in light of the temporary nature of the initial impediment.[1351]

In summary, a Singapore court may release the non-performing party from its obligations where an initial impediment in fact or in law occurred at or before the contract was formed, by declaring the contract void in common law (*e.g.* where the goods already ceased to exist),[1352] or (in contrast to the English position) avoided in equity (potentially on terms),[1353] unless the court construes the contract as placing the risk of the initial impossibility on one or both parties.[1354] Considering the more narrow requirements for common mistake at law,[1355] it is held that the aggrieved party should first plea for application of the doctrine of common mistake at law and, secondly, for application in equity.[1356] At this point, it must be noted that the doctrine of mistake and the later discussed doctrine of frustration may be pleaded by the promisor where the impediments for performance display factual similarities (section 6.2.3). However, the doctrine of mistake applies where the initial impossibility (caused by a common mistake in fact or law) occurs before the making of the contract, whereas the doctrine of frustration may discharge the obligation to perform (by bringing the contract to an end) due to an impediment to performance that occurred after the making of the contract. A contract continues to bind the parties if it is not brought to an end by frustration.

A performance obligation may also become unenforceable under Singapore contract law where a contract is declared void at common law (*i.e.* offer and acceptance do not coincide) due to a unilateral mistake of fact or law.[1357] In this situation, three requirements

1350 *Chwee Kin Keong v* Digilandmall.com *Pte Ltd* [2005] SGCA 2, (2005) 1 SLR(R) 502; Phang and Goh 2012 (n 318) para 405; Phang et al 2012 (n 112) para 10.133; It appears that English law does not accept a doctrine of common mistake in equity, see Anson's Law of Contract (n 360) 315–316 and Phang et al 2012 (n 112) para 10.133.

1351 *Chwee Kin Keong* (n 1350) SGCA 2; Phang et al 2002 (n 112) para 10.116; Phang and Goh 2012 (n 318) para 403–405; See also the considerations in the English case *Associated Japanese Bank* (n 1340) WLR 255 at 275.

1352 *Ho Seng Lee Construction Pte Ltd* (n 1338); *Associated Japanese Bank* (n 1340); Phang and Goh 2012 (n 318) paras 385, 386.

1353 *Chwee Kin Keong* (SGCA) (n 1350); Phang and Goh 2012 (n 318) paras 385, 386.

1354 Phang et al 2012 (n 112) paras 10.017–10.023; Phang and Goh 2012 (n 318) para 357; the distinction between mistake at common law and equity is especially important in cases of sub-sale due to the additional requirements for avoidance in equity.

1355 *I.e.*, at the conclusion of the contract, both parties assume that performance is possible, there must be no warranty, performance must be impossible and the parties should not be at fault of non-performance.

1356 Phang and Goh 2012 (n 318) para 404.

1357 Phang et al 2012 (n 112) para 10.142; Phang and Goh 2012 (n 318) para 418.

must be fulfilled to render an obligation permanently unenforceable because the contract simply never came into being.[1358] First, the initial impediment to perform must relate to the terms of the contract.[1359] For example, an error in the amount of goods offered which concerns a term of the contract. The second requirement is that the initial impediment must be fundamental to the contract.[1360] The third requirement is that the non-mistaken party must have actual knowledge of the initial impediment following from misapprehension as to the facts or law.[1361] Instances of constructive knowledge may be sufficient where the non-performing party seeks dismissal of performance by bringing to court the defence of a unilateral mistake in equity.[1362] Subsequently, the contract may be avoided by the court which would render the performance obligation unenforceable.

225. The contract law of China adopts an unambiguous statutory principle stipulating that enforced performance is not available in instances of impossibility in law or in fact.[1363] It appears that this provision applies in cases of initial and subsequent impossibility.[1364] The notion that enforced performance is excluded in instances of initial impossibility is, however, not sufficient to determine the actual impact on the availability to obtain an order for enforced performance once the factual or legal impediment is removed. This requires an assessment of the situations in which initial impossibility affects the existence of the obligation. The general approach taken is that a significant misconception at the beginning of a contract entitles the seller to require avoidance of the contract. In cases where the claim is granted, the performance obligation ceases to exist. For example, a commercial sales contract could be avoided due to a significant misconception as to the nature of the contract, the identity of the other party, the kind of goods, the quality, specification and quantity of the goods.[1365]

1358 Phang et al 2012 (n 112) para 10.162; Phang and Goh 2012 (n 318) para 426; It appears that English law only requires that the unilateral mistake relate to the terms of the contract and that the mistake must be fundamental; See the English case *Smiths v Hughes* [1871] LR 6 QB 597.

1359 *Chwee Kin Keong* (SGCA) (n 1350); Phang and Goh 2012 (n 318) para 427; Phang et al 2012 (n 112) para 10.163.

1360 *Chwee Kin Keong v* Digilandmall.com *Pte Ltd* [2004] SGHC 71, (2004) 2 SLR(R) 594 [107]; Phang and Goh 2012 (n 318) para 459; Phang et al 2012 (n 112) para 10.166.

1361 *Chwee Kin Keong* (SGCA) (n 1350); Phang and Goh 2012 (n 318) para 432; Phang et al 2012 (n 112) para 10.169.

1362 *Chwee Kin Keong* (SGCA) (n 1350) SLR(R) 50, [44]; *Wellmix Organics (International) Pte Ltd v Lau Yu Man,* [2006] 2 SLR(R) 117, [66]-[68]; Phang and Goh 2012 (n 318) para 433; Phang et al 2012 (n 112) para 10.171.

1363 Art 110 (1) CCL; Bing Ling 2002 (n 229) para 4.087; Lutz-Christian Wolff, 'Impossibility of Performance and Contract Validity' in DiMatteo and Chen 2017 (n 19) 290, 291.

1364 Lutz-Christian Wolff, 'Impossibility of Performance and Contract Validity' in DiMatteo and Chen 2017 (n 19) 294.

1365 Bing Ling 2002 (n 229) para 4.074; Chen-Wishart, 'Invalidity in Chinese and English Contract law' in DiMatteo and Chen 2017 (n 19) 268–273.

In certain situations of initial impossibility in law, the binding force of a contract is (entirely or partially) removed from the moment the parties entered into the contract by invalidation of the entire contract.[1366] For example, the initial impossibility is the result of an act of fraud or coercion by one party to damage the interests of the state, malicious collusion conducted to damage the interest of the state, or an illegitimate act concealed by the contract.[1367] A contractual obligation may also be removed by invalidation of the contract if the initial impossibility in law derives from a common mistake.[1368]

The category of initial impossibility at law also governs cases where the enforceability of a contract depends on government approval, albeit that it is seldom clear from the outset whether approval is a prerequisite for establishing a valid contract or that absence of approval merely bars the aggrieved party from obtaining an order for enforced performance because the contract has not obtained effectiveness (yet).[1369] An opaque legal requirement, which may amount to initial impossibility in law, is the requirement of permission of (local) authorities to enter the Chinese market because it is often not apparent whether approval ex-ante or ex-post is required. Only consultation with the relevant authorities can give a reasonable degree of certainty about the effect of the approval requirement on the enforceability of the contract. For example, if a Dutch manufacturer of vitamins and dietary supplements and a Chinese retail chain conclude a contract for the delivery of a new range of memory and immune boosting supplements, the contractual promises made by the parties may never be enforceable if it later emerges that anticipatory approval of the relevant authorities was a precondition of the validity of the contract. However, if approval is only required to obtain effectiveness, the existence of the contract is not affected and the parties may claim for enforced performance (at a later point in time). This reasoning is fully in line with the Chinese contract law approach that initial impossibility in fact or law renders performance unenforceable for the duration of the impediment, and that invalidation is a matter of exception to the security of transactions between two commercial parties.[1370]

226. *Comparative analysis* – The three subject jurisdictions all act on the notion that performance cannot be enforced in cases of initial impossibility in fact and in law. However, they all structure the applicable principles in entirely different ways, making it treacherous

1366 Art 56 CCL; Lei Chen and Larry A DiMatteo, 'History of Chinese Contract Law' in DiMatteo and Chen 2017 (n 19) 22; Shiyuan Han, 'Liabilities in Contract Law of China: Their Mechanism and Points in Dispute' (2006) 1 *Frontiers Law China* 121, 142.

1367 Arts 52 (1–3), 54(1)(2) CCL.

1368 Art 54(1) CCL.

1369 Bu 2013 (n 226) 47.

1370 Bing Ling 2002 (n 229) para 4.087; Lutz-Christian Wolff, 'Impossibility of Performance and Contract Validity' in DiMatteo and Chen 2017 (n 19) 290–291, 295

ground to determine whether there is any common core, or if and how the legal systems differ. Nonetheless, this undertaking is of paramount importance in revealing the extent to which a legal system is capable of adjusting its response and not just by invalidating a contract on the mere basis of initial impossibility. The starting point here is the simple observation that the concept of initial impossibility is not specifically regulated in the contract law of the Netherlands, Singapore and China. This does not mean that initial impossibility has no consequences in these jurisdictions. On the contrary, it is broadly accepted that there are specific situations (albeit they differ per jurisdiction) where a performance obligation ceases to exist due to an initial impossibility. Dutch and Chinese contract law follow a very straightforward approach in this regard, namely, a contract may be avoided which has been entered into under the influence of a misconception and which would have not been concluded otherwise. Putting this premise into context: where initial impossibility is caused by a substantial mistake, this could cause a commercial sales contract to be avoided, meaning in effect that any delivery obligation ceases to exist. It follows that in cases where the misconception is not substantial, both jurisdictions apply the rule that only a performance obligation is unenforceable. A similar approach is taken by the PICC, PECL and DCFR, by stipulating that a contract is not simply invalidated because performance was impossible at the time of conclusion of the contract.[1371] The same viewpoint is indirectly adopted by the CISG and draft PACL.[1372] The contract law of Singapore is stricter in its response to an initial impediment caused by a common or unilateral mistake in fact or law. In these instances, an obligation may become permanently unenforceable on application of the doctrine of mistake in common law or equity, rendering a contract void or avoided respectively. Either way, it does not leave an obligation in a place where it is merely unenforceable. However, the complexity of the doctrine of mistake at common law and its narrow scope might be considered as a drawback, although it appears that the contract law of Singapore has moved towards a less restrictive system by allowing a defence of common and unilateral mistake in equity.

In view of the considerations above, it must be noted that the rules on initial impossibility, caused by mistake, in the contract law of the Netherlands and China, puts significant emphasis on a holistic assessment of the declarations and conduct of the parties

1371 Arts 3.3.1(1), 7.2.2(a), 7.2.3 PICC, see also Vogenauer 2015 (n 19) p 891, para 18, p 890, para 9; Art 4:102 PECL and art II.–7:201 DCFR.

1372 Schwenzer 2016 (n 91) art 4 para 33, art 46 paras 12, 13, art 79 para 13; Hüseyin Can Aksoy, *Impossibility in Modern Private Law* (Springer International Publishing 2014) 117; Art 7 Draft Articles on Non-Performance PACL stipulates that an order for performance may not be required where performance is impossible in law and in fact. It may be assumed that this provision also applies in cases of initial impossibility because there are no provisions which might suggest that initial impossibility would invalidate a contract.

in light of the surrounding circumstances.[1373] In contrast, the contract law of Singapore generally protects the sanctity of the contract by following a factual assessment of the common expressed intentions of the parties.[1374] Nonetheless, common to all investigated jurisdictions, as well as the PICC, PECL and DCFR,[1375] the mistake must be relevant in order to affect the enforceability of a performance obligation, albeit the thresholds differ significantly.

The CISG did not adopt a general threshold for an initial impossibility arising from a mistake, but it entails rules for various forms of mistake.[1376] This means in effect that when a commercial sales contract is subject to the CISG, a performance obligation is only affected by domestic law where the Convention has not established rules.[1377] However, it is at this very point that things get even more complicated, because similar impediments may have a different impact on the enforceability of a performance obligation at the domestic level. For example, the distinct situation where government permission is required may call for invalidation of the contract, but this form of initial impossibility could also merely mean that performance cannot be enforced.[1378] The latter approach is useful in cases where it is possible to obtain permission at a later point in time. In this respect, it is important to recall that the CISG is not familiar with a regime for initial impossibility caused by an infringement of statutory prohibitions.[1379] To put the relevance of this lacuna in the context of an international commercial sales contract: a manufacturer in country X (seller) of raw materials for plastics and an importer in country Y conclude a sales contract for the delivery of a certain type of polyester for the production of sportswear. However, country Y renders a contractual obligation invalid if the deal entails the importation of the agreed type of polyester. This situation of the initial impossibility of performance arising from a domestic legal prohibition, rendering the contract invalid under the law of country Y, is not governed by the CISG. By contrast, the PICC innovated in 2003 in this regard by including a set of

1373 NL: *Batavus v Vriend's Tweewielercentrum* (n 307) para 3.4; *Bunde v Erckens* (n 312); *Van Beers v Van Daalen*(n 307); *ABN AMRO v Malhi* Dutch Supreme Court 5 April 2002, ECLI:NL:PHR:2002:AD8186, NJ 2003, 124; see also Tjittes 2018 (n 2) 265, 362; CHN: art 125 CCL, see also Larry A DiMatteo and Jingen Wang, 'CC and CISG: A Comparative Analysis' in DiMatteo and Chen 2017 (n 19). 480; the CISG also adopted the subjective theory (art 8 CISG).

1374 *Zurich Insurance (Singapore) Pte Ltd v B-Gold Interior Design & Construction Pte Ltd* (n 383); Phang and Goh 2012 (n 318) para 993.

1375 Art 3.2.1 PICC (erronous assumption: one party must be in error by having an incorrect or incomplete understanding of the facts or the law which already existed at the time the contract was concluded, see Vogenauer 2015 (n 19) art 3.2.1, paras 3–9; Art 4:103 PECL (fundamental mistake as to facts or law); Art II.-7:201 DCFR (mistake in fact or law must make contract fundamentally different)).

1376 Arts 8(1), 27, 71 CISG; the Convention also does not allow rescission of a sales contract on the basis of mistake as to the properties of the goods, Schwenzer 2016 (n 91) art 4 para 36.

1377 Schwenzer 2016 (n 91) art 4 para 36.

1378 *E.g.*, arts 6.1.17(1), 6.1.17(2) PICC.

1379 Schwenzer 2016 (n 91) art 4 para 39; Art 3.3.1(1) PICC; Vogenauer 2015 (n 19) 471.

rules for initial impossibility as the result of legal prohibitions.[1380] However, the PICC did not clarify the matter as it refers to the relevant mandatory domestic rules to determine the effect on the contractual obligations.[1381] Only for situations where applicable legal barriers, or any other source in the judicial system of the law of origin of the relevant mandatory rule does not prescribe the effect on a contract, the PICC indicate that the aggrieved party may seek recourse for the remedies for non-performance.[1382]

In other situations where initial impossibility is treated as a mistake by application of statutory principles or by the doctrine of mistake, the contract may be avoided or declared void, but the matter and required seriousness of the misconception differ significantly among jurisdictions. Other differences follow from the more restrictive approach of Dutch and Chinese contract law and the casuistic approach of the contract law of Singapore. Taking all these elements into consideration, it is not surprising that for the situation of initial impossibility in law and fact described under paragraph 222, different solutions may arise at the national level, depending on the seriousness of the legal and factual misapprehension of the contracting parties. Nonetheless, it can be said that the broad outlines of the mistake rules of Dutch and Singapore contract law show some similarities with the PICC,[1383] and to a certain extent with the PECL and DCFR.[1384] The rules on mistakes in the contract law of China show fewer similarities with unification instruments because it has taken an approach in this regard which is more appropriate for domestic circumstances.

6.2.3 *Subsequent impossibility*

227. *Preliminary* – Subsequent impossibility is an interesting feature from a comparative perspective because civil and common law regulate the consequences of impossibility in an entirely different way.[1385] In order to determine to what extent the three investigated jurisdictions differ in this regard, the following assesses the legal response in two scenarios of impossibility, namely, the situation where delivery of the goods is completely impossible for everybody (objective impossibility), and where delivery is only impossible for a particular seller (subjective impossibility) due to, for example, practical, moral or legal impediments. The key issue concerns the question whether a claim for enforced performance remains intact where the delivery of the goods is impossible due to an

1380 Art 3.3.1(1) PICC.

1381 *Ibid.*

1382 *Ibid.*

1383 *E.g.*, art 3.2.2(1)(a) PICC (arts. 6:228(1) DCC) and art 3.2.2(2)(b) (art 6:228(2) DCC); However, art 3.2.1(1)(b) PICC has no parallel under Dutch law.

1384 Art 4:103 PECL; Art II.-7:102 DCFR.

1385 Schwenzer, Hachem and Kee 2012 (n 13) paras 45.26, 45.42.

impediment beyond the control of the seller and which it could not reasonably be expected to have taken into account at the time of the conclusion of the contract. In other words, is enforced performance of a delivery obligation available where the seller has gained exemption for damages on the basis that the non-delivery was caused by an unforeseeable impediment beyond its control? This analysis is most relevant for instances of a subjective impossibility (*e.g.* delivery of the goods is rendered more onerous), and where delivery is temporarily impossible.

> *Illustration* – A warehouse containing a nutrition company's stock of pharmaceutical products is destroyed by fire, causing an impediment to deliver various types of vitamins which were stored at this particular warehouse. A significant part of the stock were generic vitamins, but some of the stock was specifically developed and produced for a client. For both product groups (generic and specifically produced vitamins), the nutrition company is capable of producing new vitamins, which makes it possible to fulfil its delivery obligation at a later point in time. However, the nutrition company wishes to be released from its delivery obligations due to changed market circumstances. Nonetheless, the aggrieved buyers (for a similar commercial reason) insist on performance

228. *Domestic approaches* – As previously mentioned, Dutch contract law is not familiar with a distinction between initial and subsequent impossibility. Therefore, the discussion about initial impossibility under Dutch contract law [223] should be regarded as inserted and repeated here. Nonetheless, some specific observations about a situation of subsequent impossibility are provided below. It first has to be reiterated that a contractual obligation is objectively impossible if no one would be able to perform the contract in accordance with the agreed terms, thus rendering a claim for enforced performance simply pointless. For example, the goods have perished before the agreed time for delivery (and it is not possible to deliver substitute goods),[1386] performance is legally impossible, and a failure to comply with an essential element of the agreement (compare with frustration of purpose) means that the impediment for performance goes to the root of the contract.[1387] In situations where performance is objectively impossible, it is argued that the court is entitled to deny a claim for enforced performance on its own motion on the basis that the aggrieved party

1386 De Vries 1984 (n 207) 18, 19; *Van der Leest v Gemeente Veghel* Dutch Supreme Court 4 September 2008, ECLI:NL:HR:2008:BD3127, NJ 2010, 272; De Jong 2017 (n 1321) s 9.2; The same applies for Singapore. See Phang et al 2012 (n 112) para 19.031.

1387 De Vries 1984 (n 207) 18, 19; De Jong 2017 (n 1321) s *11.3; Endlich v Construction Machinery* Dutch Supreme Court 22 October 2004, ECLI:NL:PHR:2004:AO9494, NJ 2006, 597; Sieburgh, *Asser* 6-I (n 363) para 383.

lacks sufficient interest in enforcement.[1388] It is further widely acknowledged that the court shall order the claimant to reimburse the defendant in respect of all costs incurred in the proceeding if the former lacks sufficient interest in bringing the action to court. This general practice is said to be sufficient to prevent promisees from claiming for enforced performance without realistic prospects that performance becomes possible at one point.[1389]

An example of a situation of a subjective legal impossibility is that where only one specific manufacturer of bicycles is banned from importing its products due to past violations of trade regulations or for political reasons. Although it is recognised that subjective impossibility may (temporarily) free a non-performing party from its contractual performance obligations on the basis of the principle that a person has no right of action where he lacks sufficient interest,[1390] in the case of subjective impossibility, a claim for enforced performance can also be barred by the principles of reasonableness and fairness, although the thresholds for allowing this are set very high.[1391] Moreover, if the aggrieved party claims for enforced performance in the situation that performance is merely temporarily impossible, the court may provide an order for enforced performance subject to the condition that enforcement becomes available at the moment the barrier for performance is lifted.[1392] This is understandable as Dutch contract law places the right to require enforced performance ahead of the action to obtain monetary compensation. This notion is reflected in the principle that the court is not given the discretionary power to deny a claim for enforced performance on its own motion.[1393] In view of the above, it must be mentioned that a claim for enforced performance could also be denied if performance imposes a disproportional burden on the non-performing party, which would render enforced performance unacceptable according to standards of reasonableness and fairness.[1394] This type of impediment for obtaining an order for enforced performance, however, is not a part of the concept of objective and subjective impossibility in Dutch contract law (section 6.2.4).

Where the court establishes that performance is permanently impeded, the aggrieved party only loses its right to claim enforced performance.[1395] The obligation to perform does not cease to exist on this account. This means, in effect, that the aggrieved party remains

1388 Art 3:303 DCC; Haas 2009 (n 206) 244–246; Hijma, *Asser Koop en ruil* 7-I* 2013 (n 48) 374; Sieburg, *Asser 6-II* (n 532) para 344; Jongbloed (n 530) paras 5, 6.

1389 Nispen (n 867) 27.

1390 Art 3:303 DCC; Broekema in *Groene Serie Verbintenissenrecht* (n 1324) para 7.

1391 Dutch Parliamentary History Book 6 (n 207) 262; Art 3:296(1) DCC; Stolp (n 536) 234.

1392 Art 3:296(2) DCC; De Jong, Krans and Wissink 2018 (n 194) 136.

1393 Sieburgh, *Asser 6-I* (n 363) para 372; Haas 2009 (n 206) 181; Stolp (n 536) 246.

1394 De Vries 1984 (n 207) 18; *Mulitvastgoed v Nethou* (n 568); Stolp (n 536) 238.

1395 Dutch Parliamentary History Book 6 (n 207) 486, 488; De Vries 1984 (n 207) 21; De Jong 2017 (n 1321) Ch 10; Sieburgh, *Asser 6-I* (n 363) paras 371, 373; Haas 2009 (n 206) 181; Smits 2008 (n 871) 19.

entitled to claim restitution, reversion and suspension of its own performance.[1396] More importantly, the mere removal of the right to claim enforced performance means that the goods, which may already have been delivered, cannot be reclaimed by the non-performing seller.[1397] Where performance is only temporarily impossible and the time of performance is not essential to a sales transaction, the court may allow a claim for enforced performance on the condition that enforcement is suspended for the duration of the impediment.[1398] The same applies to partial impossibility to such an extent that the right to claim enforced performance is removed for that part affected by the impediment.[1399]

In certain situations of subjective impossibility due to unforeseen circumstances, the right to enforced performance of the principal obligation may be limited by alteration of the terms of the contract or setting aside of the contract in whole or in part.[1400] The court is allowed to do so (upon the demand of one of the parties) on the basis of unforeseen circumstances of such a nature that the other party, according to standards of reasonableness and fairness, may not expect the contract to be maintained in unmodified form. The modification or termination may be given retroactive effect. Furthermore, the modification or the setting aside shall not be pronounced by the court to the extent that it is common ground that the person invoking the circumstances should be accountable for them or if this follows from the nature of the contract. Nonetheless, where non-performance is excused for damages because the cause of the impediment is not attributable to non-performance, the aggrieved party does not necessarily lose its right to claim enforced performance. This is particularly important for cases where performance is only temporarily impeded. Hence, the ability to exercise the right to claim enforced performance is not related to the statutory regime for exemption from liability in damages.[1401] In any case, where performance is subjectively impossible, the non-performing party may be released

1396 Arts 6:203; 6:262, 6:263, 6:377, 6:378 DCC; De Jong 2017 (n 1321) Ch 10; Sieburgh, *Asser 6-I* (n 363) paras 371, 373.

1397 Art 6:203 (1) DCC; Dutch Parliamentary History Book 6 (n 207) 488; De Vries 1984 (n 207) 21.

1398 Compare art 3:396 (2) DCC: Sieburgh, *Asser 6-I* (n 363) paras 372, 378; De Jong 2017 (n 1321) Ch 12; Smits 2008 (n 871) 19.

1399 Sieburgh, *Asser 6-I* (n 363) para 372; Smits 2008 (n 871) 19; J Hijma, 'Koopprijsvermindering' (2018) 7202 WPNR 566.

1400 Art 6:258 DCC; De Jong 2017 (n 1321) Ch 10.

1401 De Jong, Krans and Wissink 2018 (n 194) 95; JM Smits argues (Schelhaas 2002 (n 19) 342) that an action for enforced performance is considered as no longer useful where damages are exempted because the non-performaning party is not at fault of the impediment to performance and the impediment does not fall within its sphere of risk. It must, however, be noted that impediment to enforced performance and limitations on damages are differently framed in Dutch contract law. Furthermore, the reasoning that an action for enforced performance is no longer useful where damages are exempted does not apply where performance is merely subjectively or temporarily impossible because in these instances it could still be justified to require a non-performing party to deliver the promised goods, albeit that the court is given the discretionary power to impose certain conditions for enforcement, such as compensation of costs, or delivery at a later point in time.

from its performance obligation when it successfully seeks relief via the aforementioned actions for modification or termination of the contract.

229. The following seeks to determine and explain the response of Singapore contract law when the performance of a contractual obligation becomes objectively or subjectively impossible after the parties entered into a commercial sales contract. For the contract law system of Singapore, it is of primary significance to determine the scope of the impediment of objective impossibility by distinguishing any reasonably foreseeable or any unforeseeable cause for non-performance. A claim for enforced performance might be denied by the court based on the theory of objective impossibility, if the cause of the impediment was foreseen or reasonably foreseeable by the parties at the moment the contract was made.[1402] In this situation, the parties are not discharged from their obligations by operation of the doctrine of frustration.[1403] By contrast, it is assumed that the non-performing party provided for the impossibility of the contract, and thus accepted the risk of its occurrence. As a result, objective impossibility of performance is merely a barrier for claiming enforced performance, and the aggrieved party may sue for damages on the basis that the promisor did not fulfil its contractual obligations.

Where an unforeseeable impediment for performance arises after the contract was made, a claim for enforced performance shall not be awarded if the agreed performance is radically changed by a physical, legal or commercial impossibility.[1404] Thus, objective impossibility is not required.[1405] The decisive condition is that the purpose of the contract is frustrated due to an unforeseeable change in circumstances.[1406] For example, a claim for enforced performance of a non-monetary obligation is generally not available after the conclusion of a commercial sales contract when a timely delivery is of essence but delivery of the goods is temporarily impeded because: the subject matter of the transaction has perished;[1407] the goods are simply unavailable;[1408] or the goods cannot be obtained by both parties from the intended source.[1409] In *Alliance Concrete Singapore v Sato Kogyo*,[1410] the

1402 Phang et al 2012 (n 112) paras 19.131, 19.142.

1403 Phang et al 2012 (n 112) para 19.080 *ff.*

1404 *E.g., Glahe International Expo AG v ACS Computer Pte Ltd* [1999] 1 SLR (R) 945 (SGCA); *Win Supreme Investment (S) Pte Ltd Joharah bte Abdul Wahab* [1996] 3 SLR (R) 583 [33]; Phang et al 2012 (n 112) para 19.131 *ff*; See for the categorisation *Adani Wilmar* (n 1343) SLR(R) 216 [44]; Phang and Goh 2012 (n 318) para 1374.

1405 Phang and Goh 2012 (n 318) paras 1377, 1378.

1406 Phang et al 2012 (n 112) para 19.043; Yip Man and Goh Yihan, 'Dealing with Unforeseen Circumstances: Contractual Construction and Equitable Adjustment' (2004) 1 Journal of Business Law 89.

1407 Compare the English case *Taylor v Caldwell* [1863] 3 B & S 826; Phang and Goh 2012 (n 318) para 1378.

1408 *Lim Kim Som v Sherriffa Taibah* [1994] 1 SLR(R) 233 (SGCH); Phang and Goh 2012 (n 318) para 1379.

1409 *Alliance Concrete Singapore Pte Ltd v Sato Kogyo (S) Pte Ltd* [2014] SGCA, 35, 3 SLR 857; Phang and Goh 2012 (n 318) paras 1381–1384.

1410 (n 1409).

doctrine of frustration played a key role. In this case, a Singapore supplier for ready-mixed concrete (RMC) entered into a contract with a Singapore contractor for the purchase and sale of a certain amount of RMC. The parties contemplated that Indonesian sand would be used in the preparation of the RMC. However, after the conclusion of the contract, the Indonesian government announced a ban on the export of sand. Aside from a very limited amount of sand which was available in Singapore, the supplier had no other source of sand for the production of RMC. Given the failure of the common intended source, the Singapore Court of Appeal held that the supplier was released from its obligation to deliver RMC on application of the doctrine of frustration.[1411]

It is a question of construction of the contract whether the contract is brought to an end by frustration or continues to bind the parties. As for the operational impact, the doctrine of frustration automatically releases the parties from their performance obligations when the impediment occurs,[1412] albeit only with prospective effect.[1413] There is one noteworthy statutory provision which reflects the principles of the doctrine of frustration on the existence of the obligation to perform as set out above. This is the rule in the Singapore Sale of Goods Act which stipulates that if performance is impossible because the goods, without any fault on the part of the seller or the buyer, perished before the risk passed to the buyer, the court may refuse a claim for enforced performance on the demand of the aggrieved party.[1414]

In certain situations where the impediment to performance is caused by a legal barrier, the doctrine of frustration allows the court to discharge the obligation to performance by invalidating the contract even though there has been no total failure in consideration.[1415] The Frustrated Contracts Acts provides the principles for the situation where the promisee has (partially) paid the purchase price before the occurrence of the impediment.[1416] It does, however, not apply in the case a commercial contract for the sale of specific goods is avoided under the Sale of Goods Act because, without any fault on the part of the seller or the buyer, the goods have perished before the risk passed to the buyer, or to any other contract for the sale, of for the sale and delivery, of specific goods, where the contract is frustrated by reason of the fact that the goods have perished.[1417]

An unforeseeable event which makes performance impossible for the duration of a certain time, thereby radically changing the contract, may remove the obligation to

1411 *Alliance Concrete Singapore Pte Ltd* (n 1409) [62-65], [70], [96], [101].

1412 Phang et al 2012 (n 112) paras 19.003, 19.083.

1413 Phang et al 2012 (n 112) paras 19.028–19.042, 19.080–19.082; Phang and Goh 2012 (n 318) para 1416.

1414 SGA, s 7.

1415 *Glahe International Expo AG v ACS Computer Pte Ltd* [1998] 2 SLR(R) 764 (SGHC); Phang and Goh 2012 (n 318) para 1376, 1419, 1420.

1416 Frustrated Contracts Act, Cap. 115, 1985 Rev Ed; Phang and Goh 2012 (n 318) paras 1419-1426.

1417 Frustrated Contracts Act (n 1416), s 3(5); Section 7 Sale of Goods Act (Cap 393, 1994 Rev Ed); Phang and Goh 2012 (n 318) para 1427.

perform.[1418] A delay in performance may also result in suspension of the principal obligation until the impossibility ceases. For example, a temporary restriction of Singapore on the import of poultry and poultry products from the Netherlands due to an outbreak of Bird Flu.[1419] In cases where the non-performing party argues that performance is subjectively impossible in whole, in part or temporarily, the complete frustration of the common purpose of the contract needs to be established.[1420]

230. The contract law of China acts on the general principle that in the case a contractual obligation is not fulfilled, the aggrieved party is entitled to demand enforced performance,[1421] unless performance has become impossible in law or in fact.[1422] For example, a Chinese government ban on the importation of dairy products from the Netherlands makes it impossible for a Dutch company to deliver its cheese to a Chinese retail chain. Under Chinese contract law, the Dutch company is not entitled to claim for enforced performance. Aside from this straightforward example of an objective impossibility in law, the contract law principles do not provide detailed guidance on determining the actual fate of the right to claim enforcement where performance is rendered subjectively impossible. This requires an assessment of the legal response to various forms of impossibility. For instance, it is stipulated that the aggrieved party is not entitled to request enforced performance if the subject matter of the obligation is unfit for compulsory performance or the performance expenses are excessively high.[1423] The contract law of China also provides an exemption for enforced performance in whole or in part where the impediment could not be foreseen, avoided *and* overcome.[1424] In addition, the People's Supreme Court made it clear that a performance obligation may be modified or declared void, if requested by one of the parties, where an unforeseeable major change in circumstances, not being a business risk and not caused by *force majeure*, and, which occurred after the parties entered into the contract, would impose an obviously unfair burden on the promisor if performance is enforced, or

1418 *Chua Chay Lee v Premier Properties Pte Ltd* [2002] 2 SLR(R) 464 [25] (SGCA); *Premier Properties Pte Ltd v Tan Soo Tiong & ors*, [2000] SGHC 12, [17]-[18].

1419 <https://www.customs.gov.sg/~/media/cus/files/circulars/ca/2016/circular_ai%20the%20netherlands%20dated%2003%20nov%2016.pdf> accessed on 5 February 2018.

1420 Phang et al 2012 (n 112) para 19.051 *ff.*

1421 Bing Ling 2002 (n 229) paras 4.087, 4.090.

1422 Art 110(1) CCL; Bing Ling 2002 (n 229) para 8.072; Liming 2016 (n 224) 249; Bu 2013 (n 226) 72; Zhang 2006 (n 41) 300; Lei Chen, 'Availablity of Specific Remedies in Chinese Contract Law' in Chen-Wishart, Loke and Ong 2016 (n 156) 28; Lutz-Christian Wolff, 'Impossibility of Performance and Contract Validity' in DiMatteo and Chen 2017 (n 19) 291.

1423 Art 110(2) CCL; See s 6.2.4.

1424 Art 117 CCL; Larry A DiMatteo and Jingen Wang, 'CCL and CISG: A Comparative Analysis' in DiMatteo and Chen 2017 (n 19) 497–498.

when the promisor cannot realise the purpose of the contract.[1425] In other words, a subjective impossibility due to a change in circumstances is not an exemption for enforced performance, but it enables the parties to claim for modification and termination of the contract. This rule has its legal basis in the principle of fairness which needs to be assessed in light of the particularities of the case. The application of the latter principle is subject to the strict supervision of the Higher People's Court, and its application shall be reviewed by the Supreme People's Court where necessary.[1426] The exclusion of a *force majeure* under the change of circumstances rule gives rise to the premise that where a change of circumstance is caused by *force majeure* the right to enforced performance may be exempted under the earlier mentioned (strict) regime for *force majeure.*[1427] In other words, the contract law of China has taken the approach that a seller may be relieved from its liability (for damages and enforced performance) where the impossibility arises from a *force majeure* which was unforeseeable, unavoidable and could not be overcome. Where the impediment arises from a change of circumstances, the non-performing seller is not automatically released from its delivery obligation, but may seek relief via modification or termination of the contract.

Considering all of the above, it may be assumed, as a general rule, that a claim for enforced performance may be denied where the performance of a delivery obligation has become objectively or subjectively impossible after the formation of a commercial sales contract.[1428] This reveals that the rules on subsequent impossibility could affect the ability to claim enforced performance of the seller's delivery obligation if the purpose of a commercial sales contract cannot be achieved (*i.e.* the contract is frustrated). The legal effect of objective and subjective impossibility is that a claim for enforced performance may be denied by the court on the demand of the non-performing party.[1429] The seller is, thus, not automatically relieved from its obligations where performance is impeded. This suggests that the contractual obligation to perform continues to exist despite its

1425 Art 26 Interpretation II of the Supreme People's Court of Several Issues concerning the Application of the Contract Law of the People's Republic of China; Notice of the Supreme People's Court on Correctly Applying the Interpretation II of Several Issues concerning the Contract Law of the People's Republic of China so as to Serve the Primary Objectives of the Party and the State (Notice on Correctly Applying Judicial Interpretation II Contract Law).

1426 Notice on Correctly Applying Judicial Interpretation II Contract Law (n 1425).

1427 Art 117 CCL; Larry A DiMatteo and Jingen Wang, 'CCL and CISG: A Comparative Analysis' in DiMatteo and Chen 2017 (n 19) 499.

1428 Bing Ling 2002 (n 229) paras 8.011, 8.072; Lei Chen, 'Availablity of Specific Remedies in Chinese Contract Law' in Chen-Wishart, Loke and Ong 2016 (n 156) 28, 29; Bu 2013 (n 226) 72.

1429 The promisor is obliged to prove the existence of an impossibility of performance; Hedayatollah Shenasaei, Maggie Qin and Faramarz Shirvani, 'Limitations of Specific Performance in the China Contract Law and the Convention on Contracts for the International Sale of Goods' (2007) 5(1) International Journal of Management and Commerce Innovations 772.

unenforceability.[1430] In this light, it is held that the court may order that the right to request enforced performance is only partially or temporarily exempted.[1431] That being said, the Supreme People's Court has not yet clarified the impact of the impossibility of performance on the existence of the contractual obligation to perform and whether a contractual obligation may revive again once the impediment for performance perishes.

231. *Comparative analysis* – The contract law of the Netherlands, Singapore and China have each taken different approaches to the situation where an impossibility in performance arises after the formation of a commercial sales contract. However, where the impediment to deliver the goods is permanent and objective in nature, it is obvious that (regardless of the fault of the non-performing party) enforced performance is not available in the three jurisdictions. Nonetheless, there is an interesting divergence among the investigated legal systems with respect to the situation where performance is only temporarily impossible and where an impediment arises from a subjective impossibility. The starting point in this regard is that both Dutch and Chinese contract law act on the notion that enforced performance is not available where performance is objectively or subjectively impossible, albeit that both jurisdictions regulate the applicable principles entirely differently. Under Dutch contract law, the applicable tests for exemption of performance do not answer the question of whether the non-performing seller is released from liability in damages. In other words, the non-performing party is not automatically relieved from performance where it is exempted from liability in damages on the basis of an event which is not the fault or responsibility of the non-performing party. By contrast, the contract law of China adopts the principle that a non-performing party is not liable (for damages and enforced performance) where an impediment (objective or subjective) could not be foreseen, avoided and overcome. It appears that the CISG and PICC are more in line with Dutch contract law in this regard.[1432] The CISG has adopted the principle that application of the exemption for damages does not prevent either party from exercising any right other than to claim damages.[1433] Although this principle has no practical meaning in cases where performance is objectively impossible for everyone, it shows that an aggrieved buyer does not lose its right to delivery and, thus, may sue for enforced performance once the barrier for performance has disappeared. This viewpoint is in line with the PICC which adopted the

1430 This contrast with the current German law (the early Chinese Civil Code was modelled on the German legal code), which has taken the approach that a performance obligation is dispensed with due to performance impossibility; See Lutz-Christian Wolff in DiMatteo and Chen 2017 (n 19) 293.

1431 Bing Ling 2002 (n 229) para 8.014; Liming 2016 (n 224) 250–251; Lutz-Christian Wolff, 'Impossibility of Performance and Contract Valdity' in DiMatteo and Chen 2017 (n 19) 293.

1432 Art 79(5) CISG; Schwenzer 2016 (n 91) art 79 para 53; The question as to whether a claim for enforced performance is available in cases of *force majeure*, and performance is rendered subjective or temporarily impossible, is a matter of art 7.2.2 and not art 7.1.7 PICC; Vogenauer 2015 (n 19) art 7.2.2 para 3, 43–44.

1433 Art 79(5) CISG.

rule that the right to performance cannot be enforced for the duration of the impossibility.[1434] In cases where the impediment only effects a part of the agreed performance, or performance is only temporarily unavailable, the court applying the PICC may exclude the affected part if the obligations of the seller are divisible,[1435] or may exclude the obligation to perform for the duration of the impediment.[1436]

For situations of subjective impossibility adjudicated under the CISG, it is argued that a seller, involved in a commercial sales transaction, is only released from its obligation to perform in very specific situations since a seller bears the risk of the fulfilment of the contract.[1437] This principle was applied by the ICC Court of Arbitration in Basel, which dealt with a case where an Austrian seller of chemical fertiliser was not exempted from performance because it did not provide the Swiss buyer with the necessary instructions for the fulfilment of the contract.[1438] In a similar vein, the Schiedsgericht der Handelskammer in Hamburg (Germany) considered that the seller was not exempted from performance in case of difficulties in delivery due to the seller's financial problems, or due to financial problems of the seller's supplier (even when connected to the act of public authority in the supplier's country). These instances of subjective impossibility are not considered an impediment beyond the seller's control, but belong to the seller's area of risk.[1439] Considering the above, impossibility of performance may remove the right to require enforced performance, albeit that the threshold in case of subjective impossibility may differ according to case-specific complexities. That said, more clarity on the grounds on which a claim for enforced performance should be denied may prevent local courts from seeking recourse to their discretionary power to refuse a claim for enforced performance where national limitations apply.[1440] The latter is relevant because domestic approaches differ and, therefore, their application in cross-border sales disputes could affect the CISG objective to develop uniform law and legal certainty regarding the remedial outcome(s) for parties involved in international commercial sales transactions.

In contrast to the Dutch and Chinese impact-based approaches (*i.e.* the impact on the availability of enforced performance may differ where delivery of the goods is completely, temporarily and partially impeded), as well as the CISG and PICC, the contract law of Singapore adopts the traditional common law focus on a breach of contract and damages. Within this stance, a distinction is made between impossibility amounting to an ordinary

1434 Art 7.2.2(a) PICC; Vogenauer 2015 (n 19) art 7.2.2(a) para 15.

1435 Vogenauer 2015 (n 19) art 7.2.2(a) para 14.

1436 Vogenauer 2015 (n 19) art 7.2.2(a) para 19.

1437 Schwenzer 2016 (n 91) 739 para 12.

1438 ICC Arbitration Case n 8128 (1995) <http://www.unilex.info/case.cfm?id=207> accessed on 8 February 2018.

1439 Schiedsgericht der Handelskammer, Hamburg, Germany, 21 March 1996, <http://www.unilex.info/case.cfm?id=195> accessed on 8 February 2018.

1440 Art 28 CISG.

non-performance, and where performance is frustrated. Where the applicable requirements for frustration are met, this latter relieves the non-performing seller from liability in damages, and subsequently from its performance obligation. The contract law of Singapore is familiar with exemption for objective and subjective impossibility, but the scope of these categories is more restricted compared to the approaches taken by Dutch and Chinese contract law. For example, where the doctrine of frustration exempts a non-performing seller from liability in damages, a claim for enforced performance shares the same fate, even if the impossibility is only temporarily. The PECL and DCFR and draft PACL follow the Singapore approach in cases where performance is permanently (objective or subjective) impossible.[1441] The comments on the applicable provisions suggest that in these instances a non-performing party is excused for damages and enforced performance if the impediment to performance is not the fault or responsibility of the non-performing party.[1442]

On the basis of an overall assessment of the considerations above, it may be said that the different tests for different causes of impossibility in the contract law of the Netherlands and China provide a certain level of flexibility which is necessary to adapt adequately to today's rapidly changing cross-border trade environment. However, this approach may also lead to legal uncertainty where performance is considered subjectively impossible. Singapore contract law provides contracting parties more clarity upfront in this regard, but the narrow scope of the rules for impossibility could impair the performance interest of an aggrieved buyer where performance is merely subjectively or temporarily impossible, such as in the example mentioned under paragraph 227. In this situation, the delivery of the vitamins is temporarily impossible because the company's stock is destroyed by fire. Nonetheless, it appears that where the court establishes that delivery of the specifically developed vitamins can be delivered at a later point in time, Dutch and Chinese contract law allows for an order for delivery on the condition that, for example, performance becomes enforceable once the manufacturer has produced enough to fulfil its delivery obligation. Although Singapore contract law is not familiar with the notion of a temporary impediment, it appears that an aggrieved buyer might not lose the ability to claim for enforced performance at a later point if the time for delivery is not of the essence. Nonetheless, where the time for delivery is essential to the contract, the aggrieved buyer may claim for damages, but it loses the ability to claim for enforced performance because delivery is considered as permanently impossible. Consequently, it is submitted here that the approach taken by Dutch and Chinese contract law, as well as the unification instruments, provides the courts with a greater degree of flexibility in the sense that it

1441 Art 8:108, Comment D PECL; Art III.-3:104, Comment D DCFR; Art 29 Draft Articles on Non-Performance PACL; See Lee 2016 (n 16) 184.

1442 Art 8:108, Comment D PECL; Art III.-3:104, Comment D DCFR; Art 29 Draft Articles on Non-Performance PACL, Lee 2016 (n 16) 184.

allows for a temporarily exemption of enforced performance where this is desired by the aggrieved buyer. On the other hand, it also reinforces the buyer's right to enforced performance, which does not resonate with the Singapore favourable look on protection of the seller's interest.

6.2.4 *Hardship and performance being unreasonably burdensome or expensive*

232. *Preliminary* – The present section deals with the impact of instances of hardship and performance being unreasonably burdensome or expensive. Both concepts must be distinguished from the impediments of objective and subjective impossibility discussed above. This is because a more onerous undertaking than contemplated does not impede the execution of a contract but nonetheless may affect the availability of enforced performance, although on the basis of different conceptual foundations at the national and international levels. In the following, the exemption of an unreasonably burdensome or expensive undertaking applies where performance is so onerous that it could be contrary to good faith to require it.[1443] The term hardship used here applies where the occurrence of an event fundamentally alters (*i.e.* radically changes) the equilibrium of a contract because either the cost of performance has increased or because the value of the performance a party receives has diminished.[1444] The two situations mentioned above typically coincide, but the legal response(s) can be quite different. For instance, take a sales contract which obliges the seller to deliver a certain amount of goods each quarter for a period of five years. After one year, an unforeseeable and significant rise in the price of oil occurs which makes performance of the contract more onerous than anticipated. Suppose that no gross disproportion exists between the parties' interests in performance of the contract, although undeniably performance has become more onerous due to a change in circumstances. This situation might not render performance unreasonably expensive (which would exempt enforced performance), but it could affect the availability of enforced performance of the initial obligation by other far-reaching measures, such as judicial alteration of the terms for performance. The present section aims to provide a better understanding of the key issues of both concepts in this regard, which is of particular relevance for long-term commercial sales contracts.

1443 This definition is used here because it is in line with the approach taken by the PICC, which is regarded as a neutral instrument in the realm of international contract law; Vogenauer 2015 (n 19) art 7.2.2, para 25.

1444 This definition is used here because it is in line with the approach taken by the PICC, which is regarded as a neutral instrument in the realm of international contract law; Vogenauer 2015 (n 19) art 6.2.2, para 1.

> *Illustration* – A weaving mill of an artisanal jeans manufacturer breaks down due to an electrical short circuit. The manufacturer considers buying a similar weaving mill in Japan in order to fulfil its contractual obligations under a sales contract with an internationally renowned fashion brand. However, this would require a heavy investment of the manufacturer's money and time to deal with the supplier in Japan, to negotiate the price and to clear customs in the exporting and importing countries. On the other hand, the renowned fashion brand has a significant interest in the delivery of the jeans (albeit with delay) due to its own contractual obligations with its regional agents, which in turn have contracted with local retailers. In this situation, the question arises to what extent the availability of obtaining enforced performance may be affected by the subsequent imbalance of the equilibrium of the contract.

233. *Domestic approaches* – Under Dutch contract law, the performance of a delivery obligation is not rendered subjectively impossible where performance has become unreasonably burdensome or expensive and where an event fundamentally changes the equilibrium of the contract.[1445] Nonetheless, the right to enforced performance may not be honoured by the court where performance requires an unreasonable effort or expense, even if the promisor is responsible.[1446] A claim for enforced performance could also be denied where performance would unreasonably burden the promisor and performance is not more beneficial to the promisee than another remedy.[1447] Where an event alters the equilibrium of a contract, an order for enforced performance may also not be available where performance is excessively onerous.[1448] In the above-described scenarios, a claim for enforced performance may not be granted on the basis of the so-called derogatory effect of the standard of reasonableness and fairness if the impact is manifestly unacceptable.[1449] For example, enforced performance could be denied when performance requires disproportional offers of the promisor due to, for example, a significant increase in the manufacturing costs. This hardship principle also plays a role where an unforeseen change in circumstances has affected the monetary equilibrium of the contract in the sense that performance has become excessively expensive for the seller or the value of the bargain has diminished entirely.[1450]

1445 De Vries 1984 (n 207) 18.

1446 *Oosterhuis v Unigro* Dutch Supreme Court 21 May 1976, ECLI:NL:PHR:1976:AC5738, NJ 1977, 73; MBM Loos in Schelhaas 2002 (n 19) 354.

1447 *Multi Vastgoed* (n 568); MBM Loos in Schelhaas 2002 (n 19) 355.

1448 Arts 6:2(2), 6:248(2) DCC; Haas 2009 (n 206) 137; Hartlief and Tjittes (n 569) 1464; De Vries 1984 (n 207) 17; De Jong, Krans and Wissink 2018 (n 194) 31–33.

1449 Arts 6:2(2), 6:248(2) DCC; De Jong, Krans and Wissink 2018 (n 194) 31–33.

1450 *Kriek v Smit* Dutch Supreme Court 12 June 1987, ECLI:NL:HR:1987:AC2558, NJ 1988, 150; Sieburgh, *Asser 6-III* (n 203) 439, 441–443; P Abas, *Rebus sic stantibus: een onderzoek naar de toepassing van de clausula*

234. There are, however, no clear thresholds for determining when the costs of performance have become unreasonably disproportionate and where the financial equilibrium has changed to such an extent that enforced performance is not available. By contrast, these situations are assessed on a sliding scale of the seriousness of their impact (*i.e.* the adverse (monetary) consequences of enforced performance) in view of the seriousness of the infringement, the interest of the aggrieved party in enforced performance, the interest of the non-performing party to remedy via a less burdensome remedy,[1451] and the specific circumstances of the case (*e.g.* guarantees and the agreed price).[1452] In a well-thought out attempt to provide more clarity on the matter it is suggested that the right to enforced performance is removed where (due to an unforeseen change in circumstances) the costs of performance exceed 130% with respect to the objective interest of the aggrieved party in the performance of the contract.[1453] This is, however, not a generally accepted principle.

The aforementioned sliding scale to determine the availability of enforced performance justifies a discussion about the acceptance of the common law efficient breach doctrine. This doctrine entails the principle that an aggrieved party is only entitled to the remedy which has the least adverse impact on the agreed obligations as a whole (principle of subsidiarity) and which does not result in an imbalance between the interests of the aggrieved and the non-performing party (principle of proportionality).[1454] If strictly applied, this could enable the promisor to abandon the contract if the monetary equilibrium of the contract has changed in such a way that the execution of the contract would result in a disproportionate financial burden. It is, however, noted that the same result could be achieved by application of the derogatory effect of the standards of reasonableness and fairness,[1455] and by application of the statutory principle that a contract may be set aside, on the basis of unforeseen circumstances of such a nature that the other party, according to the standards of reasonableness and fairness, may not expect the contract to be maintained in unmodified form.[1456] Thus, aside from the earlier mentioned derogatory effect of the standard of reasonableness and fairness, the right to enforced performance could also be affected by the hardship principle through modification or (partial)

rebus sic stantibus in de rechtspraak van enige Europese landen (Kluwer 1989) 226 *ff*; P Abas, 'Enige gedachten over de gedeeltelijke ontbinding (aanpassing) in de zin van art 6:258 BW' (1998) 6307 WPNR 211.

1451 See for an example of the application of the sliding scale for determining the availability of enforced performance: *Multi Vastgoed* (n 568) para 3.6. In this case the seriousness of the failed performance was not taken into consideration by the court because the performance was contractually guaranteed and, therefore, essential to the agreement.

1452 Stolp (n 536) 241, 242.

1453 Haas 2009 (n 206) 143.

1454 Stolp (n 536) 41; L Visscher, 'De rangorde van remedies voor wanprestatie: subsidiariteit en proportionaliteit versus efficiëntie' (20017) 54(9) NTBR 385.

1455 Art 6:248(2) DCC.

1456 Art 6:258(2) DCC requires a manifestly unacceptable impact.

termination of the contract.[1457] Where the seller fails to deliver the goods in accordance with the contract and where the court most likely shall not award a claim for enforcement because this would result in an unreasonably burdensome or expensive performance,[1458] the buyer could opt for setting aside the contract in whole or in part.[1459] This legal inroad may (partially) release the buyer from its obligation to pay the purchase price.[1460] Nonetheless, a similar result can be achieved via suspension, and subsequently, termination of the contract.[1461]

That having been said, the bar for limitation of the right to enforced performance, on the basis of the principles mentioned above, is set high since a contractual promise to do something is primarily binding on the parties, and, therefore, limitation of the enforceability of a contractual obligation by the court, should not be accepted lightly.[1462] Furthermore, when considering the situation where the promisor seeks modification or setting aside of the contract on the basis of unforeseen circumstances rendering the performance (subjectively) impossible,[1463] the court needs to establish that the supervening event is not taken into account by the parties at the time of the conclusion of the contract.[1464] Moreover, the right to enforced performance may not be affected by an unforeseen change of circumstances where it is common ground that the seller is accountable for the impediment, or where it follows from the nature of the contract that the seller is responsible for the impediment for performance.[1465] Not surprisingly, the court does not readily accept that enforced performance is exempted on the mere basis that performance became unreasonably financially burdensome due to a change in circumstances, nor that enforced performance results in unreasonable hardship.[1466]

235. The common law system of Singapore is not familiar with a moral standard of good faith which limits the ability to obtain an order for enforced performance where performance has become unreasonably burdensome or expensive, or excessively onerous due to a change of circumstances. More importantly, the contract law is not familiar with a distinction in thresholds and remedial consequences in the aforementioned situations.

1457 Art 6:258(1) DCC; De Jong, Krans and Wissink 2018 (n 194) 133.
1458 Art 6:248(2) DCC; De Jong, Krans and Wissink 2018 (n 194) 31–33.
1459 Art 6:258(1) DCC; Hijma, 'koopprijsvermindering' (n 1399).
1460 *Ibid.*
1461 Arts 6:264, 6:265 DCC.
1462 Dutch Parliamentary History Book 6 (n 207) 967, 974, 979; Schoordijk (n 451) 33–43; Hofmann 1976 (n 84) 192, 208; Stolp (n 536) 246; De Jong, Krans and Wissink 2018 (n 194) 31–33, 133–135.
1463 Art 6:258(1) DCC; De Jong, Krans and Wissink 2018 (n 194) 213.
1464 Art 6:258(1) DCC; Sieburgh, *Asser 6-III* (n 203) 439.
1465 Art 6:258(2) DCC.
1466 *NVB v Helder* Dutch Supreme Court 27 April 1984, ECLI:NL:PHR:1984:AG4797, NJ 1984, 679 para 3.2; *Kriek* (n 1450); *Briljant Schreuders v ABP* Dutch Supreme Court 20 February 1998, ECLI:NL:HR:1998:ZC2587, NJ 1998,493; Dutch Parliamentary History Book 6 (n 207) 136, 969.

The most important exemption to enforced performance (in response to a subsequent imbalance of the equilibrium) follows from the earlier discussed doctrine of frustration which may also be invoked by the non-performing party against a claim for enforced performance if an unforeseen change of circumstances radically changed the purpose of the contract.[1467] For example, a seller may be released from its performance obligations on application of the doctrine of frustration if an unforeseen supervening event causes a delay in performance and enforcement of the contract, if this delay would impose a disproportional burden on the seller (*i.e.* the monetary purpose of the contract is frustrated).[1468] A promisor is, however, not easily released from its obligations by application of the doctrine of frustration where an unforeseeable change of circumstances renders performance merely financial impractical (*e.g.* increase in production costs).[1469] Only if the commercial impracticability goes beyond the normal business risks of contracting parties, can performance be regarded as frustrated, for example, by an astronomical increase in prices.[1470] The threshold in this regard is very high due to the view that the doctrine of frustration does not govern cases of economic hardship. In view of this, it is suggested that the loss must be at least 100%. It is, therefore, important to note that unacceptable hardship due to a radical change in circumstances may release the seller from its performance obligations, even if the requirements for application of the doctrine of frustration are not fulfilled.

As for the doctrine of frustration, the question is not yet answered as to when an increase in price may amount to a sufficient level of commercial impracticability in order to release the promisor from its delivery obligation. This uncertainty raises the question to what extent enforcement of non-monetary obligations is barred in the situation an unforeseen

1467 Phang et al 2012 (n 112) paras 19.040, 19.043. 19.056; Shenoy and Loo 2013 (n 13) para 17.22.

1468 Phang et al 2012 (n 112) paras 19.076, 19.077.

1469 *Holcim (Singapore) Pte Ltd v Precise Development Pte Ltd* [2011] SGCA 1 (2011) 2 SLR 106 [53]; *Oversea-Chinese Banking Corp Ltd v Daewoo Singapore Pte Ltd and another* [2000] SGHC104 (The alleged sharp devaluation of the Korean Won against the US Dollar did not brought about a situation that is fundametally different from that in which the guarantee was given. Nothing in the terms of the guarantee or of the underlying loan showed that the bank and the guarantor never agreed to be bound in the event of such devaluation as alleged or in the event of any fluctuation in the rate of exchange between the stipulated currency (US Dollar) and any other currency); *M P Bilt Pte Ltd v Edy Yumianto* [1999] 2 SLR(R) 655 [14]-[15] (The purchaser pleaded that the contract wasfrustrated by the 'runaway inflation' in Indonesia which was not foreseen by the parties when the contract was entered into. Choo JC held that there was no frustration of the contract, 'the financial capacity of the purchaser is a matter strictly of his own concern he cannot walk away from his obligations only because financial difficulties had come upon him'); an astronomical increase in price may justify a discharge of the initial obligation, *e.g., Glahe International Expo* (n 1404) SLR(R) 945 [42]; Phang et al 2012 (n 112) paras 19.068, 19.070; Phang and Goh 2012 (n 318) paras 1375, 1395, 1397, 1398, 1399; in contrast to some American common law jurisdictions, commercial impracticability under Singapore law is not regarded as a frustrating event, see Shenoy and Loo 2013 (n 13) para 17.24.

1470 See the endorsement of the Englisch case *Tsakiroglou & Co Ltd v Noblee Thorl Gmbh* (1960) 2 QB 318 in the Singapore case *Holcim (Singapore)* (n 1469).

change in circumstances makes performance merely onerous. Typically, these cases are fertile ground to discuss whether the court may limit the availability of enforced performance by modification of the terms of the contract. This solution is not available because alteration of the terms of a contract is said to result in uncertainty for the parties, and it is believed to interfere with the freedom of contracting.[1471] Considering these concerns and the absence of contradicting case law in this regard it appears that it is not at the discretion of Singapore courts to limit the availability of enforced performance by means of judicial modification of the contract if a change of circumstances has made the performance of a contract financially unfavourable.

Despite the exclusion of the doctrine of frustration in the aforementioned situations, the contract law of Singapore limits the availability of enforced performance where performance results in unacceptable personal hardship of the promisor.[1472] Be that as it may, financial distress of a promisor due to enforcement of a contract under the agreed terms does not amount to personal hardship, and, therefore, cannot be invoked by the promisor in order to be released from its obligation to perform.[1473] A clear example on this matter is provided in the case *Lim Lay Bee and another v Allgreen Properties Ltd* in which it was considered by the Singapore Court of Appeal that the personal financial hardship that the purchaser incurred due to enforcement of the contract could not be the basis for relief of performance.

Where enforced performance would result in severe hardship of the promisor due to a radical change in circumstances, an award for damages could replace an order for enforced performance in order to provide the necessary relief. For example, in *Tay Joo Sing v Ku Yu Sang* the Singapore Court of Appeal held that in awarding a claim for enforced performance of the conveyance of a half share in a property, the hardship that would be suffered by the other tenant in common resulting from such conveyance had to be taken into account. The court therefore assessed whether damages should be awarded instead of enforced performance.[1474] Hence, severe hardship may result in denial of an action for performance, even where it concerns an obligation to transfer property.[1475] By way of contrast, in *Chua Kwok Fun Kevin and another v Etons Management Consultants Pte Ltd and others* the Singapore High Court was concerned with an action for enforced performance of a settlement agreement entailing the payment of a certain sum and the

1471 Yip Man and Goh Yihan (n 1406) 90.

1472 Phang et al 2012 (n 112), para 23.133; Dora Neo, 'Specific Remedies and the Performance Interest in Singapore Contract Law' in Chen-Wishart, Loke and Ong 2016 (n 156) 206–207; Halsbury's Laws of Singapore (Contract 2016) vol 7 para 80.594; See for cases with personal services *Holiday Inns Inc v Hotel Enterprises Ltd* [1975–1977] SLR 336 (SGHC); *Pub 1997 Pte Ltd v Scorpion* (n 965); *E C Investment Holding Pte Ltd* (n 899).

1473 Hunter 2017 (n 7) 144.

1474 *Tay Joo Sing v Ku Yu Sang* [1994] SGCA 45 [33], [35], (1994) 1 SLR(R) 765.

1475 *Chung Khiaw Bank Ltd* (n 890); Phang and Goh 2012 (n 318) para 1554.

provision of a bank guarantee.[1476] The court awarded the claim for enforced performance of the settlement agreement because on the financial statements it was held that the order would not cause any personal hardship for the non-performing party.[1477] In view of the foregoing, it must be mentioned that the rules on unacceptable hardship works differently than the previously mentioned doctrine of frustration, which, simply put, discharges the non-performing party from its obligations and is, in essence, not concerned with damages. By contrast, the rules on unacceptable hardship requires an assessment as to whether damages in lieu of an award for enforced performance is a more appropriate remedy considering the circumstances of the case. Nonetheless, the promisor shall not be released from its obligations due to hardship when the disturbance of the financial equilibrium of the contract merely derives from financial issues,[1478] such as an increase in the costs of performance. By way of illustration: a manufacturer of home care products cannot avoid a claim for actual performance merely because it has sold its products in a rising market for sustainably sourced palm oil – which is the main ingredient of these products – and, therefore, finds it difficult to obtain this ingredient in the market for a competitive price.[1479] Taking the aforementioned considerations into account, it may be said that under the contract law principles of Singapore, a promisor is not able to escape from its non-monetary obligations when a foreseeable or unforeseeable increase in costs makes performance of a non-monetary obligation, deriving from a commercial sales transaction, more expensive.

Aside from the above mentioned principles, the promisor could also argue that a claim for enforced performance is contrary to the requirements of observance of accepted standards of fair dealing if enforcement would result in an unreasonable (monetary) burden and, therefore, enforcement should not be allowed.[1480] The consideration in the Singapore Court of Appeal Case of *HSBC Institutional Trust Services Ltd v Toshin Development Singapore Pte Ltd* seems to support this approach as the reasoning, in this case, opens the door for acceptance of a general good faith principle for all contracts.[1481] It is advocated that this acknowledgement of a general principle of good faith would make Singapore 'more accessible and commercially attractive to investors'.[1482]

1476 (n 967).

1477 *Ibid* SGHC [9-10].

1478 Halsbury's Laws of Singapore (Contract 2016) vol 7 para 80.594.

1479 Compare the English case *Mountford v Scott* (n 422); Halsbury's Laws of Singapore (Contract 2016) vol 7 para 80.594.

1480 Glen Ting, 'Good Faith in Contractual Agreements in Singapore' (2016) 8(17) Singapore Law Review, Juris Illuminae.

1481 [2012] SGCA 48 [40–42], [45], (2012) 4 SLR 738.

1482 Lee Shen Yang, '*A Look at "Good Faith" in the Common Law*' [unpublished, archived at CJ Koh Law Library] 12.

236. The contract law of China has adopted distinct principles and legal consequences for the scenario that performance has become unreasonably burdensome and expensive, and where the equilibrium of the contract is altered due to a drastic change of circumstances. As for the first situation of hardship, the contract law of China provides the parties to a contract with a right to performance - which may be excluded by the court if the expenses for performances have excessively increased.[1483] This statutory principle is based on the obligation that the parties to a contract shall abide by the principle of good faith in accordance with the nature and purpose of the contract and usage in practice,[1484] which ensures the parties' interest in the thing they bargained for.[1485] It is, however, not clear which standard should be used by the courts to determine that the right to performance cannot be enforced because the costs of performance have excessively increased.[1486] It is submitted that the test should consider the costs and benefits of the promisor (economic efficiency approach),[1487] but it is also held that the assessment must entail a valuation of the costs of performance to be incurred by the promisor versus the benefits of the promisee.[1488] It is also put forward that the costs of performance should be assessed in terms of the benefits of both parties when the contract is properly performed.[1489] In addition, the judges in the Economic Case Trial Division of the Supreme People's Court have stipulated that the costs of enforced performance are also regarded as excessively high if monetary compensation could provide adequate relief to the aggrieved party.[1490]

The statutory principle that enforced performance is not available if performance is unreasonably expensive was applied by the Nanjing Intermediate Court in *Xinyu House Property Development v Feng Yumei*.[1491] In this case, the company Xinyu developed a commercial shopping centre of 60,000 square metres. Approximately 6,000 square metres was partitioned into 150 small retail shops, and one shop was sold to Feng Yumei. After

1483 Art 110 CCL; Zhang 2006 (n 41) 301; Bing Ling 2002 (n 229) para 8.075; Bu 2013 (n 226) 72 para 14; Liming 2016 (n 224) 233.

1484 Art 60 CCL; Lei Chen, 'Availablity of Specific Remedies in Chinese Contract Law' in Chen-Wishart, Loke and Ong 2016 (n 156) 29; Lei Chen, 'Damages and Specific Performance in Chinese Contract Law' in DiMatteo and Chen 2017 (n 19) 399.

1485 Zhang 2006 (n 41) 302.

1486 Yang Zhen Shan, 'On the Necessity of Establishing "Principle of Changed Circumstances" In China' (1990) n 5 Chinese Legal Science 63; Ji Fang, 'Research and Analysis on Exessively High Expenses of Performance in China' (2016) Politics and Law Forum 148.

1487 Zhang 2006 (n 41) 302; Liming 2016 (n 224) 233.

1488 Lei Chen, 'Availablity of Specific Remedies in Chinese Contract Law' in Chen-Wishart, Loke and Ong 2016 (n 156) 29; Lei Chen, 'Damages and Specific Performance in Chinese Contract Law' in DiMatteo and Chen 2017 (n 19) 399.

1489 Bu 2013 (n 226) 72 para 14; Bing Ling 2002 (n 229) para 8.075.

1490 Li Guogang, *Explanation and Application of the Contract Law* (Xinghua Press, 1999) 438; Zhang 2006 (n 41) 302.

1491 *Jiangsu Nanjing Xinyu House Property Development Limited Company v Feng Yumei* [2006] Nanjing Intermediate Court 6 September (2004) SPC Gazette 2006, issue 6.

a certain period, the entire shopping mall ceased business operations due to excessively high operational costs. To make the shopping centre profitable, it was necessary to redesign the layout of the buildings and, therefore, Xinyu started to repurchase the shops. Feng Yumei refused to cooperate and claimed continuance of performance of the contract. The Nanjing Intermediate Court considered that when the purpose of the contract cannot be realised by enforcement of performance, a claim for actual performance shall not be awarded. The court held that an increase in the costs of performance would make it impossible to achieve the purpose of the contract. This means that when the costs for performance exceed the interest to be gained by both parties through the performance of the contract, the non-performing party may be allowed to avoid actual performance and pay damages instead. In this light, it was adjudicated by the court that performance of the contract would mean that Xinyu was forced to incur excessively high operational costs and that maintaining the small shop would be detrimental to the entire shopping atmosphere. Taking these negative effects into consideration, the claim for continuance of performance was refused, and Xinyu was ordered to reimburse the purchase price of the shop and pay damages.

In addition to the situation that the expenses for performance are excessively high,[1492] enforced performance is also not available where a major unforeseeable (material) change in circumstances has made enforced performance obviously unfair.[1493] Although unfairness may arise from an increase in costs of performance or decrease of the value of the counter-obligation, a gross disparity between the costs and benefits is not demanded.[1494] Nevertheless, the aforementioned exemptions are not easily applied by the court, which accords with the belief that parties conclude a contract for its actual performance and not for the monetary value of their promises.[1495]

Aside from unfairness, it is a requirement that the change in circumstances is inextricably linked with the essential elements of the contract, that it is not be a business risk and that it is not be caused by a *force majeure* which materialised after the formation of the contract by the parties.[1496] In addition, it is held that the major change of circumstances may not be caused by persons or things which fall under the responsibility

1492 Art 110(2) CCL.

1493 Art 26 Judicial Interpretation (I) Contract Law (n 173); Notice on Correctly Applying Judicial Interpretation II Contract Law (n 1425); Bu 2013 (n 226) 58, 60; Bing Ling 2002 (n 229) paras 5.091, 5.093; Chunyan Ding, 'Performance and Breach' in DiMatteo and Chen 2017 (n 19) 318; *E.g.*, a substantial change in state price of aluminium, which results in indisputable injustice or if the state policy on the real estate market is unexpectedly changed; see in this regard *Binhai Entertainment Co Ltd of Haikou City Hainan Province v Hainan Huaxin Realty Management Co Ltd* [2001] SPC 16 May 2001.

1494 Schwenzer, Hachem and Kee 2012 (n 13) para 45.104.

1495 Bing Ling 2002 (n 229) paras 8.011, 8.065.

1496 Notice on Correctly Applying Judicial Interpretation II Contract Law (n 1425); Bing Ling 2002 (n 229) paras 5.089, 5.091, 5.093; Chunyan Ding, 'Performance and Breach' in DiMatteo and Chen 2017 (n 19) 318, 319; Bu 2013 (n 226) 59 paras 26–28.

of the promisee.[1497] In this regard, it is important to mention that in light of the global financial crisis and the increase of legal issues which it has triggered, the Supreme People's Court has stipulated that a distinction between commercial risks and a change of circumstances should be made.[1498] In the view of the Supreme People's Court, commercial risks are changes in supply and demand and price changes which are not abnormal.[1499] In this light, it is held that a change in circumstances should not arise from a risk which derives from the natural operating of the specific market, or from an event which was foreseeable at the moment of conclusion of the contract, or within the reasonable expectations of a normal person.[1500]

Where a claim for enforced performance is brought to court and the promisor argues that enforcement would result in financial hardship due to a change of circumstances after the conclusion of the contract, the courts are obliged to actively direct the parties towards renegotiation of their contract.[1501] In the event the renegotiation fails, the courts are instructed to try to solve the dispute through mediation.[1502] If all measures fail and the court intends to modify the contract or to remove the right to performance by termination of the contract, the court is obliged to obtain approval of the Higher People's Court and the Supreme People's Court.[1503] The aforementioned instructions for the courts are said to protect the right to performance and, in this light, to provide a basis for balancing the interests of the parties in accordance with standards of reasonableness and fairness.[1504] Nonetheless, it should be mentioned that the limitation of the right to performance in case of hardship is merely a judiciary instruction and it is not implemented in the contract law of China. This begs the (unanswered) question to what extent the lower courts are willing to limit the right to performance if the promisor argues that due to a change of circumstances enforcement would result in hardship.[1505]

The considerations above give rise to the question of how the legal concept of *force majeure* relates to situations where hardship occurred due to an unforeseeable drastic

1497 Bing Ling 2002 (n 229) paras 5.090, 5.092; Bu 2013 (n 226) 59 para 27.

1498 Art 3 Guiding Opinions of the Supreme People's Court on Several Issues concerning the Trial of Cases of Disputes over Civil and Commercial Contracts under the Current Situation, 7 July 2009 (Guiding Opinions); Bu 2013 (n 226) 59 para 29.

1499 Art 3 Guiding Opinions (n 1498).

1500 *Ibid.*

1501 Judicial Interpretation II Contract Law (n 173); Notice on Correctly Applying Judicial Interpretation II Contract Law (n 1425); Art 4 Guiding Opinions (n 1498); Bing Ling 2002 (n 229) paras 5.088, 5.093, 8.014, 8.079; Lei Chen, 'Availablity of Specific Remedies in Chinese Contract Law' in Chen-Wishart, Loke and Ong 2016 (n 156) 31; Bu 2013 (n 226) 59.

1502 Art 4 Guiding Opinions (n 1498).

1503 Notice on Correctly Applying Judicial Interpretation II Contract Law (n 1425); Art 4 Guiding Opinions (n 1498).

1504 Art 4 Guiding Opinions (n 1498); Compare Bing Ling 2002 (n 229) para 5.093; Chunyan Ding, 'Performance and Breach' in DiMatteo and Chen 2017 (n 19) 318.

1505 Zhang 2006 (n 41) 229.

change of circumstances.[1506] The distinction with a situation of hardship was addressed in *Fuping Steel Rolling Co. of Shaanxi Longmen Iron & Steel Co, Ltd v Shaanxi Coke Chemical Co, Ltd.* In this case, it was held by the Shaanxi Higher People's Court that a situation of *force majeure* directly derives from an impossibility to perform due to a change of circumstances, while the doctrine of hardship applies where enforced performance would be severely unfavourable to the promisor.[1507] Despite this clear distinction, the exclusion of a *force majeure* from the application of the hardship doctrine leads to the question of what the impact is on the right to performance if enforcement of performance is rendered obviously unfair because a *force majeure* has made performance excessively onerous.[1508] This situation should be distinguished from cases where performance is objectively impossible due to a *force majeure.*[1509] The judiciary has solved this issue by applying the doctrine of hardship where performance is evidently unfair regardless of the cause of the hardship, that is, a change of circumstances or a *force majeure.*[1510] This shows that a situation of hardship and the legal concept of *force majeure* could coincide. This premise is confirmed by the argument that the doctrine of change of circumstances only applies if the impediment to performance is unavoidable and insurmountable, which also holds true for *force majeure.*[1511] However, in more recent literature a contradicting viewpoint is put forward which suggests that the exclusion of a *force majeure* indicates that the doctrine of a change of circumstances only applies in cases where the impediment for performance could be prevented or overcome.[1512] Given that the courts have applied the doctrine of hardship in both situations, it seems that the issue above is merely theoretical.[1513] The different views on the distinction between the two doctrines have resulted in the rule that application of the doctrine of change of circumstances by the courts is subject to examination of the Higher People's Court, and should be submitted to the Supreme People's Court for examination where necessary.[1514]

1506 Arts 94(1), 117 CCL; Bu 2013 (n 226) 60 para 31, 70 para 3.

1507 *Fuping Steel Rolling Co of Shaanxi Longmen Iron & Steel Co Ltd v Shaanxi Coke Chemical Co Ltd* [2012] Shaanxi Higher People's Court 27 November 2012.

1508 Bing Ling 2002 (n 229) para 8.051; Chunyan Ding, 'Performance and Breach' in DiMatteo and Chen 2017 (n 19) 320.

1509 Arts 94(1), 117 CCL.

1510 Chunyan Ding, 'Performance and Breach' in DiMatteo and Chen 2017 (n 19) 320.

1511 Bing Ling 2002 (n 229) para 5.090; Art 117 CCL stipulates that *force majeure* means any objective circumstances which are unforeseeable, unavoidable and insurmountable.

1512 Chunyan Ding, 'Performance and Breach' in DiMatteo and Chen 2017 (n 19) 319.

1513 *Ibid.*

1514 Notice on Correctly Applying Judicial Interpretation II Contract Law (n 1425); Lei Chen, 'Availablity of Specific Remedies in Chinese Contract Law' in Chen-Wishart, Loke and Ong 2016 (n 156) 32; Bu 2013 (n 226) 60.

237. *Comparative analysis* – The starting point for this discussion is that the contract law of the Netherlands, Singapore and China act on the universal *pacta sunt servanda* adage, which broadly means that agreements must be kept. However, the three investigated jurisdictions have taken a different approach in protecting this fundamental principle of contract law where performance causes unreasonable efforts and expenses, and where performance becomes more onerous due to a change of circumstances. It appears that the contract law of Singapore has taken the most narrow approach in this regard by following the English common law view on hardship, which does not operate as an exemption to performance, but as a relief in the form of damages in lieu of enforced performance, in exceptional situations. Nonetheless, it seems that Singapore is moving away from the restrictive English liability-based model by allowing a more flexible approach through the application of the requirements of observance of accepted standards of fair dealing. On the basis of this principle, a claim for enforced performance could be denied without directly affecting a potential liability for damages and the existence of the obligation. This adjustment is in line with the approach taken by Dutch and Chinese contract law, as well as the unification instruments.[1515]

That said, the legal systems mentioned above act on entirely different mechanisms for regulating the consequences of an unacceptably onerous performance. This means in effect that performance can be exempted where performance has become unreasonably burdensome or expensive (*i.e.* initial and subsequent imbalance), and where enforced performance has become excessively onerous due to a change of circumstances. In the latter case, the availability of obtaining performance of the initially agreed obligation under the stipulated terms, could also be affected by, for example, an imposed burden to renegotiate the terms, or by judicial modification and termination of the contract. In the latter case, the non-monetary performance obligation ceases to exist. Most unification instruments have regulated their principles for situations where performance has become excessively onerous due to a change in circumstances in a similar way.[1516] Nonetheless, at the domestic and international levels, the thresholds and available judicial instruments to correct an unacceptable change of the equilibrium of the contract vary considerably. As regards the latter point, judicial modification and avoidance of a contract are commonly adopted legal responses affecting the ability to obtain enforced performance of the obligation contemplated at the start of the contract. The contract law of China has also adopted the option of alteration of the contract by the parties as a result of court imposed renegotiation. This additional solution to restore an equilibrium disturbance is also found in the PICC,

1515 Art 79(5) CISG; Art 7.2.2 PICC; Art 9:102(2)(b) PECL; Art III.-3:302 (3)(b) DCFR; Art 7(c) Draft Articles on Non-Performance PACL.

1516 Arts 6.2.3(3), 7.2.2 (b) PICC; Art 6:111, 9:102(2)(b) PECL; Art III.-3:302, art III.1–110 DCFR: art 7(c) or expensive; Arts 7(c), 30(2) Draft PACL, Lee 2016 (n 16) 198, 212.

PECL, DCFR and draft PACL.[1517] The advantage of this practical solution is that parties remain in control, which benefits their relationship more than any judicial interference, although its disadvantages may outweigh the advantage that parties are able to regulate their contractual relationship. This is because it may be assumed that commercial parties generally are inclined to first explore the most economically advantageous route before bringing a claim to court. This route typically entails a process of communication between the parties about acceptable adjustments for each. In cases where this fails, a second round of imposed negotiations will most likely not have a material impact on the dispute, other than a significant and considerable investment in time and recourses. Compared to the above-discussed legal systems, the CISG indirectly regulates its response where performance has become more onerous, and subsequently, the promisor seeks judicial relief. In this situation, it is held that recourse may be had under the PICC and general principles of the CISG to direct the parties to renegotiation.[1518] This appears, however, to be an untenable approach when considering the principle that the exemptions from liability to pay damages due to an unforeseeable change of (*e.g.* economic) circumstances, do not affect the right to obtain enforced performance under the CISG.[1519]

On the issue of different thresholds at the domestic and international levels, the most commonly used method in determining whether enforced performance should not be granted in cases of hardship, is a calculation of the percentage increase in the cost or value of the performance for the promisor, and the decrease in the value of the performance for the aggrieved party.[1520] There is, however, no generally accepted percentage nor any guidelines for its calculation. Whereas in the Netherlands a percentage of 130% is suggested, in China the general notion applies that no gross disparity is required. The contract law of Singapore is also not familiar with predetermined percentages, but it follows that the thresholds for exemptions of liability (in damages and performance) are very high due to the narrow scope of the doctrine of frustration. As for the unification instruments, it is suggested that an increase of between 100% and 200% is required to affect the availability of enforced performance.[1521] Certainly, these viewpoints and the suggestions put forward

1517 Art 6.2.3(1)(2) PICC: the aggrieved party is entitled to request renegotiations; Art 6:111(2) PECL: the parties are bound to enter negotiations; Art III.-1:110 (3)(d) DCFR: the judicial modification and termination is only available if the non-performing party has attempted, reasonably and in good faith, to achieve by negotiation a reasonable and equitable adjustment of the terms regulating the obligation (this is not a duty to renegotiate, see Schwenzer, Hachem and Kee 2012 (n 13) para 45.112; Art 30(2) Draft Articles on Non-Performance PACL: the parties are bound to enter into negotiations with a view of adapting the contract or terminating it.

1518 Art 6.2.3(4) PICC in conjunction with art 9(2) CISG, or on the mere basis of the principle of good faith (art 7(1) CISG), or by construing it as a part of the general principles (art 7(2) CISG); Schwenzer, Hachem and Kee 2012 (n 13) para 45.115; Schwenzer 2016 (n 91) art 79 para 55.

1519 Art 79(5) CISG; Schwenzer 2016 (n 91) para 45.112.

1520 Schwenzer, Hachem and Kee 2012 (n 13) paras 45.101–45.102.

1521 Schwenzer, Hachem and Kee 2012 (n 13) paras 45.106.

in literature are valuable, but broadly accepted guidelines for commercial sales transactions are not available at national or international levels. In light of the above and for the purpose of providing more guidance for those involved in commercial sales transactions, it is recommended that clear and sound financial principles be developed to provide sufficient flexibility for the courts to protect the performance interest of the aggrieved party in view of the necessary protection of the interest of the non-performing party against unjustifiable consequences of a claim for enforced performance. Nonetheless, in light of the example mentioned under paragraph 232, it is also submitted that, in certain commercial sales contracts across civil and common law borders, financial thresholds are not appropriate to deal with an enforcement dispute. At the international level, impediments for performance may go far beyond efforts which are not quantifiable in money. In the provided example, the efforts required to obtain a similar weaving mill within a specific timeframe may result in the imposition of a burden on the manufacturer which is unacceptable in light of the contractual equilibrium. Unfortunately, there are no balanced rules at the international level for situations where performance has become excessively onerous. It is therefore of paramount importance for those involved in international commercial sales transactions to anticipate the situation where the equilibrium of the contract is altered to such an extent that both parties agree to a removal of a claim for enforced performance.

6.2.5 *Conclusions*

238. The default availability of enforced performance of non-monetary obligations under Dutch and Chinese contract law, as well as the unification instruments, and the primary focus on damages in the common law system of Singapore, results in differing legal concepts for situations where a contracting party requires protection against an order for enforced performance.[1522] This effectively means that the legal concepts for exemption from curing a non-performance is first and foremost an exemption from damages under Singapore contract law. This also holds the explanation that partial or temporary exemption from performance of non-monetary obligations are not familiar concepts under Singapore contract law.

The distinct viewpoints of the three investigated jurisdictions trace back to the underlying legal traditions which may cause significant difficulties for those involved in international commercial sales transactions. Complex issues arise from the different notions of the concept of impossibility, hardship and frustration, although there are situations where their applications coincide. Figure 15 below aims to clarify the relationship between the above-mentioned concepts.

1522 See s 4.4 for the disagreement between the subject legal systems.

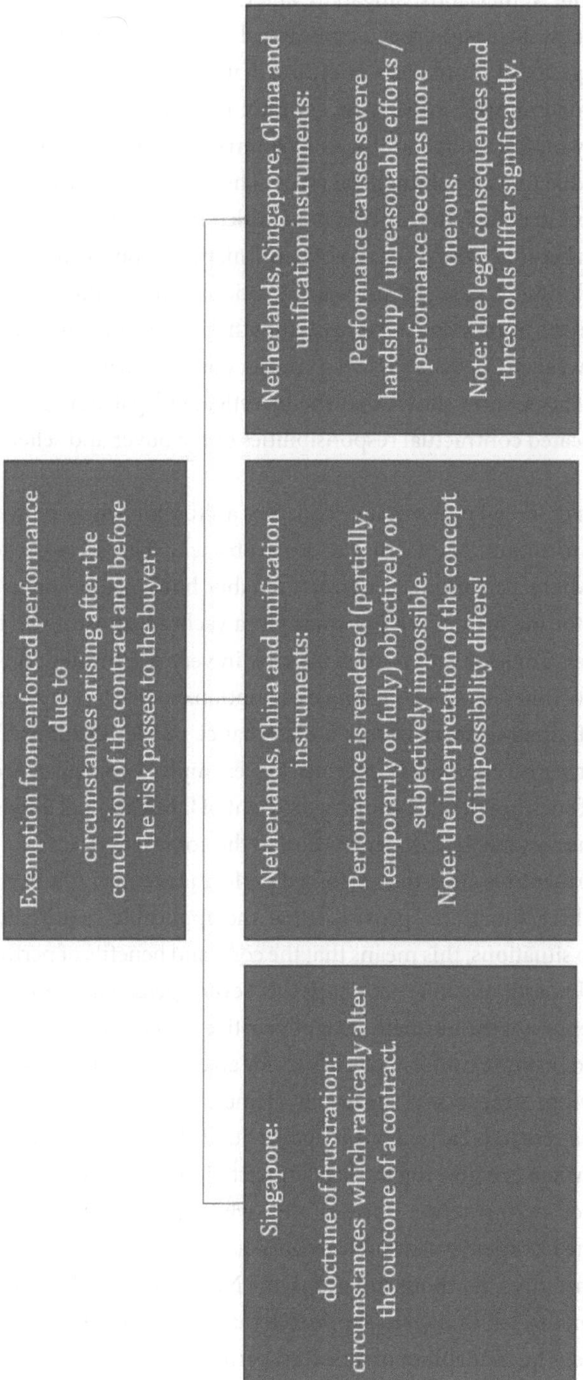

Figure 15 Exemptions from enforced performance

239. The contract law of the Netherlands, Singapore and China, as well as the unification instruments identified act on the notion that a contractual obligation must be performed even if performance brings about more costs or efforts than contemplated at the start of the contract. Consider, for example, a five-year contract in which a commercial party agrees to ship goods every month from country X to country Y at a fixed price. After one year, fuel prices increase due to a global financial crisis. The seller requests a 5% increase in the initially agreed rate. Generally, the seller is not entitled to raise the agreed price for its performance obligation because it bears the risk of performance becoming more onerous. There are however multiple other less straightforward situations in the realm of commercial sales where the court is forced, or may consider, to exempt the promisor from performance (*e.g.* when a central bank weakens/devalues its own currency and when a country abruptly imposes import tariffs). This section shows that the investigated legal systems allow the court to alter initially allocated contractual responsibilities of the buyer and seller in three situations.

The first exemption to enforced performance concerns a situation where performance is impeded due to an insurmountable factual or legal obstacle. The second exception concerns the situation where performance is unreasonably burdensome or expensive (performance is ruinous for the promisor). For example, a yacht in transit to its buyer is hit by a commercial vessel. Consequently, the yacht sank in very deep water and salvage costs would amount to fifty times its value. The third exemption entails the situation where an exceptional change of circumstances causes a disturbance of the equilibrium of the contract rendering performance excessively onerous. For example, a change of economic circumstances which is of such gravity that the procurement of fabrication of goods would cause the seller to incur unreasonable costs in relation to the contract price.

It appears from the present research that enforced performance may not be available in the above-described three situations, provided that the applicable requirements are fulfilled. For the latter two situations, this means that the costs and benefits of performance must be balanced. At the domestic and international levels, several percentages are suggested to help determine whether or not the ultimate limit of sacrifice has been exceeded. Against this background, efforts to institute uniform guidelines for an economic analysis weighing costs and benefits (leaving aside other uncertain elements) should be encouraged. Nonetheless, based on the research carried out it appears that the key issues do not arise in this regard, but rather when considering the legal impact of the discussed principles on the availability of enforced performance. For example, where performance is rendered unreasonably burdensome or expensive, or performance has become excessively onerous due to a change of circumstances. For both situations, the Netherlands and China, as well as the unification instruments, have taken the approach that the court may refuse a claim for enforced performance. The availability of enforced performance is indirectly affected where performance has merely become more onerousness due to a change of circumstances, which does not amount to an unreasonably burdensome or expensive performance. In these less severe cases, both the contract law of the Netherlands and China allow judicial modification and avoidance of the contract.

Judicial modification and avoidance are however not available by default under the contract law of China and the vast majority of unification instruments. These legal systems have adopted the prerequisite of renegotiation. Judicially imposed renegotiation of the terms for performance is not a preferable solution because the solution of renegotiations is usually already explored before commercial parties turn to court. That said, the key point here is that under the contract law of the Netherlands and China, as well as the unification instruments, a claim for enforced performance may be fully, partially or temporarily exempted where performance is subjectively impossible or has become more onerous.

In contrast, Singapore contract law is not familiar with the concept of impossibility or hardship due to its English common law foundations, which envisage damages as the preferred remedy to cure a non-performance. That said, when performance has become subjectively impossible or more onerous because of fundamentally changed circumstances (without fault of either party), the non-performing party can be released from performance under the doctrine of frustration. This legal concept contrasts strongly with the aforementioned legal systems in the sense that the only legal response is avoidance. This explains, at least in part, why the contract law of Singapore is not familiar with the concept of a temporary exemption of enforced performance, with a duty to renegotiate or with judicial interference by modification.

Given the foregoing, it follows that the contract law of the Netherlands and China, and the unification instruments, have adopted the most flexible structure, with open-ended principles, which enables the court to seek recourse to the most appropriate means where the severity of the cause renders performance more onerous than anticipated. However, this liberal approach runs counter to the need for legal certainty in international trade. For this, the unitary approach taken by the contract law of Singapore encompasses the advantage that commercial parties are able to determine in advance the enforceability of the obligations when performance has become impossible or more onerous due to a fundamental change of the equilibrium of the contract. Moreover, this solution is only available in a very limited number of cases and thus the approach taken by Singapore encourages commercial parties to take control of their relationship by constructing impossibility and hardship clauses into their contracts. Nonetheless, on an overall assessment, a combination of the approaches taken by the investigated legal systems may have most merit, to wit; an excessively more onerous performance due to a fundamental change of the equilibrium might exempt performance or give rise to judicial alteration of the contract on the demand of either party. That said, considering the universal fundamental principle of *pacta sunt servanda* in light of the necessity of legal certainty in commercial sales transactions, there should be a significantly high threshold affecting the ability to obtain the very thing parties bargained for.

At a practical level, commercial parties could circumvent the difficulties arising from the divergence between the legal systems by contractual stipulations which best fit the specific circumstances of the agreement. Such contractual stipulations should observe the operative effects and potential mandatory characteristics of the above-discussed principles. In view of this, there are three important points for consideration. Firstly, the clauses dealing with impediments for performance should entail an explanation of the employed concepts. This is necessary because (as observed in this section) the subject legal systems employ a different notion of the concepts which may exempt enforced performance. Secondly, the contractual stipulations should clarify whether the described exemptions from performance are exhaustive or indicative. The reason behind this suggestion is that it clarifies whether a potentially aggrieved party could seek recourse to legal exemption principles if the impediment is not mentioned in the contract. In view of this, the last suggestion concerns the necessity of determining the impact of contractually described impediments on the availability of enforced performance of a non-monetary obligation. That being said, the contractual allocation of the situations exempting the non-performing party from enforced performance should be read in conjunction with the discussion about the differing viewpoints on the admissibility of derogatory agreements.[1523]

6.3 DELAYED REQUEST FOR DELIVERY

240. *Preliminary* – The following provides an analysis of a very important constraint which potentially limits the availability of enforced performance of non-monetary obligations under a commercial sales contract, that is, a non-actionable duty of the buyer to require performance within a certain timeframe. This discussion is supplementary to the earlier discussed rules on inspection and notification of any defects discovered (section 5.4.4) and the limitation of a claim for enforced performance (section 6.4). The idea that the buyer is subject to a duty to request performance within a certain time limit, generally arises under hardship considerations because a delayed claim may make it significantly harder for the seller to perform its obligations. The following discusses to what extent the requirement of a timely request for performance of non-monetary obligations (in the realm of commercial sales) is adopted in the three investigated jurisdictions and how the applicable national rules relate to the approach(es) taken by the unification instruments.

1523 Ch 8.

Illustration – Company A, a manufacturer of nutritional products, located in country X, sells to Company B, located in country Y, a new type of vitamin D to be delivered on 19 March at the warehouse of Company B. The manufacturer fails to deliver the vitamins on time (*i.e.* the specified time for performance triggered the delay; a notice is not required), but Company B only requests for delivery of the vitamins six months after the agreed time for delivery. In this situation, the question arises whether the availability of enforced performance of the seller's delivery obligation is affected by the delayed request to deliver the goods, although the formal limitation period for claiming enforced performance has not yet lapsed. It should further be noted that the time of delivery was not of the essence.

241. *Domestic approaches* – Dutch contract law acts on the notion that enforced performance shall not be granted where this is unacceptable according to the requirements of reasonableness and fairness.[1524] This principle is the foundation of the doctrine of forfeiture of rights which could limit a claim for enforced performance where it is established that the aggrieved buyer neglected to pro-actively secure its right by demanding performance without undue delay.[1525] The mere passing of time, however, does not suffice to establish that the aggrieved buyer has waived its rights to enforced performance.[1526] The aforementioned principle is reflected in the rule that the aggrieved promisee may no longer invoke a defect in performance if the latter has not protested to the promisor in respect thereof promptly after it has discovered, or reasonably should have discovered the defect.[1527] The underlying idea is that the aggrieved buyer has acted in such a manner that the seller in all reasonableness cannot be expected to deliver the goods as promised, thus affecting the right of the buyer to claim for delivery of the goods in accordance with the contractual stipulations.[1528] The principle that the right to enforced performance is affected by a delay in requesting performance, however, only applies in cases of a defective delivery in fact (section 5.4.4) and where the seller fails to transfer title free from all special charges and encumbrances.[1529] In circumstances where the seller did not deliver the goods at all, the seller may seek recourse to the standards of reasonableness and fairness where an undue delay in requesting delivery brings about unacceptable hardship for the seller if an order

1524 Art 6:248(2) DCC.

1525 MBM Loos in Schelhaas 2002 (n 19) 356.

1526 *Oostenbroek v Nekami* Dutch Supreme Court 8 December 1989, ECLI:NL:HR:1989:AG6222, NJ 1990, 474; *Van den Bos v Provincial Insurance Company Limited* Dutch Supreme Court 29 September 1995, ECLI:NL:HR:1995:ZC1827, NJ 1996, 89; MBM Loos in Schelhaas 2002 (n 19) 356.

1527 Art 6:89, 7:23(1) DCC.

1528 Arts 6:89, 7:23(1) DCC; MBM Loos in Schelhaas 2002 (n 19) 357; De Jong, Krans and Wissink 2018 (n 194) 213.

1529 Arts 6:89.7:23, 7:17, 7:15 DCC; De Jong, Krans and Wissink 2018 (n 194) 213; *Brocacef v Simons* Dutch Supreme Court 23 March 2007, NJ 2007, 176, ECLI:NL:HR:2007:AZ3531.

for performance is provided. This is only conceivable in exceptional cases, as the thresholds for application of the derogatory effect of the standards of reasonableness and fairness are set very high because it results in a waiver of rights (*i.e.* the right to claim for performance of the seller's delivery obligation).[1530] As for the length of delay, it may be assumed that the guidelines for defective performance apply, that is; the aggrieved buyer has to 'promptly' inform the seller of the non-delivery after it has or should reasonably have discovered that the goods were not delivered.

242. The contract law of Singapore provides a specific solution in the form of the equitable doctrine of laches for the situation where the seller may be prejudiced if, long after the stipulated time for performance, the other party sues for enforced performance. The doctrine of laches must be considered along the lines of the principle that enforced performance is a discretionary and exceptional remedy (section 4.4.3), which allows the courts to deny a claim for enforced performance when an unjustified delay has a detrimental effect on the position of the non-performing party.[1531] The defence of laches limits the availability of equitable relief in the sense that it may be used by the courts to refuse enforced performance of non-monetary obligations (*e.g.* delivery of goods) in case of an undue delay and where this causes prejudice or injustice.[1532] In other words, the doctrine of laches applies where enforced performance would be practically unjust because the undue delay may be regarded as an equivalent to a waiver of the option to enforced performance.[1533] As for the calculation of the length of delay, it is clear that the time starts to run from the moment the aggrieved party knew or ought to have known of the non-performance.[1534] Where the promisor is notified about the failure in performance, the period starts to run from the date of the notice and not from the moment the failure in performance

1530 Art 6:248(2) DCC; De Jong, Krans and Wissink 2018 (n 194) 11–13, 289–295.

1531 Treitel 1998 (n 55) para 43.

1532 *Chng Weng Wah v Goh Bak Heng* [2016] SGCA 9, (2016) 2 SLR 464 [44]; see for the element of unreasonableness (unconscionability) *Re Estate of Tan Kow Quee* [2007] 2 SLR(R) 417 [33]; *Management Corporation Strata Title Plan No 473* (n 326) 1 SLR(R) 418 [33]; *Cytec Industries Pte Ltd v APP Chemicals International (Mau) Ltd* [2009] 4 SLR(R) 769 [46]; cited in *eSys Technologies Pte Ltd v nTan Corporate Advisory Pte Ltd* [2013] 2 SLR 1200 [37]–[38] and *Dynasty Line Ltd (in liquidation) v Sukamto Sia and another and another appeal* [2014] 3 SLR 277 [58]); Halsbury's Laws of Singapore (Civil Procedure Law 2016) vol 4, para 50.146; Phang et al 2012 (n 112) para 20.031 *ff.*; Shenoy and Loo 2013 (n 13) para 18.6; Clare Stanley and Michael J Ashdown, 'Laches and Limitation' (2014) 20(9) Trusts and Trustees 958; Note that the equitable jurisdiction to refuse performance on the ground of laches is not affected by S 32 Limitation Act (Cap 163 rev ed 1996).

1533 Report of the Law Reform Committee On the Review of the Limitation Act (Cap 163 rev ed 1996), February 2007, 10.

1534 *Lim Beng Cheng* (n 615) SGHC 282 [116]; *Management Corporation Strata Title Plan No 473* (n 326) SLR(R) 418 [33]; Phang et al 2012 (n 112) para 20.36.

occurred.[1535] The assessment of the length of the period and whether it qualifies as an undue delay varies from case to case.[1536] The same applies to the question of whether the undue delay has caused prejudice or injustice.[1537]

243. In the contract law of China, the availability of enforced performance is subject to the requirement that performance must be demanded within a reasonable time.[1538] Where the aggrieved party fails to act in accordance with this duty, its right to enforced performance is exempted but all other remedies are preserved.[1539] The rationale for this provision is threefold, namely, contracting parties should be prevented from speculating on market prices; undue delay may induce the non-performing party to believe that performance is no longer required; and the economic (efficiency) nature of concluding of a contract requires that the aggrieved party contributes to a timely settlement of a dispute over failure in performance.[1540] For example, a claim for enforced performance was rejected because the claimant had waited several years to bring this claim to court after a wrongful termination.[1541] As for the length of the period, the courts are given the discretionary power to determine the reasonable time given all the circumstances of the particular case, the principle of good faith,[1542] and the rules on limitation (section 6.4).[1543] The latter means in

1535 *Management Corporation Strata Title Plan No 473* (326) 1 SLR(R) 418 [33]; Phang et al 2012 (n 112) para 20.036; Shenoy and Loo 2013 (n 13) para 18.6.

1536 Singapore High Court in *Toh Tiong Huat v PM Gunasaykaran* [1995] 3 SLR(R) 627; In *Tay Joo Sing* (n 1474) SGCA 45 [34] the purchaser of a property brought a claim to court for enforced performance 25 months after the purchaser and the seller entered into the contract of sales. The purchaser made the seller believe that he abandoned the contract and after 25 months he demanded the transfer of the property. Since it was considered that the behaviour of the seller amounted to acquiescence, therefore, remedies of common law were the appropriate remedy instead of specific performance; Halsbury's Laws of Singapore (Contract 2016) vol 7 para 80.588; See for an undue delay of 9 years *British and Malayan Trustees Ltd v Sindo Realty Pte Ltd (in liquidation) and other actions* [1998] SGHC 92 [65], (1998) 1 SLR(R) 903.

1537 *E.g.*, where delay have resulted in a loss of evidence causing several disputes between contracting parties. See *Chng Weng Wah v Goh Bak Heng* (n 1532) SLR 464 [59].

1538 Art 6, 110(3) CCL; Lei Chen, 'Damages and Specific Performance in Chinese Contract Law' in DiMatteo and Chen 2017 (n 19) 398; Bing Ling 2002 (n 229) para 8.076; Lei Chen, 'Availablity of Specific Remedies in Chinese Contract Law' in Chen-Wishart, Loke and Ong 2016 (n 156) 30; Bu 2013 (n 226) 22, para 9.

1539 Ye Changfu 2005 (n 990).

1540 Bing Ling 2002 (n 229) para 8.076; Ye Changfu 2005 (n 990).

1541 *Wen Wufa v Guilin Commerce Bureau* [1991] Guangxi Guilin Xiufeng District Peolple's Court and Guilin Intermediate People's Court (1991) RJDC 1992, 1027; Bing Ling 2002 para 8.076, footnote 31.

1542 Art 110 (3) CCL stipulates that a promisee is not entitled to claim actual performance of a contractual obligation if it does not claim performance within a reasonable time; Arts 135–141 of the GPCL; see art 6 CCL for the obligation to act in good faith; Bing Ling 2002 (n 229) para 8.076.

1543 Art 188 *ff* GPCL; Lei Chen, 'Damages and Specific Performance in Chinese Contract Law' in DiMatteo and Chen 2017 (n 19) 399; Bing Ling 2002 (n 229) para 8.076; Lei Chen, 'Availablity of Specific Remedies in Chinese Contract Law' in Chen-Wishart, Loke and Ong 2016 (n 156). 30.

effect that the period starts to run from the time when the aggrieved party knew or ought to have known about the non-performance.[1544]

244. *Comparative analysis* – The three investigated jurisdictions, and the unification instruments recognise the possibility that a non-performing seller or buyer might be prejudiced if, long after the due date of the obligation, the aggrieved party requires performance.[1545] The subject legal systems also each act on the notion that the aggrieved party is expected to claim for enforced performance from such time as it knew or ought to have known of non-performance on the part of the other party. There is, however, a significant divergence between the legal consequences arising from the non-actionable duty of the aggrieved party to request for correct performance within a timeframe which does not unduly harm the interest of the non-performing party. The following focusses on enhancing the understanding of the differing viewpoints, since they are essential for determining the degree the non-performing party's interest is protected against abuse relative to the protection of the performance interest of the other party. In view of this, it is important to bear in mind that only the unification instruments have taken the approach that the buyer is subject to an enforceable obligation to take delivery of the goods.[1546] As previously discussed, the three investigated jurisdictions act on the notion that a failure in taking delivery (or to cooperate) results in a situation of *mora creditoris.*[1547] Hence, the following considerations are most relevant for the seller's delivery obligation, which is actionable in all the subject legal systems – provided that the applicable prerequisites are met.

245. Under Dutch contract law, the buyer is provided with a right to enforced performance of a non-monetary obligation, but it may lose all available remedies to cure the seller's non-performance when the high threshold of an unacceptable delay in requesting performance is fulfilled. The preceding sections reveal that this approach is mirrored under Singapore contract law. That is to say, the latter acts on the notion that enforced performance is only available in specific situations (and even these cases are subject to counter-exceptions), while the consequences of an undue delay of a request for performance by application of the doctrine of laches are significantly less severe. This is because the common law doctrine of laches only affects the availability of specific remedies; the aggrieved buyer may still claim for damages. Although the outcome is the same under

1544 Bing Ling 2002 (n 229) para 8.076.

1545 Art 7.2.2(e) PICC; Art 9:102(3) PECL; Art III.–3:302(4) DCFR; Art 7(e) Draft Articles on Non-Performance PACL; Under the CISG, the rule that the buyer is required to demand performance within a reasonable time is limited to cases where the buyer demands repair or replacement of non-conforming goods.

1546 S 5.3.

1547 *Ibid.*

Chinese contract law and the PICC, PECL, DCFR and the draft PACL, the legal consequence follows from different principles and distinct approaches towards balancing the interest of commercial parties. That is, an unacceptable delay in requesting performance may deprive the buyer of its right to enforced performance, but it does not affect other remedies.[1548] This rule, in effect, protects the seller against hardship deriving from a delayed request for delivery of the goods in accordance with the contractual stipulations.

With regard to the length of delay, the contract law of China, as well as the aforementioned unification instruments, adopt a straightforward starting point, which is supplemented with general guidelines. That is, the aggrieved buyer is required to claim for delivery within a reasonable time.[1549] The length of the reasonable time period depends on the nature of the non-performance, the nature of the goods (*e.g.* durable or perishable goods), the purpose of the rules (*i.e.* protection of the seller against hardship), guarantees as to the absence of defects, trade usages and practices between the parties, and all other circumstances.[1550] For example, the length of the reasonable period to demand performance may depend on the time the aggrieved party needs to determine whether it could obtain replacement goods from another source. Where this can be easily established, the time for requiring performance is shorter than when it takes a significant amount to make the necessary inquiries as to the availability of substitute goods. Furthermore, it may be assumed that for commercial sales contracts, the aggrieved buyer is required to demand delivery after it discovered or should have discovered the non-delivery.[1551]

The aforementioned elements play a key role in determining the impact of the buyer's delay in requiring delivery in the example mentioned under paragraph 240. In this example, the impact of the undue delay on the seller's interest shall be weighed against the legal detriment on the side of the buyer arising from its failure to request delivery. In view of this, the loss of all remedies under Dutch contract law, suggests that the barrier is set high for accepting the defence of the seller that enforced performance of the obligation to deliver the vitamins should not be awarded due to the detrimental effect of the delayed request on its interest. Under Chinese contract law and from the viewpoint of the vast majority of the unification instruments identified, the buyer could also lose its right to obtain delivery of the vitamins, although it is still entitled to claim for damages. It appears that Singapore

1548 The duty to request performance within a reasonable time is limited in the CISG to cases where the buyer claims for cure of fundamental defects by delivery of replacement goods or repair (art 46(2)(3) CISG). It is further important to note that the principle of observance of good faith does not directly apply between parties when their contract is governed by the CISG; Art 7.2.2(e) PICC; Art 9:102(3) PECL; Art III.–3:302(4) DCFR; Art 7(e) Draft Articles on Non-Performance PACL.

1549 Art 7.2.2(e) PICC; Art 9:102(3) PECL; Art III.–3:302(4) DCFR; Art 7(e) Draft Articles on Non-Performance PACL.

1550 Vogenauer 2015 (n 19) art 7.2.2 para 54.

1551 Art 7.2.2(e) PICC; Art 9:102(3) PECL; Art III.–3:302(4) DCFR; Art 7(e) Draft Articles on Non-Performance PACL.

courts should come to the same conclusion, as a delay in requesting delivery may result in a loss of the right to avoid the contract. However, as the aforementioned example concerns the sale of commodity goods, it appears that enforced performance of the seller's delivery obligation is not available under the Singapore sales law. Hence, for determining the actual operative effect of a specific barrier to enforced performance, it is necessary to recognise that legal principles are intimately interconnected and therefore only explicable by reference to the whole.

In view of the foregoing, it is of significant practical relevance to establish express contractual stipulations for requiring performance after the due date, in particular regarding the legal consequences arising from a total failure in performance of this duty. Nonetheless, such contractual provisions may not entirely sidestep the restrictions on the freedom of contract when they aim to interfere with statutory rules on the availability of enforced performance of non-monetary obligations. It is therefore of paramount importance that contractual provisions regulating the situation of a delayed request for performance are assessed in light of the rules on derogatory agreements.[1552]

6.4 Limitation of the action

6.4.1 *Introduction*

246. This section deals with the question of whether the availability of enforced performance is affected where such a claim is brought to court long after the stipulated time for performance (*e.g.* delivery of the goods). This issue requires an assessment of the rules on limitation periods set out by legislation.[1553] There are five issues discussed in this regard which are contrasted against the rules on limitation periods laid down in the PICC, PECL and DCFR.[1554] The first issue concerns the classification of limitation periods, to wit; procedural or substantive (section 6.4.2). The question of whether a limitation period is

1552 Ch 8.

1553 The expression 'limitation periods' will be used as a synonym for extinction of a claim or a right to enforced performance. The term prescription is also found (usually in a civil law context), but it appears that the latter term focusses on the impact of the effluxion of time on a right to ownership. Moreover, the phrase prescription often refers to substantive rules for claims being time-barred. The phrase limitation period is generally found in common law and appears to focus on the action or claim itself and is usually of procedural nature. See for interesting insights about the aforementioned distinction between precription and limitation: The Jersey Law Commission, 'Consultation Paper Prescription and Limitation' No 1/2008/CP (March 2018).

1554 The two other unification instruments examined in this research (*i.e.* CISG and the draft PACL) do not include limitation periods. The United Nations Conventions on the Limitation Period in the International Sale of Goods has not been adopted by the Netherlands, Singapore and China to date, and is, therefore, excluded from the present comparative undertaking.

of procedural or substantive nature is of significant importance for sales transactions between parties with places of business in different jurisdictions because the rules on limitation periods differ greatly.[1555] If the statutory rules on limitation periods – to be determined in light of the law governing the contract – are of a procedural nature, the question regarding whether a claim for actual performance is barred is governed by the law of the country in which the action for enforced performance is brought *(lex fori)*. In the case where the applicable limitation period is qualified as substantive law, the matter concerning the rules on limitation periods is governed by the choice of law designated in the contract *(lex contractus)*. In general, civil law countries follow the substantive approach by adopting the rules on limitation periods in the contract law principles.[1556] Common law jurisdictions generally tend to qualify the rules on limitation periods as being of procedural nature.[1557] The second issue concerns the starting point of limitation periods, the length of the relative and (if applicable) absolute maximum limitation period under the three subject jurisdictions, and whether these periods are aligned with the modern approach for commercial sales transactions as laid down in the unification instruments (section 6.4.2). The third issue concerns the question of whether contracting parties are allowed to modify a statutory time limit in their contract in the face of party autonomy (section 6.4.3). The fourth issue concerns the possibility of renewal and extension of limitation periods by conduct of contracting parties (section 6.4.4). The last issue discussed here concerns the legal consequences of not requiring performance within the applicable limitation period (section 6.4.5).

6.4.2 *The limitation period itself*

247. *Preliminary* – This section deals with the limitation regime for enforced performance of a contractual obligation. The focus is on the question of whether the investigated legal systems have adopted a uniform or two-tier system (*i.e.* a relative and absolute limitations period), and whether different rules are laid down for commercial sales contracts. Where this is the case, one must be aware of the danger of the difficulties ensuing from the borderline between commercial contracts subject to the 'standard' limitation periods and the deviating periods for sales contracts. This is particularly relevant for international commercial contracts which, for example, entail elements of sales of goods and lease, or sales of goods and services. Moreover, it is important to bear in mind that where a limitation period regime is focussed on the (legal) nature of the 'right' (*i.e.* obligation to do something, damages or unjustified enrichment), the legal position of the promisor is not always clear.

1555 Schwenzer, Hachem and Kee 2012 (n 13) para 51.01.
1556 Schwenzer, Hachem and Kee 2012 (n 13) para 51.07.
1557 Schwenzer, Hachem and Kee 2012 (n 13) para 51.09.

With this in mind, outlines of the limitation regimes adopted by the three investigated legal systems and to what extent their defined approaches align with international trends are analysed below.

> *Illustration* – Company A, a multinational technology business, located in country X, has sold 100 defibrillators to an international airline, located in country Y. The airline is required to have defibrillators available on its aircrafts as from 2017. The parties agree that the defibrillators have to be delivered on 10 June 2016. However, after two years, the airline has still not received the defibrillators and demands delivery. In this situation, the question arises whether the technology company could be protected against a delayed request for performance.

248. *Domestic approaches* – Dutch contract law does not make a distinction between limitation of a claim for monetary and non-monetary obligations under a sales contract. This means that a claim for payment of the purchase price and delivery of the goods expires after five years.[1558] The limitation period starts to run on the day following the day the promisee is entitled to enforced performance.[1559] If no term has been set for performance, the contractual obligation may be immediately performed as well as demanded, subject to due consideration of the standards of reasonableness and fairness.[1560] In this situation, the limitation period of five years starts to run from the moment the obligation could be performed. If it turns out that the contract is concluded for an indefinite period, the limitation period of five years shall not begin to run until the beginning of the day following the one on which the promisee gives notice of its intention to request the court to order the promisor to perform its contractual obligations.[1561] That said, the limitation period for

1558 Arts 3:307(1), 3:323(3) DCC; The right of action to claim performance of an obligation secured by mortgage shall not be prescribed until expiry of twenty years from the day following the one on which the mortgage has been attached to the obligation.

1559 Art 3:307(1) DCC; Sieburg, *Asser 6-II* (n 532) paras 400, 404; Hartkamp 2011 (n 80) para 195; the right to claim compensatory damages and penalties is covered by art 3:310 paragraph 1 of the DCC, which encompasses a limitation period of five years. This limitation period starts to run from the beginning of the day following the one on which the prejudiced person becomes aware of both the damage or that the penalty become exigible and the identity of the person responsible therefor, and, in any event, on the expiry of twenty years following the event which caused the damages or made the penalty exigible.

1560 Art 3:307(2), 6:38, 6:248(1) DCC; Sieburgh, *Asser 6-I* (n 363) para 240; Dutch Parliamentary History Book 6 (n 207) 170, 171; Dutch Parliamentary History Book 3 (n 204) 162 *ff*; *Visser v Erven Kroon* Dutch Supreme Court 12 November 1999, ECLI:NL:PHR:1999:AA3369, NJ 2000, 67; This principle applies, *i.a.*, to contracts whereby the promisor promises to keep safe and return a thing, which the promisee entrusts or will entrust to him or her (art 7:600 DCC) and contracts whereby one of the parties gives up a thing to another on the condition of its return by the borrower, after the latter has used it (art 7A:1777 DCC).

1561 Art 3:307(1) DCC covers contractual obligations and is in this respect the *lex specialis* of art 3:313 DCC. The latter stipulates that for an obligation to give or to do something, the prescription (in this research

the obligation to provide the source codes of customised hardware and software only starts to run from the moment the purchaser needs the codes due to obsolescence of the purchased user rights (simply put, if developed hardware and software becomes outdated).[1562]

By way of derogation from the general limitation period of five years, Dutch contract law adopts an exception for a defective performance, to wit; a limitation period of two years applies in cases of non-conformity of the goods.[1563] This period starts to run pursuant to the notification about the discovered defects.[1564] After expiry of the two-year period, the buyer may not claim that delivery does not conform to the contract.

In any event, however, the right to enforced performance of a contractual obligation and cure of a defect expires after twenty years.[1565] The final limitation period of twenty years starts to run from the beginning of the day following the one on which performance could be claimed,[1566] if necessary after a notice of termination of the contract by the promisee.[1567] This means that a contractual obligation could become time-barred, even if the promisee was not aware of the existence of its right to claim for enforced performance.[1568] However, the final limitation period does not start to run in the event the promisee is not able to claim enforced performance of the contract due to a situation of *force majeure* or a prohibition imposed by law.[1569] In other words, the promisee needs to be actually capable of requiring enforced performance of the initial obligation.

249. Under Singapore contract law the historically imposed distinction between the common law action for obtaining enforced performance of monetary and non-monetary obligations has resulted in two distinct doctrines which are, to some extent, related. The starting point is the Singapore Limitation Act, which entails the statutory principle that an action founded on a non-monetary obligation emerging from a commercial sales contract cannot be

referred to a limitation) period starts to run at the beginning of the day following the one on which immediate performance can be claimed.

1562 Sieburg, *Asser 6-II* (n 532) para 404; *Van Genk v De Wild* Dutch Supreme Court 21 June 1996, ECLI:NL:HR:1996:ZC2107, NJ 1997, 327.

1563 Art 7:23(2) DCC.

1564 S 5.4.4.

1565 Art 3:307(2) DCC.

1566 *E.g.*, if the contract entails a term which stipulates that the obligation persists for an indefinite time after a certain period has elapsed.

1567 Art 3:307(2) DCC; *Visser v Erven Kroon* (n 1560).

1568 Hartkamp 2011 (n 80) para 196; It should be noted that the Dutch Supreme Court considered that the non-performing party is not entitled to seek recourse to art 6 EVRM where the aggrieved party claims for enforced performance and the limitation periods have not yet lapsed. Art 6 EVRM brings about the principle that in the determination of civil rights and obligations, everyone is entitled to a fair and public hearing within a reasonable time by an independent and impartial tribunal established by law; Dutch Supreme Court 29 June 1990, ECLI:NL:PHR:1990:AD1189, NJ 1991, 337; Sieburg, *Asser 6-II* (n 532) para 359.

1569 Sieburg, *Asser 6-II* (n 532) para 401; Dutch Supreme Court 31 October 2003, ECLI:NL:HR:2003:AL8168, NJ 2006, 112.

brought to court after the expiration of six years, which start to run from the moment the promisor fails to perform its contractual obligations.[1570] This means that in cases of non-conformity, the limitation period generally starts to run once the goods are delivered.[1571] The same approach has been developed by the UN Limitation Convention.[1572] There is no long-stop period for non-monetary obligations arising from a contract. The limitation period of six years also starts to run as long as it can be established that the promisee knew of or could have been aware of the failure in performance but did not exercise reasonable diligence to discover it.[1573] In the case of a continuing obligation to deliver goods, the limitation period starts to run on every day the promisor fails to perform its obligation (the cause of the action) until the last day of that continuing obligation.[1574] There are no guidelines in the Singapore Limitation Act for establishing an alternative starting date for the statutory limitation period in the case a contract does not provide a specific time for performance.

With regard to the relation between the doctrine of laches and the Limitation Act, it should be noted that in *British and Malayan Trustees Ltd v Sindo Realty Pte Ltd* it was argued that the defence of laches did not apply since there are already statutory bars in the Limitation Act (Cap 163, 1996 Ed).[1575] This argument was not accepted by the Singapore High Court on the grounds of the statutory principle that nothing in the Limitation Act shall affect any equitable jurisdiction to deny a specific remedy on the ground of acquiescence, laches or otherwise.[1576] For example, in *Tay Joo Sing v Ku Yu Sang* it was held by the Court of Appeal that a delay of 25 months in bringing an action to court constitutes laches which subsequently led to a denial of an order for enforced performance of a non-monetary obligation.[1577] In a similar vein, the Singapore High Court denied in *Chew Ai Hua Sandra v Woo Kah Wai and another* a claim for enforced performance of the obligation to issue a purchase option for a property due to a delay of 16 months in bringing an action to court via a writ of summons.[1578] The court based its judgement on the view that it is commonplace that an equitable remedy, such as a claim for the performance of a non-monetary obligation, should provide relief to the aggrieved party

1570 Limitation Act (Ch 163, rev ed 1966), s 6(a)(1)(7); Halsbury's Laws of Singapore (Civil Procedure Law 2016) vol 5, para 50.148; the failure in performance is the so-called cause of the action.

1571 Limitation Act (Ch 163, rev ed 1966), s 6(1)(a).

1572 Art 8–10 UN Limitation Convention (4 years).

1573 The guideliness for establishing whether a promisee has exercised reasonable diligence are laid down in *Robert Chua Teck Chew v Goh Eng Wah* [2009] SGCA 40; Halsbury's Law of Singapore (Carriers 2016) vol 3, para 30.352.

1574 *Lim Check Meng v Orchard Credit Pte Ltd* [1997] 3 SLR 795; Halsbury's Law of Singapore (Carriers 2016) vol 3, para 30.352.

1575 *British and Malayan Trustees (* (n 1536) SGHC 92 [64].

1576 *Ibid.*

1577 (n 1474); *British and Malayan Trustees* (n 1536) SGHC 92 [65].

1578 [2013] SGHC 120 [57], (2013) 3 SLR 1088.

(*i.e.* the seller who suffered prejudice due to a lengthy delay in claiming performance) and not the party who abandoned the contract.[1579]

250. The civil law system of China is also familiar with limitation periods for enforced performance. However, recent legal reforms and the interplay between the General Principles and the General Provisions require careful consideration of the applicable rules which shape the limitation regime under Chinese law. Until 1 October 2017, the starting point was a general two year limitation period for enforced performance of contractual obligations. The General Provisions deviates from this principle by adopting a time period of three years.[1580] According to the Supreme People's Court interpretation of the latter,[1581] the limitation period of three years applies where it starts running after 1 October 2017. Where the two year period has not expired on this date, the limitation period of three years applies. As for the commencement of the general limitation period, the two year period commences on the day the promisee knows or ought to know of the infringement of its right.[1582] The limitation period of three years commences on the day the promisee knows or ought to know that its right is infringed and the identity of the promisor.[1583]

Aside from the extension of the general limitation period, the General Provisions also stipulate that a limitation period of four years applies to international commercial sales contracts, calculated from the date on which the aggrieved party knows or ought to have known about the failure in performance of the contract.[1584] This principle is limited by the rule that the courts are not able to award a claim for actual performance if twenty years have elapsed since the failure in performance.[1585]

251. *Comparative analysis* – Taking into consideration the above, three different approaches to the regulation of limitation periods can be distinguished. The first approach may be characterised as a two-tier limitation regime, which entails a general limitation period and a maximum period. This structure is adopted by the PICC which brings about a general limitation period of three years and a maximum limitation period of ten years for the enforcement of obligations arising from a commercial contract.[1586] The second approach

1579 *Ibid* SGHC 120 [56], [57].

1580 Art 188 General Provisions 2017 (n 172).

1581 Interpretation of the Supreme People's Court on Several Issues Concerning the Application of Limitation of Action Provided in the General Provisions 2017 (n 172). The aforementioned Judicial Interpretation clarifies the interplay between the GPCL and the General Provisions 2017.

1582 Art 137 GPCL.

1583 Art 188 General Provisions 2017 (n 172).

1584 Art 129 CCL.

1585 Art 137 GPCL; Art 188 General Provisions 2017 (n 172).

1586 Art 10.2(1)(2) PICC; The PECL and DCFR adopted a uniform regime of one period of three years which may be extended to a maximum length of ten (or thirty) years; Arts 14:201, 14:307 PECL; Arts III.-7:201, III.-7:307 DCFR.

follows a similar structure but has developed an exception for a defective performance. This means in effect that non-monetary obligations under a commercial sales contract is subject to a general limitation period, a specific limitation period in case of non-conformity of the goods and an absolute maximum period. This structure is adopted by Dutch and Chinese contract law, as well as the CISG (the CISG only entails a distinct limitation period for a defective performance).[1587] The contract law of Singapore follows the third approach which may be regarded as a rather simple one because it entails only one limitation period for all contractual obligations. Nonetheless, the availability of enforced performance of non-monetary obligations under a commercial sales contract can also be affected indirectly by the defence of laches and via the general principles on the discretionary power of the courts to deny or allow such a claim. In view of the aforementioned considerations, it appears that in the example mentioned under paragraph 247, the claim of the airline for delivery of the defibrillators is not affected by the discussed limitation periods due to the relatively short period between the moment the delay in performance is triggered and the request for delivery. Nonetheless, in more complicated international commercial sales contracts which entail different elements and with deliveries in different time zones, the variety of approaches at the domestic and international levels may cause significant confusion about the real length of a limitation period.

It must also be mentioned that the limitation periods discussed in this section do not rule out the possibility that enforced performance is not available in cases of any undue delay in requesting performance which causes unnecessary prejudice and injustice (section 6.3). However, difficult issues may emerge where the time allowed for demanding performance is longer than the general or maximum limitation period. This could occur where a limitation period applies, although the time for requesting performance only started to run recently because the promisee could not know or ought to have known of its right to performance at an earlier stage. As for the general limitation periods, the PICC appears to be the only instrument to have clarified this matter by adopting the principle that the reasonable time for giving notice prevails over the applicable limitation period.[1588] In other words, where the reasonable time for requiring performance is longer than the general limitation period, the former prevails. It is, however, said that this principle does not apply to the maximum limitation period.[1589]

1587 Art 39(2) CISG brings about the rule that after the expiry of two years, the aggrieved buyer is not entitled to claim for enforced performance in the form of cure by repair or replacement. Nonetheless, contracting parties may extend or shorten this period by guarantee.

1588 Art 10.1(1) PICC; Vogenauer 2015 (n 19) art 10.1 para 9.

1589 Vogenauer 2015 (n 19) art 10.1 para 9.

6.4.3 Modification by agreement

252. *Preliminary* – In cases where commercial parties to a sales contract feel the need for longer or shorter general and/or maximum limitation periods, the key question arising is whether the applicable law allows this, and if so, to what extent. The approaches taken by legal systems can be divided into three categories, to wit; (i) legal systems which prohibit agreements on limitation periods; (ii) legal systems which allow modification within certain limits, and (iii) legal systems which allow modification without restriction. The regime adopted by legal systems is generally the result of a balancing of the public interest which limitation periods are intended to serve and party autonomy.[1590] The premise here is that the public interest requires protection against a situation of legally unbridled, unknown and indefinite claims. The protection of party autonomy is based on the notion that where the promisor gives up its protection (provided by limitation periods) in the initial contract or by a later agreement, private autonomy should prevail. The discussion below shows that the three investigated legal systems have balanced these elements in entirely different ways, which brings about almost diametrically opposed limitation regimes for enforced performance of a commercial sales contract. Please note that only the fundamental principles surrounding agreements to limitation periods are relevant for the present research, and therefore, the domestic intricacies and the international viewpoints are only briefly discussed.

> *Illustration* – A producer of VR (Virtual Reality) headsets, located in country X, concludes a sales contract with a social media company, located in country Y, for the development, production and sale of 1000 VR headsets, to be delivered on 12 March 2015. The parties also agree that the obligation to deliver the VR headsets for the stipulated price cannot expire before 2025.

253. *Domestic approaches* – There is a significant difference between the three investigated jurisdictions as to the question of whether the statutory limitation periods discussed above can be modified by commercial parties. The disagreement between the legal systems generally follows from two different objectives of the rules on limitation (and prescription), that is, protection of the public interest by preventing costly and long drawn-out lawsuits,

1590 Vogenauer 2015 (n 19) art 10.3 paras 1–4; Christian von Bar, Eric Clive, Hans Schulte-Nölke et al (eds), *Principles, Definitions and Model Rules of European Private Law, Draft Common Frame of Reference (DCFR), Articles and Comments* (prepared by the Study Group on a European Civil Code and the Research Group on the Existing EC Private Law (Acquis Group)) 548–549; Schwenzer, Hachem and Kee 2012 (n 13) para 51.16.

and protection of the interest of the promisor by providing legal certainty.[1591] When considering the impact of the express provisions on limitation periods for non-monetary obligations under a commercial sales contract, Dutch contract law takes the most seller-friendly approach by permitting the parties to modify the statutory rules on limitation provided that a contractually stipulated limitation period does not exceed the statutory limitation periods or is unreasonably onerous to the other party.[1592] The rule that a contractual limitation period may not exceed the applicable statutory limitation period follows from the principle that the promisor is not allowed to waive its rights to raise the defence of limitation before the expiry of this period.[1593] In other words, contracting parties are not allowed to lengthen the limitation period by initial or later agreement (except when this follows from settlement agreements). By contrast, the contract law system of China does not permit contracting parties to reduce or extend the statutory limitation periods by party agreement.[1594] However, if the short or final limitation period has expired, the contracting parties are free to conclude a new contract, which may include enforcement of performance of the unperformed obligations.[1595] The Singapore Limitation Act makes no provisions in relation to whether it is possible for commercial parties to modify the relevant limitation period. As for English law, it is held that the parties are entitled to agree to extend and to shorten the limitation periods provided for under the Limitation Act.[1596] This raises the question of whether the courts of Singapore would also allow extension or reduction of limitation periods by agreement, express or implied.[1597] It seems that Singapore has not yet taken a position on this matter. If the position in English law is followed by Singapore courts (by the application of the English Law Act), an agreement to reduce or extend the limitation period should be possible (without limitation), although where such an agreement is not allowed, an extension can be effective when it is considered as a waiver of rights or promissory estoppel.[1598] In view of this, it must be noted that a system which

1591 D Busch and E Hondius (eds), *Principles of European Contract Law and Dutch Law (Part III). A Commentary II* (Kluwer Law International 2006) 239.

1592 Sieburg, *Asser 6-II* (n 532) para 422; Hartkamp 2011 (n 80) para 196.

1593 Art 3:322(3) DCC; Busch and Hondius (n 1591) 240.

1594 Art 197 General Provisions 2017 (n 172); Art 2 of the Provisions of the Supreme People's Court on Several Issues concerning the Application of Statute of limitations during the Trial of Civil Cases (Judicial Interpretation No. 11 [2008]); Bu 2013 (n 226) 28, para 31. The General Principles does not encompass express provision for agreements to limitation periods.

1595 Bu 2013 (n 226) 29 para 31.

1596 English Law Commission 270, *Limitations of Actions* (2001) paras 2.96, 3.170 <http://www.lawcom.gov.uk/app/uploads/2015/03/lc270_Limitation_of_Actions.pdf> accessed on 14 December 2017.

1597 English Law Commission 270, *Limitations of Actions* (2001) paras 2.96, 3.170 <http://www.lawcom.gov.uk/app/uploads/2015/03/lc270_Limitation_of_Actions.pdf> accessed on 14 December 2017.

1598 A waiver of right is a kind of promisorry estoppel. This common law device brings about that where a seller agrees to extend the limitation period, and thus induces the belief that the buyer preserves a claim for

allows for modification of limitation periods without restrictions may overshoot the mark. This is because a party with a better negotiating position may unfairly prejudice the other party by an excessive reduction or extension of the limitation periods. That having been said, where this issue is addressed by the Singapore courts, they may adopt a different viewpoint if this is required by the circumstances existing in Singapore.[1599]

254. *Comparative analyses* – The starting point for the following comparative analyses is that the applicable statutory limitation periods for claiming enforced performance of non-monetary obligations cannot be extended under Dutch and Chinese contract law. Unfortunately, the position under Singapore law is not clear on the matter. When considering the national perspectives in view of the approaches taken by the PICC, PECL and DCFR, it appears that these unification instruments have adopted a model which strikes a good balance between public interest, legal certainty, protection of performance interest and party autonomy. The essence of this model is that contracting parties are allowed to reduce and to extend the applicable limitation periods within certain limits.[1600] However, it appears that the PICC is too restrictive for commercial sales transactions (in particular where it concerns fast moving and perishable goods) because it does not allow the parties to reduce the maximum limitation period to less than four years, and the general limitation period to less than one year.[1601] To put the limitive scope of the considerations above into context, the contractual extension of the applicable limitation period in the example mentioned under paragraph 252 shall not have the desired effect under Dutch or Chinese law (it appears that the same can be assumed for Singapore law when this is appropriate in view of the circumstances existing in Singapore).

As for the discussed legal systems which disallow extension of the applicable limitation periods, it is important to note that a contractual warranty concerning any hidden defects in the goods also has the effect of lengthening the limitation periods. It is submitted here that such an option is desirable in the realm of commercial sales contracts because it allows the parties to strike a balance of interests that fit the purpose of their agreement.[1602] The same proposition applies to situations where commercial parties prefer to postpone the

enforced performance of the seller's delivery obligation, the seller is not entitled to assert the defence of limitation after the expiry of the contractual extended time period; Anson's Law of Contract (n 360) 493; Schwenzer, Hachem and Kee 2012 (n 13) para 51.18.

1599 Statutes of the Republic of Singapore, Application of English Law Act (Cap 7A Rev Ed 1994) s 3.

1600 Art 10.3(2) PICC (the parties may not shorten the general limitation period to less than one year and the maximum limitation period to less than four years; the parties may extend the maximum limitation period to more than fifteen years); Arts 14:601(2), 14:307 PECL (the limitation periods may not be reduced to less than one year or extended to more than ten years); Art III.-7:601(2) DCFR (the period of presription may not, however, be reduced to less than one year or extended to more than thirty years).

1601 The parties are allowed to extend the general limitation period, but it cannot be longer than the maximum period.

1602 Vogenauer 2015 (n 19) art 10.3, para 13; Busch and Hondius (n 1591) 239.

due date of a performance obligation in their initial or by a later contract. These legal inroads effectively circumvent the statutory restrictions for agreements to limitation periods without causing any harm on an equal level playing field. That is; for contracts between commercial parties who are competent and acquainted with the intricacies of the envisaged transactions which may require shorter or longer limitation periods. It falls, however, outside the scope of the present research to investigate whether the domestic courts would accept such agreements which in essence intend to shorten or lengthen a statutory limitation period.

6.4.4 *Renewal and extension of limitation periods*

255. *Preliminary* – As shown in the previous sections, the three investigated jurisdictions and the PICC, PECL and DCFR have taken the approach that enforced performance of a commercial sales contract is only available within certain time limits. These statutory boundaries are, however, not carved in stone. This may be justified due to the role of limitation periods in encouraging those who have claimed to materialise them in order to end a situation of legal uncertainty.[1603] This fundamental policy reason explains that, in special circumstances, limitation periods for enforced performance could be altered by conduct of the contracting parties. The two main situations considered here are: the promisor's acknowledgement (*i.e.* recognising or admitting) of its obligation to performance and commencement of a judicial proceeding. Considering that only the fundamental principles in this regard are relevant for the present research, the domestic intricacies of these situations and the international trend are jointly analysed below.

> *Illustration 1 (acknowledgement)*
> A wine producer is obliged to deliver 400 bottles of wine to B. The obligation to deliver the bottles of wine is due on 30 November 2018. On 28 November 2018, the wine producer delivers 200 bottles and confirms that it will deliver the remaining bottles as soon as it is able to. The wine producer sends a fax to B on 1 March 2019, which states that the remaining bottles of wine shall be ready for shipment on 1 August 2019.

> *Illustration 2 (commencement of judicial proceeding)*
> A is entitled to delivery of five cars by B. The delivery of the cars is due on 15 November 2013, but B fails to deliver the cars. On 1 December 2017, A commences a judicial proceeding to enforce B to deliver the cars. On 19 January 2019, the court dismissed

1603 Schwenzer, Hachem and Kee 2012 (n 13) para 51.03; Art III.–7:302 DCFR, Comment A.

the claim for enforced performance due to a subsequent objective impediment for delivery.

256. *Domestic approaches* – As for the first situation, it is recognised in the legal systems of the Netherlands, Singapore and China that the promisor's acknowledgement of its obligation to perform brings about a renewal of the general limitation period for enforced performance.[1604] As for the impact of the commencement of a judicial proceeding, it is first noted that the legal systems of the Netherlands and China classify limitation periods as substantive law (as earlier mentioned, the term prescription is commonly used in civil law jurisdictions for substantive rules that disallow an action or claim after a certain period of time). This framework of substantive principles brings about the effect of the mere interruption of the limitation periods at the commencement of a judicial procedure.[1605] The reference to interruption implies that a new limitation period starts to run when the judicial proceedings begin. This may have the unwanted consequence that the limitation period expires during the judicial proceeding.

Both legal systems forestalled this situation through different principles, although with a similar result. Under the Dutch legal system, the limitation period is considered as not interrupted in the case a claim is withdrawn or denied by the court, unless, within six months after the decision or termination of the proceeding, a new claim is filed and awarded by the court.[1606] Where a claim for enforced performance is awarded by the court, a limitation period of twenty years starts to run from the beginning of the day following that of the decision.[1607] The recent amendments in China have solved the issue by adopting an approach where the limitation period shall be recalculated from the moment of interruption and the termination of the judicial proceeding.[1608]

The current position under Singapore law is that limitation periods qualify as procedural law, bringing about that the limitation period for enforced performance ceases to run when the judicial proceeding starts.[1609] When a claim for enforced performance is awarded, a new limitation period for an action upon this judgment starts to run.[1610] Nonetheless, in the case a commercial sales contract is governed by foreign law, the law of that other

1604 NL: art 3:318 DCC; SGP: Limitation Act (Cap 163 rev ed 1996), s 26; CHN: art 140 GPCL, art 195 General Provisions 2017 (n 172).

1605 NLD: art 3:316(1) DCC; CHN: art 140 GPCL, art 195 General Provisions 2017 (n 172).

1606 Art 3:316(2) DCC; Sieburg, *Asser 6-II* (n 532) para 425; Hartkamp 2011 (n 80) para 197.

1607 Art 3:324(1) DCC.

1608 Art 195 General Provisions 2017 (n 172).

1609 Report of the Law Reform Committee on Limitation Periods in Private International Law, January 2011 <https://www.sal.org.sg/Portals/0/PDF%20Files/Law%20Reform/2011-01%20-%20Limitation%20Periods%20in%20PIL.pdf> accessed on 29 November 2018.

1610 Limitation Act (Cap 163 rev ed 1996), s 6(1)(c), (3).

country relating to limitation periods applies.[1611] This principle is necessary to prevent Singapore courts applying their own limitation periods (of procedural nature) to the exclusion of foreign limitation periods, and potentially allowing claims for enforced performance although barred elsewhere, but also potentially denying claims for enforced performance although enforceable in other jurisdictions.

257. *Comparative analyses* – The three investigated jurisdictions, as well as the PICC, PECL and DCFR, have adopted the principle that renewal of the general limitation periods for enforced performance is triggered by an acknowledgement of the obligation by the promisor.[1612] At the international level, the synonyms used for renewal are discontinuance, interruption or cessation.[1613] The question 'what constitutes an acknowledgement' should, however, be considered carefully due to the countless forms in which acknowledgement may occur in commercial trade at the national and international levels. Nonetheless, it may be assumed that the fax used in the example in paragraph 255 is sufficient acknowledgement because it shows unambiguously that the seller is aware of its delivery obligation. As a result, a new limitation period starts to run on 1 March 2019. Any further discussion about the required level of sufficient acknowledgement in the legal systems identified, does not bring about fundamental academic issues, something which cannot be said of the alteration of limitation periods by the commencement of a judicial proceeding to obtain an order for enforced performance.

The main reason is the esoteric classification of limitation periods as substantive or procedural matters, although the actual impact of the applicable rules may not differ significantly at closer look.[1614] In this regard, it is noted that the principle under Singapore law that the limitation periods of the law governing a cross-border commercial sales contract apply, brings the law of Singapore into line with the international trend of not necessarily favouring the *lex fori* in the classification of limitation periods.[1615] This, in effect, means that Singapore has simplified the matter for commercial contracts which are subject to the law of another court. In these cases, the law of the other country relating to time limits for enforced performance of a non-monetary and monetary obligation applies (*i.e. lex contractus*).[1616] Moreover, this rule provides the necessary clarity because limitation periods, their impact on party autonomy and legal consequences vary tremendously between the subject legal systems. The aforementioned approach accords with the

1611 Foreign Limitation Periods Act (Cap 111A Rev Ed 2013), s 3(3)(1)(a).

1612 NL: art 3:318 DCC; SGP: Limitation Act (Cap 163 rev ed 1996)s 26; CHN: art 140 GPCL, art 195 General Provisions 2017 (n 172); Art 10.4 PICC; Art 14:401 PECL; Art III.-7:401 DCFR.

1613 Art 10.4 PICC; Art 14:401 PECL; Art III.-7:401 DCFR.

1614 S 6.4.5.

1615 Schwenzer, Hachem and Kee 2012 (n 13) para 51.04 *ff.*

1616 Foreign Limitation Periods Act (Cap 111A Rev Ed 2013), s 3(1)(a)(b).

classification of limitation periods as a substantive matter in the legal systems of the Netherlands and China. As for the latter two, the actual impact of interruption of a limitation period is in line with the approach taken by the unification instruments, to wit; a claim for enforced performance is suspended during the proceedings.[1617] At the end of the judicial proceedings, the actual impact on the limitation period can be determined. As a general rule, the outcome differs between judgements on the merits of the case and judgments that do not relate to the merits of the case. In the latter case, it may be assumed that the initial limitation period revives once the judicial proceedings have come to an end.

To put the considerations above in the context of the second example mentioned under paragraph 255, the claim for delivery of the cars ceases to run from the commencement of the judicial procedure under the Singapore legal system. The Dutch and Chinese legal systems, as well as the unification instruments, have taken the approach that the limitation period is merely suspended by the judicial procedure. In view of the divergence between the approaches discussed above, it is submitted here that on an overall assessment of the theoretical principles, the abstruse classification of limitation periods, the legal consequences arising therefrom and the different terminology used in this regard at domestic and international levels, may cause confusion among contracting parties involved in commercial sales contracts across the borders of the three investigated jurisdictions. To forestall issues arising therefrom, contracting parties to a commercial sales contract across the borders of the investigated legal systems should consider these issues when selecting the law governing the contract with due respect for the legal boundaries discussed in section 6.4.2 and 6.4.3.

6.4.5 The effects of expiration

258. *Preliminary* – Before diving into the effects of the expiration of a limitation period on the enforceability of non-monetary obligations under a commercial sales contract, it is of paramount importance to first briefly reiterate the classification of limitation periods in the subject legal systems. This matters because cultural notions and legal traditions (*i.e.* civil and common law) underlying the three investigated jurisdictions have taken a different approach in this regard, which may cause confusion amongst those involved in commercial trade across civil and common law borders. The key point in that regard is that limitation periods can be classified as a matter of substantive or procedural law. This classification brings about that the matter is governed by the *lex contractus* or *lex fori* respectively, which in turn plays a role in determining the applicable rules on, for example, renewal and

1617 Art 10.5 PICC; Art 14:302 PECL; Art III.-7:302 DCFR.

extension (section 6.4.4) and the legal consequences of the expiry of a limitation period. In jurisdictions where the substantive approach applies, a claim for enforced performance can be extinguished (strong effect). The other option is that the existence of the obligation is not affected, but the promisor is not obliged to perform (weak effect). Legal systems which consider limitation periods as a procedural matter arrive at a similar position as the substantive weak approach, but its focus is on the action or claim.[1618] At the moment the limitation period has expired, the aggrieved party is barred from bringing a claim to court for enforcement of a contractual or statutory right to performance (*i.e.* the right has not been extinguished), provided that the claim for enforced performance is not already barred through the operation of the common law concept of the equitable doctrine of laches (section 6.3).

> *Illustration* – A manufacturer, located in country X, is obliged to deliver 10 customised 3D printers to an engineering company, located in country Y, on 12 March 2012. The manufacturer delivers five 3D printers on 10 March 2012. Concurrently, the manufacturer confirms that it shall deliver the other printers before 1 June 2012. The manufacturer fails to deliver the 3D printers due to production issues. Although the limitation period has expired, the engineering company brings a claim to court for enforced performance of the manufacturer's delivery obligation.

259. *Domestic approaches* – As for Dutch and Chinese contract law, limitation periods are of a substantive nature, which means that the *lex contractus* regulates the time permitted for obtaining an order for enforced performance. Under Dutch and Chinese contract law, these principles bring about that a court is not entitled to reject on its own motion a claim for enforced performance of a contractual obligation on the basis that a limitation period has expired.[1619] In other words, the seller has to raise the defence that the claim of the promisee cannot be allowed due to the expiry of the applicable limitation period.[1620] Until this defence is accepted by the court, the right to claim enforced performance remains available to the aggrieved buyer.[1621] At the international level, the PICC, PECL and DCFR follow the same approach.[1622] The two jurisdictions also agree on the effects of the expiry of the limitation periods, that is, the seller is provided with a right to refuse performance

1618 Vogenauer 2015 (n 19) art 10.9 para 1.

1619 Art 3:322(1) DCC; Hartkamp 2011 (n 80) para 194.

1620 Art 3:322(1) DCC; Hartkamp 2011 (n 80) para 194; Art 193 General Provisions 2017 (n 172); Bu 2013 (n 226) 20 para 2. Previously, the court was obliged to undertake a preliminary assessment of whether a claim for enforced performance should be refused on the grounds of the expiry of a limitation period; See Bu 2013 (n 226) 19–20 paras 1–2.

1621 MWE Koopmann, 'commentaar op artikel 322 Boek 3 BW' para 3 in *Groene Serie Vermogensrecht* (n 530).

1622 Vogenauer 2015 (n 19) art 10.9 para 1; Art 14:501 PECL; Art III.-7:101 DCFR.

because the right to enforced performance is time-barred (weak effect).[1623] Put differently, the performance obligation itself is not affected if the limitation period has expired; it is only the right to claim enforced performance which is not available to the aggrieved buyer.[1624] This means in effect and for example, that a promisor is not entitled to bring a claim to court for unjustified enrichment if it (accidentally) performs the initial contractual obligation and the promisee receives the thing it initially bargained for.[1625] This approach reveals the consistent emphasis on the importance of the bindingness of a contractual promise which prevails in the above mentioned legal systems.

Although the common law system of Singapore qualifies limitation periods as procedural matters for conflict of law purposes, the impact on the existence of a claim for enforced performance is not that different. This is because it only bars a claim for remedial relief (be it enforced performance or damages) under the *lex fori*.[1626] Moreover, the doctrine of laches and the discretionary power of the courts in Singapore to deny enforced performance due to an undue delay is substantive law because it affects the performance obligation itself. With regard to the procedural rules, a Singapore court is not entitled to deny a claim for enforced performance of a (non-) monetary obligation on the basis that a limitation period has expired - unless the promisor has expressly brought this defence to court.[1627] Where a seller successfully argues that the limitation period has expired, only the availability to claim for enforced performance is affected[1628] and the primary obligation to perform the contract itself is not extinguished. As a result, the performance of an expired contractual obligation does not entitle the performing party to demand monetary compensation on the basis of unjust enrichment.

260. *Comparative analyses* – Despite the significant doctrinal differences and the more subtle disparities between the rules on limitation at the national and international level, the effect of the expiry of a limitation period on a claim for enforced performance is almost similar. That is, the availability of obtaining enforced performance is only restricted by the limitation periods; the obligation itself still exists. Furthermore, the expiration of the

1623 Schwenzer, Hachem and Kee 2012 (n 13) paras 51.06–51.07; Art 14:501 PECL; Art III.–7:101 DCFR, Comment B (Principles, Definitions and Model Rules of European Private Law, Draft Common Frame of Reference (DCFR), Articles and Comments).

1624 Hartkamp 2011 (n 80) para 194.

1625 Hartkamp 2011 (n 80) para 198; Art 192 of the General Rules of the Civil Law of the People's Republic of China 2017; Bu 2013 (n 226) 20 para 3.

1626 Report of the Law Reform Committee on Limitation Periods in Private International Law, January 2011, p. 6 <https://www.sal.org.sg/Portals/0/PDF%20Files/Law%20Reform/2011-01%20-%20Limitation%20Periods%20in%20PIL.pdf> accessed on 29 November 2018.

1627 Limitation Act (Cap 163 rev ed 1996), s 4; Halsbury's Law of Singapore (Commercial Law 2014) vol 5, para 50.146.

1628 Limitation Act (Cap 163 rev ed 1996), s 6(1) stipulates that an action founded on a contract shall not be brought to court after the expiration of six years from the date on which the cause of the action accrued.

limitation period must be asserted by the court on the defence of the promisor. This approach is also followed by the PICC, PECL and DCFR.[1629] This, in effect, means that if the court asserts the expiration of the limitation period on the defence of the manufacturer, the obligation to deliver the customised 3D printers in the example mentioned under paragraph 258 still exists, although enforced performance of the obligation itself is time-barred. An important aspect of this means of regulating the impact of the expiry of a limitation period is that it protects the interest of the seller because the latter may refuse performance after a certain time. On the other hand, the fact that the obligation does not cease to exist also protects the buyer's interest against a counterclaim from a seller who cannot be forced to perform its own obligation. A similar protective effect follows from the rule that the court is only entitled to refuse a claim for enforced performance on the basis of the expiry of a limitation period if the seller has raised this defence. On this matter, too, the three investigated jurisdictions, as well as the PICC, PECL and DCFR,[1630] have adopted the same approach. Considering the observations above, it may be said that the rules on the expiry of a limitation period as adopted by the legal systems strike a good balance between the interests of the parties to a commercial sales contract.

6.4.6 *Conclusions*

261. In addition to the timeline for requesting performance in a timely manner (following from hardship considerations),[1631] all the subject legal systems have taken the approach that a claim for enforced performance of non-monetary obligations under a commercial sales contract cannot be brought to court after the expiry of a certain period. The principles considered in this section reveal that this rule is the outcome of balancing the public interest, the individual interest of contracting parties, and the general notion of party autonomy. Another important common denominator is that the subject legal systems all agree that the expiration of a limitation period merely acts as a barrier for enforced performance; the contractual right to performance underlying the claim of the aggrieved buyer is not affected. This shows that doctrinal differences (substantive *vs* procedural approach) are not necessarily reflected in the consequences of a legal principle. That said, there is considerable divergence in the ability of contracting parties to contractually alter the limitation periods. Whereas Dutch contract law only permits the parties to reduce a limitation period, Chinese contract law statutory limitation periods cannot be modified by the parties in either way. By contrast, it appears that Singapore contract law will most likely acknowledge an extension and reduction of a limitation period. Interestingly, Dutch

1629 Art 10.9(1) PICC; Art 14:501 PECL; Art III.-7:501(1) DCFR.
1630 Art 10.9(2) PICC; Art 14:501 PECL; Art III.–7:101 DCFR.
1631 S 6.3.

and Singapore contract law use the same concept to justify their approaches. Dutch contract law acts on the notion that extension is not desired because this will amount to a waiver of rights (*i.e.* the right of the seller to assert the defence of limitation). The contract law of Singapore uses the concept of a waiver of right (and promissory estoppel) to legitimise an extension of the limitation period where such a clause cannot be enforced on its own terms.

Despite the diametrically opposed viewpoints described above, it appears that the unification instruments all offer a balanced approach on their own merits, by permitting commercial parties to extend or shorten the limitation period within certain limits. National legislators seeking a similar balanced approach to accommodate and intensify commercial trade within its borders, must be aware that these limits on a reduction or extension by party agreement are inextricably linked with the length of the applicable statutory limitation period. Any undertaking to equalise the availability of enforced performance of a commercial sales contract in this regard, is also complicated when considering the fact that the contract law of Singapore only knows one limitation period for commercial sales contracts, whereas Dutch and Chinese contract law provide for a relative and maximum limitation period, and limitation periods for specific situations (*i.e.* delivery of non-conforming goods and international commercial sales contracts respectively).

That having been said, there is a silver lining when considering the rules on renewal and extension. That is, all the subject legal systems adopt the principle that the acknowledgement of the seller's or buyer's contractual right to performance triggers a renewal of the limitation period. The three investigated jurisdictions, as well as the unification instruments identified, are also aligned (from a practical viewpoint) in cases where a claim for enforced performance is awarded, that is; the promisee is provided with a new limitation period for execution of the judgement. Nonetheless, the actual impact of limitation periods on the availability of enforced performance varies enormously between the investigated legal systems due to numerous subtle differences arising from the rules on limitation, each with their own domestic rationale. To equalise the availability of enforced performance (which ultimately prevents forum shopping), national legislators may draw inspiration from the discussed unification instruments because they have significantly reduced the complexity arising from the domestic approaches. In the meantime, those involved in commercial sales contracts across the borders of the three investigated legal systems, and aiming to bring about a properly balanced set of principles regulating the impact of limitation periods, should be aware that contractual stipulations in this regard may not have the desired effect. This, in effect, means that commercial parties should be especially wary of involving themselves in sales contracts which deviate from limitation periods where this is not allowed under the law governing the contract.

6.5 Duty to mitigate in the form of a precautionary cover transaction

262. *Preliminary* – This section discusses the question of whether a buyer is subject to a duty to obtain substitute goods as a measure to mitigate damages (*i.e.* additional costs and expenses) arising from the non-delivery of goods or the delivery of non-conforming goods, where damages would be likely to increase, and the related consequences of the non-fulfilment of the duty to mitigate. This question is particularly relevant when the buyer favours having the goods delivered by the seller as stipulated in the contract and is not interested in avoidance of the contract and subsequently claiming for damages. That said, where an aggrieved buyer wants the court to order a non-performing seller to deliver the goods in accordance with the features set out in the contract, why would the buyer want to take any steps to undertake a precautionary cover purchase to mitigate damages? After all, it may be said that an action for enforced performance is usually brought to court by the buyer when it considers the goods as unique, and where there are no substitute goods available, or it requires delivery of the seller for other reasons. Nonetheless, where the buyer could obtain substitute goods without significant effort or expenses, the question arises as to whether enforced performance of the initial delivery obligation is still available where this would bring about a substantial increase in damages to be paid by the seller (*e.g.* shipment costs, customs duties and flying over of engineers from abroad to cure a defect).[1632] This assessment touches on issues such as the relationship between statutory duties to mitigate damages arising from a non-delivery and non-conforming goods in relation to the availability of obtaining an order for enforced performance, the role of the overarching principle of good faith and the standards of reasonableness and fairness.

> *Illustration* – A commercial food research company in country X purchases microscopes from a manufacturer, located in country Y, for a number of ongoing research projects. Because the delivered microscopes contain too much of highly toxic material (*i.e.* beryllium), the research company demands replacement of the microscopes of the manufacturer. However, the research company could also purchase the microscopes from a local supplier, which would have the effect that the manufacturer only has to cover the costs incurred by the research company and does not have to pay for additional shipping costs and customs duties for the delivery of the replacement microscopes. In this situation, the question arises whether the research company is still entitled to enforced delivery of the microscopes, although the former could mitigate the losses of the manufacturer fairly easily by obtaining the microscopes from another supplier.

1632 Cohen and McKendrick (n 4) 221, 227.

263. *Domestic approaches* – Dutch contract law recognises the duty of an aggrieved buyer to mitigate damages when it is able to do so and when this is reasonable in the circumstances given. This principle, however, does not by default exclude the buyer's right to enforced performance. This is because the aforementioned duty to mitigate loss relates only to damages. Nonetheless, where the aggrieved buyer unreasonably requires enforced performance of a delivery obligation when it could reasonably undertake a precautionary cover transaction, the non-performing seller may seek recourse to the Dutch contract law principle that contracting parties are bound to act in accordance with the requirements of reasonableness and fairness.[1633] This means, in effect, that an aggrieved buyer is obliged to take into account the interest of the non-performing seller when bringing a claim to court for enforced performance of the delivery obligation.[1634] In other words, the buyer could be under a duty to undertake a precautionary cover purchase when this substantially mitigates the damages of the seller in view of the costs arising from the fulfilment of an order for enforced performance of the initial delivery obligation. This premise should be viewed along the lines of the standards of reasonableness and fairness,[1635] as well as in light of the notion that a claim for enforced performance could be considered as an abuse of the right to claim for enforced performance if this would result in an imbalance between the buyer's interest in the exercise of its right and the seller's interest that would be harmed as a consequence of enforced performance of its delivery obligation.[1636] From these considerations, the conclusion may be drawn that it cannot be excluded that a claim for enforced performance of a right to delivery of the goods shall be refused by Dutch courts if such a judgement would unreasonably burden the seller, and the buyer is able to obtain substitute goods from another source, and when forcing the seller to deliver the goods would not be more beneficial to the buyer than obtaining substitute goods.

Under the contract law of Singapore, the principle of mitigation of damages in the form of a precautionary cover purchase as mentioned above is not considered as a stand-alone barrier to enforced performance of the seller's obligation to deliver the goods. This follows from the fundamental rule that enforced performance is only available in exceptional situations (section 4.4.3). The underlying principle is that damages are considered as the most adequate remedy where substitute goods are available at the marketplace. Hence, the question as to whether the buyer is obliged to undertake a precautionary cover purchase is already incorporated in the default assessment as to whether enforced performance is available. In view of the foregoing, it appears that a non-performing seller may be forced to deliver the goods as promised in the contract, if

1633 Arts 6:2(1), 6:248(1) DCC; *Baris v Riezenkamp* (545).
1634 *Multi Vastgoed* (n 568).
1635 Art 6:248(2) DCC.
1636 Art 3:13(2) DCC.

the buyer is not able to obtain substitute goods from another source – because the goods are short in supply, and damages are not adequate to provide the necessary relief. That having been said, it appears from the considerations above that Singapore courts generally shall not grant an order for enforced performance of a delivery obligation where substitute goods are available at the marketplace due to the principle that an order for damages would allow the buyer to obtain the goods itself.

Under the contract law of China, a buyer's failure to mitigate damages in instances of a non-delivery and delivery of non-conforming goods is primarily regarded as a barrier to a claim for damages and not as a limitation to enforced performance of the seller's performance obligations.[1637] However, when considering that the good faith principle aims to prevent social waste,[1638] it does not come as a surprise that it is broadly accepted amongst Chinese legal writers that enforced performance may be refused by Chinese courts where replacement goods are available at the marketplace and a cover transaction mitigates the seller's damages and equally satisfies the aggrieved buyer.[1639] In these instances, the buyer's duty to undertake a cover purchase follows from the previously mentioned overarching statutory good faith principle.[1640] Given the above, it appears that the contract law of China entails the uncodified principle that enforced performance of a delivery obligation is not available where the aggrieved buyer could reasonably obtain substitute goods.

264. *Comparative analysis* – The present section considers whether an aggrieved buyer is subject to a duty to mitigate damages deriving from the non-performance of the seller by obtaining substitute goods on the marketplace; and if so, to what extent a failure in performance of such a duty affects the availability of a claim for enforced performance of the seller's delivery obligation. The discussion in the present section reveals that three points require particular attention. The first issue concerns the uncertainty of whether a buyer is by default subject to a duty to take reasonable measures to mitigate the impact on the seller's interest by obtaining a coverage purchase. The second issue relates to the legally unframed effect for a buyer to obtain substitute goods where they are reasonably available. The third point relates to the theoretical differences between the discussed principles,

1637 Art 114 GPCL; Art, 119(1) CCL; Lei Chen, 'Damages and Specific Performance in Chinese Contract Law' in DiMatteo and Chen 2017 (n 19) 391; Lei Chen, 'Availablity of Specific Remedies in Chinese Contract Law' in Chen-Wishart, Loke and Ong 2016 (n 156) 32.

1638 Lei Chen, 'Damages and Specific Performance in Chinese Contract Law' in DiMatteo and Chen 2017 (n 19) 391.

1639 Lei Chen, 'Damages and Specific Performance in Chinese Contract Law' in DiMatteo and Chen 2017 (n 19) 400; Lei Chen, 'Availablity of Specific Remedies in Chinese Contract Law' in Chen-Wishart, Loke and Ong 2016 (n 156) 32, 33; Bing Ling 2002 (n 229) para 8.078; Lee 2016 (n 16) 323.

1640 Lei Chen, 'Availablity of Specific Remedies in Chinese Contract Law' in Chen-Wishart, Loke and Ong 2016 (n 156) 32, 33; Lei Chen, 'Damages and Specific Performance in Chinese Contract Law' in DiMatteo and Chen 2017 (n 19) 400; Bing Ling 2002 (n 229) para 8.078.

although at a practical level they appear to bring about the same impact on the availability of enforced performance when dealing with a situation where replacement goods are reasonably available in the commercial marketplace.

The first two issues come into play when considering the stance of Dutch and Chinese contract law. It can be seen from the preceding discussion that both jurisdictions are familiar with an uncodified (non-actionable) duty of the buyer to obtain substitute goods where this is required according to the standards of reasonableness and fairness, and the principle of good faith respectively. This effectively means that a claim for enforced performance of a delivery obligation shall not be granted where this would significantly burden the seller, and the aggrieved buyer could reasonably prevent this by obtaining substitute goods – as long as this would provide the aggrieved buyer with the same benefits. The CISG adopts a similar approach by excluding the right to enforced performance where it follows from the principle of observance of good faith in international trade and the buyer could reasonably obtain substitute goods from another source.[1641] In a similar vein, the DCFR limits the availability of enforced performance where a buyer unreasonably insists on delivery of the goods by the seller when the former could easily obtain the goods elsewhere, and when enforcing the seller to deliver the goods would have an unreasonable financial impact on the latter. The control over such abuse under the DCFR is that the right to enforced performance must be exercised in accordance with the principle of good faith and fair dealing.[1642] It may, however, not be assumed that enforced performance is by default excluded where the aggrieved buyer could purchase replacement goods. The prevailing principle under Dutch and Chinese contract law, as well as the CISG and DCFR, is that enforced performance is only limited where substitute goods are available in the marketplace, and the buyer may fairly be required to acquire these goods as a reasonable measure to mitigate the financial impact on the non-performing seller. The applicable assessment standards are reasonableness and fairness, and good faith. It appears, however, that there is tension between the approaches described above, and the regulation of the limitation of enforced performance through a duty to obtain substitute goods under the PICC. The latter entails the notion that if a sales contract for staple goods is not performed, a request for enforced performance from an aggrieved buyer shall not be granted if the non-performing seller proves that the aggrieved buyer may reasonably obtain substitute goods.[1643] The rationale behind this rule is that it causes the buyer not to waste time and

1641 It may, however, not be tacitly assumed that the right to claim enforced performance is affected under the CISG if substitute goods are available. See for the impact on the availability to claim damages art 77 CISG; Clayton Gillette and Steven D Walt, *The UN Convention on Contracts for the International Sale of Goods: Theory and Practice* (2nd edn, Cambridge University Press 2016) 370; Schwenzer 2016 (n 91) art 46 para 14.; Schwenzer, Hachem and Kee 2012 (n 13) para 44.262; Treitel 1998 (n 55) para 72.

1642 Art III.-3:302 DCFR Comment J (n 1590).

1643 Art 7.2.2(c) PICC.

effort in forcing the non-performing seller to deliver the goods, even if this would mean that the buyer is obliged to purchase the goods at a higher price and therefore is deprived of its right to performance.[1644] In a similar vein, the PECL codified the principle that enforced performance is excluded in the situation where the buyer, without experiencing much difficulty, may obtain the goods from another supplier.[1645] The draft articles on non-performance of the PACL have also adopted a provision which excludes enforced performance where the aggrieved buyer may reasonably obtain substitute goods from another source.[1646] The official commentary reveals, however, that this provision does not impose an actionable obligation on the aggrieved buyer to do so.[1647]

Turning to the last matter, it must first be noted that a discussion about a potential duty of the aggrieved buyer to obtain substitute goods as a reasonable measure to mitigate damages is unnecessary for the contract law of Singapore. This is because the availability of a substitute transaction is absorbed in the assessment of the court to award a claim for enforced performance of the delivery of specific or ascertained good if it thinks fit, and the overarching adequacy of damages test which applies to a claim for enforced performance of a delivery obligation which is not governed by Singapore sales law. This consideration should be viewed in light of the majority view under Dutch and Chinese contract law, as well as the unification instruments, which entails that a claim for enforced performance could be denied where the aggrieved buyer may have reasonably obtained substitute goods from another source. Thus, where Singapore law by default excludes enforced performance where substitute goods are available at the marketplace, Dutch and Chinese contract law, as well as the unification instruments, have taken a less strict approach, in the sense that a claim for enforced performance can be denied if the buyer could reasonably obtain a substitute transaction and the imposition of such a duty is appropriate in view of the circumstances of the case.

The consideration above brings about that the aggrieved buyer in the example mentioned under paragraph 262, is under a non-actionable duty to enter into a substitute transaction for mitigation purposes in the subject legal systems. Nonetheless, it appears that Dutch and Chinese contract law would only impose such a duty if this qualifies as a reasonable measure in view of the circumstances of the case. This is in stark contrast with the theoretical notion of mitigation under Singapore contract law, which lies at the very root of the limited availability of enforced performance of a non-monetary obligation. Interestingly enough, there does not seem to be much difference in the practical implications if the court asserts that the aggrieved buyer can easily obtain the microscopes from another supplier and this

1644 Vogenauer 2015 (n 19) art 7.2.2 paras 34–41.

1645 Art 9:102(2)(d) PECL.

1646 Art 7(d) Amendment Draft on Non-Performance; Lee 2016 (n 16) 198.

1647 Lee 2016 (n 16) 198.

transaction would protect the seller's financial interest in the sense that the latter is not exposed to disproportionally high costs.

That having been said, the unregulated potential obligation of the aggrieved buyer to obtain (not to find) substitute goods creates legal uncertainty and inconsistencies between the approaches taken by Dutch and Chinese contract law, and the unification instruments. For instance, it appears that an aggrieved buyer is not by default obliged to obtain substitute goods under Dutch or Chinese law. By contrast, the PICC and the PECL have explicitly excluded enforced performance where the buyer could reasonably obtain a coverage purchase. The term 'reasonably' is, however, not defined, which provides the courts with a significant degree of discretionary power. Hence, the imitating effect of a potential duty of the buyer to take reasonable mitigation measures in the form of obtaining substitute goods remains a contentious issue in the realm of commercial sales contracts. It is therefore of particular importance that contractual stipulations clarify the notion of reasonable obtainable goods and the legal consequences from a failure to obtain a coverage purchase where the seller fails to deliver the goods. Contracting parties however should bear in mind that Singapore courts do not allow contractual stipulations, indirectly coercing a party to bring about a certain state of affairs, if this would interfere with their discretionary power to deny a claim for enforced performance within the boundaries set out by the sales law principles and legal precedent.[1648]

6.6 Supervision on enforcement

265. *Preliminary* – The traditional view in the common law tradition is that where active supervision of the court is required in the form of an indefinite series of subsequent rulings to ensure the execution of its order, a request for enforced performance of a contractual obligation is not available.[1649] These subsequent rulings may amount to quasi-criminal

---

1648 Ch 8.

1649 The modern leading autority is the English case *Co-operative Insurance Society Ltd* (n 909) AC 1 [12–13]. The House of Lords held that 'the purpose of the law of contract is not to punish wrongdoing but to satisfy the expectations of the party entitled to performance... The exercise of the discretion as to whether or not to grant specific performance starts from the fact that the covenant has been broken. Both landlord and tenant in this case are large sophisticated commercial organisations and I have no doubt that both were perfectly aware that the remedy for breach of the covenant was likely to be limited to an award of damages. The interests of both were purely financial: there was no element of personal breach of faith... No doubt there was an effect on the businesses of other traders in the Centre, but Argyll had made no promises to them and it is not suggested that CIS warranted to other tenants that Argyll would remain. Their departure, with or without the consent of CIS, was a commercial risk which the tenants were able to deploy in negotiations for the next rent review; Phang et al 2012 (n 112) para 23.143; Treitel 1998 (n 55) 67; Solène Rowan, *Remedies for Breach of Contract: A Comparative Analysis of the Protection of Performance* (Oxford University Press 2012) 57.

procedure of punishment for contempt, with a potential damage to the commercial reputation of the non-performing party and the danger of heavy and expensive proceedings. For the purposes of determining as to whether the obligee has performed its obligations, it is necessary that the judicial order can be framed with precision. Jurisdictions based on the civil law tradition generally adhere to the principle that the execution of a court order for enforced performance is to be initiated and arranged by the beneficiary of the court order.[1650] Accordingly, supervision on enforcement is in most civil law jurisdictions a responsibility of the latter. Hence, the legal impediment of constant supervision of the court is generally not a familiar concept in civil law jurisdictions. Nonetheless, globalised trade necessitates looking beyond these traditional approaches and, subsequently, assessing of whether there are elements in the three investigated legal systems which might have a comparable limiting effect on the availability of enforced performance of a commercial sales contract and to what extent the domestic arguments are surmountable.

> *Illustration* – A producer of specific tomato seeds, located in country X, enters into a long-term sales contract with a tomato farming company (hereinafter buyer), located in country Y. The contract entails the obligation of the producer to deliver a specified amount of tomato seeds every month for a period of two years. The producer and the buyer agree on a base price, subject to periodic adjustments based on inflation. Then, after six months, due to an increase in costs of production, the price-adjustment provision is outpaced. Because continued performance of the delivery obligation will result in losses, the producer proposes an adjustment of the price formula. The buyer declines the proposed adjustment, and the producer refuses to deliver the tomato seeds for the remainder of the contract (*i.e.* the producer repudiates the contract). The buyer then seeks a judicial order for enforced performance for the outstanding eighteen months. In this situation, the question arises whether a potential order for enforced performance might be curtailed by the argument that policing its performance by the judiciary brings about too many costs for society.

266. *Domestic approaches* – Dutch contract law is not familiar with the objection of supervision of the court, although it is said that where the circumstances of the case may result in an indefinite series of court rulings, the court could suppress this risk by granting a claim for enforced performance under pain of a judicial penalty (section 7.4).[1651] Under Dutch contract law, the necessity of the common law supervision argument as a bar to enforced performance seems also to be overruled by the enforcement measure of authorising the aggrieved promisee to obtain the performance at the expenses of the defaulting promisor

1650 Vogenauer 2015 (n 19) 896, para 32.
1651 Mak (n 527) 104.

(section 7.3).[1652] Furthermore, the aggrieved buyer does not have to return to court to obtain payment if the promisor does not comply with the court order because an enforcement officer can step in.[1653] The imposition of a judicial penalty, however, does not guarantee that the obligation shall be performed,[1654] and subsequently, prevents additional proceedings when the promisor does not comply with the court order. This is because subsequent enforcement proceedings may be required where it concerns continuing obligations, the promisor has not enough assets to recover the forfeited judicial penalties, the promisor has brought its assets beyond the reach of the promisee, or the promisor, as a matter of principle, refuses to perform in accord with the court order and is even willing to pay the judicial penalty.[1655] Thus, following the aforementioned practical difficulties, it could be said that the availability of a judicial penalty is not sufficient to militate against the common law bar of constant supervision. Nonetheless, the justification for the constant supervision objection (the risk of an indefinite series of rulings of whether the court order is performed),[1656] is not relevant for the situation under Dutch law when considering the low thresholds for enforced performance by means of an interim relief proceeding and the enforcement measure of authorising the aggrieved party to have the obligation performed at the expense of the non-performing party.[1657]

267. Under the contract law of Singapore, a claim for enforced performance can be refused if it would demand constant supervision of the court via additional court procedures.[1658] In effect, this bar to enforced performance is appropriate where a court ruling is likely to result in a series of subsequent rulings deriving from contempt of court proceedings.[1659] The constant supervision restriction may apply when a contract entails continuous duties, such as a long-term sales contracts.[1660] In such cases where constant superintendence by the court is required, the inextricable financial burden of the judicial system (*i.e.* wasted public resources) and involved parties due to a new series of rulings may be used by the court to refuse an order for enforced performance.[1661] It is said that the argument mentioned above of wasted resources is not of relevance where the court could appoint an officer to

1652 Treitel 1998 (n 55) para 67; Rowan (n 1649) 57.
1653 Mak (n 527) 104.
1654 Smits 2008 (n 871) 23.
1655 Smits 2008 (n 871) 24, 25.
1656 See the English law case *Co-operative Insurance Society* (n 909).
1657 S 7.3.
1658 Shenoy and Loo 2013 (n 13) para 18.90; Phang et al 2012 (n 112) para 23.142.
1659 This requirement is inextricably linked with the principle that enforced performance is not available when it is difficult for the court the frame the order with precision; See the English *Co-operative Insurance Society* (n 909); Halsbury's Law of Singapore (Contract 2016) vol 7, para 80.590; Phang and Goh 2012 (n 318) para 1558.
1660 Treitel 1998 (n 55) 67.
1661 Halsbury's Law of Singapore (Contract 2016) vol 7, para 80.590.

supervise performance, or where the promisee may appoint a third party to supervise the performance of the promisor.[1662] In *Lee Chee Wei v Tan Hor Peow Victor and others and another appeal* the Singapore Court of Appeal mentioned a practical argument for application of the bar of constant supervision. The claim for enforced performance was refused, *i.a.*, on the basis that it was rendered quite impractical for the court to grant and supervise enforced performance because the buyers were serving sentences in prison.[1663] Aside from this exceptional situation, difficulties in supervision by the court are mainly expected in cases with long-running or complex contractual obligations due to the increased chance of non-compliance with an order for enforced performance.[1664] For instance, the long-running nature of a commercial sales contract to deliver certain commodity goods for an indefinite period increases the chance that the promisor fails to comply with a court order for actual performance. If subsequent supervision would significantly burden the court, it might not be willing to order enforced performance.[1665] In turn, enforcement of short-term and straightforward sales transactions will not involve great difficulties and, therefore, the constant supervision argument shall have less influence in these situations.[1666] In these cases, the adequacy of damages remains the main hurdle. In addition, contractual obligations to achieve a certain result, such as repair and replacement of defective goods, are also less affected because there is a very limited risk of repeated applications for compliance with the initial order for enforced performance.[1667] From a practical point of view, contracting parties could avoid application of the constant supervision argument by precisely stipulating the contractual obligation. The more precise an obligation is described, the less likely it is that disputes will arise over the fulfilment of the obligations. It is also less likely that a court shall refuse to order enforced performance if there has been partial performance so that supervision of delivery of only the remainder is not difficult.

268. It appears that the constant supervision objection is not exercised in Chinese courts for commercial sales contracts. Nonetheless, it is suggested that the availability of enforced performance should be limited under Chinese law if such a court order requires constant supervision of the court or in the case supervision is difficult.[1668] For instance, a sales contract for on-demand delivery of rice in a politically unstable and economically underdeveloped region. In this light, it is unsurprising that it is held that Chinese courts

---

1662 Phang and Goh 2012 (n 318) paras 1561, 1562.

1663 *Lee Chee Wei* 2007 (n 591) SGCA 22 [56].

1664 Phang et al 2012 (n 112), 23.142; See the English case *Ryan v Mutual Tontine Westminster Chambers Association* [1893] 1 Ch 116.

1665 O'Sullivan (n 861) para 18.36.

1666 Phang et al 2012 (n 112) para 23.144; See the English case *Co-operative Insurance Society* (n 909) at 12–14.

1667 *Ibid.*

1668 Zhang 2006 (n 41) 302.

are more willing to award a claim for enforced performance where the actual enforcement can be achieved without great difficulties.[1669] That said, the possibility of limiting the right to performance, if enforcement calls for constant supervision by the court or if supervision is difficult, is rebutted with the argument that the court is entitled to authorise the aggrieved party to obtain the goods at the expense of the seller (section 7.3), and to order the non-performing party to reimburse the cost incurred following from supervision on the execution of the order for enforced performance.[1670]

269. *Comparative analysis* – It appears that the constant supervision argument as a bar to enforced performance of non-monetary obligations is a fundamental principle of Singapore law. Nonetheless, a claim for enforced performance of obligations arising from a commercial sales contract has never fallen foul of the constant supervision bar. As for the legitimacy of this bar to enforced performance, it is argued (from an English law viewpoint) that the reasons for the constant supervision objection are overstated because even parties subject to an order for enforced performance of a continuous obligation generally will comply with judicial instructions.[1671] It is also argued that the availability of enforced performance should not be affected by the constant supervision objection as the court could appoint a court officer to supervise the execution of its order or to authorise the aggrieved party to obtain performance at the expense of the non-performing party. It is assumed here that the principle that the costs of this enforcement measure will be borne by the non-performing party is most likely sufficient to encourage the latter to comply with an order for enforced performance. It is also submitted that the available enforcement measures as mentioned above remove the justification for the constant supervision objection, that is; enforced performance should not be available where the general costs to society following from the continuous supervision of the court outweigh the issues arising from supervising an order for enforced performance. More importantly, parties to a commercial sales contract could limit their exposure to the constant supervision bar by precisely stipulating their contractual obligations. The more precise obligations are, the less likely it is that disputes will arise over whether or not obligations have been performed in accordance with the contractual stipulations.

These considerations should be assessed in the view that the constant supervision bar is not of any relevance in Dutch contract law. This is because the beneficiary of a judicial

1669 Lei Chen, 'Availablity of Specific Remedies in Chinese Contract Law' in Chen-Wishart, Loke and Ong 2016 (n 156) 38.

1670 Liu Tinghua, 'On Grounds for the Application and Limitations of the Specific Performance from the Law and Economics Perspective' (2010) 6 Northern Legal Science 110.

1671 Treitel 1998 (n 55) para 67; Rowan (n 1649) 57 *ff*; See for the position under English law *Beswick* (n 818); *Sky Petroleum Ltd* (n 911); A Burrows, 'Specific Performance at the Crossroads' (1984) 4 Legal Studies 102, 110; Frederick H Lawson and Harvey Teff, *Remedies of English Law* (2nd edn, Butterworths 1980) 224.

order for enforced performance is responsible for the actual execution and the expenses incurred are to be paid by the defaulting party. It also appears that in China little attention is paid to the constant supervision argument on the basis of the notion that the financial implications of disobedience against an order for enforced performance suffices to encourage defaulting promisors to perform their obligations as instructed by the court. That having been said, a potential loss of influence of the constant supervision objection in Singapore law and the willingness of Dutch and Chinese courts to award an order for enforced performance are rooted in completely different legal structures and distribution of the responsibilities of securing the enforcement of a judicial order. Nonetheless, it is submitted here that the court adjudicating the case mentioned under paragraph 265 under the law of the three investigated jurisdictions may come to the same conclusion if disobedience of the seller is not expected by the court. This could be the case if such behaviour shall affect the producer's reputation or it would expose the latter to other unacceptable commercial risks, which outweigh the losses incurred by the delivery of tomato seeds under the agreed terms. Nonetheless, in the context of commercial sales contracts, a limited number of situations where enforced performance is envisaged under Singapore contract law (*i.e.* unique and ascertained goods), can fall foul of the constant supervision bar (although it appears that this has never occurred in the Singapore context). It is therefore suggested here that contracting parties involved in commercial sales contract across the borders of the three investigated jurisdictions determine that the execution costs of a potential enforcement order are being borne by the non-performing party. Nonetheless, when dealing with a contract governed by the law of Singapore, contracting parties should be vigilant of the common law principle that the enforceability of performance obligations cannot be protected by contractual stipulations when they affect the discretionary power of the courts to disallow a claim for enforced performance (chapter 8).

In view of the dogmatic differences between the approaches taken by the three investigated jurisdictions, it appears that the PICC provides a very sound middle-ground solution by stipulating that an aggrieved party is not entitled to require enforced performance if enforcement is unreasonably burdensome.[1672] This provision aims to close the gap between the civil and common law views on the responsibility of safeguarding the execution of a court order for enforced performance by providing the court with the discretionary power to take into account that the nature of the obligation to be enforced would unreasonably burden a domestic court supervising the order.[1673] Elements that may be considered, on a case-by-case basis, to assess whether enforced performance is unreasonably burdensome or expensive are obligations arising from complex and long-term

1672 Art 7.2.2(b) PICC.
1673 Vogenauer 2015 (n 19) 896, para 32.

commercial sales contracts.[1674] Although this approach resembles the common law tradition, enforced performance of obligations arising from such contracts are not by default denied because the exclusion of enforced performance, if it is unreasonably burdensome or expensive, has to be interpreted taking into account the international character of the PICC.[1675]

6.7 Conclusions

270. All the investigated legal systems impose barriers to enforcement of performance obligations which requires the seller or buyer to bring about a certain state of affairs under a commercial sales contract. However, the method chosen by the subject legal systems varies considerably. This research reveals that this is mainly due to the different ways they have tried to strike a balance between the protection of the parties' performance interest, the protection against abuse of a claim for enforced performance, party autonomy, legal certainty for businesses and to a certain extent public interest. It appears that all these elements are inextricably linked with the legal systems' traditional views on the availability of enforced performance of non-monetary obligations. This means in effect that the findings provided in this chapter are of paramount importance to determine to what extent enforcement of a performance obligation under a commercial sales contract is effectively available to the aggrieved party. To clarify this point: a statutory right to enforced performance is valueless if the thresholds for assuming impossibility, in the sense of not being able to overcome the consequences of an impediment, are set very low. The same is true when an excessively short limitation period applies or where the aggrieved buyer is subject to a duty to find a cover purchase, even in the case of a tight market. Conversely, the viewpoint that enforced performance is only allowed in specific circumstances may have limited impact where case law shows that this notion is interpreted liberally by the adjudicators and counter-exceptions are restricted.

The present chapter has shown that the considerations above are to a certain extent true for the three investigated jurisdictions. To put this in context, Dutch and Chinese contract law have a favourable outlook on enforced performance in the form of a cure by making (a fresh) delivery or repair, although they show a great willingness to accept subjective impossibility and hardship as a barrier to enforced performance. In the realm of commercial sales, the default contract law regime of Singapore only envisages enforced performance of non-monetary obligations in exceptional situations. Nonetheless, the protection of the seller's interest is not unlimited as the traditional understanding of the

1674 Vogenauer 2015 (n 19) 896, para 32.
1675 Art 1.6(1) PICC; Vogenauer 2015 (n 19) 183, para 5.

concept of hardship (*i.e.* increase in costs due to a change in circumstances) generally does not amount to frustration of a contractual obligation and thus does not impair the availability of enforced performance. The differing principles discussed above may cause controversy between commercial parties from different legal backgrounds. The same holds true when considering the dogmatic basis of the three investigated legal systems and the extent that they accept notions of temporary or partial impediments. While Dutch and Chinese contract law (as well as the unification instruments) preserve the right to enforced performance to the extent that its availability can be temporarily suspended or that a claim is only partially awarded, the contract law of Singapore has taken an all-or-nothing approach. In light of the foregoing, it may appear that the civil law roots of Dutch and Chinese contract law bring about a similar structure of barriers to enforced performance. At a practical level, these differing viewpoints may result in significant interpretation issues. It is therefore suggested that the contractual stipulations describe and explain the scope of the situations arising after conclusion of the contract which exempt enforced performance, whether it concerns a comprehensive or indicative list, and the impact of the contractual stipulations in this regard on the legal response to a claim for enforced performance under the law governing the contract. These clauses should observe at all times the differing viewpoints on the admissibility of derogatory agreements.[1676] In view of this, contracting parties should also take note of the significant differing consequences of a failure to request for delivery on a timely manner. Whereas the buyer is possibly exempted from all available remedies under Dutch contract law when it has not protested to the seller promptly after it has discovered, or should reasonably have discovered a defect,[1677] the buyer is potentially only deprived of the ability to obtain an order for enforced performance under Chinese and Singapore contract law. There is, however, an immense difference between the both jurisdictions when considering the impact on the availability of enforced performance. This is because under Chinese contract law, the buyer is provided with a right to enforced performance which can be exempted if the latter fails to request for enforced performance. This stands in stark contrast with the exceptional nature of enforced performance under Singapore contract law which is further limited if the buyer fails to demand delivery of the goods within a reasonable time after the agreed time for performance. Contracting parties involved in sales contracts which are partially or fully affected (in substance and procedural) by two or more of the investigated legal systems could circumvent difficulties arising from the differing approach by establishing a contractual requirement for demanding performance within a stipulated time frame and for the legal consequences deriving from a failure in performance. As earlier mentioned,

1676 Ch 8.
1677 Arts 6:89(1), 7:23(1) DCC.

such contractual provisions should always be drafted in view of the admissibility of derogatory agreements under the law governing the contract.[1678]

A similar consideration applies to the situation where a delayed request for performance (after the due date) is expected to significantly harm the interest of the non-performing party. Nonetheless, the success of contractual provisions dealing with such a situation depends on the degree contracting parties have familiarised themselves with the underpinnings of the applicable legal principles and the extent to which contractual deviation is allowed. In view of this, it should dawn on contracting parties that the legal consequences of an undue delayed request for performance follows from balancing the performance interest of the aggrieved party and the necessary measures to protect the non-performing party against abuse; understanding the interaction between these elements, however, does not suffice to safeguard contractual provisions dealing with undue delay. For this, the rules on the admissibility of derogatory agreements come into play.[1679] That said, the starting point is that Chinese contract law, as well as the PICC, PECL, DCFR and draft articles of the PACL, require that performance is demanded within a reasonable time after the aggrieved party has or should have discovered the non-performance on loss of the right to enforced performance. This principle aims to protect the non-performing party against hardship. Nonetheless, the aggrieved party's interests are not seriously affected by this limitation to enforced performance because other remedies are still available. Although Singapore contract law strikes the balance differently and relies on the common law doctrine of laches when faced with an undue delayed request for performance, there is reason to believe that the results in practice are similar when comparing the time for making a request and the consequences deriving from a delayed request under Chinese contract law and the aforementioned unification instruments. Interestingly, Dutch contract law regulates the protection of contracting parties in a similar fashion as Chinese contract law and the unification instruments mentioned above, yet the time for requesting performance and the legal consequences arising from a failure to make a request for performance are significantly stricter. Nonetheless, the very high threshold for depriving the buyer from all the available remedies as a response to an undue delayed request for performance provides a sufficient counterbalance at a domestic level. However, for those involved in commercial sales contracts across the borders of the three investigated legal systems, the divergence between the time for requesting performance (*i.e.* reasonable period *v* prompt) and legal consequences when the buyer fails to make a timely request raises the question as to whether the differing approaches should be harmonised under the CISG.

1678 Ch 8.
1679 *Ibid.*

Comparison of the rules on limitation periods and ability of contracting parties to deviate from the applicable principles results in even greater divergence between the three investigated jurisdictions. At one end of the spectrum is the Singapore contract law, in which contracting parties are entitled to interfere with the availability of enforced performance by shortening or lengthening the limitation period. At the other end of the spectrum there is the contract law of China which does not allow interference with the statutory boundaries to enforced performance in this regard. Dutch contract law is somewhere in the middle by not allowing contracting parties to extend the statutory limitation periods. The above approaches are not harmonised at the international level. It is therefore of paramount importance for those involved in commercial sales transactions across the borders of the subject jurisdictions to take into account the legal boundaries of contractual interference with the applicable limitation periods. Moreover, for bringing about a truly balanced set of provisions, the impact of contractual stipulations on limitation periods should be drafted in view of the barrier to enforced performance deriving from the rules on a timely notification of a non-conforming performance and a timely request for performance in the case of a complete non-performance.

That said, there is an important similarity found in the notion that enforced performance is not available in the case where the aggrieved buyer could have mitigated the impact on the seller by taking reasonable measures in the form of a substitute transaction. Nonetheless, there is a significant difference when taking into account that the availability of replacement goods is only considered as a limitation to enforced performance under Dutch and Chinese contract law where this follows from the principle of reasonableness and fairness, and good faith respectively, while it is a part of the default notion of the reluctance to award a claim for enforced performance under the contract law of Singapore. The practical solution lies in the regulation of the notion of reasonably obtainable goods in the contractual stipulations and the legal consequences deriving from a failure of the buyer to obtain these goods where this is required. The operative effect of this route is, however, significantly limited where a contract is governed by Singapore contract law and the court establishes that the buyer is indirectly enforced (by means of contractual stipulations) to bring about a certain state of affairs.

A similar complexity arises from the common law barrier of constant supervision, although it appears that this doctrine is losing its influence in Singapore. Nonetheless, constant supervision may still be imposed by the court as a counter-exemption to the already limited availability of enforced performance of non-monetary obligations arising under a commercial sales contract. This may result in complicated situations in the context of international commercial sales transactions which involve parties from the civil and common law traditions, in particular when it concerns a sales contract across the borders of the three investigated jurisdictions. This is undesirable and, more importantly, it contradicts the objective of the three investigated jurisdictions to bring about a trade-friendly contract law regime. It is, therefore, advocated here that those involved in commercial sales contracts across civil and common law borders, and national legislators, pay more attention to the middle-ground position adopted by the unification instruments, in particular, the CISG and DCFR. It is demonstrated that these legal instruments employ a balanced structure which recognises the necessity of protection of the performance interest and protection of the interest of the non-performing party against abuse, and they provide sufficient flexibility for the dynamics of international trade. Moreover, they bring about a middle-ground which addresses civil and common law fundamental principles, especially the PICC. Nonetheless, this research also shows that every unification instrument offers a unique framework of interwoven principles, which makes it impossible to employ a cherry-picking approach. Moreover, the way the unification instruments have structured the barriers to enforced performance is not flawless. It is also for this reason that the principles cannot simply be copied or mixed,[1680] without taking account of the details discussed in this section.

1680 *E.g.* the text of the CISG appears to indicate that a claim for enforced performance is available where damages are exempted, although this effect is not intended.

7 Enforcement measures

7.1 Introduction

271. *Preliminary* – From a comparative perspective, it is also of significant importance to consider the enforcement measures to help determine to what extent enforced performance of a commercial sales contract is effectively available. This assessment is directly related to the view of Dutch, Singapore and Chinese contract law on the extent the law is entitled to interfere with the freedom of commercial parties by compelling performance under the contract. This is obviously treacherous ground because the degree of personal involvement of the seller to a commercial sales contract may vary considerably, although it may be assumed that this argument is less relevant in an international commercial context where parties contracted for the delivery of goods.

The following discussion about the available enforcement measures revolves around four instruments to provide the aggrieved party with the very thing it bargained for. First, enforcement by seizure of the goods (section 7.2), which is most suitable where the goods still exist and cannot be obtained from another source. The second instrument entails judicial leave to acquire substitute goods at the expense of the seller (section 7.3). This alternative method of enforcement is particularly appropriate where delivery by the seller has become impossible. The third instrument concerns a method of securing compliance by means of a judicial penalty (*i.e. astreinte*) (section 7.4). As for the latter, the PICC entails an option to impose a monetary fine in order to secure the compliance with a court order for enforced performance.[1681] However, the procedure for the levying of this financial sanction, as well as its admissibility, is left to the discretion of the national court adjudicating the dispute.[1682] It is also important to bear in mind that even if the national court of the *lex fori* (the law of the jurisdiction in which the action for enforced performance is brought) imposes a monetary fine, this may cause significant difficulties where the country, other than the *forum* state, does not recognise this measure to secure obedience.[1683] In addition to the three judicial instruments mentioned above, the fourth enforcement measure concerns the ability of contracting parties to compel each other to performance of the contract by stipulating that, upon a failure in performance of the contract (*e.g.* non-delivery of the goods), a stipulated amount of money is owed to the aggrieved party (section 7.5). In this context, specific attention is paid to the importance of distinguishing the meaning

---

1681 Art 7.2.4(1) PICC.

1682 Vogenauer 2015 (n 19) art 7.2.4 para 2; Smits 2008 (n 871) 19, s 3.1.1.3.

1683 Vogenauer 2015 (n 19) art 7.2.4 para 2.

of penalty and liquidated damages clauses in a commercial sales contracts involving parties from the three investigated jurisdictions and, more generally, when commercial parties are trading across civil and common law borders.

7.2 Action for handing over the goods

272. *Preliminary* – This section briefly discusses to what extent the aggrieved buyer is capable of compelling the seller to deliver the goods as instructed by the court. This, in effect, means that the focus is put on the specific rules to provide operative effect to an order for enforced performance. The outcome of this discussion is used to determine the extent to which the subject legal systems are truly capable of protecting an aggrieved buyer's performance interest after its entitlement to delivery is established by the court.

> *Illustration* – Suppose that a technology company (seller) concludes a contract with an international consultancy firm (buyer) for the delivery of 500 smartphones by 1 September 2018. The seller fails to deliver the smartphones and the buyer brings a claim to court for enforced performance of the seller's delivery obligation. The court provides the latter with an enforcement order, but the seller is not willing to comply with the award.

273. *Domestic approaches* – Under Dutch law, the process of enforcement of the obligation to deliver the goods as stipulated in the contract, starts with a judgement for performance of the delivery obligation. On the basis of this title of enforcement, the bailiff makes an 'attachment' (in Dutch this is called an 'exploot') of execution.[1684] In order to actually enforce the court's judgement, the bailiff (on request of the aggrieved buyer) must serve the title of enforcement to the non-performing seller.[1685] Simultaneously or subsequently, the bailiff must demand compliance with the court's judgement within a designated period.[1686] In the case where the seller does not deliver the goods to the buyer within the stipulated period for delivery, the bailiff may 'attach' the goods in order to execute the judgement.[1687] In other words, the bailiff may take away the goods from the seller and subsequently hand them over to the buyer.[1688] This form of attachment in execution does not require a preceding leave of the court to levy such an attachment.

1684 Art 440(1)(b) Dutch Code of Civil Procedure.
1685 Art 430(3) Dutch Code of Civil Procedure.
1686 Art 439(1)(2) Dutch Code of Civil Procedure.
1687 Art 439(1) Dutch Code of Civil Procedure.
1688 Smits 2008 (n 871) 21.

274. Singapore law is familiar with a form of direct execution of an order for the supply of specific or ascertained goods, albeit within the boundaries discussed in section 4.4.3. This means, in effect, that an aggrieved buyer should first obtain a court order for enforced performance of the seller's obligation to deliver the goods as stipulated in the contract. Following this procedure, the buyer may claim for judicial leave for enforcement, by means of a writ of execution in the form of an order for the delivery of goods (*i.e.* writ of specific delivery). However, enforcement is only available where the initial judgement does not give the seller the alternative of paying the assessed value of the goods.[1689] Where a writ of specific delivery is provided, an enforcement officer of the court may seize the specified or ascertained goods and deliver them to the buyer.[1690]

275. In line with the Dutch and Singapore approach, Chinese law also entails a multi-step process, albeit that the actual undertaking follows a different path. The general starting point, consistent with the law of the Netherlands and Singapore, is that the aggrieved buyer must first obtain an order for enforced performance of the seller's obligation. Under the law of China, the enforcement of this judgement refers to the conduct of the enforcement organ of the court, which is carried out according to legal procedure and within the power of the state to compel the seller to fulfil its obligations as specified in the court's order.[1691] When the seller does not comply with the judgement for performance, the aggrieved buyer may apply to the court for execution of the judgement for performance of the seller's obligation, or the judge may refer the matter to the execution officer.[1692] Once the adjudicating court provides its ruling, the execution officer, after receiving the court's order, shall issue an enforcement notice to the non-performing seller, requiring it to deliver the goods within a designated period. In the case the seller fails to deliver the goods within this period, the enforcement officer may take enforcement measures.[1693] The measure of enforcement taken by the court is to conduct enforcement if the seller fails to deliver the goods specified in the judgement.[1694] This means that where the goods subject to enforcement are specified in its initial order, the delivery of these goods shall be enforced.[1695] If the goods have been destroyed or extinguished, compensation may be made by converting the goods (as described in the contract) into money with the consent of both parties. Where the two parties fail to reach a consensus on the converted compensation through

1689 <https://www.supremecourt.gov.sg/rules/court-processes/civil-proceedings/post-trial-matters/enforcement-proceedings> accessed on 30 October 2018.

1690 *Ibid.*

1691 Shizhou Wang, *Civil Procedure in China* (Kluwer Law International 2014) para 420.

1692 Art 236 Civil Procedure Law of the People's Republic of China (2017); Shizhou Wang 2014 (n 1691) para 426.

1693 Art 240 Civil Procedure Law of the People's Republic of China (2017); Shizhou Wang 2014 (n 1691) para 431.

1694 Art 252 Civil Procedure Law of the People's Republic of China (2017); Shizhou Wang 2014 (n 1691) para 439.

1695 Art 4 Interpretation of the Supreme People's Court on the Application of the Civil Procedure Law of the People's Republic of China (2015).

negotiation, the court shall terminate the enforcement procedure, and the aggrieved buyer may claim for a separate lawsuit.[1696]

276. *Comparative analyses* – The Netherlands, Singapore and China all envisage a situation where a judicial order for enforced performance amounts to an action for the delivery of the goods to the buyer, although the illustration below shows that the process to achieve this result varies considerably between the three jurisdictions. The text boxes in red entail a step requiring judicial interference, and the text boxes in blue represent an action taken by an enforcement officer. From this overview it follows that under Dutch law, an order for the delivery of goods is self-executing, in the sense that it can be directly enforced by an enforcement officer. Hence, an additional court ruling is generally not required. This form of direct execution is not a familiar concept in the contract law of Singapore and China, because in both legal systems a judicial order for the delivery of goods still requires a separate ruling of the court in order to bring about the actual result of the initial judgement.

The above considerations bring about the notion that the dogmatic basis from which the three legal systems approach the availability of enforced performance is not necessarily reflected in the ability of the aggrieved buyer to actually obtain the goods. In other words, it is advocated here that the actual availability of enforced performance can only be determined after a detailed assessment of the applicable enforcement rules. In view of this, it should be noted that the present section reveals that the significant strong protection of the buyer's performance interest under Dutch contract law is not counterbalanced by restrictions on the ability of the buyer to effect enforced performance. The opposite is true for the contract law of China: the ability of the aggrieved party to give effect to a judicial order for enforced performance depends on the outcome of two additional legal steps. It appears that the contract law of Singapore occupies an intermediate position in this regard. Nonetheless, it may be assumed that (compared to Dutch and Chinese contract law) greater protection of the seller's interest is offered when taking into account that enforced performance of non-monetary obligations arising from a commercial sales contract is blocked when continued supervision of the court is necessary in order to ensure fulfilment of the contract.

At a practical level, the performance interest of the buyer in the example provided in paragraph 272 appears to be best protected by Dutch contract law because a judicial order for enforced performance suffices to directly acquire the goods, by means of an enforcement officer without any additional court ruling. Nonetheless, the court may frustrate enforcement by the seller in a summary proceeding, if on demand of the latter, the court

1696 Art 494 Interpretation of the Supreme People's Court on the Application of the Civil Procedure Law of the People's Republic of China (2015).

establishes that enforcement is not justified.[1697] Under Singapore or Chinese law such a procedure is not necessary since the aggrieved buyer is obliged to take additional steps to give effect to the judicial order for enforced performance. Despite the differences in the procedures set out above, the legal systems share the fundamental notion that the seller's interests against abuse requires judicial protection. This takes the form of summary proceedings under Dutch law, and the imposition of additional judicial actions under Singapore and Chinese law.

Enforced performance, by obtaining the goods from the seller, may be barred by the courts where the initial order is based on factual and legal errors, or when there is proof of new facts or circumstances which emerged subsequent to the judgement and rendering performance subjectively or objectively impossible. On a practical note, those involved in commercial sales involving perishable goods across the borders of the subject legal systems may benefit substantially from giving due consideration to the actual effect of a judicial order for enforced performance and the timeframe within which actual execution is available.

1697 *Ritzen v Hoekstra* Dutch Supreme Court 22 April 1983, ECLI:NL:PHR:1983:AG4575, NJ 1984, 145.

Figure 16 Action for the actual delivery of the goods as stipulated in the contract

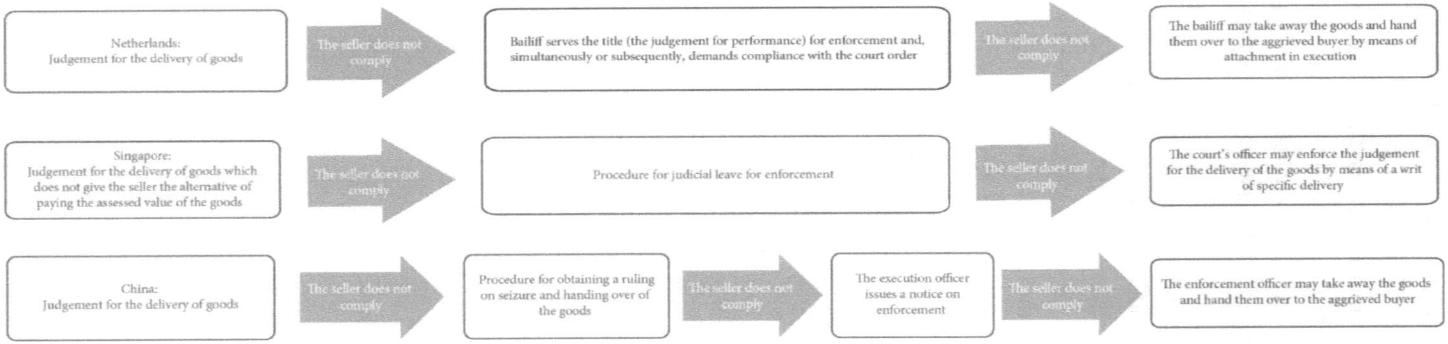

7.3 OBTAINING SUBSTITUTE GOODS AT THE EXPENSE OF THE SELLER

277. *Preliminary* – Where delivery of goods is barred (section 6.2) or non-conforming goods are delivered, but the buyer is able to procure substitute goods from another supplier, the question arises as to whether the buyer may do so at the expense of the seller if the former does not wish to avoid the contract, or where the requirements for avoidance are not fulfilled. The buyer may also be interested in obtaining substitute goods and having the costs covered by the non-performing party where the process of forcing the non-performing seller to deliver the goods takes a lot or just too much time in view of the perishability of the goods concerned, or is undesired for other reasons. The aforementioned objections are especially true in the case of a delivery obligation under an international commercial sales contract. It is questionable, however, to what extent the CISG can be of help in this regard since it is not clear whether the Convention allows an aggrieved buyer to obtain substitute goods and claim for the expenses incurred where the buyer is not entitled to avoidance of the contract.[1698] Therefore, the following draws attention to the ability of the three investigated jurisdictions to provide more satisfactory and less complicated solutions to circumvent the questionable legal inroads to deal with the uncertainties arising under the CISG in this regard.[1699]

> *Illustration* – An international semiconductor company located country X, purchases specific equipment for the development of a chipmaker. The equipment is necessary to complete a collaborative research project with a client, which is conducted at the facilities of the latter. Because the delivered equipment does not meet the relevant safety standards, the client announces that it will cancel the contract with the semiconductor if the equipment is not replaced within two weeks. The latter explains the situation to the manufacturer (*i.e.* seller) of the equipment and demands replacement in accordance with the contractual stipulations. The manufacturer refuses to comply with this request and the question arises whether the semiconductor may purchase substitute equipment from another supplier and claim for the payment of incurred expenses by the manufacturer.

278. *Domestic approaches* – In addition to the enforcement instrument of seizure discussed above, Dutch law adopted the principle that where a seller does not deliver the goods in accordance with the contract (due to an attributable or non-attributable cause) a Dutch

1698 See the comparative analyses in paragraph 281 for a discussion about the solutions to circumvent this issue; Eric E Bergsten and Stefan Kröll, *International Arbitration and International Commercial Law: Synergy, Convergence, and Evolution: Liber Amicorum Eric Bergsten* (Wolters Kluwer 2012), 588, 589.

1699 *Ibid.*

court may, on request of the aggrieved buyer, authorise the latter to procure replacement goods.[1700] This means that the buyer may obtain substitute goods itself, or ask a third party to do so, at the expense of the seller. In anticipation of a seller's failure to comply with an order for enforced performance, the buyer may combine its request for judicial leave with a claim for enforced performance, but this is not required. Hence, the aggrieved buyer may ask for authorisation to procure the goods without obtaining an order for enforced performance. This method of enforcement is appropriate where the buyer has a significant interest (*e.g.* in subsequent sales) in obtaining the goods from another source as soon as the seller fails to comply with its delivery obligation. It may also be helpful where the aggrieved buyer is not entitled to claim for damages because the non-performing party is not at fault for its failure to deliver the goods. Also in these instances, the aggrieved buyer may ask the court to provide judicial leave to obtain substitute goods at the seller's expense. The buyer can limit the risk that the incurred costs of this undertaking cannot be recovered from the seller, by ordering the payment of such expenses directly when claiming for authorisation.[1701] In instances where such a claim is granted, the aggrieved buyer is provided with an enforceable court order (*i.e.* additional judicial intervention is not required after the aggrieved buyer obtained the substitute goods and requires payment of the costs incurred). Aside from an order authorising the buyer to buy the goods at the seller's expense, the buyer may also obtain the goods when the seller is not able to deliver the goods due to *force majeure*.[1702] Insofar as international trade is concerned, the aforementioned option is most helpful when a legal impediment (*e.g.* criminalising the sale of certain products to a foreign party) makes it impossible for the seller to deliver the goods, but the buyer is able to obtain the goods by execution because they already arrived at the port of destination.[1703] In this situation, the availability of obtaining the goods by execution is based on the notion that a contractual obligation does not cease to exist in the situation where *force majeure* makes it objectively impossible for all time or temporarily impossible for the promisor (or a third party) to perform the contract.[1704]

279. Singapore law is not familiar with the instrument of judicial leave for obtaining substitute goods at the expense of the seller as an alternative for enforced performance. This may not even be necessary due to the ability of the aggrieved party to obtain substitute

---

1700 Art 3:299(1)(2) DCC; De Jong, Krans and Wissink 2018 (n 194) 97.

1701 Art 3:299(1) DCC

1702 Art 6:79 DCC deals with the consequences of non-performance. See in this regard art 491 Dutch Civil Procedure; Smits 2008 (n 871) 19; De Jong 2017 (n 1321) para 36; Sieburgh, *Asser 6-I* (n 363) paras 360, 376.

1703 Dutch Parliamentary History Book 6 (n 204) 275, 486; Sieburgh, *Asser 6-I* (n 363) paras 360, 376.

1704 Haas 2009 (n 206) 288.

goods and to claim the expenses incurred as a form of damages.[1705] This self-help method of obtaining the thing the buyer bargained for follows directly from the default principle that the courts in equity generally do not intervene when alternatives are available on the market at an ascertainable price (section 4.4.3). It is also an easily accessible remedy as damages, as a cure for a failure in performance, are available as of right. It is also important to note that the buyer is not obliged to claim for enforced performance simultaneously or subsequently with an order for judicial leave, but is free to acquire the promised goods itself and claim for payment of the costs incurred. In other words, the undertaking of obtaining the goods at the expense of the seller is not regarded as an enforcement method, but as a self-help remedy which results in a claim for damages.[1706]

280. The law of China takes a civil law inspired approach by adopting the instrument of judicial leave to obtain the goods as promised under a commercial sales contract. This means in effect that where the non-performing seller, against whom enforcement is sought, fails to deliver the goods as specified in the judgement, as required by a notice of enforcement, the court may authorise the buyer or any other person (in a separate procedure) to obtain the goods at the expense of the seller.[1707] The amount of expenses shall be determined by the court according to the circumstances of the case, and they need to be prepaid by the seller within the designated time limit. If the latter fails to make payment, the court may enforce the payment of the expenses.[1708]

281. *Comparative analysis* – Where a commercial sales contract entails the delivery of goods which can be obtained from another source, the law of the Netherlands, Singapore and China each aim to provide the buyer with the very thing it bargained for, albeit that they significantly differ in the way this result can be achieved. The divergence directly follows from diametrically opposed viewpoints on the availability of enforced performance of a non-monetary obligation. This means in effect that where a commercial sales contract entails the delivery of goods which can also be obtained from another source, and Dutch contract law applies, the buyer may demand judicial leave for obtaining substitute goods at the expense of the seller.[1709] Chinese contract law does not qualify the undertaking of obtaining substitute goods as a separate enforcement measure, but has taken the approach that this action (obtaining authorisation of the court) is a method of executing a court

1705 Treitel 1998 (n 55) 64.

1706 Treitel 1998 (n 55) 64.

1707 Art 252 Civil Procedure Law of the People's Republic of China 2017; Shizhou Wang 2014 (n 1691) para 439.

1708 Art 504 Interpretation of the Supreme People's Court on the Application of the Civil Procedure Law of the People's Republic of China 2015.

1709 See for the position in French law: Treitel 1998 (n 55) 57.

order for enforced performance.[1710] Despite these differences (which can be explained by analysing the influence of the French civil law tradition in the Netherlands and the German civil law tradition in China),[1711] the process of obtaining substitute goods and claiming for the expenses incurred under the law of the Netherlands and China is considered a direct enforcement method which lies within the discretionary power of the courts.[1712] Nonetheless, it appears that the power of Dutch and Chinese courts to refuse an aggrieved buyer to obtain substitute goods at the expense of the seller is limited due to the default principle that enforced performance of (non-) monetary obligations is available as of right.

The Singapore view on the matter is slightly different due to the way this legal system regulates the relationship between the availability of enforced performance and damages. This means in effect that the aggrieved buyer is as of right entitled to demand payment of the costs incurred for obtaining substitute goods as damages where the seller failed to deliver the goods in accordance with the contract. When assessing the above considerations in the view of the example mentioned under paragraph 277, it may be assumed that the three subject jurisdictions allow the semiconductor to obtain the equipment from another supplier at the expense of the manufacturer. Nonetheless, there appears to be an uneven distribution of risks when considering the effect of the applicable principles. As for Dutch contract law, the aggrieved buyer can be provided with a court order entailing authorisation to procure the goods from another source and to obtain the payment of the expenses when incurred. Although Singapore law is not familiar with such a direct enforcement instrument, it acts on the notion that the aggrieved buyer may recover the expenses as damages after procuring the promised goods from a third party. Thus, in both situations the aggrieved buyer is entitled to payment when the costs have actually incurred. By contrast, the courts of China adopted the approach that the amount of the expenses (to be determined by the court) are to be paid by the seller in advance. From a practical perspective, the aggrieved buyer involved in commercial sales transactions across the borders of the three investigated legal systems may be forced to seek recourse to an action for damages, although it only has an interest in obtaining the goods elsewhere without affecting the existence of the contract. It is therefore submitted here that when obtaining the goods directly from the seller is factually troublesome or disruptive, the buyer could benefit from contractual stipulations which take into account a potential situation of non-delivery, forcing the buyer to obtain the goods from another supplier and obtaining payment from the initial seller.

In view of the above suggestion, it is important to draw attention to the fact that where the buyer claims for damages on the basis of a cover purchase, the question arises of whether

1710 See for the position in German law: Treitel 1998 (n 55) 57.

1711 Treitel 1998 (n 55) 57.

1712 The text of the civil procedure law of the Netherlands and China both stipulate the the court may authorise the aggrieved party; Art 3:299(1)(3) DCC and art 252 Civil Procedure Law of the People's Republic of China 2017 respectively.

the CISG requires avoidance of the contract.[1713] It appears that the CISG allows the buyer to demand payment of the costs of a substitute transaction, in instances of (partial) non-delivery and non-conformity, without avoidance of the contract. There are two lines of thought in this regard. The first approach entails the notion that the aggrieved buyer is entitled to claim for payment of expenses incurred as damages as a compensation of the seller's failure in performance.[1714] If the buyer is still in possession of the non-conforming goods, the value must be deducted from the costs of the substitute goods. The second approach is based on the idea that the buyer, without avoidance of the contract, is entitled to bring a claim to court for the costs of the cover transaction as expenses for mitigating losses.[1715] In view of both approaches, it appears that in the situation where the requirements for avoidance are not fulfilled or avoidance is not desired, the CISG allows an aggrieved buyer to obtain substitute goods and claim for the expenses incurred.[1716] Nonetheless, contracting parties should give due consideration that there are two crucial differences between both approaches. In instances where the aggrieved buyer claims for payment of the cover transaction as a measure to prevent or mitigate losses, the former bears the proof of the damages incurred if it would have not entered into a substitute transaction. In instances where a buyer claims for payment of the cover purchase as a compensation for the seller's failure in performance (without avoidance of the contract), the recoverable costs are limited to compensation of foreseeable losses. In view of these considerations, the preferable approach is to allow the aggrieved buyer to claim damages under the compensation provision (which does not require avoidance) for recovery of the costs of a substitute transaction when this is necessary to prevent or mitigate damages. From a practical viewpoint, allowing the aggrieved buyer to obtain payment of a substitute transaction without avoidance of the contract is of particular importance to protect the buyer with a legitimate interest in performance of, for example, a subsequent delivery obligation which becomes due in the following period. The notion that avoidance is not required also protects the buyer when unwinding of the contract results in unnecessary costly actions. For those seeking an alternative to the above, it is noted that the PICC, PECL, PECL, DCFR and draft PACL do not provide an express provision which allows the aggrieved party to claim for recovery of the costs of a cover transaction without avoidance of the contract. In view of the foregoing comments and the practical implications of the discussed conceptual differences, contractual stipulations dealing with the admissibility of conducting a cover purchase and claiming the price as damages may prove to be most useful.

1713 Art 75 CISG.

1714 Art 74 CISG; Bergsten et al (n 1698) 585–590.

1715 Art 77 CISG; Bergsten et al (n 1698) 588, 589.

1716 Art 74 CISG; Schwenzer 2016 (n 91) para 23.

7.4 Judicial penalty

282. *Preliminary* – In addition to the direct enforcement of an order for performance discussed above, civil and common law systems have also adopted (indirect) enforcement instruments to encourage a promisor to comply with an order for enforced performance. The most common measures are the imposition of a penal sum, and committal. The latter may result in imprisonment or a monetary fine for disobedience of a judgement for enforced performance. The potentially far-reaching (personal) impact of punishment for contempt of court is said to be one of the reasons that the courts in common law jurisdictions are reluctant to provide an order for enforced performance.[1717] In the following, a judicial penalty is to be understood as an order for payment of a fixed sum for each period (usually a day) of non-performance. This indirect enforcement instrument is independent of damages. In the realm of commercial sales, a judicial penalty is the most important instrument to ensure performance, and could be most useful to secure delivery of the goods (or to compel a buyer to take delivery where this is legally required or follows from the contractual stipulations).[1718] Therefore, the focus of the present section is on exploring some central aspects of judicial penalties to encourage performance. Generally, two categories of judicial penalties can be distinguished. Firstly, the *provisional* monetary penalty, which can only be recovered by the aggrieved buyer by means of a fresh application to the court. Secondly, the *definitive* monetary penalty which is not subject to revision of the court. The following discusses to what extent the means by which the enforcement instrument of a judicial penalty operates in the Netherlands, Singapore and China, and to what extent the approaches of the three jurisdictions differ. These findings are contrasted against the PICC which, unlike the other supranational legal instruments under consideration, entails the possibility to order a party to pay a judicial penalty as a coercive measure.

> *Illustration* – A company specialised in nutrition products, located in country X, sells a recently developed vitamin supplement to a producer of healthy snacks, located in country Y. The seller fails to deliver the vitamins on the agreed day and does not provide any clarity about the expected delivery date. The buyer has contributed to the development of the vitamins and its production process has been redesigned in such a way that the vitamins can easily be added to the products. In view of these considerations, the buyer has a specific interest in prompt delivery of the vitamins and, therefore, claims for enforced performance of the seller's delivery obligation. Simultaneously, the question

1717 Rowan (n 1649) 45.
1718 S 5.3.

arises to what extent compliance with such an order can be secured with a judicial penalty payable for each day of delay.

283. *Domestic approaches* – The procedural law of the Netherlands is only familiar with a definitive judicial penalty as a method to enforce compliance with an order for enforced performance of non-monetary obligations to do or not to do something. For example, the aggrieved buyer may claim for enforced performance in the form of a cure by making a fresh delivery, combined with an *astreinte* (judicial penalty). On demand of the aggrieved buyer, the court could also order the seller to allow the buyers on its premises and to take away the goods identified in the contract, combined with a judicial penalty of, for example, €2,500 for each week that the seller fails to comply with the court order, with a maximum of €10,000.[1719] The applicable statutory principles enable the court, on the demand of the aggrieved party, to fix a judicial penalty for each specified period (*e.g.* day, week, month or year) that the party who is ordered to perform does not comply with the judgement.[1720] The courts are given the discretionary power to determine the amount of the judicial penalty.[1721] It is important to note that although the imposition of a judicial fine is entirely regulated by the state, the judicial penalty incurred must be paid to the aggrieved party,[1722] and therefore, could be considered as a form of private fine.

284. A judicial penalty as a coercive device seems to have no corresponding instrument in the Singapore legal system, although it recognises the concept of compulsion by means of a civil contempt proceeding which is appropriate where a person intentionally disobeys a court order to do or not to do something.[1723] A contracting party who commits contempt of court shall be liable to be punished with a fine to be paid to the court, or imprisonment for a specific term. The amount of the fine and the duration of the imprisonment depends on the court exercising the power to punish for contempt.[1724] The High Court and the Court of Appeal may impose a fine not exceeding S$100,000, while the State Court and any other court can mete out a maximum fine of S$20,000.[1725] It is held that the aforementioned fines should not be used where the sanction is ineffective in securing

1719 *Pluto Sport v VOF Marber et al* District Court 's-Gravenhage 22 November 2011, ECLI:NL:RBSGR:2010:BO4625.

1720 Art 611a *ff* Dutch Code of Civil Procedure; Hijma and Olthof 2017 (n 248) para 94(1).

1721 Hijma and Olthof 2017 (n 248) para 94(1).

1722 Smits 2008 (n 871) 23; M B Beekhoven van den Boezem 'commentaar op artikel 611c' in P Vlas and TFE Tjong Tjin Tai (eds), *Groene Serie Burgerlijke Rechtsvordering* (Wolters Kluwer 2017).

1723 Administration of Justice (Protection) Act 2016 (19), s 4(1)(a).

1724 Administration of Justice (Protection) Act 2016 (19), s 12(1).

1725 Administration of Justice (Protection) Act 2016 (19), s 12(1)(a)(b).

compliance.[1726] This is the case where performance is impossible. It appears that the imposition of a monetary fine is also not available when it undermines the freedom of contract (*i.e.* certainty which parties are entitled to expect of the law).

285. To fully grasp the enforcement scheme of civil judgements under the law of China, it is important to start with the earlier discussed principle that the aggrieved party to the contract must apply for enforcement of an order for performance.[1727] The actual enforcement shall be carried out by a special enforcement officer from the court.[1728] After receiving the application for enforcement, an enforcement notice is sent to the non-performing party encompassing the demand to comply with the judgement for enforced performance.[1729] If the non-performing party fails to fulfil the obligations specified in the notice, it is required to report its property situation.[1730] Where the non-performing party refuses to report its property situation or makes a false report, the People's Court may impose a fine or detention on the person to be enforced, to be paid to the state.[1731] In addition, the refusal to carry out legally effective judgements or rulings of the courts are regarded as an obstruction of civil proceedings. This means in effect that where a seller fails to deliver the goods as specified in the judgement, the court may impose a fine by a written decision.[1732] To date, the amount of a fine on a commercial party shall not be less than 50,000 yuan but it cannot exceed 1 million yuan.[1733]

286. *Comparative analysis* – While the legal basis of an order for delivery of goods is a part of the contract law of the Netherlands, Singapore and China, the instruments to put pressure on the non-performing seller to comply with the court's order is not necessarily considered as substantive law. Consequently, a claim for financial sanctions to compel the other party to perform the contract is subject to the *lex fori* (*i.e.* the law of the court adjudicating the dispute) where the contract is governed by supranational principles of substantive law, such as the CISG. An exception to this is the situation where a commercial sales contract is governed by the PICC. The latter entails a possibility to force the non-performing party to comply with an order for enforced performance of (non-)monetary obligations arising from the contract by directing that the former is obliged to pay a judicial penalty if it does

1726 Micheal Chesterman, 'Contempt: In the Common Law, but Not the Civil Law' (1997) 46(3) The International and Comparative Law Quarterly 521.
1727 Art 236 CPL (2017).
1728 Art 240 CPL (2017).
1729 *Ibid.*
1730 Art 241 CPL (2017).
1731 *Ibid.*
1732 Arts 111(6), 114(4), 116 CPL (2017); Shizhou Wang 2014 (n 1691) para 159.
1733 Art 115 CPL (2017); Shizhou Wang 2014 (n 1691) para 162.

not comply with the order.[1734] This means in effect that a seller can be ordered to pay a judicial penalty when it does not adhere to an order for delivery of the goods in accordance with the agreed features, but also when a party is obliged to pay a certain amount to a third party or to open an escrow account. Under the PICC, the incurred judicial penalties have to be paid to the aggrieved party (equivalent of the *astreinte* under French law).[1735] This rule however does not apply if the law of the forum has adopted the rule that the penalty is paid to the state.[1736]

The above-described principle (of procedural nature) for monetary fines under the PICC stands in stark contrast with the scope and impact of a judicial penalty under Dutch, Singapore and Chinese contract law. A key difference with the approach taken by the PICC is that the three jurisdictions only allow the method of securing enforced performance by the imposition of a judicial fine for non-monetary obligations. Despite this similarity, the three investigated jurisdictions differ significantly in the way they have regulated the imposition of a judicial penalty. That is, under Dutch contract law, a judicial penalty is only available when it is requested by the aggrieved party, and incurred penalties are to be paid to the aggrieved party, which makes it a private fine. The court is only given discretionary power to determine the amount of the judicial fine. The Dutch law approach described above is completely unknown in Singapore and China as both legal systems adopt the principle that the courts are provided with the discretionary power to order a judicial fine to be paid to the state. This is a valid approach when considering the fact that the state is responsible for enforcement of the decision of the court. Nonetheless, where protection of the seller's interest is favoured, providing the court with so much discretionary power might result in a significant legal detriment for the buyer. This impairing effect is aggravated under the common law system of Singapore, because the imposition of a judicial fine is only available as a separate form of a judgement (*i.e.* committal for contempt), which suggests that its availability is significantly limited. Moreover, leading case law reveals that the courts follow the premise that the purpose of the law is not to punish wrongdoing but to satisfy the expectations of the party entitled to performance. This suggests that penal consequences of non-compliance with an order for enforced performance are not easily accepted by the court.

When placing the considerations above in the context of the example mentioned under paragraph 282, it appears that only under Dutch law is the court entitled to impose a judicial penalty on the request of the buyer. This is understandable as the latter is responsible for the actual enforcement. Where the contract is governed by Singapore or Chinese law,

1734 Art 7.2.4(1) PICC; Vogenauer 2015 (n 19) art 7.2.4 para 4.

1735 Art 7.2.4(1) PICC.

1736 Art 7.2.4(2) PICC; Ingeborg Schwenzer, 'Specific Performance and Damages according to the 1994 UNIDROIT Principles of International Commercial Contracts' (1998) 1(3) European Journal of Law Reform 289, 302.

it is not necessary to request a judicial penalty as this is autonomously decided by the court as an instrument to enforce its decision to deliver the vitamins to the buyer. Apart from the coercive effect of a judicial penalty in the two jurisdictions, the buyer lacks a substantive interest in the imposition of a penalty as it is not the ultimate beneficiary.

In the realm of international commercial sales contracts, parties could significantly benefit from a system which bridges the gap between the divergence in the availability of judicial penalties to compel the promisor to perform, in particular in view of the almost diametrically opposed discretionary power of the national courts to allow or disallow financial sanctions. However, the discussion in this section reveals that the regulation of monetary pressure to compel performance varies considerably between the two most important unification instruments for commercial sales transactions across civil and common law borders (*i.e.* the CISG and PICC). Nonetheless, at a practical level difficulties can be minimised by contractual stipulations which provide for sufficient financial pressure for performance of non-monetary obligations which give due consideration to the common law prohibition of coercive measures which might force a contracting party to bring about a certain state of affairs.

In view of the foregoing, it should be noted that the possibility of ordering a judicial fine as a method of securing compliance with an order for the delivery of goods may affect the legitimacy of the (common law) constant supervision argument, which is used to justify the narrow scope of an order for enforced performance.[1737] The rationale is that a judicial fine, as a coercive measure, does not impose stringent constraints on the court, nor does it affect the liberty of the non-performing party. Furthermore, the inapplicability of contempt proceedings in the case of sale transactions between two commercial parties, and the deterrent effect of the imposition of monetary fines payable to the court (to remove the objective of unjust enrichment) makes the latter an appropriate alternative.[1738] The positive side-effect of a judicial penalty as a coercive measure in the civil procedure law of the Netherlands and China is found in its ability to lessen the caseload of the courts dealing with claims for enforced performance of a commercial sales contract because it encourages the non-performing party to act in accordance with the judgement.[1739]

7.5 Contractual penalty

287. *Preliminary* – This section focuses on the ability of contracting parties to protect their performance interest by means of a contractual penalty clause compelling the promisor

1737 S 6.6.
1738 Rowan (1649) 59.
1739 Smits 2008 (n 871) 19; Hofmann 1976 (n 84) 126.

to perform the thing it promised to do. A discussion about the enforceability of contractual penalty clauses is particularly relevant when it concerns, for example, arrangements for the delivery of goods accompanied by certain documents essential for customs clearance, when timely delivery is essential due to other transport arrangements, or when it is required that the goods are accompanied with a legalised document that they are manufactured in accordance with particular producing standards. In these situations where there is a special interest in performance, contractual provisions in the form of penalty clauses may play a significant role in protection of the parties' performance interest. In view of this, the following is concerned with determining the enforceability of contractual penalty clauses as an enforcement measure and how the approaches taken by the subject legal systems relate to their primary understanding of the necessity to protect the enforceability of non-monetary obligations under a commercial sales contract. This analysis is indicative for the widespread influence of the primary difference between the civil and common law traditional understanding of the enforceability of non-monetary obligations as found in the three investigated jurisdictions and the approach taken by the unification instruments in this regard. The following discussion is of particular importance for those involved in international commercial sales contracts who seek to influence the default response of the subject legal systems.

> *Illustration* – A manufacturer located in country A concludes a sales contract with a collaborative of the ten largest research hospitals located in country B, for the sale of customised MRI equipment. The sales contract provides that, in the event the manufacturer fails to deliver the equipment by 26 December 2018, a fixed sum shall be payable at a stipulated rate per week irrespective of the actual harm caused by the delay. In this situation the question arises whether the aforementioned contractual provision is enforceable in court and thus capable of protecting the buyer's performance interest.

288. *Domestic approaches* – Dutch contract law entails the principle that any clause, which provides that a promisor must pay a sum of money or perform another obligation, should it fail in the performance of its obligation, is considered to be a penalty clause – irrespective of whether this is to repair damages or only to encourage performance.[1740] Coupled with the default availability of enforced performance of non-monetary obligations, the enforceability of a contractual penalty clause is in full accord with the fundamental notion of Dutch contract law that the purpose of the contract is performance.

The enforceability of a contractual penalty clause is limited by three principles. Firstly, the promisee is not entitled to demand performance of both the penalty clause and the

1740 Art 6:91 DCC.

obligation to which the penalty clause relates.[1741] However, penalties for delay in performance would allow the aggrieved buyer to sue for delivery of the goods and payment of penalty, potentially on pain of an additional judicial penalty for non-compliance.[1742] Secondly, whatever is due pursuant to a penalty clause takes the place of statutory damages.[1743] In the alternative, contracting parties could include a clause which stipulates that the aggrieved party is entitled to choose between the contractual penalty or statutory damages.[1744] The parties could also agree that contractual penalties and statutory damages will be payable to the aggrieved party in the case of non-performance.[1745] Thirdly, contractual penalty clauses do not result in payable penalties where the failure in the performance of the obligation cannot be attributed to the promisor.[1746] Another important point is that commercial parties are entitled to deviate from the statutory limitations on penalty clauses in their sales contract.[1747]

The impact of a contractual penalty clause can be reduced by the court if it is evident that fairness so requires. The court, however, may not award the promisee less than the damages due by law for failure in performance.[1748] Moreover, the court may award supplementary damages on the demand of the aggrieved party if it is evident that fairness so requires; these are in addition to the stipulated penalty intended to take the place of damages by law.[1749] Importantly, contracting parties are not allowed to derogate from the power of the court to reduce a penalty clause or award supplementary damages.[1750] Nonetheless, the risk of reduction of contractual penalties by the court can be reduced by stipulating that the occurrence of certain situations (described in the contract) are at the buyer's or seller's risk.[1751]

289. Singapore contract law does not allow enforcement of contractual provisions regarding the payment of an agreed sum when the clause is found to be penal in nature; an agreed sum that qualifies as liquidated damages, on the other hand, is considered as a valid method of protecting the parties' performance interest. The traditional (narrow) test for determining whether an agreed sum is penal or qualifies as a valid liquidated damages clause requires an assessment of the question whether the stipulated sum is a pre-estimate of loss; if the

1741 Art 6:92(1) DCC.
1742 De Jong, Krans and Wissink 2018 (n 194) 216.
1743 Art 6:92(2) DCC.
1744 De Jong, Krans and Wissink 2018 (n 194) 216.
1745 De Jong, Krans and Wissink 2018 (n 194) 216.
1746 Art 6:92(3) DCC.
1747 De Jong, Krans and Wissink 2018 (n 194) 216.
1748 Art 94(1) DCC.
1749 Art 94(2) DCC.
1750 Art 94(3) DCC.
1751 De Jong, Krans and Wissink 2018 (n 194) 219.

stipulated amount is not a pre-estimate of loss, but so extravagant and unconscionable in comparison with the greatest loss that could conceivably prove to have followed from the failed performance, the agreed sum is considered to be penal in nature and thus unenforceable.[1752] The question of whether a contractual provision is a penalty clause or qualifies as a valid liquidated damages clause should be answered in light of the case *Philips Hong Kong Limited v The Attorney General of Hong Kong*, which brings about the principle that an agreed sum does not necessarily qualify as a penalty just because there are situations where the stipulated amount to be paid upon a failure in performance might be higher than the actual loss of the aggrieved party.[1753] This viewpoint is followed by Singapore courts and clearly reflected in *CLAAS Medical Centre Pte Ltd v Ng Boon Ching*.[1754] In this case, the Singapore Court of Appeal held that the question is 'whether the sum is so extravagant, having regard to the range of damages which the innocent party was likely to suffer, that it could not constitute a genuine estimate of the damages that he could have suffered'. The English case *Cavendish Square Holding BV v Makdessi* reveals a more cautious approach towards qualifying an agreed sum as a penalty clause.[1755] From this case derives the principle that the test for determining whether a contractual provision is a penalty is premised on whether the sum or remedy stipulated as a consequence of breach of contract is 'extravagant, exorbitant or unconscionable' with regard to the innocent party's legitimate interest in the performance of the contract. From the *Cavendish* case it follows that an agreed sum is considered to be a penalty clause when the stipulated amount is out of proportion (*i.e.* unconscionable, exorbitant or extravagant) to the plaintiff's legitimate interest. In other words, the *Cavendish* case implies a liberal view on the mechanism to determine the enforceability of agreed sums by considering the plaintiff's legitimate interest in enforcing the initial obligation to bring about a certain state of affairs in view of the stipulated amount payable by the non-performing party. The considerations in the *Cavendish* case are followed in Singapore,[1756] but there is also case law according to which

1752 *Dunlop Pneumatic Tyre Co Ltd v New Garage and Motor Co Ltd* [1915] AC 79; *Phoenix Heights Estate (Pte) Ltd v Lee Kay Guan* [1981–1982] SLR(R) 484; *Orchard Twelve Investments Pte Ltd v Golden Bay Realty Pte Ltd* [1985–1986] SLR(R) 723; *Hong Leong Finance Ltd v Tan Gin Huay* [1999] 1 SLR(R) 755 (SGCA); *CLAAS Medical Centre Pte Ltd v Ng Boon Ching* [2010] SGCA 3, (2010) 2 SLR 386 [67]; *Xia Zhengyan v Geng Changqing* [2015] 3 SLR 732; Phang et al 2012 (n 112) paras 23.019, 23.023; Phang and Goh 2012 (n 318) paras 1541–1548; Dora Neo, 'Specific Remedies and the Performance Interest in Singapore Contract Law' in Chen-Wishart, Loke and Ong 2016 (n 156) 209-210.

1753 [1993] 1 HKLR 296.

1754 *Hong Leong Finance v Tan Gin Huay* (n 1752); *T2 Networks Pte Ltd v Nasioncom Shn Bhd* (n 373); *CLAAS Medical Centre Pte Ltd v Ng Boon Ching* (n 1752).

1755 [2016] AC 1172.

1756 *iTronic Holdings Pte Ltd v Tan Swee Leon* [2016] SGHC 77; *Allplus Holdings Pte Ltd and others v Phoon Wui Nyen (Pan Weiyuan)* [2016] SGHC 144; *CIFG Special Assets Capital I Ltd v Polimet Pte Ltd* [2017] SGHC 22; *Seraya Energy Pte Ltd v Denka Advantech Pte Ltd and another suit (YTL PowerSeraya Pte Ltd, third party)* [2019] SGHC 2.

the *Cavendish* reformulation of the earlier mentioned genuine pre-estimate of loss test is not a part of the law of Singapore.[1757] Nonetheless, the Singapore cases following the *Cavendish* approach support the premise that contracting parties have a considerable leeway to encourage proper performance by putting economic pressure on the promisor. However, the Singapore Court of Appeal have not yet approved the *Cavendish* approach. It is, therefore, of paramount importance that contracting parties give due consideration to the above discussed boundaries of securing the parties' performance interest by agreed sums payable upon a failure in performance. In this context, another important point is that where the court finds reason to classify an agreed sum as a legally unenforceable penalty, the aggrieved party could alternatively sue for unliquidated damages rather than relying on the contractual clause or to frame its initial claim in unliquidated damages.[1758] In view of the aforemetioned freedom to claim for the most suitable remedy, it goes without saying that a claim for unliquidated damages is the best option where the stipulated sum is lower than the actual losses incurred by the aggrieved party.[1759]

290. The starting point under Chinese contract law is that contracting parties are allowed to include a penalty clause in their contract on the basis of the principle of freedom of contract and because it is held that, in a commercial context, such a clause is necessary to overcome potential difficulties to prove the extent of loss incurred.[1760] From this reasoning and the applicable statutory provision it follows that Chinese courts shall allow a penalty clause which is compensatory in nature.[1761] This is, however, not necessarily the case where the aggrieved party seeks to compel the other party to performance of the contract by means of a punitive penalty clause.[1762]

The disagreement follows from the notion that the statutory principle entailing the rules on penalty clauses is merely concerned with compensation of damages and, therefore, punitive penalty clauses are not enforceable.[1763] However, it is also submitted that the permissibility of punitive penalty clauses follows from the statutory principle of freedom of contract,[1764] although they are considered as an exemption to the rule that only

1757 *Hon Chin Kong v Yip Fook Mun* [2017] SGHC 286.

1758 Phang et al 2012 (n 112) para 23.021.

1759 Phang et al 2012 (n 112) para 23.021.

1760 Lei Chen, 'Damages and Specific Performance in Chinese Contract Law' in DiMatteo and Chen 2017 (n 19) 394.

1761 Art 114 CCL; Lei Chen, 'Damages and Specific Performance in Chinese Contract Law' in DiMatteo and Chen 2017 (n 19) 394.

1762 Lei Chen, 'Damages and Specific Performance in Chinese Contract Law' in DiMatteo and Chen 2017 (n 19) 394–395.

1763 Lei Chen, 'Damages and Specific Performance in Chinese Contract Law' in DiMatteo and Chen 2017 (n 19) 395; Bing Ling 2002 (n 229) paras 31, 445.

1764 Art 4 CCL; Lei Chen, 'Damages and Specific Performance in Chinese Contract Law' in DiMatteo and Chen 2017 (n 19) 394.

compensatory penalty clauses are allowed.[1765] It is further held that fault of the non-performing party can be required on the basis of the coercive nature of a penalty clause.[1766] This is an important deviation of the strict-liability approach of Chinese contract law. Nonetheless, it accords with the approach taken by the PICC which was a source of great inspiration for Chinese legislators in drafting the current contract law of China.[1767] The relevant principle enshrined in the PICC in this regard is that the aggrieved party is entitled to recover the agreed sum irrespective of the harm suffered, except where the sum payable is grossly excessive in relation to the harm resulting from the non-performance and to the other circumstances.[1768] In the case it is accepted that punitive penalty clauses are legitimate, it may be assumed that the aggrieved party may claim for enforcement of the penalty clause in conjunction with a claim for enforced performance or damages.[1769]

Considering the fact that there is no consensus on the question as to whether a punitive penalty clause shall be allowed by the court, the enforceability of a performance obligation is currently best protected by a compensatory penalty clause for a delay in performance of the contract.[1770] For determining the amount owed, contracting parties may include a clause which brings about the obligation to pay a fixed sum on a failure in performance or a method for the calculation of the amount of monetary compensation. Where the amount agreed on is lower than the damages incurred, the aggrieved party may petition the People's Court or an arbitration institution to make an increase. Where the stipulated amount is significantly higher than the damages incurred, the non-performing party may petition the People's Court or an arbitration institution to make an appropriate reduction.[1771] Nonetheless, it cannot be predicted with any degree of certainty that a compensatory penalty clause, which also encourages performance of the contractual obligations, can be used to strengthen or secure the default availability of enforced performance of non-monetary obligations under a commercial sales contract.

1765 Han Shiyan, 'The Performance Interest in Chinese Contract Law: Monetary Awards' in Chen-Wishart, Loke and Ong 2016 (n 156) 56.

1766 Han Shiyan, 'The Performance Interest in Chinese Contract Law: Monetary Awards' in Chen-Wishart, Loke and Ong 2016 (n 156) 56.

1767 André Janssen and Samuel C K Chau, 'CCL and Unidroit Principles' in DiMatteo and Chen 2017 (n 19) 449.

1768 Vogenauer 2015 (n 19) art 7.4.13 paras 15–16.

1769 Han Shiyan, 'The Performance Interest in Chinese Contract Law: Monetary Awards' in Chen-Wishart, Loke and Ong 2016 (n 156) 57.

1770 Art 114 CCL.

1771 Art 114 CCL.

Figure 17 Enforceability of penalty clauses

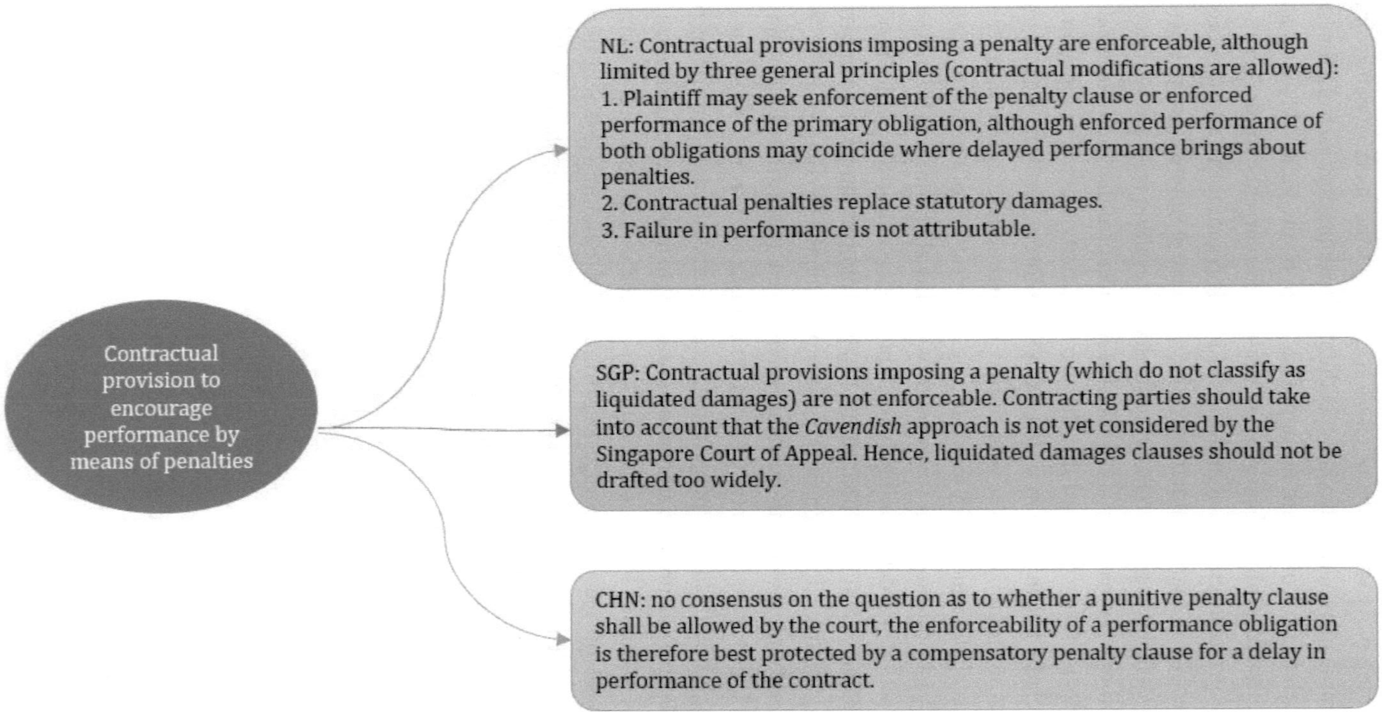

291. *Comparative analyses* – The preceding discussion reveals that there are basically three approaches towards the permissibility of a contractual penalty clause to compel the promisor to perform. The first approach entails the notion that a contractual penalty clause is allowed regardless of its compensatory or punitive nature, although excessive sums can be subject to judicial reduction and the occurrence of a non-excused failure in performance. This approach is adopted by Dutch contract law, as well as by the PICC, PECL and DCFR.[1772] Moreover, the legitimacy of a penalty clause, irrespective of its nature and the harm incurred, is in full accord with the default availability of enforced performance of non-monetary obligations, provided that the prerequisites are fulfilled and enforcement of the principal obligation is not barred.[1773]

The second approach entails the notion that punitive and compensatory penalty clauses derive from different statutory sources which could bring about a certain hierarchy, with compensatory penalty clauses the general rule and punitive penalty clauses the exception, which can be reduced by the court if the agreed sum is deemed excessive. It is suggested that this approach is adopted by the contract law of China, although the opposite can also be advocated. It is furthermore important to note that it is not clear as to whether fault is required or that the rules on contractual penalty clauses follow the strict-liability nature of the Chinese contract law remedial regime. It is suggested here that the differing opinions on the matter (and thus a potential unenforceable penalty clause) require close attention by those not familiar with the distinction between punitive and compensatory penalty clauses and when involved in cross-border commercial sales contracts which are governed by Chinese contract law.

The third, and most restrictive, approach can be found in the contract law of Singapore which adopted the common law principle that an agreed sum payable upon a failure in performance is not enforceable when it is found to be penal in nature. However, if the agreed sum qualifies as liquidated damages the courts will enforce the clause. The dividing line between these categories is not completely clear in the Singapore context. It appears that the courts have adopted a more cautious approach towards the qualification of an agreed sum as a penalty clause, but a departure from the traditional (narrow) test of a genuine pre-estimate of loss is not yet confirmed by the Singapore Court of Appeal. Nonetheless, there is sufficient support for the premise that the courts have adopted a more relaxed approach towards the rules against penalties in order to allow the parties to protect their performance interest by a clause for the payment of a fixed sum upon a failure

1772 Art 7.4.13 PICC; Art 9:509 PECL; Art III.-3:712 DCFR; The CISG and the draft PACL do not entail an express provision for contractual penalty clauses; It must be noted that Dutch contract law expressly stipulate that the obligee may not demand performance of the penalty clause where the failure in performance of the obligation cannot be attributed to the obligor. This a departure from the approach taken by the PICC, PECL and DCFR which limit the recovery of a specified sum to cases of non-performance.

1773 S 4.4 and Ch 6.

in performance. That said, there is still a strict judicial control present. This runs counter to the significant freedom of contracting parties to protect their performance interest under the contract law of the Netherlands (and to a certain extent China) by agreed sums which are only subject to reduction in exceptional situations.

The example provided earlier helps to illustrate the practical impact of the aforementioned considerations. Suppose that the manufacturer fails to deliver the customised MRI equipment before the agreed time for delivery. In this situation, Dutch contract law, as well as the PICC, PECL and DCFR appears to allow contractual stipulations for the payment of a fixed rate per week, irrespective of the actual harm caused by the delayed performance. This is a significant departure from the approach taken by Singapore courts following the traditional genuine pre-estimate of loss test as set out in *Dunlop Pneumatic Tyre Co Ltd v New Garage and Motor Co Ltd*, but also from the reformulated rule in the *Cavendish* case which requires the court to consider whether the consequence of a failure in performance is out of all proportion or 'unconscionable' or 'extravagant' having regard to the legitimate interest of the aggrieved party in enforcement of the primary obligation (*e.g.* timely delivery). This means in effect that Singapore courts will not enforce the clause when the agreed sum is found to be penal in nature because the stipulated amount is out of proportion to the legitimate interest of the aggrieved party.

On an overall assessment, it is submitted here that the approach taken by Dutch contract law, as well as the unification instruments identified, is in full accord with the adage *pacta sunt servanda* which is reflected in the right of contracting parties to enforced performance of a non-monetary obligation. In other words, the right to enforced performance can be further strengthened by contracting parties by means of appropriate penalty clauses. Today it seems that there is no consensus on the matter in China. Nonetheless, it is indicative that Chinese contract law specifically considers a contractual penalty clause as a part of its damages regime, and that the legitimacy of a punitive penalty clause must be inferred from the principle of freedom of contract. In other words, it is not axiomatic that the right to proper performance of a non-monetary obligation under a commercial sales contract can be strengthened by putting monetary pressure on the party who is obliged to perform. Similar to Dutch contract law, the approach taken by Singapore contract law also derives from its traditional understanding of the remedial instrument to protect the position of the aggrieved party; though, in contrast to the Dutch approach (and the PICC, PECL and DCFR), Singapore contract law considers damages as the primary measure to provide contracting parties with the very thing they bargained for. Unsurprisingly, contracting parties are not allowed to circumvent this fundamental principle by a contractual penalty clause in order to compel the promisor to perform as stipulated in the contract. The principle that a Singapore court relegates the aggrieved party to a claim for damages where a clause classifies as punitive, is also out of step with Dutch and Chinese contract law, as well as the PICC, DCFR and PECL, which allow for a reduction of the agreed sum if it is excessive in the circumstances.

Aside from these technical legal considerations, it is important to note that those working in the realm of international commercial sales should act with due care when drafting contractual provisions to compel the parties to do exactly what they promised to by the imposition of a fixed sum payable upon a failure in performance. It is, therefore, that specific attention should be paid to the discussed protection mechanisms and the ability of the court to control the impact of agreed sums (*i.e.* reduction *v* invalidation) in order to determine whether the parties' performance interest is sufficiently protected. As for the impact on the availability to claim damages and to circumvent the risk that the actual damages of the aggrieved buyer are higher than the agreed financial incentive for the seller to perform its obligations, parties may consider to stipulate that the right to claim payment is without prejudice to the buyer's right to claim damages (or similar wording). However, the question whether such a clause is of any effect should always be determined in light of the law governing the contract.

7.6 CONCLUSIONS

292. This chapter reveals that the availability of enforced performance is significantly influenced by the national rules which enable the aggrieved buyer to give effect to such an order. The discussed disparity is related to the views of the three investigated jurisdictions on the party's interest which deserves most protection. It is, therefore, advocated here that every attempt to bridge the gap between the fundamental principles underlying the availability of enforced performance should be assessed in light of the following four issues. These considerations are of significant importance for those involved in commercial sales transactions across the borders of the three subject jurisdictions and those seeking legal inroads to overcome practical difficulties arising from the discussed conflicting principles at the national and international levels.

The first major difference to take into consideration is the complexity of effectively obtaining the goods after an order for enforced performance is provided under Singapore or Chinese contract law. Their procedures are less efficient and more expensive in comparison to the significantly liberal and straightforward rules under Dutch contract law, which encompasses hardly any barriers to giving effect to a judicial order for enforced performance. Consequently, the performance interest of a party to a commercial sales contract is fully protected. Nonetheless, it is questionable whether this progressive approach strikes the correct balance between the interests of both parties to a commercial sales contract involving perishable commodity goods which are easily obtainable by the buyer in the marketplace. Nonetheless, in instances where a change of circumstances would make it particularly difficult for the seller to deliver substitute goods, the latter could frustrate execution by means of summary proceedings. It is however questionable whether such efforts to bar actual enforcement are always justified. Nonetheless, the reverse can be said from the thresholds for compelling the promisor to perform under Singapore and Chinese law. In view of the immense impact of the differing approaches and the lack of uniform principles in this regard, it is of paramount importance to regulate the thresholds for actual execution of an order for enforced performance in the contractual stipulations in order to bring about an enforcement regime which accords with the specifics of the agreement, in particular the nature of the goods.

Where the option of actually enforcing the judgement for performance takes too much time or is too costly for the aggrieved buyer, the latter could opt for obtaining substitute goods at the seller's expense, albeit that thresholds differ significantly in the investigated legal systems. This divergence requires the careful attention of contracting parties. The main point is that the option of obtaining substitute goods is a fundamental factor underlying the significantly limited availability of enforced performance in the contract law of Singapore. Put differently; it is a preliminary question, rather than a rule which enables the aggrieved buyer to give effect to a judicial order for enforced performance, as is the case in the Netherlands and China. Consequently, the availability of enforced performance is directly affected by the possibility of obtaining a cover purchase under Singapore contract law. This stands in stark contrast with the Netherlands and China, which have taken the approach that the buyer's right to obtain substitute goods at the expense of the seller is a question of giving effect to a judicial order for enforced performance.[1774] Considering the lack of clarity on this matter under the CISG, contractual stipulations can be particularly helpful to sidestep the differences by regulating the situation where the seller fails to deliver the goods or delivers non-conforming goods and the buyer desires to obtain substitute goods at the expense of the seller without unwinding the contract.

The third major disagreement which impacts the ability to give effect to a judicial order for enforced performance arises from the ability of the courts to impose financial sanctions to compel the promisor to perform. Whereas Dutch and Chinese contract law (as well as the PICC) have taken the approach that the courts are entitled to impose financial sanctions, the legal system of Singapore is unfamiliar with such a legal device. Nonetheless, a similar repressive effect may follow from the possibility of contempt of court proceedings. This is, however, a very indirect method compared to the Dutch and Chinese approaches. As

1774 It is recalled that the buyer may be subject to a duty to acquire replacement goods to mitigate the impact of an order for enforced performance (s 6.5). This duty is not related to the right of the buyer to obtain substitute goods at the expense of the seller once the claim for enforced performance is awarded, although there is an interesting link between the two concepts.

for the latter two, it remains at the discretion of the courts to impose financial sanctions. This brings about the necessary flexibility to deal with situations where the protection of the parties' interest is tipped to the wrong side given the circumstances of the case. That said, the contract law of Singapore has built-in flexibility allowing the courts to balance the interests of both parties. Nevertheless, it appears that the default reluctance against enforced performance and the presence of specific common law counter-exceptions brings about a regime overly protective of the seller's interest. This raises the question of whether or not a correction is required to bring about a more balanced system in view of the approach taken by the unification instruments and the diversity of interests and dynamics in international commercial sales transactions.

The aforementioned undertaking is of significant importance as the last section of this chapter reveals a related disagreement between the investigated legal systems which demands close attention from contracting parties. That is, a fixed sum payable upon a failure in performance may not be of particular help for those seeking a middle-ground solution when taking into account the judicial reduction mechanism adopted by Dutch and Chinese contract law, as well as by the PICC, PECL and DCFR, and the ability of Singapore courts to exercise judicial control by invalidation of agreed sums when they are found to be penal in nature. As a result, contracting parties to a commercial sales contract should be aware that they may be not allowed to circumvent the availability of enforced performance by coercing performance by contractual stipulations for the payment of a specified sum upon a failure in performance.

8 Derogatory agreements

293. *Preliminary* – The findings in the preceding chapters show vivid contrasts between the availability of enforced performance at a practical and theoretical level in the three subject jurisdictions. The different approaches by the legal systems are fundamental to their default responses to a claim for enforced performance of obligations to bring about a certain state of affairs under a commercial sales contract. Suggestions have been made as to how the investigated legal systems could narrow the gap between their approaches in light of solutions offered by the unification instruments. The present-day reality is, however, that the availability of enforced performance of non-monetary obligations owed under a commercial sales contract differs dramatically between the three investigated jurisdictions. This raises the question of whether or not contracting parties to a commercial sales contract are permitted to agree to an enforced performance clause which excludes, restricts or expands the availability of enforced performance beyond the default control mechanism of the law governing the contract. In answering this question, the focus is not on exemption clauses specifically, because such a narrow approach would not provide any guidance in determining the position of Singapore law. Accordingly, this chapter discusses the legal acceptability of clauses (individually negotiated or by means of standard terms), which may frustrate the discretionary power of the courts to assess their appropriateness along the lines of the freedom of contracting and legal restrictions.

> *Illustration* – An importer of beverages, located in country X, and a trading company in country Y conclude an annual sales contract for a specific beer brand. The trading company guarantees that it shall deliver 20–25 40-foot containers of pilsner and lager beer on a monthly basis. The parties also agree that the trading company shall increase the supply of beer prior to other buyers, if the supply capacity of the importer expands. After six months, the importer notifies the trading company that it requires an additional supply of lager beer in the form of 2–5 foot containers every month. The trading company refuses to deliver the requested quantity due to delivery obligations in respect of other buyers. Subsequently, the importer brings a claim to court for the enforcement of the seller's delivery obligation. The trading company argues that the buyer's claim cannot be awarded because the parties agreed to damages, to the exclusion of enforced performance, as a remedy for a failure in delivery of the goods as stipulated in the contract.

294. *Domestic approaches* – The leading principle in Dutch law is that parties to a commercial sales contract are entitled to exclude or reinforce the aggrieved party's right

to enforced performance of an obligation to bring about a certain state of affairs under a commercial sales contract.[1775] This includes the right of the parties to a commercial sales contract to impose a financial fine on non-delivery and for non-conforming delivery. Aside from strengthening a contractual right to enforced performance, contractual stipulations may also exclude the buyer's right to claim for a cure by repair and replacement under the statutory regime for a defective performance.[1776] Dutch courts may, however, strike down such clauses when they are contrary to the *boni mores* (*i.e.* standards of good behaviour in the realm of commercial contract law),[1777] and when they are the result of duress, fraud or undue influence.[1778] Furthermore, a clause in standard terms which excludes or restricts the availability of enforced performance may be nullified when the clause is unreasonably onerous,[1779] and if the user of the standard terms has not given the other party a reasonable opportunity to take note of the general terms and conditions.[1780] In addition to the limitations set out above, the courts will also not uphold clauses which exclude or restrict enforced performance when they are not in accord with the standards of reasonableness and fairness (threshold for application of the derogatory effect of the standards of reasonableness and fairness are very high).[1781] It follows from the considerations above that Dutch courts (in exceptional situations) may override the principle that enforced performance is not available where this follows from a juridical act, that is; a derogatory agreement for the exclusion of the right to enforced performance.[1782] That having been said, contracting parties are entitled to agree that the aggrieved party may only pursue damages, thereby implicitly renouncing its right to obtain enforced performance. This premise is founded on the freedom of contract and fundamental notion of the bindingness of a contractual promise.

1775 Nispen (n 867) para 12, confirmed in Jongbloed (n 530) para 7; See also TFE Tjong Tjin Tai, 'Garantie, nakoming en schadevergoeding' (2004) 6577 WPNR 363–386; Dutch Parliamentary History Book 3 (n 204) 896; JM Smits in Schelhaas 2002 (n 19) 345.

1776 The principle that commercial parties are entitled to exclude the buyer's right claim for a cure by repair or replacement under the statutory regime for sales contracts also applies where the shares of a business are the subject matter of a sales contract; *Equinix v Rooq et al* District Court Overijssel 7 January 2015, ECLI:NL:RBOVE:2015:363, JOR 2015, 96; Contracting parties should be aware not to merely exclude the sales law provisions, but also general statutory provisions such as art 3:296 DCC for the right to demand performance and art 6:89 DCC which entails a limitation regime for defective performance.

1777 Art 3:40 DCC; JM Smits in Schelhaas 2002 (n 19) 345.

1778 Art 3:44 DCC; Hartkamp 2011 (n 80) paras 87, 218; Sieburgh, *Asser 6-I* (n 363) para 364; Jongbloed (n 530) para 7.

1779 Art 6:233(a) DCC; JM Smits in Schelhaas 2002 (n 19) 345.

1780 Art 6:233(b) DCC; JM Smits in Schelhaas 2002 (n 19) 345.

1781 Art 6:248(2) DCC; Hartkamp 2011 (n 80) para 31; JM Smits in Schelhaas 2002 (n 19) 345; De Jong, Krans and Wissink 2018 (n 194) 11–13.

1782 Art 3:396(1) DCC.

295. It appears that Singapore (case) law has not yet paid attention to the admissibility of clauses which interfere with the availability of enforced performance of an obligation to bring about a certain state of affairs under a commercial sales contract. Determining the position of Singapore law is therefore difficult. Nonetheless, an assessment of cases outside the realm of commercial sales law may provide some helpful guidance to determine, obliquely, the potential judicial response to enforced performance clauses in commercial sales contracts. The starting point is that Singapore courts have taken the approach that contracting parties are bound by the discretionary power of the courts.[1783] This means in effect that the discretionary power of the courts to deny or to allow the exceptional measure of enforced performance in principle cannot be fettered by a contractual clause. The likely reluctance of Singapore courts towards clauses which affect the equitable function of its courts is also reflected in the case *Tay Ah Poon and another v Chionh Hai Guan and another.* It was considered by the Court of Appeal that the liquidated damages clause in question did not exclude a claim for enforced performance, and the defaulting party could still be forced to perform the contract.[1784] The case *Govindaraju v Ganasen* also assists in determining how enforced performance clauses in commercial sales contracts might be approached in Singapore. In this case, the Court of Appeal considered that the clause to elect repudiation of the contract in case of failure in performance did not exclude the general (equitable) right of the purchasers to claim for enforced performance of the contract.[1785] The notion that the discretionary power of the courts cannot be constrained by derogatory agreements also derives from the case *Pub 1997 Pte Ltd v Scorpion.*[1786] It follows from this case that a Singapore court most likely would not enforce a clause stipulating that the seller is not entitled to sell the goods specified in the contract to other parties for the duration of a certain period. This is because enforcement of this negative obligation (*i.e.* injunction) would effectively result in an award for enforced performance of a positive obligation because it would compel the seller to deliver the goods to the initial buyer. This runs counter to the discretionary power of the courts to direct, if it thinks fit, that a contractual obligation to deliver specific or ascertained goods shall be performed specifically. For the sake of clarity; clauses excluding or restricting the availability of enforced performance arising from individual negotiations or standard terms are not governed by the Unfair Contract Terms Act.[1787]

1783 See the English case *Quadrant Visual Communications Ltd v Hutchison Telephone (UK) Ltd* [1993] BCLC 422 at 451 in conjunction with *Tay Ah Poon v Chionh Hai Guan* (n 589) [19].

1784 *Tay Ah Poon v Chionh Hai Guan* (n 589) [18]; Dora Neo, 'Specific Remedies and the Performance Interest in Singapore Contract Law' in Chen-Wishart, Loke and Ong 2016 (n 156) 211, 212.

1785 *Govindaraju and another v Ganasen and another* [1994] SGCA 125 [15, 18], (1994) 3 SLR(R) 815.

1786 *Pub 1997 Pte Ltd* (n 965) [21]; Phang et al 2012 (n 112) para 23.174.

1787 SGA, s 55(1) in conjunction with Unfair Contract Term Act (1999), s 6; Chong et al 2016 (n 125) paras 10.3.17–10.3.19.

296. Chinese scholars have made some interesting observations regarding the admissibility of clauses affecting the availability of enforced performance of contractual obligations. The starting point in this regard is the broadly accepted notion that commercial parties are entitled to fashion their agreement to their needs, which brings about that clauses reinforcing and excluding the aggrieved party's statutory right to enforced performance are valid and enforceable.[1788] The premise that such clauses are permitted in principle also follows from the statutory provision that a lawfully established contract shall be binding on the parties.[1789] However, Chinese courts are reluctant to allow contracting parties to interfere with the statutory control mechanism for enforced performance.[1790] In other words, Chinese courts could show some reticence when confronted with clauses in commercial sales contracts regulating the availability of enforced performance, which go beyond, or simply ignore, the statutory limitations. It appears that the assessment made by Chinese courts will be in line with the principle position that the contracting parties shall adhere to the principle of fairness,[1791] and that private parties are not at liberty to interfere with the discretionary power of courts to award or deny a claim for enforced performance of an obligation under a commercial sales contract.[1792] Where a clause in standard terms interferes with the statutory control mechanism for enforced performance, additional barriers apply. That is, the user of the standard terms is obliged to inform about the exclusion or restriction of the availability of enforced performance.[1793] Furthermore, Chinese law invalidates exemption clauses when they follow from fraud, intentional or gross negligence.[1794]

297. *Comparative analysis* – A significant controversy between the three investigated jurisdictions becomes apparent when considering their approaches towards contractual stipulations which in essence depart from their legal control mechanisms for enforced performance. Where the focal point in the Netherlands, China, as well as the (vast) majority of the unification instruments (*i.e.* PICC, PECL, DCFR)[1795] lies on the validity of clauses exempting or restricting enforced performance, the discussion in Singapore centres around the question of whether parties should be permitted to agree on clauses for enforced

1788 Bing Ling 2002 (n 229) para 8.003.
1789 Art 8 CCL.
1790 Lei Chen, 'Availability of Specific Remedies in Chinese Contract Law' in Chen-Wishart, Loke and Ong 2016 (n 156) 38.
1791 Arts 5, 6 CCL.
1792 Lei Chen, 'Availability of Specific Remedies in Chinese Contract Law' in Chen-Wishart, Loke and Ong 2016 (n 156) 38.
1793 Art 40 CCL; Bing Ling 2002 (n 229) para 4.058.
1794 Arts 52, 53 CCL: Bing Ling 2002 (n 229) para 4.058.
1795 Art 7.2.2 PICC; Art 4:110 PECL (clauses not individually negotiated); Art 8:109 PECL (indivually negotiated clauses); Art II.-9:-401 -II.-9:411 DCFR (clauses not individually negotiated).

performance. It may, therefore, appear to be problematic if not impossible to draw any conclusions. Nonetheless, the assessment of the domestic viewpoints in the present section provides (to a certain degree) general guidelines for determining the admissibility of clauses which deviate from the availability of enforced performance under the default systems of the three investigated jurisdictions.

The starting point is that Dutch and Chinese contract law allow clauses which restrict or allow a claim for enforced performance (the latter is less relevant), although in both jurisdictions the effect of this principle is limited. This is due to the fact that contractual stipulations dealing with the availability of enforced performance may be struck out by Dutch and Chinese courts where, for example, the operative effect of the clause is contrary to the principle of good faith, or when it arises from intentional or gross negligence. Furthermore, specific barriers are put in place in Dutch and Chinese law when clauses dealing with enforced performance are not individually negotiated but are a part of standard terms. This is not surprising as commercial parties do not always conclude contracts on an equal footing. Therefore, a certain degree of protection is offered by Dutch and Chinese contract law to eliminate undesirable results which follow from an imbalance of bargaining power between commercial parties. Chinese contract law has adopted another fundamental barrier which appears to be the result of the efforts of Chinese law to narrow the gap with the common law tradition, albeit with a completely different effect. It follows that Chinese courts are likely to be reluctant to allow clauses interfering with the statutory limitations to enforced performance because this would directly affect the discretionary power of the courts to allow or deny enforced performance. It is for the same reason that Singapore courts will most likely show a discernible judicial reluctance to uphold a contractual clause which allows enforced performance beyond the legal control mechanism for the enforcement of positive obligations to bring about a certain state of affairs. Hence, where the hesitation of Chinese courts to allow clauses affecting the default system for enforced performance brings about a significant freedom to protect the performance interest of the parties, the disinclination of Singapore contract law to allow clauses expanding the availability of enforced performance brings about the notion that contracting parties are not entitled to protect their performance interests. This, in effect, means that clauses which indirectly coerce performance of non-monetary obligations to bring about a certain state of affairs shall not be honoured if enforced performance is not envisaged in the case at hand.

To put these considerations into the context of the example mentioned under paragraph 293, it appears that the buyer's claim for the delivery of the beer shall be awarded under Dutch and Chinese law, as there are no indications that one of the previously mentioned limiting elements apply nor that the contractual stipulations for damages would rule out a claim for enforced performance. The outcome under Singapore contract law is probably diametrically opposed considering the notion that the existence of the equitable remedy of enforced performance of non-monetary obligations cannot depend on the presence of a contractual term expressly providing that the aggrieved party has such a right. Another important principle in this regard is that protection of performance interest is, generally, not allowed when it would directly or indirectly coerce performance of a non-monetary obligation which is not granted protection under Singapore contract law. Hence, those involved in commercial sales contracts across the borders of the subject jurisdictions should give due consideration to the above-described diametrically opposed viewpoints in order to determine the value of any contractual stipulations regulating the availability of enforced performance to, for example, delivery or the taking delivery of goods.

In view of the above, it appears that the ability of contracting parties to protect their performance interest differs significantly between, on one hand, Dutch and Chinese contract law, and on the other hand, Singapore contract law. That said, there is also an important common denominator; that is, the domestic courts will subject clauses dealing with enforced performance to (careful) examination, be it on the basis of general legal principles, specific provisions for standard terms or uncodified doctrinal viewpoints. This premise also applies where the parties have shaped the availability of enforced performance along the lines of the preferred remedy of the law governing the contract.

Unfortunately, the drafters of the CISG have not addressed the legal uncertainty arising from the disagreement between the subject legal systems which in essence represents a fundamental point of divergence between the civil and common law traditions. The CISG takes the approach that clauses deviating from the default regime for enforced performance are subject to domestic law.[1796] This raises the question: can commercial parties doing business across civil and common law borders take their lead from the approach taken by the PICC, PECL or DCFR in order to obtain a middle-ground solution which serves the interest of both legal traditions?[1797] The answer appears to be in the negative, because these unification instruments have taken the approach that enforced performance is generally available, unless limitations apply. This runs counter to the arguments underlying the unwillingness in the common law tradition to allow clauses providing for enforced performance; that is, inadmissible interference with the discretionary power of the courts. That having been said, it may not be that difficult to sidestep the perceived inadequacies of the investigated legal systems to respect the foundations of the civil and common law without undermining the wishes of the parties to deviate from the legal controlling mechanism to enforced performance. The solution submitted here for the domestic courts is to adjudicate such clauses in international commercial sales contracts in line with the uniform notion of freedom of contract and the principle of reasonableness. It may appear

1796 Schwenzer 2016 (n 91) art 46 para 48.

1797 Art 7.1.6 PICC; Art 4:110 PECL (clauses in standard terms); Art 8:109 PECL (individualy negotiated terms); Art II.-9:401 *ff* and II.-3:105 DCFR.

that this would require Singapore courts to overcome a major doctrinal hurdle, but it is not that controversial when considering the available safeguards to prevent injustice.

9 Conclusions and recommendations

300. *Preliminary remarks* – This chapter is not a repetition of what has already been stated. Instead, it ties up the conclusions provided in the preceding chapters to determine the extent to which the contract law of the Netherlands, Singapore and China balance out the interests of parties to a commercial sales contract in the principles surrounding the enforceability of non-monetary obligations, and how the domestic solutions relate to the approaches taken by the unification instruments. The key focus points are the legal limitations where the default regime entails a right to enforced performance, and counter-exceptions where the default regime only allows enforced performance in specific situations. On that note, the findings in the previous chapters reveal that under the subject legal systems, the principles surrounding the constitution, the actual performance of non-monetary obligations and the substantive rules on enforced performance are intricately interwoven elements of systems that aim to balance different interests (*i.e.* interest of the state, of contracting parties and of market actors). The impact of the discussed principles on the enforceability of contractual rights is, therefore, only explicable with reference to the whole. This means that the larger framework of historical and modern contract law principles is taken into consideration rather than simply focusing on the statutory provisions dealing with the availability of enforced performance of non-monetary contractual obligations arising from a commercial sales contract.

The starting point of this undertaking is that the legal principles encompassing the actual performance of the seller's and buyer's performance obligations and the ability of the parties to enforce those obligations are firmly rooted in cultural notions of the value of the act of promise making, legal traditions and general contract law principles. The differences arising therefrom can be traced back to the way the interests of contracting parties are balanced against each other in view of the weight attached to the concept of party autonomy and the role of public interest. At a practical level, the competing viewpoints are (after countless hours of negotiations) generally accommodated and accomplished in overly lengthy and dense contractual stipulations in order to bring about a contract that parties feel as comfortable as possible in signing. This costly endeavour might not be necessary when commercial parties and those working in an international sales context are provided with more in-depth insights about the actual enforceability of the contractual obligations. In more practical terms, to be forewarned is to be forearmed.

In view of the above, the present conclusion is concerned with three inextricably linked focus points. Firstly, the extent to which the legal systems are able to safeguard the performance interest of parties to a commercial sales contract. Secondly, the extent to which the interest of the non-performing party is protected against unjustifiable consequences in light of the concept of freedom of contract. And lastly, with what degree of flexibility might courts grant a claim for enforced performance in order to provide the most effective response in consideration of the complexities surrounding international commercial sales contracts. In paragraph 316, these three key elements are evaluated in light of the following comprehensive conclusions of the analyses provided in the preceding chapters.

301. Before diving into the above-mentioned elements, it is reiterated that the efforts of the three investigated jurisdictions to position themselves as legal hubs are not reflected in their traditional view on enforced performance of non-monetary obligations under a commercial sales contract (with the exception of the contract law of China). China has achieved something which is broadly perceived as almost impossible for domestic legal systems. That is, the contract law of China narrows the gap between the civil and common law traditions on a domestic level, by adopting a middle-ground solution which is, *i.a*, inspired by the approach taken by the CISG and PICC. The result, however, is not completely flawless when observing all the relevant provisions affecting the availability of enforced performance. Another interesting point in the context of determining the legal roots of the availability of enforced performance of non-monetary obligations is that the Singapore courts are provided with the discretionary power to adopt appropriate modifications to suit local circumstances. However, the observations in the preceding chapters reveal that, although changes are visible, this has not led to a major shift from the English law position. That said, the Singapore case law discussed shows the increasing willingness of courts to look beyond common law borders. In any case, this does not necessarily mean that Singapore contract law is moving towards a broader notion of the availability of enforced performance, which would enable contracting parties to obtain the very thing they bargained for and not to be forced to settle for monetary relief in the form of damages. As far as the contract law of the Netherlands is concerned, the (French) civil law tradition is strongly embedded in the principles underlying the availability of enforced performance. Alteration, therefore, seems unlikely given that these principles are the very foundation of Dutch contract law.

302. *Recommendations* – The above-described divergence between the three investigated jurisdictions on this matter vividly portrays the unresolved misalignment between the civil and common law traditions. Should there be a desire to narrow the gap between the two major legal families, it might be helpful to move towards an overarching solution at the international level, recognizing that the divergence is deeply entrenched in principles dealing with contractual obligations, from the very moment they are supposed to come into existence until their execution. The suggestion for such a consolidation takes into account the key differences affecting the actual value commercial parties may attach to a

contractual right to be provided with the goods in the quantity and quality as stipulated. The disagreement among the investigated legal systems derives from the thresholds for bringing about enforceable obligations and the limitations imposed for execution,[1798] the goods subject to enforcement measures under the sales law provisions,[1799] the judicial measures available for enforced performance and the admissibility of contractual stipulations that interfere with the default systems for enforced performance.[1800]

The insights gained in this research may provide the judiciary, legislators and commercial parties (doing business across the borders of the three investigated jurisdictions, and in general parties with a civil and common law background) with new perspectives for determining the degree of flexibility by which a claim for enforced performance of non-monetary obligations, under a commercial sales contract, can be granted and given effect in the subject legal systems. The aforementioned undertaking requires balancing the interests of contracting parties in view of the elements identified in this study. Based on this consideration, seven inextricably linked recommendations are formulated below as a model for enhancing the understanding of the need for the adoption of a more holistic approach, that is, evaluation of the larger framework of legal principles surrounding a performance obligation in order to bring about new insights, rather than focusing on the default regime for enforced performance of non-monetary obligations.

303. The first recommendation calls on those involved in drafting international contract law instruments to open the door for legal consolidation of the different ways of structuring the contract and sales law provisions and the distinct interpretation of the basic elements that bring about a commercial sales contract. A one-sided or overly restrictive attitude in this regard could lead to an imbalance in the protection of the performance interests of commercial market actors involved in trading relationships across the borders of the three investigated jurisdictions and, in general, when it concerns commercial sales contracts concluded between parties located in separate civil and common law jurisdictions.

The starting point of the divergence is the distinct structure of a dualistic and unitarian system as adopted by Dutch and Chinese contract law respectively,[1801] and the imposition of an individual act for the sale of goods in Singapore contract law. With the exception of the DCFR, most unification instruments take a uniform approach. As a result, the scope of goods subject to sales law provisions differs significantly in each of the legal systems discussed. The divergence is further aggravated by the disagreement related to the level of

1798 S 3.4.6.
1799 S 3.3.
1800 Chs 7 and 8.
1801 The contract law of the Netherlands consists of a *lex generalis* for obligations and a *lex specialis* for sales contracts; the contract law of China incorporates sales law provisions into the general rules on contracts.

the actual required monetary reciprocity of non-monetary obligations to bring about a certain state of affairs.

If there is a desire to bridge the gap between civil and common law notions of the enforceability of non-monetary obligations, starting with the issues set out above, we must ask first: is it necessary to reform the ambit of a commercial sales contract? In view of findings discussed in preceding chapters, the answer appears to be in the positive when taking into account the fact that contract law principles are merely an instrument to regulate and facilitate transactions in light of the parties' performance interest and protection against unjustified consequences. This is true for all three investigated jurisdictions, as well as for the unification instruments identified. On that account, a progressive attitude towards the applicability and scope of rules concerning the ambit of a commercial sales contract would be beneficial for all the subject legal systems. It is, therefore, suggested here to work towards a comprehensive notion of the concept of a commercial sales contract which employs a restrictive negative definition of the concept of goods and requires a tolerant view among the courts on the rules on formation.[1802] Dutch and Chinese contract law, as well as the CISG and DCFR, already display such an attitude, although there are pronounced differences. By adopting strict rules on contract formation and interpretation of the goods subject to sales law, Singapore contract law is significantly less protective towards the performance interest of the promisee in this regard. Although when considering the guidelines formulated for the protection of the interest of the promisor against abuse, in the following part, Singapore legislators might find sufficient positive guarantees to agree to a solution at the international level, which does not necessarily reflect their English law tradition.

304. That being said, uniform solutions to the issues discussed above are not expected in the foreseeable future. It is therefore important for those involved in international commercial sales contracts to carefully consider the different mechanisms to fill the gap where an offer, and thus the commercial sales contract deriving therefrom, is not sufficiently clear in determining the quantity and quality of the goods to be delivered by the seller and the price owed for the goods, or rules for determining the price.[1803] Any misunderstanding in this regard could have substantial implications if, after a considerable time, it is asserted by the court adjudicating a dispute between the parties that an enforceable sales contract has not come into existence or that the scope of the assumed obligations significantly differ. This research demonstrates that the investigated legal systems deploy different principles and rules for the interpretation of the terms of an offer in order to determine whether an enforceable contract has come into existence.

1802 As for the concept of concept of goods, inspiration may be drawn from the DCFR.
1803 S 3.4.

The practical recommendation to bring about an offer that is sufficient for determining the obligations of the parties should be applied in view of the aforementioned considerations, as well as the necessity of balancing the interests of both parties in contractual stipulations. The latter point is especially important for commercial sales contracts governed by Dutch and Chinese contract law and where inspiration is drawn from the PICC, PECL or DCFR. This is because the courts are allowed to act (on the request of a contracting party) where from the start of the contract there is a gross disparity between the purchase price as assumed by the parties (and asserted by the court) and the quantity and quality of the goods to be delivered by the seller.[1804] The freedom of the contracting parties to prevent issues in this regard is, however, limited under Chinese contract law if adoption of a price commissioned by the government or based on government-issued pricing guidelines is required by law.[1805] The foregoing pragmatic considerations on bringing about a clear offer entailing all details necessary for the final contract, appears to be of less importance under the contract law of Singapore. That is, to constitute enforceable obligations, it is not required that the consideration of the buyer (*i.e.* payment of the purchase price) is adequate in view of the seller's obligation to deliver the stipulated goods.[1806] This brings about the notion that, at one end of the spectrum, Chinese contract law provides for significant freedom of the court to interfere with the seller's and buyer's obligations deriving from the accepted offer in the case of a substantial inconsistency between the monetary value of the assumed obligations, while at the other end, Singapore contract law is not concerned with a monetary disparity between the buyer's and seller's obligations in order to bring about an enforceable contract. Dutch contract law holds an intermediate position between the Chinese and Singapore approaches.

Notwithstanding this divergence between the three subject jurisdictions, each of the legal systems is familiar with a mechanism to interfere with the obligations of the parties assumed in an offer. Careful consideration, therefore, must be given to the terms of an offer and the legal limitations of the undertaking of an offer, which (on acceptance) serves as the basic reference point for the court in establishing whether parties are subject to an enforceable sales contract, together with defining the scope of the obligations arising therefrom. In view of these considerations, it is submitted here that the universal principle of freedom of contracting is not fully protected when the parties have differing viewpoints

1804 NL: art 3:54 DCC; CHN: art 54 CCL; Art 3.2.7 PICC; Art 4:109 PECL; Art II.-7:207 DCFR. The contract law of Singapore is based on English law, which is not familiar with the notion that a gross disparity between the obligations assumed by the parties may give rise to judicial interference by, e.g., declaring a contract void, avoided or adaption of contractual stipulations such as modification of the contract price. See for a detailed discussion about the complexities of the concept of gross disparity Schwenzer, Hachem and Kee 2012 (n 13) Ch 21.

1805 Art 62(2) CCL.

1806 S 3.4.5.

about the meaning of the stipulations and the extent to which they represent the parties' intentions. The view of contract law that emerges from the discussed materials on the formation of contracts is that, in comparison to Dutch and Chinese contract law, the thresholds for judicial interference are significantly higher under Singapore contract law. That is to say, in the contract law of the Netherlands and China, the starting point is a holistic approach for determining the intentions of the parties. This, in effect, means that the courts shall not necessarily give effect to the literal language of the terms of the contract; they may take into account contextual elements to determine the intentions of the parties. Where appropriate, the courts may also have recourse to the standard of reasonableness and fairness and the principle of good faith respectively. In practice, the courts in Singapore may arrive at a similar outcome by invoking implied terms and through the exceptions to the parol evidence rule as accepted under Singapore law, but the effective scope of these measures should not be overestimated in a commercial sales context. That is to say, the terms of a commercial sales contract are generally understood to reflect the intentions of the parties, which are established by determining what a reasonable outside observer (*i.e.* abstract person) would have taken them to be. Nonetheless, it appears that the flexibility offered by Singapore case law, provides sufficient latitude to deal with CISG-contracts which requires that the courts give due consideration to all relevant circumstances in determining the intentions of the parties.

305. In deviation from the key focus of the present work on protection of the buyer's expectation of performance, the second recommendation deals first with protection of the seller's performance interest when the buyer fails to fulfil its obligations. The underlying notion of this undertaking is that a legal principle generally favours either the buyer's or seller's interest. It is seldom possible to protect the buyer's performance interest and the seller's interest in a single legal principle. In Dutch and Chinese contract law, as well as in the five identified unification instruments, the rules on enforced performance of obligations arising from a commercial sales contract and the obligation to put a defect right focus on protection of the buyer's performance interest. Therefore, the second recommendation advocates for more attention in protecting the seller's performance interest in view of two important difficulties arising from a situation of partial payment, and where payment of the purchase price is inextricably linked with the buyer's obligation to take delivery of the goods. A discussion about the different approaches in both scenarios is necessary because it is generally assumed that civil and common law are on the same page when considering the availability of enforced performance of the buyer's obligation to pay the purchase price, that is, the seller is provided with a *legal right* to obtain payment.

This research reveals that the investigated legal systems deploy very different principles when the seller accepts a partial payment and then subsequently claims for the outstanding amount. Although, it appears that the difference lies not so much in the actual outcomes, the impact of the discussed principles is arguably far more significant when considering the thresholds for application. The underlying reason for the distinct approaches found in the legal systems is rooted in the civil and common law interpretations of the impact of the seller's acceptance of a partial performance by the buyer. The starting point is that the investigated legal systems all act on the notion that the seller is obliged to make full delivery of the goods and the buyer is obliged to make full payment of the agreed purchase price. Unsurprisingly, the seller is entitled to reject payment of a lesser sum than agreed. However, where the seller accepts partial payment that is not provided for in the contract, the assessment of the question as to whether the seller is allowed to sue for the outstanding amount reveals a fundamental divergence between the legal systems. The Dutch and Chinese contract law take the approach that the seller is entitled to claim for the outstanding amount, unless the seller's conduct leads the buyer to reasonably believe that the partial payment has discharged the obligation to pay the outstanding balance. In the Singapore common law system, the seller's acceptance of a lesser sum for the delivered goods results in a modification of the sales contract when consideration for this adjustment is provided. If consideration for the partial payment is not found, the obligation to pay the agreed purchase price still exists. Nonetheless, a claim for the balance can be refused upon the doctrine of promissory estoppel when this follows from the seller's conduct, but the requirements are significantly higher in comparison to the approach taken by Dutch and Chinese contract law. In Singapore law, the buyer is only relieved from its obligation to pay the outstanding purchase price when both parties have acted in reliance on the seller's promise to accept a lesser sum and that in the general circumstances it would be inequitable to permit the seller to go back on its promise. The unification instruments favour the civil law's less strict approach in this regard, which means, in effect, that acceptance of a part payment does not require good consideration (hence, it is not considered as a modification of the contract), but it needs to be established that the seller's conduct has led the buyer to believe that the part payment would release the former from its obligation to pay the outstanding amount. The differences in approaches can be overcome at a practical level by making explicit contractual stipulations regarding a situation of a partial payment in view of the approach taken by the law governing the contract. It is, however, of significant importance that due consideration be given to the later discussed legal boundaries for contractual interference with the default system for enforced performance and the discretionary power of the courts to deviate from contractual modifications.

Where the buyer's obligation to pay the purchase price becomes due on delivery, but the buyer refuses to take delivery, unjustified consequences for the seller may emerge when considering the risk of loss and the incurrence of expenses related to prolonged storage, and where the seller is under a legal duty to preserve the goods. In view of these considerations, and the non-actionable nature of a duty to take delivery under the subject legal systems, and in order to balance the discussed divergence between the civil and common law views on the potential role of good faith in this regard, it is suggested here to enable the seller (as of right) to claim for enforced performance of the buyer's obligation to pay the purchase price where the latter fails to take delivery on improper grounds. The need for this rule is already recognized since the PECL and DCFR are familiar with a similar principle to protect the seller's performance interest. However, there is currently no universally accepted view on the dogmatic qualification of the buyer's obligations (*i.e.* enforceable obligations or non-actionable duties) and the legal impact of a failure to take delivery. This may result in a disagreement between parties from different legal backgrounds, due to a misunderstanding of the enforceability of the contractual obligations.

In order to manage potential difficulties arising from this situation, a simple solution can be found in a contractual stipulation entailing the express obligation of the buyer to pay the purchase price, regardless of the acceptance or refusal of the goods, unless payment cannot reasonably be required, the contract is void or avoided, or the parties are released from their obligations on the occurrence of certain situations to be determined by the parties. Such a precautionary contractual clause significantly lowers the risk that a seller is forced to sell the goods on the market and subsequently has to sue for monetary relief where the buyer fails to take delivery. Hence, with the proposed solution, it can be reasonably expected that the buyer shall take delivery (unless one of the stipulated exceptions apply), meaning that the seller is directly entitled to payment of the purchase price.

306. The third recommendation focusses on the primary notion of the availability of enforced performance of non-monetary obligations in the realm of the sale of goods and the practical implications of divergence. The most obvious example of a non-monetary obligation arising from a commercial sales contract is the delivery of goods in accordance with the contractual stipulations. The difficulties in safeguarding the performance interests of the buyer in this regard are rooted in the favourable civil law view on enforced performance of non-monetary obligations, which is diametrically opposed to the common law reluctance to award enforced performance, instead favouring the award of damages.

These conceptually distinct notions of the enforceability of non-monetary obligations are also found in the three subject jurisdictions. Whereas the dogmatic underpinnings of Dutch contract law allow for enforced performance of contractual obligations (regardless of their nature and occurrence of a failure in performance), Singapore contract law does not envisage enforced performance of non-monetary obligations in the realm of commercial sales, with the exception of specific situations (*e.g.* the delivery of specific and ascertained goods, and when substitute goods are (practically) unobtainable), which are further subject to counter-exceptions. The position of Chinese contract law is somewhat unclear because the statutory principles suggest that a right to enforced performance of a non-monetary obligation is available on a failure in performance. Nonetheless, from a purely theoretical point of view, it can be argued that such a claim does not depend on the occurrence of a non-performance. That having been said, the prevailing legal opinion under Dutch and Chinese contract law is that an award for enforced performance only enables the buyer to give effect to the judicial enforcement order as soon as there is an actual non-performance. This notion fully aligns with the approach taken by the unification instruments, but stands in stark contrast to the approach taken by Singapore contract law, which allows only for enforced performance of commercial sales contracts in very limited situations.

When considering the desired scope of the availability of enforced performance, the importance of the buyer's performance interest in the realm of commercial sales transactions should not be underestimated, due to the potential presence of ancillary performance obligations of the seller, such as the handing over of safety certificates, declarations of origin and the continuous availability of spare parts. Under Dutch and Chinese contract law, as well as the PICC, PECL and DCFR, enforced performance of ancillary obligations is possible on the basis of the standards of reasonableness and fairness, and the good faith principle. This legal escape route is not available in the common law system of Singapore due to a different view on the imposition of good faith in commercial sales contracts.

Based on an overall assessment of the observations provided above, it is submitted here that a universally acceptable solution for the protection of the buyer's performance interest can be best found in the formulation of the buyer's right to performance as a remedial instrument for the seller's delivery obligation, and the intricately interwoven ancillary obligations and duties. This basic understanding of the concept of enforced performance shall not cause major concerns when taking into account the fourth recommendation, which aims to provide sufficient countervailing power to substantially constrain unjustifiable consequences and also to prevent abuse of a right to enforced performance.

A more practical solution to overcome the consequences of the divergence can be found in contractual stipulations that give due consideration to the fact that the concept of delivery encompasses various obligations under the investigated legal systems, such as physical or constructive delivery of the goods and even deemed delivery. Particular attention should also be given to the differing viewpoints on the legal (and thus practical) consequences of a failure to deliver the goods at an agreed time. Depending on the law governing the contract, delivery of the goods can be inextricably linked with the transfer of risk of the seller to the buyer and potentially with the transfer of title. In view of the immense differences in this regard at national and international levels, Incoterms® might be helpful in circumventing and overcoming potential difficulties. This suggestion is also of particular relevance for commercial sales contracts involving carriage of goods in combination with the agreement that the purchase price becomes due during transit. For those involved in such contracts it is of significant practical importance to take note of the full scope of the concept of delivery under the law governing the contract, in particular when the dispatch of the goods brings about legal delivery, including the passing of risk.[1807] Determining the time of the legal delivery of the goods is also important for safeguarding the availability of a cure for non-conformity. This is because under the three investigated jurisdictions, as well as the CISG and DCFR, the time at which conformity of the goods must be determined is inextricably linked with the time the goods are considered as delivered to the buyer (delivery of the goods does not necessarily coincide with the transfer of property in the goods).

307. The objective of the fourth recommendation is to concentrate on bringing about sufficient counterweight to the right to enforced performance versus protecting the non-performing party against unjustifiable consequences (*i.e.* to mitigate the effects of unfettered rights). The suggested counterbalance consists of five elements which are necessary to generate contractual stipulations that sufficiently satisfy the differences in approaches towards appropriate means to protect the interests of contracting parties under the contract law of the subject jurisdictions. This undertaking could be helpful in consolidating the fundamental differences between the civil and common law traditions (at the international level) by taking into account the approaches developed in the three jurisdictions.

308. In view of the above, the first counterweight entails the imposition of an express requirement of a request for enforced performance within a reasonable time from the moment the buyer ought to be aware of the non-delivery. This restriction on the availability of enforced performance is laid down in Chinese contract law and is broadly adopted at the international level, with the exception of the CISG, which is only familiar with examination and notification requirements for non-conforming performance. Under Dutch and Singapore contract law, a failure to demand performance within a specific timeframe is also penalized with legal consequence(s) for the party that fails to make the request in due time, but the timeframe and scope of the legal detriment differ significantly. Although a uniform set of principles would do justice to the civil and common law understanding of the necessity to protect a seller against stale claims, any form of harmonization in this regard requires an assessment of the impact of the legal system as a whole, in order to offset an imbalance in the protection of the interests of contracting parties. In particular, attention should be paid to the differing provisions in the subject legal systems for examination of the goods and notification of the seller about any non-conformities therein. The same consideration applies when bringing about a practical solution in the present situation, where the most important sales law instrument does not follow the approach taken by the PICC, PECL, DCFR and draft PACL. It is therefore

1807 S 5.3.

suggested here that those involved in commercial sales contracts across the borders of the three subject jurisdictions seek recourse to contractual provisions to specify the legal consequences of a delayed request for performance and the applicable period imposed by the law governing the contract. This must be done with an awareness of the legal framework of time limits for examination and notification of a non-conforming performance, and the admissibility of contractual interference with the rules on the availability of enforced performance of a non-monetary obligations arising from an agreement between commercial parties.

309. The above considerations are inextricably linked with the second counterweight, which entails the notion that enforced performance is not available if the aggrieved buyer is able to mitigate the impact on the seller by acquiring (*i.e.* not a duty to find) substitute goods, provided that the goods are readily available in the marketplace. A uniform approach in this regard is necessary when taking into account the legal uncertainty deriving from the significantly different value attached to the availability of replacement goods in view of the enforceability of the seller's delivery obligation at the national and international levels. The practical impact of the divergence between the subject legal systems cannot be overestimated in the context of international commercial sales transactions. This is because the ability of the buyer to obtain substitute goods in the marketplace in the case of a complete non-delivery plays a role in the Dutch and Chinese contract law standards of reasonableness and fairness, and good faith respectively. This stands in stark contrast to the notion that the availability of a substitute transaction is essential to the default rules on enforced performance under Singapore contract law. It appears that the PICC and PECL bring about a reasonable middle ground solution, although difficulties in practice could be expected due to the arbitrary threshold of reasonably obtainable goods. The usefulness of contractual stipulations in this regard is limited where a commercial sales transaction involves the contract law of Singapore. This is because the latter does not allow the parties to (in)directly coerce the buyer into performing a non-monetary obligation that cannot be enforced under the default system.

310. The third counterweight, in the form of hardship as an exemption from enforced performance, is related to the restrictive impact of the doctrine of frustration and a radical change in circumstances employed by Singapore contract law, in view of the concepts of subjective impossibility and hardship adopted by Dutch and Chinese contract law as well as by the unification instruments. Although the limited impact of the common law doctrine of frustration is not surprising, given the way that the availability of enforced performance is structured under Singapore law, the constantly changing elements affecting international commercial sales contracts may require a more flexible and transaction context specific approach. Considering that the importance of the limiting effect of a situation of hardship

is broadly recognised by the unification instruments, as well as by Dutch and Chinese contract law, major obstacles for the acceptance of a broader notion of the concept of hardship are not expected. In particular, when taking into account the earlier discussed situation of a delayed request for performance that may also be barred when enforced performance brings about unacceptable hardship for the seller.

311. The fourth counterweight entails the discretionary power of the court to temporarily or partially deny a claim for enforced performance. The necessity of the imposition of this limitation to the right to enforced performance is also rooted in the argument that adjudicators should be provided with sufficient flexibility to deal with the present day dynamics of international commercial trade. It is, therefore, of little surprise that partial and temporary exemptions from enforced performance are well-known judicial measures at the international level. The advantages of these solutions for certain impediments are also recognised in Dutch and Chinese contract law. However, the all-or-nothing approach of the applicable common law principles in this regard brings about the premise that Singapore courts do not have the same flexibility. From a practical perspective, commercial parties could seek recourse to contractual stipulations to overcome potential difficulties arising from the discussed differences. In order to avoid interpretation issues, the contractual solution should entail (at the very minimum) an extensive description and explanation of the meaning of the impediments triggering exemption from enforced performance, qualification of the listed impediments (whether it is a comprehensive list, or the described impediments are merely indicative) and to what extent the contractual stipulations affect the legal principles regulating the availability of enforced performance under the law governing the contract.

312. The fifth counterweight aims to reduce clear and subtle differences between the ways the three subject jurisdictions have structured the rules on limitation. In this regard the discussed divergence also relates to legal traditions and cultural interpretation of the impact of concluding a contract, and to the extent contractual stipulations may result in a waiver of rights deriving from the agreement and the applicable legal principles. Taking this, and the need to balance the interests of contracting parties in view of the universal concept of party autonomy and legal certainty into account, it is suggested here to allow a reduction and extension of a general limitation period with a floor and cap based on a maximum limitation period. Essential to this attempt to bring about a universally acceptable structure is to allow for renewal of the limitation periods for enforced performance by an acknowledgement of the obligation by the promisor, to allow for suspension of the limitation periods during proceedings (when it relates to the merits of the case) and to acknowledge that on the expiry of a limitation period only the right to claim for enforced performance is removed; the obligation itself should not be affected. However, a harmonised

set of principles is not anticipated in the foreseeable future due to the legal and cultural underpinnings of the discussed limitation periods. It is therefore suggested here that contracting parties agree to a balanced scheme of contractual stipulations entailing the regulation of the limitation of enforced performance in view of the discussed legal boundaries, as well as the rules on the applicable time limits for requesting performance and to cure a non-conforming performance. This undertaking however requires particular scrutiny as an erroneous interpretation of the statutory principles governing the contract may have an immense impact on the availability of enforced performance.

313. The fifth recommendation aims to balance the generous approach of Dutch and Chinese contract law, and the unification instruments, towards the availability of enforced performance in the form of repair and replacement to cure a delivery of an *aliud* (*i.e.* goods different in nature) or *peius* (*i.e.* defective goods) against the reluctance of Singapore contract law to recognise these specific forms of enforced performance in the realm of commercial sales contracts. The disagreement between the subject legal systems is inextricably linked to the extent to which they adopt civil and common law traditional views on enforced performance of non-monetary obligations.

At the international level, it is broadly recognised that a seller to a commercial sales contract can be forced to make a fresh delivery or repair where the seller delivers goods that do not possess the features agreed in the contract. Importantly, the limitations on enforced performance in the form of cure by repair and replacement also apply in cases of a shortfall in goods under the (most important unification instruments in the field of commercial sales contracts) CISG and DCFR, and also under the draft PACL. Considering this significant level of consensus, it is proposed here to strive for a solution that provides the courts with the flexibility to grant a claim for enforced performance to cure a seller's failure to deliver the goods in conformity with the contractual stipulations when the court establishes that this brings about the most appropriate and effective response in view of the buyer's performance interest and protection of the seller's interest against hardship.

The recognition of the availability of enforced performance in the form of repair and replacement should not be limited to unique or difficult to obtain goods. This is because an action for repair and replacement could also be the most appropriate response in the case of non-conforming delivery of commodity goods if, for example, the initial seller observes specific standards in its manufacturing process which are not yet followed by competitors. In view of the foregoing, the buyer should be entitled to express and to substantiate its preference, although the court should not be bound to this choice where the failure in performance is fundamental to the contract. In the latter situation, the distorting effects of enforced performance on the seller's interest could potentially justify a judicial deviation of the freedom of contract. This seller-friendly approach should be balanced with a requirement of giving notice of the non-performance within a reasonable time.

On one hand, the solution suggested above satisfies the civil law strict interpretation of the bindingness of a contractual promise, entitling the aggrieved buyer to claim for enforced performance in the form of cure by repair and replacement. On the other hand, this attempt to narrow the gap between the two major legal traditions reflects the common law concept of a fundamental breach and the buyer-friendly requirement of a reasonable period of time in which to give notice. More importantly, the aforementioned elements are of significant importance in providing the courts sufficient latitude to deal with the complexity of commercial sales transactions across the borders of the subject jurisdictions, and in general when a contract is concluded between parties with respective civil and common law backgrounds. In this situation, contracting parties could expressly stipulate that the buyer is provided with a right to claim for enforced performance in the form of cure by repair and replacement. Although such a provision reflects the civil law tradition, it is accepted under the Singapore regime for consumer sales. In this context, another important aspect is that the consumer sales law, in certain circumstances, allows for the qualification of a business purchasing goods as a consumer. Significantly, the aforementioned considerations may cause a Singapore court to deviate from the traditional narrow interpretation of enforced performance (in the realm of commercial sales) when it concerns a non-conforming unique item and the buyer does not have the financial resources to obtain a similar product in the marketplace.[1808]

314. The sixth recommendation aims to regulate the rules which enable an aggrieved buyer to give effect to a judicial order for enforced performance in the context of commercial sales contracts. This suggestion entails a set of three inextricably linked principles. The starting point is the recognition of the ability of the buyer to obtain the goods from the seller with support of a public enforcement officer whereby the costs of enforcement shall be borne by the non-performing party. In view of the general reluctance against direct execution (with the exception of the Netherlands), the second (subsequent) principle entails the notion that the aggrieved party is only allowed to execution once the court provided the latter with judicial leave for giving effect to its order. The third principle is necessary for dealing with situations where the court establishes that obtaining the goods directly from the seller is not possible or requires more than reasonable efforts. In these cases the buyer should be allowed to obtain the goods from another source at the expense

1808 See the US case *Stephan's Machine & Tool* (n 1223). In this case it was considered that a degree for specific performance may include such terms and conditions as to payment of the price, damages, or other relief as the court may deem just.

of the seller. When this is not possible or appropriate, the aggrieved buyer should be allowed to compel the seller to deliver the goods by means of a financial sanction (*astreinte pénale*).

For the aforementioned suggested principles to be laid down in an international contract law instrument, however, requires a significantly liberal attitude by Singapore courts when a contract is governed by this instrument, in particular when considering the way Singapore contract law regulates enforced performance of a non-monetary obligation. A less obvious but important element for complex commercial sales transactions is the common law constant supervision argument, which is rooted in the principle that the court is responsible for safeguarding the correct execution of its order for enforced performance. The element of sufficiently precise terms and the penal consequences of non-compliance with an order for enforced performance plays an important role in the application of the constant supervision bar. To overcome this barrier, it is suggested here that allocation of the responsibility of enforcement to the party provided with an order for enforced performance (with the support of an enforcement officer that is subject to government regulation), and the costs of enforcement to the non-performing party, affect the relevance of the counter-exception of constant supervision.

At a practical level, it is of significant importance that those involved in commercial sales contracts across the borders of the subject legal systems take into consideration the fact that Singapore contract law does not allow the parties to circumvent the rules on enforced performance of non-monetary obligations. In view of this, contractual stipulations affecting the underlying principles of the constant supervision argument and the allocation of the responsibility of enforcement may not have the desired effect when the court asserts that they indirectly coerce performance.

315. The objective of the seventh recommendation is to balance the protection of the buyer's and seller's interests by contractual modification of the default rules dealing with the availability of enforced performance of non-monetary obligations. The complexity of this matter traces back to the limitations on the freedom of contract; that is, contractual (substantive) unfairness under Dutch contract law,[1809] the protection of the principle of good faith and the state's interest under Chinese contract law, and protection of the discretionary power of the courts under Singapore contract law.

In view of the above, the seventh recommendation encompasses a general permission of clauses affecting the availability of the right to claim for enforced performance to cure a non-delivery or non-conforming delivery. This may concern a positive clause which provides the buyer with the freedom to choose between the various forms of enforced performance in the case the seller fails to provide the goods in accordance with the terms

1809 Substantive unfairness can be remedied (in exceptional situations) by application of the derogatory effect of the standards of reasonableness and fairness.

of the contract. The parties could also entirely exclude the buyer's right to enforced performance. A key element of the suggested approach is that the courts are provided with the discretionary power to strike out a clause affecting the availability of enforced performance when it establishes that it brings about a contractual (substantive) unfairness with insurmountable consequences, which could not have been foreseen by the aggrieved party at the time of conclusion of the contract.

To achieve a pragmatic solution that does not require intervention in existing legal principles is much more difficult. This is due to the fact that Singapore contract law does not honour contractual protection of the performance interest of the party to a commercial sales contract if enforced performance of the subject matter is not available under the default system. Consequently, for those involved in commercial sales contracts across the borders of the subject jurisdictions, and in general for parties with a civil and common law background, it is of immense importance to give due consideration to the limited effect of contractual protection of the interest of the parties in actual performance of the assumed obligations when this is not envisaged by the law governing the contract.

316. *On balance* – In the realm of commercial sales contracts, the level of protection of the buyer's performance interest varies significantly. At one end of the spectrum, a directly enforceable right for non-delivery and non-conforming delivery is provided by Dutch and Chinese contract law, as well as by the identified unification instruments. At the other end, enforced performance of an obligation to bring about a certain state of affairs under a commercial sales contract is a severely restrictive exception to the primary right to damages under Singapore contract law. This distinction, however, is less clear cut when considering the discussion in the preceding chapters about the various options to protect the parties' performance interest (*e.g.* specific performance, (interlocutory) mandatory injunctions, contractual penalties and liquidated damages), the different situations of non-performance and the bars to enforcement of obligations arising from a commercial sales contract.

It appears that Dutch and Chinese contract law, in line with the unification instruments, provide the buyer with a significant level of protection of its expectations of the seller's performance obligations. This, in effect, means that the aggrieved buyer is provided with a statutory right to enforced performance of the seller's obligation to deliver the goods in accordance with the contractual stipulations. Where the seller fails to fulfil this obligation, the aggrieved buyer may claim for delivery in the case of non-delivery, and has a right to demand a fresh delivery and to put a defect right in the case of a non-conforming delivery. This liberal approach towards the concept of enforced performance stands in stark contrast with the default response to a failure in performance of non-monetary obligations under Singapore contract law; that is, damages. Only when it concerns the delivery of specific and ascertained goods, when substitute goods are only obtainable with great difficulty, and the court thinks it fit in view of the adequacy of damages bar, can enforced performance of the seller's delivery obligation be granted in the absence of counter-exceptions. Important exceptions to this already limited availability of enforced performance are the bar of constant supervision, vagueness, lack of mutuality, and unfairness following a lack of monetary consideration or adequate consideration, the clean-hands doctrine and potential hardship for the seller following the enforced performance. The degree of protection of the buyer's performance interest is further limited under Singapore contract law due to the nature of the judicial measures to give actual effect to an order for enforced performance (*i.e.* contempt of court procedure which may result in monetary fines imposed by the court and even an order for imprisonment of the non-performing party) which are considered draconian measures. This research reveals that Dutch and Chinese contract law, as well as the unification instruments identified, also impose limitations on the right to enforced performance under, at first glance, similar principles. For example, legitimate interest as a bar against abuse, undeterminable substance, substantive unfairness, subjective impossibility of performance resulting in an unacceptable change of the equilibrium and a duty to mitigate losses by obtaining substitute goods. However, the actual impact of these legal limitations on the availability of enforced performance is significantly less severe. This reiterates that the buyer is provided with a much greater degree of protection for its expectation of performance under the aforementioned legal systems than under Singapore contract law which favours damages over enforced performance.

There is also a significant variation in the admissibility of contractual stipulations (indirectly) regulating the availability of enforced performance where enforcement of the subject matter is not envisaged by the law governing the contract. It is here where the concept of freedom of contract brings about fundamental differences between the three investigated jurisdictions. Whereas Dutch and Chinese contract law, and the unification instruments identified, appear to honour freedom of contract within general legal boundaries (*e.g.* reasonable and fairness, and good faith considerations), Singapore contract law follows the common law approach by not honouring contractual clauses regulating the protection of the buyer's expectation of performance if this would (indirectly) coerce performance of non-monetary obligations that are not enforceable under the default system. Nonetheless, the above-described limiting factors are merely considerations in the exercise of the court's discretion to award a claim for enforced performance. In other words, the vast majority of the discussed limiting factors are not necessarily a bar to enforced performance. This suggests that the flexibility of the Singapore courts to grant an order for enforced performance does not differ that much from the flexibility provided to the courts under Dutch and Chinese contract law, and the approach taken by the unification instruments. Nonetheless, the restrictive concept of enforced performance and the number of different bars to enforced performance suggest that the buyer's contractual right to delivery of commodities, does not play a meaningful role under Singapore contract law when substitute goods are available at the marketplace. Hence, the balance of approach is clearly in favour of the seller's interest where it otherwise would be forced to performance under Dutch and Chinese contract law, as well as under the unification instruments. There is, however, an important argument in favour of the restricted common law view on the concept of enforced performance, which may counterbalance the overwhelming representation of the civil law approach at the international level. That is, for situations where a non-performance follows from a change of mind, enforced performance should not be readily available because it may unduly interfere with the party's freedom.[1810] The same freedom also underlies the ability to enter into a contract in the first place.[1811] This reasoning is rooted in the well-known common law principle that commercial parties bargain for monetary considerations and not to obtain the actual subject matter, and the inextricably linked efficient breach theory.[1812]

Nonetheless, for those currently working in the realm of international commercial sales transactions it is of paramount importance to bear in mind that the discussed legal systems, in favouring protection of the interest of the aggrieved party in performance, are not on the same page when considering the impact of the principles protecting the non-performing party against abuse and unjustifiable consequences of enforcement of its performance obligations. That said, the diametrically opposed doctrinal viewpoints on the availability of enforced performance could (theoretically) converge when considering the discretionary power of Singapore courts to decree enforced performance, the overarching principle of reasonableness and fairness under Dutch contract law, the principle of good faith under Chinese contract law, and similar standards under the unification instruments identified. Ergo, the flexibility of the courts to deal with a claim for enforced performance varies according to the circumstances of the case. It is, therefore, quite impossible to define standard rules for the degree of protection of the buyer's performance interest and protection of the seller's interest against unacceptable consequences of enforced performance. Notwithstanding the above observations, the civil and common law traditions still have a significant impact on the question as to whether performance obligations under a commercial sales contract can be ordered by the court when considering the divergence in the notion of the scope of enforced performance and the limitations on the freedom of contract to protect a buyer's performance in any of the subject legal systems.

317. *On a final note* – This comparative work does not advocate that the three subject legal systems should adopt a uniform response to a claim for enforced performance of non-monetary obligations arising from a commercial sales contract, because domestic rules surrounding the concept of enforced performance are intricately interwoven with

1810 Chen-Wishart 2017 (n 26); Virgo and Worthington 2018 (n 29) 98–126.
1811 *Ibid.*
1812 *Ibid.*

general contract law principles which are developed in a national context. As a result, it is submitted here that to embrace legal solutions available at the international level (in order to equalise and overcome the most fundamental divergence between civil and common law traditional views on enforced performance) would disrupt the legal structure of the subject jurisdictions when the impact on other provisions and rules are not taken into account. It is, therefore, of paramount importance that the concept of enforced performance be treated holistically, in order to find common ground and overcome fundamental differences, and to obtain new insights and find new ways to deal with allegedly insurmountable disagreements between the two major legal traditions. In this regard, it is not appropriate to focus merely on the primary principles that allow or disallow enforcement of the buyer's and seller's performance obligations under a commercial sales contract. Considering the ambitions of the Netherlands, Singapore and China,[1813] legislators in the three jurisdictions may draw inspiration from the findings of the present work to move towards a form of convergence that does not distort the balance between protection of the parties performance interest, the necessity of protection against abuse and the notion of freedom of contracting as a barrier to contractual (substantive) unfairness. It will be particularly interesting to see if and how the draft PACL develops further in view of the ambition to harmonize the contract law of various jurisdictions in Asia, which are founded on Dutch, French and German based civil law, to legal systems which are rooted in centuries-long legal traditions, from jurisdictions with a common law background.

1813 Ch 1.

Bibliography

A – Attributed works

Abas P, *Rebus sic stantibus: een onderzoek naar de toepassing van de clausula rebus sic stantibus in de rechtspraak van enige Europese landen* (Kluwer 1989)

- 'Enige gedachten over de gedeeltelijke ontbinding (aanpassing) in de zin van art. 6:258 BW' (1998) 6307 *WPNR* 211

Adams M and Heirbaut D (eds), *The Method and Culture of Comparative Law: Essays in Honour of Mark Van Hoecke* (Hart Publishing 2014)

Ahmad Tajudin A, 'Article 55 on Open-Price Contract: A Wider Interpretation Necessary?' (2014) 3(3) Journal of Arts and Humanities 38

Aksoy HC, Impossibility in Modern Private Law (Springer International Publishing 2014)

Asser C and Vranken JBM, *Mr. C. Assers handleiding tot de beoefening van het Nederlands burgerlijk recht: Algemeen deel.* (W.E.J. Tjeenk Willink 1995)

Bakels F, 'Ontbinding van wederkerige overeenkomsten' (Dphil thesis, Leiden University 1994)

Baker JH, *Introduction to English Legal History* (4th edn, Oxford University Press 2007)

Ballantine HW, 'Mutuality and Consideration' (1914) v 28 n 2, I, *Harvard Law Review* 121-134

Bar C von, Clive E, Schulte-Nölke H et al (eds), Principles, Definitions and Model Rules of European Private Law, Draft Common Frame of Reference (DCFR), Articles and Comments (prepared by the Study Group on a European Civil Code and the Research Group on the Existing EC Private Law (Acquis Group)

Bartels SE and Mierlo AIM van, *Mr. C. Assers Handleiding tot de beoefening van het Nederlands Burgerlijk Recht. 3. Vermogensrecht algemeen. Deel IV. Algemeen goederenrecht* (Kluwer 2013)

Bartels SE and Velten AA van, *Mr. C. Assers Handleiding tot de beoefening van het Nederlands Burgerlijk Recht. 5. Zakenrecht, Eigendom en beperkte rechten* (Wolters Kluwer 2017)

Beaton J, Burrows A and Cartwright J, *Anson's Law of Contract* (30th edn, Oxford University Press 2016)

Beekhoven van den Boezem MB, 'commentaar op artikel 611c' in Vlas P and Tjong Tjin Tai TFE (eds), *Groene Serie Burgerlijke Rechtsvordering* (Wolters Kluwer 2017)

Bell GF, 'Why should Singapore withdraw its reservation to the United Nations Convention on Contracts for the International Sale of Goods (CISG)' (2005) 9 Singapore Year Book of International Law

Berg MAMC van den and Gulijk S van, *Mr. C. Assers Handleiding tot de beoefening van het Nederlands Burgerlijk Recht. 7.*

Bijzondere overeenkomsten. Deel VI. Aanneming van werk (Wolters Kluwer 2017)

Berg MAMC van den, 'De keuze tussen nakoming, schadevergoeding of ontbinding en de belangen van de crediteur' (2001) 6439 WPNR 299

- 'Crediteursverzuim: relict van een verouderd rechtsdenken', in Dijck G van, Gestel R van, Giesen I and Hammerstein F (eds), *Cirkels. Een terugblik op een vooruitziende blik* (Kluwer 2013)

Bergsten EE and Kröll S, *International arbitration and international commercial law: synergy, convergence, and evolution: liber amicorum Eric Bergsten* (Wolters Kluwer 2012)

Birks P, 'Rights, Wrongs, and Remedies' (2000) v 20 n 1 Oxford Journal of Legal Studies

Blei Weissmann YG, 'commentaar op artikel 127 Boek 6 BW' in RJQ Klomp and HN Schelhaas (eds), *Groene Serie Verbintenissenrecht* (Wolters Kluwer 2018)

Bowen HS, *Outlines of Specific Performance* (HeinOnline legal classics library, William S. Hein & Company 2018)

Broekema-Engelen BJ, 'commentaar op artikel 74 Boek 6 BW' paras 2-4 in Klomp RJQ and Schelhaas HN (eds), *Groene Serie Verbintenissenrecht* (Wolters Kluwer 2011)

Bu Y (ed), *Chinese Civil Law* (Beck and Hart Publishing 2013)

Burrows A, 'Specific Performance at the Crossroads' (1984) 4 Legal Studies 102

Burrows JF, Finn J and Todd S, *Law of Contract in New Zealand*, (8th edn, Butterworths 1997)

Busch D and Hondius E (eds), Principles of European Contract Law and Dutch Law (Part III). A Commentary II (Kluwer Law International 2006)

Butler P, 'The Doctrines of Parol Evidence Rule and Consideration -- A Deterrence to the Common Law Lawyer?' in *Celebrating Success: 25 Years United Nations Convention on Contracts for the International Sale of Goods* (Collation of Papers at UNCITRAL, SIAC Conference 22-23 September 2005, Singapore) <https://www.cisg.law.pace.edu/cisg/biblio/butler4.html#46>

Carter JW, Phang A and Phang SY, 'Performance Following Repudiation: Legal and Economic Interests' (1999) v 15 n 2 The Journal of Contract Law 97

Cartwright J, 'Redelijkheid en billijkheid: a view from English law', <https://openaccess.leidenuniv.nl/bitstream/handle/1887/42938/02-Cartwright_bwkj_30.pdf?sequence=1>

Chan HHM, The Legal System of Singapore (Butterworths Asia 1995)

Chan SK, 'A New Charter of Justice' in Goh Y, Tan P (eds), *Singapore Law, 50 Years in the Making*

Chang H, 'The legal history of contemporary China' (Zhongguo Jindai Fazhishi) (1973) Tapei: The Commercial Press, 283

Cheah WL and Goh Y, 'An empirical study on the Singapore Courts of Appeal's citation of academic works: Reflections on the Relationship between Singapore's Judiciary and Academia' (2017) 3 Singapore Academy of Law Journal <http://academypublishing.org.sg/

Journals/Singapore-Academy-of-Law-Journal/e-First/ctl/eFirstPDFPage/mid/519/ArticleId/1090/Citation/eFirstPDF>

Chen J, *Chinese Law, Towards an Understanding of Chinese Law, Its Nature and Development* (The Londen-Leiden Series on Law, Administration and Development, v 3, Kluwer Law International 1999)

– Chinese Law, Context and Transformation (Martinus Nijhoff Publishers, 2008)

Chen L (Lihu) and Zhu P, 'On the Actual Performance System in International Contract Law (2008) issue 1 Present-day Law Science 94 (陈立虎，朱萍．国际合同法上的实际履行制度研究．时代法学)

Chen L, 'The Historical Development of the Civil Law Tradition in China: A Private Law Perspective' (2010) 78 Tijdschrift voor Rechtsgeschiedenis, 159

Chen-Wishart M, 'Contractual Remedies: Beyond Enforcing Contractual Duties' (2017) George Washington Law Review, 85(6) 1617-1624

Chen-Wishart M, Loke A and Ong B (eds), *Remdies for Breach of Contract: Studies in the Contract Law of China* (Oxford University Press 2016)

Cheshire GC, Furmston MO, Fifoot CHS, Phang A, *Cheshire, Fifoot and Furmston's Law of Contract: Singapore and Malaysian Ed.* (Buttersworths Asia 1994)

Chesterman M, 'Contempt: In the Common Law, but Not the Civil Law' (1997) v 46 n 3 The international and comparative law quarterly 521

Chong S, Cavinder Bull SC (eds) and a team of expert contributors, *Law Relating to Specific Contracts in Singapore* (2nd edn, Sweet & Maxwell 2016)

Chow KF, *Law and Practice of Construction Contracts* (v 1, 4th edn, Sweet & Maxwell Asia 2004)

Cohen N and McKendrick E (eds), *Comparative Remedies for Breach of Contract: International Studies in the Theory of Private Law* (Hart Publishing 2005)

Davies PS, Penner J, *Equity, trusts and commerce* (vol 24 Hart studies in private law, Hart Publishing 2017)

DiMatteo LA and Chen L (eds) *Chinese Contract Law, Civil and Common Law Perspectives* (Cambridge University Press, 2017)

Edward F, A treatise on the specific performance of contracts, including those of public companies (2nd edn, W.C. Little 1861)

Eisenberg MA, 'Actual and Virtual Specific Performance, the Theory of Efficient Breach, and the Indifference Principle in Contract Law' (2005) 93 California Law Review 975

Eisenberg MA, 'The Bargain Principle and Its Limits' (1982) 95 Harvard Law Review 741

Elizalde F de (ed), *Uniform Rules for European Contract Law?: A Critical Assessment* (Hart Publishing 2018)

Fandl KJ, 'Cross-Border Commercial Contracts and Consideration' (2016) 34 Berkeley J. Int'l Law 1

Farnsworth EA, 'Legal Remedies for Breach of Contract' (1970) 70 Colum. L. Rev. 1145

– 'A Common Lawyer's View of His Civilian Colleagues' (1996) 57 Louisiana Law Review 227

Feenstra AJ, 'Het aanbod tot betaling van schadevergoeding en kosten in art 6:86: harmonie- of conflictmodel?' (1998) WPNR 6319

Feinman JM, 'Good Faith and Reasonable Expectations' (2013) Arkansas Law Review <http://media.law.uark.edu/arklawreview/files/2015/02/525-570-Feinman.pdf>

Feng C, Nelson LP and Simon TW, *China's Changing Legal System, Lawyers & Judges on Civil & Criminal Law* (Palgrave Macmillan 2016)

Florijn, EOHP, Ontstaan en ontwikkeling van het nieuwe Burgerlijk Wetboek (Dphil thesis, Universitaire Pers Maastricht 1994)

Fried C, *Contract as Promise: A Theory of Contractual Obligation* (Oxford University Press 2015)

Fu J, *Modern European and Chinese Contract Law, A Comparative Study of Party Autonomy* (Wolters Kluwer Law & Business 2011)

Gillette C and Walt SD, The UN Convention on Contracts for the International Sale of Goods: Theory and Practice (2nd edn Cambridge University Press 2016)

Giuliano AM, 'Nonconformity in the Sale of Goods between the United States and China: The New Chinese Contract Law, the Uniform Commercial Code, and the Convention on Contracts for the International Sale of Goods' (2006) v 18 n 1 Florida Journal of International Law 331

Goetz C and Scott R, 'Enforcing Promises: An Examination of the Basis of Contract' (1980) 80 Yale L. J. 1261

Goh Y and Tan P, 'An Empirical study on the development of Singapore Law' (2011) 28 (Singapore Academy of Law Journal) 176

Goh Y and Yip M, 'Past consideration or unconnected consideration?' (2012) SAL Ann Rev 553

Goh Y, Koh P, Lee PW, Phang A and Tham CH, *The Law of Contract in Singapore* (Andrew Phang Boon Leong (ed) Academy Publishing 2012)

Greuter-Vreeburg YMI and Gessel-de Roo MJEG van (eds), Verbintenissenrecht, 1798–1814 (Werken der Stichting tot uitgaaf der bronnen van het oud-vaderlandse recht no 2002)

Haas D, 'De grenzen van het recht op nakoming' (Dphil thesis, Vrije Universiteit Amsterdam 2009)

Haazen OA, 'Precedent in the Netherlands' (2019) vol. 11.1 Electronic Journal Of Comparative Law <http://www.ejcl.org/111/article111-12.pdf>

Han S, 'Liabilities in Contract Law of China: Their Mechanism and Points in Dispute' (2006) 1 Frontiers Law China 121

Hao Liyan (郝丽燕), 'On Delivery of Substitute Goods in the Case of Defective Performance of Sales of Specific Goods' (论特定物买卖瑕疵履行时的交付替代物), Jinan University School of Political Science and Law (济南大学政法学院) (2017) issue 9 Journal of Politics and Law 86

Harris D, Campbell D and Halson R, *Remedies for Breach of Contract* (2nd edn, Cambridge University Press 2002)

Hartkamp AS and Sieburgh SH, *Mr. C. Assers Handleiding tot de beoefening van het Nederlands Burgerlijk Recht. 6. Verbintenissenrecht. Deel IV. De verbintenis uit de wet* (Wolters Kluwer 2015)

Hartkamp AS, *Mr. C. Assers Handleiding tot de beoefening van het Nederlands Burgerlijk Recht. 3. Vermogensrecht algemeen. Deel I. Europees recht en Nederlands vermogensrecht* (Wolters Kluwer 2018)

Hartkamp AS, Tillema MMM, Heide ter AEB, 'Contract Law in the Netherlands' (Kluwer Law International 2011)

Hartlief T, Tjittes RPJL, 'Kroniek van het vermogensrecht' (2001) v 76 Nederlands Juristenblad 1459

He Q, *Chinese legal history* (3rd edn, Legal Press China 2002)

He Xu Xu (贺栩栩), 'Improvement of Rules on Continuous Performance in Sales Contracts' (论买卖合同法中继续履行规则的完善) issue 12 Political Science and Law 94 (政治与法律)

Hendrikx A, 'Het aanvullen van een leemte in de overeenkomst naar Nederlands en Engels recht' Een Kwart Eeuw : Privaatrechtelijke Opstellen, Aangeboden Aan Prof. Mr. H.J. Snijders Ter Gelegenheid Van Zijn Emeritaat (Wolters Kluwer 2016) 155

Herman S, 'Specific Performance: a Comparative Analysis' (2003) v 7 issue 1 Edinburgh Law Review 5

– 'Specific Performance: a Comparative Analysis' (2003) v 7 issue 2 Edinburgh Law Review 194

Hijma J and Olthof MM, *Compendium van het Nederlands vermogensrecht* (13th edn, Wolters Kluwer 2017)

Hijma J, 'Koopprijsvermindering' (2018) 7202 WPNR 566

Hijma J, *Mr. C. Assers Handleiding tot de beoefening van het Nederlands Burgerlijk Recht 7-I* Bijzondere overeenkomsten: Koop en ruil 8th edn* (2013)

Hoecke M van, 'Methodology of Comparative Legal Research' (2017) 1 Comparative Law Methodology 127

Hofmann LC and Opstall SN van, *Het Nederlands verbintenissenrecht: De algemene leer van de verbintenissen: Eerste gedeelte* (9th edn, Tjeenk Willink 1976)

Holthöfer E, 'Niederlande' in Coing H, *Handbuch der Quellen und Literatur der neueren europäischen Privatrechtsgeschichte* 3: Das 19 Jahrhundert 1: Gesetzgebung zum allgemeinen Privatrecht (C.H. Beck Verlag 1982)

Honnold JO, *Uniform Law for International Sales under the 1980 United Nations Convention* (3rd edn, Kluwer Law International 1999)

Hunter H, *Law of Sales in Singapore* (Singapore Academy of Law, Academy Publishing 2017)

Husa J, *A New Introduction to Comparative Law* (Hart Publishing, 2015)

Hynes JD, 'Freedom of Contract, Fiduciary Duties, and Partnerships: The Bargain Principle and the Law of Agency' (1997) 54(2) Wash & Lee L Rev

Jansen N and Zimmerman R (eds), *Commentaries on European Contract Law* (Oxford University Press 2018)

Janssen JFM, 'De levering bij voorbaat van toekomstige goederen' (2006) 6685 WPNR

Ji F, 'Research and Analysis on Excessively High Expenses of Performance in China' (2016) Politics and Law Forum 148

Jiang H, 'Enlarged State Power to Declare Nullity, 'The Hidden State Interest in the Chinese Contract Law' (2014) vol 7, 1 *Journal of Civil Law Studies*

Jiang H, 'Freedom of Contract Under State Supervision' (2015) SSRN Electronic Journal

Jones W, 'Some questions regarding the significance of the general provisions of Civil Law of the People's Republic of China' (1987) 28 Harvard International Law Journal 313

Jong GT de, *Niet-nakoming van verbintenissen* (Monografieën BW n B33, Kluwer 2017)

Jong GT de, Krans HB and Wissink MH, *Verbintenissenrecht algemeen* (Studiereeks Burgerlijk Recht, 5th edn, Wolters Kluwer 2018)

Jongbloed AW, 'commentaar op artikel 296 Boek 3 BW' in Hijma J (ed), *Groene Serie Vermogensrecht* (Wolters Kluwer 2018)

- 'commentaar op artikel 303. Vereiste van voldoende belang' in Hijma J (ed), *Groene Serie Vermogensrecht* (Wolters Kluwer 2018)

Jongbloed AW and Struik H, 'Vooruilopen op tekortkoming bij niet-opeisbare verbintenissen volgens het NBW' (1983) AA 704

Kantor M, 'The Convention on Contracts for the International Sale of Goods: An International Sales Law, 1 International Law Practicum (NYS Bar Assoc. Autumn 1988)

Kim SY, 'All in Good Faith: Recognising the Doctrine of Good Faith in Singapore's International Sales Law' (2016) (http://www.singaporelawblog.sg/blog/article/168)

Kimel D, 'Neutrality, Autonomy, and Freedom in Contract' (2001) 21 OJLS 473

- 'Remedial Rights and Substantive Rights in Contract Law' (2002) 8 Legal Theory 313
- *From Promise to Contract: towards a liberal theory of contract theory of contract* (Hart Publishing 2003)

Koopmann MWE, 'commentaar op artikel 322 Boek 3 BW' in Hijma J (ed), *Groene Serie Vermogensrecht* (Wolters Kluwer 2019)

Koot RMChM, 'commentaar op artikel 38 Boek 6 BW' in Klomp RJQ and Schelhaas HN (eds), Groene Serie Verbintenissenrecht (Wolters Kluwer 2011)

Kruisinga SA, 'The Impact of Uniform Law on National Law: Limits and Possibilities – CISG and Its Incidence in Dutch Law' (2009) vol 13.2 Electronic Journal of Comparative Law <https://www.ejcl.org/132/art132-2.pdf> accessed on 2 January 2019

Lawson FH and Teff H, Remedies of English Law (2nd edn, Butterworths 1980)

Lee SY, 'A Look at "Good Faith" in the Common Law' [unpublished, archived at CJ Koh Law Library]

Lee YJ (ed), *A Study on Draft Articles Principles of Asian Contract Law: Performance & Non-Performance II* (Asia Private Law Review No. 7 special 2016)

Legrand P, 'Comparative legal Studies and Commitment to Theory' (1995) 58, 2 Modern Law Review 262

Li G, Explanation and Application of the Contract Law (Xinghua Press, 1999)

Liang H, 'On Contract Liability' (1982) 1 Study and Inquiry 62

– 'Problems on Changes of Circumstance in Contract Law'(1988) in 6 Studies in Law 40

Liming W, 'Specific Performance in Chinese Contract Law: An East-West Comparison' (1992) v 1 issue 2 Asia Pacific Law Review 18

– *Breach of Contract Theory* (China University of Political Science and Law Press 2003)
– *Contract Law of China* (China Law & Society Library, William S. Hein & Co., Inc 2016)

Ling B, *Contract Law in China* (Sweet & Maxwell Asia 2002)

Liu T, 'On Grounds for the Application and Limitations of the Specific Performance from the Law and Economics Perspective' (2010) 6 Northern Legal Science 110.

Loke AFH, 'The Lemon Law and the Integrated Enhancement of Consumer Rights in Singapore' (2014) Singapore Journal of Legal Studies 285-306

Lorenzon F, Baatz Y, Nicoll C and Sassoon DM, *C.I.F. and F.O.B. Contracts* (5th edn, Sweet & Maxwell 2012)

Lu Chen, 'Specific Performance and Its Limits' (2007) issue 4 Journal of Comparative Law 98 (芦谌, . 履行请求权及其界限.比较法研究. 2007年. 期号 4. 页码 98)

Luca V de, 'The Conformity of the Goods to the Contract in International Sales' (2015) v 27 n 1 Pace International Law Review 163

Luo W and Liu J, *A Complete Research Guide to the Laws of the People's Republic of China (PRC)* (2003) Law Library Resource Xchange <http://en.pkulaw.cn.ezproxy.leidenuniv.nl:2048/Article/Article1.aspx>

MacMillian C, 'From Promise to Contract: towards a liberal theory of contract' (2004) 15 no 1 King's Law Journal 202

Mak V, *Performance-Oriented Remedies in European Sale of Goods Law* (Studies of the Oxford Institute of European and Comparative Law, Hart Publishing 2009)

Man Y and Goh Y, 'Dealing with unforeseen circumstances: Contractual construction and equitable adjustment' (2004) 1 Journal of Business Law 89

Mattei U, 'Comparative Law and Critical Legal Studies' in Mathias Reimann and Reinhard Zimmerman (eds), *The Oxford Handbook of Comparative Law* (Oxford University Press 2006)

Mayne JD and McGregor H, *Mayne and McGregor on Damages* (18th edn, Sweet & Maxwell, 2009)

McMahon JP, 'Review' (1990) 21 Journal of Maritime Law and Commerce

Meng Z, 'Party Autonomy, Private Autonomy, and Freedom of Contract' (2014) 10(6) Canadian Social Science 212-216 <http://www.cscanada.net/index.php/css/article/view/5155 DOI: http://dx.doi.org/10.3968/5155>

Michaels R, 'The Functional Method of Comparative Law' in Mathias Reimann and Reinhard Zimmerman (eds), *The Oxford Handbook of Comparative Law* (Oxford University Press 2006)

Muñoz DR, 'The Rules on Communication of Defects in the CISG: Static Rules and Dynamic Environments. Different Scenarios for a Single Player' (2005) Pace essay <http://www.cisg.law.pace.edu/cisg/biblio/munoz.html#389>

Murray P and Lin J, International Trade and Maritime Law in China (Thomson Reuters 2017)

Narasimhan S, 'Of Expectations, Incomplete Contracting, and the Bargain Principle' (1986) 74(4) California Law Review 1123

Nispen CJJC van, Sancties in het vermogensrecht (serie Mon. NBW deel A11, Kluwer 2003)

Oosterhuis J, *Specific Performance in German, French and Dutch Law in the Nineteenth Century: remedies in an age of fundamental rights and industrialisation* (Brill Academic Publishers 2011)

O'Sullivan J and Hilliard J, *The Law of Contract* (6th edn, Oxford University Press 2014)

Peerenboom R, 'Judicial Independence in China: Common Myths and Unfounded Assumptions' (2010) Cambridge University Press 69

Phang ABL, *The Development of Singapore Law Historical and Socio-Legal Perspectives* (Butterworths 1990)

- 'Liquidated Damages in a Statutory Context' (1992) v 5 n 1 Journal of Contract Law 74
- 'Specific Performance – Exploring the Roots of "Settled Practice"' (1998) 61 Modern Law Review 421
- Contract Law (2003) 4 Singapore Academy of Law Annual Review of Singapore Cases 127
- *From Foundation to Legacy: The Second Charter of Justice* (Singapore Academy of Law 2006)
- Phang ABL and Goh Y, Contract Law in Singapore (Wolters Kluwer 2012)

Pollock F, Maitland FW, *The History of English Law before the Time of Edward I* (2nd edn, Liberty Fund 2010)

Raz J, *The Morality of Freedom* (Clarendon Press 1986)

Remien O, 'Enforced Performance in European Contract Law' in Boele-Woelki K, Grosheide FW and Hondius EH (red), *The Future of European Contract Law : Essays in honour of*

Ewoud Hondius to commemorate his retirement as professor of civil law at the University of Utrecht (Kluwer Law International 2007)

Reynolds D, *China, 1898–1912: the Xinzheng Revolution and Japan* (Harvard University Press for the Council on East Asia Studies 1993)

Rossum MM van, 'commentaar op artikel 17 Boek 7 BW' CG Breedveld-de Voogd and SE Bartels (eds), *Groene Serie Bijzondere overeenkomsten,* (Wolters Kluwer 2017)

Rowan S, 'The new French law of contract' (2017) International & Comparative Law Quarterly

- *Remedies for Breach of Contract A Comparative Analysis of the Protection of Performance* (Oxford University Press 2012)

Schaick AC van, *Mr. C. Assers Handleiding tot de beoefening van het Nederlands Burgerlijk Recht. Procesrecht. 2. Eerste aanleg* (Wolters Kluwer 2016)

Schelhaas HN (general ed), Busch D, Hondius E, Kooten H van and Schrama W (eds), *The Principles of European Contract Law and Dutch Law: A Commentary* (Kluwer Law International 2002)

Schelhaas HN , Verheij AJ and Wessels B, *Bijzondere overeenkomsten* (Studiereeks Burgerlijk Recht 4th edn, Wolters Kluwer 2016)

Schmidt auf Altenstadt PJM von, Vermeulen FE and Wiel BTM van der (eds), *Middelen voor Meijer. Liber amicorum mr. R.S. Meijer* (Boom Juridische Uitgevers 2013)

Schmiegelow M, Schmiegelow H (eds), *Institutional Competition between Common Law and Civil Law, Theory and Policy* (Springer 2014)

Schollmeyer M, Utlu A, 'Die Nacherfüllung im Kauf' (2009) v 31 issue 10 JURA 721

Scholten P, *Mr. C. Assers Handleiding tot de beoefening van het Nederlands Burgerlijk Recht. Algemeen Deel* (W.E.J. Tjeenk Willink 1974)

Schoordijk HC, *Het algemeen gedeelte van het verbintenissenrecht naar het nieuw burgerlijk wetboek* (Kluwer 1979)

Schüller CL, *Het Burgerlijk Wetboek, met Aanteekeningen* (Utrecht, Schultze en Voerman 1841)

Schwenzer I (ed), Commentary on the UN Convention on the International Sale of Goods (CISG) (4th edn, Oxford University Press 2016)

Schwenzer I, 'Specific Performance and Damages According to the 1994 UNIDROIT Principles of International Commercial Contracts' (1998) v 1 n 3 European Journal of Law Reform 289

Schwenzer I, Hachem P and Kee C, *Global Sales and Contract Law* (Oxford University Press 2012)

Shen J, 'The Remedy of Requiring Performance under the CISG and the Relevance of Domestic Rules [particulary in the context of China-related sales transactions]' (1996) *Arizona Journal of International & Comparative Law* 253-306 <https://www.cisg.law.pace.edu/cisg/biblio/shen1.html>

Shenasaei H, Qin M, Shirvani F, 'Limitations of Specific Performance in the China Contract Law and the Convention on Contracts for the International Sale of Goods' (2007) v 5 issue 1 International Journal of Management and Commerce Innovations 772

Shenoy GTL and Loo WL (eds) *Principles of Singapore Business Law* (2nd edn, Cengage Learning 2013)

Shiffrin SV, 'The Divergence of Contract and Promise' (2007) 120 Harv. L. Rev. 708

Sieburgh CH, *Mr. C. Assers Handleiding tot de beoefening van het Nederlands Burgerlijk Recht. 6. Verbintenissenrecht. Deel I. De verbintenis in het algemeen, eerste gedeelte* (Wolters Kluwer 2016)

- *Deel II. De verbintenis in het algemeen, tweede gedeelte* (Wolters Kluwer 2017)
- *Deel III. Algemeen overeenkomstenrecht* (Wolters Kluwer 2018)

Smith SA, *Contract Theory* (Oxford University Press 2004)

- 'Duties, Liabilities, and Damages' (2012) 125 Harvard Law review 1727

Smits J, Haas D and Hesen G (eds), *Specific Performance in Contract Law: National and Other Perspectives* (Intersentia 2008)

Stanley C and Ashdown MJ, 'Laches and limitation' (2014) v 20 issue 9 Trusts and Trustees 958

Stolp MM, 'Ontbinding, schadevergoeding en nakoming. De remedies voor wanprestatie in het licht van de beginselen van subsidiariteit en proportionaliteit' (DPhil thesis Radboud University Nijmegen 2007)

Stoyanov D, 'Causa and Consideration – A Comparative Overview' (2016) 23 Lex ET Scientia Int'l J. 14

Tan Ling, 'Actual Performance Responsibility and its Legal Application' (2000) 5 Modern Law 85 (谭玲．实际履行责任及其法律适用[J]．现代法学)

Ter KL, 'Good Faith in the Performance of Commercial Contracts Revisited' (2014) n 26 Singapore Academy of Law Journal 111

Thomas K, 'Analysing the Notion of 'Consumer' in China's Consumer Protection Law' (2018) Vol 6 n 2 The Chinese Journal of Comparative Law

Ting G, 'Good Faith in Contractual Agreements in Singapore' (2016) v 8 n 17 Singapore Law Review, Juris Illuminae

Tjittes RJ, *Commercieel Contractenrecht: Deel I: Totstandkoming en inhoud* (Boom juridisch 2018)

Tjong Tjin Tai TFE, 'Garantie, nakoming en schadevergoeding' (2004) 6577 WPNR 363

Treitel GH, *Remedies for Breach of Contract: A Comparative Account* (Oxford University Press 1998)

Valcke C, 'Contractual Interpretation at Common Law and Civil Law: An Exercise in Comparative Legal Rhetoric' in Neyers JW, Bronaugh R and Pitel SGA (eds), Exploring Contract Law (Hart Publishing 2009)

Veen TJH, *En voor berisping is hier ruime stof: over codificatie van het burgerlijk recht, legistische rechtsbeschouwing en herziening van het Nederlandse privaatrecht in de 19de en de 20ste eeuw* (Cabeljauwpers 2001)

Veldman M, 'Grenzen aan het recht op nakoming' (2001) 6455 WPNR 736

Virgo G and Worthington S (eds), *Commercial Remedies: Resolving Controversies* (Cambridge University Press 2018)

Visscher, 'De rangorde van remedies voor wanprestatie: subsidiariteit en proportionaliteit versus efficiëntie' (20017) 54 n 9 NTBR 385

Vogenauer S (ed) *Commentary on the UNIDROIT Principles of International Commercial Contracts (PICC)* (2nd edn, Oxford University Press 2015)

Vriend M, 'commentaar op artikel 248 Boek 6' in Klomp RJQ and Schelhaas HN (eds), *Groene Serie Verbintenissenrecht* (Wolters Kluwer 2018)

Vries GPJ de, *Recht op nakoming en schadevergoeding, excepties en ontbinding volgens NBW en BW* (Studiepockets privaatrecht nr 32, Tjeenk Willink 1984)

Wang L, 'The reception of German civil law via Japan in late Qing period' (1997) 1 Law Science (faxue)

Wang S, *Civil Procedure in China* (Kluwer Law International 2014)

Wang Z, *Textbook of Chinese Civil Law* (1982)

Webster A, *The Richest East India Merchant: The life and business of John Palmer of Calcutta 1767–1836* (The Boydell Press 2007)

Wessels B, *Koop: algemeen* (Monografieën BW B65a, Kluwer 2015)

Wessman MB, 'Should we fire the Gatekeeper? An Examination of the Doctrine of Consideration' (1993) 48 U. Miami L. Rev 48

Winship P, 'Aircraft and the International Sales Convention', 50 Journal Air Law & Commerce (1985)

Wunschheim C von, Tercier P and Ajani G, *Enforcement of commercial arbitral awards in China: business laws of China* (West 2017)

Xu G, 'An Introduction to the Structures of three major Civil Code Projects in nowadays China' (2004) 19 Tulane European and Civil Law Forum 37, 54 <http://biblio.juridicas.unam.mx/libros/4/1943/33.pdf>

Yang ZS, 'On the Necessity of Establishing "Principle of Changed Circumstances" In China' (1990) n 5 Chinese Legal Science 63

Yao H, The modernization of Chinese civil law and the contemporary tasks, Gansu Social Science (Gansu shehui kexue) 3 (2008) 127

Ye Changfu, 'On Judgement and Choice of the Value of Specific Performance of Contract' (2005) issue 2 Modern Law Science Xiandai Faxue 152 (叶昌富. 论强制实际履行合同中的价值判断与选择. 现代法学. 2005年. 期号 2. 页码 152)

Zayani N, 'The Doctrine of Good Faith in China: A Tool to Correct the Contractual Behaviour or a Serious Restriction to the Freedom of the Contract and Individual Interests' (2016) v 1 issue 10 Dama International Journal of Researchers 13-19 <http://www.damaacademia.com/issue/volume1/issue10/DIJR-O-003.pdf>

Zhang J, *On the Qing Civil Law* (Qingdai minfa zonglun) (Chinese University of Political Science and Law Press 1998)249

Zhang M, *Chinese Contract Law: Theory and Practice* (Martinus Nijhoff Publishers 2006)

Zheng Xiaochuan and Lei Mingguang, 'Reconsideration of Continuous Performance' (2003) issue 3 Habei Law Science 67 (郑小川， 雷明光. 对"继续履行"的再思考. 河北法学)

Zheng YL, 'It's Not What Is on Paper, but What Is in Practice: China's New Labor Contract Law and the Enforcement Problem' (2009) v 8 issue 3 Washington University Global Studies Law Review 596

Zhong J and Yu G, 'China's Uniform Contract Law: Progress and Problems' (1999) Volume 17/1 Pacific Basin Law Journal <http://escholarship.org/uc/item/97t9s6th> accessed on 9 May 2016

Zwalve WJ, *C.Æ. Uniken Venema's Common Law & Civil Law: Inleiding tot het Anglo-Amerikaanse vermogensrecht* (Boom Juridische uitgevers 2008)

B – Other relevant materials

Commission Directive 1999/44/EC of the European Parliament and of the Council of 25 May 1999 on certain aspects of the sale of consumer goods and associated guaranteed, (1999) OJ, L171/12

De toekomst van de nationale rechtsstaat [The future of the national rule of law], Scientific Council for Government Policy Rapport nr. 270, 2002b and *Nederland Handelsland: het perspectief van de transactiekosten* [The Netherlands a trading country: the perspective of transaction costs], Scientific Council for Government Policy Rapport 2003 nr 66

Dutch Parliamentary History Book 3 (Kluwer 1981)

- Book 6 (Kluwer 1981)
- Book 7 (Kluwer 1991)

Halsburys Laws of Singapore

Kamerstukken II 2015–2016, nr. 1553

The Columbia Encyclopedia (Columbia University Press, 2015)

The Educational Central of High Judges, *The Collection of Civil Cases* (1989) [1]

The Jersey Law Commission, 'Consultation Paper Prescription and Limitation' No 1/2008/CP (March 2018)

C – Online resources

<https://www.artsbeat.blogs.nytimes.com/2015/12/02/danh-vo-and-bert-kreuk-settle-legal-dispute-over-artwork>

<http://www.cisgw3.law.pace.edu/cases/050803g1.html>

<https://www.cisgw3.law.pace.edu/cisg/text/commentary2.html#f8>

<https://www.cisg.law.pace.edu/cisg/biblio/southerington.html>

<https://www.cisg.law.pace.edu/cisg/countries/cntries-China.html>

<https://www.customs.gov.sg/~/media/cus/files/circulars/ca/2016/circular_ai%20 the%20netherlands%20dated%2003%20nov%2016.pdf>

<http://www.iicl.law.pace.edu/cisg/page/cisg-list-contracting-states>

<https://www.nccih.nih.gov/health/asianginseng/ataglance.htm>

<https://www.sal.org.sg/Portals/0/PDF%20Files/Law%20Reform/2011-01%20-%20Limitation %20Periods%20in%20PIL.pdf>

<http://www.singaporelaw.sg/sglaw/laws-of-singapore>

<https://www.singaporelawwatch.sg/About-Singapore-Law/Overview>

<https://www.singstat.gov.sg/modules/infographics/economy> accessed on 28 January 2019>

<https://www.supremecourt.gov.sg/rules/court-processes/civil-proceedings/post-trial-matters/ enforcement-proceedings>

<http://www.uncitral.org/pdf/english/texts/sales/cisg/V1056997-CISG-e-book.pdf>

<http://www.unidroit.org/english/principles/contracts/main.htm>

<http://www.unilex.info>

Index

T

V

W

9 789462 369870